NORTHERN
MEXICO
HANDBOOK

THE SEA OF CORTEZ TO THE GULF OF MEXICO

D1232511

NORTHERN
MEXICO
HANDBOOK

THE SEA OF CORTEZ TO THE GULF OF MEXICO
FIRST EDITION

JOE CUMMINGS

MOON
PUBLICATIONS, INC.

NORTHERN MEXICO HANDBOOK
THE SEA OF CORTEZ TO THE GULF OF MEXICO

Published by
Moon Publications, Inc.
P.O. Box 3040
Chico, California 95927-3040, USA

Printed by
Colorcraft Ltd.

Please send all comments,
corrections, additions,
amendments, and critiques to:

**NORTHERN MEXICO HANDBOOK
MOON PUBLICATIONS, INC.
P.O. BOX 3040
CHICO, CA 95927-3040, USA**

Printing History
   1st edition—August 1994

Library of Congress Cataloging-in-Publication Data

   Northern Mexico Handbook: the Sea of Cortez to the Gulf of Mexico
   Joe Cummings
      p.   cm.
   Includes bibliographical references and index.
   ISBN 1-56691-022-6
   1. Mexico, North—Guidebooks.   I. Title.
F1314.C86   1994   94-9389
917.2'104835—dc20   CIP

Editor: Gina Wilson-Birtcil
Copy Editors: Elizabeth M. Kim, Nicole Revere
Production & Design: David Hurst
Cartographers: Bob Race, Brian Bardwell
Index: Deana Corbitt

Front cover photo by Richard Fisher, Sunracer Photography and Publishers

All photos by Joe Cummings unless otherwise noted.

Distributed in the United States by Publishers Group West

Printed in Hong Kong

CONTENTS

MAPS

MAP SYMBOLS

- MEX. FEDERAL HIGHWAY
- MEX. STATE HIGHWAY
- U.S. STATE HIGHWAY
- U.S. HIGHWAY
- U.S. INTERSTATE
- PEMEX GAS STATION
- AIRPORT

- DIVIDED HIGHWAY
- MAIN ROAD
- OTHER ROAD
- UNPAVED ROAD
- TRACK / TRAIL
- BRIDGE
- RAILROAD
- STATE BORDER
- INTERNATIONAL BORDER

- HOTEL / ACCOMMODATION
- POINT OF INTEREST
- TOWN / VILLAGE
- CITY
- MOUNTAIN
- WATERFALL
- WATER

CHARTS AND SPECIAL TOPICS

ABBREVIATIONS

a/c—air-conditioning
ATV—all-terrain vehicle
B&B—bed and breakfast
C.E.—*clase económica*
Chih.—Chihuahua
Coah.—Coahuila
COTP—Captain Of The Port
d—double occupancy
Dgo.—Durango
FNM—*Ferrocarriles Nacionales de Mexico*
G.T.—*gran turismo*
km—kilometers
N.L.—Nuevo Leon
Nte.—*norte* (north)
NP—new pesos
Ote.—*oriente* (east)

OW—one-way
pp—per person
Pte.—*poniente* (west)
q—quadruple occupancy
RT—roundtrip
RV—recreational vehicle
s—single occupancy
s/n—*sin número,* used for street addresses
    without building numbers
Sin.—Sinaloa
S.L.P.—San Luis Potosí
Son.—Sonora
t—triple occupancy
Tamps.—Tamaulipas
Zac.—Zacatecas

RESTAURANT RATINGS KEY

$	Less than US$4 per meal
$$	US$4-8 per meal
$$$	US$9-16 per meal
$$$$	Over US$16 per meal

Ratings are based on the average
price of an entree.

ACKNOWLEDGMENTS

Researching and writing this guidebook would have been a nigh impossible task without the generous assistance of the following people and organizations in Mexico: Guillermo Alvarez, Pilar Alvarez, Roberto Balderrama, María Barriga, Walter Bishop V., Silvestre Carbajal, Statia Carey, Alonso Enriquez, Javier Esquivel L., Barranca Bob Francis, Yasmin García and Jaime Guerrero González of Hotel Paraíso Radisson, Cristina Muñoz de García, Philippe Gentges, José Salcido Gómez, Nancy Heredia, Dr. César Hernández, Rafael Mendoza Kaplan, Angel Fco. Leal, Sergio Centeno Macias, Rockin' Chef Memo, "El Minero y El Músico" in Cerocahui, Margarita Roblada Moguel, José Saucedo Morales, Norma Nuñez, Luz Carmen Parra, Sigfrido Paz Paredes, Blanco Potisek, Juana Nava Prez, Alvaro Quezada, Juan Quezada, Sandra Luz Reyna, Ramón Quintana, Alejandro Rivera, Gilberto Limón de la Rocha, Martha Munguía Rojo, Norma Rodríguez, Ana Luz Sacramento, Adolfo Salido, Doris Martell Santos, Katherine Renpenning Semadeni, Isabel Siqueiro, Modesto Lozano Taylor, Miguel Terrones, José Trinidar, Margarita Zaragosa, and Ignacio Zepeda.

Extra special gold points to Sonia Estrada of the Chihuahua tourist office, who went out of her way to make sure my visit to Mexico's largest state was fruitful, and to Mauro Alfredo and Kathryn Pabst Rodríguez, who did the same for Alamos.

In the U.S., the following individuals and organizations also deserve mention: Judy Almeranti and Copper Canyon Lodges, Sue Brush and Elizabeth Basie of Westin Hotels, Marshall Burgamy, Sioux Colbourne, Rick Fisher, Rolando García, Julie Holmes-Chalpan of Holiday Inn International, research assistant and *béisbol* aficionado Tom Huhti, research assistant Chris Humphrey, Christina DeLeón and The Atkins Agency, Robert "Take-Me-To-The-Desert" Kay, Harry Lewellyn, Wendy Luft, Chicki Mallan, Mexico Mike Nelson, Michael Persh, Barbara Pierce, Ed Herschman, Valentino Rojas and Amy Bortz of Edelman Public Relations International, and Doug "Diego" Rhodes of Adobe Tours.

IS THIS BOOK OUT OF DATE?

Between the time this book went to press and the time it got onto the shelves, hotels have opened and closed, restaurants have changed hands, and roads have been repaired (or fallen into disrepair). Also, prices have probably gone up; because of this, all prices herein should be regarded as approximations and are not guaranteed by the publisher or the author.

We want to keep this book as accurate and up-to-date as possible and would appreciate hearing about any errors or omissions you may encounter while using *Northern Mexico Handbook*.

If you have any noteworthy experiences (good or bad) with establishments listed in this book, please pass them along to us. If something is out of place on a map, tell us; if the best restaurant in town is not included, we'd like to know. Found a new route to a hidden canyon or historic mining town? Share it with other Northern Mexico travelers. All contributions will be deeply appreciated and properly acknowledged. Address your letters to:

Northern Mexico Handbook
c/o Moon Publications
PO Box 3040
Chico, CA 95927-3040

BOB RACE

INTRODUCTION

Much of the wilderness once associated with the American Southwest lives on in the sparsely populated Northern Mexico mainland. Here *vaqueros* still cobble their own boots, and horses and burros remain an important form of transport. Yet in many of the nine northern states—Sonora, Sinaloa, Chihuahua, Durango, Zacatecas, San Luis Potosí, Coahuila, Nuevo León, and Tamaulipas—new four-lane highways have recently cut road travel in half, creating established corridors that connect border towns with formerly remote destinations in the interior, as well as Mexico's two main coastlines (Sea of Cortez and Gulf of Mexico).

Despite the northern mainland's accessibility from the U.S.-Mexico border, it remains largely undiscovered. Consequently, a world of travel possibilities, only partially obscured by legends of silver barons, bandidos, revolutionaries, lost gold mines, and ancient Amerindian cities, is open to anyone willing to take the transborder plunge.

Cloud forests, canyons inhabited by Tarahumara Indians, tropical lagoons, state-of-the-art museums, deep limestone caves, precipitous waterfalls, austere Mennonite colonies, chile farms, and beach resorts are just a taste of what Northern Mexico has to offer. The uniquely *norteño* culture that has developed over the centuries endows the top half of Mexico with a spirit that may seem both familiar and surprising to first-time visitors, a mixture of tranquillity and independence that brings many of us back time after time.

THE LAND

Northern Mexico sits firmly over the major part of continental Mexico, distinguishing it from isthmic, peninsular, and insular Mexico. Because of its vast continental mass, traveling from east to west or north to south one crosses at least 15 totally different terrains—a jumble of mountain ranges, plateaus, basins, plains, and wetlands that give the region its highly variable character.

GEOGRAPHY

Mainland Northern Mexico's nine states extend approximately 1,040,000 square km, or about 52% of the total surface area of the Republic of Mexico. Of Mexico's 31 states, the four largest are northerners—Chihuahua, Sonora, Coahuila, and Tamaulipas—a fact that proud Northern Mexicans are quick to point out.

Northern Mexico's border with the U.S. extends for 3,133 km from the Gulf of Mexico in the east to Río Colorado in the west, a dammed-to-a-trickle river that forms the state border between Baja California Norte and Sonora. To the east, more than half of the U.S.-Mexico border is formed by the Río Bravo, better known in the U.S. as the Rio Grande.

Mountain Ranges

Three major cordilleras (mountain chains), each of which is comprised of numerous smaller sierras (mountain ranges), dominate the Northern Mexican landscape and determine much of the region's climatic variation and biodiversity. Together the three encircle a major system of plateaus and basins known in Mexi-co as the Altiplano or "High Plains," thus forming the basic topographic framework for all of Northern Mexico.

Two of these cordilleras constitute the Sierra Madre or "Mother Range," so called because the two arms reach down the east and west flanks of continental Mexico as if to cradle the vast center. In many ways, life in these northern mountain chains represents Mexico at its most traditional. In the Sierras Madre most people still use the horse or burro for transport and farm work, plow their fields with oxen, and grind their own corn and wheat for handmade bread and tortillas. The vagaries of 20th-century Mexican politics have largely eluded the Madreans, simply because the highlands are less arable than the plains below; hence fighting for land—the source of most political conflict in Mexico—is historically less common.

The western Sierra Madre or **Sierra Madre Occidental,** Mexico's most extensive cordillera, runs 1,300 km (800 miles) along a northwest-southeast axis more or less parallel to the Sea of Cortez and Pacific Ocean coastlines. Basically a continuation of a chain that begins with Alaska's Endicott Mountains and extends through the Rocky Mountains of the U.S. and Canada,

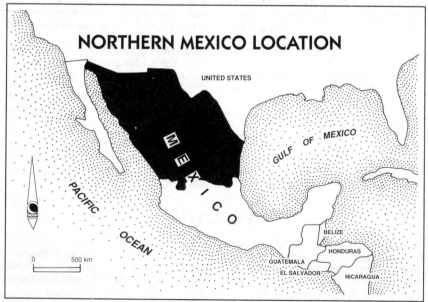

NORTHERN MEXICO LOCATION

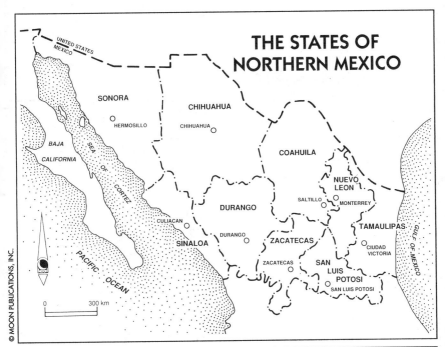

© MOON PUBLICATIONS, INC.

the Sierra Madre Occidental reaches a breadth of 300 km in places, and is interspersed with peaks over 3,000 meters (9,800 feet) high.

This cordillera is volcanic in origin, with rugged cliffs, steep canyons, and high waterfalls along the eastern escarpment and gentler slopes descending the western side toward the coastal plains. Extensive pine and oak forests blanket the uppermost

THE STATES OF NORTHERN MEXICO

STATE	CAPITAL	SIZE (IN SQ. KM.)	POPULATION (1990)
Chihuahua (Chih.)	Chihuahua	244,938	2.4 million
Sonora (Son.)	Hermosillo	182,052	1.8 million
Coahuila (Coah.)	Saltillo	149,982	1.9 million
Durango (Dgo.)	Durango	123,181	1.3 million
Tamaulipas (Tamps.)	Ciudad Victoria	79,384	2.2 million
Zacatecas (Zac.)	Zacatecas	73,252	1.2 million
Nuevo León (N.L.)	Monterrey	64,924	3.1 million
San Luis Potosí (S.L.P.)	San Luis Potosí	63,088	2.0 million
Sinaloa (Sin.)	Culiacán	58,328	2.2 million

elevations. Suspended between the western and eastern flanks is an interior savanna that has been used as a natural highway for human and animal migration since prehistoric times.

By contrast, the **Sierra Madre Oriental,** extending roughly 1,200 km parallel to the Gulf of Mexico coast, is a sedimentary chain of predominantly limestone peaks that are pocketed with caves and vertical pits called *sótanos,* some as deep as 1,400 feet. Although averaging only 150 km in width, the Oriental cordillera reaches heights in excess of 3,800 meters (12,000 feet).

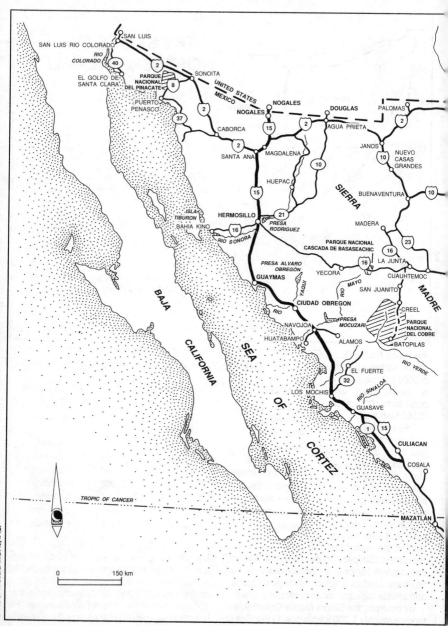

© MOON PUBLICATIONS, INC.

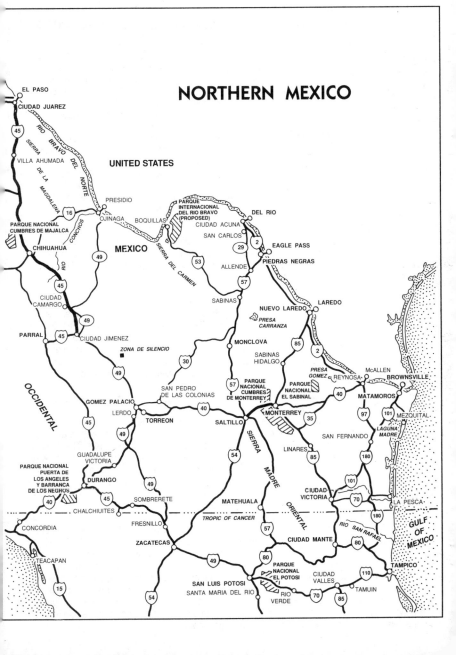

NORTHERN MEXICO

Humid winds from the Gulf of Mexico coil off the Oriental peaks and condense to provide lush, semitropical vegetation along the Sierra Madre Oriental's eastern escarpment, while the western side receives the desertic influences of the arid central plains. As a result of these weather patterns, one of the more remarkable features of the Oriental chain is an extensive cloud forest (see "Reserva de la Biosfera, El Cielo," p. 474) on Gulf-facing slopes south of Ciudad Victoria.

Linking the lower portions of both Sierra Madre cordilleras is a lesser chain of mountain ranges known as the Sierra Transversal de Zacatecas, La Breña y San Luis Potosí. Running west to east across the states of Zacatecas and San Luis Potosí, this largely volcanic chain divides the northern Altiplano from its counterpart in the south. The highest peaks here top out at 2,500-3,000 meters.

PRINCIPAL PEAKS OF NORTHERN MEXICO

NAME	HEIGHT	STATE
San Rafael	3,770 m (12,366 ft)	Coahuila
El Potosí	3,810 m (12,496 ft)	Nuevo León
El Morro	3,710 m (12,170 ft)	Nuevo León
Picacho San Onofre	3,554 m (11,657 ft)	Tamaulipas
El Jabalí	3,409 m (11,182 ft)	Coahuila
Epazote	3,227 m (10,585 ft)	Durango
La Ascensión	3,210 m (10,530 ft)	Tamaulipas
Grande	3,190 m (10,463 ft)	San Luis Potosí
El Oso	3,170 m (10,398 ft)	Durango
Páfilo	3,168 m (10,390 ft)	Durango
Las Nopaleras	3,130 m (10,266 ft)	Coahuila
Alto las Taunitas	3,110 m (10,200 ft)	Chihuahua
Las Chorreas	3,070 m (10,070 ft)	Durango

Altiplano

The vast plateau between the Sierra Madre Occidental and Sierra Madre Oriental is commonly known as the Altiplano, or less commonly as the Altiplanicie Septentrional or Llanuras Boreales—both of which roughly translate as "northern high plains." After Tibet and Bolivia, it is the third highest inhabited plateau in the world. At its northern end the Altiplano averages 1,000 meters above sea level, but as it moves south toward the Sierra Transversal de Zacatecas, La Breña y San Luis Potosí, the plateau ascends to around twice that height. Much of the Altiplano is comprised of interior chaparral, grassland (savanna), scrubland, or desertland.

The central plains also encompass a number of large depressions or basins called bolsones (Spanish for "bags" or "purses"). These basins hold rainwater that flows down mountainsides and forms shallow lakes—possibly the only source of surface water on the Altiplano during long periods between rains. A lack of rivers also means a lack of drainage for the plains, so minerals suspended in the runoff—mainly gypsum and salt—tend to collect in the lowest points of a bolsón. During times of sparse precipitation and hot weather, these lakes evaporate, leaving behind the gypsum dunes of Cuatrociénegas or the salt flats of El Salado de San Luis.

The configuration of mountains, rivers, and bolsones outlining the Altiplano divides the plateau into a number of subregions. South of Big Bend, Texas, the Río Bravo (Rio Grande) owes most of its volume to Mexico's Río Conchos. The latter has also transformed a portion of the Chihuahuan Desert into a verdant oasis called the **Cuenca del Río Conchos,** an area now supporting the cities of Chihuahua, Jiménez, Camargo, and Delicias in the state of Chihuahua.

The **Región Lagunera** occupies parts of Durango and Coahuila where the Nazas and Aguanaval rivers fill several large lakes. The damming of this hydraulic system provides major water resources for the area and has drained a portion of the lakes, leaving behind a fertile plain where wheat, corn, cotton, and vinifera are cultivated in abundance.

Part of the larger Chihuahuan Desert (see "Deserts," below), **El Bolsón de Mapimí** straddles the states of Chihuahua and Coahuila in the center of the Altiplano and is characterized by a stark flatness and desert climate. Superficial streams formed by intense, sporadic precipitation is quickly lost to subsurface infiltration and evaporation. Gypsum, one of the principal precipitates left behind, has been exploited economically.

El Salado de San Luis, a *bolsón* system centered in San Luis Potosí, extends into parts of Coahuila, Tamaulipas, and Zacatecas. It is similar in climate to Mapimí. As the name El Salado suggests, the primary precipitate is salt, which is collected from salt wells at its southern edge. In both Mapimí and El Salado, abundant lechugilla, yucca, and candelilla are important desert plants in the daily lives of local campesinos. These campesinos utilize the plants to make fiber products and candle wax.

To the west of the Bolsón de Mapimí is the **Comarca de los Indios Pueblos** ("Pueblo Indian District"), a desert area that is nonetheless irrigated by several rivers originating in the Sierra Madre Occidental. The valleys lining the Río Casas Grandes, in particular, have become thriving agricultural centers.

Gulf Coastal Plains

These plains form a wide coastal belt along the Gulf of Mexico from the Río Bravo delta to the port of Veracruz. Blessed with a mild and moist climate, the inland plains are traversed by several rivers that feed into the Gulf, creating a major agricultural and ranching center.

Coastal Features: Most of the Gulf coast from the U.S. border to Tampico is fringed by sandy barrier islands and peninsulas, a result of gradual coastal erosion. Even the short stretch south of La Pesca to Tampico not protected by barrier islands is blanketed by broad, straight, low-relief beaches.

Openings between barrier islands are known as *bocas* (mouths). Major openings along the Gulf coast north of Tampico are Boca de Sandoval (or Boca Madre), Boca de San Antonio, and Boca de Jesús María. These openings introduce saltwater from the Gulf of Mexico into the **Laguna Madre de Tamaulipas,** a 230-km-long intracoastal waterway enclosed by barrier islands.

Laguna Madre's brackish waters mingle with flows from the ríos San Fernando and Soto la Marina to provide an unusually rich environment of saltmarshes and softshore biomes. Just north of Tampico, the Río San Rafael feeds the small Lago San Andrés, while the city itself sits on the northern edge of Lago Pueblo Viejo, an intracoastal lagoon formed by a meeting of the Gulf and Río Pánuco.

Sea Of Cortez Coastal Plains

Wedged between the Sea of Cortez and the Sierra Madre Occidental, these narrow coastal plains extend from the Río Colorado delta in Sonora south to just north of Tepic, Nayarit. Although the Sea of Cortez coast is drier than its Gulf counterpart, irrigation systems utilizing the Concepción, Sonora, Yaqui, Mayo, and Fuerte rivers have created highly productive farming centers near Caborca, Hermosillo, Ciudad Obregón, Navojoa, and Los Mochis.

Deserts

Deserts are loosely defined as those areas averaging fewer than 25 cm (10 inches) of rain per year; by this definition, certain portions of nearly every state north of the Isthmus of Tehuantepec can be classified "desert," although rainfall varies considerably between locales.

Nearby desert regions in the U.S. are even more extensive and cover large parts of Nevada, California, New Mexico, Arizona, and Texas—thus forming the core of the great American Southwest. In distinguishing a "natural Southwest region," biologists at the University of Arizona allocate roughly half the area to Northern Mexico and the other half to the United States. In Mexico this area is known as *el Gran Suroeste,* "the Grand Southwest."

The North American desert regions can be divided into four major deserts: the Great Basin, Mojave, Sonoran, and Chihuahuan. The first two are entirely located within U.S. boundaries, while two-thirds of the Sonoran Desert and three-fourths of the Chihuahuan Desert lie in Northern Mexico.

Chihuahuan Desert: The largest of the North American deserts (covering approximately 453,000 square km or 36% of the total desert area) is centered between the Sierra Madre Occidental and Sierra Madre Oriental cordilleras in the great central plateau or Altiplano. It is a high desert in which the lower basins average over 700 meters above sea level, with surrounding areas commonly 1,400-1,500 meters (as high as 2,200 meters/7,200 feet at the southern end).

Rainfall—most prominent in the winter months—ranges from just under 20 cm (eight inches) a year at lower elevations to 25 cm (10 inches) or more in desert grasslands near mountain ranges. This makes the Chihuahuan Desert one of the "wetter" North American deserts. Temperature ranges are extreme, varying from 40° C (104° F) in midsummer to well below freezing in winter. Citing these weather patterns, desert specialists typically classify the Chihuahuan Desert as a "warm-temperate desertland" comparable to the Saharan, Arabian, Indian, Mojave, and Iranian deserts.

Most of this desert is underpinned by a layer of hard limestone commonly known as caliche, and covered by a thin soil that supports over a thousand plant species endemic to this desert, predominantly grasses, yuccas, and agaves.

The general topography encompasses alluvial plains, *bajadas* (outwash plains), and low mountains which combine to form three distinct subdivisions: Trans-Pecos (overlapping southern New Mexico, far west Texas, northeastern Chihuahua, and northwestern Coahuila); Mapimian (eastern Chihuahua and western Coahuila); and Saladan (mostly northern San Luis Potosí).

Indicator plants—dominant species which occur only or mostly in the Chihuahuan Desert—include creosote bush, tarpaper bush, whitethorn acacia, lechuguilla, peyote cactus, candelilla, and

THE SEA OF CORTEZ

The Sea of Cortez was named by Spanish explorer Francisco de Ulloa after he sailed its entire perimeter in 1539 and 1540 at the command of the most infamous of all Spanish conquistadors, Hernán Cortés (who had himself sailed the sea in an aborted attempt to colonize the Baja California peninsula four years earlier). The name Mar de Cortés henceforth appeared on regional maps until the Mexican government officially renamed it the Gulf of California (Golfo de California) early in this century. Sailors, writers, and other assorted romanticists, however, have continued to call it by its older name, the Sea of Cortez.

The sea is roughly 1,125 km (700 miles) long, with an average width of 150 km (93 miles). Oceanographers have divided it into four regions based on the prominent characteristics—depth, bottom contours, and marine productivity—of each zone. The northern quarter of the gulf, between the Colorado River delta and the Midriff Islands, is shallow in relation to the zones further south because of silt deposited by the Colorado River. The sea here is highly saline due to evaporation, and there is an unusually wide tidal range of up to 9.5 meters (31 feet). Before the Colorado River was dammed, the tidal bore created when the seaward river currents met the incoming tide was powerful enough to sink ships.

The second region south encompasses the Midriff Islands, where basins reach depths of 900 meters (2,700 feet) and strong currents bring nutrients up from the bottom while aerating the water. This leads to a very high level of biological productivity, otherwise known as "good fishin'."

From the Midriff Islands to Culiacán, basin depth doubles, silting is minimal, and water temperatures begin decreasing dramatically. The final sea zone below Culiacán, where the Sea of Cortez meets the Pacific Ocean, is "oceanic" in nature, with trenches

and submarine canyons that are 3,600 meters (12,000 feet) deep.

Of the 25 named islands in the Sea of Cortez, the largest is Isla Tiburón (Shark Island), a geological remnant of the mainland with an area of around 1,000 square km. Because of their isolation, the Cortez islands feature a high number of endemic natural species; at least half of the 120 cactus varieties found on the islands are endemic. The Sea of Cortez is biologically the richest body of water on the planet, with over 800 species of marine vertebrates at last count (the number rises with the publication of each new study).

In order to protect the Cortez ecosystem from coastal industries and overfishing, the Mexican government plans to ask the United Nations for International Biosphere Reserve status for the northern Sea of Cortez and its surrounding shores. Whether or not the request is granted, the government has stated it will take steps to upgrade protection for the sea, which is finally being recognized as one of Mexico's greatest natural assets.

Two species native to the Cortez, **totoava** and **vaquita dolphin,** are of particular concern. According to government sources, gill-netting for the totoava (with a 70- to 100-ton yearly harvest) has severely threatened the vaquita, which is now thought to be the most endangered marine mammal in the world. The current vaquita population is estimated at only 200-500 individuals. Since the passage of new Mexican laws in 1993, the use of gill nets in the upper Sea of Cortez has become illegal. If the law is fully enforced, the vaquita may be able to bounce back as successfully as the California gray whale has (from around 250 worldwide in the 1930s to over 20,000 in the 1990s) since the U.S. Marine Mammal Protection Act of 1972.

NORTH AMERICAN DESERTS

UNITED STATES

0   500 km

PACIFIC

SEA OF CORTEZ

M E X I C O

GULF OF MEXICO

OCEAN

∅ = GREAT BASIN
⬚ = MOJAVE DESERT
≡ = SONORAN DESERT
⊞ = CHIHUAHUAN DESERT

© MOON PUBLICATIONS, INC.

crucifixion thorn. Although cactus species are common, they tend to be outnumbered by other desertscrub vegetation. There is a noticeable lack of the various columnar cacti normally associated with the Sonoran Desert to the west; locally dominant cacti include prickly pear, cane cholla, and other low-growing varieties. In spite of their low profile, the Cactaceae of the Chihuahuan Desert number some 250 species, more than in any other North American desert.

Sonoran Desert: The third largest North American desert occupies about 221,000 square km or 21.5% of the total desert area, extending 12° latitude from the upper California-Nevada border south to the tip of the Baja California peninsula. On mainland Mexico it is limited to the coastal plains and the Río Colorado-Río Sonora alluvial plains of Sonora. Essentially it is cur-

tained from the Chihuahuan Desert by the Sierra Madre Occidental.

Like the Kalahari, Central Australian, and Patagonian deserts, the Sonoran is classified as "tropical-subtropical" due to the relatively narrow differential between average summer and average winter temperatures. Rainfall is heaviest at the western edge of the Plains of Sonora and Arizona Upland subdivisions.

The surface of the Sonoran Desert features a mix of volcanic, sedimentary, and metamorphic rock. Volcanic activity from as recent as 1,300 years ago has left a number of striking craters and lava fields in the Pinacate region of northern Sonora. The topography is also unique for the number of year-round rivers traversing the desert from the Sierra Madre Occidental to the Sea of Cortez.

CLIMATE

Temperatures

Mexican geographers sometimes divide their nation into three broad climatic zones: *tierra caliente* (hot land), sea level to 900 meters (3,000 feet); *tierra templada* (temperate land), 900-1,800 meters (3,000-6,000 feet); and *tierra fría* (cold land), over 1,800 meters (6,000 feet).

This schema is accurate for most of Northern Mexico. The Gulf of Mexico and Sea of Cortez plains are the lowest points and also have the warmest average year-round temperatures; the coolest average temperatures are found in the Sierra Madre Occidental and Sierra Madre Oriental mountain ranges. For temperature extremes, the elevation model (see below) works well. In January, snow is not uncommon in the Sierra Madre Occidental above 1,800 meters.

Although the hottest summers are generally found on the coastal plains, temperatures in the Altiplano—particularly in parts of Coahuila, Nuevo León, and Tamaulipas—often exceed 40° C (104° F) in July and August.

A model that takes into consideration regional differences in precipitation, atmospheric pressure, winds, and humidity, along with elevation, divides Northern Mexico into four major thermal zones. South of the Tropic of Cancer (23° latitude) in areas under 1,000 meters (in Northern Mexico this includes the Pacific coast from just north of Mazatlán to Teacapán and the Gulf coast plains south of La Pesca to Tampico), temperatures stay above 20° C (68° F) year-round, with a variation between annual temperature extremes of less than 10° C (50° F). Thus temperatures seldom drop below 15° C (59° F) or ascend beyond 34° C (93° F).

RIO GRANDE/BRAVO

The fifth longest river in North America, the Rio Grande—called Río Bravo in Mexico—has its source at 3,660 meters (12,000 feet) in Colorado's Rocky Mountains, from whence it flows southeast through Colorado and New Mexico, then along the Texas-Mexico border for more than half its length until it empties into the Gulf of Mexico, for a total distance of 3,025 km (1,880 miles). Its principal tributaries include the Pecos, Devil, Chama, and Puerco rivers in the U.S. and the Salado, San Juan, and Conchos rivers in Mexico, all of which are important sources of water in a region that generally receives little rainfall. The major portion of the river's volume, however, is provided by Mexican tributaries; the only U.S. affluent of significance is the Pecos River in Texas.

Archaeological evidence indicates that Amerindian groups had inhabited rock shelters along the river for 10,000-12,000 years before the Spanish *entrada*. Still-visible Coahuiltecan pictographs on the walls of Seminole Canyon near Ciudad Acuña are at least 4,000 years old. The Upper Rio Grande Valley near Ciudad Juárez is the oldest irrigated region in Mexico and the oldest continually cultivated area in North America. The Patarabueyes, a Pueblo Indian group, had been tilling the flood plains since at least A.D. 1200 when the Spanish arrived at La Junta in the 1600s.

The Spanish first explored the river (which they originally called Río de las Palmas) in the 1500s and settled on the riverbanks in the 17th and 18th centuries. By the mid-19th century, steamboat traffic extended northwestward from the Gulf of Mexico as far as Camargo, roughly 170 km (105 miles) upriver.

Nowadays water from the river is so heavily diverted for agricultural use on both sides of the border near Ciudad Juárez/El Paso that the Rio Grande just about comes to a halt until it is joined farther down by Mexico's Río Conchos at Ojinaga, Chihuahua. Then for 150 km (93 miles) or so, the Rio Grande follows the southern boundary of Big Bend National Park, flowing through three high-walled canyons (the Santa Elena, the Mariscal, and the Boquillas) that are favorite destinations of river runners.

Major cities along the Rio Grande/Río Bravo's course include Albuquerque, El Paso, and Brownsville in the U.S., and Ciudad Juárez, Nuevo Laredo, Reynosa, and Matamoros in Mexico. Two major international dams, the Presa Amistad (near Ciudad Acuña) and Presa Falcón (near Nuevo Laredo), have been built along the river to provide water storage through protracted dry periods and to prevent flooding downriver during heavy rains.

Above 1,000 meters in the Sierra Madre Occidental of western Chihuahua, northwestern Durango, and eastern Sonora, the average temperature is less than 20° C (68° F) with an annual variance of 10-20° C (50-68° F). At higher altitudes in both Sierra Madre cordilleras, the median annual temperature is 10° C (50° F) with a thermal fluctuation below 10° C (50° F); annual highs average 18° C (64.5° F), annual lows around 0° C (32° F). The hottest zones are found in the interior Sonoran Desert and in the Chihuahuan Desert's Bolsón de Mapimí, where annual extremes are over 38° C (100° F) apart.

Precipitation

Generally, the highest rainfall in Northern Mexico occurs at the southern edge of the Sierra Madre Oriental, where the cordillera intersects

---

ESTIMATING TEMPERATURE CHANGES

For every degree of latitude farther south you travel, figure a temperature increase of 2° C (3.5° F). For each 100-meter increase in altitude, figure a temperature drop of 2° C.

---

with the Gulf coastal plains below the Tropic of Cancer, i.e., from the Huasteca region of San Luis Potosí east to Tampico, Tamaulipas. Here annual precipitation usually exceeds 150 cm (58.5 inches), most of this occurring in the late summer. A similar weather pattern occurs on the Pacific coast in the vicinity of Mazatlán.

A dry, steppe climate dominates major parts of Zacatecas, Coahuila, Nuevo León, north-

AVERAGE TEMPERATURES AND PRECIPITATION FOR SELECTED CITIES

CITY	JAN.	APRIL	JULY	OCT.
Chihuahua, Chih.	9.4°C/49°F 25 cm/.1 in	18.3°C/65°F .76 cm/.3 in	25°C/77°F 7.9 cm/3.2 in	18.3°C/65°F 3.6 cm/1.4 in
Ciudad Obregón, Son.	18.3°C/65°F .69 cm/.27 in	25°C/77°F .41 cm/.16 in	33.9°C/93°F .69 cm/.27 in	29.4°C/85°F 1.45 cm/.57 in
Creel, Chih.	5°C/41°F 4.83 cm/1.9 in	10°C/50°F 1.4 cm/.55 in	17.2°C/63°F 13.5 cm/5.3 in	12.2°C/54°F 6.6 cm/2.6 in
Culiacán, Sin.	19.4°C/67°F 1 cm/.4 in	23.3°C/74°F 0 cm/0 in	28.3°C/83°F 14.7 cm/5.8 in	26.7°C/80°F 4.06 cm/1.6 in
Durango, Dgo.	11.7°C/53°F 1.3 cm/.05 in	18.3°C/65°F .25 cm/.01 in	20.6°C/69°F 12.5 cm/4.9 in	17.8°C/64°F 3 cm/1.2 in
Guaymas, Son.	17.8°C/64°F .76 cm/.3 in	22.8°C/73°F .25 cm/.1 in	30.5°C/87°F 4.57 cm/1.8 in	27.2°C/81°F 1.02 cm/.4 in
Hermosillo, Son.	15.5°C/60°F .25 cm/.1 in	22.7°C/73°F .25 cm/.1 in	32°C/90°F 7.1 cm/2.8 in	26°C/°79°F 4 cm/1.6 in
Mazatlán, Sin.	19.4°C/67°F 1.3 cm/.5 in	21°C/70°F 0 cm/0 in	27.2°C/81°F 16.7 cm/6.6 in	26°C/79°F 6.1 cm/2.4 in
Monterrey, N.L.	15°C/59°F 2.03 cm/.8 in	23.3°C/74°F 2.8 cm/1.1 in	27.2°C/81°F 7.4 cm/2.9 in	22.2°C/72°F 11 cm/4.3 in
San Luis Potosí, S.L.P.	12.8°C/55°F 1.3 cm/.5 in	20.6°C/69°F .51 cm/.2 in	19.4°C/67°F 5.8 cm/2.3 in	17.2°C/63°F 1.8 cm/.7 in
Tampico, Tamps.	18.3°C/65°F 5.3 cm/2.1 in	25°C/77°F 1 cm/.4 in	27.8°C/82°F 14.7 cm/5.8 in	25.5°C/78°F 17.8 cm/7.0 in
Torreón, Coah.	12.2°C/54°F 1.3 cm/.5 in	21°C/70°F .51 cm/.2 in	26.6°C/80°F 5.3 cm/2.1 in	23.3°C/74°F 2.3 cm/.9 in
Zacatecas, Zac.	9.4°C/49°F 1 cm/.4 in	15°C/59°F .25 cm/.1 in	13.9°C/57°F 8.9 cm/3.5 in	13.3°C/56°F 2.3 cm/.9 in

western San Luis Potosí, northern Durango, and the western Sierra Madre Oriental, with less than 75 cm (29 inches) annual precipitation below the Tropic of Cancer and less than 60 cm (23 inches) above the parallel. Most of this rainfall occurs during the summer months.

The Sonoran and northern Sinaloan plains and the center of the Altiplano (eastern Chihuahua and most of Coahuila) feature a dry, desertic climate with annual rainfall of fewer than 25 cm (10 inches). Rains are sporadic and intense, usually occurring in the early fall and spring.

Light, sporadic rains distributed year-round are typical in central and northwestern Tamaulipas and in northern Nuevo León. In the southern half of Tamaulipas rainfall tends to be more concentrated in the summer months. Throughout this zone the average annual precipitation is around 60 cm (23 inches). A similar pattern occurs on the lower western slopes of the Sierra Madre Oriental and lower eastern slopes of the Sierra Madre Occidental.

The higher elevations (coniferous zones) of the Sierra Madre cordilleras receive up to 120 cm (47 inches) of annual rainfall, most of it falling during the summer months.

BIOTIC COMMUNITIES

Although Northern Mexico is often described simply as a region of "mountain islands and desert seas," the geographic interplay of mountains, valleys, basins, seas, and rivers—not to mention nearly 10 degrees variation in latitude and 16 degrees in longitude—has formed over 30 major biomes (separate, ecosystem-based biotic communities) that can be broadly grouped into five biogeographic provinces: Chihuahuan, Tamaulipan, Madrean, Sonoran, and Sinaloan. The vegetational zones across these divisions encompass forests and woodlands, scrublands, grasslands, desertlands, and wetlands.

Forests And Woodlands

In Northern Mexico, forests and woodlands are for the most part found in the Sierra Madre cordilleras. At the higher elevations in Coahuila, Durango, and Chihuahua, two types of **Madrean montane conifer forests** are common: ponderosa pine and, on scattered peaks in the 2,000- to 3,000-meter range, a mixed conifer forest of Douglas fir, white fir, limber pine, and aspen.

At 1,000-2,000 meters along these same slopes, **Madrean evergreen woodland** is encountered. Mild winters and wet summers produce several varieties of evergreen oaks (live oaks) at this elevation, along with alligator-bark juniper, one-seed juniper, and piñon pine (Mexican pinyon). Although often called a "transition" forest, the Madrean evergreen woodlands are florally distinct from the vegetational zones above and below them. In Mexico these areas are sometimes called *encinal,* meaning woodlands dominated by evergreen oaks (encinos). Another commonly heard term is "pine-oak woodland."

Tropical-subtropical deciduous forests occur on the lower (300-1,050 meters) and warmer foothills of the sierras Madre. On the Occidental side, the **Sinaloan deciduous forest** is mostly confined to steep canyon areas in southern Sonora and northern Sinaloa, and is particularly profuse in the vicinity of Alamos, Sonora. Usually bordered by Madrean evergreen woodland, the forest is characterized by tropical elements, including hydromorphic fig, lianas, orchids, and bromeliads; common trees include Coulter acacia, bursera (torote), palo colorado, copalquín, cassia, and several trees endemic to Sinaloa whose names only keen botanists and locals know, such as Jarilla chocola, a semitropical tree common in the sierra foothills. Most of these plants are drought-deciduous; that is, they alternate periods of growth with periods of dormancy through two wet and two dry seasons. Hence the Sinaloan deciduous forest typically features a heavy summer foliage while looking rather bare during the arid winter months.

The Sierra Madre Oriental's counterpart is the **Tamaulipan semi-deciduous forest,** which extends from the Rio Grande Valley in Texas southward to Ciudad Victoria, Tamps., along the lower eastern escarpment of the cordillera. Common vegetation includes honey mesquite, Texas ebony, granjeno, winged elm, hackberry and huisache. In many areas tree branches are festooned with Spanish moss, especially near rivers where Montezuma bald cypress (called sabino in Mexico) is the dominant tree.

A bit further south along the eastern Sierra Madre Oriental is the little-known **Tamaulipan**

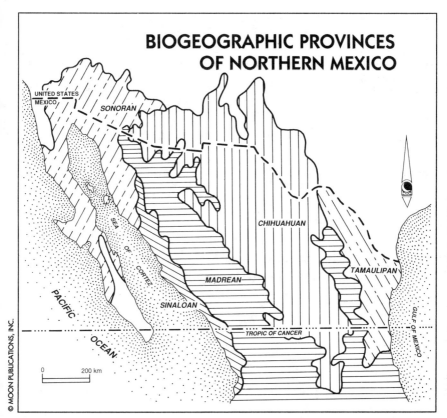

BIOGEOGRAPHIC PROVINCES OF NORTHERN MEXICO

SONORAN

CHIHUAHUAN

TAMAULIPAN

MADREAN

SINALOAN

TROPIC OF CANCER

PACIFIC OCEAN

SEA OF CORTEZ

GULF OF MEXICO

UNITED STATES
MEXICO

0   200 km

© MOON PUBLICATIONS, INC.

cloud forest, the northernmost cloud forest habitat in the Americas. (Mexico has two more cloud forests further south, one each in Veracruz and Chiapas.) It lies just above the southern reaches of the Tamaulipan subtropical deciduous forest in the area of Goméz Farías, Tamps., at an elevation of 900-1,500 meters (3,000-5,000 feet). As its name suggests, this forest receives much of the water necessary for growth from cloud cover (formed by moist air from the Gulf) that blankets the area for most of the year. Dominant trees here are evergreen oaks, sweet gum, wild cherry, magnolia, maple, hickory, beech, and Mexican alder.

Scrublands

Drier mountain slopes in northeastern Chihuahua, Coahuila, and Nuevo León feature interior chaparral (sometimes described as "Mediterranean-type" terrain) at elevations of around 1,500-2,450 meters (5,000-8,000 feet). Occasionally chaparral occurs along the lower borders of Madrean evergreen woodlands. Typical interior chaparral species encountered near the Sierra Madre Occidental include shrub live oak, manzanita, mountain laurel, hollyleaf buckthorn, and desert olive; these are often mixed with Sonoran thornscrub elements such as catclaw and mesquite as well crucifixion thorn, jojoba, yucca, and other desertland species.

In Coahuila and Nuevo León, interior chaparral near the Sierra Madre Oriental is typically dominated by various shrub live oaks (Coahuila shrub oak, Pringle oak, Vasey oak), Texas madrone, silktassel, sugar sumac, chaparral ash, and various sages. As in the Occidental ranges, thornscrub and desertland species often find minor distribution in these eastern chaparrals.

Tropical-subtropical scrublands at lower elevations toward or below the Tropic of Cancer usually take the form of thornscrub (also known as thorn forest or, in Mexico, as *matorral*). A transitional community between desertscrub and woodlands, thornscrubs are characterized by thorny, multitrunked trees and shrubs with a canopy between two and eight meters in height.

As with interior chaparral, separate versions exist for the Sea of Cortez and Gulf of Mexico sides of the continent. The west coast version, **Sinaloan thornscrub** (or Sinaloan thorn forest), covers much of southern Sonora and north-

ern Sinaloa with brasil, torote, acacia, palo verde, hopbush, brittlebush, guayacán, tree ocotillo, and palo blanco, interspersed with cactus (particularly pitahaya or organ-pipe cactus, hecho, and prickly pear) and herbaceous shrubs. Many Sinaloan thornscrub species are drought-deciduous, alternating periods of growth with periods of dormancy through two wet and two dry seasons.

Tamaulipan thornscrub (Tamaulipan thorn forest) is centered in northern Tamaulipas but now extends into southern Texas, where it has invaded former grasslands destroyed by overgrazing. Like its Sinaloan counterpart, Tamaulipan thornscrub is found below 1,000 meters between desertscrub communities and either

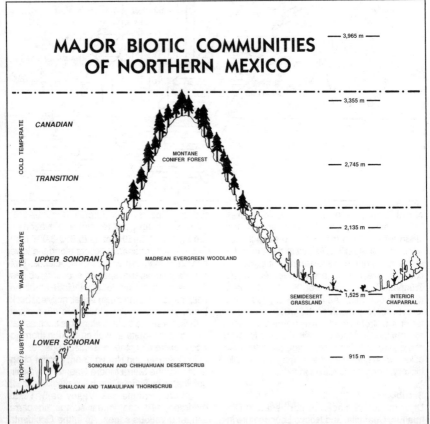

MAJOR BIOTIC COMMUNITIES OF NORTHERN MEXICO

© MOON PUBLICATIONS, INC.

NORTHERN MEXICO WILDLIFE[†]

Common Name; *Scientific Name;* Common Habitat

MAMMALS

antelope jackrabbit; *Lepus alleni;* Sinaloan thornscrub, savanna grassland

Apache squirrel; *Sciuris nayaritensis;* Madrean evergreen woodland

Arizona pocket mouse; *Perognathus amplus;* Sonoran desertscrub

big brown bat; *Eptesicus fuscus;* Madrean conifer forest, riparian tropical-subtropical deciduous forest

blacktailed jackrabbit; *Lepus californicus;* semidesert grassland, Sonoran desertscrub

bobcat; *Felis rufus baileyi;* Sinaloan thornscrub

cactus mouse; *Peromyscus eremicus;* Sonoran desertscrub

California myotis; *Myotis californicus;* Sonoran desertscrub

cliff chipmunk; *Eutamias dorsalis;* interior chaparral

coati; *Nasua nasua;* Madrean evergreen woodland, Sinaloan deciduous forest, Sinaloan riparian evergreen forest/woodland

coyote; *Canis latrans;* semidesert grassland, Sonoran desertscrub

deer mouse; *Peromyscus maniculatus;* Madrean conifer forest

desert bighorn sheep; *Ovis canadensis mexicana;* Chihuahuan desertscrub

desert cottontail; *Sylvilagus auduboni;* Chihuahuan and Sonoran desertscrub, Chihuahuan and Sonoran riparian scrubland

desert muledeer; *Odocoileus hemionus crooki;* Chihuahuan and Sonoran desertscrub

eastern cottontail; *Silvilagus floridanus;* Madrean conifer

elk; *Cervus elaphus;* Petran and Madrean conifer forests, Madrean evergreen woodland, interior chaparral

feral burro; *Equus asinus;* Sonoran desertscrub

gray fox; *Urocyon cinereoargenteus;* Sonoran desertscrub

gray wolf; *Canis lupus;* Madrean conifer forest

jaguar; *Felis onca;* riparian tropical-subtropical deciduous forest, Sinaloan riparian evergreen forest/woodland

jaguarundi; *Felis yagouraoundi;* Sinaloan and Tamaulipan thornscrub

javelina (collared peccary); *Dicotyles tajacu;* Sinaloan thornscrub, semidesert grassland, savanna grassland, Sonoran desertscrub

kit fox; *Vulpes macrotus;* Sonoran desertscrub

margay; *Felis weidii;* Sinaloan deciduous forest

Merriam's kangaroo rat; *Dopodomys merriami;* semidesert grassland, Chihuahuan and Sonoran desertscrub

Mexican cottontail; *Sciurus truei;* Sinaloan deciduous forest

Mexican grizzly bear; *Ursus arctos;* Madrean evergreen woodland

Mexican longnosed bat; *Leptonycteris nivalis;* Madrean evergreen woodland

mule deer; *Odocoileus hemionus;* Madrean conifer forest, interior chaparral, semidesert grassland

ocelot; *Felis pardalis;* Sinaloan and Tamaulipan thornscrub, Sinaloan riparian evergreen forest/woodland

[†]Rather than an exhaustive listing, this is a selective presentation of noteworthy (either very common or very unusual) fauna found throughout Northern Mexico. *(continued)*

NORTHERN MEXICO WILDLIFE

Common Name; *Scientific Name;* Common Habitat

MAMMALS (continued)

pronghorn; *Antilocapra americana;* semidesert grassland

raccoon; *Procyon lotor;* riparian scrubland, riparian tropical-subtropical deciduous forest

ringtailed cat; *Bassariscus astutus;* Sonoran desertscrub

Sonoran pronghorn; *Antilocapra americana sonorensis;* Sonoran desertscrub

Texas antelope ground squirrel; *Ammospermophilus interpres;* Chihuahuan desertscrub

white-tailed deer; *Odocoileus virgianus;* Madrean conifer forest, Madrean evergreen woodland, Sinaloan deciduous forest, semidesert grassland, montane riparian wetland

BIRDS

bald eagle; *Haliaeetus leucocephalus;* riparian tropical-subtropical deciduous forest

belted kingfisher; *Megaceryle alcyon;* montane riparian wetland

black-bellied tree duck; *Dendrocygna autumnalis;* Sinaloan riparian evergreen forest/woodland

black brant; *Branta nigricans;* interior and maritime marshlands

black-crowned night heron; *Nycticorax nycticorax;* interior and maritime marshlands

blue-winged teal; *Anas discors;* interior and maritime marshlands

broad-tailed hummingbird; *Selasphorus platycercus;* montane riparian wetland

burrowing owl; *Athene cunicularia;* semidesert grassland, Sonoran desertscrub

bushtit; *Psaltriparus minimus;* interior chaparral

cactus wren; *Campylorhynchus brunneicapillus;* semidesert grassland, Chihuahuan and Sonoran desertscrub

canyon wren; *Catherpes mexicanus;* interior chaparral

caracara; *Caracara cheriway;* savanna grassland

Colima warbler; *Vermivora crissalis;* Madrean evergreen woodland

curved-bill thrasher; *Toxostoma curvirostra;* semidesert grassland, Chihuahuan and Sonoran desertscrub

eared trogon; *Eupilotis neoxenus;* Madrean conifer forest

elf owl; *Micrathene whitneyi;* Sonoran desertscrub

emerald toucanet; *Aulacorhynchus prasinus;* cloud forest

Gould's turkey; *Meleagris gallopavo mexicana;* Madrean conifer forest, Madrean evergreen woodland

goshawk; *Accipter gentilis;* Madrean conifer forest

great blue heron; *Ardea herodias;* riparian tropical-subtropical deciduous forest

greater yellowlegs; *Totanus melanoleucus;* interior and maritime marshlands

green parakeet; *Aratinga holochlora;* Sinaloan riparian evergreen forest/woodland

Harris' hawk; *Parabuteo unicinctus;* Sinaloan thornscrub, Sonoran desertscrub

imperial woodpecker; *Campephilus imperialis;* Madrean conifer forest

ladder-backed woodpecker; *Picoides scalaris;* semidesert grassland, Sonoran desertscrub

lilac-crowned parrot; *Amazonia finschi;* Sinaloan riparian evergreen forest/woodland

long-billed marsh wren; *Cistothorus palustris;* interior and maritime marshlands

mangrove cuckoo; *Coccyzus minor;* mangrove

NORTHERN MEXICO WILDLIFE

Common Name; *Scientific Name;* Common Habitat

BIRDS (continued)

masked bobwhite; *Colinus virgianianus ridgwayi;* savanna grassland, Sonoran desertscrub

Mexican duck; *Anas platyrhynchos diazi;* interior and maritime marshlands

Mexican jay; *Aphelocoma ultramarina;* Madrean evergreen woodland

military macaw; *Ara militaris;* Sinaloan riparian evergreen forest/woodland

Montezuma quail; *Crytonyx montezumae;* Madrean evergreen woodland

mourning dove; *Zenaida macroura;* semidesert grassland, Chihuahuan and Sonoran desertscrub, Chihuahuan and Sonoran riparian scrubland, riparian tropical-subtropical deciduous forest

pectoral sandpiper; *Calidris melanotos;* interior and maritime marshlands

roadrunner (paisano); *Geococcyx californianus;* semidesert grassland, Chihuahuan and Sonoran desertscrub

prairie falcon; *Falco mexicanus;* semidesert grassland

pygmy owl; *Glaucidium gnoma;* Madrean conifer forest

roseate spoonbill; *Ajaia ajaia;* mangrove, tidal scrubland

sandhill crane; *Himantopus mexicana;* interior and maritime marshlands

Scott's oriole; *Icterus parisorum;* Chihuahuan desertscrub

Sinaloa wren; *Thryothorus sinaloa;* Sinaloan thornscrub

snow goose; *Chen caerulescens;* interior and maritime marshlands

thick-billed parrot; *Rhyncopsitta pachyrhyncha;* Madrean conifer forest

violet-crowned hummingbird; *Amazilia violiceps;* Madrean evergreen woodland

warbling vireo; *Vireo gilvus;* montane riparian wetland

white-necked raven; *Corvus cryptoleucus;* Chihuahuan desertscrub

white-winged dove; *Zenaida asiatica;* Sinaloan and Tamaulipan thornscrub, Sonoran desertscrub, riparian tropical-subtropical deciduous forest, riparian scrubland

wild turkey; *Meleagris gallopavo;* montane riparian wetland

willet; *Catotrophorus semipalmatus;* interior and maritime marshlands

yellow-billed cuckoo; *Coccyzus americanus;* riparian tropical-subtropical deciduous forest

AMPHIBIANS & REPTILES

Arizona alligator lizard; *Gerrhonotus kingi;* Madrean conifer forest, interior chaparral, montane riparian wetland, interior and maritime marshlands

Arizona coral snake; *Micruriodes euryxanthus;* Sonoran desertscrub, semidesert grassland

beaded lizard; *Heloderma horridum;* Sinaloan deciduous forest

boa constrictor; *Constrictor constrictor;* Sinaloan deciduous forest, Sinaloan riparian evergreen forest/woodland

bolson turtle; *Gopherus flavomarginatus;* Chihuahuan desertscrub

canyon treefrog; *Hyla arenicolor;* montane riparian wetland

chuckwalla; *Sauromalus obesus;* Sonoran desertscrub

Coahuila box turtle; *Terrapene coahuila;* interior and maritime marshlands

desert box turtle; *Terrapene ornata luteola;* semidesert grassland

(continued)

NORTHERN MEXICO WILDLIFE

Common Name; *Scientific Name;* Common Habitat

AMPHIBIANS AND REPTILES (continued)

desert iguana; *Dipsosaurus dorsalis;* Sonoran desertscrub
desert striped whipsnake; *Masticophis taeniatus;* interior chaparral
desert tortoise; *Gopherus agassizi;* Sonoran desertscrub
fringe-toed lizard; *Uma notata;* Sonoran desertscrub
giant toad; *Bufo marinus;* Sinaloan riparian evergreen forest/woodland
gila monster; *Heloderma suspectum;* Sonoran desertscrub
iguana; *Iguana iguana;* Sinaloan deciduous forest
leopard frog; *Rana pipiens;* Sinaloan riparian evergreen forest/woodland
Mexican garter snake; *Thamnophis eques;* montane riparian wetland
Mohave rattlesnake; *Crotalus scutulatus;* Chihuahuan desertscrub
mountain skink; *Eumeces callicephalus;* Madrean conifer forest
mountain treefrog; *Hyla eximia;* montane riparian wetland
red diamondback rattlesnake; *Crotalus ruber;* Sonoran desertscrub
regal horned lizard; *Phrynosoma solare;* Sonoran desertscrub
reticulated gecko; *Coleonyx reticulatus;* Chihuahuan desertscrub
reticulated gila monster; *Heloderma suspectum suspectum;* Sonoran desertscrub
rosy boa; *Lichanura trivirgata;* Sonoran desertscrub
roundtail horned lizard; *Phrynosoma modestum;* Chihuahuan desertscrub
sidewinder; *Crotalus cerastes;* Chihuahuan and Sonoran desertscrub
softshell turtle; *Trionyx ater;* interior and maritime marshlands
Sonoran green toad; *Bufo retiformis;* savanna grassland, Sonoran desertscrub
Sonoran mountain kingsnake; *Lampropeltis pyromelana;* Madrean conifer forest, interior chaparral
southwestern earless lizard; *Holbrookia texana scitula;* semidesert grassland

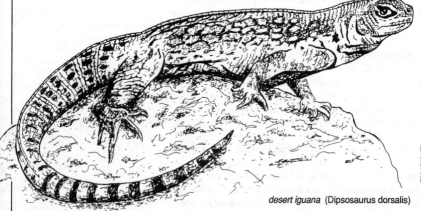

ERIN DYWER

desert iguana (Dipsosaurus dorsalis)

NORTHERN MEXICO WILDLIFE

Common Name; *Scientific Name;* Common Habitat

AMPHIBIANS AND REPTILES (continued)

Tarahumara salamander; *Ambystoma rosaceum;* montane riparian wetland

Texas banded gecko; *Coleonyx brevis;* Chihuahuan desertscrub

Texas lyre snake; *Trimorphodon biscutatus vilkinsoni;* interior chaparral

Trans-Pecos rat snake; *Elaphe subocularis;* Chihuahuan desertscrub

tree lizard; *Urosaurus ornatus;* Sinaloan thornscrub, Sonoran desertscrub, riparian tropical-subtropical deciduous forest

western diamondback rattlesnake; *Crotalus atrox;* Chihuahuan desertscrub

western rattlesnake; *Crotalus viridis;* Madrean conifer forest, interior chaparral

FISH††

blue catfish; *Ictalurus furcatus;* riparian scrubland

channel catfish; *Ictalurus punctatus;* riparian scrubland

Chihuahua chub; *Gila nigresens;* interior and maritime marshlands

Chihuahuan shiner; *Notropis chihuahua;* riparian scrubland

desert pupfish; *Cymatogaster macularius;* interior and maritime marshlands

European brown trout; *Salmo trutta;* montane riparian wetland

gila trout; *Salmo gilae;* montane riparian wetland

golden shiner; *Notemigonus crysoleucus;* montane riparian wetland

largemouth bass; *Micropterus salmoides;* riparian tropical-subtropical deciduous forest, Sinaloan riparian evergreen forest/woodland

Mexican golden trout; *Salmo chrysogaster;* montane riparian wetland

Mexican stoneroller; *Campostoma ornatum;* riparian scrubland, riparian tropical-subtropical deciduous forest, Sinaloan riparian evergreen forest/woodland

mosquitofish; *Gambusia affinis;* riparian scrubland, riparian tropical-subtropical deciduous forest

rainbow trout; *Salmo gairdneri;* montane riparian wetland

smallmouth bass; *Micropterus dolomieui;* riparian tropical-subtropical deciduous forest

speckled chub; *Hybopis aestivalis;* riparian scrubland

striped bass; *Morone saxatilis;* riparian tropical-subtropical deciduous forest

Tamaulipan shiner; *Notropis braytoni;* riparian scrubland

tilapia; *Tilapia* various species; Sonoran riparian deciduous forest

††For saltwater fish see "Fishing," p. 44

tropical deciduous forests or Madrean evergreen woodlands. Because the coastal plains of Tamaulipas receive significantly more rainfall than the western plains of Sonora and Sinaloa, fewer of the Tamaulipan species are drought-deciduous. Dominant trees and shrubs include mesquite, acacia, cenizo, huisache, hackberry, strangler fig, and breadnut tree, interspersed with small cactus species.

Grasslands

Large tracts of land in the Altiplano consist of **semidesert grasslands** (often incorrectly called desert grassland, or in Mexico *pastizal*), a transitional zone of dominant perennial grass-scrub that occurs between desertscrub and either chaparral or evergreen woodland. This type of grassland is mostly found within Chihuahuan Desert areas of 1,100-1,400 meters (3,600-4,600 feet)

JOE CUMMINGS

cirio

in Chihuahua, western Coahuila, Nuevo León, and Zacatecas. In northeastern Sonora, it also occurs just above Sinaloan thornscrub.

Toboso grass and black grama are major indicators for semidesert grassland, often mixed in with other grasses (buffalo grass, various other gramas), scrub (acacia, mesquite), and various cacti and succulents (particularly ocotillo, yucca, sotol, barrel cactus, and prickly pear).

In areas where rainfall is more plentiful, usually farther south toward the Tropic of Cancer, grasses intensify to produce **savanna grassland.** Perennial grasses are thicker in a savanna and are interspersed with woody trees and shrubs.

Desertlands

It isn't mere aridity that makes a desert most distinctive but rather the range of biologic responses to aridity. Because periods of rain are so infrequent, resident species must make use of "ephemeral habitats"—those that exist only temporarily—to carry out the breeding and feeding necessary to survival. Only organisms specially adapted to these conditions of desert living can survive as a species; typically desert plants and animals are dormant or torpid between seasons of activity. What distinguishes one desert from another is the range of endemic and/or predominant biological entities present.

Below semidesert grasslands, the driest areas of the warm, temperate Chihuahuan Desert between the Sierras Madre produce low **Chihuahuan desertscrub,** typified by lechugilla, tarpaper bush, creosote bush, ocotillo, shrub mesquite, various yuccas and agaves, saltbush, sandpaper bush, cholla, acacias, sage, and a number of Cactacaea that grow close to the ground such as barrel cactus (biznaga), rainbow cactus, hedgehog cactus, peyote cactus, prickly pear, and desert Christmas cactus. Tall cacti tend not to take part in the Chihuahuan desertscape.

West of the Sierra Madre Occidental and north of Guaymas, the subtropical Sonoran Desert features **Sonoran desertscrub.** Like their Chihuahuan neighbors, the Sonoran desertlands feature a number of agaves, yuccas, acacias, ocotillos, and barrel cacti. Because of longer wet seasons and warmer temperatures, most of the Sonoran varieties of these plants are larger; this is especially true of ocotillos and yuccas. The peculiar cirio or "boojum tree," a 12- to 15-meter (40- to 50-foot), candle-shaped succulent related to the ocotillo, is a Sonoran endemic that grows only in a limited area north of Bahía Kino (and across the Sea of Cortez in Baja California). Sonoran desertlands also produce numerous endemic tree species, including torote blanco (elephant tree), palo verde smoke tree, and ironwood (palo fierro).

For many visitors, Sonoran desert vegetation is generally typified by three large, tall, columnar cacti species that impart the classic Southwestern desert look: pitahaya or organpipe cactus; sahuaro or saguaro; and cardón. As the world's tallest cactus, the cardón can reach as high as 18 meters (60 feet) and weigh as much as 12 tons, though more commonly it tops out at 7.5-9 meters (25-30 feet). The giant, pale-green trunks feature 11-17 vertical ribs and sometimes measure three feet thick. The cardón is often confused with the smaller saguaro cactus; one major difference is that the branches of the cardón tend to be more vertical than those of the saguaro.

THE BURRO

Long-eared, slow-plodding, dim-witted—the quintessential beast of burden: this is the city person's image of *Equus asinus*. But to rural Mexicans the donkey or burro is an image of strength and sure-footedness. Compared to the horse, its taller, more graceful-appearing cousin, the burro is a far more useful animal in mountainous or arid domains. On slopes, rocky surfaces, or sand it moves with more agility and is able to keep a load—whether human or inanimate—more balanced. Standing only about 3¹/2 feet high at the shoulder, burros can also cover greater distances on less water and food than horses; they actually seem to prefer rough forage such as dead cactus or thorny palo verde over nutrient-rich grasses.

Although a burro's coloring may vary from light to dark brown, its withers are almost always marked with a cross of darker hair. This cross is said to be a symbol of divine protection for having carried Mary and the infant Christ from Egypt to the Holy Land. Amid the arid plains of Northern Mexico, a burro certainly takes on a biblical aura.

Unknown numbers of wild burros roam northwestern Mexico, particularly in desertscrub areas of the Sonoran Desert and in the canyons of the Sierra Madre Occidental. Ranchers or campesinos will occasionally capture a wild burro for domestic use as they are fairly easy to tame (the burro's legendary stubbornness can often be attributed to mistreatment by its owner; a well-cared-for animal is usually quite loyal). The wild male burro or "jack" is considered the best stud for producing a mule, so ranchers occasionally turn mares loose to breed with them. Mules produced from such a union are especially hardy.

Trekkers occasionally hire burros or mules as pack animals in Northern Mexico's canyons and sierras. For long forays, it is sometimes cheaper to purchase one outright rather than pay a daily hire rate; prices range from around US$40 for a poor animal to around US$75 for an exemplary one—if you can find a rancher willing to sell one. If the price doesn't include a *burriqueta* (or *aparejo*), a leather-and-wood frame for carrying cargo, you'll have to buy one or have one made—they're quite inexpensive. If possible, have a veterinarian inspect the animal for diseases before agreeing on a purchase.

Wetlands

Although Northern Mexico is generally thought of as arid territory, a remarkable number of wetland habitats exists wherever the land meets rivers, sea coasts, lakes, underground springs, *tinajas* (rock pools), or seasonal streams and basins. In fact, for every type of terrain described above, there exists a corresponding riparian, maritime, or interior-marshland environment (sometimes all three).

Hence you'll find **montane riparian wetlands** along mountain rivers of the Sierras Madre; **riparian deciduous forests** and **riparian evergreen woodlands** along lower slope riverbanks; **riparian scrublands** where streams run through scrublands; **maritime marshlands** along the Gulf of Mexico and Sea of Cortez coasts; and **interior marshlands** surrounding lakes and desert *bolsones* (drainage basins). The Gulf coast also has areas where interior and maritime marshlands comingle along barrier-island lagoons.

The topology of wetland vegetation is extremely complex; saltmarshes, for example, represent the most concentrated biomass on the planet (exceeding even tropical rainforests). To begin to enumerate even the basic indicator species for each of these habitats is well beyond the scope of a travel guidebook. Certain characteristics for some of these biomes are described under the corresponding destination sections later in this guide; readers with a keen interest in Northern Mexico wetlands should scan "References" on p. 486 for further sources.

THE HISTORY

PRE-CORTESIAN HISTORY

Paleo-Indian And Desert-Archaic Cultures
Scattered evidence of human habitation in Northern Mexico dates back at least 10,000 years. Human skeletons, metates (grinding stones), and pictographs found in parts of Mexico near the Río Bravo river system and further west in Chihuahua indicate a Paleo-Indian (or Clovis-Folsom) presence—among the earliest known cultures in North America. The Paleo-Indians of Northern Mexico are believed to be descendants of Asian tribes that migrated across the Bering Strait to North America from the Asian continent some 50,000 years ago.

The distribution of artifacts suggest that the Paleo-Indian groups were nomadic and small in number, and that they relied on small game and forage for food. It isn't known whether their cultures later evolved into more advanced cultures or whether they were supplanted by other migrants, but by the time the Ice Age ended around 5000 B.C., the slightly more advanced Desert Archaic culture had developed in pockets across the north.

Archaic Indian groups such as the San Dieguitos of the Río Colorado delta or the Chihuahua Cochise of the northern Sierra Madre Occidental spent much of the year wandering in small migratory bands of 15 to 20, guided by freshwater sources and the availability of game. Their simple economy was based on hunting, fishing, and the gathering of edible wild plants. Archaeological remains include circles of stones, stone tools—choppers, raspers, knives, spear points, axeheads, mortars (metates)—and simple pottery.

Gradually the Amerindian cultures of Northern Mexico breached a cultural watershed as the development of agriculture allowed nomadic groups to slow or halt their wanderings. Ceramic technology evolved to the point that pottery became a commerce item between tribes. It is still a matter of regional debate whether these changes were native to Northern Mexico or whether they came from present-day Arizona and New Mexico (which until less than 150 years ago were part of Mexico anyway), but by the early centuries of this millennium a number of groups in northwestern Mexico were actively engaged in these more advanced technologies.

Oasis And Arido America
Mexican historians generally divide Northern Mexico's Amerindian history (as opposed to prehistory) into four phases: Old (A.D. 700-1060), Middle (1060-1340), Late (1340-1519), and Spanish period (1519-1821). The first three phases are conceptually (though not chronologically) analogous to the preclassic, classic, and postclassic system employed in Mesoamerican studies; and for North American scholars, the "Old" phase roughly corresponds to "Agricultural" or "Proto-historic" periods in the development of Amerindian cultures according to their general classification system.

Current evidence indicates that the earliest agriculture in Northern Mexico or the U.S. Southwest can be traced to the La Junta culture centered around present-day Ojinaga, Chihuahua, in the upper Río Bravo (Rio Grande) valley. Cultivated by a little-understood Indian group (known as the Patarabueyes when the Spanish arrived in the 1500s), the flood plains here are considered to be the oldest agricultural region in North America. Early agricultural and ceramic techniques were also developed by the Río Sonora culture in the extensive Sonora River valley.

The most abundant evidence of early cultures in Northern Mexico dates to Oasis America, a term Mexican archaeologists commonly use to categorize the loose association of Indian groups centered around Chihuahua's Río Casas Grandes from as early as A.D. 900 through the Spanish *entrada*. A huge area encompassing the southwestern Pueblo cultures along with northwest Mexico's Paquimé (Casas Grandes) culture, Oasis America was distinct from Arido America—the Desert-Archaic cultures that remained in northeastern Mexico and Texas through the Spanish *entrada*—as well as the advanced Mesoamerican cultures of Southern Mexico and Central America.

Hallmarks of Oasis America included the construction of multistory, cubelike houses in mountain caves or on semidesert plains. Oasis American cultures also produced beautiful ceramics that were prized by neighboring Mesoamericans. The cultural chronology of Oasis America is thought to have included the Hohokam, Mogollon, and Anasazi cultures along with many other lesser-known sedentary groups in northwest Mexico and the American Southwest. In Mexico, the major remains of this period are found in the state of Chihuahua at Paquimé (Casas Grandes), Cuarenta Casas, and the Río Papigochic area.

Some Mexican archaeologists include Oasis America and the earlier Arido America within the larger "Gran Chichimeca," a proto-historic Amerindian diaspora that extended from southern Kansas to the Tropic of Cancer and from the Sea of Cortez to the Gulf of Mexico. (Chichimeca is actually a derogatory Aztec term meaning "sons of dogs" and is employed by Mexico City historians with an Aztec bias—a bias that colors all official, i.e., Mexico City-centered, history.) Between Oasis America-Arido America and the Aztec- and Mayan-dominated Mesoamerica was a belt termed Mesoamerica Marginal which extended across southern Durango, Zacatecas, San Luis Potosí, and Querétaro. As cultural/commercial liaisons developed between Oasis America and Mesoamerica, the cultures here blended characteristics of both north and south. Archaeological remains of Mesoamerica Marginal include the ruins of Chalchihuites (Zacatecas), La Quemada (Zacatecas), and Tamuín (San Luis Potosí).

By the 11th century, contact with Mesoamerica had advanced to the point that the Paquimé Indians of western Chihuahua were incorporating the ceremonial platforms and I-shaped ball courts of the Central Mexico Aztec and the Southern Mexico Maya into their capital city. Oasis American cultures in northwest Mexico continued to expand and flourish well into the 13th century, then gradually began to stagnate and decay as all civilizations inevitably do. By the time the Spanish arrived in the early 16th century, much of Oasis America was either in a state of decline or had disappeared. Arido America, on the other hand, never developed much beyond the Desert-Archaic stage.

SPANISH CONQUEST OF MEXICO

Following 700 years of conflict with the Moors over control of the Iberian peninsula, Spain emerged in the 15th century as the most powerful nation in Europe. Convinced that a Roman Catholic God was destined to rule the world with Spain as His emissary, the Spanish monarchy sent Christopher Columbus in search of a new route to the Far East. His mission was to establish contact with a mythical "Great Khan" in order to develop an alternate trade route with the Orient, since the Arabs (Moors) controlled the overland route through the Middle East. Along the way as many pagans as possible were to be converted to Christianity. Once the Arab trade monopoly was broken, the Holy Land would be returned to Christian control.

Columbus's landing in the West Indies in 1492 was followed by Pope Alexander VI's historic 1493 decree which gave the Spanish the rights to any new land discovered west of the Azores, as long as the Spanish made "God's name known there." Hence, the Spanish conquest of the New World started as a roundabout extension of the Holy Crusades.

A succession of Spanish expeditions into the Caribbean and Gulf of Mexico led to the rapid conquest of Mexico and Central America. Conquistador Hernán Cortés subdued the Valley of Mexico Aztecs in three years (1519-21), and the allegiance of other Aztecs and Mayans followed quickly. At first the Indians were enslaved, but another papal bull issued in 1537 by Pope Paul III discouraged slavery. Consequently Spain's policy changed from "conquest" to "pacification"—an ambiguous policy all too often abused.

Basically, the Spanish mission system worked thus: The padres, always in the company of armed escorts, approached groups of natives and offered them the protection of the Church and the Spanish crown in return for a willingness to undergo religious instruction. Those who agreed were congregated at a suitable spot and directed to build a mission. The mission in turn became both a refuge and a place for natives to learn European farming techniques and other trades, as well as Catholic ways. Those who rebelled were punished, and those who organized rebellions were executed. Once pacification was complete, the mission became a secularized church community (pueblo) and the missionaries moved on to new areas. The system worked well among the docile cultures of Central Mexico but was often unsuccessful among the nomadic, fiercely independent Indians of Northern Mexico.

Northern Mexico Colonization

Missionary zeal wasn't the only motive driving the Spanish conquistadors. The rugged terrain of the conquered New World was thought to contain vast mineral caches, perhaps even gold and silver. When a substantial vein of silver was discovered at Taxco, Gro., in 1522, Spanish hopes seemed confirmed and an all-out effort to find more of the precious metal—often under the guise of missionization—began less than a year after Cortés's arrival.

As the conquistadors took control of Central Mexico, the indigenous populations fed them myths about cities of gold and silver to the north, an obvious ploy (which the Spanish leadership never fully seemed to recognize) to rid themselves of the conquistadors. The mythical cities were never found, but during one push northward a huge silver deposit called La Bufa—much larger than the one found at Taxco—was discovered in Zacatecas in 1540.

After the opening of La Bufa mine in 1546, Zacatecas became an important point of departure for further exploration and missionization of the North. So thorough was their hunt for silver that the Spanish uncovered every large deposit in Mexico, and soon New Spain was minting its own silver coins and financing the colonization of the entire continent.

Many of the largest silver caches—along with gold deposits—were found in the Sierra Madre Occidental regions of western Chihuahua, Durango, and eastern Sonora. The Spanish crown took one-fifth (the origin of the popular term "El Quinto") of all treasures, and the Spanish officers in charge of mining the silver usually took a fifth for themselves as well.

Meanwhile, the missionization of northeast Mexico was proceeding poorly. The nomadic people of Arido America were no more susceptible to Spanish rule than they had been to Aztec rule. This was due partly to hostility toward outsiders, and partly because the people of the northeast were much less homogeneous in culture, language, and dialect. The Spanish had managed to gain a foothold on the Río Pánuco near Tampico, but two Cortés expeditions into the Río Bravo area in 1528 were forced to return south the same year.

Sometime in the late 1520s (the exact date is unknown), the legendary Alvar Nuñez Cabeza de Vaca and a Moorish slave named Esteban (considered the first black to arrive in the New World) departed from Cuba to explore the Gulf of Mexico coast. After their ship ran aground on the Florida coast, they attempted to reach New Spain on animal-hide boats and became stranded on Galveston Island, Texas. Although their reception by the Karankawa of Galveston Island was less than warm, Cabeza de Vaca and Esteban ended up living with various Amerindian tribes throughout the American Southwest as they traveled westward on foot for the next nine years.

During this remarkable journey De Vaca learned six Amerindian languages and developed a widespread reputation among the Indians as a healer, but in 1536 he headed south into Sonora and rejoined his own people. He later became an outspoken critic against the Spanish treatment of Amerindians and was eventually banished by the colonial administration to a remote Latin American outpost.

Tantalized by Cabeza de Vaca's secondhand stories of gold cities, the colonial government commissioned Francisco Vasquez de Coronado to explore the lands to the north. Coronado's explorations (as far north as Oklahoma and Kansas) never yielded any gold or silver, but along the way he left missionaries in the upper Rio Grande valley to "pacify" the people. This eventually led to the discovery of El Paso del Norte, the "northern pass" in the mountains of northern Chihuahua, through which a well-worn trade route eventually developed (culminating in the booming El Paso-Juárez transborder metropolis).

Other Spanish settlements in northwest Mexico followed. Italian-born Padre Eusebio Francisco Kino managed to establish 25 missions in Sonora and Arizona, where he is said to have converted thousands of Amerindians to the one true faith, Roman Catholicism. In 1701 Kino accompanied an expedition from northwestern Sonora to the mouth of the Río Colorado, confirming an earlier claim that Baja California was

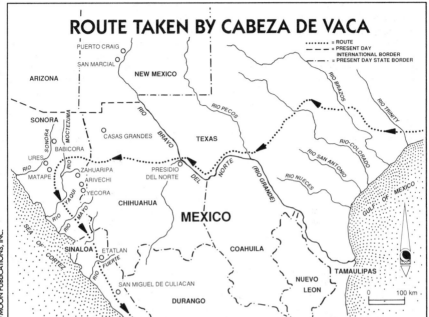

ROUTE TAKEN BY CABEZA DE VACA

a peninsula. Around this same time, missionaries in northeastern Mexico were able to push northward into Coahuila, Nuevo León, and Tamaulipas (and beyond into Texas and Louisiana). No gold or silver was discovered in this region, but Spanish settlers found the terrain well-suited to large-scale farming and cattle ranching, ultimately more stable and profitable than prospecting for shiny metals.

In 1746 José de Escandón, a highly regarded military officer and colonial administrator, received an assignment to survey the Gulf of Mexico coastal plains from Río Pánuco north to the Nueces River in Texas. The following year Escandón began sending colonists to the area and named it the state of Nuevo Santander after his home province in Spain. Other Spanish *empresarios* established similar colonies in the northeast, which soon became Mexico's cattle kingdom.

The New World's first cowboys or *vaqueros* (those who work with *vacas* or cows) bred horses to use in ranch work. Although the colonists had met with hostile Indians from time to time, the population (or what was left of it after disease

decimated a large portion) in this area wasn't a major problem until Spanish horses got into the hands of the Plains Indians to the north. With the increased mobility, Comanches began moving southward from the Rocky Mountains. They displaced the Apaches, who moved deeper into Northern Mexico, displacing in turn the more peaceful Jumano and Coahuiltecan tribes. Although some Apache groups were lured into the mission system, the Spanish continued to battle the Apaches right up until Mexican independence.

INDEPENDENCE AND CHANGING BORDERS

Independence From Spain

By the end of the 18th century the Catholic Church in Mexico had amassed huge amounts of wealth and had become a lender to the colony's growing entrepreneurial class. At the other end of the economic spectrum, the increasing numbers of mestizos (Mexican-born residents of mixed Spanish and Amerindian ancestry) were denied land ownership and other rights, and generally were treated as second-class citizens.

Fearing that the Church was becoming too powerful, King Charles III of Spain decreed in 1804 that all church funds were to be turned over to the royal coffers. As padres all over Mexico were forced to comply with the decree (calling back large sums of money that had been lent out to entrepreneurs), economic chaos ensued. Mexicans blamed their economic and social problems on Spain's remote rule; when Napoleon invaded Spain in 1808, limiting authority to Spanish loyalists in Mexico City, the disaffected clergy began planning a revolt.

Mexico's struggle for independence from Spain began on 16 Sept. 1810 (celebrated annually as *diez y seis* or Mexican Independence Day), when mestizo Padre Miguel Hidalgo y Costilla issued a call for independence known as the *Grito de Dolores* ("Cry of Dolores") in Guanajuato. Although the rebels who gathered around Hidalgo soon captured Zacatecas, Valladolid, and San Luis Potosí, Mexico wasn't completely free of Spanish rule for another 11 years. When Hidalgo was captured and executed by loyalists, another padre took his place and the fighting continued until Mexico City acceded to the demands of the rebels in 1821.

The Plan De Iguala And
The Constitution Of 1824

The 1821 Plan de Iguala treaty between Spain and Mexico guaranteed three political underpinnings of the new regime: the religious dominance of the Catholic Church, a constitutional monarchy, and equal rights for mestizos as well as Mexican-born Spaniards. Former Viceroy Agustín de Iturbide was appointed emperor of the new republic but his reign lasted only two years before he was overthrown by another junta that established a short-lived federal republic called Los Estados Unidos de México— the United States of Mexico—in 1824.

Over the next six years the Mexican republic endured two more coups and it wasn't until 1829 that all Spanish troops were expelled from Mexico. In 1832 all non-Dominican missions were secularized and converted to parish churches. Another change in policy involved the encouragement of Anglo-American immigration to the northeastern Mexican state of Coahuila y Texas (actually one state).

Santa Anna And
The Republic Of Texas

In 1833 Antonio López de Santa Anna, a megalomaniac general in charge of enforcing the expulsion of Spanish troops, seized power and revoked the Constitution of 1824, thus initiating a series of events that eventually led to a war with the United States and the resultant loss of huge amounts of Mexican territory (see "The Mexican-American War and the Gadsden Purchase," below).

Mexican citizens everywhere were angry at the revocation of their republican constitution by a self-appointed dictator who called himself the "Napoleon of the West." Particularly upset were the Anglo-American immigrants who had voluntarily left behind their U.S. citizenship in order to take Mexican citizenship under that constitution and live in the northern half of Coahuila y Texas. In 1836 the "Texicans" declared an independent Republic of Texas, fought and lost San Antonio's infamous Battle of the Alamo, and then routed Santa Anna's defending troops in San Jacinto, Texas.

Defeated and captured, Santa Anna signed an independence treaty in which he reportedly agreed to the Rio Grande border between Mexico and the new Texan republic. He then was allowed to return to Mexico City. There matters lay until the U.S. granted statehood to the near-bankrupt Texan republic in 1845. Later the Santa Anna government claimed that they had never recognized the Río Bravo (Rio Grande) as the Texas-Mexico border and that Texas only extended as far south as the Nueces River (about 160 km/100 miles north of the Rio Grande at the widest gap). In addition, Mexico claimed that Texas had been granted independence in 1836 with the condition that its government never seek annexation to the United States.

The Mexican-American War And
The Gadsden Purchase

Which side violated the independence treaty? Modern history books on each side of the Rio Grande tell the story differently; yet neither wields a copy of the treaty as proof. Logic suggests both parties violated the treaty, the Mexicans by changing the agreed border, the Texans by ignoring the promise to remain independent of the United States. At any rate, when the U.S. Army moved in to claim the area south of the

Nueces River (and west, including about half of present-day New Mexico and Colorado), Santa Anna retaliated by sending troops across the Río Bravo/Rio Grande, thus starting the Mexican-American War.

After a series of skirmishes along the Río Bravo (during which 200 Texans of Irish descent from San Patricio, Texas, deserted the U.S. Army and fought for the Mexican army), U.S. President James Polk ordered the army to invade Mexico. Mexico City finally fell to U.S. troops in Sept. 1847 and Santa Anna signed the Treaty of Guadalupe Hidalgo in Feb. 1848. In the treaty, Mexico conceded not only the Río Grande-Nueces River area of Texas but also the territories of Nuevo México and Alta California—which together included the present-day states of Colorado, Nevada, and California, and parts of New Mexico, Arizona, Utah, and Wyoming—for a payment of US$25 million and the assumption of US$3 million in claims lodged against the Mexican government by citizens living in these territories.

In retrospect, it is likely that the annexation of Texas was part of a U.S. plan to provoke Mexico into declaring war so that the U.S. would have an opportunity to gain more of the Southwest. The war so damaged Mexico's already weakened economy that in 1853 Santa Anna sold southern Arizona and a section of New Mexico's Mesilla Valley to the U.S. for another US$10 million as part of the Gadsden Purchase (known in Mexico as el Tratado de Gadesden or Venta de la Mesilla). Altogether Mexico lost 51% of its territory as a result of the war; U.S. President Abraham Lincoln later called it "the most unjust war there ever was." Moral recriminations aside, the ultimate political cause for Mexico's loss of territory in the 19th century was a lack of national cohesion (coups d'état were putting a new Mexican president in office an average of every 7½ months) at a time when its more powerful northern neighbor was engaged in active expansion.

For the Mexican population, already strongly dissatisfied with Santa Anna, this additional loss and threatened further loss of territory (at least three postwar American filibuster groups tried to take additional lands from Baja California and Sonora) was the final straw; in 1855 Santa Anna was overthrown by populist Benito Juárez.

CIVIL WAR, REVOLUTION, AND REFORM

Benito Juárez And The War Of Reform

The second half of the 19th century was to be even more turbulent for Mexico than the first. A civil war (the "War of Reform") erupted in 1858 following the removal of Santa Anna in which self-appointed governments in Mexico City and Veracruz vied for national authority. Once again, Church wealth was the principal issue. The liberals, under Zapotec Indian lawyer Benito Juárez, had promulgated a new constitution in 1857 and passed a law further restricting the financial powers of the Church (all Church property, save for church buildings, had to be sold or otherwise relinquished). A reactionary opposition group took control of Mexico City, and fighting continued until 1861, when the liberals won and Juárez was elected president.

Juárez immediately had to deal with the 1862 French invasion of Mexico, which came in response to Mexico's nonpayment of debts to France. Napoleon III's first invading force was defeated at Puebla on the Gulf of Mexico coast, but the following year the French captured the port and continued onward to take Mexico City, where they installed Austrian Ferdinand Maximilian and his wife Carlotta as emperor and empress of Mexico. Under U.S. pressure, the French gradually withdrew from Mexico, Maximilian was executed (Carlotta returned to Europe, widowed and estranged), and Juárez was back in power by 1867.

Over the next four years Juárez initiated many economic and educational reforms. Upon his death in 1872, Juárez's political opponent, Porfirio Díaz, took over and continued those reforms, albeit in a much more authoritarian manner. Díaz (or his cronies) would rule Mexico for the next 28 years, suspending political freedoms such as open elections and a free press but modernizing the country's education and transportation systems.

Foreign Investment In Northern Mexico

Díaz and the "Porfiriato" encouraged foreign investment on a large scale, and in the 1880s vast land tracts in the north were sold to American or European mining, farming, manufacturing, oil, and railway concessions. Mineral ex-

TERRITORIAL LOSSES

MEXICO BEFORE 1836

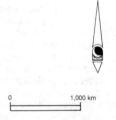

0 — 1,000 km

MEXICO FROM 1836 TO THE PRESENT

1836 : TEXAS DECLARES INDEPENDENCE.
1845 : ANNEXED BY THE UNITED STATES.

1848 : TREATY OF GUADALUPE HIDALGO - CEDED TO THE UNITED STATES.

1848 : NUECES RIVER/RIO BRAVO TERRITORY DISPUTE.

1853 : GADSDEN PURCHASE.

PRESENT MEXICO/UNITED STATES BORDER.

cavation in turn-of-the-century Northern Mexico boomed—gold, silver, copper, lead, zinc, and gypsum were the main finds, along with graphite, mercury, nickel, and sulfur. Foreign oil companies established themselves in Tamaulipas, Veracruz, and Tabasco, and employed large numbers of expatriates. A large proportion—perhaps most—of the income generated by these operations left the country. This money was then used by foreigners to purchase more mines, oil rigs, plantations, and textile factories in Mexico. By 1920, an estimated 75% of Mexico's industrial wealth was concentrated in the hands of foreigners.

The Mexican Revolution
And U.S. Prohibition

By the early 1900s, it was obvious that the gap between rich and poor in Mexico was becoming increasingly wide due to the extreme pro-capitalist policies of the Díaz regime and the total lack of a political voice for workers and peasants. In response to the situation, a liberal opposition group formed (in exile, using Texas as a base) and organized strikes throughout the country, which forced Díaz to announce an election in 1910. His opponent was Francisco Madero, a liberal from Coahuila who was educated in the U.S. (Berkeley, California). But as it became clear that Madero was garnering mass support, Díaz imprisoned him on trumped-up charges June 21, 1910—election day.

Following Díaz's reelection, Madero was released on bail with the provision that he remain in the city of San Luis Potosí. He did—until October—at which time he fled to Texas and began organizing the overthrow of the Díaz government. The rebels, with the assistance of Chihuahua's colorful bandit-turned-revolutionary Francisco "Pancho" Villa and peasant-hero Emiliano Zapata, managed to gain control of the northern Mexican states of Sonora and Chihuahua. Unable to contain the revolution, Díaz resigned in May 1910 and Madero was elected president. The opposition, however, broke into several factions—the Zapatistas, Reyistas, Vasquistas, Villistas, and Felicistas (named for the leaders of each movement)—and Madero was executed in 1913.

For the next six years the various factions played musical chairs with national leadership and Mexico remained extremely unstable. The U.S. supported the Constitutionalist Army Commander-in-Chief, Venustiano Carranza, who formed a government in Veracruz. The notorious Pancho Villa (born Doroteo Arango in Durango) opposed Carranza from his own provisional capital in Guanajuato.

Angered by U.S. support of Carranza, Villa began raiding American border towns. The U.S. response was to send Gen. "Blackjack" Pershing and nearly 5,000 U.S. Cavalry troops into Mexico in an attempt to roust Villa. This "punitive expedition" lasted from March 1916 through

Joining Pancho Villa and Zapata in Mexico City is John (Jack) Reed, the gringo in the back wearing the sombrero and wire-rim glasses. You know, Warren Beatty in Reds.

Feb. 5, 1917; Villa eluded General Pershing but Carranza finally emerged as president.

Carranza then held a historic convention that resulted in the Constitution of 1917 (the current Mexican constitution). It established the *ejido* program, which returned to local communities lands traditionally cultivated by the peasantry, but taken away by rich ranch and plantation owners under Díaz. Three years later opponent Alvaro Obregón (a Sonoran who had served as army chief of the División Noroeste during the revolution) and his supporters overthrew Carranza, who later was assassinated while attempting to flee Mexico City.

Obregón managed to hang onto the office for four years and establish important educational reforms. He was followed by Sonoran Plutarco Elías Calles in 1924. Calles instituted wide-reaching agrarian reforms, including the redistribution of three million hectares of land. He also participated in the establishment of the National Revolutionary Party (PNR), the forerunner of the Institutional Revolutionary Party (PRI), Mexico's dominant party today. In 1928, just as Obregón was elected to serve in the presidency a second time, he was assassinated by a religious fanatic.

In the same year that Obregón originally took power in Mexico City, the U.S. government amended its own constitution to make the consumption, manufacture, and sale of alcoholic beverages a federal offense. This proved to be a disastrous experiment for the U.S. (ushering in an era of organized crime), but was a boon to Mexican border development as Americans rushed into Northern Mexico border towns to buy booze from the restaurants, cantinas, and liquor stores.

American dollars flowed into Mexico as the border towns added casinos and brothels to the assortment of liquor venues. On the negative side, U.S.-Mexico border towns became world-renowned as sleaze capitals. The reputation persisted long after Prohibition ended in the U.S. in 1933 and long after the Mexican government outlawed gambling (but not prostitution, which is still legal in proscribed districts) in 1938, even though the cities wisely managed to channel some of their unexpected revenue into manufacturing, agriculture, and other non-tourist-related development.

Nationalist Reforms And World War II

The year 1934 proved a turning point in modern Mexican history as PNR candidate Lázaro Cárdenas ascended to the presidency. (With Mexico's legacy of election-fixing, it's difficult to use the word "elect" in the usual democratic sense— see "Government," below, for further explanation.) Cárdenas instituted the most sweeping social reforms of any national leader to date, effecting significant changes in education, labor, agriculture, and commerce.

His land reforms included the redistribution of nearly 50 million acres among newly created *ejidos* or agricultural collectives in which land is owned jointly by peasant communities—a legacy that is as hot a debate topic today as it was then. Foreign-owned oil interests were expropriated and a national oil company, Petróleos Mexicanos (PEMEX), was established. Even though foreign investors were compensated for expropriations at fair market value (under a treaty signed by both the U.S. and Mexico), these reforms frightened off prospective investors for many years. It has been only recently that Mexico has been able to reattract foreign capital. Cárdenas also reorganized the PNR as the Mexican Revolution Party (PRM— Partido de la Revolución Mexicana), which soon changed its name to the current-day Institutional Revolutionary Party (PRI—Partido Revolucionario Institucional).

Since the Cárdenas period, Mexican political history has been characterized by comparatively subtle shifts. Mexican leadership succession also has stabilized, a process often referred to as the "institutionalization of the revolution" (meaning the PRI wins every national election). The economy went for a roller-coaster ride in the '70s and early '80s when the government nationalized banks and devalued the peso, but during the two most recent presidencies the economic picture has brightened considerably.

CONTEMPORARY NORTHERN MEXICO

Northern Mexico only began to emerge from its provincial past with the construction of a national railroad system in the late 19th century, when communications between the central and northern states expanded rapidly. During WW II, the Mexican economy was boosted by increased U.S. demand for materials and labor, and also by the scarcity of imported goods in Mexico, which forced the nation to increase domestic production. In addition, Mexican troops fighting in the Pacific for the Allies needed materials, both imported and domestic. This exchange of products between the U.S. and Mexico favored the development of Northern Mexico by sheer virtue of proximity.

Northerners took advantage of their increasing prosperity to reinvest in regional human resources by building Mexico's top universities and technological research centers. Today these educational centers train many of the best and brightest from all over the country.

Another boost to Northern Mexican political and economic development came along in the '80s when former Pres. Miguel de la Madrid proclaimed a new era of modernization and plupartyism—equivalent in word if not in deed to Gorbachev's perestroika/glasnost proclamation. The already-modernizing north and the stronghold of PAN (Partido Acción Nacional, the nation's main opposition party) can only benefit from a relaxation of PRI's hold. The era of optimism was extended by current Mexican Pres. Carlos Salinas, who is a strong supporter of the much-debated NAFTA (North American Free Trade Agreement, see "Economy," below, for more information on the treaty).

In the '90s Northern Mexico is clearly poised to take further advantage of upward shifts in the economy. In 1880 only three northern cities were among Mexico's 25 largest: Monterrey, Saltillo, and Hermosillo. By the '60s, ten of Mexico's 25 largest cities were located in the north.

GOVERNMENT

Political System

Mexico's federal system (Estados Unidos Mexicanos or "United Mexican States") allows for some degree of autonomous rule by state governors and their legislatures. The nine states of mainland Northern Mexico, along with Baja California Norte and Baja California Sur, are considered among the most politically progressive states in the nation. Several northern gov-

ernors and big-city mayors are members of the nation's main opposition party, PAN (Partido Acción Nacional or National Action Party), particularly in Chihuahua, Tamaulipas, San Luis Potosí, and Sinaloa. However, PRI (Partido Revolucionario Institucional or Institutional Revolutionary Party) continues to win every national election.

PAN is sometimes described as a conservative party because of its pro-business stance, yet in the context of Mexican politics it is more reform-minded than PRI. As elsewhere in the world, labels and their meanings shift with time. Many *norteños* are skeptical, and see PRI losses in the north as anomalous. President Salinas's economic successes have also strengthened PRI support among PAN's traditionally northern base.

In spite of PAN victories in the north, Mexican politics has been notorious for election fraud ever since it adopted a republican system in 1917. Hard-boiled cynics insist that all high political offices are part of a ruling dynasty extending outward from the presidency in Mexico City (even municipal mayors in Mexico are called *el presidente* and the local seat of government is the *palacio municipal*). Wags point out other symbolic evidence—the president wears an imperial sash and sits upon a throne when making official proclamations—and the fact that whichever candidate the incumbent endorses always wins the next election.

The *presidentes municipales* appoint city *delegados* to represent federal power at the local level; smaller communities may even have *subdelegados*. These *delegados* and *subdelegados* are the highest authority within their jurisdictions and are part of a chain of command that reaches back to the president of Mexico.

Pres. Carlos Salinas De Gortari

Elected in 1988 by the slimmest margin in PRI history (if in fact the announced election results were accurate), Salinas is considered one of the best and most active presidents Mexico has ever had. He has been involved in government since 1971, and has held posts in both finance and economics; he also directed the campaign of former president Miguel de la Madrid, and served as minister of planning and the budget under the de la Madrid administration.

Salinas's major accomplishment was the adroit application of badly needed economic reforms. This is his strong suit; both his mother and father were economists, and Salinas has an economics degree from UNAM in Mexico City, plus two master's degrees and a Ph.D. from Harvard University in Cambridge, Massachusetts. Mikhail Gorbachev has referred to Salinas's reforms as "Salinastroika," while the Mexican press sometimes calls him *Hormiga Atómica* (Atomic Ant) in reference to his energy and short stature. The president's six-year term ends in 1994; since re-election is not permitted by the Mexican constitution, the hope among his supporters is that the next president will keep the nation on the same reform-minded path.

ECONOMY

Production, Resources, And Income

Per capita income figures for the northern states are well above the Mexican national average (which is US$3950 per year, just ahead of per capita figures for Malaysia, about 30% behind South Korea's). Northerners have a saying to explain their higher productivity: "In Southern Mexico the people want; in Central Mexico they think; in Northern Mexico we work." While this folk axiom may be partially true, the added reality is that Northern Mexico is blessed with a variety of natural resources that are either absent or less accessible in other regions.

Agriculture, ranching, timber, mining, fishing, and manufacturing are Northern Mexico's main revenue-earners. In all of these sectors, Northern Mexico leads the nation in production statistics. Sinaloa, for example, grows over 75% of Mexico's soy and virtually all of its *córtamo* (safflower); the Región Lagunera (Torreón-Lerdo-Gómez Palacio) produces about a third of the nation's cotton; Sonoran fisheries lead the entire Mexican Pacific Ocean and Sea of Cortez coasts (including those surrounding Baja California) in annual fishing takes; Coahuila and San Luis Potosí lead in horse breeding; and Durango and Chihuahua account for half the nation's timber output. In mineral production, Sonora is first in copper (producing nearly all of the nation's output); Zacatecas leads in silver (a third of national output); and Chihuahua produces the most lead and zinc.

The timber industry is limited to the higher slopes of the sierras Madre Oriental and Occidental; mining is limited to the mid-level slopes. Fishing boats work both coasts, but the Sea of Cortez produces the largest catch and Guaymas is the main fishing center. Shrimp, oysters, and tuna are the major money-makers here, followed by seabass and lobster; on the Gulf of Mexico coast, oysters, sardines, and red snapper are the most important. Agriculture and ranching are dispersed more evenly.

Manufacturing is mostly concentrated in the Saltillo-Monterrey area and larger border towns. The latest stars of the manufacturing sector are the *maquiladoras* or in-bond industries, which combine third-world labor costs with first-world capital and management. These are predominantly located in former special export-processing zones along the border, although since 1988 the *maquila* program has been expanded to all of Mexico. Gradually such joint-venture enterprises are distributing themselves farther south into the interior, relieving some of the social and environmental pressures concentrated along the border (see "*Maquiladoras* and the Free Trade Agreement" below).

Border Economy

The border is also the focus of a mostly undocumented shadow economy supported by both legal and illegal migrant Mexican labor in the United States. Mexican labor migration has become so integrated into the regional economy that it is now considered largely responsible for the competitive and stable pricing of U.S. consumer goods. Economists use the term "commodity migrants" to describe social behavior in which labor transports itself to where capital demands it.

That Mexican labor is essential to U.S. production is also indicated by the cyclical nature of migration statistics relative to upturns and downturns in the U.S. economy. Intertwined with the shadow economy, the entire border economy tends to move with the U.S. economic tide.

The System

On a macroeconomic level, Northern Mexico finds itself caught between two economic systems. Because of its proximity to the U.S., the regional economy has tended to be American-influenced yet subject to the same vicissitudes of the national Mexican economy as the rest of the country, most pointedly a weak currency and steady inflation. Although the country's current-account balance rose from a deficit US$6.2 billion in 1982 to a surplus of US$4 billion in 1987, the inflation rate that same year hit 146%. Because of its regional ties to the U.S., particularly Texas and the Southwest, Northern Mexico's economy weathered this period better than many other areas in Mexico.

However, since the election of President Salinas the nation has moved closer to U.S.-style, growth-led economics, thus lessening the schizoid nature of the North's regional economy. In 1988—the year Salinas was elected—the Bank of Mexico was able to slow the runaway devaluation of the Mexican peso to almost a halt; it's now on a steady keel with the U.S. dollar, a considerable improvement over the 1976-87 period in which the currency slid from eight pesos to the dollar to over 2000.

One of the biggest steps taken by the Salinas government was the reprivatizing of the national banking system, the telephone system, and several other state industries (PEMEX is the major exception). Still, the eight largest employers in Mexico are government agencies connected with education, social security, PEMEX, or defense. Among private corporations, the largest employers are General Motors (58,000 employees) and TelMex (49,900).

National inflation is now running at about 12-18% per annum, down from 20-25% in 1991. Foreign exchange reserves are rising; from 1990 to 1991 Mexico's foreign reserves doubled from US$8.4 billion to US$16.7 billion, the highest in the country's history. Exports for 1992 totaled US$27.3 billion; foreign debt as a percentage of exports is 20%, less than half of what it was in 1983. GNP growth is a very respectable four percent per annum and an increase to five to six percent is a reasonable projection by 1996 or so. Remarkably, the national budget deficit hit zero in 1992 and at the end of 1993 ran a surplus for the first time in Mexican history.

Some optimistic economists predict that if Mexico continues its current economic reforms, it may become the world's fastest-growing economy by the year 2000. Growth in Northern Mexico will probably be slower, however, since much of the current and projected growth is in areas of Mexico that are "catching up" with the North.

Ejidos

One of the most unique features of the Mexican economy is the *ejido* institution. An *ejido* is a land tract held in common by a peasant community that includes not only cultivated fields but also school properties, urban zones, water and forest resources, and any other facilities or resources either native to the land or produced by collective efforts. *Ejidos* are granted to *ejidatarios* by the government without rents or fees of any kind and originally were nontransferrable, nonattachable, and inalienable, i.e., *ejido* lands couldn't be sold, used as loan collateral, or taken away by local, regional or national legal bodies.

According to Mexican law, *ejidos* are considered neither state property nor private property but are entities of the "social interest sector." How they are used is solely the concern of the peasant communities that hold them, but around 95% of them are "individual" *ejidos* in which the common holdings are divided into individual plots and cultivated by individual *ejidatarios* and their families. The remaining five percent are "collective" *ejidos* that pool all land resources for collective production.

The *ejido* came into being under the Constitution of 1917 as a way of restoring lands that had been taken from the native people by rich *hacendados* (big ranchers and plantation owners) during Spanish colonization and early Mexican independence. The number and total acreage of Mexico's *ejidos* is not well documented but by 1970 they were estimated to encompass around 46% of national farmlands.

Various bits of legislation enacted since the *ejido's* 1917 inception have alternately strengthened and weakened the program. In the '80s laws were passed that allowed *ejidatarios* to lease their lands to neighboring private estates for agricultural or livestock purposes. Recently established regulations now permit the sale of *ejido* lands.

Has the *ejido* program been successful? On the one hand, it has kept hereditary lands in the hands of peasant communities who have worked them for hundreds of years—without them, many *ejidatarios* would probably become landless migrant workers. On the other hand, because *ejido* production is notoriously low (as are fixed prices for agricultural products), the need for cash to survive in Mexico's cash economy has forced many *ejidatarios* to work as laborers on private neighboring lands. As a result, it has been estimated that *ejidatarios* are among the poorest and most exploited of Mexico's rural workers.

All *ejidatarios* are automatic members of PRI's peasant division, but because of their overall lack of education and political experience, they're easily manipulated by PRI leaders in Mexico City and hence are relatively powerless. The selling of *ejido* lands, as is now permitted, may gradually erode the *ejido* system, although it will certainly enrich many *ejidatarios* in the short term.

Maquiladoras
And The Free Trade Agreement

Since 1974 the *maquiladora* (also called "twin-plant" or "in-bond" factory) industry—in which foreign-owned companies build manufacturing facilities in Mexico, train Mexican workers, and export the profits—has grown at an average annual rate of approximately 17%. According to Wharton Econometrics, around 200 new *maquiladora* plants were established in Mexico in 1991, bringing the total to around 2,250. Most recently, the benefit to Mexico had been direct employment for 560,000 Mexicans along with the generation of around $3 billion in annual revenue—a sum second only to PEMEX revenue as a source of national income.

Maquilas were once restricted to special "export processing zones" within 12.5 miles of the border, but the Mexican government has extended the geographic zone of eligibility for *maquilas* to include the entire country in order to compete with other world labor markets (primarily Asia). *Maquila*-made products enjoy duty-free status when imported to the foreign company's country. Conversely, parts and raw materials imported into Mexico for use by the *maquiladoras* are tax exempt.

One of the intentions of the *maquila* program has been to slow the flow of migrant labor to the U.S. and Canada by enticing Mexicans to stay at home and work at foreign-owned companies. By allowing foreign (primarily U.S.) capital to use inexpensive Mexican labor without paying taxes on the export of finished products, it's supposed to be a win-win situation; Mexico gets jobs and U.S. business makes a profit. But as long as the apparent standard of living is

higher in *El Norte, maquila* jobs are not going to satisfy everybody.

NAFTA: Enter the much ballyhooed North American Free Trade Agreement, called El Tratado de Libre Comercio in Mexico. Finally ratified by the U.S. Congress in January 1994—and by the Canadian and Mexican governments much earlier—NAFTA will gradually drop nearly all taxes and tariffs on goods exchanged between the U.S., Canada, and Mexico. Supporters say the treaty will stimulate the economies of all three countries by lifting trade barriers and taking full advantage of the comparative production strengths in each country.

NAFTA opponents in the U.S. and Canada claim that as the treaty goes into effect, North American jobs will be lost to Mexico as American and Canadian companies rush to set up shop in Mexico, leaving closed factories behind. Industrial flight is already in full swing without the treaty, respond the treaty's supporters, since many North American companies have been moving manufacturing operations to Mexico (and elsewhere) to take advantage of the large, inexpensive, and productive labor force as well as the growing demand for imported goods. Neither Mexican nor U.S. law forbids this. With or without NAFTA, Mexico will continue to attract foreign manufacturers, traders, and investors.

Without NAFTA, however, North American-made products have difficulty competing in the Mexican market due to high tariffs and other trade barriers, or in the world market due to high labor costs. Hence capital (and jobs) flow to Mexico, creating a foreign market North America is unable to tap as long as trade barriers remain in place. Mexico is a ready-made market; many Mexican-made consumer goods cost more than their North American counterparts but are of lesser quality.

Furthermore, say NAFTA supporters, North American jobs are lost not only to the *maquiladoras*, but also to immigrant Mexican labor flooding north of the border. If the U.S. were to liberalize trade restrictions on Mexican products, the Mexican economy would presumably improve and *maquilas* would become unnecessary from the Mexican perspective.

With the treaty now in effect, Mexico expects the short-term, direct creation of 260,000 new jobs, plus 650,000 indirect jobs. As the economic gap between the two countries diminishes, say NAFTA advocates, illegal immigration to the U.S. will become less and less of a problem. As President Salinas has said: "I want to export goods—not people; if I do not create jobs for Mexicans in Mexico, they will merely walk across the border looking for jobs in the U.S., and then the American worker may lose *his* job."

The expanding Mexican consumer market brought on by an increased standard of living should further strengthen a hitherto untapped demand for North American products, thus increasing jobs in the U.S. and Canada. The point many people seem to be missing is the fact that even if Americans could keep all U.S. investment within the country, they would still lose jobs to illegal (and nontax-paying) migrant labor from Mexico. History shows that labor follows capital, in spite of all attempts to separate the two.

In many ways, NAFTA recognizes an already existing economic reality, namely the "silent commercial integration" that Mexico and the U.S. have cultivated over the past 150 years as a result of sharing a 3,000-km border. In spite of Mexico's number-three ranking among international trade partners, it has yet to be offered "most favored nation" status by the United States.

American exports now account for 75% of Mexico's total imports while 80% of Mexico's exports go to the United States. The advantage to NAFTA is that it adds Canada to the equation, thus increasing three-way trade shares. With competitive trade blocs emerging in East Asia and the European Community, a North America-wide trade alliance makes good long-range economic sense.

One of the more sobering objections to NAFTA comes from environmentalist groups. Pointing to *maquila*-linked pollution in Mexico, environmentally conscious critics fear that the expansion of Mexico's industrial sector will increase the threat to the country's air, soils, and waterways.

If NAFTA leads to increased Mexican prosperity, the local and national governments will theoretically have more funds to spend on environmental protection and enforcement than they have now. As with the employment issue, however, the potential for industrial abuse exists with or without NAFTA.

THE PEOPLE

North Vs. South

Northern Mexicans see themselves as almost a breed apart from their compatriots to the south. They're proud of being *norteños* (northerners), and this pride is evident in the many ways they manage to declare their northern-ness through language, dress, food, and custom.

First, some stereotypes: northerners wear wavy-brimmed, Texas-style Stetson headgear and boots; southerners wear flat-brimmed *sombreros* and sandals; northerners eat wheat tortillas; southerners prefer corn; northerners are comparatively punctual; southerners pay no attention to time; northerners are tall and fair-skinned; southerners are short and dark. Such statements are often heard in Mexico, but any foreign visitor traveling cross-country will quickly note both the relative inaccuracy of these stereotypes as well as the kernels of truth that have propagated them.

Ask a *norteño* what separates the northern character from the southern and the most common answer will be that northerners are more hardworking, more self reliant, and better looking! To the average *norteño*, southerners seem to rely excessively on fate and the Mexican government to see them through their lives. A special scorn is reserved for *chilangos*, a derogatory term used by *norteños* in reference to Mexico City politicians or businesspeople who come and try to tell the northerners how to run things. Ask a northerner to imitate *chilango* speech and they'll mimic a high, mincing voice.

The reciprocal view from the south—heavily influenced by the Mexican academic bias toward the pre-Cortesian cultures of Southern Mexico—is keyed to the superiority southerners feel in being descended from the Aztecs and Mayans. Many Mexico City scholars still refer to the pre-Cortesian Amerindian cultures of the North as *los bárbaros del norte*, viewing them as the least civilized of Mexico's ancient cultures. To southerners, *norteño* speech sounds like a low growl.

AMERINDIANS OF NORTHERN MEXICO

GROUP	PRIMARY LOCATION	CURRENT APPROXIMATE POPULATION
Huastec	San Luis Potosí, Hidalgo, Tamaulipas, Veracruz	91,000
Tarahumara	Sierra Madre Occidental, Chih. & Dgo.	62,000
Mayo	Sonora	56,600
Tepehuan	Durango, Chihuahua, Zacatecas	17,600
Huichol	southeast Durango, Nayarit, Jalisco	14,800
Cora	southern Durango, Nayarit	10,200
Yaqui	Sonora	9,700
Seri	coastal Sonora	500
Papago & Pima	Sonora, Sinaloa	490
Kikapú (Kickapoo)	Coahuila	200

A more significant difference between North and South is the average standard of living. With the exception of Mexico D.F., Northern Mexico states have a higher degree of literacy—as high as 95% in Nuevo León—than those of the South. (In contrast, such southern states as Chiapas, Oaxaca, and Guerrero have literacy rates under 70%.) The average number of households with running water and electricity is also greater in the North, and the incidence of malnutrition is far less.

Criollo Vs. Mestizo

The tension between North and South dates to a caste system that existed in colonial New Spain and that to some degree still exists in a subtler and more simplified form throughout modern Mexico. In colonial Mexico the most privileged were the *gachupines* (pure-blooded Spaniards born in Spain), followed by criollos (pure-blooded Spaniards born in Mexico), mestizos (mixed Indian-Spanish born in Mexico), and *indios* (pure-blooded Indians). In many cases the Spanish lumped together *indios* and mestizos as simply *indígenas*. One of the ironies of the colonial caste system was that the *gachupines* themselves were descended from a 700-year mixing of Moors and Iberians, the conquerors and the conquered—a pattern the Spaniards repeated in the New World.

Their profound knowledge of how to survive in the desert made the Amerindian cultures of Northern Mexico more difficult for the Spaniards to subdue than any other indigenous groups in continental Mexico. Nevertheless, by the late colonial era, when Spaniards and criollos were settling the north in larger numbers, most of the Indian population of the region (which had been sparse to begin with) had been eliminated through disease or colonial violence. Hence a relatively larger proportion of Northern Mexico's population traces its ancestry to criollo or Spaniard (rather than mestizo or Indian) origin. Today the average *norteño* physiognomy tends to be more European than Amerindian.

To at least some degree, these physical differences play into the racial prejudices held by North and South. The Mexican government recognizes *mestizaje* ("mestizo-ism," or "mixing") as the root cultural characteristic of Mexico, yet distinguishes between two kinds of mestizos, the *indomestizos* of the South ("in whom indigenous characteristics predominate") and the *euromestizos* of the North ("in whom European traits prevail"). Also recognized are smaller groups of *afromestizos* in the southern Gulf coastal regions (particularly Veracruz), where African slaves were brought in by the Spanish to fill labor shortages caused by the rapidly shrinking indigenous population toward the end of the colonial era.

In many ways the schism between mestizos and Spaniards (and/or criollos) that led to the Mexican independence struggle (see "The History," pp. 22-35) was less of an issue in the North than in the South because of the northern frontier context. In addition to coping with the rugged terrain, Northern Mexicans have borne the brunt of the nation's Indian wars, revolutions, and U.S. invasions. This almost continual confrontation with the outside world has engendered a high degree of self-reliance and solidarity among *norteños*.

This self-reliance contrasts strongly with the traditional paternalism of southern Mexico, where each person tends to participate in a web of "patron-client" relationships in which one is either taking care of someone or being taken care of—in either case for reciprocal services rendered. (This relationship is mirrored in the enormous faith Southern Mexicans show for their patron saints and the relative importance of *compadrazgo* or "godparenthood.") Although the North-South differences are not nearly as strict as this sociological explanation may imply, the tendencies are nevertheless observable.

Population Density And Growth
One reason highway traffic in Northern Mexico is pleasantly light compared to that farther south is simply that the northern states are the nation's least densely populated. Eight out of nine states fall below the national average of 41.3 persons per square km, ranging from a low of 10 persons per square km in Sonora to a high of 38 in Sinaloa; Nuevo León slightly exceeds the national average at 48 persons per square km. Most of the latter state's population is found in the metropolitan Monterrey area.

Mexico's population growth rate is currently estimated at 1.9% per annum, relatively low for a developing country. The overall rate for the North is even lower, perhaps due to the relatively higher levels of income and education.

Indígenas
Of the estimated nine million Amerindians who inhabited Mexico when the Spanish arrived in 1518, only a relatively small proportion survived the conquest. The principal causes of their decline in absolute numbers as well as in cultural varieties and cultural vitality include: the sudden changes in the socioeconomic and cultural order brought about by the conquest; the onslaught of diseases (smallpox, chicken pox, measles, malaria) brought from Europe and Africa, against which the indigenous populations had no natural defense; the violent form in which the conquest was accomplished and the local populations were kept under control; and the exploitation and marginalization to which the Indians were subjected for over 300 years.

By 1568, only 47 years after the defeat of the Aztecs, the Indian population had declined to an estimated 2.5 million. Later, at the beginning of the 17th century, the total population of New Spain was approximately 7.6 million, of which the predominant proportion were mestizos; the indigenous population had shrunk to just 750,000.

Today the Mexican government classifies as *indígena* those persons: 1) who are monolingual in an "aboriginal" language; 2) whose first language is aboriginal but who also speak Spanish; or 3) who speak no aboriginal languages but whose "physical and cultural characteristics are aboriginal." According to this classification system, there are 56 indigenous groups (with 90 indigenous languages) in Mexico today, most of whom live in the southern states, with a total population of approximately 5.2 million (six percent of the nation's total population).

Around 240,000 *indígenas* reside in the nine states of Northern Mexico (not counting the Cora and Huichol, who reside in southern Durango in small numbers—perhaps as many as 2,000—but who, for the most part, are centered in Nayarit and Jalisco). Most numerous are the Huastecs of San Luis Potosí; the Tarahumaras of the Sierra Madre Occidental; the Tepehuanes of Durango, Chihuahua, and Zacatecas; and the Yaquis of Sonora. The Papagos, Pimas, Mayos, and Seris of Sonora, along with the Kikapús of Coahuila, are fewer in number (500 or less per group) and are considered in danger of cultural extinction.

Immigrants
For Northern Mexicans, *mestizaje* is more than a blend of Spanish and Indian heritages. The mix is typically more complicated, mainly because Northern Mexico remained a frontier area much longer than most of the nation and hence has attracted people who arrived in the New World long after the Spanish first colonized the Mexican mainland. Transmigration via the U.S. has also had a substantial influence on Northern Mexico's ethnic makeup.

During the late 19th and early 20th centuries, large groups of Mennonites and Mormons, fleeing religious persecution in the U.S. and Canada, immigrated to the fertile plains of the North.

These groups—for the most part of Northern European descent—have had a huge impact on Mexican farming practices and have become somewhat integrated into the overall social fabric, particularly in Chihuahua and Nuevo León.

Other immigrants who pioneered the Northern Mexican frontier included: Chinese laborers who came to work in 19th-century mines and railroad camps and many of whose descendants are now successful city merchants; Greek farmers who turned the Valle de Culiacán into one of the most productive farm areas in all of Mexico; and Mexican intellectuals, artists, and dissidents fleeing political oppression in the South (and gravitating toward Chihuahua, Hermosillo, Durango, Mazatlán, Monterrey, or Tampico). Many of these newcomers intermarried and their descendants have added much to Northern Mexico's multicultural spirit.

RELIGION

The original inhabitants of Mexico were indoctrinated in the ways of Roman Catholicism by Spanish missionaries between the 16th and 19th centuries. That Catholicism is now the majority religion in Mexico (around 90%) is an amazing achievement considering that it was laid over a vast variety of native belief systems in existence for perhaps thousands of years, and also given the fact that the Mexicans eventually forcefully expelled the Spanish from their country.

Of the small existing Protestant population, most are Indians in the South who were missionized by North Americans in the 19th and 20th centuries. A few colonies of Mormons and Mennonites also thrive in the state of Chihuahua. Although many Spanish Jews arrived in the early European migration to Mexico, the Spanish Inquisition forced a preponderant number to convert to Catholicism.

Mexican Catholicism

In contrast to their Christian counterparts in North America and northern Europe, who are mainly Protestant, Mexican Catholics tend to be devout practitioners of their faith. Mexican Catholicism, however, has its own variations that distinguish the religion from its European predecessors. Some of these variations can be traced to preexisting Indian spiritual traditions that were absorbed by the Catholic faith, and as such are localized according to tribe.

One variation that is common to all of Mexican Catholicism is the Virgin of Guadalupe cult, which began in 1531 when a dark-skinned Virgin Mary appeared before the peasant Juan Diego in a series of three visions at Tepeyac, near Mexico City (which coincidentally was a sacred Aztec site dedicated to the goddess Tonantzin). Many Mexican churches are named for Our Lady of Guadalupe, who has become so fused with Mexican identity that the slogan ¡Viva Guadalupe! is commonly used at political rallies. The official feast day for Guadalupe, Dec. 12, is fervently celebrated throughout the country.

At one time most of Northern Mexico was under the ecclesiastical jurisdiction of the Guadalajara diocese; now there are regional dioceses centered in many Northern Mexican cities. Since there are fewer churches per capita in rural areas of Northern Mexico than farther south, a church (iglesia) will sometimes hold as many as 18 masses a day.

Roadside Religion

Occasionally along Mexico's roadways you'll see small roadside crosses (sometimes in clusters) or shrines. Often placed at fatal accident sites, each cross marks a soul's point of departure from this world. Larger shrines containing Christ or Virgin figures have been erected to confer blessings or protection on passing travelers. They can vary from simple enclosures made of vegetable-oil cans to elaborate sculptural designs.

BOB RACE

OUT AND ABOUT

SIGHTSEEING ITINERARIES

Many of the places described in this guide can be reached within one or two days by car or bus from the U.S. border. Still, the total area covered encompasses over half of Mexico's surface area; time and money constraints will compel most of us to make advance decisions as to which parts we're going to see and which parts will have to be left out.

Most visitors entering Northern Mexico by road approach either from the northwest (San Luis Río Colorado, Nogales, Agua Prieta) or from the northeast (Piedras Negras, Nuevo Laredo, Matamoros), hence the following suggested itineraries are divided by angle of entry. Persons with more money than time can fly to any of Northern Mexico's many airports, thus avoiding the northwest-northeast thoroughfares. Road travel, however, is the top choice of those who really want to experience the most of what these regions have to offer.

These are only suggested itineraries, to be adjusted according to individual tastes and energy. Some people are content to spend two weeks or more in one place; others prefer to see and experience as many different places as they can, regardless of time spent in each locale. In Mexico it usually pays to be a little underambitious with your travel plans; don't try to see too much in too short an interval or your travels may quickly become a tedious chore.

Northwest

If you have only five days to spend, consider staying within the state of Sonora, where you can explore Pinacate National Park, the historic Jesuit missions, the beaches of Bahía Kino and San Carlos, or the colonial city of Alamos. Or head straight for the state of Chihuahua's *barrancas* (canyons) if hiking or canyoneering is your particular interest, and—if time permits—stop off in the state capital of Chihuahua on your way out for a little culture and history.

With eight days to explore, you could add parts of Sinaloa, including colonial El Fuerte, the former Sierra Madre mining center of Cosalá, and the beaches of Mazatlán.

Ten days would allow the addition of a foray into Chihuahua's Sierra Tarahumara (Copper Canyon) area via the spectacular Chihuahua al Pacífico rail journey from Los Mochis, Sinaloa.

If you have two weeks for the northwest, consider making a Sonora-Sinaloa-Durango-Chihuahua loop, taking in the best along the way: the Sonora missions and Alamos; Mazatlán; the scenic Mazatlán-Durango mountain highway; historic Parral; and the Copper Canyon. The scenery along this loop encompasses parts of the Sonoran Desert, the Pacific Ocean, the Sierra Madre Occidental, and the Chihuahuan Desert.

Northeast

For the naturalist, a five-day trip would allow plenty of time to explore the Gulf of Mexico coast from Matamoros, N.L., to Tampico, Tamps., an area known for good fishing, deserted beaches, intracoastal lagoons, marshes, and barrier islands. Depending on your interests, an enjoyable five-day sojourn alternatively could be spent exploring the Monterrey-Saltillo area in Nuevo León—shopping in the markets and malls of these two very different cities and visiting the Cumbres de Monterrey National Park (which includes Horsetail Falls, the caves of Villa de García, and Huasteca Canyon).

With eight days to spend, the above Gulf Coast and Monterrey-Saltillo itineraries could be combined. A good 10-day trip might include these along with a visit to Ciudad Valles and the lush Huasteca region of San Luis Potosí. If colonial architecture is of major interest, substitute the city of San Luis Potosí for Monterrey in your 10-day trip.

If you have two weeks, consider a loop which takes in the Gulf of Mexico coast, Monterrey-Saltillo (and/or Cumbres de Monterrey National Park), the Región Huasteca, San Luis Potosí, and the exquisitely restored silver city of Zacatecas.

North Central

Road entry into Mexico via Ciudad Juárez or Ojinaga (opposite the West Texas towns of El Paso or Presidio) misses out on the coastal attractions along the Sea of Cortez or Gulf of Mexico. Nevertheless, this is the most direct route to Casas Grandes, the Sierra Tarahumara (Copper Canyon area), Parral, Durango, and the Región Lagunera. Any of these destinations could be accomplished within a a five- to seven-day trip.

An ambitious 8- to 10-day circuit from Juárez/El Paso or Ojinaga/Presidio might head south to Chihuahua's state capital, then to the Sierra Tarahumara, Durango, and Zacatecas, returning north through Saltillo, Las Cumbres de Monterrey National Park, and Monterrey to Laredo, Texas. From Juárez/El Paso, you could also toss in a stop at the Paquimé ruins in Casas Grandes.

A desert-mountain-sea alternative along the same route might divert west from Durango to Mazatlán, then up the Sea of Cortez coast to Hermosillo, from where it is possible to return by road to El Paso via Agua Prieta. This loop takes in the Chihuahuan Desert, the Sierra Madre Occidental, the Sea of Cortez, and the Sonoran Desert.

The Grand Tour

Road warriors with flexible schedules can drive through all nine states of Northern Mexico from coast to coast—taking in all the sights mentioned above—comfortably within a month. A schedule of five or six weeks would allow more time to explore sidetrack destinations like Real de Catorce, S.L.P. and Coahuila's Sierra del Carmen, as well as more time for resting and soaking it all in.

An itinerary that would lead you through the best of Northern Mexico would include: Pinacate National Park, Son.; the Sierra Tarahumara (Urique and Copper Canyons, Basaseachic Falls), Chih.; the Paquimé ruins at Casas Grandes, Chih.; Alamos, Son.; Mazatlán, Sin.; the Mazatlán-Durango drive along Mexico 40; Zacatecas and Guadalupe, Zac.; San Luis Potosí, S.L.P.; El Potosí National Park, S.L.P.; the Región Huasteca, S.L.P.; La Pesca, Tamps. (plus Tampico for seafood lovers); El Cielo, Tamps., Monterrey, N.L.; Cumbres de Monterrey National Park, N.L.; Saltillo, Coah.; and the Colombia-Matamoros drive parallel to the Río Bravo/Rio Grande along Mexico 2.

OUTDOOR RECREATION

Some of Northern Mexico's major attractions fall under this heading—from hiking in the sierras Madre Occidental and Oriental to marlin fishing in Mazatlán. For the most part, Northern Mexico's outdoor recreation can be enjoyed at little or no cost simply because user demand is so low; when fees are involved they're usually quite reasonable.

HIKING AND BACKPACKING

National Parks And Natural Areas
Northern Mexico has a number of officially designated *parques nacionales* (national parks) and *parques naturales* (literally "natural parks," a designation similar to that of "natural area" or nature reserve in the United States).

Chihuahua: Parque Nacional Basaseachic Falls, Parque Nacional Cumbres de Majalca, and Parque Natural Barranca del Cobre

Nuevo León: Parque Nacional Cumbres de Monterrey and Parque Nacional El Sabinal

Durango: Parque Nacional Raymundo, Parque Nacional Puerta de los Angeles y Barranca de los Negros, and Parque Natural La Ciudad.

Coahuila: Parque Nacional de los Novillos and Parque Natural la Amistad

San Luis Potosí: Parque Nacional El Gororrón and Parque Nacional El Potosí

Tamaulipas: Parque Natural Camargo

Sonora: Parque Nacional El Pinacate

In addition, Isla Tiburón, Son., and Rancho Nuevo, Tamps., are considered wildlife sanctuaries for birds and sea turtles respectively, while the cloud forest at El Cielo, Tamps., has been honored with International Biosphere Reserve status by the United Nations. An international park is under discussion for an area along the Texas-Coahuila border that would link the U.S.'s Big Bend National Park with that of Mexico's Sierra del Carmen.

At most of these officially protected areas, public facilities are few and rudimentary—in some cases ("natural parks" or *parques natu-*

rales) they're virtually nonexistent. These public lands are described in some detail in later sections of this guidebook.

Trails
Hiking trails are plentiful in the sierras Madre Occidental and Oriental, from fairly wide, 150-year-old paths created by Indians or immigrant shepherds to smaller, more recent trails worn by hikers. In the lower, subtropical slopes toward both coast lowlands, trails are much more scarce—it's a good idea to scout an area first and ask questions locally about the best way to get from point A to point B. Although it's sometimes tempting to venture off established trails, this is a good way to get lost; it can also add to the destruction of delicate ecosystems. Light trails that don't seem to go anywhere may be animal trails that connect surface water sources.

Maps
Topographic maps, which chart trails and elevation differential, are essential for extended hiking and backpacking. **Map Link** (tel. 805-965-4402, fax 805-962-0884, 25 E. Mason, Santa Barbara, CA 93101, U.S.A.) carries a fairly complete line of Mexico topographic maps in two scales, 1:250,000 (contour lines every 50 meters on plains and every 100 meters in mountains), and 1:50,000 (contour lines every 10 meters and 20 meters), that are sold separately (around US$6 each) according to region. Map Link will mail out a catalog on request.

These same topographic maps are also available in Mexico from any Instituto Nacional de Estadística Geografía e Informática (INEGI) office (see "Maps and Information," p. 82, for further details) for US$3.30 per sheet. Some topos may be out of print, in which case you can usually obtain a photocopy of archival prints from an INEGI office for US$8.30. These maps not only show trails and contour lines, but villages not normally marked on other maps. In Mexico they're mostly used by the military, *narcotraficantes*, and surveyors.

Although you won't need a great deal of Spanish to read the INEGI maps, you might need to know the following translations for the map legend:

brecha: gravel road

vereda: path

terracería transitable en todo tiempo: all-weather dirt road

terracería transitable en tiempo de secas: dirt road passable only in dry weather

carretera pavimentada: paved highway

carretera de más de dos carriles, caseta de pago: toll highway of more than two lanes

Equipment

Day Hikes: For hikes of a day or less, all you need are sturdy footwear (light, high-topped hiking boots are preferable to sneakers in rocky terrain) and whatever food or water you plan to consume for the day (count on a half-gallon of water per person for chaparral or lower sierra hiking, more if the weather is hot).

Overnight Hiking/Backpacking: Longer hikes obviously require more preparation and more equipment. Whether in the desert or the mountains, bring enough clothing to remain comfortable at both ends of the thermometer—Northern Mexico days tend to be warm, nights cool. A sleeping bag (for temperatures down to 25° F/-4° C in the high sierras) and a backpacking tent (with plenty of ventilation for camping at lower elevations) are necessities for coping with potentially harsh environments.

Good hiking boots are essential. Thick lug soles are preferable, as they provide protection from sharp rocks and desert plants. Bring along a first-aid kit that includes an elastic bandage for sprains and snakebite treatment (see special topic "Snakebite Prevention and Treatment" on p. 108 for more detail) and a pair of tweezers for removing thorns and cactus spines. Also bring a flashlight, compass, waterproof matches, knife, flashlight with extra batteries, foul-weather gear, and a signal device (mirror or whistle). If you'll be hiking along the coast, a "telescoping" fishing rod and light tackle are handy additions, as surf fish are usually plentiful (see "Fishing," below, for details on what to catch).

Water: Always carry plenty of water—a minimum of one gallon per person per full day of walking during hot weather, three quarts in winter. Although there are streams and springs in the sierras, the water level varies considerably and you shouldn't count on finding year-round sources of water along the way except in canyon bottoms. If you need drinking water from one of these sources, always boil it first for at least 10 minutes or treat it with iodine or with a water filter designed to remove impurities. Whether or not you know of reliable water sources along the trail, it's a good idea to bring along a water purification system (tablets, iodine crystals, or a reliable filter) just to be sure. Bring enough food for the duration of your hike, plus one or two days extra.

Campsites: In addition to all the usual rules for choosing campsites, add: Don't camp beneath coconut palms (a falling coconut could knock your tent in or fracture your skull) or in arroyos (danger of flash floods).

Fires and Waste Disposal: Open fires are permitted just about anywhere in Mexico except within city limits. Even in the desert, fuel is plentiful (dried ocotillo and cactus skeletons make excellent fuels), but imitate the locals and keep your fires small so as not to waste any. Never leave hot coals or ashes behind—smother with sand (or water if you can spare it) till cool to the touch.

Pack out all trash that won't burn (including cigarette butts—they take 10-12 years to decompose), bury human waste six inches down, and don't use soap in streams or springs.

Desert Hiking: For hikes in the Sonoran or Chihuahuan deserts, special precautions are appropriate in addition to those outlined above. Water is the number-one concern; desert hiking requires at least one gallon of water per day per person—some people recommend at least two gallons per day if you plan to hike while the sun is high. On extended excursions of more than a night or two, the weight of anything beyond two gallons (water weighs about 3.7 kilograms per gallon) is prohibitive and it will be necessary to ascertain water locations from reliable sources in advance. While hiking, keep your mouth closed and breath through your nose to keep the mouth and throat from drying out. This will also keep you cooler, as the nasal cavities are designed to moderate outside air temperatures as the air passes into your lungs.

Sun protection is especially essential in the desert. Wear long-sleeved clothing with light, reflective colors (white is best), sunglasses, a wide-brimmed hat, and sunscreen. Between 11 a.m. and 3 p.m., it's best to take shelter from the sun if possible, especially during the hotter months. Most of Mexico's deserts have a modicum of shade available in the form of mesquite trees, overhanging cliffs, or leaning boulders. But it's also a good idea to carry your own shade—a light, opaque tarp (a poncho can double as a tarp and rain protection—yes, it does rain in the desert occasionally).

Anyone contemplating an extended desert hike for the first time might consider reading at least one of the books on desert travel listed in the "References" on p. 486. These contain important information on a variety of desert survival topics, from how to test the edibility of plants to making your own water with an improvised solar still.

HUNTING

The Mexican government allows licensed hunting in season, as regulated by the Secretaría de Desarrollo Social (SEDESOL). Hunting is popular in Northern Mexico among foreigners and Mexicans alike but is for the most part restricted to various species of rabbit, quail, dove, pheasant, and waterfowl (ducks, widgeons, and geese). White-tailed deer and mule deer are also hunted but permits are limited in number and quite expensive by Mexican standards. Occasionally a special hunt for the rare desert bighorn sheep (*borrego cimarrón*) is held; bighorn permits cost as much as US$5000 and aren't usually issued to foreigners (earlier in this century, bighorn hunting by foreigners nearly wiped out the entire population).

Permits come in six types: Type I - waterfowl, Type II - doves, Type III - other birds, Type IV - litter mammiferous, Type V - limited, and Type VI - specials. Hunting regulations, which include bag (size and number) limits, are strictly enforced. Signs that say *Prohibido Cazar* mean "Hunting Prohibited." Hunting seasons vary according to game, but no hunting is permitted anywhere in May, June, and July. Current SEDESOL hunting season calendars can be obtained through any Mexican embassy or consulate abroad.

To apply directly to the Mexican government for a permit, contact SEDESOL (Aquiles Serdán 28, piso 7, Mexico, D.F. 06500). Permits are valid for only one Mexican state at a time; allow at least two months for processing. In addition to the SEDESOL hunting permit, foreign hunters need a consular certificate, special visa, and military gun permit. The consular certificate may be obtained from any Mexican embassy or consulate upon presentation of a letter from the hunter's local police or sheriff's office verifying that the hunter has no criminal record. This certificate is also necessary for obtaining the military gun permit, which can be issued by army garrisons at these border crossings: Mexicali, Nogales, Ciudad Juárez, and Nuevo Laredo. A maximum of two rifles per hunter is allowed, along with two boxes of American shells per gun (additional shells may be purchased in Mexico).

A new regulation requires that all foreign hunters be accompanied by a licensed Mexican hunting guide. If this whole process sounds daunting (it is actually very time consuming, even if you speak perfect Spanish), you'd be much better off arranging the guide and all the necessary paperwork through a U.S. broker service or Mexican hunting outfitter; a list of the latter can be requested from any Mexican consulate. This costs a bit more than applying directly through SEDESOL because you have to pay either membership dues or a surcharge, but the procedure is guaranteed to be much smoother and quicker.

Organizations dedicated to helping hunters obtain Mexican permits include: **Mexican Hunting Association** (tel. 213-421-1619), 3302 Josie Ave., Long Beach, CA 90808; **Joan Irvine Travel** (tel. 714-548-8931), 1600 West Coast Hwy., Newport Beach, CA 92663; and **Sunbelt Hunting and Fishing** (tel. 210-546-9101, 800-876-4868), P.O. Box 3009, Brownsville, TX 78520. (The California outfits specialize in northwestern Mexico trips while the Texas agency focuses on northeast Mexico.) Certain hotels and sporting goods stores in regions near well-known hunting grounds—e.g., Ciudad Victoria, Tamps.; Hermosillo, Son.; Chihuahua, Chih.; Los Mochis, Sin.; Torreón, Coah.—also outfit hunters.

FISHING

Mexico's reputation as one of the best sport-fishing regions in the world is well deserved. Although it's most famous for the acrobatic billfish (marlin, sailfish, and swordfish) of Mazatlán and other deep-sea fishing, Northern Mexico also has opportunities for surf casters, lake trollers, small boaters, and sport divers as well as for folks who don't know a rod from a reel.

Onshore Fishing

Onshore or surf fishing can be enjoyed anywhere along the coast where you can get a line into the water (unless you see a rare *Prohibido Pescar* sign). It is the most accessible to travelers since it doesn't require a boat. Surf fishing is good along the Gulf of Mexico coast between Playa Bagdad and Lago Morales (La Pesca), and on the Sea of Cortez and Pacific Ocean south of Los Mochis, but fish can be taken in just about any surf zone along either coastline. Common onshore fish along the Sea of Cortez and Pacific coast include surfperch, cabezón, sand bass, ladyfish, halibut, corvinas, opaleye, leopard shark, triggerfish, and croakers. On the Gulf of Mexico side, look for flounder, croakers, redfish (red drum), sand seatrout, ladyfish, and black drum. All of these are excellent food fishes.

Note: One fish commonly caught along the Sea of Cortez/Pacific is the puffer; the meat of the puffer is in fact toxic to humans and can cause poisoning. There are two species common to the Sea of Cortez and Pacific, both of whose bodies expand like balloons when they're disturbed, which is the easiest way to identify them. Further identifiers: the bullseye puffer has a brownish body with black spots; depending on its stage of maturity, the golden puffer is either all golden or a dark purple-black with white spots and white fin trim. In Mexico this fish is called *bolete.*

Inshore Fishing

Anyone with access to a small boat, either a skiff trailered in or a rented *panga* (an open fiberglass skiff that's usually five to six meters/ 18-20 feet long and powered by a 40- to 50-horsepower outboard motor—this is the most popular Mexican fishing boat) can enjoy inshore fishing at depths of around 50-100 fathoms. Common inshore catches on the lower Sea of Cortez/Pacific coast include many of the surf fishes mentioned above, plus various kinds of groupers, Mazatlán jack, seabass, bonito shark, sculpin (scorpionfish), barracuda, rockfish, lingcod, sierra, pompano, amberjack, red and yellow snapper, pargo, and cabrilla (cabrilla must be released if caught, however—see "Legal Requirements," below). Larger gamefish that may occasionally be taken inshore are the bluefin and yellowfin tuna, yellowtail, dorado, jack crevalle, and roosterfish.

Inshore fishing on the Gulf of Mexico coast includes the excellent bay, *boca,* and lagoon fishing along the barrier islands between Tampico and the U.S. border, where the onshore Gulf fish listed above are common along with snooker. Farther off the windward side of the barrier islands, typical Gulf catches include silver and spotted seatrouts, sheepshead, ling, kingfish, skipjack, bonito, tarpon, Florida pompano, blue runner, and mackerel. Again, all fishes mentioned here are good eating.

Offshore Fishing

The bigger game fish are found in deeper waters —over 100 fathoms (about 15 meters or 600 feet)—and require bigger tackle and more technique, e.g., specialized trolling methods prescribed for each type of fish. Larger boats—fishing cruisers—are usually necessary simply because of the distances involved from shore to fishing areas.

Because of the special tackle and techniques involved in offshore fishing, many visitors hire local fishing guides (who usually provide boats and tackle) to take them to offshore fishing grounds. A sometimes less expensive alternative is to sign up for fishing cruises that take out groups of tourist anglers on a big powerboat.

Mazatlán is the west coast center for offshore fishing. Most offshore anglers are after striped, blue, or black marlin, sailfish, swordfish, wahoo, dorado, roosterfish (papagallo), yellowtail, and tuna. Offshore fishing on the Gulf of Mexico side brings in sailfish, blue marlin, barracuda, red snapper, grouper, amberjack, and warsaw. All of these fish are large, powerful fighters and require a certain skill in handling rod and line. The billfish are known as the most acrobatic, performing high leaps and pirouettes when hooked, although the wahoo and roosterfish will also "greyhound," performing a series of long, low jumps while swimming rapidly in one direction.

Of the billfish, none except the swordfish are considered particularly good eating; the other billfish are thought of as traditional trophies to be stuffed and mounted in someone's den or living room. To their increasing credit, many sportfishers these days are releasing billfish after the fight is over; many sportfishing outfitters, in fact, discourage (or even forbid) the taking of these beautiful creatures unless a fish has been badly damaged in the fight. The wahoo, dorado, roosterfish, yellowtail, and various tunas all make excellent eating.

Fishing Seasons

Fish bite somewhere in Mexico waters year-round. Water temperature, ocean currents, weather patterns, fish migrations, and other changing variables, however, mean that you usually won't find the same type of fish in the same spot in December, say, as in July. All the variables interact to provide a complex set of fishing conditions that not only vary from month to month but also from year to year. An unusually dry year in the American Southwest, for example, can lessen the outflow of nutrients from the Colorado River into the Sea of Cortez, thus diminishing the proliferation of plankton and other small marine creatures at the bottom of the Cortez food chain. This, in turn, will affect populations of larger fish from seabass to whale sharks (a Cortez resident and the largest fish on the planet).

All the various "fishing calendars" in print (including the ones in this book) can serve only as general guidelines. The happiest sportfishers drop line with the knowledge that a certain amount of luck is always involved. It also helps to ask around once you've arrived at a fishing area—try local sporting goods stores, bait shops, and other anglers. In the most popular fishing areas, professional guides are available.

A few generalizations with regard to fishing seasons are possible. The greatest variety and number of offshore, onshore, and inshore fish are swimming the widest range of Mexican waters between April and October, when the water temperatures are relatively warm. During the winter, many Sea of Cortez/Pacific species migrate south and are available only in the Mazatlán area.

Fortunately for winter anglers farther north, however, exceptions abound. The widely distributed California yellowtail, for example, is present year-round, migrating up and down the Sea of Cortez (Altata to Mazatlán in the winter, central to northern Cortez in the summer) as well as the lower Pacific coast. Wahoo generally spend Dec.-April near Mazatlán, moving up towards the southern Cortez in the warmer months. On the Gulf of Mexico coast, redfish, black drum, and sheepshead are plentiful Jan.-Feb., flounder and speckled trout Oct.-November. Most other Gulf of Mexico species are present in some numbers year-round.

As a final caveat, remember that an unusually warm winter will mean better fishing all along the Sea of Cortez/Pacific coast; likewise a particularly cold winter will force many fish quite far south, making even Mazatlán and the Gulf of Mexico less productive than average.

Equipment

Although bait and tackle are available at shops in Hermosillo, San Carlos, Los Mochis, Mazatlán, La Pesca, and Tampico, you can't count on finding exactly what you want, as supplies vary. Therefore you ought to have your gear squared away, according to the type of fishing you plan on trying, before arrival in Northern Mexico.

A full fishing kit containing tackle for every conceivable Mexico sportfishing possibility would probably weigh in excess of 150 pounds. Seasoned Mexico anglers, however, claim you can get by in just about any situation with four basic rigs: two trolling rods with appropriate reels and 50- to 80-pound test monofilament line (for offshore fishing), one medium-duty eight- or nine-foot rod and spinner with 20- to 30-pound mono (for surf casting and onshore fishing), and a six-foot light spinning rig loaded with four- to eight-pound line (for bait fishing, freshwater fishing, or light surf casting). Two trolling rigs are recommended because these are the ones used against the fish most likely to yank your outfit into the sea; it's always best to have a spare. For freshwater angling, a 20- to 30-pound line will do for virtually all situations.

Bait

What a fish will take at any given moment is highly variable, hence the properly equipped angler is ready with an array of natural and artificial bait. Live or frozen bait (including everything from squid to mackerel to clams) is usually available near the more frequented fishing areas; you can also catch your own quite easily with a light rig. A cooler is necessary for keeping bait fresh—hired boats will usually supply these. Among the vast selection of artificial lures available, the most reliable seem to be those perennials that imitate live bait, such as spoons, leadheads, candybars, swimmers, and, for offshore fishing, trolling heads. Bring along a few of each in different colors and sizes and you'll be ready for just about anything. A few highly specialized lures, such as marlin heads and "wahoo specials," can be purchased in San Carlos, Mazatlán, and La Pesca.

Tide Tables

Serious onshore-inshore anglers will want to bring along a set of current tide tables so they can decide what time to wake up in the morning. (For information on where to obtain Pacific and Cortez tables, see "Charts and Tide Tables" under "Boating," below.)

Freshwater Fishing

Arid Northern Mexico has a surprising number of lakes, rivers, and streams with angling opportunities. Common catches throughout the region include catfish, crappie, largemouth and smallmouth bass, sunfish, trout, walleye, and white bass. Particularly good fishing venues are found in the lakes formed by dammed rivers draining the western Sierra Madre Occidental in northwestern Mexico and in similar lakes of the lower Río Bravo and Río Soto de la Marina valleys in northeastern Mexico. State governments periodically stock many of these lakes with gamefish. Presa Vicente Guerrero (Lake Guerrero) in Tamaulipas is known throughout North America for its excellent largemouth bass fishing. More detail on inland fishing is given in the destination chapters.

Small- to medium-size spoons, plastic worms, and spinners are the basics for Mexico lake fishing—bring a wide selection for experimentation.

Legal Requirements

The red tape surrounding fishing in Mexico is minimal. The basic requirement is that anyone over 16 who intends to fish must have a Mexican fishing license; technically, this includes all persons aboard boats equipped with fishing tackle, whether they plan to fish or not. This is important to remember for anyone going along on fishing trips as a "spectator."

A single license is valid for all types of fishing, anywhere in Mexico, and is issued for periods of one week (US$20), one month (US$25), or one year (US$32). A license is usually included in the price of sportfishing cruises but not necessarily on **panga** trips—if you don't have a license, be sure to ask if one is provided before going out on a guided trip. The cost of the Mexican license has been rising steadily over the last few years but it remains less expensive than most fishing licenses in the U.S. or Canada. Rates are reviewed quarterly and adjusted accordingly, so those given above could rise or decrease a bit every three to six months.

Fishing licenses are available from a number of sources, including tackle shops and Mexican insurance companies near the U.S.-Mexico border. They can be obtained by mail from the Secretaría de Pesca (tel. 619-233-6956, fax 619-233-0344; 1010 Second Ave., Suite 101, San Diego, CA 92103) or from California branches of the American Automobile Association (AAA). ClubMex (tel. 619-585-3033, fax 619-422-2671; P.O. Box 1646, Bonita, CA 91908) also issues Mexican fishing licenses as well as boat permits.

Mexican Regulations

The general daily bag limit is 10 fish per person, limited to no more than five fish of any one species. Exceptions include perch and carp, of which up to 20 a day can be taken. Certain fish varieties are further protected as follows (per day limits): one full-grown billfish (marlin, sailfish, or swordfish) and two of each of tarpon, shark, halibut, roosterfish, and dorado. For inland fishing the limit is five fish per day, whether one or more species.

Bag limits are the same for divers as for rod-and-reelers; only hand-held spears and band-powered spearguns (no gasguns or powerheads) are permitted. The use of gill nets, purse nets, and every other kind of net except handling nets by nonresident aliens is prohibited, as are traps, explosives, and poisons.

The taking of shellfish (clams, oysters, abalone, shrimp, and lobster) by nonresident aliens is also officially prohibited; however, it is generally recognized that taking a reasonable amount of these (no more than can be eaten in a meal or two) is permitted by custom. This regulation is in place to protect the Mexican fishing unions; even buying shellfish from local sources is prohibited unless purchased from a public market or *cooperativa*, in which case you should obtain a receipt to show in the event of an inspection.

Totuava, sea turtles, and cabrilla are protected species which cannot be taken by anyone. Mexican fishing regulations are subject to change at any time—be sure to check with the Mexico Department of Fisheries for the latest version before embarking on a fishing expedition.

Other Precautions

Fishing, boating, diving, and other aquatic activities can have long-term effects in lagoons and on delicate shore ecologies—use special care when traversing these places. Never drop an anchor or a fishing line on a coral reef, as such contact can cause irreversible damage to reef systems.

U.S. Customs And California State Regulations

Once you've bagged a load of fish in accordance with Mexican fishing limits, you still have to conform to U.S. Customs regulations if you cross the U.S.-Mexico border with your catch. Fortunately, the U.S. regulations conform with Mexican bag limits, so that whatever you've legally caught south of the border may be transported north of the border. The state of California further requires anyone transporting fish into the state to present a completed "California Declaration of Entry" form, which is available at the border. In order to facilitate the identification of the transported fish, some part of each fish—head, tail, or skin—must be left intact (in other words, you can't just show up at the border with a cooler full of anonymous fish fillets).

BOATING

An extremely wide range of pleasure boats is in use at any one time in Northern Mexico, from sea kayaks to huge motor yachts. The most heavily navigated area is the Sea of Cortez/Pacific Ocean coast between Bahía Kino and Mazatlán, but even these waters are relatively uncrowded compared to the marinas and bays of the United States. Along the Gulf of Mexico, pleasure boating is much less popular in spite of the many opportunities offered by the barrier island system running from the U.S. border south to Tampico.

Because of the relative safety of Sea of Cortez boating, this is the most popular coast, particularly for smaller crafts—kayaks, skiffs, and motor- or sail-powered vessels under 35 feet. The Cortez waters are relatively calm most of the time, late summer and early fall being the exceptions, when *chubascos* or hurricanes can whip up sizable and sometimes treacherous swells. South of Mazatlán in the open Pacific, and anywhere along the Gulf of Mexico coast, high winds and challenging swells come and go year-round.

The major difference between the two coasts is the number of available, safe anchorages. The Gulf of Mexico side features only four anchorages that provide protection when onshore winds prevail: Mezquital in the northern Laguna Madre, La Pesca at the southern tip of the Laguna Madre barrier island system, Lomas del Real in Lago San Andrés, and Tampico. Over on the Cortez side, however, dozens of protected anchorages line the east coast as well as the Cortez islands. The Sea of Cortez thus offers not only safer boating waters but a wider selection of places to drop anchor on a whim.

Open-ocean Pacific or Gulf of Mexico sailing is not for the novice and it shouldn't be attempted along either coast without plenty of prior open-ocean experience. The relative absence of assistance and boat-repair facilities (see "Emergencies," below) along the Gulf coast make it an especially risky venture for first-timers.

It is now possible for boaters to navigate from ports in California, British Columbia, or Alaska to Baja California's Ensenada marina and then arrange for overland transport of their boats (on hired trailers) from Ensenada to San Felipe on the Cortez side. From San Felipe you can then undertake a crossing to San Carlos on the mainland. The Ensenada tourist office (tel. 667-2-30-22, fax 2-30-81, Blvd. Costero and Calle Rocas, Ensenada, Baja California Norte) has details on this newly established service.

Car-Topping: The most popular boats for short-range cruising, fishing, and diving are those that can be transported on top of a car, RV, or truck, e.g., aluminum skiffs in the 12- to 15-foot range. The primary advantage of this type of boat is that it can be launched just about anywhere. Larger, trailered boats are restricted to boat launches with trailer access. The most appropriate outboard motor size for a 12- to 15-footer is 15- to 20-horsepower—larger motors are generally too heavy to be carried separately from the boat (a necessity for car-topping).

If you decide to transport a skiff (or sea kayak) on top of your vehicle, be sure to use a sturdy, reliable rack or loader with a bow line to the front bumper and plenty of tie-downs. The rough road surfaces typical of Mexico's highways (even its best) can make it difficult to keep a boat in one place; crosswinds are also a problem in many areas. Frequent load checks are necessary.

Trailering

Larger boats that must be trailered because of their weight and then floated from the trailer at a launch site are much less versatile than car-top boats. Along the Cortez coast there are fewer than 25 launches with trailer access. Another disadvantage to boat trailering is that Mexican road conditions can make towing a slow, unpleasant task. On the other hand, if one of these spots happens to be your destination and you plan to stay awhile, then the added cruising range of a larger vessel might be worthwhile.

Charts And Tide Tables

The best nautical charts available for Mexico waters are those originally published by the U.S. government. The nautical surveys that resulted in this series were carried out between 1873 and 1901—as a result, many place-names are out of date.

The charts can be purchased individually from the Defense Mapping Agency (tel. 800-826-0342 or 301-227-2495), Washington, DC 20315-0010. Two of the Coastal Series are out of print, however, and only the Pacific and Sea of Cortez charts are readily available. A less expensive source of these charts is *ChartGuide: Mexico West,* a compilation of all the nautical charts from San Diego to Guatemala, including those currently unavailable from the DMA. Chart-Guide has extensively updated the charts by marking anchorages, boat ramps, hazards, even fishing and diving spots. The spiral-bound volume costs US$58 and can be ordered from U.S.-based ChartGuide (tel. 714-891-5779, fax 714-892-7510), Charlie Davis and Assoc., 5151 Oceanus Dr., No. 107, Huntington Beach, CA 92649. It is also available in some California marine supply stores. Charts for the Gulf of Mexico are quite difficult to come by—try asking around at marine supply stores along the Texas Gulf coast.

Tide tables are published annually; to cover the entire Mexico coastline you'll need three sets, one each pertaining to the Pacific, Sea of Cortez, and Gulf of Mexico tides. The Pacific/Sea of Cortez tables can be purchased from marine supply stores in California, the Gulf tables in Texas. Map Link (tel. 805-965-4402, fax 805-962-0884; 25 E. Mason, Santa Barbara, CA 93101) may also be able to order charts and tide tables.

Boat Permits

A temporary import permit is required if you plan to take a boat to mainland Mexico, whether by land or water. The permit can be obtained from the Registro Federal de Vehículos office at each of the major border crossings.

In addition, any nonresident foreigner operating a boat in Mexican waters who intends to fish from the boat is required to carry a Mexican fishing permit. Even if you transport a boat to Mexico with no fishing tackle and no plans to fish, it's a good idea to obtain a permit anyway: first, because you might change your mind when you see all the fish everyone else is pulling in, and, second, because you never know when you might end up carrying a passenger who has fishing tackle. *All* boats used for fishing require a permit, whether car-topped, trailered, deflated and carried inside a motor vehicle, or sailed on the open seas. The permits can be obtained by mail from the Mexico Department of

Fisheries (*Secretaría de Pesca*) or from the ClubMex (see "Legal Requirements" under "Fishing," above, for the phone numbers and addresses of each). A boat permit is valid for 12 months; fees vary according to the length of the craft.

Fuel, Parts, And Repairs
Only San Carlos and Mazatlán on the west coast, and La Pesca and Tampico on the Gulf of Mexico coast, have permanent marinas that offer fuel year-round. Elsewhere you must count on your own reserves or try your luck at canneries, boatyards, and fish camps along the way (prices at these sources will probably be well above the official PEMEX rates). Often you'll have to go ashore at places other than marinas and haul your own fuel back to the boat —come prepared with as many extra fuel containers as you can manage.

Finding marine supplies and repairs in Mexico is much more challenging than finding fuel. San Carlos, Mazatlán, La Pesca, and Tampico are the best places for both—there's usually someone around who can work minor miracles. To a limited extent, parts (but not necessarily competent repair) are also available for established-brand (e.g., Johnson, Mercury, Evinrude) outboard motors in smaller ports. As with all other motorized conveyances in Mexico, it's best to bring along plenty of spare parts (especially props, filters, water pumps, shear pins, hoses, and belts) to avoid getting stuck "in the middle of nowhere." Don't forget to bring along at least one life jacket per person—statistics show that in 80% of all boating fatalities, the victims weren't wearing PFDs (personal flotation devices).

Watermakers
Ocean cruisers might consider equipping their boats with a desalinator in order to avoid relying totally on stored fresh water. Recovery Engineering (tel. 800-548-0406 in the U.S. and Canada) has developed a new line of reverse-osmosis desalinators that run off 12-volt power sources and produce as much as 3.3 gallons of drinking water per hour from seawater. For life rafts they also manufacture a hand-pumped survival version that weighs only 2.5 pounds.

Emergencies
In the north end of the Sea of Cortez, the Cholla Bay Sportsmen's Club in Puerto Peñasco, Sonora can respond to pleas for emergency assistance on VHF 16 with their own search-and-rescue team. Elsewhere along the Cortez coastline, many Mexican agencies also monitor this channel, including the Mexican navy, all COTPs, ferry vessels, and commercial ships.

Citizen-band (CB) radio is commonly used as a substitute for a telephone system in the remoter marine areas; it's also heavily used by RVers, the Green Angels, CB clubs, and other boaters, so it's one of the quickest ways to get attention. As in the U.S. and Canada, channel 9 is the most used, and channels 1, 3, 4, 7, 9, and 10 are also monitored. Special radio permits for foreign visitors are no longer required for CB radios with a transmission power of five watts or less.

SEA KAYAKING

Kayaking is one of the best ways to experience coastal Mexico, bar none. Coves, inlets, water caves, and beaches that are inaccessible to skiffs or 4WD vehicles are easily approached in a kayak, especially on the Sea of Cortez. The Cortez is, in fact, a truly world-class sea kayaking environment, as more and more kayakers are discovering every year. It's also an excellent place to learn sea kayaking skills, since the seas are generally calm.

The most popular kayaking areas along the Cortez coast are still on the Baja California side. (Moon's *Baja Handbook* contains detailed information on Baja kayaking.) However, a growing number of kayakers have launched from the eastern Cortez shore, particularly in the Bahía Kino and San Carlos areas. The Gulf Current, which runs counterclockwise around the Cortez, favors trips planned in a south-north direction if you launch from the east coast, with pickup arranged at the north end. A few intrepid kayakers have accomplished voyages across the currents from Bahía Kino, Son., to Bahía de los Angeles on the Baja side by using the "Stepping Stones" route from island to island (the Seris once followed the same route in reed canoes). Extended Cortez trips are fairly easy when the weather's good, since campsites can be chosen from a huge selection of beaches. If you bring along some light fishing gear, you're virtually guaranteed not to go without food.

For now the main kayaking areas on the Sea of Cortez's east coast are Bahía Kino and San Carlos, both in the upper Cortez along Sonoran shores. Several other areas along the Sonora and Sinaloa coasts have strong, untapped potential as kayaking destinations, especially Bahía San Jorge and the Río Concepción estuary between Puerto Peñasco and El Desemboque, Son., and the series of river estuaries, bays, and islands west of Culiacán, Sinaloa. Another potential kayak playground, especially for novice paddlers, is the Laguna Agua Brava, a lovely 110-km-long lagoon that is part of a *marismas nacionales* (national marine reserve) south of Mazatlán at Teacapán.

The coastal islands near Mazatlán are well worth paddling to, but kayaking in the Pacific is for the experienced sea paddler only. The high surf and strong currents require equal quantities of strength and expertise.

Open-sea kayaking in the Gulf of Mexico is almost as challenging as in the Pacific, though surf zones tend to be tamer. Kayakers will find paddling on the massive Laguna Madre between Mezquital and La Pesca very similar to paddling in the barrier island lagoon of the same name that extends from Corpus Christi to South Padre Island in Texas. This is a good area for less experienced kayakers, yet the variety of wildlife will keep almost any kayaker enthralled.

Maps And Tide Tables
Nautical charts are of little use for kayak navigation—a better choice would be 1:50,000-scale topographic maps, available from Map Link (see "Maps" under "Hiking and Backpacking," p. 41, for phone number and address). Tide tables are also invaluable (see "Charts and Tide Tables" under "Boating," p. 48, for sources).

WINDSURFING

Both of Northern Mexico's coasts offer outstanding windsurfing possibilities. The Sea of Cortez is a high-wind paradise Nov.-March, particularly from the central coast southward. As with kayaking, the favorite spots are Bahía Kino and San Carlos in Sonora, where conditions are perfect for beginning and intermediate boardsailors. Any of the channels between the Sea of Cortez coast and the larger offshore islands (e.g., Canal Infiernillo opposite Isla Tiburón) usually see good sideshore wind action, although sometimes that's coupled with strong currents—if you don't see other sailboards out, try to find someone who knows the currents before launching.

Farther south, the surf and open-ocean blasts of Mazatlán will delight those in the advanced class. The Pacific shoreline generally demands a more experienced boardsailor, although there are bays near Mazatlán suitable for almost any level. Novices and intermediate boardsailors can also enjoy the lagoons and river estuaries along the northern and central Sinaloa coast or the lengthy Laguna Agua Brava south of Mazatlán. Boardsailors with sturdy transport—4WD or high-clearance trucks—can choose from dozens of smaller bays that pocket the entire Sea of Cortez/Pacific coast and are connected to Mexican highways by dirt roads of varying quality.

The best windsurfing area along the entire Gulf of Mexico coast is the extensive barrier island-lagoon system between the U.S. border and Tampico. This region offers open-sea windsurfing on the windward side of the barrier islands—complete with surf and high winds—combined with the calmer pleasures and long runs of the intracoastal Laguna Madre.

SURFING

Mexico is one of the last refuges of "soul surfing," an experience that has all but disappeared from the crowded surfing beaches of North America. Instead of fighting for a wave, Mexican surfers will typically take turns, making sure that everyone gets a ride now and then. Two reasons persist for the laid-back atmosphere: Mexico attracts a lot of older North American surfers who are either fed up with the agro scene up north or are simply investigating new territory (or both); and there are many fewer surfers on Mexican beaches, hence heated competition is simply less imperative.

Northern Mexico surfing is mostly restricted to points south of Culiacán, Sin., where the Sea of Cortez meets the Pacific Ocean, and to the

surfing at Mazatlán

plored, Texas surfers agree the best action is off the jetties near La Pesca. Why would Texans head hundreds of miles south to La Pesca from their home surf in Port Aransas, Mustang Island, and Galveston Island? Simply because La Pesca is more pristine in every way—fewer people, less trash, and cleaner water.

Equipment

Fortunately, surfing is one of the more low-tech sports of modern times, so the fact that surf shops are scarce in Mexico is not a major problem. For any extended trip down the Sea of Cortez/Pacific coast, carrying both a short- and a longboard would prepare you for the wide variation in surf. Besides wax and a cooler, about the only other items you need bring are a first-aid kit for routine surf injuries (most surf spots are far from medical assistance—don't forget butterfly bandages) and a fiberglass-patching kit for bad dings. Boards can also be repaired at just about any boatyard on the coast, since most Mexican *pangas* are made of fiberglass and require a lot of patching. Mazatlán has a couple of surf shops where boards can be rented or repaired.

northern Gulf of Mexico coast. On the Sea of Cortez/Pacific side, most of the best surf areas are below *puntas* that offer right point breaks stoked by prevailing northwesterlies during the winter months. Interspersed with the point action are plenty of reef and beach breaks, some of which arrive with the southwestern summer swells. As with all other coastal recreation, more places are accessible to those with high clearance vehicles or 4WD, although so many good surf spots are easily accessible by ordinary passenger cars that a heavy-duty rig isn't obligatory.

In the summer the Sea of Cortez/Pacific surf is mostly small to flat except when a tropical storm comes up from the south. When this happens, there's usually high wave action at Mazatlán. Mazatlán, in fact, is the focus of most surfing activity in Northern Mexico, although plenty of other good surf areas lie between Altata to the north and San Blas, Nay., to the south.

Tropical depressions coupled with strong south winds can bring high surf to the Gulf of Mexico coast any time of year. Although the surfing possibilities here are vastly underex-

SNORKELING AND SCUBA DIVING

The Sea of Cortez/Pacific coast has opportunities for diving, but they are not as well known or as well promoted as those on the Baja California side of the Sea of Cortez. The best diving is in the Mazatlán area where rock and island reefs are fairly common. The west and southwest sides of these islands offer the greatest proliferation of sealife, including kelp beds, coral reefs, and encrusted sea pinnacles amid scenic sand flats. The fast-running currents mean that visibility is usually quite good in offshore areas, but heavy swells and surging along the Pacific coast mean that it should only be tackled by experienced scuba divers or with an experienced underwater guide.

Because the Sea of Cortez has one of the richest marine ecosystems in the world, the underwater scenery can be especially vivid and varied. Sea lions, numerous whale and dolphin varieties, colorful tropical species, manta rays, and schooling hammerhead sharks are all part of a thick food chain that is stimulated by cold-water upwellings amid the over 100 islands and islets that dot the Cortez. The largest proportion of Cortez sealife are species of tropical Panamic origins that have found their way north from Central and South American waters.

With the exception of Puerto Peñasco, the northern Cortez is avoided by many divers because of strong tidal surges, speedy currents, and overall lack of underwater marine variety (relative to the central and southern Cortez). A dive shop in Puerto Peñasco rents diving equipment and organizes trips to nearby Isla San Jorge, a little-known dive destination in the northern Cortez.

The next northernmost diving area is Bahía Kino and San Carlos, where tidal conditions and visibility are suitable for recreational diving. The Midriff Islands are the main attractions here. Isla Tiburón and smaller islets nearby are the most accessible of these; others require long-range boats and an experienced appraisal of local currents and tidal changes. Rock reefs are abundant throughout these islands.

Below the Midriffs, tidal conditions calm down considerably and the water is generally warmer. Marine varieties began multiplying, and spearfishing is excellent in many areas. Coastal islands, bays, and points here are suitable both for snorkeling and scuba diving; rock reefs, boulders, volcanic ridges, and sand flats are common throughout. The southern Cortez features vast submarine canyons as well as more remote volcanic and continental islands that are best explored by experienced scuba divers.

Above Mazatlán, onshore water temperatures usually hover between 21° C (70° F) and 29° C (85° F) year-round; farther south, as the warm Cortez meets the cool Pacific, temperatures drop a few degrees. Water visibility is best July-Oct., when it exceeds 100 feet; however, this is also when the air temperature is warmest, often reaching well over 32° C (90° F). In Mazatlán, several dive operations offer trips and equipment rental.

Equipment

Divers shouldn't count on finding the equipment they need in Mexico, even in the resort areas—most equipment sold or rented at the dive shops is imported from the U.S., so stock can vary from season to season. Purchase prices are also generally higher in Mexico than north of the border. Average equipment rental fees are: mask and snorkel US$5, fins US$5, belt US$5, buoyancy compensator vest US$10, regulator US$15, tank rental US$8, air refills US$4.

For Pacific and central Cortez diving, a light wetsuit may be needed late Nov.-April, shorties or ordinary swimsuit the rest of the year. From the Midriff Islands north in the Sea of Cortez, heavier suits are necessary Dec.-March.

Because divers and anglers occasionally frequent the same areas, a good diving knife is essential in case you have to deal with wayward fishing line; in fact, bringing two knives would be a good idea so you'll have a spare. Bring extra CO_2 cartridges for flotation vests, rubber slings for spear guns, O-rings, and a wetsuit patching kit.

Air

Dependable air for scuba tanks is usually available in Puerto Peñasco, San Carlos, and Mazatlán. Always check the compressor first, however, to make sure it's both well maintained and running clean. This will lessen the risk of a contaminated air supply. Divers with extensive Mexico experience will usually carry a portable compressor not only to avoid contaminated air but also so that they can travel to areas where tank refills aren't available.

ENTERTAINMENT

BASEBALL

El béisbol is the most popular spectator sport in the northwest (Sonora, Sinaloa) and northeast (Nuevo León, Tamaulipas), where you'll typically find more (and larger) community fields and stadiums than in many areas of the United States. Baseball was first brought to Mexico by U.S. railroad workers working along the Sonoran/Sinaloan coast and today several Northern Mexican cities have professional teams. The Latin American World Series between Mexico's Pacific Coast League and the Caribbean League (Puerto Rico, Dominican Republic, Cuba) is held each February; the event has alternated between Hermosillo, Son., Culiacán, Sin., Mazatlán, Sin., and various Caribbean capitals. Several famous ballplayers on professional U.S. teams (e.g., Fernando Valenzuela, Teddy Higuera) have come from Mexican teams.

The regular Pacific Coast League season runs Oct.-Jan., perfect timing for visiting American farm-leaguers who want to stay in shape between the end of U.S. baseball season and spring training, while the larger Mexican League plays during the summer. Although the nation's hottest teams (usually made up of Northern players based in Mexico City) play in the Mexican League, the overall quality of PCL ball is reputedly better. The atmosphere at a typical game is reminiscent of North American ball, with *tacos y cerveza* replacing hotdogs and beer.

Tickets for baseball games are usually easy to obtain at the stadium on game day (exceptions include play-off and Latin American World Series games). Inquire at local tourist offices for playing schedules and stadium locations.

BULLFIGHTING

La corrida de toros ("the running of bulls") is especially popular in the north central-states of Zacatecas and San Luis Potosí, and in Ciudad Juárez (which has the best of the border corridas). Aficionados agree that the finer bullfights in the country are typically seen in Zacatecas, San Luis Potosí, Aguascalientes, Guadalajara, and Mexico City. Mazatlán has a *plaza de toros* (bullring) but it is kept in business mostly as a tourist attraction (Sinaloans prefer baseball!).

Regular bullfight columns appear in the sports sections of Mexican newspapers. Before a big corrida, these columns will critique the bulls as much as—or even more than—the matadors themselves, assessing weight (the average is over 500 kilograms), bloodlines, and other variables. Local tourist offices are good places to find the current corrida schedule; in most areas of Mexico, summer is the bullfight season (an exception is Mazatlán, where the bulls run during winter and spring to coincide with the tourist season).

SOMBRA Y SOL

Alternately called *la corrida de toros* ("the running of bulls"), *la fiesta brava* ("the brave festival"), *la lidia de toros* ("the fighting of bulls"), or *sombra y sol* ("shade and sun," in reference to the stadium seating), the bullfight can be perceived as a sport, an art, or a gory spectacle, depending on the social conditioning of the observer.

To the aficionado, the *lidia* is a ritual drama that rolls together courage, fate, pathos, and death in one symbolic event. But no matter how you may feel toward the bullfight, it is undeniably an integral part of Mexican history and culture. Every town of any size has at least one *plaza de toros* or bullring; occasionally a small bullring will be improvised for a rural fiesta. In Northern Mexico you'll find major stadiums in Ciudad Juárez, Mazatlán, Monterrey, Zacatecas, and San Luis Potosí. Of these five cities, the latter two are considered the heartland of the Mexican bullfight in terms of both bulls and toreros (bullfighters). *continued*

History

Ritualistic encounters with bulls have been traced as far back as 3000 B.C. when, on the Greek island of Crete, the Minoans would perform ritual dives over the horns of attacking wild bulls. A closer antecedent developed around 2000 B.C. on the Iberian peninsula, where a breed of fierce, wild bulls roamed the plains. Iberian hunters—ancestors of the Spanish and Portuguese—figured out how to evade the dangerous bulls at close quarters while delivering a fatal blow with an axe or spear. When the Romans heard about this practice they began importing wild Spanish bulls and accomplished bullfighters for their Colosseum games—possibly the first public bullfights.

During the Middle Ages, bullfighting became a royal sport that was practiced on horseback by the Spanish and the occupying Moors, who both used lances to dispatch the wild bulls. As the toreros began dismounting and confronting the bulls on the ground, the game eventually evolved into the current corrida as performed in Spain, Portugal, Mexico, and throughout much of Latin America.

In the early years the only payment the torero received was the bull's carcass after the event. Nowadays bullfighters receive performance fees that vary according to their status within the profession.

El Toro

The bulls used in the ring, *toros de lidia* ("fighting bulls"), are descendants of wild Iberian bulls that for over four centuries have been bred especially for their combative spirit. They're not trained in any way for the ring, nor goaded into viciousness, but as a breed are naturally quick to anger. The fighting bull's neck muscles are much larger than those of any other cattle breed in the world, making the animal capable of tossing a torero and his horse into the air with one upward sweep.

Bulls who show an acceptable degree of bravery by the age of two are let loose in huge pastures (averaging 10,000 acres per animal) in Zacatecas, San Luis Potosí, or Guanajuato to live as wild beasts until they reach four years, the age of combat. By the time *el toro* enters the ring, he stands around 127 cm (50 inches) high at the withers (higher at the shoulder, but they aren't measured there because the neck muscle expands to varying degrees when the bull is preparing to attack) and weighs 500 kilograms (1,100 pounds) or more.

The carcass of a bull killed in the ring does not go to waste, at least not from a meat-eater's perspective. Immediately after it's taken from the ring, it's butchered and dressed, and the meat is sold to the public.

El Torero

The bullfighter is rated by his agility, control, and, as surprising as it may seem to the uninitiated, his compassion. The torero who teases a bull or who is unable to kill it quickly when the moment of truth arrives is considered a cruel brute. In order to be judged a worthy competitor by the spectators, he must excel in three areas: *parar*, or standing still as the bull charges (as opposed to stepping away from the bull, even as little as an inch)—only the cape and the torero's upper body should move; *templar*, or timing and grace—the movements must be smooth, well timed, and of the right proportion; and *mandar*, or command, the degree to which he masters the entire *lidia* through his bravery, technique, and understanding of the bull, neither intimidating the animal nor being intimidated by it.

Standard equipment for the torero is the *capote de brega*, the larger cape used in the first two-thirds of the *lidia;* the *muleta*, a smaller cape used during the final third; the *estoque* or matador's sword; and the *traje de luces* or "suit of lights," the colorful torero's costume originally designed by the Spanish artist Goya.

La Lidia

The regulated maneuvers or *suertes* followed in a bullfight date from 18th-century Spain. Anywhere from four to eight bulls may appear in a corrida (typically six), and one torero is on hand for every two bulls scheduled. The order of appearance for the toreros is based on seniority. Toreros who have proven their skills in several bullfighting seasons as *novilleros* (novice fighters) are called *matadores de toros* (bull killers). Ordinarily each torero will fight two bulls; if he is gored or otherwise put out of action, another torero will take his place even if it means facing more than his allotment of bulls.

Each *lidia* is divided into three *tercios* or "thirds." In *el tercio de varas*, the bull enters the ring and the matador performs *capeos*, a cape maneuver that doesn't expose the matador's body to the bull's horns, but is meant to test the bull or lead it to another spot in the ring. He then "lances," a cape maneuver that exposes the matador's body to the horns and brings the bull closer to him, while two horsemen receive the bull's charge with eight-foot *varas* or lances. The *varas* have short, pyramid-shaped points that are aimed at the bull's neck muscle but which do not penetrate very deeply on contact.

The purpose of the encounter is 1) to punish the neck muscle so that the bull lowers its horns; and 2) to give the bull the confidence of meeting something solid so that it won't be frustrated by the emptiness of the cape as the *lidia* proceeds. Usually only two *vara* blows are administered but more are permitted if necessary to produce the intended effect (the lowering of the head). The crowd protests, however, when more than two are administered, as they want the matador to face a strong bull.

In *el tercio de banderillas,* the bull's shoulders receive the banderillas—26-inch wooden sticks decorated with colored paper frills, each tipped with a small, sharp, iron barb. They can be placed by the matador himself or more often by hired assistant toreros (called banderilleros when performing this function). The purpose of the banderilla placement is to "correct" the bull's posture; the added punishment also reportedly makes the bull more "crafty" in his charges. Placed in pairs, up to six banderillas may be applied to the bull, varying in number and position according to the needs of the individual animal.

At the end of the *tercio de banderillas,* signaled by a bugle fanfare, the matador takes up his *muleta* and sword and walks before the box of the *juez* or judge presiding over the *lidia.* He looks to the *juez* for permission to proceed with the killing of the bull and, after receiving a nod, offers his *brindis* or dedication. The *brindis* may be made to an individual spectator, to a section of the plaza, or to the entire audience. If the dedication is to an individual, he will present his *montera* (matador's hat) to that person (who will return it, with a present inside, to the matador after the *lidia*). Otherwise, he tosses his hat onto the sand after waving it at the crowd; he remains hatless for the final *tercio,* a gesture of respect for the bull during its last moments alive.

The final round of the lidia is called *el tercio de muerte,* "the third of death." The main activity of this *tercio* is *la faena,* "the work" involving cape and sword, during which a special set of passes leads to the killing of the bull. For the first two *tercios* there is no time limit; for the last, however, the matador has only 15 minutes within which to kill the bull, or else he is considered de-

feated and the bull is led from the ring (where it is killed immediately by the plaza butcher).

In a good *faena,* a matador will tempt fate over and over again, bringing the bull's horns close to his own heart. The time for the kill arrives when the bull has so tired from the *faena* that it stands still, forelegs squared as if ready to receive the sword. Then, with his cape the matador must draw the bull into a final charge while he himself moves forward, bringing the sword out from under the cape, sighting down the blade, and driving the blade over the horns and between the animal's shoulders. A perfect sword thrust severs the aorta, resulting in instant death. If the thrust is off, the matador must try again until the bull dies from one of the thrusts.

It is not necessary to kill the bull in one stroke (quite an extraordinary accomplishment); the matador's honor is preserved as long as he goes in over the horns, thus risking his own life, every time. If the bull falls to its knees but isn't dead, another torero on hand immediately comes forward and thrusts a dagger (*puntilla*) behind the base of the skull to sever the spinal cord and put the beast out of its misery. When the bull is dead, the *lidia* is over. If the matador has shown bravery and artistry, the crowd will let him know with their applause; an unusually dramatic performance will see lots of hats and flowers thrown into the ring.

Practicalities

It's usually a good idea to buy tickets for a corrida in advance if possible—check with the local tourist office to find out where they're available—since it's not unusual for an event to sell out (in which case you might still be able to buy a ticket—at higher prices—from a scalper or *revendedor*). In a large stadium, the spectator sections are divided into the *sol* (sunny side) and *sombra* (shaded side), then subdivided according to how close the seats are to the bullring itself. The *sol* tickets aren't bad, since the corrida usually doesn't begin until around 4 p.m., as long as you bring a hat, sunglasses, and sunscreen, plus plenty of pesos for beverages (tequila and beer are usually available, along with soft drinks).

CHARREADAS

Decreed the national sport of Mexico in a 1933 presidential edict, the *charreada* or Mexican-style rodeo is quite popular throughout Northern Mexico. *Charreadas* are held in *lienzos charros* or *charro* rings by private *charro* associations to demonstrate equestrian and ranching skills, much like its U.S. counterpart (which was originally inspired by the Mexican version). Though open to everyone, *charrería* (the *charro* art) is a rather expensive pastime requiring the maintenance of trained horses and elaborate clothing—somewhat analogous to polo in the Anglo world.

Unlike in American rodeo, *charros* and *charras* (gentleman and lady riders) compete for team, not individual, awards. Each team fields six to eight persons, who singly or in combination perform a series of nine *suertes* (maneuvers or events); upon completion of all *suertes,* the team with the most points wins. Another difference is that *charreada* points are usually scored for style rather than speed. Live mariachi music adds drama and romance to the events.

One of the more thrilling *suertes* is the *paso de la muerte* in which a *charro* leaps from the back of a horse onto the back of an unbroken mare—while both horses are at full gallop! Also striking is the *escarmuza charra,* a women's event featuring rapid, precision-timed, and carefully executed equestrian moves by a group of 6-10 riders. In the *coleadero,* a *charro* leans down from his horse and throws a steer by catching its tail with his leg. For a *terna en el ruedo,* three mounted *charros* rope a wild bull and bring it to the ground within 10 minutes or three casts of la reata (origin of the English word "lariat"); points are scored for complexity and style of the rope work, not speed.

In the bull-riding event or *jinete de toro,* the rider must stay atop the bull until it stops bucking, then dismount with the cinch in hand, landing on both feet simultaneously. By contrast, the American rodeo counterpart to this event only requires a cowboy to stay mounted eight seconds or more.

A serious *charreada* regular maintains four *charro* suits: the *traje de faena* or plain working outfit; the *traje de media gala,* a semi-formal suit with embroidery; and two *trajes de gala*—the silver-buttoned *traje de etiqueta* or "dress suit" and the *traje de ceremonia,* an elegant tuxedo outfit for special ceremonies. Each *traje* consists of a broad-brimmed sombrero, tight-fitting trousers of cloth or leather, a short-waisted jacket, boots, and—when the *charro* is mounted—deerskin *chaparreras* ("chaps"). *Charras* generally dress in outfits of the *china poblana* style with full, embroidered blouses and long, billowing, brightly colored skirts.

MUSIC

When most North Americans think of Mexican music they think of brass-and-violins mariachi music, which is a style from the state of Jalisco in Central Mexico. In Northern Mexico, mariachi music is generally reserved for weddings and tourists. By far the most commonly heard music in Northern Mexico is *la música norteña,* a style that's representative of ranchero life yet has a wide appeal throughout Northern Mexico and beyond, including as far north as Chicago and as far south as Colombia and Venezuela.

Norteña music shares common roots with the Tex-Mex *conjunto* music enjoyed in Texas and New Mexico and made famous by Flaco Jimenez (from Texas), Ramón Ayala (Monterrey, Mexico), Los Tigres del Norte (California) and, most recently, the Grammy-winning Texas Tornadoes (a group comprised of Flaco, Freddie Fender, and the remnants of Doug Sahm's Sir Douglas Quintet).

In Mexico this music is typically played by an ensemble led by an accordion and *bajo sexto,* a large Mexican 12-string guitar. Originally, these two instruments were supported by a string bass and sometimes a trap drum set; later, electric bass and guitar were occasionally added, along with alto sax and keyboards (though most *norteña* bands maintain the traditional accordion, bajo sexto, and acoustic bass lineup). The music itself encompasses an exciting mix of Latinized polkas and waltzes, *rancheras* (similar to American country and western), and *corridos* (Mexican ballads), as well as modern Latin forms like *cumbias* and salsa.

The most popular *norteña* band among Northern Mexicans in recent years has been Los Tigres del Norte. Although based in San José, California, most of the band members were born

BOB RACE

in Sinaloa. Like many *norteña* bands, Los Tigres sing songs that reflect the daily lives and sentiments of northern Mexican peasants, sometimes with a political edge. In 1988 Los Tigres won a Grammy award in the U.S. for best Mexican-American album for *¡Gracias!... America... Sin Fronteras* ("Thank You!... America... Without Borders"). Some of the songs recorded by Los Tigres and other *norteña* groups have been banned by the Mexican government and can only be heard from bootleg tapes that circulate at cantinas or local fiestas.

The major recording and touring center of *norteña* music is an area that stretches across Tamaulipas, Nuevo León, Coahuila, Chihuahua, Durango, and southern Texas, but live *norteña* music often can be heard at fiestas throughout Northern Mexico and in bars and cantinas in larger towns and cities. In districts where bars tend to cluster, you'll find *trobadores* strolling from bar to bar most evenings playing *norteña* music—usually not the nicest area of town to hang out, but it's an opportunity for the curious to hear some local sounds.

FESTIVALS AND EVENTS

Mexicans love a fiesta and *norteños* are no exception. Any occasion will suffice as an excuse to hold a celebration, from a birthday or promotion to a chile harvest. Add to all the civic possibilities the vast number of Mexican Catholic religious holidays, and you've got the potential for some kind of public fiesta at least every week of the year, if not all 365 days. Besides the national religious holidays, 115 Catholic saints are honored each year on individual feast days (nine or 10 each month). Any town, pueblo, *ejido,* or colonia named for a saint (e.g. Santa Ana, Villa de Santiago, San Fernando, etc.) will usually hold a fiesta on the feast day of its namesake. Individuals named for saints, too, will often host parties on their *día de santo* (saint's day).

The primary requisites of a fiesta are plenty of food (especially tamales, considered a festive dish), beer, liquor, music, and dancing. More elaborate celebrations will include parades, exhibitions, *charreadas* (Mexican rodeos), and occasional fireworks.

Following are some of the more memorable yearly events and public holidays observed throughout Northern Mexico. Smaller festivals and events that are held only locally are mentioned later in the text with respect to the destination. Actual dates may vary from year to year, so be sure to check with the appropriate tourist office in advance if you need current dates for the time of your visit.

Government offices and some businesses close on national holidays. These closings are not always mentioned in the text; you may want to call ahead to find out.

January
New Year's Day: January 1 (official holiday)
Día de los Santos Reyes: January 6—see "Las Posadas" under "December"

February
Constitution Day: February 5 (official holiday)
Carnaval: This pre-Lenten festival is held in late February or early March as a last celebration of the carnal pleasures that Catholics are supposed to forego during the 40-day Lent season

preceding Easter (the fiesta's name derives from the Italian *carne vale,* "flesh taken away"). In Mexico, Carnaval is traditionally observed only in port towns; in Northern Mexico the festival is celebrated most grandly in Mazatlán and Tampico. Like New Orleans's Mardi Gras, Carnaval features lots of music, dancing, costumes, parades, and high-spirited revelry. See the Mazatlán section for more information.

Flag Day: February 24 (official holiday)

March
Birthday of Benito Juárez: March 21 (official holiday)

Spring Break: Not a Mexican holiday at all, but an annual ritual for North American college and university students (mostly Southern Californians and Arizonans) who go on the rampage in Puerto Peñasco, San Carlos, and Mazatlán. The spring break season usually straddles late March and early April. Unless you're one of the revelers, these towns should be avoided at all costs during these weeks.

April
Semana Santa: Easter Week or "Holy Week" (the third week in April) is second only to Christmas as the most important holiday period of the year. One of the most prominent Semana Santa customs is breaking *cascarones,* colored eggs stuffed with confetti, over the heads of friends and family. Besides attending mass on Good Friday and Easter Sunday, many Mexicans take this opportunity to go on vacations. Mexican beach resorts can be overcrowded this week with the large influx of both Mexicans and North Americans.

May
International Worker's Day: May 1 (official holiday)

Cinco de Mayo: Held on May 5, this festival commemorates the defeat of an attempted 1862 French invasion at Puebla de los Angelos on Mexico's Gulf of Mexico coast. Features music, dance, food, and other cultural events.

Mother's Day (Día de las Madres): May 10

June
Navy Day: June 1 (official holiday)

September
Mexican Independence Day (Fiesta Patria de la Independencia): Also called *diez y seis,* since it falls on the 16th of September, this holiday celebrates the country's independence from Spain, as announced in 1821 in the town of Dolores. Festivities actually begin on the 15th and last two days. The biggest celebrations are centered in the state capitals, and include fireworks, parades, *charreadas,* music, and folk-dance performances.

October
Día de la Raza: Celebrated as Columbus Day north of the border, the 12th of October in Mexico commemorates the founding of the Mexican race (as heralded by the arrival of Columbus in the New World).

November
Día de los Muertos: The "Day of the Dead" is Mexico's third most important holiday, corresponding to Europe's All Saints Day except that it's celebrated on the first and second days of November instead of only the first. Some of the festivities are held in cemeteries where children clean the headstones and crucifixes of their deceased relatives (*los difuntos*) and play games that are unique to this fiesta. In some areas the faithful will spend an entire day and night beside the family graves in a cemetery. Even roadside shrines throughout Mexico are laid with fresh flowers and other tributes to the dead. Offerings of *pan de los muertos* ("bread of the dead") and food and liquor are placed before family altars on behalf of deceased family members along with papier-mâché skulls and skeletons. Also referred to as Fiesta de Todos los Santos (All Saints Festival) and Festival de los Fieles Difuntos (Festival of the Deceased Faithful).

Anniversary of the 1910 Revolution: November 20 (official holiday)

December
Día de Nuestra Señora de Guadalupe: The feast day of the Virgin of Guadalupe, Mexico's patron saint, is December 12; special masses are held that day throughout Mexico. The nearest Sunday to the 12th will also feature special events such as mariachi masses, food booths,

Day of the Dead, Durango

and games. The celebrations at the border city of Ciudad Juárez are particularly well attended.

Las Posadas: Beginning on the 16th of December, Mexicans hold nightly *posadas*—candlelight processions terminating at elaborate, community-built nativity scenes—in commemoration of the Holy Family's search for lodging. The processions continue for nine consecutive nights. Other activities include piñata parties where children break open hanging papiermâché figures filled with small gifts and candy. Churches large and small hold continuous Christmas masses beginning at midnight on the 25th (Día de la Navidad).

Las Posadas culminates on January 6, which is Día de los Santos Reyes (literally "Day of the King-Saints," referring to the story of the Three Wise Men). On this day Mexican children receive their Christmas gifts and family and friends gather to eat a wreath-shaped fruitcake called *rosca de reyes* (wreath of the kings) baked especially for this occasion. Hidden inside each *rosca* is a small clay figurine (*muñeco*) that represents the infant Jesus. While sharing the *rosca* on this day, the person whose slice by chance contains the *muñeco* is obliged to host a *candelaría* or Candlemas party on February 2 for everyone present.

At the *candelaría* (which commemorates the day the newborn Jesus was first presented at the temple in Jerusalem), the host traditionally displays a larger Christ-infant figure and serves tamales and *atole* (a thick, hot grain drink flavored with fruit or chocolate).

SHOPPING

You'll have ample shopping opportunities while traveling through Northern Mexico, from roadside craft vendors to bustling municipal markets and big-city department stores. A few things to remember: *Solo mirando* means "just looking." Prices are sometimes marked in old pesos, sometimes in new pesos, sometimes in U.S. dollars—when in doubt, ask. In shops that take credit cards, you'll get a better rate of exchange by charging your purchases.

Markets

One of the main shopping venues in Mexico is *el mercado,* the market. Virtually every town and city has at least one, sometimes housed in a centrally located *mercado municipal* building provided by the city government. Stalls within the municipal market are rented by vendors hawking everything from fresh meat to furniture. Sometimes smaller street vendors cluster near the municipal market. Large cities like Monterrey have several daily markets scattered around the city; smaller village communities may have only an open space or plaza where vendors gather one day per week or on weekends. Even if you're not looking to buy anything in particular, Mexican markets are worth strolling through for their color and ambience.

Market goods sometimes have price tags attached, sometimes not. When price tags are absent, you can usually expect to haggle a bit. Even when a price tag is apparent, it doesn't hurt to try for a lower price by bargaining. Generally speaking, you'll have much better luck if you make an effort to negotiate in Spanish, however poorly. Usually more than one vendor in the same market will be purveying the same wares; comparing prices at different stalls can help you determine the best price.

Department Stores

Among the several Mexican department store chains found in Northern Mexico, once of the best is **Sanborn's** (no relation to the Texas insurance company of the same name). Along with the usual department store fare, the typical Sanborn's contains a pharmacy with common North American brand medicines, a selection of English-language books and magazines, a *cafetería* with good Mexican food, and clean restrooms. **Woolworth Mexicana** is found in several Northern Mexican cities and is a more downscale alternative to Sanborn's with many of the same features.

Purchasing something at a Mexican department store is usually a two-step process. First you present the item(s) to a uniformed attendant, who rings it up at a cash register. Then the cashier hands you a receipt (but not the item) and takes the purchase to another counter where you must show your receipt in order to receive your purchase.

Unlike in Mexican markets, where price-haggling is expected, department store prices are always fixed.

Good Buys

Contrary to myth, the ubiquitous **designer goods** seen in the downtown shopping districts of major cities as well as in larger border towns are usually legally licensed products. Gucci, Fila, Ralph Lauren, Ellesse—among other well-known labels—have granted permission for the manufacture of such items in Mexico; retail prices are typically 30-40% less than in the label's country of origin. Some world shoppers say they can tell the difference between, for example, a Ralph Lauren shirt made in Mexico and one made in the U.S. (or more likely Hong Kong, Thailand, Malaysia, etc.), but for most of us the money saved tends to outweigh these small variations.

Silver and gold jewelry are bargains in Mexico, mainly due to lower labor costs rather than lower costs per ounce. Well-crafted silver (*plata*) pieces are particularly plentiful and relatively inexpensive throughout Northern Mexico. Look for .925 stamped into silver products; this means they're 92.5% silver, the highest quality. You will also come across *alpaca,* an alloy of copper, nickel, and zinc that looks like silver and costs a third to a half less than real silver. Zacatecas has the best silver selection and prices in Northern Mexico.

The states of Zacatecas, Durango, Nuevo León, and Tamaulipas are known for producing the finest *charreada costumery*—sequined sombreros, embroidered *charro* jackets, fancy spurs and saddles—in Mexico. **Leatherwork** in general is good throughout Northern Mexico but is especially well regarded in Zacatecas, Coahuila, Nuevo León, and Tamaulipas.

Among the various kinds of Indian arts and crafts available throughout the region, look for high-quality **baskets** (*cesta, canasta*) handwoven by the Seris, Yaquis, and Papagos of Sonora or by the Tarahumara of the Sierra Madre Occidental; **ceramics** fashioned by the Guarijíos (near Alamos, Sonora) and from the Casas Grandes area of Chihuahua; and **woodcarvings** by the Seris and Guarijíos. Handwoven *sarapes* ("serapes"), *jorongos* ("ponchos"), blankets, and rugs can be found in many Northern Mexican states, but Saltillo, Coah., is known to have the best quality and variety. For **rebozos and shawls** (*chales),* the state of San Luis Potosí is the best, particularly the small town of Santa María del Río.

Folk and religious art can be found in the former colonial provincial capitals of Mazatlán, Chihuahua, Zacatecas, and San Luis Potosí. *Retablos,* religious paintings on wood or tin, cost US$6-10 new, US$15-75 for older pieces. Now that folk art has become a standard element of modern Mexican interior design, some of the larger department stores carry limited folk art selections. FONART stores in the larger border cities usually offer a wider variety than department stores, but quality varies greatly from year to year.

Generally speaking, **liquor** is significantly less expensive in Mexico than in the U.S. or Canada. Quality liquors typically cost around US$9 per liter (as low as US$5 for a fifth); the best buys are tequila, rum, and brandy. Top brands include Herradura (the only tequila still made entirely by traditional methods), Bacardi Añejo (an aged rum usually not available north of the border), and Don Pedro Reserva Especial brandy.

Vanilla, extracted from the seed pod of the orchid *Vanilla planifolia* (first cultivated by Mexico's Aztecs), goes for around US$10-15 a liter. If you see vanilla that costs less than US$10 per liter, it probably isn't genuine vanilla but rather tonka bean extract, which has a very similar taste and smell. The cheaper tonka bean substitutes may contain traces of kumarin, a blood thinner used (in larger amounts) as rat poison and banned for human consumption in the United States. "Tropical World" is the most reliable brand of genuine vanilla—look for the Vanilla Association stamp.

Mexican coffee costs around US$5 per kilo, or even less in the Huasteca coffee-growing region in southeast San Luis Potosí. A reliable Mexican coffee brand called Café Combate is sold in whole-bean or ground form at stores of the same name in some cities.

Many **pharmaceuticals** that would ordinarily require a doctor's prescription in the U.S., Canada, or Europe are readily available over the counter in Mexico. It is perfectly legal to purchase Mexican drugs over the counter and consume them in Mexico; however, once you return home you're subject to the drug laws of your home country. Popular over-the-counter purchases by visiting Americans include Minoxidil (for baldness), Retin-A (acne, face wrinkles), isoprinosine (herpes), and ribavirin (herpes again). It's not a good idea to purchase or use any over-the-counter drug in Mexico without a doctor's counsel.

Complaints

The **Procuraduría Federal del Consumidor** or Consumer Protection Agency solicits complaints about purchases and contracts and will defend consumer rights through legal action if deemed necessary. Branch offices in Northern Mexico include Ciudad Juárez (tel. 16-12-39-70), Ciudad Victoria (tel. 131-2-96-82), Culiacán (tel. 67-3-35-55), Chihuahua (tel. 14-13-47-70), Durango (tel. 181-8-07-21), Hermosillo (tel. 62-4-75-17), Mazatlán (tel. 69-2-52-00), Monterrey (tel. 83-40-50-73), Reynosa (tel. 2-77-70), Saltillo (tel. 84-5-55-44), San Luis Potosí (tel. 48-2-18-02), Tampico (tel. 12-12-22-52), Torreón (tel. 17-2-64-06), and Zacatecas (tel. 492-2-04-60).

Complaints can also be made by mail directly to the central office in Mexico City at Carmona y Valle 11, Col. Doctores. Complaints need not be filed in Mexico.

ACCOMMODATIONS

Places to stay in Northern Mexico run the gamut from hostels to plush resort hotels. Commercial campgrounds are not as numerous but visitors who bring along the appropriate gear will find camping opportunities in wilderness areas. RVers can avail themselves of almost any open space as well as the occasional RV/trailer park.

HOTELS AND MOTELS

Rates

Hotel and motel rates throughout Northern Mexico are moderate to begin with, but you can save money by planning your stay by the times of year and week. At hotels and motels in tourist areas, particularly beach destinations, midweek rates are lower than weekend rates. Conversely, in business destinations such as Hermosillo, Chihuahua, Durango, and Monterrey, hotel rates are lower on weekends.

In the sierras, some places charge high season rates May-Oct.; along the Sea of Cortez/Pacific coast it's generally the opposite (Dec. 15-Apr. 15 rates are highest). To save money on accommodations, try traveling in the off-season for each region; except for the inland deserts and coastal plains, much of the region is livable year-round (37° C/100° F summer temperatures on the Cortez coast are usually mitigated by sea breezes and relatively low humidity).

Whatever the rack rate is, you can usually get the price down on a hotel room by bargaining (except during peak periods, e.g., Christmas, spring break, or Easter). Be sure to clarify whether or not the room rate includes meals when checking in—occasionally it does. Asking for a room without meals (*sin comidas*) is an easy way to bring the rate down, or simply ask if there's anything cheaper (¿*Hay algo más barato?*).

Rating System: Each state in Mexico uses a SECTUR rating system to classify all accommodations by price and facilities. Potentially there are seven classes, from *clase económica* (C.E.) to *gran turismo* (G.T.), but the majority of places fall in the one- to five-star classes between these extremes. Except for five-star and

G.T.-class hotels, which have no upper rate limit, the rating system limits the maximum room tariff that a hotel, motel, or guesthouse may charge. Two-star hotels in Nuevo León, for example, have an upper rate cap of US$28, three-star places can charge up to US$53, and four-star establishments are limited to a maximum of US$82. One-star places are capped at US$20; *clase económica* rates aren't monitored.

In reality, hotels/motels charge whatever the market will bear, which is usually less than the maximum allowable rate. These maximums vary from state to state, so the system isn't that useful for pinning down the exact rates if all you have to go on is the star rating; however, the ratings do give an idea of the relative price ranges for each category.

Trying to judge the facilities using the rating system is even more difficult. While the facilities of a two-star hotel are always significantly fewer than those of a five-star, I've found that in some instances the difference between a two-star and a three-star or a three-star and a four-star isn't readily apparent.

Economic

Hotels and motels in Northern Mexico are considerably less expensive than their counterparts in the U.S., Canada, or Europe. In the economic range (one- to two-star according to most state rating systems), you'll find simple but clean rooms with private bath and double bed for around US$20-30 a night. Soap, towels, toilet paper, and purified drinking water are usually provided, but in some places you may have to ask. Rooms in this price range may not have air conditioners or heaters (you can often obtain a *calentador* or space heater on request for especially cool nights). In cities and large towns, the cheaper hotels tend to be found near the *mercado municipal,* railway station, or inter-city bus terminal.

In rural areas and small towns, room rates in very basic C.E. hotels may be as low as US$8-15. City lodging under US$15 per night is rare unless you stay at a youth hostel, *casa de huéspedes,* or *pensión* (described separately below), where bathrooms are usually shared.

Shared bathroom facilities are usually indicated by the term *baño colectivo.*

Medium-priced

The largest number of hotels and motels in Northern Mexico fall into the US$30-60 range. Government ratings for this price range may vary from two to four stars depending on the state. Some are older Mexican-style hotels that are just a bit larger than those in the economic range, while others are American-style motels; most everything in this range will come with heating and a/c.

Luxury And Resort Hotels

Higher-end places (five-star and G.T. classes) are found mostly in state capitals and in the beach resorts of San Carlos and Mazatlán. Prices for "international-class accommodation" average US$75-120. Some of these places are good values in this range, while others are definitely overpriced.

The most reputable luxury chain in Northern Mexico is Westin's Camino Real, which has hotels in Saltillo, Monterrey, Mazatlán, and Tampico. Holiday Inn International appeals to the upper-middle price range and has hotels in Monterrey (three locations), Mazatlán, and Hermosillo.

BUYING OR LEASING PROPERTY IN MEXICO

The Mexican government allows both resident and nonresident foreigners to own Mexican real estate—both land and buildings—within certain restrictions. Under the Constitution of 1857, land ownership by direct title is only permitted in areas that are more than 100 km (62 miles) from any international borders and 50 km (31 miles) from any sea coasts.

However, since 1973 the Mexican government has offered a way for foreigners to acquire lots that fall outside the geographic limits, including coastal property. For property of this nature, the Ministry of Foreign Affairs issues permits to foreigners allowing them to create limited real estate trusts, administered by Mexican banks, with themselves as beneficiaries. Originally, these trusts were valid for 30-year nonrenewable terms only. In 1989 the government further liberalized real estate regulations so that the trusts (called *fideicomisos)* can be renewed at the end of each 30-year term for an additional 30-year term, with no limit on the number of renewals. In December 1993 the basic term for bank trusts was lengthened to 50 years, a period that may be long enough to attract U.S. housing lenders. Until now U.S. lenders have remained aloof from the fideicomiso market. Fideicomisos can be bought and sold among foreigners—at market rates—just like fee-simple property.

Before you rush off to acquire Mexican land by purchase or bank trust, you should be aware that a lot of people get burned in Mexican real estate deals. It's best to negotiate through an established, reputable real estate agent. Local or state tourist offices in Northern Mexico often carry information on residential property and can assist with locating real estate agencies.

Time-Shares

Time-share salespeople have become the scourge of Mexico's resort areas (including Northern Mexico's Mazatlán), where they hang out on street corners and in hotel lobbies, hounding every tourist who passes by. These hustlers, who are often gringos, will try almost anything to convince you to sign on the dotted line, on the spot (including denying that what they're selling is a time-share). It pays to hold off on any decision until you've made inquiries among current time-share residents at the development and checked with your consulate to see if there have been any complaints. Time-share developments typically begin selling when construction has just begun—sometimes they don't get finished, or when they do they may not shape up as promised. Also, keep in mind that from an investment perspective, time-shares don't appreciate in value (if they appreciate at all) as much as single-owner properties.

Other problems: Because there aren't any permanent residents at time-shares, they usually lack a sense of community as well as any sense of responsibility toward the local environment. For the developer, time-shares mean huge profits since the same space is sold repeatedly in one-week segments. Since land in coastal Mexico is relatively inexpensive considering the charming scenery and climate, it seems to attract a get-rich-quick type of developer who shows a decided lack of respect for fragile coastal environments.

This is not to say that there aren't any good time-share opportunities. But in general, as with any real estate deal, it pays to proceed very cautiously—don't be cajoled into buying without considering all the options.

GUESTHOUSES AND HOSTELS

Casas De Huéspedes And Pensiónes

The *casa de huéspedes* (guesthouse) and *pensión* (boardinghouse) are the cheapest places to stay in Mexico (aside from youth hostels or very basic campgrounds), but unfortunately for budgeters they aren't very plentiful. The typical *casa de huéspedes* offers rooms with shared bath for US$5-8 or US$8-12 with private bath. A *pensión* costs about the same but may include meals. At either, most lodgers are staying for a week or more, but the proprietors are usually quite happy to take guests by the night.

The main difference between these and budget hotels/motels (besides rates) is that they are usually located in old houses or other buildings that have been converted for guesthouse use. Soap, towels, toilet paper, and drinking water are usually provided, but as with budget hotels and motels, you may have to ask.

Youth Hostels

Northern Mexico has youth hostels (*villas deportivas juveniles*) in Ciudad Obregón, Durango, Monterrey, Zacatecas, and San Luis Potosí. Accommodation is in shared dormitory-style rooms where each guest is assigned a bed and a locker. Bathing facilities are always communal and guests must supply their own soap and towels. Rates are only US$1.30-$1.50 per bed per night, and food is available at hostel cafeterias (except Monterrey) for around US$2-2.50 per meal.

Staying at youth hostels is a great way to meet young Mexicans and improve your Spanish (English is rarely spoken). About the only drawback is that the hostels tend to be inconveniently located some distance from the center of town, so transport can be a problem if you don't have your own wheels. City buses, however, are usually available.

In spite of their nomenclature, youth hostels welcome travelers of all ages. All that's required is membership in any national hostel association affiliated with Hostelling International, formerly known as the International Youth Hostel Federation (IYHF). Temporary or yearly memberships are available directly from individual youth hostels, or you can contact the relevant organi-zation in your home country for membership information in advance. Hostelling International can provide an international directory that lists all hostels operated in Mexico; those relevant to this guidebook are listed under the appropriate destinations.

CAMPING

Northern Mexico has plenty of space for campers. Because the population density of the region as a whole is low, it's fairly easy to find off-the-beaten-track campsites that offer idyllic settings and precious solitude (often for free). For travelers who like the outdoors, it's also an excellent way to slash accommodation costs.

Campgrounds And RV Parks

Campgrounds charge fees ranging from around US$1.50 for a place with virtually zero facilities to a high of US$15 for a developed RV park with full water, electrical, and sewage hookups plus recreation facilities (e.g., boat ramps). Most campgrounds charge around US$3-5 for tent camping, US$6-12 for full hookups.

Many motels and hotels will allow RVers to park overnight for a minimal fee. For US$10 or more you should be allowed to use showers and toilets in any unoccupied rooms.

If you can forego permanent toilet and bathing facilities, you won't have to pay anything to camp in wilderness areas since there's a virtually limitless selection of free camping spots, from beaches to deserts to mountain slopes. You won't necessarily need 4WD to reach these potential campsites, as there are plenty of turnouts and graded dirt *ramales* (branch roads) off the main highways that can be negotiated by just about any type of vehicle.

RV Electrical Problems: Mexican circuits are rarely grounded and two-prong electrical outlets are the norm. Bring adapters to convert three-prong plugs to two-prong. To guard against electrical shock, always ground your unit by attaching a piece of wire between a metal part of your rig and a a metal stake in the ground. If the power doesn't work or you get a shock from touching the exterior of your rig, reverse the plug in its outlet.

Always check with the management to confirm voltage before plugging in; in some parks you may find outlets with a 220V (rather than the usual 110V) source. This is relatively rare, and most parks supply transformers to step voltage down from 220V to 110V. If you have a 220V/110V transformer, bring it along just in case.

FOOD AND DRINK

Many of the most popular Mexican dishes worldwide (especially in Texas and the American Southwest) are actually from Northern Mexico, where ranch-style cooking tends to prevail. *Huevos rancheros, burritos, chiles rellenos, frijoles a la charra, fajitas, cabrito, carne asada, filet tampiqueña (carne a la tampiqueña), tacos al carbón*—all are part of *cocina típica norteña.*

But Northern Mexican food isn't a single, monolithic cooking style. Each state has its local specialties that form recognizable subregional cuisines. Areas along the Sea of Cortez/Pacific and Gulf of Mexico coasts produce delectable seafood dishes, while in the Altiplano beef and *cabrito* reign supreme. And as you would expect, the farther south you go the more Southern Mexican influences you will find. By the time you reach Zacatecas and San Luis Potosí, the local cooking styles are a full blend of North and South.

WHERE TO EAT

Your selection of eating venues depends largely on where you are in Northern Mexico at any given moment. You'll find the greatest range of places to eat in the larger towns and cities, which offer everything from humble sidewalk taco stands to five-star hotel restaurants.

In small towns there may be only two or three restaurants (*restaurante, restorán*) that serve basic Mexican dishes (see "What to Eat" below) or, if near the coast, seafood. Most hotels also have restaurants and in small towns they may be among the best choices. Sometimes the best meals on the road will come from what you improvise after a visit to a local *tienda de abarrotes* (see "Buying Groceries" on p. 71).

Back in the city, one of the main nonrestaurant choices is the *taquería,* a small, inexpensive diner where tacos are assembled before your eyes (sort of the Mexican equivalent of the old-fashioned American hamburger stand). Taquerías tend to be found in areas where there's much foot traffic (near bus terminals, for example); the good ones will be packed with taco-eaters in the early evening.

Another economic choice is any *lonchería,* a small, cafe-style place that usually serves *almuerzo* (late breakfast/early lunch) and *comida* (the main, midday meal). *Lonchería* hours are typically 11 a.m.-5 p.m. Municipal markets will often have a row of *loncherías* where basic meals and *antojitos* (snacks or one-plate dishes) are quite inexpensive. Some *loncherías* offer *comida corrida,* a daily fixed-price meal that includes a beverage, an entree or two, plus side dishes and possibly dessert.

A *comedor* is usually a more basic version of a *lonchería.* Cafes are similar to *loncherías* except that they may open earlier and serve *desayuno* (breakfast) in addition to other meals. A

JOE CUMMINGS

cafetería is a larger coffee shop (often attached to a large department store or pharmacy) with a full menu. Table service is the norm; Mexican *cafeterías* rarely serve food in what North Americans might call "cafeteria-style."

Ordering And Paying

You really don't need that much Spanish to get by in a Mexican restaurant. Stating what you want, plus *por favor* (please), will usually do the trick (e.g., *dos cervezas, por favor,* "two beers, please"). The menu is called *el menú* or, much less commonly in Northern Mexico, *la carta*. As a last resort, you can always point to what you want on the menu.

La cuenta is the bill. A tip (*la propina*) of 10-15% is expected at any restaurant with table service; look to see if it has already been added to the bill before placing it on the table.

WHAT TO EAT

Tortillas

A Mexican meal is not a meal without tortillas, the round, flat, pancakelike disks that are eaten with nearly any nondessert dish, including salads, meats, seafood, beans, and vegetables. Food experts have cataloged 166 kinds of tortillas in Mexico. Very large, thin wheat tortillas known as *tortillas de agua,* for example, are a favorite in Sonora; Durango's *gorditas* are the opposite—small and thick. In some places—especially Sonora and Chihuahua—you may encounter *coyotas,* thick wheat tortillas similar to *gorditas.*

Corn tortillas (*tortillas de maíz*) are more common in Southern Mexico, where Indian populations (the first corn cultivators) are larger and the climate is well suited to growing corn. In the North the geography is more conducive to wheat cultivation, which requires less rain than corn. Culturally, wheat ties the *euromestizos* of the North to their European roots, while corn is identified more with Mesoamerica and the *indomestizo* culture.

Both corn and wheat tortillas, however, are consumed in great quantity throughout the North. Among *norteños* it is said that meat and poultry dishes taste best with flour tortillas while vegetable dishes go best with corn. Some restaurants will offer a choice of the two (if you

order tortillas without specifying, you may get *¿De harina o de maíz?* as a response).

Although prepackaged tortillas are available in *supermercados,* most Mexicans buy them fresh from neighborhood *tortillerías* (see "Buying Groceries," p. 71) or make them at home. Many restaurants and cafes, and virtually all *loncherías* and *taquerías,* serve only fresh tortillas (tortillas made the same day or the night before they're served). If you're used to prepackaged tortillas (which is what most Mexican eateries in the U.S. or Canada serve), you're in for a pleasurable surprise when you raise a fresh, hot, homemade tortilla to your nose for the first time.

Incidentally, there are two sides to a tortilla, an inside and an outside, that dictate in which direction the tortilla is best folded when wrapping it around food. The side with the thinner layer (sometimes called the *pancita* or belly) should face the inside when folding the tortilla. If you notice that the outside of your tortilla is cracking and pieces are peeling off onto the table, it's probably because you've folded it with the *pancita* outside instead of inside (where the food would have kept it from flaking off).

Antojitos

This word literally means "little whims," thus implying "snacks" to many people. However, it also refers to any food that can be ordered, served, and eaten quickly, in other words Mexican fast-food (like burgers and hot dogs in North America). Typical *antojitos* include *tamales, enchiladas, burritos, chivichangas, flautas, chiles rellenos, chalupas, picadillo, quesadillas, tortas,* and *tacos.*

Visitors who identify these terms with dishes at Mexican restaurants in their home countries are sometimes confused by the different shapes and forms they may take in Mexico. Tacos can be rolled as well as folded, and enchiladas can be folded (or stacked) as well as rolled; shape is irrelevant. An "enchilada" (literally "chilied") is any *antojito* made with a tortilla that has been dipped or cooked in a chile sauce; an "entomada" (or "entomatada") is the equivalent made with tomatoes. A "taco" is any type of plain tortilla that surrounds other ingredients. In some eateries you can order tacos either *suave*—heated but soft tortillas stuffed with meat and vegetable fillings—or *dorado* ("golden")—

ANTOJITOS (COMIDA TIPICOS)

burrito—(also *burro* or *burra*) a flour tortilla rolled around meat, beans, or seafood fillings. Most common in Sonora and Chihuahua, where *carne machaca* (shredded, dried meat) is the most popular filling

chalupa—also known as a *tostada;* a crisp corn tortilla topped with beans, meat, etc.

chiles rellenos—mild poblano chiles stuffed with cheese, deep-fried in egg batter, and served with *ranchero* sauce (tomatoes, onions, and chiles)

chivichanga—sometimes spelled *chimichanga;* a Sonoran tortilla doubled over, filled with meat and/or vegetables, rolled (or folded again), then deep-fried. Found almost exclusively in Sonora

enchilada—a corn tortilla dipped in chile sauce, then folded or rolled around a filling of meat, chicken, seafood, or cheese and baked in an oven

flauta—a small corn tortilla roll, usually stuffed with beef or chicken and fried

picadillo—also known as *salpicón;* a spicy salad of chopped or ground meat with chiles and onions

quesadilla—a flour tortilla folded over sliced cheese and grilled; ask the cook to add *rajas* (pepper strips) for extra flavor

taco—a corn tortilla folded or rolled around anything and eaten with the hands; *taco dorado* is the fried version

tamal—plural *tamales;* cornmeal (*masa*) dough wrapped in a corn husk and steamed; sometimes stuffed with corn, olives, pork, or turkey. Common in San Luis Potosí

torta—a sandwich made with a Mexican-style roll (*bolillo* or *birote*); one of the most popular is the *torta de milanesa,* made with breaded, deep-fried veal or pork

BOB RACE

thin corn tortillas stuffed tightly with meat, then deep-fried whole and served with lettuce and grated cheese.

Breakfasts

Menus at tourist restaurants are sometimes confusing because some of the same "breakfast" dishes may end up on more than one section of the menu. This is because Mexicans have two kinds of breakfasts, an early one called *desayuno,* eaten shortly after rising, and a second called *almuerzo* that's usually taken around 11 a.m. To further confuse the issue, Spanish-English dictionaries usually translate *almuerzo* as "lunch," while bilingual menus often read "breakfast."

The most common Mexican *desayuno* is simply *pan dulce* (sweet pastry) and/or *bolillos* (torpedo-shaped, European-style rolls) with coffee and/or milk. Cereal is also sometimes eaten for *desayuno,* e.g., *avena* (oatmeal), *Crema de Trigo* (Cream of Wheat), or *hojuelas de maíz* (corn flakes).

The heavier eggs-and-frijoles dishes known widely as "Mexican breakfasts" in the U.S. and Canada are usually taken as *almuerzo,* the late breakfast (which is most typically reserved for weekends and holidays). Eggs come in a variety of ways, including *huevos revueltos* (scrambled eggs), *huevos duros* (hard-boiled eggs), *huevos tibios* (coddled eggs—but not "soft-boiled" as sometimes translated), *huevos escafaldos* (soft-boiled eggs), *huevos estrelladas* or *huevos fritos* (eggs fried "sunny side up"), *huevos a la mexicana* (also *huevos mexicanos,* eggs scrambled with chopped tomato, onion, and chile), and *huevos rancheros* (fried eggs served on a tortilla). Eggs also come *con chorizo* (eggs scrambled with ground sausage), *con machaca* (with dried, shredded meat), *con tocino* (with bacon), or *con jamón* (with ham). All egg dishes usually come with frijoles and tortillas. The biggest *al-*

muerzo package on the menu is typically called almuerzo albañil ("brickmason's almuerzo") or huevos albañil ("brickmason's eggs"); this means eggs with one or more varieties of meat on the side.

One of the cheapest and tastiest almuerzos is chilaquiles, tortillas chips in a chile gravy with crumbled cheese on top. Eggs and/or chicken can be added to chilaquiles as options. Visitors from Texas (especially Austin) will notice a strong similarity to Tex-Mex cafe-style migas ("crumbs"), though the latter always includes eggs. Another economical choice is molletes, a split bolillo spread with mashed beans and melted cheese, served with salsa on the side. Molletes are usually only US$0.75-1.50 an order; they're often served with juice and coffee as a "university breakfast" (desayuno universitario) for US$2 or less.

Entrees

The main dish or el plato fuerte of any meal can be a grander version of an antojito, a regional specialty from another part of Mexico (mole poblano, for example), or something the cocineros (cooks) have dreamed up themselves. The most typical entrees are centered around meats, seafood, or poultry.

Meat and Poultry: Common meats include carne de res (beef), puerco (pork), and cabrito (kid goat). Jamón (ham), chorizo (sausage), and tocino (bacon) are usually reserved for almuerzo. Throughout the northwest, machaca or dried, shredded meat is very popular. Steak may appear on menus as bistec, bistek, biftec, or "steak." Venado (deer meat or venison), liebre (hare), and conejo (rabbit) are commonly served in the sierras. Poultry dishes include pollo (chicken), pavo (turkey), and, less frequently, pato (duck) and codorniz (quail). Quail is particularly popular in the northeast.

Cabrito or kid goat is an almost exclusively Northern Mexican dish which is most popular in Nuevo León (and to a lesser extent in Coahuila and Chihuahua). Restaurants which specialize in cabrito are easy to spot because their windows will display several cabritos in a row roasting on vertical spits. Spit-roasted kid (cabrito al pastor) is by far the most common way this delicacy is served. Of the several cuts offered on a typical menu, most aficionados agree the pierna or leg is the best overall, followed by

riñon or kidney. Many a visiting gringo, intent on trying cabrito but not wanting to spend much the first time out (and not really knowing the difference between one cut or another), has chosen to order cabecita because it's the cheapest cut on the menu (typically around US$3). Surprise of surprises, cabecita ("little head") is the goat's head! The minimal meat on this cut consists of the cheeks, brain, and tongue (all very tasty). In the Nuevo Laredo area of northern Tamaulipas, machitos—sort of a goat tripe burrito—is quite popular.

Fajitas, the latest fad to sweep Mexican restaurants in the U.S., are strips of meat cooked in a style that originated in the Nuevo Laredo area of Tamaulipas. The name means "little belts" or "little skirts" and refers to a beef cut known in English as "skirt steak," often considered an unusable cut by butchers outside Mexico. In Northern Mexico, ranchero cooks usually slice skirt steaks into strips, grill them quickly over a very hot fire, and serve them with fresh flour tortillas, salsa fresca (called pico de gallo in some parts of Northern Mexico), grilled onions (cebollas asadas), guacamole, and beans. Restaurants in Nuevo Laredo often sell fajitas by the kilo.

Outside of Nuevo León fajitas are sometimes called arracheras; Coahuila restaurants occasionally distinguish between skirt steaks cooked in strips and those cooked whole, calling the former "fajitas" and the latter "arracheras." As fajitas gain in popularity throughout Northern Mexico (partly as a result of their increasing popularity in the U.S.), the presentation is becoming more sophisticated. Most cooks now marinate skirt steaks briefly before cooking in order to tenderize the naturally tough meat. In resort areas, restaurants catering to tourists now offer chicken, shrimp, and sirloin fajitas, so the original meaning of the term "fajita" is changing to indicate any meat, poultry, or seafood cooked in this style—marinated, quickly grilled, and served with tortillas and salsas.

Seafood: Pescado (fish) entrees on the menu are often seasonal or dependent on the "catch of the day." Often just the word "pescado," along with the method of cooking (e.g., pescado al mojo de ajo), will appear. If you need to know exactly what kind of fish, just ask, "¿Hay cuál tipo de pescado?", although in some cases the only response you'll get is something generic like "Pescado blanco" ("white fish").

On the Sea of Cortez/Pacific coast *tacos de pescado* (fish tacos) are popular. If you haven't ever tried one, you're most likely wondering, "What's the big deal—a fish taco?" Eat one, though, and you're hooked for life. Short, tender, fresh fish fillets are quickly dipped in batter and fried, then folded into a steaming corn tortilla with a variety of condiments that include *salsa fresca* (chopped tomatoes, onions, chiles, and lime juice), marinated cabbage (similar to coleslaw in the U.S.), guacamole, and sometimes a squirt of mayonnaise (*mayonesa*). ¡La última! Any kind of white-fleshed fish can be used—the best fish tacos are those made from yellowtail (*jurel*). In Mazatlán a fish taco may be made with shredded fish prepared in a ceviche or *picadillo* style instead of fried fish fillets.

Shellfish (*mariscos*) is quite popular on both coasts but especially along the Gulf of Mexico: *ostiones* (oysters), *almejas* (clams), *callos* (scallops), *jaibas* (small crab), *cangrejo* (large crab), *camarones* (shrimp), *langosta* (lobster, Sea of Cortez/Pacific only), *langostina* (crayfish, also called *cucarachas*), and *abulón* (abalone, Sea of Cortez/Pacific only). These can be ordered as *cocteles* (cocktails—steamed or boiled and served with lime and salsa), *en sus conchas* (in the shell), or *ceviche* (marinated raw in lime juice, onions, and chiles until "cooked" by the acidic juices); or ordered in many of the ways listed below.

Entree items, whether meat, poultry, or seafood, are most commonly prepared in one of the following styles:

adobo, adobada—marinated or stewed in a sauce of vinegar, chiles, and spices

al pastor—roasted on a spit (usually goat)

a la parilla—broiled or grilled

albóndigas—meatballs

al carbón—charcoal-grilled

a la veracruzana—seafood (often *huachinanga* or red snapper) cooked with tomatoes, onions, and olives

al mojo de ajo—in a garlic sauce

al vapor—steamed

asada—grilled

barbacoa—pit-roasted

con arroz—steamed with rice

encebollado—cooked with onions

entomado—cooked with tomatoes

enchilada—cooked with chiles

empanizada—breaded

frito—fried

guisado—in a spicy stew

machaca—dried and shredded

Carnitas: This dish from the state of Michoacán belongs in a category all its own and is usually sold only at butcher shops or at specialty restaurants. The usual method for producing *carnitas* is to slowly braise an entire pig in a huge pot, along with a variety of flavorings (a closely guarded secret among *carnitas* purveyors). The result is chopped into thin slices and eaten with stacks of tortillas, pickled vegetables and chiles, guacamole, and various salsas.

Carnitas are always sold by weight, even in *carnitas* restaurants. You can order by the *kilo,* (one kilogram, about 2.2 pounds), *medio* (half kilo), or *cuarto* (one-fourth kilo), or sometimes in *cien gramos* (100-gram increments). Figure on a quarter kilo (about a half pound) per hungry person and you shouldn't have much left over.

Other Dishes

Beans: The beans most preferred in Northern Mexico are pinto beans, usually dried beans (*frijól*) that are boiled until soft, then mashed and fried with lard or vegetable oil (usually the former) to make frijoles. Often this preparation is called *frijoles refritos* or "refried beans," although they're not really refried except when reheated! Sometimes the beans are served whole, in their own broth, as *frijoles de ollas* (boiled beans) or with bits of roast pork as *frijoles a la charra* (ranch-style beans). Frijoles can be served with any meal of the day, including breakfast. In San Luis Potosí black beans are almost as common as pintos and are always served with *platillos huastecos* (Huasteca dishes).

Cheese: Even the lowliest restaurant or cafe will usually have some cheese (*queso*) around, so if your appetite isn't stimulated by the *guisada de iguana* simmering on the hearth, you can usually ask for *chiles rellenos* (mild poblano chiles stuffed with cheese and fried in an egg batter) or quesadillas (cheese melted in folded flour tortillas). A meal of beans, tortillas, and cheese provides a complete source of protein for travelers who choose to avoid meat, poultry, or seafood for health, economic, or moral reasons.

Northern Mexico is famous for its cheeses, the most common of which are Sonora's *queso cotijo* (also called *queso añejo*), Chihuahua's *queso menonita* (called *queso chihuahuense* outside the state), and *queso asadero* (produced in several states but most common in eastern Chihuahua). All three cheeses can usually be found in supermarkets throughout Northern Mexico.

Queso menonita (Mennonite cheese) is a mild, white cheddar produced in wheels by Mennonite colonists in Chihuahua, while *queso asadero* ("griller cheese") is a braided cheese (somewhat similar to mozzarella or Armenian string cheese) made by combining sour milk with fresh milk. The former is a common ingredient in dishes stuffed with cheese, such as enchiladas or *chiles rellenos*, which won't receive high, direct heat. *Asadero* melts well (without burning or separating) at high temperatures, and as such is well suited to *chile con queso* (hot, blended chile-cheese dip) or *queso fundido* (hot melted cheese topped with chorizo or mushrooms) and other dishes in which the cheese is directly exposed to high heat.

Cotija or *añejo* is a crumbly, aged cheese that resists melting and is commonly used as a topping for enchiladas and beans; the flavor and texture are what you might expect from a cross between feta and Parmesan.

Many ranchos produce their own *queso fresco*, "fresh cheese" made from fresh cow's, goat's, or sheep's milk. To make *queso fresco*, the rancheros first cure the milk with homemade rennet (from a calf's fourth stomach) until the milk separates, and then press the curds with weights (sometimes under flat rocks lined with cloth) to remove excess moisture. In more elaborate operations, the initial pressing is then ground up and repressed into small, round cakes. This type of cheese is not usually found in stores; if you want to buy some, look for *Hay queso* signs as you pass ranchos. If you're very fortunate, you might even come across *queso de apoyo*, an extra-rich cheese made from heavy cream.

Vegetables: Although vegetables are sometimes served as side dishes with *comidas corridas*, with restaurant entrees, or in salads (*ensaladas*), they're seldom listed separately on the menu. When they do appear on menus it's usually at restaurants in towns that are near farming areas. The best place to add vegetables to your diet is at a market or grocery store (see "Buying Groceries," below).

Soup: The general menu term for soup is *sopa*, although a thick soup with lots of ingredients is usually a *caldo* or *caldillo. Menudo*, a soup made with hominy (*nixtamal*) and cow's feet and stomach (or, less commonly, intestine) in a savory, reddish-brown broth served with chopped onions, chiles, and crumbled oregano, is seen throughout Northern Mexico and is highly prized as a hangover remedy. *Pozole* is a similar soup with a much lighter-colored broth; some varieties of *pozole* are made with chicken instead of tripe.

Other tasty soups include *sopa de tortillas, sopa azteca,* and *sopa tlapeño,* all variations of artfully seasoned chicken broth garnished with *totopos* (tortilla wedges) and sliced avocado.

Salsas And Condiments

Any restaurant, cafe, *cafetería, lonchería, taquería,* or *comedor* will offer a variety of *salsas* or sauces with their food. Sometimes only certain salsas are served with certain dishes, while other times one, two, or even three salsas are stationed on every table. Often each place has its own unique salsa recipes—canned or bottled salsas are rarely used. The one ingredient common to all salsas is chile peppers, though these vary in heat from mild to incendiary.

There are as many types of salsas as there are Mexican dishes—red, green, yellow, brown, hot, mild, salty, sweet, thick, thin, blended, and chunky, to name a few. It would take a separate book to describe them all. The most typical is the *salsa casera* or "house salsa," a simple, fresh concoction of chopped chiles, onions, and tomatoes mixed with salt, lime juice, and cilantro. This is what you usually get with the complimentary basket of *totopos* (tortilla chips) served at the beginning of every Mexican meal (including *almuerzo*). Another common one is *salsa verde,* "green sauce," which is made with a base of tomatillos (small, tart, green, tomatolike vegetable). Some salsas are quite *picante* (spicy hot—also *picosa*), so it's always a good idea to test a bit before pouring it over everything on your plate.

Whole pickled chiles are sometimes served on the side as a condiment, especially with tacos and *carnitas*. On Sonoran tables it's common to see a bowl of *chiltepines,* small, round, fiery red peppers. Salt (*sal*) is usually on the table, although it's rarely needed since Mexican dishes tend to be prepared with plenty of it. Black pepper is *pimiento negro,* and if it's not on the table it's normally available for the asking. Butter is *mantequilla,* sometimes served with flour tortillas.

In *taquerías,* guacamole—mashed avocado blended with onions, chiles, salt, and other optional ingredients—is always served as a condiment. In restaurants it may be served as a salad or with tortilla chips. In Sinaloa and Durango, "guacamole" sometimes refers to a very spicy paste of tomatillos and green chiles that may resemble avocado guacamole—always taste before heaping it on your plate. Toasted and ground avocado leaves are also used as a seasoning in Sinaloa and San Luis Potosí.

Desserts And Sweets

The most popular of Mexican desserts, or *postres,* is a delicious egg custard called *flan.* It's listed on virtually every tourist restaurant menu, along with *helado* or ice cream. Other sweet alternatives include pastries found in *panaderías* or bakeries (described under "Buying Groceries," below), and the frosty offerings at the ubiquitous *paleterías.* Strictly speaking, a *paletería* serves only *paletas,* flavored ice on sticks like American popsicles except in a much wider range of flavors, but many also serve *nieve* (snow), which is flavored grated ice served like ice cream in bowls or cones.

Another common street vendor food is *churros,* a sweet fried pastry something like a donut stick sprinkled with powdered sugar. Perhaps Northern Mexico's best *churros* are those sold by vendors in the city parks of Torreón, Coahuila.

Dulcerías are candy shops where a huge variety of sticky Mexican sweets, usually wrapped individually, is sold. Often brightly decorated, *dulcerías* are oriented toward children and sometimes carry inexpensive toys as well as sweets. The larger ones sell piñatas, colorful papier-mâché figures that are filled with candy and small gifts and hung at parties; on special occasions, children are allowed to break them with sticks, thus releasing all the goodies inside. Traditionally, piñatas are crafted to resemble common animals, but these days you'll see all kinds of shapes, including "Teenage Mutant Tortugas de Ninja."

BUYING GROCERIES

The cheapest way to feed yourself while traveling in Mexico is the same way you save money at home: Buy groceries at the store and prepare your own meals. While they may not have any dining spots to speak of, even the smallest towns in Northern Mexico will have at least a small grocery store or corner market. A ripe avocado (*aguacate*), a chunk of *queso,* and a couple of *bolillos* can make a fine, easy-to-fix meal.

The humblest stores are the small, family-owned *tienda de abarrotes,* which are usually recognizable by the single word *abarrotes*— "groceries"—printed somewhere on the outside (*tienda* means "store"). These will have the basics—tortillas, dried beans, flour, herbs and spices, bottled water, a few vegetables, possibly *bolillos* and cheese—as well as limited household goods like soap and laundry detergent. As at the 7-Eleven back home, the food at the average *tienda de abarrotes* is not particularly inexpensive.

A better deal, when you can find it, is the government-sponsored CONASUPO (an acronym for Compañía Nacional de Subsistencias Populares). CONASUPOs carry many of the same items as a *tienda de abarrotes* but at government-subsidized prices. Not every item is cheaper, however, so it pays to shop around. Larger, supermarket-style CONASUPOs are called CONASUPER.

Privately run supermarkets can be found in larger towns and are usually called *supers* or *supermercados.* Like their North American counterparts, they're usually well stocked with a wide variety of meats, baked goods, vegetables, household goods, beer and liquor, and so on. Supermarket prices are often better than in smaller grocery stores.

Most towns and cities have *mercados municipales* (municipal markets), large, warehouse-type structures where meat, fruit, and vegetable producers sell their goods directly to the public. Prices are often very good at these markets but it really helps if you speak some Spanish and know how to bargain. Although they're usually centrally located, municipal markets are sometimes difficult to find simply because they look so inconspicuous on the outside—you may have to ask around.

Another common *tienda* is the *ultramarinos,* which is primarily a place to buy beer and liquor but which also sells a few deli-style food items.

Panaderías

Although a few bakery items can often be purchased at all of the above-named stores, the best place to buy them, naturally, is at their source—a *panadería* or bakery. Many of the *panaderías* in rural Northern Mexico still used wood-fired *hornos* (ovens), which make the *bolillos* (Mexican rolls), *pastels* (cakes), and *pan dulce* (cookies and sweet pastries) especially tasty. *Pan de barra,* American-style sliced bread, is also occasionally available but it never measures up to crusty *bolillos.* To select bakery items from the shelves of a *panadería,* simply imitate the other customers—pick up a pair of tongs and a tray from the counter near the cash register and help yourself, cafeteria-style.

Tortillerías

Unless you make them yourself, the best place to buy tortillas is where they make them fresh every day. Restaurants, *tiendas,* and home cooks will purchase from the local *tortillería* to avoid spending hours at a *metate* (grinder) or *comal* (griddle). The automated process at a *tortillería* uses giant electric grinders and conveyor belts to transform whole corn into fresh tortillas, which you purchase by weight, not number. A kilo will yield about 40 average, five-inch tortillas; you can order by the *cuarto* or *medio* (quarter or half kilo). The government-subsidized prices are quite low.

Prices

Here are some sample grocery prices taken from a supermarket in Guaymas, Son. in late '92 (in U.S. dollars-per-kilogram—2.2 pounds—unless otherwise specified):

> whole chicken: 2.50
> ground beef: 4.60
> *queso cotijo añejo:* 4.00
> *queso chihuahuense:* 4.60-5.60
> *queso asadero:* 7.00
> San Miguel avocados: .70

papayas: 1.50
tomatoes: 3.00
bananas: .83
onions: .76
broccoli: 1.86
corn on the cob: .28
rice: .66
milk, 2 liters: 1.00
18 eggs: 1.15
purified water, one gallon: .92
tequila, most brands: 9.00/liter

WHAT TO DRINK

Nonalcoholic Beverages

Cold Drinks: The water and ice served in restaurants in Northern Mexico are always purified—it's not necessary to order *agua mineral* (mineral water) unless you need the minerals. Likewise, the water used as an ingredient in "handmade" drinks, e.g., *licuados* or *aguas frescas,* is also from purified sources.

Licuados are similar to American "smoothies"—fruit blended with water, ice, honey or sugar, and sometimes milk or raw eggs, to produce something like a fruit shake. In Northern Mexico, *tuna* (not the fish but the prickly pear cactus fruit) *licuados* are particularly delicious. Other tasty and nutritious additives include oats (*avena*) and wheat germ (*trigo*). Any place that makes *licuados* will also make orange juice (*jugo de naranja*).

Aguas frescas are the colorful beverages sold from huge glass jars either on the streets of larger cities or at carnivals, usually during warm weather. They're made by boiling the pulp of various fruits, grains, or seeds with water, then straining it and adding sugar and large chunks of ice. *Arroz* (rice) and *horchata* (either melon or pumpkin seeds, or almonds) are two of the tastiest *aguas; cebada,* a concoction of barley mixed with cinnamon and vanilla, is also good and is a specialty of Sinaloa. *Licuados* and *aguas frescas* are often sold from colorful storefronts invariably named "La Flor de Michoacán" or "La Michoacana."

U.S. soft drinks (*refrescos*), like 7-UP, Coke, and Pepsi, are quite common; Mexico has

⟨⟨⟨⟨⟨⟨⟨⟨⟨⟨⟨⟨⟨⟨ TEQUILA ⟩⟩⟩⟩⟩⟩⟩⟩⟩⟩⟩⟩⟩⟩⟩

Mexico's national drink has been in production since at least the time of the Aztecs (the Spaniards levied a tax on tequila as early as 1608). The liquor's name was taken from the Ticuila of Jalisco who mastered the process of distilling an extract from the *Agave tequiliana* or blue agave, a process still employed by tequila distilleries today. Native to Jalisco, this succulent is the only agave that produces true tequila as certified by the Mexican government (look for the initials DGN—Dirección General de Normas—on the label).

Much of the tequila-making process is still carried out *a mano* (by hand). In the traditional method, the mature heart of the tequila agave, which looks like a huge pineapple and weighs 50-150 pounds, is roasted in pits for 24 hours, then shredded and ground by mule- or horse-powered mills. After the juice is extracted from the pulp and fermented in ceramic pots, it's distilled in copper stills to produce the basic tequila, which is always clear and colorless, with an alcohol content of around 40%. "Gold" tequilas are produced by aging the tequila in imported oak barrels.

José Cuervo, Sauza, and Herradura are well established tequila labels with international notoriety. Of these three, Herradura is said to employ the most traditional methods and hence tequila connoisseurs generally prefer it over the other two. But don't take their word for it; try a few *probaditos* ("little proofs" or shots) for yourself.

Mezcal And The Worm

The distillate of other agave plants (also known as magueys or century plants) is called mezcal. The same roasting and distilling process is used for mezcal as for tequila. (Tequila, too, is a mezcal, but no drinker calls it that, just as no one in a U.S. bar orders "whiskey" when they mean to specify scotch or bourbon.) The caterpillarlike grub you see floating at the bottom of a bottle of mezcal is the *gusano de maguey* ("maguey worm"), which lives on the maguey plant itself. They're safe to eat (just about anything pickled in mezcal would be) but not particularly appetizing. By the time you hit the bottom of the bottle, though, who cares?

Tequila Drinks

The most common way to drink tequila is straight up, followed by a water or beer chaser. Licking a few grains of salt before taking a shot and sucking a lime wedge afterwards will make it go down smoother (the salt raises a protective coating of saliva on the tongue while the lime juice scours the tongue of salt and tequila residues). In Chihuahua the ordeal is simplified in a drink called the "Pancho Villa," simply chilled tequila mixed with salt and lime.

Tequila con sangrita, in which a shot of tequila is chased with a shot of *sangrita* (not to be confused with *sangria,* the wine-and-fruit punch), is a slightly more elegant way to accomplish the same process. *Sangrita* is a bright red mix of orange juice, lime juice, grenadine, red chile powder, and salt. A drink called the *vampiro* ("vampire")—quite popular in Nuevo León, Coahuila, and Chihuahua—takes this a step further, mixing tequila and *sangrita* together in the same glass with a wedge of lime.

An old tequila standby is the much-abused margarita, a tart Tex-Mex cocktail made with tequila, lime juice, and Cointreau (usually "Controy" or triple-sec in Mexico) served in a salt-rimmed glass. A true margarita is shaken and served on the rocks, rather than blended with ice in the "frozen" style. Crushed or blended ice tends to kill the flavor.

Vampiro
Sangrita:

1½ cups fresh orange juice

juice of one lime

2 tbsp. grenadine

¼ to ½ tsp. red chile powder *(not* "chili powder," but pure ground, dried red chiles), depending on taste

1½ tsp. salt

Use the above ingredients to prepare *sangrita,* then mix approximately 1½ parts *sangrita* to one part tequila in a glass of ice and garnish with a wedge of lime.

equivalent beverages that are just as good. An apple-flavored soft drink called Manzanita is quite popular.

Hot Drinks: Coffee is served in a variety of ways. The best (when you can find it) is traditional Mexican-style coffee, which is made by filtering near-boiling water through fine-ground coffee in a slender cloth sack. Instant coffee (*nescafé*) is often served at small restaurants and cafes—a jar of instant coffee may be sitting on the table for you to add to hot water. When there's a choice, a request for *café de olla* ("boiled coffee") should bring you real brewed coffee. One of the better Mexican brands found in supermarkets is Café Combate.

Café con leche is the Mexican version of café au lait, i.e., coffee with hot milk in near-equal proportions. Coffee is particularly good in San Luis Potosí, where *café con leche* is a local specialty. *Café con crema* (coffee with cream) is not as available—when it is, it usually includes non-dairy powdered creamer.

Hot chocolate (*chocolate*) is fairly common on Mexican menus. It's usually served very sweet and may contain cinnamon, ground almonds, and other flavorings. A thicker version that is made with cornmeal—almost a chocolate pudding—is called *champurrado* or *atole*.

Black tea (*té negro*) is not popular among *norteños* although you may see it on tourist menus. Ask for *té helado* if you want iced tea. At home many Mexicans drink *té de manzanilla* (chamomile tea) or *té de yerba buena* (mint tea) in the evenings. In Sinaloa *té de damiana* is popular. Some *norteños* claim the herb *damiana* has aphrodisiac qualities; others say it's a sedative.

Alcoholic Beverages

Drinking laws in Mexico are minimal. The legal drinking age in Mexico was recently raised from 15 to 18 years, and it's illegal to carry an open container of alcoholic beverage in a vehicle. That's about it—liquor of every kind is widely available in bars, restaurants, grocery stores, and *licorerías* or liquor stores.

Cerveza: In northwest Mexico, particularly Sonora, the most popular (and most available) beer brand is Tecate (brewed in Tecate, Baja California Norte), while farther south toward Mazatlán it's Pacífico (from Mazatlán). Both are good-tasting, light- to medium-weight brews, with Tecate holding a slight edge (more hops) over Pacífico. You can't compare either of these with their export equivalents in the U.S., since Mexican breweries produce a separate brew for American consumption that's lighter in taste and lighter on the alcohol content—it's always better in Mexico.

As you move east to the more populated areas of Northern Mexico, a greater variety of labels is available, including such major Mexican brands as Corona (now partially owned by Anheuser-Busch), Dos Equis (XX), Superior, Carta Blanca, Bohemia, and Negro Modelo. It's really a matter of personal taste as to which of these brands will most satisfy a visiting beer drinker; beer connoisseurs most often cite Bohemia as the country's best brew. To order Dos Equis, *norteños* usually ask for "lager."

The cheapest sources for beer are the brewery's agents or distributors (look for signs saying *agencia, cervezería,* or *depósito*), where you can return deposit bottles for cash or credit. You can buy beer by the bottle (*envase*), can (*bote*), six-pack (*canastilla*) or case (*cartón*). Large, liter-size bottles of Tecate are called *caguamas* or "sea turtles" and are quite popular. The Pacífico equivalent is known as a *ballena* or "whale." When buying beer at an *agencia* or *depósito*, specify *fría* if you want cold beer; otherwise you'll get beer *al tiempo* (at room temperature).

Wine: Northern Mexico—particularly the Región Lagunera and Zacatecas—is one of Mexico's major wine production areas, and regional wines are commonly served in restaurants. A broad selection of varietals is available, including cabernet sauvignon, chardonnay, chenin blanc, Pinot noir, barbera, and zinfandel. These and other grapes are also blended to produce cheaper *vino tinto* (red wine) and *vino blanco* (white wine). When ordering wine in Spanish at a bar, you may want to specify *vino de uva* ("grape wine"), as *vino* alone can be used to refer to distilled liquors as well as wine. *Vino blanco,* in fact, can be interpreted as cheap tequila.

Liquor: Tequila is Mexico's national drink and also the most popular distilled liquor in Northern Mexico (see special topic "Tequila," above). The second most popular is brandy followed closely by *ron* (rum), both of which are produced in Mexico for export as well as for domestic consumption. Among brandies, Presidente is the biggest seller, but Don Pedro Reserva Especial is better quality. A favorite rum drink is the *cuba libre* ("free Cuba"), called *cuba* for short—a mix of rum, Coke, and lime juice over ice. An alternative made with Mexican brandy is called *cuba de uva* ("grape cuba"). Other hard liquors—gin, vodka, scotch, etc.—may only be available at hotel bars and tourist restaurants. Drinks that contain imported liquor typically cost about twice as much as those that contain domestic (*nacional* or "national" on most bar menus) liquor.

In rural areas of Chihuahua and Coahuila, a contraband liquor called lechugilla, illegally distilled from the heart of the *Agave lechugilla* (a succulent considered an indicator plant for the Chihuahuan Desert), is quite common. Clear and colorless, lechugilla (or *"leche"* as it is sometimes nicknamed) can register a strength of nearly 100 proof, with a flavor that resembles a mix of tequila and grain alcohol. Good-quality lechugilla may taste no stronger than tequila at first swallow, but the fire in the belly and resultant intoxication are always more intense. In "dry" areas of the Sierra Tarahumara where alcoholic beverages are prohibited by law (e.g., Urique, Batopilas), it may be the only liquor available.

In northern Chihuahua a similar liquor called sotol (from a desert succulent of the same name in the *Agave* family) is the moonshine of choice. Sinaloans make their own moonshine called *caña* ("cane") from sugarcane; the taste, as might be expected, is similar to that of high-proof rum. *Bacanora* is the Sonoran equivalent, made from mezcal or hearts of Sonoran agave. The generic term for all contraband liquors is *aguardiente.*

Cantinas and Bars: Traditionally speaking, a true cantina is a Mexican-style drinking venue for males only, but in modern urban Mexico the distinction between "bar" and "cantina" is becoming increasingly blurred. In large cities, an upscale bar-restaurant with "cantina" in its name may have plenty of women downing drinks with the *machos.*

In small, rural towns, the more traditional cantina is the kind of place you'll occasionally stumble upon, usually on the outskirts of town, where blinking Christmas lights festoon a *palapa* roof and palm-thatch or ocotillo walls. Inside are a few tables and chairs—and a handful of *borrachos;* generally the only women present will either be serving the booze or serving as hired "dates." The only drink choices will be beer, Mexican brandy, and cheap tequila or *aguardiente* (often when you order tequila in a place like this, you'll be served a large glass of *aguardiente,* considered an acceptable substitute).

Bars, on the other hand, will only be found in hotels and in the larger cities or resort areas. They have developed largely as social venues for tourists or for a younger generation of Mexicans for whom the cantina is passé. A bar, in contrast to a cantina, will offer a variety of beers, wines, and distilled liquors. By Mexican standards, bars are considered very upmarket places to hang out, so they aren't extremely popular—many young Mexicans would rather drink at a disco where at least the drinking is accompanied by dancing.

A sign outside a bar reading "ladies bar" means that the bar admits women. This doesn't always mean the bar in question is a place a lady would want to enter; a peek inside will usually tell the tale.

Bar Lingo
bartender—*cantinero*
beer—*cerveza* (*una fría*—"a cold one")
bottle—*envase, botella* (*casco*—empty bottle)
a drink—*una copita, uno tragito*
drunk, drunkard—*borracho*
glass—*vaso, copa*
hangover—*la cruda*
no ice—*sin hielo*
with ice—*con hielo*
snacks—*botanas*

GETTING THERE

BY AIR

Mexico is ranked eighth in the world—right between China and Japan—for the number of airports (78) in the country that can be reached by scheduled commercial flights. Major international airline connections into Northern Mexico are handled by **Alaska, Aeroméxico** (on some routes in conjunction with American Airlines), **Aero California,** and **Mexicana** via several major U.S. cities, as well as major cities worldwide. (See "Airlines Serving Northern Mexico," below.)

Direct flights to Northern Mexico destinations are substantially less expensive than those that connect through Mexico City. For convenience and price, the best U.S. cities from which to fly to Northern Mexico are Los Angeles, Phoenix, Tucson, El Paso, Harlingen (Texas), Houston, McAllen (Texas), and San Antonio. Sample roundtrip international fares for nonstop flights (figure just over half the roundtrip fare for the equivalent one-way fare) include: Los Angeles-Chihuahua US$343; Los Angeles-Monterrey US$495; Tucson-Los Mochis US$224; Tucson-Mazatlán US$328; McAllen-Tampico US$196; McAllen-Monterrey US$128; San Antonio-Monterrey US$152; Phoenix-Guaymas US$216; El Paso-Chihuahua US$201.

Other international departures require connections through Mexico City in which the total fare is the sum of the ticket price to Mexico City plus the fare from Mexico City to your Northern Mexico destination. Thus, if you can get a cheap flight to one of these six U.S. cities and use it as a gateway, you'll probably save a considerable sum.

Note that air tickets to Mexico that are purchased in the U.S. are guaranteed (by U.S. federal law) against fare increases no matter which carrier you use. On the other hand, for tickets

---

AIRLINES SERVING NORTHERN MEXICO

* = nonstop flight
Note: All routes are subject to change; call the airlines for the latest information.

AERO CALIFORNIA (tel. 800-237-6225 in the U.S. and Canada)

Flights to **Culiacán** from Aguascalientes, Ciudad Juárez, Colima, Guadalajara*, La Paz*, Los Angeles*, Los Mochis*, Mexicali, Mexico City*, Puebla, Tijuana*, and Torreón

Flights to **Ciudad Juárez** from Culiacán, Durango, Guadalajara, La Paz, Mexico City, and Torreón

Flights to **Durango** from Ciudad Juárez, Guadalajara*, Puebla, Tijuana, and Torreón*

Flights to **Los Mochis** from Aguascalientes, Culiacán*, Durango, Guadalajara*, Los Angeles, Mexico City*, Puebla, Tijuana*, and Torreón

Flights to **Mazatlán** from Guadalajara, La Paz*, Mexico City*, and Tijuana

Flights to **Torreón** from Ciudad Juárez*, Culiacán, Durango*, Guadalajara, La Paz, Mexico City*, Puebla, and Tijuana*

Flight to Hermosillo from Mexicali*

AEROMÉXICO (tel. 800-237-6639 in the U.S. and Canada)

Flights to **Chihuahua** from Acapulco, Cancún, Ciudad Juárez*, Culiacán*, Durango, Guadalajara, Harlingen (Texas), Hermosillo*, Ixtapa/Zihuatanejo, Los Angeles*, Los Mochis, Madrid (Spain), Manzanillo, Mazatlán, McAllen (Texas), Mérida, Mexico City*, Monterrey*, Morelia, New York, Oaxaca, Paris (France), Puerto Vallarta, Rome (Italy), San Luis Potosí, Tampico, Tijuana, Torreón, Veracruz, and Villahermosa

AIRLINES SERVING NORTHERN MEXICO
continued

Flights to **Ciudad Juárez** from Acapulco, Aguascalientes, Cancun, Chihuahua*, Durango, Frankfurt (Germany), Guadalajara, Ixtapa/Zihuatanejo, La Paz, Madrid (Spain), Manzanillo, Mazatlán*, Mérida, Mexico City*, Monterrey, Paris (France), Puerto Vallarta, Rome (Italy), San Luis Potosí, Torreón, Veracruz, and Villahermosa

Flights to **Ciudad Obregón** from Acapulco, Aguascalientes, Culiacán*, Guadalajara*, Hermosillo*, Los Angeles, Madrid (Spain), Mazatlán, Mérida, Mexico City, Monterrey, Morelia, Tepic, and Tijuana

Flights to **Ciudad Victoria** from Acapulco, Ixtapa/Zihuatanejo, Los Angeles, Mexico City*, and Villahermosa

Flights to **Culiacán** from Acapulco, Aguascalientes, Chihuahua*, Ciudad Obregón*, Durango*, Guadalajara*, Guaymas, Hermosillo, Ixtapa/Zihuatanejo, La Paz*, Los Angeles, Los Mochis*, Madrid (Spain), Manzanillo, Mazatlán*, Mérida, Mexico City*, Monterrey, Oaxaca, Puerto Vallarta, Rome (Italy), San Luis Potosí, Tepic, Tepic*, Tijuana, and Tucson

Flights to **Durango** from Acapulco, Cancún, Chihuahua, Ciudad Juárez, Culiacán*, Frankfurt (Germany), Guadalajara*, Harlingen (Texas), Ixtapa/Zihuatanejo, Los Angeles, Madrid (Spain), Mazatlán, Mazatlán*, McAllen, Mérida, Mexico City*, Monterrey*, Morelia, Oaxaca, Paris (France), Rome (Italy), Salina Cruz, San Antonio, San Luis Potosí, Tampico, Tijuana, Torreón, Torreón*, Veracruz, and Villahermosa

Flights to **Guaymas** from Culiacán, La Paz*, Los Angeles, Mexico City and Tucson*

Flights to **Hermosillo** from Acapulco, Chihuahua*, Ciudad Juárez, Ciudad Obregón*, Culiacán, Guadalajara*, Ixtapa/Zihuatanejo, Los Angeles*, Los Mochis*, Mazatlán, Mérida, Mexico City*, Monterrey*, San Diego*, San Luis Potosí, Tampico, Tijuana*, and Tucson*

Flights to **Los Mochis** from Chihuahua, Culiacán*, Guadalajara, Hermosillo*, La Paz*, Mazatlán*, Mexico City, Monterrey, and Tucson

Flights to **Matamoros** from Acapulco, Guadalajara, Mérida, and Mexico City*

Flights to **Mazatlán** from Acapulco, Chihuahua, Ciudad Juárez*, Ciudad Obregón, Culiacán*, Durango*, Guadalajara*, Hermosillo, Los Angeles, Los Cabos*, Los Mochis*, Mérida, Mexico City, Monterrey, Morelia, San Luis Potosí, Tijuana*, Tucson, and Veracruz

Flights to **Monterrey** from Acapulco, Aguascalientes*, Bahías de Huatulco, Campeche, Cancún, Chihuahua*, Ciudad Juárez, Ciudad Obregón, Culiacán, Durango, Frankfurt (Germany), Guadalajara, Harlingen (Texas)*, Hermosillo*, Ixtapa/Zihuatanejo, La Paz, Los Angeles, McAllen (Texas), Mérida, Mexico City, Miami, Morelia, New York, Oaxaca, Paris (France), Puerto Vallarta, Rome (Italy), San Antonio*, San Diego, San Luis Potosí*, Tampico*, Tapachula, Tepic, Tijuana, Torreón, Uruapan, Veracruz, and Villahermosa

Flights to **San Luis Potosí** from Acapulco, Bahías de Huatulco, Cancún, Chihuahua, Ciudad Juárez, Culiacán, Durango, Guadalajara*, Guaymas, Harlingen (Texas), Hermosillo, Houston, Ixtapa/Zihuatanejo, La Paz, Los Angeles, Mazatlán, McAllen (Texas), Mérida, Mexico City, Mexico City*, Monterrey*, New York, Oaxaca, Puerto Vallarta, Rome (Italy), San Antonio*, Tampico, Tapachula, Tijuana, Tucson, Veracruz, and Villahermosa

Flights to **Tampico** from Acapulco, Aguascalientes, Campeche, Cancún, Chihuahua, Durango, Frankfurt (Germany), Guadalajara, Harlingen (Texas), Hermosillo, Ixtapa/Zihuatanejo, La Paz, Los Angeles, McAllen (Texas), Mérida, Mexico City*, Monterrey*, Paris (France), Poza Rica*, Puerto Vallarta, Salina Cruz, San Antonio, San Luis Potosí, Tapachula, Torreón, Uruapan, Veracruz*, and Villahermosa

Flights to **Torreón** from Acapulco, Aguascalientes, Campeche, Cancún, Chihuahua*, Ciudad Juárez, Durango*, Frankfurt (Germany), Guadalajara*, Hermosillo, Ixtapa/Zihuatanejo, Los Angeles, Madrid (Spain), Manzanillo, McAllen (Texas), Mérida, Mexico City*, Miami, Monterrey*, Morelia, Paris, Poza Rica, Puerto Vallarta, Rome (Italy), Salina Cruz, San Antonio, San Luis Potosí, Tampico, Tapachula, Tijuana, Uruapan, Veracruz, and Villahermosa *continued*

AIRLINES SERVING NORTHERN MEXICO
continued

ALASKA AIRLINES (tel. 800-426-0333 in the U.S. and Canada)

Flights to **Mazatlán** from Anchorage, Fairbanks, Juneau, Los Angeles*, Portland, San Francisco*, and Seattle

LEO LOPEZ AIRLINES (tel. 915-778-1022 in the U.S. and Canada)

Flights to **Chihuahua** from El Paso* and Los Mochis

MEXICANA AIRLINES (tel. 800-531-7921 in the U.S. and Canada)

Flights to **Hermosillo** from Acapulco, Bahías de Huatulco, Guadalajara*, Ixtapa/Zihuatanejo, Mexico City*, Oaxaca, Tampico, Tuxtla Gutiérrez, and Veracruz

Flights to **Mazatlán** from Acapulco, Caracas (Venezuela), Chicago, Denver*, Guadalajara*, Ixtapa/Zihuatanejo, Los Angeles*, Los Cabos, Los Cabos*, Mérida, Mexico City*, New York, Oaxaca, Puerto Vallarta, Puerto Vallarta*, San Francisco*, Tampico, and Veracruz

Flights to **Monterrey** from Acapulco, Bahías de Huatulco, Cancún, Caracas (Venezuela), Chicago*, Guadalajara, Havana (Cuba), Mérida, Mexico City*, New York, Oaxaca, Puerto Escondido, Puerto Vallarta, San Antonio*, San Francisco, San Luis Potosí*, Tampico*, Tuxtla Gutiérrez, Veracruz, and Villahermosa

Flights to **Nuevo Laredo** from Guadalajara and Mexico City*

Flights to **San Luis Potosí** from Acapulco, Cancun, Chicago, Guadalajara, Mérida, Mexico City*, Monterrey*, Oaxaca, Puerto Vallarta, Veracruz, and Villahermosa

Flights to **Tampico** from Acapulco, Bahías de Huatulco, Cancún, Chicago, Guadalajara, Havana (Cuba), Hermosillo, Ixtapa/Zihuatanejo, Los Angeles, Los Cabos, Mazatlán, Mérida, Mexico City*, Monterrey*, New York, Oaxaca, Puerto Escondido, Puerto Vallarta, San Antonio, San Francisco, San José (California), Tijuana, Veracruz*, and Villahermosa

Flights to **Zacatecas** from Chicago*, Los Angeles, Mexico City, and Tijuana*

NOROESTE (tel. 800-6-21-26 in Mexico)

Flights to **Ciudad Obregón** from Culiacán*, Durango, Hermosillo*, Mazatlán, Mexicali, Monterrey, and Torreón

Flights to **Culiacán** from Ciudad Obregón*, Durango, Hermosillo, Mazatlán*, Mexicali, Monterrey, and Torreón

Flights to **Durango** from Ciudad Obregón, Culiacán, Hermosillo, Mazatlán*, Mexicali, Mexico City*, Monterrey, Torreón* and Torreón

Flights to **Hermosillo** from Ciudad Obregón*, Culiacán, Durango, Hermosillo, Mazatlán, Mexicali*, Mexico City, Mexico City*, Monterrey, and Torreón

Flights to **Mazatlán** from Culiacán, Culiacán*, Ciudad Obregón, Durango*, Hermosillo, Mexicali, Monterrey, and Torreón

Flights to **Monterrey** from Ciudad Obregón, Culiacán, Hermosillo, Mexicali, Monterrey, Torreón, and Torreón*

Flights to **Torreón** from Ciudad Obregón, Culiacán, Durango*, Hermosillo, Mexicali, Mexico City, Monterrey, and Monterrey*

SARO (Servicios Aereos Rutas Oriente, tel. 800-JET-SARO in the U.S. and Canada)

Flights to **Culiacán** from Mexico City, Monterrey, Tepic*, Tijuana*, and Torreón*

Flights to **Mazatlán** from Monterrey and Torreón*

AIRLINES SERVING NORTHERN MEXICO
continued

Flights to **Monterrey** from Acapulco, Cancún, Culiacán, Mazatlán, Mexico City, Puebla, Tijuana, and Torreón

Flights to **Torreón** from Culiacán*, Mazatlán*, Mexico City*, Monterrey, Puebla, and Tepic*

TAESA (tel. 512-725-8414 in the U.S. and Canada)

Flights to **Chicago** from Ciudad Juárez*, Durango, Guadalajara*, Mexico City, Morelia, and Zacatecas*

Flights to **Chihuahua** from Mexico City*

Flights to **Ciudad Juárez** from Acapulco, Cancún, Chicago*, Cozumel, Durango*, Ixtapa/Zihuatanejo, Mérida, Mexico City, and Zacatecas*

Flights to **Durango** from Chicago, Ciudad Juárez*, and Mexico City

Flights to **Hermosillo** from Mexicali* and Mexico City

Flights to **Saltillo** from Mexico City*

Flights to **Zacatecas** from Chicago*, Ciudad Juárez*, Mexico City, Morelia*, and Tijuana

---

purchased in Mexico you're liable for price increases before departure—these may be collected at airport check-in. Hence if you plan to fly within Mexico and have a good idea of your itinerary, you may want to consider buying the tickets in the U.S. in advance to guard against this.

BY LAND

Most foreign visitors to Northern Mexico arrive via one of the many border gateways along the U.S.-Mexico frontier between Yuma, Arizona, and Brownsville, Texas. The major crossings connect with major Mexican highways: Nogales, Arizona-Nogales (Mexico 15); El Paso-Ciudad Juárez (Mexico 45/49); Eagle Pass-Piedras Negras (Mexico 57); Laredo, Texas-Nuevo Laredo (Mexico 85); McAllen-Reynosa (Mexico 97/101); and Brownsville-Matamoros (Mexico 101). Interspersed between these are at least a dozen smaller, less-used crossings which make perfectly good gateways. For information on border formalities, see individual states and "Entry Regulations," p. 100.

Reaching The Border
Those who plan to use public transport in Mexico can easily reach the U.S.-Mexico border by bus or train. Inter-city buses in the U.S. generally depart more frequently and are less expensive than trains. **Continental Greyhound Bus Lines**

is the major carrier; a bus pass may be more economical than buying single-journey tickets. Outside the U.S., a Greyhound *Ameripass,* which allows unlimited bus travel within specified dates, can be purchased from travel agencies at a discount (e.g., a seven-day pass bought outside the U.S. costs around US$100; in the U.S., around US$135-150). Several smaller, regional bus lines also provide service to U.S. border towns.

Local express buses at large border towns provide convenient connections between the downtown areas on both sides of the border. El Paso's "Border Jumper," for example, links downtown El Paso with downtown Ciudad Juárez. For information on these kinds of bus services, refer to the appropriate city section.

U.S. Rail
The only long-distance passenger rail line in the U.S. is **Amtrak,** which brings passengers very close to the border at San Diego, California, and El Paso, Texas. Connections with a number of other Amtrak lines to points in the U.S. farther north or east can be arranged. Amtrak has special one-way, roundtrip, or excursion fares on occasion—always ask before booking.

Outside North America, some international travel agencies sell a **USA Railpass** which allows unlimited U.S. rail travel within specified dates. A rail pass called *All Aboard America* is sold inside the U.S. at slightly higher prices. For schedule information or bookings inside the U.S., call (800) 872-7245 (800-USA-RAIL).

Mexican Rail

Mexico's national rail service has its westernmost terminus in Mexicali, Baja California Norte. The Mexicali line connects with the Mexico City-Nogales, Son., line at Benjamin Hill—an alternative way to get to mainland Mexico from Baja (this can also be accomplished farther south in Baja via one of the ferry services—see "By Ferry from Baja," below). In the U.S., **Mexico By Rail** (tel. 800-228-3225) specializes in booking train trips from Chihuahua, Eagle Pass, and Nuevo Laredo into the interior (MBR also sells tickets on other major routes) for a surcharge above the normal first-class fares. Information on rail travel from these and other Mexican border cities can be found under "Getting Around," below, as well as under the appropriate destination sections.

Driving To Northern Mexico

Most people visiting Northern Mexico by land (except border day-trippers) drive their own vehicles. The red tape for driving into Mexico is fairly minimal and shouldn't prevent or discourage anyone from attempting it. If you find the traffic at the larger border gateways daunting, consider using one of the many smaller crossings available. An easy-to-obtain temporary vehicle import permit is required for stays of longer than 72 hours. See "Entry Regulations," p. 100, for more details on red tape, and "Driving in Northern Mexico," pp. 90-99, for important information on road travel inside the country.

BY FERRY FROM BAJA

Three ferry services currently run to mainland Mexico from Baja California—one each from La Paz to Topolobampo and Mazatlán, and one from Santa Rosalía to Guaymas.

The old passenger-vehicle ferries are still a good way for anyone driving on the mainland to reach southern Baja without having to make a time-consuming U-turn at the top of the peninsula. It's also a way for drivers from the U.S. West Coast to return from mainland Mexico's Sea of Cortez/Pacific coast without covering the same territory twice. In the reverse direction, many West Coasters use the ferry services as an alternative way of reaching the mainland since it allows them to see Baja on the way to Mazatlán or other points farther east or south.

The ferry system was privatized a few years ago and is now operated by Grupo Servicios Maritimos y Turísticos (SEMATUR). As service continues to evolve, we can expect classes, fares, and departure schedules to change regularly. Keep this in mind when making plans according to the below-mentioned information.

Fares And Classes

Passenger fares are based on class: *salón* (reclining seats in various general seating areas), *turista* (shared bunk rooms), and *cabina* (private cabins with toilet facilities). Some ferryboats also have an additional *especial* class that features larger deluxe cabins. Fares for children under 12 are 50% of adult fares.

Vehicle fares are based on the vehicle's length—the longer the rig, the higher the fare. Sample tariffs range from US$10 for a motorcycle on the La Paz-Topolobampo route to as much as US$430 for a trailer rig over nine meters (30 feet) long from La Paz to Mazatlán. Passenger and vehicle fares are separate.

Note: Signs at the ferry ticket offices warn that passenger tickets will not be issued to pregnant women.

Reservations

Whether it was the fare increases or the reorganization of management under private auspices, ferry reservations are now somewhat easier to make than they were several years ago. *Salón* seats are sold on a first-come, first-served basis; *turista* can be reserved three days (or more) in advance; a *cabina* can be reserved a month (or more) in advance. During holiday periods (especially Semana Santa, when you might want to avoid ferry service altogether), you should try to arrive as early as possible during the allowable booking period for advance tickets. Reservations must be confirmed 15 days before departure date for the La Paz-Mazatlán and La Paz-Topolobampo routes, 10 days before departure for the Santa Rosalía-Guaymas route.

SEMATUR operates ticket offices at each of its ferry piers for advance as well as day-of-departure sales. A number of Mexican travel agencies have also been authorized to handle ticket reservations and sales in Ciudad Constitución, Baja California Sur (Viajes Pedrín, tel. 113-2-01-12); Guerrero Negro; Baja California Sur (Viajes Mario's, tel. 7-07-88); La Paz, Baja California Sur (Viajes Transpeninsulares, tel. 112-2-03-99; Viajes Perla, tel. 2-86-66; Viajes Cabo Falso, tel. 2-41-31); Los Mochis (Viajes Paotam, tel. 681-5-19-14); and Mazatlán (Turismo Coral, tel. 69-81-32-90; Marza Tours, tel. 86-08-96; Viajes Attiq, tel. 84-24-00). SEMATUR also has a toll-free information and reservation telephone number in Mexico: 800-6-96-96 (this number can be accessed from the U.S. and Canada by adding a 91 prefix).

Santa Rosalía-Guaymas
Ferries depart Santa Rosalía for Guaymas every Tuesday and Friday at 8 a.m. In the opposite direction, ferries leave on the same days at 9 a.m. The westbound crossing takes approximately eight hours and the eastbound about nine.

Passenger fares are US$11.50 *salón,* US$23 *turista. Cabina* and *especial* aren't usually available on this route, but occasionally a larger ferry from another route will be used. When available, a *cabina* costs US$35, *especial* US$46.

Autos/trucks under five meters (15 feet) cost US$88 on this route, US$115 for over five meters. Buses and motorhomes are charged US$130, trailer rigs US$160-300 depending on length. You can wheel the Harley on for US$13 (US$22 with sidecar).

La Paz-Topolobampo
Topolobampo is a small port town that serves the Los Mochis area. An interesting way to reach the Barranca del Cobre (Copper Canyon) area from Baja California is to ride this ferry to Topolobampo, then take a half-hour bus ride to Los Mochis, where you can catch the *Chihuahua al Pacífico* train to the canyons (or farther on to Chihuahua). Ferries on this route are mostly devoted to cargo, with a smaller *salón* section. During holiday periods, more passenger space is usually made available.

The ferry usually leaves La Paz Mon.-Fri. at 8 p.m. and arrives in Topolobampo about 6 p.m. Westbound, the ferry departs Topolobampo Sun.-Thurs. at 9 a.m., arriving at La Paz around 6 p.m. The *salón* fare is US$11.50. When other classes are made available, *turista* costs US$23 and *cabina* US$35.

Buses and motorhomes on this route are charged US$130; autos under five meters (15 feet) cost US$77, over five meters US$100. Motorcycles pay US$10 (US$16 with sidecar). Trailer rigs cost US$139-261.

Mazatlán-La Paz
At the moment this is the most full-service passenger-vehicle ferry available between Baja and the mainland. Each of the three craft that regularly ply this route offer *salón, turista, cabina,* and *especial* classes plus a restaurant-bar, disco, video lounge, and cafetería.

Ferries depart both ports daily except Saturday at 3 p.m., arriving on the other side at around 9 a.m. Fares are US$18 *salón,* US$35 *turista,* US$52 *cabina,* and US$69 *especial.*

Vehicle tariffs are: autos under five meters (15 feet) US$126; buses and motorhomes US$214; motorcycles US$16 (US$28 with sidecar); trailer rigs US$228-430.

GETTING AROUND

MAPS AND INFORMATION

Maps

Among the many Mexico maps available to visitors, two are particularly well suited to general-purpose Mexico road travel.

One is published by the American Automobile Association (AAA) and is available free to members from most AAA offices (if you're not a member, ask someone to obtain one for you). While lacking the topographic shading of AAA's Baja California map, the excellent graphics on the Mexico map nonetheless make it easy to read, and it's accurate and detailed enough for most Northern Mexico auto trips. The map's coverage extends well into the U.S. border states to aid drivers in navigating toward the Mexico gateway of their choice. Distances on the AAA map are marked in km for Mexico, miles for the U.S. portion (scale: one inch=93.3 km or 58 miles).

For those planning to spend much time on Northern Mexico's back roads, a Mexican road atlas is recommended. The best one currently available is the Pronto Atlas, published in Mexico but available through Treaty Oak (tel. 512-326-4141; P.O. Box 50295, Austin, TX 78763) and Map Link (tel. 805-965-4402, fax 805-962-0884; 25 E. Mason, Santa Barbara, CA 93101) as well as many travel bookstores abroad. This spiral-bound atlas contains 36 foldout maps (maps 5-27 cover the North) with a scale of 1:1,000,000 (one inch:25 km), along with color graphics to indicate forests and woodlands, desertlands, marshlands, and 1,000-meter contour increments. Best of all, the atlas includes a fairly complete network of unpaved roads, villages, and ejidos that don't appear on the AAA or any other large-scale, single-page maps.

Two map companies in Mexico City produce individual state maps oriented toward highway travel. The easiest to find (in Mexico as well as bookstores abroad) are the 1:800,000 scale Guia Roji maps, which are easy to read and adequate for most purposes. More detailed but less commonly seen are the 1:100,000 scale HFET maps, which include some topographic shading and contour lines, plus regional inset maps, a town and city index, and annotations on history, culture, and economics.

HFET (the intitials stand for Hector F. Esparza Torres, a one-man map company) also produces many city maps as well as the handy little Microatlas de los Estados de la República Mexicana, a handy shirt-pocket atlas that contains separate maps showing the major paved roads in every state. Both Guia Roji and HFET are generally available through Treaty Oak (which specializes in maps of Mexico and Latin America) or Map Link.

Topographical Maps

Since differences in elevation often determine backcountry route selection, hikers, kayakers, mountain bikers, and off-highway drivers should consider using topographic maps. These can be obtained in advance from Treaty Oak or Map Link in the U.S. (see "Hiking and Backpacking," p. 41), or in Mexico from any regional office of the Instituto Nacional de Estadística Geografía e Informática (INEGI). In Northern Mexico, INEGI maintains major offices in Durango, Hermosillo, Monterrey, and San Luis Potosí (addresses and telephone numbers vary; refer to individual cities throughout handbook); each of these regional offices stocks maps for at least three contiguous states. INEGI also has smaller offices in every state capital and even in some smaller towns, especially along the border. The INEGI office in Piedras Negras, Coah., for example, carries useful topographic maps for northern Coahuila (along with maps for the rest of the state, Nuevo León, and Tamaulipas).

For more information on what's available in topographic maps, see "Maps" under "Hiking and Backpacking," p. 41.

Tourist Information

Mexico's federal tourist bureau, the Secretaría de Turismo (SECTUR), has offices in every state capital. These in turn have federal representatives in some smaller towns where tourist traffic is considered significant. The tourist offices usually stock a variety of free brochures, maps, hotel and restaurant lists, and information on local activities, but some offices are better staffed

MEXICAN GOVERNMENT TOURISM OFFICES ABROAD

USA*

10100 Santa Monica Blvd., Los Angeles, CA 90067; tel. (310) 203-8191, fax (310) 203-8316

405 Park Ave., Suite 1002, New York, NY 10022; tel. (212) 755-7621, fax (212) 753-2874

70 E. Lake St., Suite 1413, Chicago, IL 60601; tel. (312) 606-9015, fax (312) 606-9012

Centre Plaza Bldg., 45 N.E. Loop 410, Suite 125, San Antonio, TX 78216; tel. (210) 366-3242, fax (210) 366-1532

2707 North Loop West, Suite 450, Houston, TX 77008; tel. (713) 880-5153, fax (713) 880-1833

128 Aragon Ave., Coral Gables, FL 33134; tel. (305) 443-9160, fax (305) 443-1186

Mexican Embassy, 1911 Pennsylvania Ave., Washington, D.C. 20036; tel. (202) 728-1750, fax (202) 728-1758

*Toll-free number for MGTO in the U.S.: (800) 446-3942

CANADA

999 W. Hastings #1610, Vancouver, B.C. V6V 2W2; tel. (604) 669-2845

2 Bloor St. West, Toronto, Ontario M4W 3E2; tel. (416) 925-1876, fax (416) 925-6061

1 Place Ville Marie, Suite 4029, Montreal, Quebec H3B 3M9; tel. (514) 871-1052, fax (514) 871-3825

UK

7 Cork St., London, WIX 1PB; tel. (441) 734-1058, fax (441) 437-6265

JAPAN

2-15-1 Nagata-cho, Chiyoda-ku, Tokyo 100; tel. (813) 358-12-110, fax (813) 350-35-643

GERMANY

Wiesenhuettenplatz 26, 6000 Frankfurt, AM Main 1; tel. 4969-25-3414, fax 4969-25-3755

to handle visitor queries than others. Each state also maintains its own state tourism office, often a better source of destination-specific information than SECTUR. Mazatlán, Chihuahua, Monterrey, and Ciudad Juárez have city visitors bureaus in addition to the federal and state offices, so they are particularly well stocked with useful information. The addresses, phone numbers, and hours of each office are listed under the appropriate destination sections of the book.

If you would like to contact the national office directly, you can call or write the Secretaría de Turismo de Mexico (tel. 05-250-01-51, 05-250-01-23, 05-250-04-93), Presidente Mazaryk No. 172, Mexico, D.F. 11570.

Outside Mexico the government maintains 12 Mexican Government Tourism Offices (MGTO) to handle requests for tourist information. Seven of these are located in the U.S.; see the chart above for contact information.

Travel Clubs

The popularity of Baja California and northwest Mexico as vacation destinations has spawned **ClubMex,** a long-lived travel club that specializes in recreational travel on the peninsula as well as along the Sea of Cortez/Pacific coast of mainland Mexico. Membership benefits include discounts (usually 10-20%) at various hotels, restaurants, and other tourist-oriented establishments in Mexico; discounted group auto and boat insurance; the opportunity to participate in club events (e.g., tours, fiestas); a telephone information "hotline"; and a monthly newsletter that contains tips from other club members, short travel features, and the latest information on road conditions and Mexican tourism policy. The ClubMex can also arrange tourist cards, boat permits, and fishing licenses by mail. Contact ClubMex (tel. 619-585-3033, fax 619-422-2671; P.O. Box 1646, Bonita, CA 92002-1646).

Sanborn's Insurance operates its own **Sanborn's Mexico Club** (tel. 210-682-1354; P.O. Box 310, McAllen, TX 78502), which offers 10-20% discounts on hotels and restaurants throughout Mexico (especially the northeast), a quarterly newsletter, a list of RV parks in Mexico, and a health guide.

Newsletters
In addition to the U.S.-published travel club newsletters mentioned above, two published in Mexico are worth a look. **Travelmex** (A.P. 31-750, Guadalajara, Jal. 45050) publishes an eight-page newsletter containing travel features and road reports 10 times per year; an annual subscription costs US$15.

AIM, an acronym for Adventures in Mexico, issues a homespun bimonthly newsletter (from Guadalajara) which, although aimed mostly at North American retirees living in Mexico—or those considering such a move—contains a good deal of practical information on Mexico travel. For subscription information, see the section on "Estimating Costs," p. 113.

BY PLANE

Domestic air travel in Mexico is generally less expensive than international flights from the U.S. to Mexico flown over comparable distances. The "Airlines Serving Northern Mexico" chart on pp. 76-79 will give you an idea of the possible connections. In many cases you can save money by flying in and out of a Mexican border city like Ciudad Juárez or Tijuana rather than the closest U.S. cities, El Paso and San Diego.

Following are several sample one-way economy fares on domestic flights: Ciudad Juárez-Torreón US$176; Hermosillo-Monterrey US$220; Durango-Mazatlán US$62 (US$53 on Noroeste); Monterrey-Tampico US$125; Ciudad Obregón-Durango US$190; Reynosa-Tampico US$112.

Private Flights
Northern Mexico is dotted with a couple hundred or more airstrips—many of them unpaved—that are used by privately owned and/or small commercial aircraft. Air traffic over the North is light, and the paperwork for crossing the border is minimal. As if that weren't enticing enough, aviation gas is sometimes cheaper in Mexico

than in the U.S. or Canada. Many pilots land immediately after crossing the border in order to fill up on the less expensive stuff and then stop again before leaving Mexico. Keep in mind, however, that fuel is available at or nearby only a fraction of these airstrips—careful itinerary planning is crucial.

An outfit calling itself Baja Bush Pilots (tel. 619-297-5587 in San Diego) publishes a 384-page guide, *Airports of Baja California and Northwest Mexico* by Arnold Senterfitt (P.O. Box 34280, San Diego, CA 92163), that contains aerial photos, sketch maps, and descriptions of virtually every landing strip in Sonora and Sinaloa. While some pilots fly to northwest Mexico without this book, they're few and far between. The guide can be ordered by mail from Baja Bush Pilots for US$37 plus US$2 shipping and handling.

Nothing similar yet exists for the north-central and northeastern regions, where foreign pilots rely on word of mouth. Smaller Texas or New Mexico airfields are a good place to begin inquiries about these less-explored (by plane) regions.

BY BUS

Inter-city Buses
Transportation in Northern Mexico is quite reliable and covers virtually every town and city in the region. On long-distance trips, many buses offer a/c and reclining seats, sometimes even hostess service. Shorter trips may or may not have a/c, but the buses are always tolerably comfortable—toilets are available on-board and seats usually recline. Schedules are often scrupulously kept and even smaller bus terminals may feature public phones, restrooms, and cafes.

Between state capitals and other large cities, a faster class of service called *expreso* or "express" is available for about 25-35% above the cost of ordinary first class. Even more elite are the newer *ejecutivo* ("executive") buses, which feature more sophisticated suspension systems, wider, plusher seats, on-board TV, and express service for about double the usual first-class fare.

In more remote areas, inter-city buses may consist of old school buses in questionable mechanical condition—they function but you can't count on strict time schedules. Terminals on these routes may be little more than a wooden stall or just a worn patch by the side of the road. Mexicans sometimes refer to this type of bus as a *pollero* or "chicken bus," both because the passengers are packed in like chickens in a coop and because it's not unusual for rural passengers to be accompanied by a live chicken or two. For visitors who want to see and experience back-road Mexico, the *polleros* provide an excellent opportunity to get to know local villagers and campesinos.

All fares—from express buses to *polleros*—are inexpensive by most international standards. For most routes you can expect to pay less than US$0.05 per km for a basic first- or second-class ticket. A ticket on a first-class bus from Chihuahua to Parral (a distance of 300 km), for example, costs just US$8.30 first class, US$6 second class; a more basic, rural bus along the Mazatlán-Teacapán route (about 100 km) costs only US$2.50.

Reservations aren't accepted for many buses—you simply show up at the bus terminal around the time you want to leave (several departures a day are usually available). All the Spanish you need for riding a bus is *boleto* (ticket), the name of your destination (have a map handy just in case), and a reasonable command of spoken numbers for when they quote the fare (although the fare is always posted somewhere on the ticket office wall). (Refer to the "Spanish Phrasebook" at the back of this handbook.)

City Buses And *Colectivos*
Larger towns and cities have comprehensive city bus systems with fares averaging US$0.15-$0.35 (collected in pesos only). City buses come in a variety of sizes and shapes, from 12-passenger vans (usually called *colectivos*) to huge modern vessels with automatic doors. In some cities, painted school buses are the norm. The destination or general route (typically a street name) of the bus is usually painted somewhere on the front or displayed over the front windshield.

Printed bus schedules are hard to come by or may be nonexistent. If you can't figure out which bus to take by comparing the destination sign with a map, ask other waiting bus passengers. If your Spanish isn't up to that, make inquiries at the tourist office.

BY TAXI

Route Taxis
These same cities may also have *taxis de ruta*, specially licensed cars (usually large American station wagons that hold up to 12 passengers) that follow set routes similar and often paralleling the bus routes. Unlike the city buses, they can be flagged down anywhere along their route. The destination is usually painted in whitewash on the windshield, but the locals often distinguish the route by the taxis' two-tone color scheme (e.g., a *roja y crema* may run from the central bus station to a market on the outskirts of town, while a *negro y azul* may go from the cathedral to the main shopping district). Other than the terminating points of the route at either end, there are no predetermined taxi stops, so passengers must let the driver know where they want off. As on the city buses, route taxi fares are the same no matter where you disembark, but they're usually a bit higher than bus fares.

Hire Taxis
Regular hire taxis usually congregate at hotels and designated taxi stands. Sometimes fares are posted at the hotel or taxi stand, but often you'll have to ask for fare quote. If possible, try to find out the fare (from hotel staff or a friendly resident) in advance of approaching a taxi driver so you'll feel more secure about not getting ripped off. If the quoted fare doesn't match what you've been told in advance, you have the options of negotiating for something closer to the correct fare or trying another taxi driver. The author's experience, however, has been that city taxi drivers in Mexico usually quote the correct fare immediately.

In smaller towns there are no buses or route taxis, but sometimes you'll find a few regular hire taxis hanging out by the town plaza. They're generally used for reaching out-of-town destinations, since anyplace in Mexico without a city bus system is small enough to get around on foot. Although the locals pay a set fare based on distance, gringos are sometimes quoted a much higher fare. Dig in and negotiate until it's reasonable—even if you can afford the higher fare, you owe it to other foreign visitors not to encourage price-gouging.

BY TRAIN

Mexico's national railway (Ferrocarriles Nacionales de Mexico or FNM) had its beginnings in the late 19th and early 20th centuries, when various U.S. companies built lines along and leading to the Sea of Cortez/Pacific coast (the country's first rail line ran between Culiacán and the small seaport of Altata) with imported materials. All railways were nationalized during the '30s and until recently Mexican trains had a rather shabby reputation. During the last few years, FNM has renovated 14 train routes that feature Servicio Estrella Azul (Blue Star Service), an all-first-class service divided into *primera regular* (first-class coach), *primera especial* (first-class reserved, air-conditioned), *camarote* (single sleeper with toilet facilities), and *alcoba* (double sleeper with toilet facilities).

First-class passengers may arrange stopovers en route (maximum two per ticket) for a 15% surcharge over the regular fare. Children under 12 are eligible for a 50% discount on all fares.

Luggage allowances for rail passengers are 50 kilograms (110 pounds) per adult ticket holder,

---

RAILWAY SCHEDULE

Arrival/departure for the following rail lines may change at any time. Only major first- and second-class routes are listed. To follow routes, read downward on the left time column, and upward on the right time column to return (e.g., depart on Train No. 1 from Guadalajara at 9:30 a.m.; arrive Nogales at 10:50 a.m. To return, depart on Train No. 2 from Nogales at 2:30 p.m.; arrive Guadalajara at 7:00 p.m.)

DEL PACIFICO (SPECIAL 1ST-CLASS RESERVED), GUADALAJARA/NOGALES/GUADALAJARA

	TRAIN NO. 1		TRAIN NO. 2	
Depart	9:30 a.m.	Guadalajara	7:00 p.m.	Arrive
	1:35 p.m.	Tepic	1:30 p.m.	
	5:30 p.m.	Mazatlán	7:15 a.m.	
	8:44 p.m.	Culiacán	4:26 a.m.	
	11:45 p.m.	Sufragio	1:15 a.m.	next day
next day	2:57 a.m.	Ciudad Obregón	10:24 p.m.	
	4:40 a.m.	Empalme	9:55 p.m.	
	6:45 a.m.	Hermosillo	6:45 p.m.	
	8:25 a.m.	Benjamin Hill*	4:44 p.m.	
Arrive	10:50 a.m.	Nogales	2:30 p.m.	Depart
		Connecting to:	•	
Depart	9:45 a.m.	Benjamin Hill*	4:10 p.m.	Arrive
	11:20 p.m.	Caborca	2:37 p.m.	
	1:10 p.m.	Puerto Peñasco	12:20 p.m.	
Arrive	4:55 p.m.	Mexicali	8:00 a.m.	Depart

CHIHUAHUA AL PACIFICO (SPECIAL 1ST-CLASS RESERVED), LOS MOCHIS/CHIHUAHUA/LOS MOCHIS

	TRAIN NO. 73		TRAIN NO. 74	
Depart	6:00 a.m.	Los Mochis	8:50 p.m.	Arrive
	6:43 a.m.	Sufragio	7:59 a.m.	
	7:26 a.m.	El Fuerte	6:16 p.m.	
	11:11 a.m.	Témoris	4:30 p.m.	
	12:12 p.m.	Bahuichivo	3:32 p.m.	
	1:30 p.m.	Posada Barrancas	2:10 p.m.	
	1:35 p.m.	Divisadero	1:45 p.m.	
	3:14 p.m.	Creel	12:26 p.m.	
	6:25 p.m.	Cuauhtémoc	9:15 a.m.	
Arrive	8:50 p.m.	Chihuahua	7:00 a.m.	Depart

RAILWAY SCHEDULE
(continued)

CHIHUAHUA-LOS MOCHIS (TARAHUMARA) (2ND CLASS), LOS MOCHIS/CHIHUAHUA/LOS MOCHIS

	TRAIN NO. 75		TRAIN NO. 76	
Depart	7:00 a.m.	Los Mochis	10:25 p.m.	Arrive
	8:45 a.m.	Sufragio	10:25 p.m.	
	1:45 p.m.	Bahuichivo	5:25 p.m.	
	3:10 p.m.	Posada Barrancas	3:58 p.m.	
	3:25 p.m.	Divisadero	3:30 p.m.	
	5:05 p.m.	Creel	2:00 a.m.	
Arrive	11:25 p.m.	Chihuahua	8:00 a.m.	Depart

EL REGIOMONTANO (SPECIAL 1ST-CLASS RESERVED OR SLEEPER), MEXICO CITY/MONTERREY/MEXICO CITY

	TRAIN NO. 71		TRAIN NO. 72	
Depart	6:00 p.m.	Mexico City	10:00 a.m.	Arrive
next day	12:11 a.m.	San Luis Potosí	3:55 a.m.	next day
	5:44 a.m.	Saltillo	10:00 p.m.	
Arrive	8:10 p.m.	Monterrey	7:50 p.m.	Depart

	TRAIN NO. 181		TRAIN NO. 182	
	SALTILLO/PIEDRAS NEGRAS/SALTILLO			
Depart	8:15 a.m.	Saltillo	6:55 p.m.	Arrive
Arrive	5:35 p.m.	Piedras Negras	9:15 a.m.	Depart

EL TAMAULIPECO (RESERVED SEAT AND 2ND CLASS), MONTERREY/MATAMOROS/MONTERREY

	TRAIN NO. 141		TRAIN NO. 142	
Depart	10:30 a.m.	Monterrey	4:00 p.m.	Arrive
	3:05 p.m.	Reynosa	11:05 a.m.	
Arrive	4:00 p.m.	Matamoros	9:20 a.m.	Depart

DIVISION DEL NORTE (SPECIAL 1ST-CLASS RESERVED* OR 2ND CLASS), MEXICO CITY/CIUDAD JUAREZ/MEXICO CITY

	TRAIN NO. 7		TRAIN NO. 8	
Depart	8:00 p.m.	Mexico City*	9:30 a.m.	Arrive
	11:30 p.m.	Querétaro*	5:40 a.m.	next day
next day	6:50 a.m.	Aguascalientes*	10:30 p.m.	
	9:30 a.m.	Zacatecas*	8:05 p.m.	
	5:10 p.m.	Torreón	12:00 p.m.	
	9:20 p.m.	Jimenez	7:40 a.m.	
next day	1:20 a.m.	Chihuahua	3:15 a.m.	next day
Arrive	6:45 a.m.	Ciudad Juárez	10:00 p.m.	Depart

NUEVO LAREDO-MONTERREY-MEXICO CITY (SPECIAL 1ST-CLASS RESERVED* OR 2ND CLASS), MEXICO CITY/NUEVO LAREDO/MEXICO CITY

	TRAIN NO. 1		TRAIN NO. 2	
Depart	9:00 a.m.	Mexico City*	7:00 p.m.	Arrive
	12:56 p.m.	Querétaro*	2:42 p.m.	
	2:35 a.m.	San Miguel Allende*	1:09 p.m.	
	5:10 p.m.	San Luis Potosí*	10:05 a.m.	
	11:55 p.m.	Saltillo	2:35 a.m.	next day
	2:20 a.m.	Monterrey	11:30 p.m.	
Arrive	7:20 a.m.	Nuevo Laredo	6:30 p.m.	Depart

NORTHERN MEXICO RAIL NETWORK

25 kilograms (55 pounds) for children ages 5-11. Excess baggage and cargo charges are reasonable.

Although the national routes are fairly extensive, they are actually of limited use to travelers except for long overnight hauls, when a train bunk is definitely more comfortable than a reclining bus seat. For short to medium hauls, buses are much faster and departures are much more frequent; most train routes offer only one departure per first-class bus; from Monterrey to San Luis Potosí, for example, it costs around US$15 whether by reserved first-class seat on the Regiomontano train or by *expreso* bus. The Regiomontano takes nearly eight hours to complete this route (departing at 7:50 p.m. and arriving at 3:45 a.m.), while an express bus takes less than six (with several day or evening arrival times to select from).

However, for train enthusiasts or for those who aren't in a hurry, Mexican trains provide a pleasant alternative to road travel. The scenery along the railroads is typically better than that along highway routes, and you'll have more of an opportunity to meet Mexican passengers than on a bus since you can walk around comfortably on the train.

Even if you're not a train fan, one rail trip that shouldn't be missed is the Chihuahua al Pacífico route between Chihuahua's state capital and Los Mochis on the Sea of Cortez coast. This 13-hour journey across the Sierra Madre Occidental winds through spectacular vistas of craggy mountain peaks, conifer forests, piñon-oak woodlands, precipitous cliffs, plummeting canyons, and sparkling rivers—easily among the top five rail trips in the world. For details on the trip, refer to the Sierra Tarahumara ("Copper Canyon") section.

For overnight trips (only necessary if you're heading for Mexico City) in the winter, bring along a blanket or sleeping bag for added warmth. Toilet tissue is another handy item to have, as train restrooms are sometimes short.

The most useful lines in Northern Mexico include: **El Pacífico** (special first-class reserved) from Nogales to Guadalajara with stops in Hermosillo, Ciudad Obregón, Navojoa, Culiacán, and Mazatlán among others (this train also connects with a shorter line from Mexicali and Puerto Peñasco); **El Sinaloense** (second class) from Los Mochis to Guadalajara with stops in Culiacán and Mazatlán; the **Chihuahua al Pacífico** (special first-class reserved) from Los Mochis to Chihuahua via several stops in the Copper Canyon area; the **Chihuahua-Los Mochis,** a slower second-class version of the Chihuahua al Pacífico (also known as *el pollero*); **El División del Norte** (special first-class reserved and second-class coach) from Ciudad Juárez to Mexico City via Chihuahua, Torreón, and Zacatecas; **El Regiomontano** (special first-class reserved, single and double sleepers) from Monterrey to Mexico City via Saltillo and San Luis Potosí; **El Coahuilense** (special first-class reserved) from Piedras Negras to Saltillo (connects with the Regiomontano); **El Tamaulipeco** (reserved seat) along the Monterrey-Reynosa-Matamoros route (also connects with the Regiomontano); and the **Nuevo Laredo-Mexico City** (special reserved first class and second class) via Monterrey, Saltillo, and San Luis Potosí.

Reservations And Information
First-class seats and bunks can be reserved in advance by writing to the Chief Commercial Passenger Department, FNM, Gran Estación Central de Buena Vista, Mexico City, D.F. 06358 (tel. 05-547-86-55). Upon receipt of your reservation, a time limit for purchasing your ticket(s) will be assigned; the purchase can be made in person at the departure station or by mail with a cashier's check or international money order (in Mexican currency) for the amount due.

In the U.S., tickets for the Regiomontano, Coahuilense, Pacífico, and Chihuahua al Pacífico lines can also be reserved and purchased through **Mexico By Rail** (tel. 800-228-3225), though surcharges are steep (e.g., a roundtrip Nogales-Mazatlán first-class ticket costs US$140 through Mexico by Rail, but only US$36 if you purchase the ticket on your own in Mexico; for the Chihuahua al Pacífico the fares are US$120 vs. US$54).

For current fares and schedules, you can request a copy of the "General Information and Condensed Schedules of Main Trains" from La Gerencia de Tráfico de Pasajeros, FNM (see above address).

CYCLING

Plenty of cycle touring and mountain biking opportunities are available in Northern Mexico, though it seems that North American cyclists have yet to discover them. The interior of the region in particular—from the western escarpment of the Sierra Madre Occidental all the way across to the eastern edge of the Sierra Madre Oriental—is a potential recreational cycling mecca. The traffic is relatively light, the scenery is striking (which helps fight boredom), and cyclists can pull over and camp just about anywhere.

Touring or mountain biking? If you're only heading straight down the flat, paved roads of the Sea of Cortez or Gulf of Mexico coastal plains, a touring bike would be the best choice for weight and speed. Other appropriate routes for tour biking include the border trip along Mexico 2 from San Luis Río Colorado to Ciudad Juárez (crossing the northern Sonoran Desert, the Continental Divide, and nearly half the northern Chihuahuan Desert) or from Ciudad Acuña to Playa Bagdad on the Gulf of Mexico coast in Tamaulipas (through Chihuahuan Desert grasslands and Tamaulipan thorn forest to the beach).

On the other hand, the mountain-fringed interior has so many great offroad rides that anyone who really wants to see Northern Mexico (and has the time) should consider the mountain-bike option, since offroad riding requires a stronger frame, higher clearance, and wider tires.

Equipment And Repairs
Whether you're riding a mountain or a touring bike, you'll need the same basic essentials to handle long-distance riding in Northern Mexico. If you plan to camp along the way, you'll need the usual camping and first-aid gear, selected to fit your panniers. Helmets are particularly important since a head injury can become even more serious when you're "in the middle of

nowhere," and it will also keep direct sun off the top of your skull. Don't forget to bring sunglasses and plenty of high-SPF sunscreen.

A rearview mirror is a must for keeping an eye on motorists coming from behind on narrow roads. A locking cable is preferable to a clunky U-lock for long-distance trips since they weigh less—bicycle theft isn't much of a problem in most areas. The only other security you might need is a removable handlebar bag for carrying camera and valuables—the bag can be taken with you when stopping off at restaurants or *tiendas* (it's also a reachable spot for on-the-fly snacks).

Water will be an uppermost consideration on overnight trips. No matter what the time of year (spring and fall are the best pedaling seasons), cyclists should try to carry about a gallon of water a day, divided among four one-liter bottles —so if one is punctured, all your water won't be lost (the one-liter bottles used for cycling are also more puncture resistant than the typical water containers designed for camping). Punctures are of particular concern in Northern Mexico because of spine-bearing trees and plants.

Tires: The aforementioned puncture threat means that your bike should be outfitted with heavy-duty tires and tubes. Bring along two or three spare tubes, one spare tire, a tire gauge, and a complete tire repair kit. You should also carry duct tape and moleskin to use as booting material against sidewall cuts (often caused by sharp rocks along the road).

Rack: Check nuts and bolts daily and retighten as necessary. Applying Loctite should lessen the need for retightening—carry a small supply along with extra nuts and bolts. Bailing wire can be used for improvised repairs if you run out of nuts and bolts or get a minor break—carry eight or 10 feet along with wire cutters.

Other Repairs: You'll find bike shops in most major cities. Although the Mexicans who run these shops can sometimes perform miraculous repairs using nothing that resembles the bike's original parts, it's safer to come prepared with spares, especially for parts that aren't easily jury-rigged. At a minimum, carry a spare freewheel, a rear derailleur, and all the wrenches and screwdrivers necessary to work on your bike. If in addition you bring along several extra spokes, cables, and a spare chain, you'll be ready for just about any repair scenario.

Bicycle Transport
Most bus lines will take the bikes of paying passengers in their luggage compartments for no additional cost, but bikes may have to be boxed. For return trips from Mexico to your home country, you should be able to pick up a box from a larger Mexican bicycle shop along the way (or build your own from discarded cardboard boxes).

DRIVING IN NORTHERN MEXICO

Millions of North Americans (about 3.2 million at last count) drive in Mexico every year without so much as a fender-bender or parking ticket. Sanborn's Mexican Insurance of McAllen, Texas (one of the largest insurers in the Mexican insurance business) says the percentage of claims reported by its clients represents a mere 2% of the auto policies issued by the company. By contrast, the national average for U.S. auto insurance is two to five times this amount.

This is not to say that driving in Mexico is totally free from anxiety. But drivers who prepare themselves and their vehicles, and who take appropriate precautions while driving Mexican roads, will probably discover that Mexican driving is for the most part a comfortable proposition.

The Mexican government is currently seeking to increase the number of visitors entering the country by land by upgrading facilities and highways along the following corridors and circuits: Nogales-Mazatlán, Ciudad Juárez-Creel (Copper Canyon)-Topolobampo, Colombia-Matamoros (Lower Rio Grande/Río Bravo Corridor), and Nuevo Laredo-Monterrey-Saltillo-Reynosa. The announced goal is to provide 2,338 km of better highways in the North by the year 2000. State governments are also engaged in promoting "two-nation vacations" through logistical partnerships between U.S. and Mexican border states, especially between Sonora and Arizona, and among Coahuila, Nuevo León, Tamaulipas, and Texas.

INSURANCE

One legal preparation that should be undertaken before driving into Mexico is acquiring Mexican vehicle insurance. No matter what your own insurance company may tell you, the Mexican authorities don't recognize foreign insurance policies for private vehicles in Mexico.

While vehicle insurance isn't required by law in Mexico, it's a good idea to carry a Mexican policy anyway; without it, a minor traffic accident can turn into a nightmare. Short-term (as little as one day's worth) insurance can be arranged at any of several agencies found in nearly every border town between the Pacific Ocean and the Gulf of Mexico.

One of the most popular, and reliable, Mexico insurers is **Sanborn's Mexico Insurance** (tel. 210-686-0711 or 800-222-0158, fax 210-686-0632; P.O. Box 310, McAllen, TX), which has offices in virtually every town along the U.S.-Mexico border. For short visits Sanborn's offers a combination of service and convenience that's hard to beat. For long-term visits, however, better deals can usually be negotiated from other sources, especially for drivers who will be making more than one trip into Mexico each year. Some agencies in Mexico offer annual policies in which you're only charged for those days you're actually in Mexico. Of course, this requires a trip south of the border in order to obtain such a policy in the first place, so you'll need a day or two's worth of border insurance for the trip.

One U.S. agency that can arrange Mexican liability insurance on a per-use basis is **Anserv Insurance Services** (tel. 800-262-1994 in California, 800-654-7504 elsewhere, fax 619-296-4715; 1761 Hotel Circle South, Suite 250, San Diego, CA 92108). Their rates are as low as $61 per year for 60 days of use per year.

The **ClubMex** (see "Travel Clubs," p. 83, for addresses and phone numbers) offers low group insurance rates (for members only) that range from US$100 a year for liability only to US$135 a year for US$5000 worth of collision, fire, theft, and glass insurance (add another US$15-20 for each additional US$5000 in coverage). These group policies are offered on a yearly basis only (i.e., they can't be purchased by the day, week, or month).

Another good source of Mexican insurance is **International Gateway Insurance Brokers** (tel. 800-423-2646), whose premiums for a multiple-entry, one-year, comprehensive policy start at US$160 for under US$5000 in coverage to US$355 for US$30,000-35,000 in coverage. Their "Tour Aid" service includes US$3000 accident coverage; emergency towing up to US$100 for autos or up to US$200 for motorhomes; emergency road service to US$100; hospital guarantee to US$500; parts service (they ship parts from the U.S. to Mexico for the cost of parts only); and legal service. Tour Aid is available for US$20 a year or is included with their insurance.

Most companies (including all of the above) have lower premiums for "limited territory" trips that stay within Baja California (Norte and Sur), Sonora, Chihuahua, and Durango. If you plan to confine yourself to this area, you should consider a limited-territory policy. International Gateway, for example, charges only US$172 for a one-year, multiple-entry, limited-territory policy covering US$25,000.

Whichever policy you choose, always make photocopies of the policy and keep originals and copies in separate, safe places. It's also a good idea to carry a photocopy of the first page (the "declaration" or "renewal of declaration" sheet) of your home country policy, as Mexican customs law requires that you cross the border with at least six months' worth of home country insurance.

CHOOSING YOUR WHEELS

Trailers And RVs Vs. Campers And Vans

Mexico is a popular destination among the trailer/RV crowd because you can pull off the road and "camp" just about anywhere outside the cities, with few restrictions. The restrictions that do exist are largely physical—numerous places simply can't accommodate a wide trailer or motorhome due to narrow roadways, steep grades, or sharp curves.

Probably the rig most suited to Mexico travel is a well-equipped camper or van. With a bed, two five-gallon water containers, a small propane stove and refrigerator, and a portable toilet, you can travel just as independently as someone driving a 40-foot motor home. Add a deep-cycle RV battery under the hood and you can run a

RVers can traverse the Sierra Madre Occidental by hiring a flatcar on the Chihuahua al Pacifico train.

variety of electrical appliances for at least a week without running your engine. For extra power, a solar panel can be mounted on top of the cab or camper.

As long as you're tricking out your rig, consider installing oversized tires to get more traction and road clearance, overload shocks to protect your vehicle and its contents on rough roads, and a rollbar over the front seats. Whether or not you've got high clearance, skid plates under your fuel tank, engine, and transmission are items to consider.

What's the perfect Mexico rig? Such a beast doesn't really exist, of course, since we all have individual needs, but probably the nearest-to-perfect rig for enjoying most of what Northern Mexico has to offer would be one that combines features of a self-sufficient camper (as described above) with a rugged 4WD vehicle that has a turning circle of 20 feet or less. To achieve this kind of optimal functionality, ambitious drivers have successfully tried everything from jeeps to three-ton diesel cabs (which have a remarkably short turning radius) as bases for custom-built campers.

Motorcycles

Parts of Northern Mexico are excellent for motorcycle touring. The winding sierra roads are especially challenging and since traffic is generally light you can really stretch out and enjoy the ride.

As with automotive travel in Mexico, predeparture planning is very important. You should be able to carry enough gear in two panniers and a backpack (tied down on the rear) for a transcontinental trip. Motorcycle mechanics aren't easily found outside larger towns, so it's best to be as self-reliant as possible for a safe and successful trip. Besides the usual camping and first-aid gear, bikers should carry any tools needed for routine maintenance, as well as spare brake shoes, a tire repair kit, spare levers, an extra battery, a clutch cable, spare light bulbs, a one-gallon reserve gas can, and a spare helmet visor.

For a transcontinental trip, any bike smaller than 600cc is too small. A four-stroke gets better mileage than a two-stroke, an important consideration given the situation with gas stations in Mexico. Experienced Mexico bikers replace standard fuel tanks with larger five-gallon tanks to extend their fuel range.

All of the same driving precautions that apply to four-wheel driving should be followed by bikers as well. Special care should be taken when negotiating blind curves, since buses and trucks in Mexico aren't used to seeing motorcycles on the highway.

Car Rentals

Cars can be rented in any state capital, in Mazatlán, and in the border cities of Ciudad Juárez and Nuevo Laredo. Various Volkswagen models are usually the only choice; most rental places charge a daily rate of around US$26 for a VW bug, US$45-48 for a VW Jetta or Nissan Tsuru II (Sentra), US$48-55 for a VW combi (van), plus per-km fees ranging US$0.18-$0.30 per km. The bug, incidentally, is one of the best non-4WD passenger cars for Mexico travel since the engine is air-cooled (no radiator boil overs) and the road clearance is just a bit above average.

If you're planning on driving long distances, you can save money by arranging a flat rate with no per-km costs *(kilometraje ilimitado)*. If you can rent by the week, the savings increase considerably. A new, made-in-Mexico VW bug (no a/c or radio) rents for as little as US$159 per week, with unlimited free kilometers—but only in larger cities. In smaller cities, rates are high. Some companies also charge extra for a/c or automatic transmissions.

Avis International (tel. 800-331-1212 in the U.S./Canada; 91-800-70-777 in Mexico) often has the best deals on weekly rentals in Mexico out of large border cities like Tijuana, Ciudad Juárez, Nuevo Laredo, and Monterrey. Advance bookings made in the U.S. seem to be less expensive than those made in Mexico.

Rentals from the U.S. side are sometimes a bit cheaper but there may be a geographic limit, e.g., the lower state lines of Sonora, Chihuahua, Coahuila, or Tamaulipas—beyond which the rental vehicle is prohibited.

HAZARDS AND HIGHWAY SIGNS

Driving Precautions

The number-one rule for Mexico driving, no matter what kind of road you're on, is: *Never* take the road for granted. Any highway in Mexico, including toll roads, can serve up 100 meters of smooth, seamless blacktop followed immediately by 100 meters of contiguous potholes or large patches of missing asphalt. A cow, horse, or burro could be right around the next curve, or a large dog can leap out in front of your vehicle just as you fasten your eyes on a turkey vulture drying its wings on top of a tall saguaro cactus.

The speed limits set by the Mexican government—80 kph (about 50 mph) on most highways, 110 kph (about 68 mph) on some four-lane highways—are very reasonable for highway conditions. Obey them and you'll be much safer than if you try to keep the speedometer needle in the spot you're accustomed to. Wandering livestock, relatively narrow highway widths on two-laners (19-25 feet), and lack of consistent highway maintenance mean that you simply can't drive at U.S.-Canada speeds in this neck of the woods.

You'll notice a conspicuous lack of shoulders along many roadways. This doesn't mean turnouts don't exist—gravel turnouts are fairly regular and in many areas you can drive directly onto the roadside from the highway—it just means that you can't count on a safe margin at one side of the highway or the other in an emergency situation. At the very least, an emergency turnout will raise a lot of rocks and dirt—small dangers in themselves. In some spots (e.g., in the Sierras), leaving the highway might launch you and your vehicle into a 1000-foot (or greater) freefall—guardrails may be flimsy or nonexistent.

Yet another reason not to take the road for granted is the high number of blind curves (sometimes unmarked) and blind hilltops in areas of varied elevation. Never assume a clear path around a curve or over a hilltop—potential obstructions include an 18-wheeler or bus passing in the opposite direction (oblivious to the risk of passing blind), wandering livestock, a rockslide, or a road washout. To be on the safe side, keep toward the outside edge of your own lane. Some commercial trucks in Mexico drive as if they're exempt from all speed limits, flying at least 40 km over the posted limit.

Rule number two: Never drive on the highways at night. Except in metropolitan areas, lighting is nonexistent along the highways. In addition, reflectors and even painted lines are absent from many highway sections; even if no other vehicles besides your own occupy the road at night, you could easily overshoot an unexpected curve. Add to this the fact that many poorly maintained local vehicles have nonfunctioning headlights, taillights, or brakelights, and it should be obvious that trying to make highway miles after sundown is crazy. Local drivers may do it, but they're used to local conditions and know the roads relatively well (still, a high proportion of car accidents in Mexico—around 80% according to insurance companies—occur at night in spite of local savvy).

Specific Hazards

Vados: When you see road signs marked *Vado* or *Zona de Vados,* slow down. *Vado* is most often translated as "dip," but in Northern Mexico it can mean more than a simple dip in the road—it's any place where the road intersects an arroyo or dry stream wash. The danger lies not only in the sudden grade drop but in the potential for running into a recently accumulated body of water. Some *vados* have a measuring stick (marked in meters) next to them so that if water is present, you'll know roughly how deep it is. If you come to a *vado* full of water and no measuring stick is in place, get out of your vehicle and measure the depth yourself using an ocotillo branch or other suitable object before attempting to cross.

Vados aren't always signposted, so keep an eye out for them—they can appear in relatively flat terrains. Even in dry weather, some *vados* are particularly treacherous while others are quite mild. The *vados* in rural northwest Mexico are particularly hazardous—driving over them at a high rate of speed can severely damage the undercarriage of a passenger car.

Topes: In towns, pueblos, *ejidos,* or anywhere else people live in Mexico, you'll also encounter *topes* or speed bumps. Often they're unpainted and unposted, and can really sneak up on a driver. Some *topes* are real industrial-strength tire-poppers, so always take it very slow when traversing them. *Topes* in northeast Mexico are sometimes labeled *boyas* ("buoys"). Similar in purpose are *vibradores,* a section of raised ribs across the road.

Highway Signs

One of the pleasures of driving in Northern Mexico is the relative absence of signs cluttering the roadside—in fact, billboards are virtually nonexistent. The Mexican government does have a system of highway signs, however, based on common international sign conventions followed throughout most of the world (except the U.S.), and these can be very helpful as long as you know what they mean. Most symbols are self-explanatory, e.g., a silhouette of a man holding a shovel means "men working."

Along major highways as well as on many secondary roads, driving progress can be measured with the assistance of regularly spaced **kilometer markers** (usually black lettering on a reflective white background). These are normally calibrated according to distance intervals between two towns, so that sometimes

the numbers run only as far as the next town and then start over. The markers can be a significant navigational aid, especially when you want to take note of a remote off-highway spot for a future trip.

Cautionary sign captions that are especially helpful include: Curva Peligrosa (Dangerous Curve), Despacio (Slow), Camino Sinuoso (Winding Road), Grava Suelta (Loose Gravel), Zona de Baches (Pothole Zone), and Zona de Vados (Dip Zone—see "Specific Hazards," above). If you're having tire trouble, look for homemade signs reading *llantera, desponchadora,* or *vulcanizadora,* all of which indicate tire repair shops. My favorite Mexican traffic sign is *No maltrate las señales*—"Don't mistreat the signs!"

ON THE HIGHWAY

Mexican Highways And Tolls

Much of the time Mexican roads appear similar to two-lane roads in less populated areas of the American Southwest. The two main differences are: 1) road conditions vary (sometimes a lot) from one section of highway to another; and 2) once you're away from towns and cities, you're often farther from any significant population centers than on any comparable section of U.S. highways, so accidents or errors of judgment may have more ramifications. Drivers from western Canada may feel more at home on desolate sections of Mexican highways than Americans—except that the terrain is completely different from anything in Canada!

Another difference is that two-lane (and even some four-lane) routes often lead through small and medium-sized towns rather than employ a bypass. In more populated regions of Mexico this means slowing down to a 30 kph (18 mph) crawl every 20 km or so; fortunately the North has far fewer of these areas than the South.

Mexican highways often present an intriguing mixture of old and modern. Horse-drawn cart tracks sometimes parallel four-lane highways, and cattle may roam freely across rural blacktops. The best roadways are the *autopistas* or freeways, which are multiplying in number each year. Also known as *carreteras rojas* or *red highways* (for the color usually assigned them on highway maps), most are financed by long-term private investment projects that are repaid through public tolls. Toll roads usually have phone boxes placed at intervals; from these boxes stranded drivers can call the nearest *caseta de cobro* or toll booth and request assistance. The larger toll operations may have their own ambulances and/or mechanics; others will relay calls for assistance to the appropriate authorities.

Tolls: At the moment there are major toll freeways from Nogales to Mazatlán (Mexico 15), Ciudad Juárez to San Luis Potosí via Torreón and Zacatecas (Mexico 49), and Nuevo Laredo to Monterrey (Mexico 40). All of these, not coincidentally, run a basic north-to-south course; the highway investors realize a significant portion of the tolls will be paid by foreign visitors from the U.S. and Canada, as well as by transport companies moving goods back and forth between Mexico and North America. The toll rate structure usually charges a basic auto fee (e.g., US$2.30 or the peso equivalent), with an extra charge amounting to the same base toll for every axle beyond two on that vehicle; a triple-axle rig, for example, would pay US$4.60, four axles US$6.90, and so on.

The base toll rate isn't necessarily the same for equivalent distances on different toll roads. The La Gloria-Monterrey basic auto toll costs a whopping US$21 for 139 km (86 miles), or about US$0.15 per km; other toll roads cost just US$0.03-0.10 per km (e.g., the 26-km Fresnillo-Zacatecas toll highway costs only US$1). U.S. dollars, old pesos, and new pesos (see "Money," p. 111) are equally acceptable for toll charges, but your change due may be paid in a combination of all three currencies—you don't have a choice.

Mexico 15-D, a 1274-km (791-mile) four-lane highway between Nogales and Mazatlán, is often cited as the most expensive toll road in the country. On a price-per-kilometer basis, however, it's actually one of the least expensive; at US$74 for the basic car/van toll, it works out to US$0.058 per kilometer.

When deciding between *cuota* (toll) and *libre* (free) highways, remember that the four-lane tollways offer a considerable savings in time and gas over their nontoll, two-lane equivalents.

Note: On the highway, a left-turn signal from the vehicle immediately in front of you usually means it's okay for you to pass, rather than in-

dicating a left turn (which the driver would indicate by sticking out his left arm while activating the turn signal).

OFF THE HIGHWAY

Like the highways, Mexico's unpaved roads vary considerably, from rutted jeep tracks to elevated, graded, gravel boulevards—the trouble with the latter is that they tend to degenerate rather quickly between gradings into "washboard" surfaces that can be impossible to drive on at anything but very low speeds (5-10 mph), unless you want to risk crushed vertebrae and a dropped transmission.

The effect of these unpaved roads on you and your vehicle depends a lot on what kind of vehicle you're driving. Some off-highway navigators drive pickups with customized shocks and suspension that enable a driver to "float" over even the worst washboard surfaces (see "Choosing Your

---

OFF-HIGHWAY VEHICLE (OHV) DRIVER RESPONSIBILITIES

In order to help preserve Northern Mexico's wilderness areas, consider these *Tread Lightly!** guidelines when operating your 4x4, dirt bike, ATV (all-terrain vehicle), or mountain bike:

Travel only where you and vehicles are permitted. Never blaze your own trail.

Respect the rights of hikers, campers, and others to enjoy their activities undisturbed.

Educate yourself by obtaining travel maps and regulations from public agencies, complying with signs and barriers, and asking owners' permission to cross private property.

Avoid streams, lakeshores, meadows, muddy roads and trails, steep hillsides, and animals.

Drive and travel responsibly to protect the environment and preserve opportunities to enjoy recreation on wildlands.

*Tread Lightly! is a U.S. Forest Service-sponsored program established to promote the environmentally responsible use of OHVs. For information, contact Tread Lightly! Inc. (tel. 801-627-0077, fax 801-621-8633; 298 24th St., Suite 325-C, Ogden, UT 84401).

Wheels," above, for more on this topic). Other drivers, like many of the local residents, can't afford heavy-duty, customized rigs, so they learn to drive slowly and appreciate the scenery.

The best unpaved roads in Northern Mexico are probably those that have evolved more or less naturally (i.e., with little or no grading). When the weather's right (not wet), some of these roads ride better than a run-of-the-mill, potholed highway. Roads like this, however, will sometimes start out quite nicely but get increasingly worse with each passing mile to the point that even the most intrepid explorers are forced to turn around. At other times, a road will suddenly improve after a long stretch of cavernous potholes and caved-in sides. Weather is a big determining factor; even the best ungraded, unpaved roads are often impassable during or following a hard rain.

How do you know when to turn around? It helps to ask others before embarking on a road that doesn't see much traffic, even though the element of risk is always present when driving down a dirt road for the first (or even the hundredth) time. A good road map can also assist with such decisions. The Pronto Road Atlas (see "Maps," p. 82) classifies unpaved roads into three categories: graded, all-weather dirt roads; graded dirt roads that can be driven in dry weather; and unimproved dirt roads. Although neither of these maps is entirely up-to-date (no published map could be) or 100% accurate, using one or the other in conjunction with local input will greatly enhance the decision-making process with regard to off-highway travel. A topographic map could be of considerable value to a 4WD navigator as well, since sometimes it's the steep grades that call up defeat.

Getting Stuck

Even with the best planning, there always exists the possibility of getting stuck in muddy or sandy areas. Anyone engaging in serious off-highway driving should carry along a sturdy shovel for digging out mired wheels. You can also try jacking the vehicle just high enough so that you can fill in the hole created by a spinning wheel—or simply push the vehicle off the jack so that the stuck wheel lands slightly ahead of the hole. Another handy trick for negotiating soft ground is to let the air out of your tires to a pressure of around 12-15 pounds per square inch. This re-

ally works, but you should also carry along a 12-volt air compressor (one that will plug into the cigarette lighter) for pumping the tires back up after you're on firm ground again.

CITY DRIVING

Towns founded during the Spanish colonial era were invariably constructed in a grid-pattern design, as decreed in the king of Spain's *Royal Ordinance for the Laying Out of New Cities, Towns or Villages*. This design continues to be followed by Mexican city planners and makes it easy to navigate no matter what the size of the city—if, that is, you have a map in hand and can tell the difference between north, south, east, and west.

Larger cities make use of diagonal streets that cut across the grid at 45-degree angles. These diagonals help drivers traverse the city more quickly but also pose the greatest potential for confusion if you're unfamiliar with the city; you might consider avoiding the diagonals until you're sure you've got your bearings.

Traffic Offenses

Although Mexican traffic police really don't go out of their way to persecute visiting foreign drivers, it may appear that way when you're the foreigner being stopped. As a rule of thumb, the more cautiously you drive, the less likely it is that you'll inadvertently transgress local traffic codes. But if you're caught in the act of violating a traffic law, what can you expect?

If you are stopped by a *tránsito* or traffic cop, the first rule is to behave in a patient, civil manner—the cop just might let you off with a warning. Usually, if the officer decides to make a case of it, he will ask you to follow him to the nearest police post or station, where a fine will be assessed and collected on the spot—a request that's perfectly legal. If the cop suggests (or hints at) being paid on the spot, he's going for *la mordida,* the minor bribe.

In Mexico, requests for *mordida* from foreigners—for traffic offenses, at least—have become increasingly rare (the government is trying hard to stamp it out altogether). But if you are confronted with such a situation, you have two choices. First, Mexico's Attorney General for the Protection of Tourists recommends that you insist on going to the nearest station to pay the fine, and that as you pay you request a receipt. Such a request may result in all charges being dropped. Your second choice (if you don't feel like taking a trip to the station) is to negotiate the "fine" on the spot. Doing so, however, won't contribute to the shrinking of the *mordida* phenomenon.

In the author's experience, turning the wrong way on one-way streets and running stop signs are the two most common traffic violations among foreign drivers in Mexico. In some towns the stop (*Alto*) signs seem almost intentionally hidden. Also, vertical signs aren't posted at many intersections; only a broad stripe painted on the pavement indicates where vehicles are supposed to stop. The best practice is to assume that you're supposed to stop at every single intersection in a city (which is pretty close to the truth), except at green traffic lights. This can be generalized for most other urban areas.

Another common offense is going the wrong way on an unmarked, one-way street. Always look carefully at the cars driving or parked on a street to determine which direction is legal before turning.

A few other things to be aware of:

It is illegal to turn left at a traffic light that is equipped with a left-turn arrow unless this arrow is lit (even if the arrow isn't red and the straight-ahead light is green).

At urban traffic circles, drivers turning left usually do so in front of the circle instead of going around counterclockwise from the right as they would in the United States.

In situations where you have parked illegally, the police may remove your license plates, forcing you to come to the station to pay the parking fine.

FUEL, PARTS, AND REPAIRS

Fuel

The only automotive fuel commercially available in Mexico is that sold at government-owned PEMEX stations. The total number of PEMEX stations in Mexico increases each year, but they're still somewhat scarce outside large cities. A good rule of thumb is to top off your tank whenever: 1) it reaches the half-empty mark; and 2) a PEMEX station is at hand.

Three kinds of fuel are available: a leaded fuel rated at octane 81 ("Nova"); an unleaded with an octane rating of 87 ("Magna Sin"); and diesel. All three are priced by PEMEX according to standard rates and shouldn't vary from station to station. All three are slightly more expensive in Mexico than their U.S. or Canadian equivalents; the price is usually marked (in pesos) on the pump. The pump readout often accommodates only three or four digits, so a 25,000-peso (or NP$25) sale may appear as 2500, 25.00, 250, or 25.0 (although this sounds like it could be a problem when paying up, it's not once you're used to seeing it).

Take care not to be cheated—make sure the pump is zeroed before the attendant starts pumping your gasoline/diesel. This seems to be less of a problem than in previous years; stations in the border towns are still the most likely places to overcharge. It helps if you get out of your vehicle and keep an eye on the pumping procedures; if you're confused by the pump readout, currency conversion, and price per liter, carry a handheld calculator to make sure it all adds up—a calculator held in clear view will deter most potential grifters. As new pumps are added, they will be calibrated to read in nuevo pesos to conform to the new currency system instituted in Jan. 1992 (see "Money," p. 111). This should make calculations considerably easier (and is one of the reasons the government decided to knock three zeros off the currency).

At press time, PEMEX prices were US$0.40 per liter for Magna Sin, US$0.37 per liter for Nova, and US$0.27 per liter for diesel. Since PEMEX is government-owned, you don't see the week-to-week price fluctuations common in countries where oil companies are privately owned and where rates are influenced by small changes in international oil prices. According to recent Mexican government announcements, both Magna Sin and Nova are scheduled to increase by less than 1% a month, for a total price increase of about 10% by the end of each year. Diesel is supposed to rise just NP$0.01 per month.

Fuel must be paid for in cash. Mexican currency is the overwhelming preference of most PEMEX stations; some stations near the U.S.-Mexico border take U.S. dollars, but the rate is always rounded down. Carnet, a popular credit card issued in Mexico, is now being accepted at a few stations in Monterrey. It's probably only a matter of time before Carnet acceptance at PEMEX stations spreads to other cities across the nation, with perhaps Visa and MasterCard close behind. For the moment, however, be sure to carry plenty of pesos for fuel purchases.

Rumors about the quality of PEMEX fuels sometimes suggest that an extra fuel filter or an additive are necessary. This may have been the case 10 or more years ago, but nowadays PEMEX fuel seems to perform well with all types of vehicles, without such measures. The main problem with PEMEX fuel remains its availability. Stations are sometimes widely spaced (or abandoned), and not all stations carry unleaded gasoline. Generally speaking, the more affluent a town is, the more PEMEX stations it will have. You can further judge the prosperity of a town by the number of PEMEX stations offering Magna Sin—to feed the late-model American cars that wealthier Mexicans tend to purchase.

A new federal law in Mexico requires that all cars manufactured after 1991 be fitted with catalytic converters. As the decade wears on, this should mean a rapid increase in the availability of Magna Sin, especially in relatively affluent Northern Mexico.

At the moment Magna Sin seems to be readily available in the more populated areas of Northern Mexico. The most obvious lack of unleaded—from the average visitor's perspective—is in the Copper Canyon area, where the nearest PEMEX station with Magna is in La Junta, Chihuahua. Creel residents say they expect a Magna pump to be installed in their town sometime in the next year or two; in the meantime, be sure to top off in La Junta on the way in.

In a pinch, leaded gas can be used in vehicles that are supposed to take only unleaded (i.e.,

GREEN ANGELS

The Secretaría de Turismo operates a fleet of 1,030 green trucks called Angeles Verdes (Green Angels) that patrol Mexico's highways and offer professional assistance to anyone with automotive problems. This is the only such highway assistance program in the world.

Each truck carries a first-aid kit, shortwave radio, and a variety of common auto parts as well as extra gasoline; they are usually staffed by two uniformed employees, one of whom may speak some English. The drivers will perform minor repairs for the cost of the parts and can provide towing for distances up to 15 miles. If they can't remedy the problem or tow your vehicle to a nearby mechanic, they'll give you a lift and/or arrange for other assistance. They can also radio for emergency medical assistance if necessary.

The trucks patrol their assigned highway sections (a total of 234 routes nationwide) at least twice a day. The Mexican government has announced plans to triple the number of Green Angel trucks by the end of the decade.

Although the Green Angels patrol only during daylight hours, the following telephone numbers can be called day or night, 24 hours a day.

Coahuila
Piedras Negras: (84) 3-01-37
Saltillo: (84) 14-31-75, 12-21-82
Chihuahua
Ciudad Juárez: (16) 14-66-92, 14-06-70
Chihuahua: (14) 17-89-72
Durango
Gómez Palacio: (17) 14-44-74, 14-07-31
Durango: (181) 1-56-81
Nuevo León
Guadalupe: (83) 67-12-05
Monterrey: (83) 40-31-14, 40-21-13
San Luis Potosí
Ciudad Valles: (138) 2-29-49
Matehuala: (488) 2-08-58
San Luis Potosí: (48) 14-09-06, 12-21-78
Sonora
Agua Prieta: (633) 8-09-34
Caborca: (641) 6-48-50
Ciudad Obregón: (641) 6-48-50, 6-77-93
Hermosillo: (62) 14-63-04, 15-31-97
Nogales: (631) 3-12-66
Puerto Peñasco: (638) 3-41-29
Zacatecas
Fresnillo: (408) 2-25-75
Zacatecas: (492) 2-68-24
Toll-free from anywhere in Mexico: 91-800-9-03-29

those fitted with anti-smog catalytic converters) without an appreciable difference in performance. You shouldn't be forced to burn more than a tankful of leaded here and there, if at all, since roughly every other PEMEX station seems to dispense unleaded. Many auto experts advocate adding a can of octane booster to your tank in cases where you have to run a tank of leaded in an unleaded-only vehicle. (The author has occasionally burned a tank or two of Nova, with octane booster, in his unleaded-only vehicle without noticeable ill effects.) **Note:** If you're driving a new car still under warranty, using leaded fuel may void the warranty. If this is a potential concern, check your car's warranty before making the decision to use Nova in the more remote areas of Northern Mexico. Carrying a spare five-gallon can will get you through most situations where fuel is tight.

Other availability-related problems include long lines at small-town stations and the occasional selling out of one or all types of fuel at a particular station. To notify customers, the hose will usually be draped over the top of a pump when it's empty. If you're low on fuel and all of the nearest stations are empty, ask if there's a *bodega* (storage facility) nearby. Foreign visitors are legally permitted to buy gasoline directly from a *bodega* in such a situation.

Oil

Motor oil is widely available at *tiendas, supermercados,* and PEMEX stations throughout Northern Mexico. If your vehicle takes anything lower than 30-weight, however, you had better bring along your own, since most places stock only 30- or 40-weight oil.

Parts And Repairs

Good auto shops and mechanics are available in all larger towns and cities and especially in the state capitals. Elsewhere, if you have a breakdown, it's either do-it-yourself or rely on the mercy of passing drivers. In areas where you can find a mechanic, the following makes can usually be serviced: Chevrolet, Dodge, Ford, Nissan, Toyota, and Volkswagen. For anything other than these makes—even for short trips—you should carry spare filters, plugs, points, hoses, belts, and gaskets.

Diesel mechanics can be harder to find. A list of qualified diesel shops in Mexico can be obtained by contacting San Antonio's Mexican Government Tourism Office (MGTO, Centre Plaza Bldg., 45 N.E. Loop 410, Suite 125, San Antonio, TX 78216; tel. 210-366-3242 or 800-232-4MEX), an office which specializes in Mexican road tourism.

Although plenty of visitors drive the length and breadth of Mexico without so much as a spare tire, anyone driving long distances should consider bringing the following extras, regardless of the vehicle type:

- ✔ air filters
- ✔ battery cables
- ✔ brake, steering, and transmission fluids
- ✔ fan belts
- ✔ fuel filters
- ✔ funnel
- ✔ fuses
- ✔ lug wrench and jack
- ✔ radiator hoses
- ✔ spare tire
- ✔ spark plugs
- ✔ water filters
- ✔ one or two five-gallon gas cans
- ✔ one five-gallon container of fresh water
- ✔ two or three cans octane booster
- ✔ emergency flares
- ✔ all-weather tarp or "space blanket"
- ✔ fire extinguisher
- ✔ 60-foot tow rope
- ✔ tire gauge
- ✔ tube repair kit
- ✔ 12-volt air compressor

(For a glossary of Spanish automotive terms, see the "Spanish Phrasebook" at the back of this book.)

IMMIGRATION, CUSTOMS, AND CROSSING THE BORDER

ENTRY REGULATIONS

U.S. And Canadian Citizens

U.S. and Canadian citizens visiting Mexico solely for tourism, transit, or study purposes are not required to obtain a visa. In fact, for Mexico visits of less than 72 hours all that's needed is one proof of citizenship—an original birth certificate (or certified copy), an original voter's registration card, a certificate of naturalization, or a passport. Driver's licenses aren't accepted as citizenship proof.

All U.S. or Canadian citizens crossing the Mexican border for more than 72 hours or going farther south than border checkpoints (20-40 km/12-25 miles south of the border in most places) must have in their possession a validated "tourist card" (Form FMT), which isn't actually a card but a slip of paper. These are available free of charge at any Mexican consulate or Mexican tourist office, from many travel agencies, on flights to Mexico, or at the border. (Exceptions to the tourist card requirement include visits to anywhere on the Baja California peninsula as well as Golfo de Santa Clara and Puerto Peñasco in the state of Sonora.)

The tourist card is valid for stays of up to 180 days and must be used within 90 days of its issuance. Your card becomes invalid once you exit the country (you're supposed to surrender it at the border), even if your 180 days hasn't expired. If you'll be entering and leaving Mexico more than once during your trip, you should request a multiple-entry tourist card (usually available from Mexican consulates only).

Validation: Once you cross the border with your tourist card, it must be validated by a Mexican immigration officer. This can be arranged at any *migración* office in Mexico (all *municipio* seats have them), but is most conveniently accomplished at the border crossing.

Minors: Until 1991, Mexico had a regulation requiring children under the age of 18 who crossed the border without one or both parents to carry a notarized letter granting permission from the absent parent(s). This regulation is no longer in effect, but we've heard that some Mexican border officers (as well as airline check-in crews) are still asking for the letter, unaware that the regulation has been rescinded. Unaccompanied minors or minors traveling with only one parent should be prepared for all situations by carrying a notarized letter. In cases of divorce, separation, or death, the minor should carry notarized papers documenting the situation.

In reality, minors with tourist cards are rarely asked for these documents. Children under 15 may be included on their parents' tourist card but this means that neither the child nor the parents can legally exit Mexico without the other.

Citizens From Other Countries

Tourists from countries other than the U.S. or Canada may need visas in advance of arrival in Mexico. Citizens of Australia, New Zealand, and most West European countries can usually obtain free, no-photo visas at the Mexican border, but be sure to check with a Mexican embassy or consulate first—visa regulations change from year to year.

If you apply in person at a Mexican consulate, you usually can obtain a tourist visa on the same day of application.

Foreign visitors who are legal permanent residents of the U.S. do not need visas to visit Mexico for tourist purposes. A free tourist card can be obtained by presenting your passport and a U.S. residence card to any travel agency or at the airport or border crossing.

Pets

Dogs, cats, and other pets may be brought into Mexico if each is accompanied by a **vaccination certificate** (which must show that the animal has been vaccinated or treated for rabies, hepatitis, pip, and leptospirosis) and a **health certificate** (International Health Certificate for Dogs and Cats). The latter must be issued no more than 72 hours before entry and signed by a registered veterinarian.

Since 1992 the requirement that the health certificate be stamped with a visa at the border or at a Mexican consulate has been repealed. The certificate is still necessary; the "visa" isn't.

When you recross the border into the U.S., the U.S. Customs Service will ask to see the vaccination certificate.

Inmigrante Rentista Visas

Special visas (FM-2 status) are issued to foreigners who choose to reside in Mexico on a "permanent income" basis. This most often applies to foreigners who decide to retire in Mexico, though it is also used by artists, writers, and other self-employed foreign residents. With this visa you're allowed to import one motor vehicle as well as your household belongings into Mexico tax-free.

The basic requirements for this visa are that applicants must forego any kind of employment while residing in Mexico and must show proof (bank statements) that they have a regular source of foreign-earned income amounting to at least US$1500 per month (plus US$500 for each dependent over the age of 15, e.g., US$2000 for a couple). A pile of paperwork, including a "letter of good conduct" from the applicant's local police department, must accompany the initial application, along with an immigration tax payment (currently US$121) and various applications fees totaling around US$75.

The visa must be renewed annually but the renewal can be accomplished at any immigration office in Mexico (every *municipio* has one). After five years in Mexico, an *inmigrante rentista* is eligible to apply for *inmigrado* status, which confers all the rights of citizenship (including employment in Mexico), save the rights to vote and hold public office.

Many foreigners who have retired in Mexico manage to do so on the regular 180-day tourist visa; every six months they dash across the border and return with a new tourist card (issued at the border) on the same day. This method bypasses all the red tape and income requirements of the retirement visa.

Retirees disinclined to make a run for the border every six months can alternatively obtain an FM-3 *visitante rentista* visa, which allows one-year stays with none of the privileges (i.e., tax-free importation of vehicle and household goods) of the FM-2 visa. FM-3 status does,

however, carry the same minimum income requirements as the FM-2, and it must be renewed annually. For most people the FM-3 visa isn't worth the hassle of application and annual juggling of financial statements, especially since the tourist card is freely available at the border.

CUSTOMS

Entering Mexico

Officially, tourists are supposed to bring into Mexico only those items that will be of use during their trip. This means that you can bring in practically anything as long as it doesn't appear to be in large enough quantities for resale. Firearms and ammunition, as well as boats, however, require special permits (see "Outdoor Recreation," p. 39, for permit information).

Auto Permits

Foreign-registered motor vehicles (cars, trucks, RVs, motorcycles, etc.) do not require permits for border town visits of less than 72 hours. For longer visits, however, you *must* obtain a **temporary vehicle importation permit** at the border if you're going anywhere besides Baja California, Puerto Peñaso, or Golfo de Santa Clara. To receive this permit, you simply drive your vehicle to a Mexican customs office at an official border crossing and present the following: a valid state registration for the vehicle (or similar document certifying legal ownership), a driver's license, and a credit card (Visa, MasterCard, American Express, or Diner's Club) issued outside Mexico.

If you are leasing or renting the vehicle, you'll also have to present a leasing or rental contract made out to the person bringing the vehicle into Mexico. If the vehicle belongs to someone else (e.g., a friend or relative), you must present a notarized letter from the owner giving you permission to take the vehicle to Mexico. Contrary to rumor, you aren't required to present the "pink slip" or ownership certificate unless the state registration certificate is for some reason unavailable.

Once the Mexican customs officials have approved your documents, you'll proceed to a Banjército (Banco del Ejército or Military Bank) office attached to the customs facilities, where your credit card account will charged US$10

MEXICAN CONSULATES

UNITED STATES

Alabama: 801 Sullivan Ave., Mobile, AL 36609 (tel. 205-653-4560)
Arizona: 135 Terrace Ave., Nogales, AZ 85621 (tel. 602-287-2521)
  1990 West Camelback, Suite 110, Phoenix, AZ 85015 (tel. 602-242-7398)
  553 S. Stone Ave., Tucson, AZ 85701 (tel. 602-882-5595)
California: 331 W. Second St., Calexico, CA 92231 (tel. 619-357-3863)
  905 N. Fulton St., Fresno, CA 93728 (tel. 209-233-3065)
  2401 W. Sixth St., Los Angeles, CA 90057 (tel. 310-351-6800)
  Transportation Center, 201 E. Fourth St., Oxnard, CA 93030 (tel. 805-483-4684)
  9812 Old Winery Pl., Suite 10, Sacramento, CA 95827 (tel. 916-446-9024)
  588 W. Sixth St., San Bernardino, CA 92401 (tel. 714-889-9836)
  610 A St., San Diego, CA 92101 (tel. 619-231-8414)
  870 Market St., Suite 528, San Francisco, CA 94102 (tel. 415-392-5554)
  380 N. First St., Suite 102, San Jose, CA 95112 (tel. 408-294-3415)
Colorado: 707 Washington St., Suite A, Denver, CO 80203 (tel. 303-830-0601)
District of Columbia: 1911 Pennsylvania Ave., Washington, D.C. 20036 (tel. 202-728-1750)
Florida: 780 N.W. LeJeune Rd., Suite 525, Miami, FL 33126 (tel. 305-441-8780)
  1717 W. Cass St., Tampa, FL 33606 (tel. 813-254-5960)
Georgia: 410 South Tower, One CNN Center, Atlanta, GA 30303 (tel. 404-688-3258)
Illinois: 300 N. Michigan Ave., 2nd Fl., Chicago, IL 60601 (tel. 312-855-1380)
Louisiana: 1140 World Trade Center Bldg., 2 Canal St., New Orleans, LA 70130 (tel. 504-522-3596)
Massachusetts: 20 Park Plaza, Suite 321, Boston, MA 02116 (tel. 617-426-8782)
Michigan: Book Bldg., Suite 1515, 1249 Washington Blvd., Detroit, MI 48231 (tel. 313-965-1868)
Missouri: 1015 Locust St., Suite 922, St. Louis, MO 63101 (tel. 314-436-3233)
New Mexico: Western Bank Bldg., 401 Fifth St. NW, Albuquerque, NM 87102 (tel. 505-247-2147)
New York: 8 E. 41st St., New York, NY 10017 (tel. 212-689-0456)
North Carolina: P.O. Box 19627, Charlotte, NC 28219 (tel. 704-394-2190)
Oregon: 545 N.E. 47th Ave., Suite 317, Portland, OR 97213 (tel. 503-233-5662)
Pennsylvania: Bourse Bldg., Suite 525, 21 S. Fifth St., Philadelphia, PA 19403 (tel. 215-922-4262)
Texas: 200 E. Sixth St., Suite 200, Austin, TX 78701 (tel. 512-478-2866)
  P.O. Box 1711, Elizabeth and E. Seventh Sts., Brownsville, TX 78520 (tel. 210-542-4431)
  Shoreline Plaza One, 410 North Tower, Corpus Christi, TX 78401 (tel. 512-882-3375)
  1349 Empire Central, Suite 100, Dallas, TX 75247 (tel. 214-630-7341)
  1010 Main St., Del Rio, TX 78841 (tel. 210-774-5031)
  140 Adams St., Eagle Pass, TX 78832 (tel. 210-773-9255)
  910 E. San Antonio St., El Paso, TX 79901 (tel. 915-533-3644)
  4200 Montrose Blvd., Suite 120, Houston, TX 77006 (tel. 713-524-4861)
  1612 Farragut St., Laredo, TX 78040 (tel. 210-723-6360)
  1418 Beech St., Suites 102-104, McAllen, TX 78501 (tel. 210-686-0244)
  511 W. Ohio, Suite 121, Midland, TX 79701 (tel. 915-687-2334)
  127 Navarro St., San Antonio, TX 78205 (tel. 210-227-9145)
Utah: 182 S. 600 E, Suite 202, Salt Lake City, UT 84102 (tel. 801-521-8502)
Washington: 2132 Third Ave., Seattle, WA 98121 (tel. 206-448-6819)

CANADA

British Columbia: 1130 W. Pender St., Vancouver, B.C. VGE 4A4 (tel. 604-684-3547)
Ontario: 60 Bloor St. W, Suite 203, Toronto, Ont. M4W 3B8 (tel. 416-922-2718)
Quebec: 2000 Mansfield St., Suite 1015, Montreal, Que. H3A 2Z7 (tel. 514-288-2502)

for the permit fee. **Note:** This fee must be paid by credit card; cash is not accepted. If you don't have a credit card, you'll have to post a bond (one to two percent of the vehicle's blue-book value) issued by an authorized Mexican bond company, a very time-consuming and expensive procedure. Banjército is the bank used for all Mexican customs charges; the operating hours for each module are the same as for the border crossing at which it's located.

Once the US$10 fee has been charged to your credit card, the permit is issued, with a validity period equal to that shown on your tourist card or visa. You may drive back and forth across the border—at any crossing—as many times as you wish during the permit's validity. You are supposed to surrender the permit at the border when your trip is over, however.

Always carry your vehicle import permit with you when driving your vehicle in Mexico. The permit may be checked at interior immigration checkpoints; and the police may ask to see it during routine checks, or if you've been stopped for a traffic offense.

In the U.S., further information on temporary vehicle importation can be obtained by calling (800) 446-8277 (toll free). Under a new agreement between the American Automobile Association (AAA) and the Mexican government, U.S. motorists with credit cards will be able to obtain both tourist cards and auto permits from AAA offices in Texas, New Mexico, Arizona, and California. As of May 1994, these offices can also assist with all other vehicle border documentation

Insurance: Although it's not yet required by Mexican law, any visitors planning to drive their own vehicles in Mexico should carry Mexican vehicle insurance. Foreign insurance policies aren't valid in Mexico; without insurance, if you get in an accident that's judged your fault, you can be jailed until you pay damages. See "Driving in Northern Mexico," p. 90, for details on how to obtain Mexican insurance.

Returning To The U.S.
Visitors returning to the U.S. from Mexico may have their luggage inspected by U.S. Customs officials. The hassle can be minimized by giving brief, straight answers to their questions (e.g., "How long have you been in Mexico?" "Do you have anything to declare?") and by cooperating with their requests to open your luggage,

vehicle storage compartments, and anything else they want opened. Sometimes the officers use dogs to sniff luggage and/or vehicles for contraband and illegal aliens.

Customs Duties: Nearly 3,000 items (including all handicrafts) made in Mexico are exempt from any U.S. Customs duties. Adults over 21 are allowed one liter (33.8 fluid ounces) of alcoholic beverages and 200 cigarettes (or 100 cigars) per person. All other purchases or gifts up to a total value of US$400 within any 31-day period can be brought into the U.S. duty-free.

Plant and Animal Prohibitions: The following fruits and vegetables cannot be brought into the U.S. from Mexico: oranges, grapefruits, mangoes, avocados (unless the pit is removed), and potatoes (including yams and sweet potatoes). All other fruits are permitted (including bananas, dates, pineapples, cactus fruits, grapes, and berries of all types).

Other prohibited plant materials are straw (including packing materials and items stuffed with straw), hay, unprocessed cotton, sugarcane, and any plants in soil (this includes houseplants).

Animals and animal products that cannot be imported include wild and domesticated birds (including poultry, unless cooked), pork or pork products (including sausage, ham, and other cured pork), and eggs. Beef, mutton, venison, and other meats are permitted at up to 50 pounds per person.

Customs regulations can change at any time, so if you want to verify the regulations on a purchase before risking duties or confiscation at the border, check with a U.S. consulate in Northern Mexico before crossing.

BORDER CROSSINGS

Between San Luis (Yuma), Arizona, and the Gulf of Mexico are 21 official U.S.-Mexico border crossings (not counting Tijuana, Tecate, and Mexicali in Baja California). Border facilities at most gateways are open 24 hours, although the smaller crossings (Sasabe, Naco, Palomas, Colombia, Ojinaga, Piedras Negras, Nueva Ciudad Guerrero, Camargo, Dí Ordaz, Nuevo Progreso) maintain more limited schedules—usually weekdays 7 a.m.-9 p.m., Sat.-Sun. 8 a.m.-5 p.m.—depending on size and border traffic.

Nuevo Laredo is the largest port of entry along Mexico's entire border and also the most heavily used commercially since it connects Mexico with U.S. Interstate 35, which extends north through the middle of the U.S. to Dallas, Kansas City, Minneapolis, Duluth, and the Canadian border. Ciudad Juárez is the second most used gateway. At any of the border crossings, you'll find the shortest waits (15-30 minutes at Ciudad Juárez or Nuevo Laredo) are between 10 a.m. and 3:30 p.m. or after 7-8 p.m. on weekdays. Weekends are the worst days in either direction, except late at night or before dawn. If you're on your way out of Mexico and find yourself near the border during rush hours, it might be best to find a restaurant or other spot on the Mexico side and wait it out. Waits are always longer going north.

If you're on foot, crossing is usually a breeze. Public and chartered buses also get through more quickly than private vehicles because of special traffic lanes provided them.

At all other crossings, wait times are rarely more than 5-15 minutes.

Unofficial Crossings

All along the lengthy U.S.-Mexico border are places where locals cross back and forth at will without immigration checks on either side. Some of these spots are deliberately tolerated by immigration officials of both nations. The rowboat crossings at Paso Lajitas, Chih., opposite Lajitas, Texas, next to Big Bend National Park, and at Boquillas del Carmen, Coah., opposite the park itself, have long been places where park visitors and local tradespeople have been allowed to

---

OFFICIAL U.S.-MEXICO BORDER CROSSINGS

The following list includes only those crossings with U.S. and Mexican immigration posts. Hours of operation were current as of May 1993.

San Luis Río Colorado, Son. (road; opposite San Luis, AZ): 24 hrs.

Sonoyta, Son. (road; opposite Lukeville, AZ): 24 hrs.

Sasabe, Son. (road; opposite Sasabe, AZ): 8 a.m.-8 p.m. Mon.-Fri., 10 a.m.-2 p.m. Sat.-Sun.

Nogales, Son. (road; opposite Nogales, AZ): 24 hrs.

Naco, Son. (road; opposite Naco, AZ): 8 a.m.-midnight daily

Agua Prieta, Son. (road; opposite Douglas, AZ): 24 hrs.

Palomas, Chih. (road; opposite Columbus, NM): 24 hrs.

Ciudad Juárez, Chih. (bridge; opposite El Paso, TX; there are also three bridge crossings southeast of El Paso near Fabens and Fort Hancock): 24 hrs.

Ojinaga, Chih. (bridge; opposite Presidio, TX): 7:30 a.m.-9 p.m. Mon.-Fri., 8 a.m.-4 p.m. Sat.-Sun.

Ciudad Acuña, Coah. (bridge; opposite Del Rio, TX): 24 hrs.

Piedras Negras, Coah. (bridge; opposite Eagle Pass, TX): 24 hrs.

Nuevo Laredo, Tamps. (bridge; opposite Laredo, TX; plus second crossing northeast at Colombia, Tamps.): 24 hrs.

Nueva Ciudad Guerrero, Tamps. (bridge; opposite Salineno, TX): 7:30 a.m.-9 p.m. Mon.-Fri., 8 a.m.-4 p.m. Sat.-Sun.

Ciudad Miguel Alemán, Tamps. (bridge; opposite Roma, TX): 24 hrs.

Camargo, Tamps. (bridge; opposite Rio Grande City, TX): 7:30 a.m.-9 p.m. Mon.-Fri., 8 a.m.-4 p.m. Sat.-Sun.

Díaz Ordaz, Tamps. (ferry; opposite Los Ebanos, TX; bridge to be constructed): 7:30 a.m.-9 p.m. Mon.-Fri., 8 a.m.-4 p.m. Sat.-Sun.

Reynosa, Tamps. (bridge; opposite Hidalgo/McAllen, TX): 24 hrs.

Nuevo Progreso (Río Bravo), Tamps. (bridge; opposite Progreso, TX): 7:30 a.m.-9 p.m. Mon.-Fri., 8 a.m.-4 p.m. Sat.-Sun.

Matamoros, Tamps. (bridge; opposite Brownsville, TX): 24 hrs.

cross without any border formalities. (If the proposed international park linking Big Bend with Mexico's Sierra del Carmen is ever realized, Boquillas del Carmen, Coah., will become the main gateway to the Mexican half of the park.) Northeast of Ojinaga, Coah. is a small Mexican town where the residents regularly collect their mail at the Ruidoso, Texas post office.

HEALTH

By and large, Northern Mexico is a healthy place —sanitation standards are relatively high compared to those in many other parts of Mexico, and the water quality in many areas is superior. The visitor's main health concerns are not going to be with food or water sources, but with avoiding mishaps while driving, cycling, hiking, boating, diving, surfing, or otherwise enjoying Mexico's great outdoors. Health issues directly concerned with these activities are covered under the relevant sections in this book.

Food- And Water-related Illnesses
Visitors who use common sense will probably never come down with food- or water-related illnesses while traveling in Northern Mexico. The first rule is not to overdo it during the first few days of your trip—eat and drink with moderation. Shoveling down huge amounts of tasty but often rich Mexican foods along with pitchers of margaritas or strong Mexican beer is liable to make anyone sick from pure overindulgence. If you're not used to the spices and different ways of cooking, it's best to ingest small amounts at first.

Second, take it easy with foods offered by **street vendors,** since this is where you're most likely to suffer from unsanitary conditions. Eat only foods that have been thoroughly cooked and are served either stove-hot or refrigerator-cold. Many gringos eat street food without any problems whatsoever (the author included), but it pays to be cautious, especially if it's your first time in Mexico.

Doctors usually recommend that you avoid eating peeled, raw **fruits and vegetables** in Mexico. Once the peel has been broken, it is virtually impossible to disinfect the produce. As long as unpeeled fruits and vegetables are washed in purified water and then dried with a clean cloth before eating, they're usually okay (plenty of Mexican fruit is consumed daily in Canada and the U.S., after all).

Hotels and restaurants serve only purified drinking water and ice to their customers (whether Mexican or gringo), so it's unnecessary to ask for mineral water or to refuse ice. **Tap water,** however, should not be consumed, except in hotels where the water system is purified (if so, a notice will be posted over the washbasin in your room). Most **grocery stores** sell bottled, purified water if you need it for the road. Water purification tablets, iodine crystals, water filters, etc. aren't necessary for Mexico travel unless you plan to do extensive backpacking (see "Hiking And Backpacking," p. 41, for details).

Turista
People who have never before traveled to a foreign country may experience a significant period of adjustment to the new gastrointestinal flora that comes with the territory—the differences wrought by distances are really unavoidable. Sometimes the adjustment is unpleasant.

Mexican doctors call gastrointestinal upset of this sort *turista* since it affects tourists but not the local population. The usual symptoms of *turista* (also known by the gringo tags "Montezuma's Revenge" or the "Aztec Two-Step") are nausea and diarrhea, sometimes with stomach cramps and a low fever. Again, eating and drinking in moderation will help prevent the worst of the symptoms, should they begin to appear. These symptoms rarely persist more than a day or two. (If it's any consolation, Mexicans often get sick when they go abroad, too.)

Prevention and Treatment: Many Mexico travelers swear by a preventive regimen of Pepto-Bismol begun the day before arrival in the country. Opinions vary as to how much of the pink stuff is necessary to ward off or tame the evil flora, but a person should not exceed the recommended daily dosage—taper off use throughout the second week until you stop using it altogether.

Another regimen that seems to be effective is a daily tablet of 100-milligram doxycycline (sold as Vibramycin in the U.S.), a low-grade antibiotic that requires a prescription in most countries. It works by killing all the bacteria in your intestinal tract—including the ones that reside there naturally and help protect your bowels from outside intruders as well as new arrivals. It's available without a prescription in Mexican *farmacias,* but you should check with your doctor first to make sure you're not sensitive to it—some people have problems with sunlight or upset stomach while taking doxycycline. (Also be sure to take it with plenty of water and/or a meal.) Some physicians believe that when you stop taking this drug, you're particularly susceptible to intestinal upset because no protective bacteria is left to fight off infections.

Note: According to *Staying Healthy in Asia, Africa, and Latin America* (Moon Publications), the U.S. Public Health Service does not recommend either of the aforementioned preventive practices for travelers planning trips for more than three weeks.

If you come down with a case of *turista,* the best thing to do is drink plenty of fluids (adults should drink at least three quarts or liters a day, a child under 80 pounds/37 kilos at least a liter a day—but no tea, coffee, milk, fruit juices, or booze), eat only bland foods (nothing spicy, fatty, or fried), and take it easy until it passes. Pepto-Bismol or similar pectin-based remedies usually help. Some people like to mask the symptoms with a strong over-the-counter medication like Immodium AD (loperamide is the active ingredient); however, though it can be very effective, it isn't a cure—only time will cure traveler's diarrhea.

If the symptoms are unusually severe (*especially* if there's blood in the stools or a high fever) or persist more than one or two days, you should see a doctor. Most hotels can arrange a doctor's visit or you can contact a Mexican tourist office or U.S. consulate for recommendations.

Sunburn And Dehydration

Northern Mexico visitors are probably afflicted more by sunburn than by all other illnesses and injuries combined. The sunlight in Mexico can be quite strong, especially in the Altiplano and along the Sea of Cortez/Pacific coast. For outdoor forays, sun protection is a must, whatever the activity—the longer you'll be in the sun, the more protection you'll need.

A hat, sunglasses, and plenty of sunscreen or sunblock make a good start. Bring along a sunscreen with a SPF (sun protection factor) of at least 25 (even if you don't plan to use it all the time) for when your skin has had enough toasting. Apply it to *all* exposed parts of your body—don't forget hands, tops of the feet, neck, tops of the ears, any thinned-out or bald areas on your scalp, and places where you part your hair. Sunscreen must be reapplied after swimming (no matter what the label says) or after heavy perspiring.

If you're going boating, don't leave shore with only a bathing suit—bring an opaque shirt, preferably with long sleeves, along with a pair of long pants for when the sun gets to be too much. Since you can never know for certain whether your boat might get stranded or lost at sea for a period of time (if, for example, the motor conks out and you get caught in an offshore current), you shouldn't be without extra clothing for emergencies.

It's also important to drink plenty of water and/or nonalcoholic, noncaffeinated fluids when spending time in the sun, to avoid dehydration (alcohol and caffeine—including the caffeine in iced tea and cola—only increase your potential for dehydration). Symptoms of dehydration include darker-than-usual urine (or inability to urinate), a flushed face, profuse sweating or an unusual lack thereof, and sometimes a headache, dizziness, and general feeling of malaise. Extreme cases of dehydration caused by hot weather can lead to heat exhaustion or, less commonly, heat stroke, in which the victim may become delirious and/or convulse. If either condition is suspected, get the victim out of the sun immediately, cover with a wet sheet or towel, and administer a rehydration fluid that replaces lost water and salts (sodium, potassium, chloride, and bicarbonate). If you can get the victim to a doctor, all the better—heat stroke can be very serious.

Rehydration Formula: If Gatorade or a similar rehydration fluid isn't available you can mix your own by combining the following ingredients: 1 quart (4 cups or 1 liter) purified water or diluted fruit juice; 2 tablespoons sugar or honey; 1/4 teaspoon salt; and 1/4 teaspoon baking soda (if soda isn't available, use another 1/4 teaspoon salt). A dehydration victim should drink this mixture at regular intervals until symptoms have subsided substantially—four or more quarts/liters may be necessary in moderate cases, more in severe cases.

Motion Sickness

Visitors with little or no boating experience who join fishing cruises in Northern Mexico are sometimes prone to motion sickness. This happens when the repeated pitching and rolling over ocean swells affects a person's sense of equilibrium to the point of nausea. Commonly known as "seasickness" (*mareado* in Spanish), it can be a very unpleasant experience not only for the green-at-the-gills but for fellow passengers (who will be anxious lest the victim spew on them at any moment).

The best way to prevent motion sickness is to take one of the preventives commonly available from a pharmacist: promethazine (sold as Phenergan in the U.S.), dimenhydrinate (Dramamine), or scopolamine (Transderm Scop). The latter is available as an adhesive patch worn behind the ear—the time-release action is supposed to be more effective than tablets. These medications should be taken *before* boarding the vessel rather than after one feels seasick. It's also not a good idea to eat a large meal before getting on a boat.

If you start to feel seasick while out on the bounding main, certain actions can lessen the likelihood that it will get worse: 1) do not lie down, since often the first symptom of motion sickness is drowsiness—if you give in to the impulse you'll almost certainly guarantee a worsening of the condition; 2) stay in the open air rather than below decks—fresh air usually helps; and 3) fix your gaze on the horizon—this will help steady your disturbed inner ear, which is the proximate cause of motion sickness in the first place.

Bites And Stings

Mosquitoes and *Jejenes:* Mosquitoes breed in standing water and since standing water isn't that common in arid Northern Mexico, neither are mosquitoes (exceptions include estuaries and marshes when there isn't a strong enough breeze around to keep them at bay). The easiest way to avoid mosquito bites is to apply insect repellent to exposed areas of the skin and clothing whenever they're out and biting (for most species, this means between dusk and dawn).

The most effective repellents are those that contain a high concentration of DEET (N,N-diethyl-metatoluamide). Those with an aversion to applying synthetics to their skin can try citronella (lemon-grass oil), which is also effective but requires more frequent application. Carl Lumholz, while traveling in northwestern Mexico in the early 1900s, successfully used a French-Canadian recipe consisting of 17 parts olive oil, two parts oil of pennyroyal, and one part carbolic acid.

Some of the same conditions that bring out the mosquitoes will produce *jejenes,* tiny flying insects also known as "no-see-ums" among North Americans because you almost never see them while they're biting. The same repellents that are effective for mosquitoes will usually do the trick for *jejenes.*

For relief from the itchiness of mosquito bites, try rubbing a bit of hand soap on the affected areas. *Jejene* bites will usually stop itching in less than 10 minutes if you refrain from scratching them. Excessive scratching of either type of bite can lead to infection, so be mindful of what your fingers are up to—scratching never helps.

Wasps, Bees, and Hornets: Although stings from these flying insects can be very painful, they aren't of mortal danger to most people. If you're allergic to such stings and plan to travel in remote areas of Northern Mexico, you should consider requesting anti-allergy medication from your doctor before leaving home. At the very least, carry a supply of Benadryl or a similar over-the-counter antihistamine. Dramamine (dimenhydrinate) also usually helps mitigate allergic reactions.

Relief from a wasp-bee-hornet sting can be achieved by applying a paste of baking soda and water to the area. Liquids that contain ammonia, including urine, are also helpful in relieving pain. If a stinger is visible, remove (by scraping if possible, or with tweezers if not) before applying any remedies. If a stung limb becomes unusually swollen or if the victim exhibits symptoms of a severe allergic reaction (difficulty breathing, agitation, hives), seek medical assistance.

Ticks: If you find a tick embedded in your skin, don't try to pull it off—this may leave the head and pincers under your skin and lead to infection. Covering the tick with petroleum jelly, mineral oil, alcohol, gasoline, or kerosene will usually cause the tick to release its hold in order to avoid suffocation.

Burning the tick with a cigarette butt or hot match usually succeeds only in killing it—when you pull the tick out, the head and pincers may not come with it. Stay with the suffocation method and if it doesn't come out, use tweezers and twist slowly counterclockwise.

Scorpions: Scorpions (*alacranes*) vary in the strength of their venom from individual to individual and species to species, but the sting is rarely dangerous to adults. It can be very painful, however, and can result in partial numbness and swelling that lasts up to several days. In Mexico, the small yellow scorpions inflict a more painful sting than the larger, dark-colored ones.

The best treatment begins with having the victim lie down and relax to slow the spread of the venom; keep the affected area below the level of the heart. Ice packs on the sting may relieve pain and mitigate swelling—aspirin also helps.

Children who weigh less than about 30 pounds (13 kilos) should receive medical attention if stung by a scorpion. Doctors in Mexico usually have ready access to scorpion antivenin (*anti-alacrán*), but it should only be administered under qualified medical supervision.

Avoiding Scorpions: Scorpions prefer damp, dark, warm places—e.g., dead brush, rockpiles, and fallen logs—so exercise particular caution when placing your hands in or near such areas (hands are the scorpion's most common target on the human body). In fact, campers should wear gloves while handling firewood as an extra precaution against scorpion stings.

SNAKEBITE PREVENTION AND TREATMENT

Although 13 rattlesnake and one coral snake species can be found in Northern Mexico, the overall risk of being bitten by a poisonous snake while hiking in Northern Mexico is quite low, mainly because such creatures avoid contact with all large mammals, including humans. Most of the unfortunate who are bitten by snakes in Mexico are local ranchers who spend a great deal of time in snake habitats, or small children who may not know to retreat from a coiled rattler.

Nonetheless, anyone spending time in the Northern Mexican outback, including campers and hikers, would be well-advised to follow a few simple precautions.

Prevention
First of all, use caution when placing hands or feet in areas where snakes may lie. This primarily includes rocky ledges, holes, and fallen logs. Always look first, and if you must move a rock or log, use a long stick or other instrument. Wear sturdy footwear when walking in possible snake habitats. High-top leather shoes or boots are best. Rancheros wear thick leather leggings when working in known snake territory; these are sometimes available for purchase at *zapaterías* (shoe stores) or at leather and saddle shops.

Most snakes strike only when they feel threatened. Naturally, if you step on or next to a snake, it is likely to strike. If you see or hear a rattlesnake, re-main still until the snake moves away. If it doesn't leave the vicinity, simply back away slowly and cautiously. Sudden movements may cause a snake to strike; rattlers rarely strike a stationary target. Remember also that a rattler can't strike a target that is farther away than three-fourths of its body length. Use this rough measure to judge when it may be safe to move away from one, leaving plenty of room for error.

If you'll be hiking in wilderness areas far from professional medical treatment, by all means carry an elastic bandage or two, the type used for sprains. The old "slice and suck" method of treating snakebite has been discredited by most medical experts.

Don't attempt to kill a rattler unless you have a genuine need to use it as food (great barbecued)—as nasty as they may seem, snakes are as important to the desert ecosystem as the most beautiful flowering cactus.

Treatment
If bitten by a snake, it is important that you remain calm in order to slow the potential spread of venom in your body until you are able to discern whether the snake in question is a rattler, and so that you can follow the necessary steps for treatment in a cool-headed manner if it is.

First, immediately following the bite, try to identify the snake—was it a rattler or a coral snake? At the very least, memorize the markings and physical

Other favorite spots for scorpions are crumpled clothing and bedding. In desert areas of Northern Mexico, always check your bed sheets or sleeping bag for scorpions before climbing in. In the same environments, shake out your shoes and clothing before putting them on.

Centipedes: Called *cientopiés* ("100 legs") in Spanish, these slow-moving insects aren't as common as scorpions but have a similarly painful bite. Unlike scorpions, they prefer dry, rocky realms; you're most likely to see them when hiking in the desert. They're also less quick to inflict their bite except when mightily disturbed. Treatment is the same as for scorpions; none of the species in Northern Mexico are known to be deadly, but some people react more strongly than others.

Poisonous Sea Creatures

Various marine animals carry poisons that can inflict painful stings on humans. Along the coasts, such creatures include jellyfish, Portuguese men-of-war, cone shells, stingrays, sea urchins, and various fish with poisonous spines.

The best way to avoid jellyfish and Portuguese men-of-war is to scope out the water before going in—if you see any nasties floating around, look for another beach. Stingrays can be avoided by shuffling your feet in the sand as you walk in shallow surf—this will usually cause rays resting in the sand to swim away.

To avoid cone-shell and sea-urchin stings, wear shoes in the water (several sport-shoe manufacturers now produce specialized water shoes, e.g., Nike's Aqua Socks). You can also often spot cones and urchins in clear waters, especially if you're wearing a diving mask.

---

characteristics so that a physician can administer the most appropriate antivenin. If you can kill the snake and bring it to the nearest treatment center, all the better, but this could expose you or your fellow hikers to the risk of another bite (not to mention the exertion of energy—that alone could cause the venom to spread faster).

Second, examine the bite for teeth marks. A successful bite by a poisonous pit viper (which includes copperheads, cottonmouths, and rattlesnakes) will have one or two large fang punctures in addition to smaller teeth marks, while a bite by a nonpoisonous snake will not feature fang punctures. A coral snake bite will usually feature a series of small, closely spaced punctures made by the "chewing" motion of smaller fangs (coral snakes have to chew or bite their victim's flesh repeatedly in order to inject sufficient quantities of venom). In general, nonpoisonous bites cause relatively small, shallow marks or scratches.

If you suspect that the bite is poisonous, *immobilize the affected limb and wrap tightly in an elastic bandage.* This will slow the spread of venom through the lymph system and mitigate swelling. Be careful that the bandage isn't wrapped so tightly that it cuts off circulation—you should be able to insert a finger under it without difficulty. Keep the arm or leg below the level of the heart. The victim should avoid all physical activity if possible since increased circulation will accelerate the absorption of the venom. For this same reason, aspirin, sedatives, and alcohol should be avoided. Do not apply cold therapy—ice packs, cold compresses, and so on—to the bite area or to any other part of the victim's body.

Get the victim to a hospital or physician if possible. Where feasible, carry the victim to restrict physical exertion. Even when wrapping the limb appears successful in preventing symptoms, the bite will need medical attention and a physician may decide that antivenin treatment is necessary. (However, it's possible for a poisonous snake to bite without injecting any venom—up to 20% of reported bites are "dry bites" like these.)

Snakebite victims who require antivenin treatment will usually receive the broad-spectrum North American Antisnakebite Serum for pit viper poisoning (or a similar antivenin for coral snake poisoning)—where available. Your home physician may able to provide a prescription for the serum in advance of your outdoor trip if convinced that you'll be in areas where antivenin is unavailable or medical treatment is inaccessible.

In cases where it's been determined that a bite is venomous and the serum isn't available, the best you can do is follow the treatment outlined above and keep the victim immobile and cool until the symptoms—pain in the affected limb, abdominal cramps, headache—have subsided. (For some bites, wrapping the limb in an elastic bandage will avoid all or most of the worst symptoms.) The victim should drink plenty of water. Don't panic—remember that few rattlesnake or coral snakebites turn out to be fatal, even when untreated.

centipede

JOE CUMMINGS

Anglers should take care when handling landed fish to avoid poisonous spine wounds. If you don't know how to avoid the spines while handling a fish, let someone who is more experienced show you how.

The treatment for stings from all of the above is the same: Remove all tentacles, barbs, or spines from the affected area; to remove as much venom as possible, wash with rubbing alcohol or diluted ammonia (urine will do in a pinch) and wrap the area in cloth to reduce the flow of oxygen to the wound until pain subsides. If an acute allergic reaction occurs, get the victim to a doctor or clinic as quickly as possible.

Medical Assistance
The quality of basic medical treatment, including dentistry, is of a relatively high standard in Mexico's cities and larger towns—ask at a tourist office or at your consulate for recommendations. Every state capital has good hospitals, as well as public clinics or Red Cross (Cruz Roja) stations in nearly every other town.

Emergency Evacuation: Critical Air Medicine (tel. 619-571-0482; 95-800-010-0268 toll free from Mexico) and **Air-Evac International** (tel. 619-571-0482), both in San Diego, California, can provide emergency 24-hour airlift service (accompanied by licensed physicians and nurses) from anywhere in Mexico to U.S. hospitals. Both outfits will accept collect calls; payment for the service can be made with a credit card or through your health insurance company.

A company that provides a similar air evacuation service—but only through membership in an affiliated insurance program—is **Medical Air Services Association** (tel. 817-430-4655, fax 817-491-1368; 9 Village Circle, Suite 540, Roanoke, TX 76262). MASA policies cost around US$70 per individual per year (family rate US$130) and cover unlimited emergency air transport from Mexico. For higher premiums, coverage can be extended to include the U.S. and Caribbean.

MONEY

NEW PESOS VS. OLD PESOS

The unit of exchange in Mexico is the peso, which under the "old peso" system appears either in coins of 50, 100, 500, and 1000 pesos, or in bills of 1000, 5000, 10,000, 20,000, 50,000, and 100,000.

In January 1993 the government introduced the *nuevo peso* or "new peso" (N$). These notes are exact copies of old peso notes, less the three zeros (e.g., "10,000 pesos" now reads "10 pesos" but otherwise looks exactly the same), and come in denominations of N$10, N$20, N$50, and N$100. The latter two denominations (equivalent to 50,000 and 100,000 old pesos) can be difficult to break, so try to get them changed at every opportunity in order to have a good supply of smaller notes.

For currency denominations of N$10 and less, new peso and centavo coins have been issued in denominations of 5 cents, 10 cents, 20 cents, 50 cents, N$1, N$2, N$5, N$10, and N$20.

Until the older currency passes from circulation, *both* kinds of pesos, in any combination, are legal tender throughout Mexico. In remote villages where the new peso isn't commonly seen yet, you might encounter some initial reluctance to accept new pesos, but usually someone is around who can vouch for the validity of the new currency. As of mid-1993, old pesos were still more commonly seen than new pesos—even in larger cities.

The "$" symbol is often used for indicating old peso as well as dollar prices. New peso prices are indicated by the symbol N$. While it is highly unlikely that you would ever confuse the two—since the exchange ratio is so high for old pesos—you should ask if in doubt. New peso prices are much closer to what dollar prices might conceivably be, creating more potential for confusion between dollars and new pesos. Sometimes the abbreviation m.n. will appear next to a price—this means *moneda nacional* ("national money") and refers to old pesos.

When quoting prices verbally, Mexican vendors will ordinarily refer to new peso prices. Even under the old peso system, they often abbreviated a verbal price quote by omitting the word *mil* (thousand), since few things cost less than 1000 pesos. Thus *doce cinco* meant *doce mil cinco cien* (12,500 old pesos) and under the new system means 12 new pesos plus 50 centavos or N$12.50. (More correctly, this would be spoken as *"doce cincuenta"* or "twelve fifty.")

Since the smallest new peso coin is five centavos, all payments are rounded off to the nearest multiple of five centavos. For a marked price of N$8.52 (8,520 old pesos), for example, you actually pay N$8.50; for a N$8.53 price you would pay N$8.55.

Many commercial establishments in Northern Mexico—especially in border towns and beach resorts—will take U.S. dollars as well as pesos. Paying with pesos, however, usually means a better deal when the price is fixed in pesos; if you pay in dollars for a purchase quoted in pesos, the vendor can determine the exchange rate. For example, if a can of motor oil is marked at N$6, and the bank rate is N$3 per dollar, you'll pay only US$2 for the oil with pesos changed at the bank. However, if you ask to pay in dollars, the vendor may charge US$2.50 since vendors have the "right"—by custom rather than law—to charge whatever exchange rate they want. On the other hand, if you're bargaining for a price, it really doesn't matter which currency you use.

Stores in smaller towns generally prefer not to take dollars, since this means keeping track of two currencies and makes banking more complicated. PEMEX stations typically refuse dollars (attendants are usually too busy to stop and calculate the rates).

Since the official exchange rate can vary from week to week, check before crossing the border. (See also "Exchange Rates" and "Estimating Costs," below for caveats.)

Deflation
The Mexican peso has been in a deflationary spin since 1976, when the government decided to allow the national currency to "float" on the international money market. From 1976-87 the exchange rate slid from eight pesos to the dollar to over 2,000. In 1988 the Bank of Mexico insti-

tuted measures to slow the decline to less than a centavo per day (more like two centavos per week) by the end of 1992. Since the switch to the new peso in 1993, the peso has actually gained a bit in value against the U.S. dollar. All indications point to a more stable Mexican currency in the coming years.

The relatively stable exchange rate means that changing money in Mexico is much less stressful now than just a few years ago—it's unnecessary to check the exchange rate every day.

EXCHANGE RATES

Banks

Banks offer the best exchange rate for buying pesos and they all offer the same rate, as set by the Bank of Mexico. This rate is usually posted behind the counter where foreign exchange is handled. They also accept a wide range of foreign currencies, including Swiss francs, German marks, English pounds, Japanese yen, and Canadian dollars. Either cash or traveler's checks are accepted, though the latter usually get a slightly better exchange rate. The main drawbacks with banks are the long lines and short hours (Mon.-Fri. 9 a.m.-1:30 p.m., but the foreign exchange service usually closes around 12-12:30 p.m.).

Moneychangers

The second best rate is at the *casa de cambio* or private moneychanging office. The *casa de cambio* (also called *servicio de cambio*) will either knock a few centavos off the going bank rate or charge a percentage commission. It pays to shop around for the best *casa de cambio* rates since some places charge considerably more commission than others. The rates are usually posted; *compra* refers to how many pesos you'll receive per dollar, while *venda* determines how many pesos you must pay to receive a dollar. As with banks, the difference between the buying and selling rates is the moneychanger's profit (unless they charge a commission on top of it).

Moneychangers are usually open much longer hours than banks; some even have evening hours, which makes them immeasurably more convenient than banks. U.S. dollars are generally preferred, though many *casas* will also accept Canadian dollars. However, Cana-

dians should always keep a reserve supply of U.S. dollars for instances where Canadian currency isn't accepted. Moneychangers will usually accept traveler's checks; some of the border-town *casas,* however, only take cash.

Only the larger towns and tourist centers have moneychanging offices. In smaller towns you'll have to resort to a bank or local merchant. Many store owners will be glad to buy dollars at a highly variable and sometimes negotiable rate. Few will take traveler's checks, however, unless you make a purchase.

Moneychangers at Mexican airports offer notoriously low rates. Try to buy pesos in advance of your trip if arriving by air, or pay with dollars until you can get to a bank or reasonable *casa de cambio.*

Hotels

Hotels, motels, *pensiones,* and other lodging places generally offer the worst exchange rates. If you're trying to save money, avoid changing currency where you stay, and pay for your room in pesos if possible, since the same low rate often applies to room charges paid in dollars.

Credit Cards

Plastic money (primarily Visa and MasterCard) is widely accepted at large hotels, at restaurants catering to tourists or businesspeople, at car rentals (you can't rent a car without a credit card), and at shops in tourist centers or large cities. Usually card displays at the cash register or on the door will announce that *tarjetas de crédito* (credit cards) are accepted. If in doubt, flash one and ask *"¿Se acepta tarjetas de crédito?"* or simply *"¿Está bien?"* A reference to *efectivo* means "cash." Credit cards are not accepted at PEMEX stations.

Paying for goods and services in Mexico with credit cards that are paid through U.S. or Canadian banks can save you money, since the exchange rate will usually have dipped further in the dollar's favor by the time the transaction is posted at your bank. Many shops and some hotels, however, will add a three to six percent surcharge to bills paid with a card, which more than offsets the exchange rate differential.

Cash advances on credit card accounts—a very useful service for emergencies—are available at Mexican banks.

MONEY MANAGEMENT

Estimating Costs

Inflation in Mexico is currently running at around 12-18% per annum, in large part due to the continued weakening of the peso on international markets but also because of a slight relaxation of wage and price controls. This means that when estimating your travel costs based on prices quoted in this book, some allowance must be made for ongoing inflation. Although peso prices will increase in direct proportion to the inflation rate, this isn't necessarily so for prices figured in dollars, since the dollar is continuing to gain in value against the peso.

Because of fluctuations in the peso-dollar ratio, and in an effort to keep prices up-to-date, all prices in this book are quoted in U.S. dollars. This doesn't mean, however, that there won't be any increase in prices by the time you arrive, book in hand. A couple of phone calls to hotels or other services for price quotes should give you an idea of rate increases, if any, and you can apply this difference as a percentage to all other prices for a rough estimate of costs.

Overall, the cost of living in Mexico is 30-50% lower than in most parts of the U.S. and Canada. Spending is virtually limitless while traveling, however; the key to keeping expenses down is to live as much like the locals as you can. If you're contemplating a long-term stay in Mexico, you might try reading a few issues of *AIM (Adventures in Mexico),* a bimonthly "newsletter on retirement and travel" that devotes a lot of space (almost every paragraph!) to analyzing and comparing prices in various Mexican cities. Subscriptions are US$16 (C$19 in Canada) for one year (Write to AIM, A.P. 31-70, Guadalajara, Jal. 45050).

Tipping And Taxes

A tip of 10-15% is customary at restaurants with table service unless a service charge is added to the bill. Luggage handling at hotels or airports warrants a tip of US$0.50, or the equivalent in pesos, per bag (a few hotels have a no-tipping policy, which will be posted in your room). The tipping of chambermaids is apparently optional according to Mexican custom—some guests tip and some don't.

PEMEX station attendants don't need to be tipped unless they wash your windows, check the oil, or perform other extra services beyond pumping gas—the equivalent of US$0.25-$0.50 in pesos is sufficient. When the change due on a gasoline purchase is less than N$1 (1000 old pesos), however, it's customary to let the attendant keep the change.

The Mexican government collects an *impuesta al valor agregado* (IVA) or "value added tax" on all goods and services, including hotel and restaurant bills as well as international phone calls. Before 1992 the IVA was 15%, but in an effort to boost consumption, the tax has since then been reduced to 10%. Hotels and restaurants are supposed to pass the five percent tax savings on to the consumer by dropping their prices accordingly; as a result you may see menus that read, "Five percent solidarity discount included."

Bank Accounts

For long-term stays in Mexico—six months or more—visitors might consider opening a Mexican bank account. Now that peso deflation has been virtually halted, a peso account is quite safe; Mexico, in fact, hasn't had a single bank failure in 60 years. Interest earnings are refreshingly high compared to current rates in the U.S., up to 14% per annum on money market accounts, 17% for certificates of deposit. Bancomer will accept personal checks drawn on U.S. banks from their account-holders and usually has the greatest number of branches in any given city. Probably the biggest advantage is that you won't have to worry about the short foreign-exchange hours kept by Mexican banks; you can bank right up till closing or use an ATM card.

COMMUNICATION

THE MEDIA

Newspapers

Every state capital in Northern Mexico publishes at least one Spanish-language daily newspaper. Monterrey's *El Norte* is widely recognized as being the best and is available in cities throughout the North. Even if your Spanish is minimal, city newspapers are worth looking at for current information on museum exhibits and local cinema. Check the comics section for American comic strips with translated dialogue balloons and titles—Lorenzo y Pepita (Blondie), El Fantasma (The Phantom), and Hombre Araña (Spiderman) are Mexican favorites.

Along the border and in Mazatlán, English-language dailies from nearby U.S. states are sometimes sold in hotel lobbies or city newsstands. Elsewhere, *USA Today* and the *International Herald Tribune* are occasionally available. You may also come across *The News,* an English newspaper published in Mexico City and heavily oriented toward Mexico City residents.

Radio And Television

In the border area, radios and TV pick up local broadcasts from both sides of the border. Further south the U.S. stations begin to fade, and in the more remote areas you may find yourself out of range of even Mexican broadcast media. Consider bringing along a shortwave radio if you're a news fanatic.

Many hotels and motels have their own satellite dishes with as many as 50 channels from Mexico and the U.S. on tap. In urban areas, a variety of radio stations can be picked up.

COMMUNICATION SERVICES

Postal Service

The Mexican postal service is quite reliable, though relatively slow. Most towns in Mexico have a post office (*correo*) where you can receive general delivery (*poste restante*) mail. Have correspondents address mail in your name (last name capitalized), followed by a/c Lista de Correos, the town name, and the state, e.g., Joe CUMMINGS, a/c Lista de Correos, Alamos, Sonora, Mexico. The usual post office hours are Mon.-Fri. 9 a.m.-2 p.m. and 4-6 p.m., Sat.-Sun. 9 a.m.-noon.

In small towns and villages, residents don't often use street addresses, simply the addressee's name followed by *domicilio conocido* ("known residence") and the name of the town or village. Even in large towns and cities, addresses may use the name of the street without a building number (*sin número,* abbreviated as "s/n"), or will mention the nearest cross streets (e.g., *ent. Abasolo y Revolución,* or "between Abasolo and Revolución").

Many foreigners who are seasonal residents have their mail sent in care of a hotel or RV park. You can rent boxes at larger Mexican post offices but the initial application process often takes several weeks. Some towns have private mail companies (e.g., "Mail Boxes, Etc.") that also rent boxes but with minimal red tape.

The Mexican post office offers an express mail service (EMS) called Mexpost. International rates are relatively high; a Mexpost express letter to the U.S. or Canada, for example, costs US$18.

Telephone Services

The national telephone company, TelMex, has improved its services considerably over the last few years. Local phone calls are relatively cheap—a 100 old-peso coin, about US$0.03, will pay for a phone-booth call—as are long-distance calls *within* Mexico. Connections are usually good, though you may have to wait a while to get through to the operator during busy periods (e.g., Sundays and holidays).

If you don't want to use a phone booth or hotel phone (hotels usually add their own surcharges to both local and long-distance calls), you can make a call during business hours from a TelMex office. Only large towns have TelMex offices with public telecommunications facilities, however; a small town may have a private telephone office (usually called *caseta de teléfono*),

TELEPHONE CODES

Information (national): 01
Long-distance operator (national): 02
Time: 03
Information (local): 04
Mexico City area code: 05
Police: 06
Spanish-English emergency information: 07
International operator: 09
Long-distance direct dialing from Mexico:
  station to station (in Mexico): 91 + area code + number
  person to person (in Mexico): 92 + area code + number
  station to station (to U.S. & Canada): 95 + area code + number
  person to person (to U.S. & Canada): 96 + area code + number
  station to station (to other countries): 98 + area code + number
  person to person (to other countries): 99 + area code + number
Northern Mexico area codes (see individual destination descriptions for other towns and cities):

Chihuahua, Chih.: 14	Monterrey, N.L.: 83
Ciudad Juárez, Chih.: 16	Nogales, Son.: 631
Ciudad Victoria, Tamps.: 131	Nuevo Laredo, Tamps.: 871
Culiacán, Sin.: 67	Saltillo, Coah.: 84
Durango, Dgo.: 181	San Luis Potosí, S.L.P.: 48
Guaymas, Son.: 622	Tampico, Tamps.: 12
Hermosillo, Son.: 62	Torreón, Coah.: 17
Mazatlán, Sin.: 69	Zacatecas, Zac.: 492

Mexico country code: 52

To call Mexico direct from outside the country, dial: 011 + 52 + area code + number. Example: to call the number 20-03-61 in Chihuahua from the U.S., dial 011 (international code) + 52 (Mexico country code) + 14 (Chihuahua area code) + 20-03-61 (the phone number in Chihuahua).

Help: SECTUR (the Ministry of Tourism) maintains a 24-hour traveler's aid "hotline" for emergencies of all kinds: 91 (5) 250-0123, 250-0151.

often set up in the corner of a local shop, where you can make calls. Like hotels, private telephone offices add surcharges to calls.

Bus terminals often have operator-staffed TelMex *casetas* that are open daily 9 a.m.-9 p.m.

A public pay phone service called LADATEL (acronym for "Larga Distancia Teléfono") offers phone booths where local and/or long-distance calls can be paid for with coins, credit cards, or debit cards (depending on the type of booth). The only credit cards accepted so far are those issued by Banamex, Bancomer, or Carnet in Mexico. Debit cards can be purchased in denominations of N$5, N$10, N$20, N$30, and N$50 at many pharmacies, convenience stores (such as Oxxo, the Mexican equivalent of 7-Eleven), supermarkets, bus terminals, and airports.

International Calls: To direct-dial an international call to the U.S. or Canada, dial 95 plus the area code and number for a station-to-station call, or dial 96 plus area code and number for a person-to-person call. For other countries besides Canada and the U.S., dial 98 and 99 respectively. Long-distance international calls are heavily taxed and cost more than equivalent international calls from the U.S. or Canada.

To reach toll-free (800) numbers in Mexico from the U.S. or Canada, dial 91 first. From Mexico, AT&T can be reached by dialing 95-800-462-4240, a toll-free call that connects you with a USADirect system. For MCI the number is 95-800-950-1022 and for Sprint 95-800-977-8000. The appropriate long-distance operator can then place a collect call on your behalf or, if you have an AT&T, MCI, or Sprint phone card, charge the call to your account. If you try these numbers from a hotel phone, be sure the hotel operator realizes it's a toll-free call; some hotel operators use their own timers to assess phone charges. Another way to reach AT&T is to push "*01" on the tan-colored LADATEL phones (the ones which accept LADATEL phone cards) or on blue pay phones.

Collect: For international service, calling collect saves money and hassles. In Spanish the magic words are *por cobrar,* prefaced by the name of the place you're calling (e.g., *"A los Estados Unidos, por favor—por cobrar"*). This will get you connected to an English-speaking international operator (speak slowly and clearly for best results). You're supposed to be able to obtain an international operator directly by dialing 9, but this number doesn't always work.

An alternative way to make collect calls to the U.S. is to dial an AT&T operator (push "*01") as described above.

Local Numbers: Most telephone numbers in Mexico consist of five or six digits. There's no standard way of hyphenating the numbers; a five-digit number may appear as 211-13, 2-1113, or 2-11-13, and a six-digit number may be written 341720, 341-520, 34-1720, or 34-17-20. For the sake of consistency, the forms with three dashes are used in this book since they seem to be the most commonly used in Mexico.

CROSS-CULTURAL CONSIDERATIONS

Time And Appointments

Of the many common myths about Mexican culture, the one that says the Mexican sense of time is highly flexible is probably the most accurate. The whys and wherefores attached to this concept are too numerous and too complex for the context of this book (read Octavio Paz's *The Labyrinth of Solitude* for a glimpse

of an explanation). However, it's important to realize that the so-called *mañana* attitude is nothing more than a generalization and that in many cases Mexican individuals may be every bit as punctual as North Americans (especially when it comes to doing business with North Americans). *Norteños,* it is said, tend to be more punctual than their southern counterparts.

If you make an appointment with a northerner for dinner, a party, or other social engagement, you should figure that the actual meeting time will be around two hours later than actually scheduled. As with business engagements, if the person involved has dealt frequently with North Americans, this might not *always* be the case. Also, Mexicans will typically accept an invitation rather than say no, even if they don't plan to attend the scheduled event. This is because, within the Mexican social context, it is usually worse to refuse an invitation than it is not to show up. To avoid disappointment, prepare yourself for any of these scenarios.

When hiring a fishing boat or any sort of guide in Northern Mexico, you can expect a modicum of punctuality since Mexicans in the tourist industry have usually adapted themselves to the expectations of North American and European tourists. Again, business and social appointments differ.

Siesta: The stereotypical siesta, in which everyone goes off to sleep for a couple of hours in the afternoon, is fast becoming history throughout Mexico. Nevertheless, a vestige of the siesta has been preserved in the hours kept by offices and small businesses, which are typically closed from 2-4 p.m. or 3-5 p.m. The first hour is reserved for *comida,* the mid-day meal, while the second hour is for relaxing or taking care of personal business. While to North Americans two hours may seem like a long lunch hour, the fact is that Mexican offices and businesses stay open much later than in the U.S. or Canada (until seven or eight in the evening).

No matter what hours are posted for small businesses, the actual opening and closing times may vary with the whims of the proprietors. This is also true for tourist information offices, but banks usually follow their posted hours to the minute.

Meal Times: If you'll be meeting Mexican acquaintances for meals, whether at a restaurant or in their homes, you should be aware that customary eating times differ from those in North America or northern Europe.

The first meal of the day, *desayuno* (breakfast), is usually taken at about the same time as the average North American breakfast, say 6-8 a.m. On a working weekday, another light breakfast/early lunch (*almuerzo*), might be eaten around 11 a.m. (on weekends and holidays this may be a much larger feed), or nothing at all until around 2-3 p.m., when the *comida* or largest meal of the day is eaten. In small towns, workers will often go home for this meal and not return to the workplace until around 4-5 p.m.

After work, around 8-10 p.m., *la cena,* the final meal of the day, is eaten. *Cenas* are usually as light and informal as *desayunos,* so it is not often that guests are invited to a home for this meal. On weekends and holidays, the *cena* may become a grander occasion, however.

For information on what Mexicans typically eat at these meals, see "What to Eat," p. 66.

Terms Of Address

Mexicans frequently use titles of respect when addressing one another. At a minimum, *señor* will do for men, *señora* for married women, and *señorita* for unmarried women or girls. When in doubt about a woman's marital status, *señora* can be used.

Professional titles can also be used for variety and to show additional respect. *Maestro* (master) or *maestra* (mistress) are common and can be used to address skilled workers (cobblers, auto mechanics, seamstresses, etc.) and any teacher except those at secondary schools and college or university (who are *profesores*). Attorneys are *licenciado* (men) or *licenciada* (women), while doctors are *doctor* or *doctora*.

Body Language

Mexicans tend to use their arms and hands more during verbal communication than do their North American or northern European counterparts. Learning to "read" the more common gestures (but not necessarily to imitate them) can greatly enhance your comprehension of everyday conversations, even when you don't understand every word being spoken.

One of the more confusing gestures for North Americans is the way Mexicans beckon to other persons by holding the hand out, palm down, and waving in a downward motion. This looks

similar to a farewell gesture in the U.S. and Canada but means "come here" in Mexico. Holding the palm upward and crooking the fingers toward the body, the typical North American gesture for "come here," is a vaguely obscene gesture in Mexico.

Extending the thumb and forefinger from a closed hand and holding them about a half-inch apart means "a little bit" in North America but in Mexico usually means "just a moment" or "wait a minute" (often accompanied by the utterance *"Momentito"* or *"Poquito"*).

The wagging of an upright forefinger means "No" or "Don't do that." This is a good gesture to use when children hanging around at stoplights or gasoline pumps begin wiping your windshields and you don't want them to. Don't overdo it, though—they only need to see a few seconds of the wagging finger (otherwise you'll look out of control!).

Handshakes and Abrazos: Mexicans commonly greet one another with handshakes, which are used between the sexes and among children and adults—in fact, with everybody. Mexican males who are friends will sometimes greet one another with an *abrazo* (embrace) and urban women may kiss one another on the left cheek. Foreigners should stick to the handshake until they establish more intimate relationships with *norteños*. Handshakes are also used upon parting and saying farewell.

Dress

Compared to their southern counterparts, who tend to be more conservative, *norteños* are relatively tolerant about the way visitors dress. Nonetheless, invisible lines exist that, out of respect for Mexican custom, shouldn't be crossed.

In Town: Number one is that beachwear is not considered suitable dress for town visits. Beach resorts are the most obvious exception to this general rule since during peak seasons tourists may outnumber the locals in these towns, so the locals are quite habituated to gringo immodesty. In downtown Mazatlán, however, beachwear will result in indignant stares if you wander far from the beach strip.

Churches: Upon entering a church or chapel in Mexico, men are expected to remove their hats (many Mexican males will also remove their hats when passing in front of a church). More tradition-minded Mexican women will cover their heads when inside a church, but younger women usually don't and foreign females aren't expected to. Shorts, sleeveless shirts/blouses, sandals, or bare feet are considered improper dress (for both men and women) in churches, even for brief sightseeing visits.

MEASUREMENTS AND TIME

Electricity
Mexico's electrical system is basically the same as that in the U.S. and Canada: 110 volts, 60 cycles, alternating current (AC). Electrical outlets are of the North American type, designed to work with appliances that have standard double-bladed plugs. Small towns in some rural areas may experience brief interruptions of electrical service or periods of brownout (voltage decrease). In a few villages, gasoline-powered generators are the only source of electricity and they may be turned off during the day.

Measurements
Mexico, like most countries in the world, uses the metric system as the official system of weights and measures. This means that the distance between Nogales and Mazatlán is measured in kilometers, cheese is weighed in grams or kilograms, a hot day in Monterrey is 32° C, gasoline is sold by the liter, and a big fish is two meters long. A chart at the end of this book will help Americans make the conversions from pounds, gallons, and miles to kilos, liters, and kilometers (or vice versa) when necessary.

Norteños who are used to dealing with American tourists will often use the Anglo-American and metric systems interchangeably. Even rancheros in remote areas occasionally use *millas* (miles) as a measure.

In this book, distances will be given in kilometers (for the benefit of metrically oriented readers and for checking against local estimates), followed by miles in parentheses (for visiting Americans). Heights are given in meters—American users can simply multiply by three for a close equivalent in feet.

Time
The states of Sonora and Sinaloa belong to the Mountain Time Zone, as followed in the U.S. and Canada. The rest of the mainland to the east follows Central Time (Greenwich Mean Time + 7). This means you should set your timepieces an hour ahead when crossing the Sonora or Sinaloa state lines going east, or an hour back when crossing west.

The time in Mexico is commonly expressed according to the 24-hour clock, from 0001 to 2359 (one minute past midnight to 11:59 p.m.) rather than the Anglo-American 12-hour system. A restaurant that posts hours of 1100-2200, for example, is open 11 a.m.-10 p.m. Signs may be posted using either system.

Business Hours
The typical small business will be open Mon.-Fri. (Saturday for retail businesses) 9 a.m.-2 p.m., closed until about 4-5 p.m., and then reopened until about 7-8 p.m. Official government offices typically maintain an 8:30 a.m.-3 p.m. schedule (although Secretary of Tourism offices will usually open again 5-7 p.m.).

Banks are open Mon.-Fri. 8:30 a.m.-1:30 p.m., but remember that the foreign exchange service usually closes down around noon (probably to lock in the exchange rate before afternoon adjustments).

(top) Chihuahua al Pacífico train; (bottom) Barranca de Urique (photos by Joe Cummings)

(top) burro driver, Sierra Tarahumara; (bottom, left) *vaquero;* (bottom, right) gold prospector, Cerocahui
(photos by Joe Cummings)

SAFETY AND LEGALITIES

Safety

Statistics clearly show that violent crime is much less common in Mexico than anywhere in the country to its immediate north, the United States. According to Interpol statistics, U.S. murder figures, for example, are 14% higher than Mexico's as of 1991. Yet Americans themselves seem to be the most paranoid of all visitors to Mexico.

History recounts the reasons for this paranoia (although Mexicans historically have even more reason to fear Americans), the primary one being the general border lawlessness that was the norm very early in this century. The turn of the century and the early 1900s was an era of border disputes and common banditry on both sides of the frontier all the way from the Texas Gulf coast to California's Pacific coast. Americans living in these areas came to fear the *bandidos* who stole livestock and occasionally robbed the Anglo ranchers themselves, while the Mexicans in turn feared American cattle rustlers, horse thieves, gunslingers, and the infamous Texas Rangers (known as *rinchos* in Northern Mexico), a private militia whose conduct at the time fell somewhere between that of the Hell's Angels motorcycle gang and the L.A. police force.

Soon after this era had begun to cool down, and as politics on both sides of the border stabilized, the U.S. Prohibition experiment sent millions of Americans scrambling into Mexican border towns to get the booze they weren't legally permitted in their own country. In the illicit atmosphere, boozers were soon rubbing elbows with gamblers and pimps, and it wasn't long before Mexican border towns gained an even more unsavory reputation.

Once Prohibition was lifted, Americans no longer had reason to come to Mexico solely for drinking purposes, and the border towns began cleaning up their acts. Among the ignorant and inexperienced, however, the border-town image not only remains but also sadly mixes with the equally outdated *bandido* tales, preventing many Americans from enjoying the pleasures of life south of the border.

To add a personal testimony to statistics, neither the author nor anyone in the author's ac-

quaintance has ever been robbed anywhere in Mexico. On one occasion, however, the author left two shirts and a pair of slacks in a hotel closet in Loreto, Baja California Sur, one morning and didn't remember leaving them until arriving in La Paz in the evening. A phone call that same day and a visit to the hotel a week later were unsuccessful in retrieving the clothes—the management claimed they were never turned in by the cleaning staff. The moral of the story is that the author now tries to be extra careful to not leave things behind in hotel rooms.

Precautions

In general, visitors to Mexico should take the same precautions they would when traveling anywhere in their own countries or abroad. Keep money and valuables secured, either in a hotel safe or safety deposit box, or in a money belt or other hard-to-get-at place on one's person. Keep an eye on cameras, purses, etc., making sure you don't leave them behind in restaurants, hotels, or campgrounds. At night, lock the doors to your hotel room and vehicle.

Private campgrounds usually have some kind of security (if only a night watchman) to keep out intruders. Secluded beach or wilderness campsites seem to be safe due to their very seclusion—in Mexico it is very rare for any crime to occur in such areas. Nonetheless, don't leave items of value lying around outside your tent, camper, or RV at night.

Help: SECTUR maintains a 24-hour traveler's aid "hotline" for emergencies of all kinds: tel. 91 (5) 250-0123, 250-0151.

Legal Codes And Enforcement

All foreign visitors in Mexico are subject to Mexican legal codes, which are based on Roman and Napoleonic law. The most distinctive features of the Mexican judiciary system, compared to Anglo-American systems, are that the system doesn't provide for trials by jury (instead, the judge decides) nor writs of habeas corpus (though you must be charged within 72 hours of incarceration). Furthermore, bail is rarely granted to an arrested foreigner—for many offenses, not even Mexican nationals are allowed bail. Hence, once you are arrested and jailed for a serious offense, it can be very difficult to arrange release. The lesson here is: Don't get involved in matters that might result in your arrest—this primarily means anything having to do with drugs or guns.

The oft-repeated cliché that in Mexico an arrested person is considered guilty until proven innocent is no more true south of the border than north. As in Canada and the U.S., an arrested person is considered a criminal *suspect* until the courts confirm or deny guilt. You have the right to notify your consulate if detained.

Mexican federal police or *federales* occasionally set up roadblocks to conduct searches for drugs, mostly under pressure from the United States. Such roadblocks have become increasingly rare, however, due to complaints from North American tourists who drive regularly in Mexico. If your vehicle is stopped by a roadblock, it's best to be as cooperative as possible. If you notice any irregularities or if you object to the way in which the procedure is carried out, make note of the incident (including whatever badge numbers, names, or license tag numbers you can obtain *discreetly*) and later file a report with the Mexican Attorney General for Tourist Protection (see "In Case of Arrest," below, for more detail).

La Mordida

In the past, Mexican police had a reputation for hassling foreigners, especially those who drove their own vehicles in Mexico. Tales of the legendary *mordida* or minor bribe (literally "bite"), supposedly a necessary part of navigating one's way around Mexico, swelled way out of proportion to reality but were nonetheless based on real incidents. (See also "Driving in Northern Mexico.")

For several years now, however, the Mexican police have for the most part ceased singling out foreigners for arrest, partly as a result of anti-corruption efforts by the federal government but, more importantly, because of a conscious effort to attract more tourists. The vast majority of foreign visitors who drive in Northern Mexico these days complete their trips without any police hassles (see "Traffic Offenses," p. 96, for tips on traffic laws and dealing with traffic police).

Drugs

Marijuana, and to a lesser extent opium, is cultivated in remote areas of the Sierra Madre Occidental in the states of Sinaloa, Chihuahua, and Durango. For the most part, such drug "plantations" are well hidden from the view of tourists, hikers, and other passersby, hence there is little danger in traveling in these areas if you don't poke your nose too far off the beaten path.

The main area where you need to be careful not to stray off the main trails is between Urique and Batopilas in Barranca del Cobre National Park. In recent years Mexican soldiers have patrolled this area regularly, however, so the fields are being pushed farther back into seldom-visited areas. Occasionally an over-zealous hiker in the Sierra Tarahumara region may stray far from the trail and stumble onto a pot patch; the best thing to do if this happens is immediately leave the vicinity. Should you be accosted by a grower or guard, make it clear that you're merely a *turista* and didn't intend to disturb the farm; better yet, pretend you don't know what the stuff is.

Given the stiff penalties for contraband drug possession in Mexico, it would be very foolish of any foreign visitor to attempt to purchase either marijuana or opium in Northern Mexico.

In Case Of Arrest

If you get into trouble with the Mexican law, for whatever reason, you should try to contact your nearest consulate in Mexico (when there is one—embassies and consulates for each town are listed under the respective destinations). SECTUR and state tourist offices can also be of help in some instances. These agencies routinely handle emergency legal matters involving visiting foreigners; you stand a much better chance of resolving legal difficulties with their assistance.

THE STATE OF SONORA

Unsuccessful early Spanish incursions into the area now encompassed by the state of Sonora left it terra incognita until the 17th and early 18th centuries. For much of this period Sonora remained a province of little importance; the discovery of gold in Alamos brought a steady stream of settlers from the south and by 1824 the former province of Sonora y Sinaloa had become the state of Occidente. During Occidente's eight-year existence, the capital alternated between the important mining centers of Alamos, El Fuerte (Sin.), and Cosalá (Sin.). Occidente was eventually divided into the separate states of Sonora and Sinaloa. In both states the main centers of activity tended to be the lower western slopes of the Sierra Madre Occidental, a storehouse of mineral wealth.

Luckily, at about the time the mines played out, agriculture in the Yaqui and Sonora river plains expanded to support the local economy together with Sea of Cortez fishing. Today the state is a leader in both, producing about a third of Mexico's annual *ajonjalí* (sesame) crop; an assortment of grains, vegetables, grapes, oranges, and olives; and the nation's most important fisheries. Sonorans also take pride in the fact that three ex-presidents were born in their state: Alvaro Obregón, Abelardo Rodríguez, and Plutarco Elías Calles.

The focus of economic and cultural activity has thus moved from the mountains of eastern Sonora to the alluvial and coastal plains. More recently, tourism has become an important contributor to the state economy, supported by a warm climate year-round, 916 km of coastline, and an average of 360 days of sunshine per year.

SAN LUIS RIO COLORADO
TO PUERTO PEÑASCO

Sonoita-San Luis Río Colorado

On Mexico 2 between Sonoita and San Luis Río Colorado is an agricultural checkpoint for "white mosquito plague." Here a Mexican official may check your papers, then use a vacuum cleaner-type contraption to blow compressed air beneath the dashboard of your vehicle—ostensibly to destroy white mosquito larvae. In spite of this slight red tape, the Sonoita-San Luis Río Colorado drive is very worthwhile as it crosses prime Sonoran Desert scenery, with views of the Sierra del Pinacate to the south and easy access to El Pinacate National Park.

El Pinacate National Park

Marked on some maps as "Parque Natural del

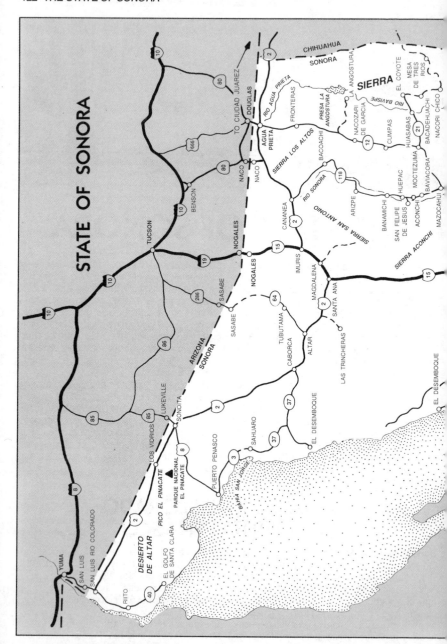

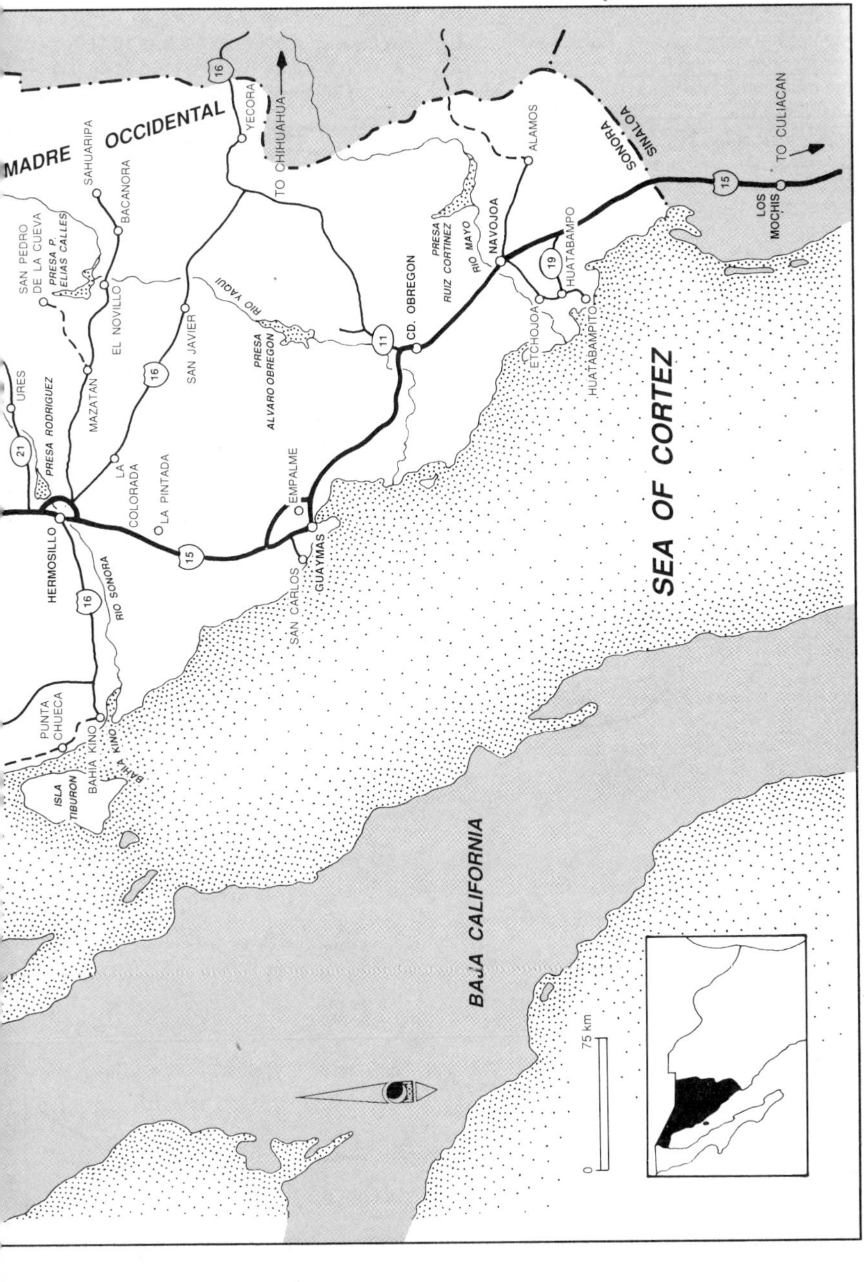

SAHUARIPA

MADRE OCCIDENTAL

BACANORA

SAN PEDRO DE LA CUEVA

PRESA P. ELIAS CALLES

EL NOVILLO

URES

MAZATAN

PRESA RODRIGUEZ

HERMOSILLO

RIO SONORA

LA COLORADA

LA PINTADA

SAN JAVIER

RIO YAQUI

PRESA ALVARO OBREGON

EMPALME

SAN CARLOS

GUAYMAS

PUNTA CHUECA

BAHIA KINO

ISLA TIBURON

16

16

21

16

15

16

YECORA

TO CHIHUAHUA

CD. OBREGON

11

PRESA RUIZ CORTINEZ

RIO MAYO

NAVOJOA

ALAMOS

ETCHOJOA

HUATABAMPO

HUATABAMPITO

19

SONORA

SINALOA

TO CULIACAN

LOS MOCHIS

15

SEA OF CORTEZ

BAJA CALIFORNIA

75 km

0

© MOON PUBLICATIONS, INC.

Gran Desierto del Pinacate," this 2,000-square-km natural area between San Luis Río Colorado, Sonoita, and Puerto Peñasco is one of the more dense volcanic regions in the Americas. More than 10,000 volcanic apertures, of which only about 500 have been studied and classified, dot the terrain along with extensive lava fields and huge craters. The volcanic desert landscape, which is nothing short of spectacular, has inspired at least three early 20th-century western novels: *Desert Gold* (Zane Grey, 1913), *Dust of the Desert* (R.W. Ritchie, 1922), and *The Devil's Highway* (Harold Bell Wright and John Lebar, 1932).

The park is named for the 1,270-meter (4,235-foot) **Pico El Pinacate** (named for the *pinacate,* an endemic beetle that sits vertically on end when threatened), part of the Sierra del Pinacate, a mountain range that follows a northwest-to-southwest axis roughly 24 km long and about half as wide; the second tallest peak is Pico Carnegie (1,254 meters/4,180 feet) just southwest of Pico El Pinacate. These peaks are actually the erosional remnants of a great volcano dubbed Volcán Santa Clara by Padre Kino, who visited the area in 1701 and 1706.

Though no one yet knows for sure, Santa Clara may have erupted as far back as 10,000 years ago. Pinacate's most recent volcanic eruption— relatively small—took place in 1935 near Cráter El Elegante.

Following Kino's visit, Pinacate wasn't visited by another European until 1882, and the first extended exploration of Pinacate was carried out by the MacDougal-Hornaday expedition in 1907. Although Volcán Santa Clara was the first extinct volcano recognized in North America, it is the last to be studied in detail; much about the area remains a geological mystery.

Features: Pinacate's remarkable landscape varies wildly from sand dunes to black cinder cones to red-rimmed craters, interspersed with classic Sonoran Desert vegetation (in Mexico this area is known as El Desierto de Altar). The largest sand dunes are found to the south and west, the most impressive lava fields to the northeast. To the north are the most significant craters and cinder cones: **El Elegante, Cerro Colorado, MacDougal, Sykes,** and **Molina.** So otherworldly is the landscape that U.S. lunar missions have trained here to simulate lunar landings. Electrical discharges from sierra sum-

mits, appearing as weak lights ("St. Elmo's Fire"), are not uncommon.

As forbidding as the terrain may sound, it has been inhabited by Amerindians for at least 10,000 years. Stone sleeping circles (low, hemispheric walls used as windbreaks) and ground mesquite beans found in lava caves suggest Pinacate was a habitat for the paleolithic San Dieguitos. The later Sand Papagos believed the larger craters to be an abode of the god of fire. When Padre Kino crossed Pinacate, the Papago residents he encountered wore rabbit fur and lived on roots, insects, fishing, and sand-flat farming of corn, tubers, and beans.

Today a few Papagos live on *ejido* lands adjacent to park boundaries, along with a small number of hardy Mexicans. Houses are typically a patchwork construction of discarded pieces of wood, cardboard, and corrugated metal, along with various desert materials such as ocotillo or sotol branches.

Biosphere Reserve Status: Since 1979 Pinacate has been a U.N.-designated Biosphere Reserve, an internationally recognized honor bestowed on natural environments considered of global significance. Among the species protected here are the rare Sonoran antelope and desert bighorn sheep, who take shelter (and water) in volcanic craters during the winter. *Paisanos* (roadrunners) are common and are typically among the biggest specimens seen in Mexico or the U.S. Southwest. Since annual rainfall averages a scant 7-10 cm (three to four inches) a year, the only year-round source of water is **Papago Tanks,** a set of *tinajas* (rock pools) along the park's west side near the sand dunes.

The six largest craters—**Elegante, Sykes, Molina, Cerro Colorado, Celaya,** and **Badilla**—are fairly accessible from the north entrance to the park off Mexico 2. Cráter El Elegante is the largest (1,440 meters/4,800 feet rim to rim, 240 meters/800 feet deep) and most visited of these. You can walk Elegante's rim in two to three hours; get an early morning start as the very exposed trail tends to get quite warm, even in winter. The view into the crater is stupendous. Along the way you'll see exemplary cholla, mesquite, ocotillo, saguaro, cenizo, palo verde, torote, and perhaps bighorn sheep tracks. The sheep themselves are quite shy and only rarely spotted by human visitors.

Although it's thrilling to imagine you're strolling along the edges of extinct volcanoes, the visible crater rims are not actually the edges of the original calderas but rather are "rim beds" formed by falling debris after eruption. The "craters" are depressions left after the cone collapsed and all the gases had been expelled.

The massive **dune fields** are best accessed via a 3.7-km (six-mile) unpaved road that heads west from Mexico 8 near Km 73. Don't try driving on the dunes and don't lose sight of your parked vehicle unless you bring a compass and take a cautionary heading.

Between Cráter El Elegante and the Sierra del Pinacate lies the youngest and visually most spectacular **lava fields** in the region. The terrain here is typical flow breccia, in which lava hardened on top while remaining molten below, so that the surface still has a "fluid" appearance. Contrary to popular myth, the lava fields here are crossable on foot, although the 16-km (10-mile) hike will totally ruin all but the sturdiest footwear.

Practicalities: A **permit** is required to legally visit the park. It's available for free at the Sonoita border crossing. Many people, however, visit Cráter El Elegante without a permit. **Camping** is permitted anywhere in the park, but probably the safest area to camp is at one of the *ejidos* along the park's north edge on the south side of Mexico 2—ask for permission first. A night spent under the stars in Pinacate is a special experience—coyotes and cactus owls provide the soundtrack; kangaroo rats dance in the moonlight.

The main road into El Pinacate National Park from Mexico 2 (near Los Vidrios at Km 51) is black cinder, passable by ordinary passenger car for the first 6.5 km (four miles). Here the road jogs right at a quarry (a small wooden sign reads "Elegante/Puerto Peñasco") and becomes rougher and sandier. Vehicles without high road clearance should be left here—the deep, sandy *vados* ahead can be tough going. Though it's not absolutely necessary, 4WD certainly comes in handy. From this junction it's 9.5 km (six miles) to another right turn toward Elegante—look for white road markers—then less than a kilometer more to the base of the cone. It's worth the hike (if your vehicle can't make the drive and you're well prepared for desert hiking) to view the gigantic, four-meter chollas along the way, plus stands of torote, creosote bush, saguaro, and biznaga.

This same road connects with Mexico 8, the highway to Puerto Peñasco from Sonoita, between Km 51 and 52. The route isn't straightforward, however, and the selection of branch roads along the way has caused many a driver to get lost or end up back on Mexico 2—a compass helps. If you're coming from Puerto Peñasco, look for the water tower on the left.

The most colorful time to visit Pinacate is in the spring when the sand verbena, cactus, and palo verde trees are in bloom.

SAN LUIS RIO COLORADO

Compared to Nogales or Agua Prieta to the east, few North Americans enter Northern Mexico via the border town of San Luis Río Colorado—all the more reason to choose this gateway if you're coming from the U.S. West Coast and prefer to avoid heavier border traffic (this border crossing is open 24 hours). Squeezed into the northwesternmost corner of the state on the east bank of the Río Colorado, the town itself is essentially a collection of shops catering to local cotton farmers and border traders.

Originally settled by boat via the Río Colorado and Sea of Cortez, the vast river delta that once watered the entire region has been slowed to a trickle by 10 dams erected upriver along the U.S. portion of the river. Although the entire river originally belonged to Mexico, local farmers now depend on metered flows from the U.S. side to irrigate their fields.

On the immediate U.S. side of the border is San Luis, Arizona. San Luis is even smaller than its Mexican counterpart, little more than a farming community. If you're planning to stock up on **food** or other supplies for a Sonora road excursion, you'll do better to make Yuma your last stop as there are a couple of large supermarkets there. Opposite the smaller Del Sol supermarket in San Luis, Arizona, is an agency that sells **Mexican insurance.**

Once across the border, be sure to check in at the **customs office** if you need a temporary vehicle permit (see "Auto Permits," p. 101). This is also a good place to change money, as Calle 2, the main north-south street, has a string of *casas de cambio* along it; **Servicio de Cambio San Luis Río Colorado Viejo** is the most efficient.

Three **banks** can also be found along Calle 2.

The **San Luis Turf and Greyhound Club**, a block west of the border, offers off-track betting (on televised greyhound and horse racing throughout the U.S. and Mexico) and sports book along with full bar and food service.

Accommodations And Food
Should you need to stay in San Luis Río Colorado, several hotels and motels are available. The best is **Hotel San Angel Valle Grande** (tel. 653-4-01-01), at Av. Obregón 1050, which offers a/c, satellite TV, pool, and Jacuzzi for around US$40. Also on Av. Obregón are **Motel Continental** (tel. 4-23-86) and **Motel Río Colorado,** both in the US$20-30 range.

Since this town doesn't really get any border tourists—most people who enter here are heading straight for El Golfo de Santa Clara—few eating places offer the kinds of facilities designed to attract gringos. For steak and Sonora's famous *carne asada,* locals recommend **Restaurante El Herradero** (tel. 4-40-60) at Av. Obregón between Calle 11 and 12. For Mexican fare **Restaurante Tres Amigos** (tel. 4-13-86) at Obregón and Morelos is also good. If you're in the mood for something quick and cheap, look for the street vendors and burrito stands along Calle 2 and Av. Obregón.

Transport
San Luis Río Colorado is the western terminus of national highway Mexico 2, pieces of which extend all the way eastward to the Gulf of Mexico. Between here and Caborca (352 km/218 miles southeast), Mexico 2 runs roughly parallel to an old Indian trail that was used to link a permanent water source in Sonoita with settlements at the junction of the Gila and Colorado rivers.

The trail was later used by Spanish explorers during the 16th and 17th centuries to travel between Northern Mexico and Alta California. It was called Camino del Diablo ("Devil's Road") by the Spanish; as many as 500 European travelers died of thirst or heatstroke along its inhospitable cinder tracks before the road was finally paved between 1955-60. Today the San Luis Río Colorado-Caborca stretch is a comfortable drive that passes through prime Sonoran Desert scenery.

Fuel

Whether you're heading south or east, San Luis Río Colorado is a good place to top off with Magna Sin (unleaded gas). Although several PEMEX stations in town post Magna Sin signs, the only place that consistently carries unleaded fuel is the station at Calle 4 and Revolución.

EL GOLFO DE SANTA CLARA

This little-known spot doesn't appear in any state-published tourist brochures but has almost a "cult" status among a small group of repeat visitors. Poised at the northernmost tip of the Sea of Cortez near the mouth of the dried-up Río Colorado, El Golfo is a true oddity, a fishing village at the edge of one of North America's driest desertlands.

Although the 114-km road from San Luis Río Colorado to El Golfo is paved all the way, the village itself has only a small network of sand roads (drivers with non-4WD vehicles should deflate their tires to 10-12 pounds per square inch). Southeast of town via one of these roads is the main attraction, a long stretch of sandy beach with well-spaced *palapas*. Dunes in this area are popular with ATV riders. At high tide, the dunes become sandy beaches; at low tide, broad mudflats are exposed and large clams are plentiful. The difference between high and low tides extends up to 7.5 meters (25 feet)—which at most local beaches translates to roughly a mile between high and low tidelines—among the highest tidal variations in the world.

On the way to El Golfo you'll pass a brick-works and several small farming towns. About halfway from San Luis Río Colorado to El Golfo, **Riito** offers a few *tiendas* with classic Sonoran storefronts, a CONASUPO, and a leaded-only PEMEX station. You can cut across to/from Baja California at Riito via a paved east-west road that runs between Mexico 5 (Baja) and the road to El Golfo. El Golfo is, in fact, a favorite side destination for Baja hands coming up or down Mexico 5 between Mexicali and San Felipe.

Just north of El Golfo is an intriguing area of mesa-type lava and ash formations left from Pinacate's oldest volcanic outflow (see "El Pinacate National Park," above).

Climate

From May through mid-Sept., this desert delta becomes an inferno, with temperatures soaring over 38° C (100° F); heavy evaporation from the Sea of Cortez produces yet another El Golfo anomaly—a humid desert. Best time to visit: Nov.-April.

Accommodations And Food

At the beach southeast of town are a couple of rustic campground/RV parks and restaurants, including the well-run **El Capitán.** Rates are a uniform US$3 for tents/campers, US$10 for trailers/RVs. Basic rooms are available in town for around US$15.

The best seafood in El Golfo is served at the simple but very clean **El Delfín.** Don't miss the delicious *burritos de machaca de manta raya,* fresh flour tortillas wrapped around dried and shredded manta ray. **Casa de Mariscos** is similar. You can also fix your own meals with supplies from **Mercado Las Brisas** or the town's **CONASUPO.**

Events

Visitors come from far and wide for Día de la Marina (Marine Day), held annually on June 1 in coastal towns all over Mexico. This is El Golfo's biggest celebration of the year, and the sand streets are crammed with food vendors hawking *mariscos,* cold beer, fresh fruit, and other snacks as mariachi and *norteña* musicians stroll by.

Driving

The PEMEX station here usually has Magna Sin. Auto service is available at the **Off Road Tire Shop,** which is also a good spot for local information; Jesús, the proprietor, speaks excellent English.

Even if you have a 4WD, take care exploring the area as the deep sand here can mire just about any vehicle. Anyone trailering a boat to El Golfo should bring along a current set of Cortez tide tables, as the tidal range is extensive.

Border Formalities

Neither tourist cards nor temporary vehicle import permits are required for visits to El Golfo, which is part of the little-publicized Sonoran Free Trade Zone. If you plan to fish in El Golfo, however, you will need a Mexican fishing permit (see "Fishing" under "Outdoor Recreation," p. 44, for details).

If you will be proceeding farther east than Puerto Peñasco or Sonoita, you will also need the proper tourist and vehicle papers; see the "Entry Regulations" section, p. 100, for details on Mexican immigrations and customs requirements.

SONOITA

In 1698 the Spanish founded Misión San Marcelo de Sonoyta here next to an oasis known to the Papago as "Sonoydag." Although the mission was destroyed in a 1751 Pima revolt, Sonoita remained the only dependable source of water for travelers along the harsh Camino del Diablo, a vital overland link between California and Central Mexico until well into the 19th century. On some maps, the town name is still spelled "Sonoyta."

With all the facilities today available in Lukeville, Arizona (see "Puerto Peñasco," below), few North American travelers stop off in Sonoita for more than the usual border formalities. **Motel Nora** (tel. 651-2-10-12), on the east side of town on Mexico 2, has rooms in the US$22-28 range; the motel also provides a few spaces with **full hookups** for RVs and campers (around US$10 a night).

Magna Sin gasoline is available at a PEMEX station on Mexico 2 in town. The Sonoita **crossing** is open daily 8 a.m.-midnight.

PUERTO PEÑASCO

Known as "Rocky Point" to thousands of Arizonans, Puerto Peñasco (Spanish for "rock port") is a curious amalgam of Mexican fishing port and American beach playground. As at El Golfo de Santa Clara, the beaches here tend to be very flat and desert-sandy, with extreme tidal variation. Unlike tiny El Golfo, however, this is a "real" town in terms of population, with a reported 40,000 residents (although it really feels more like 4,000) and several distinct districts. As part of the Sonoran Free Trade Zone, Puerto Peñasco can be visited without a tourist card or temporary vehicle import permit.

The original Puerto Peñasco, founded as a fishing village in the 1920s, sits atop a broad, rocky cape (a basaltic lava flow from Pinacate) overlooking the Sea of Cortez on one side and a small natural harbor on the other. Urban features include a small fish market, a couple of charming hotels and restaurants, a simple malecón (waterfront promenade) and a sprinkling of older Mexican homes. Along the highway from Sonoita is a newer, larger commercial district with stores, offices, more restaurants, and railway and bus stations, all mixed in with newer, less well-built houses. Puerto Peñasco's Mexican population is mostly restricted to these two urban districts, while North American tourists and retirees are congregated in nearby beach areas.

Just west of the commercial district are **Playa Hermosa** and **Playa Bonita**, sandy, northern extensions of the harbor with three beach hotels and a couple of RV parks. After about eight km (five miles), the north end of Playa Hermosa/ Bonita runs into the even longer **Sandy Beach**, access to which is controlled by a gringo consortium at Cholla Bay, an expatriate community at Sandy's north end.

Climate And Seasons
The primary tourist season here runs Nov.-May, when U.S. snowbirds take refuge from the cold north. The winter months are generally quite comfortable, with daytime temperatures averaging around 18-24° C (65-75° F). The occasional two- or three-day cold snap causes temperatures to plummet as low as 6° C (43° F).

Although summers can be quite hot (over 38° C/100° F), the normal daily high July-Sept. is around 30-35° C (86-95° F). Puerto Peñasco usually isn't as hot as El Golfo or the Baja coast opposite simply because of prevailing winds and currents that tend to move counterclockwise around the Sea of Cortez; each degree in latitude north and longitude west the currents move increases the water and air temperatures. Although summers are generally too warm for long-term residents, weekend visitation is common year-round.

PUERTO PEÑASCO

© MOON PUBLICATIONS, INC.

SIGHTS

For most visitors, **Cholla Bay** is either love or hate at first sight. Largely responsible for the gringoization of Puerto Peñasco (starting with the Anglicizing of local place-names), the Cholla Bay enclave is made up of mostly seasonal residents who have built a ragtag collection of beach homes that run from tacky to charmingly rustic. Access to both Sandy Beach and Cholla Bay is via a 6.5-km private road flanked by signs that make it clear you're entering a quasi-colony. Although one gets the overall impression that at least some residents have chosen this spot as an escape from zoning and environmental laws in the U.S., several Cholla Bay residents have volunteered time and money to Puerto Peñasco social services.

On weekends and holidays Nov.-May the Sandy Beach area is jammed with visiting Arizonans who park their campers and RVs in long rows along the beach; the sand dunes behind the beach are buzzing with ATVs and dune buggies. During the week, however, Sandy Beach is nearly empty. To get to Cholla Bay/ Sandy Beach from Puerto Peñasco, take Calle 26 east off Blvd. Juárez opposite the baseball stadium; this road meets the private Cholla Bay access road. A road also runs southwest directly from Mexico 8 north of town.

Another gringo enclave spreads southeast of town from **Playa Miramar.** Several modest RV parks line the shore here, flanked by the beach housing developments of Las Conchas and the newer Estero La Pinta. The **Desert and Ocean Studies Center** (CEDO) at Las Conchas displays a skeleton of a fin whale as well as other marine and desert artifacts.

The area's most pristine and least-visited beaches will be found southeast of Miramar off the road between Puerto Peñasco and Sahuaro (on the way south to Caborca). Only the first 18 km (11 miles) of this road are paved, after which it's 26.5 km (16.5 miles) of sand, dirt, and gravel. Deserted beaches are only 15-20 minutes from the main road via rough vehicle tracks leading to the coastline.

Sunsets over the Sea of Cortez can be spectacular from any west-facing point in Puerto Peñasco. On clear days you may be able to spot 3,000-meter (10,000-foot) Picacho del Diablo, the highest peak in Baja California's Sierra de San Pedro Mártir, on the other side.

ACCOMMODATIONS AND FOOD

Hotels And Motels

Each district in Puerto Peñasco is represented by a smattering of hotels. Some close June-Sept., so be sure to call or write in advance if you plan to attempt a summer visit. Those hotels that stay open in summer usually slash their rates by 30-50%.

Most visitors interested in staying on the beach head for the Playa Hermosa/Bonita area, where there are two decent places to choose from. **Hotel Playa Hermosa** is the nearest to town and has basic rooms with a/c and TV for US$25 s/d weekdays, US$30 weekends. A new high-rise wing is under construction adjacent to the single-story wing; when finished, rates will be slightly higher. A bit north of here is the efficient and clean **Hotel Playa Bonita** (tel. 638-3-25-86), US$55 weekdays, US$65 weekends, oceanfront rooms US$65. All rooms have TV and a/c; common facilities include tennis courts and a swimming pool. During the summer Playa Bonita runs a special in which for

INDIAN CULTURES OF NORTHWEST MEXICO

	NORTE	CENTRO SUR	NORESTE
A.D. 1700-?	Pima	Mayo, Seri, Yaqui	Apache, Opata
A.D. 400-1100	Trincheras		Paquimé (Casas Grandes)
A.D. 0-200		Huatabampo	
400-200 B.C.	San Dieguito Río Sonora		
6,000-4,000 B.C.		Clovis-Folsom	
10,000 B.C.	Clovis		Clovis

every three-night stay you get a fourth night free.

In the "old town" near the harbor are a couple of good choices for visitors who care more about being in Mexico than they do about getting a suntan. The four-story **Hotel Costa Brava** (tel. 3-41-00, fax 3-36-21) overlooks the *malecón* and is within walking distance of the fish market and a couple of seafood restaurants. All rooms have Sea of Cortez sunset views; rates are US$35-40 s/d, US$40-45 t/q (some views are better than others, hence the rate spread). Parking is enclosed; service is friendly and efficient.

Perched high above everything else in Puerto Peñasco is the nearby **Hotel Viña del Mar** (tel. 3-36-00; 602-327-2059 in Arizona), where rates run US$40-55. For sunset views the Viña del Mar is tops. Facilities include enclosed parking and a pool.

In the commercial district are several moderately priced hotels, only one of which is overwhelmingly commendable. The top choice, not only because of overall value but because it's within walking distance of Playa Hermosa, is **Motel Señorial** (tel. 3-20-65), Calle 3 and Av. Armada Nacional. Large, clean rooms with satellite TV and a/c cost US$35. The recently renovated restaurant and piano bar add a touch of class. Summer rates here are as low as US$18 per night for a double room.

Just off the highway into town, at Calle Constitución and Calle Morua, is the **Hotel Paraíso del Desierto** (tel. 3-21-75), an adequate place to stay if you're stopping over on the long route to/from Caborca, if your first accommodation choice isn't available, or if you're counting pennies. Simple rooms with a/c and TV cost US$22-28 and there's a pool on the premises. Farther north along the highway at Km 94, **Hotel Mar y Sol** (tel. 3-31-90) has satellite TV and a/c; rates are on a par with Paraíso del Desierto.

More in the center of the commercial district are **Hotel Villa Granada** and **Motel El Cid**, each costing around US$25 d plus US$3 for each additional person. Both are on the rundown side, best considered as backup when all else is full (as is often the case during spring break).

Down at Playa Miramar the two-story, characterless **Hotel Granada del Mar** has clean, simple rooms (no TV) for US$44 s/d in back, US$55 for oceanfront s/d, or US$66 with kitchen.

The adjacent beach disco might annoy guests seeking a quiet beach holiday. **Manny's Beach Club** (tel. 3-36-05; 602-387-6921 in Arizona) at Playa Miramar also rents a few small, a/c rooms behind the club for around US$50. At the west end of the beach, **Alma Marina Suites and Hotels** looks like a new development but was closed when I visited.

El Reef/Sandy Beach Club, an all-around recreational facility at Sandy Beach, rents a few beachfront rooms for around US$50.

According to the SECTUR office in Hermosillo, a franchise of the Super 8 Motel chain should be opening soon in Puerto Peñasco.

RV Parks And Camping
As there are more camping/RV facilities in the beach areas than hotels or motels, this is Puerto Peñasco's main accommodation mode. The highest concentration of RV slots is at Playa Miramar, where you'll find full hookups for a uniform US$12 per vehicle with two persons, beachfront spaces for US$15, plus US$1-2 per extra person per day. Weekly rates of US$72 (US$90 beachfront) and monthly rates of US$240 (US$300 beachfront) are available. Seniors may be able to get a 10% discount at some places. Rates typically include utilities, though hot showers may be metered. When no boat ramps are available, a boat launch will cost around US$10. As with hotels, some of these parks close June-Sept., so be sure to call or write in advance if you plan to attempt a summer visit.

The largest facility at Playa Miramar is **Clomar Trailer Park** (tel. 3-32-91), which offers a coin laundry, hot showers, billiards, and a restaurant/bar. Also large and probably the most popular park is **Playa de Oro RV Park** (tel. 638-3-26-68; A.P. 76, Puerto Peñasco, Son. 83550); facilities include a convenience store, restaurant/bar, boat ramp, and boat storage.

Other Playa Miramar parks include **San Rafael RV Park** (tel. 3-26-81; A.P. 58); **Playa Miramar Trailer Park** (tel. 3-25-87; A.P. 2); **El Señorial RV Park** (no phone); and **Playa Elegante RV Park** (tel. 3-37-12; A.P. 101).

Attached to Hotel Playa Bonita at the beach of the same name is **Playa Bonita RV Park** (tel. 3-25-96; A.P. 34, Puerto Peñasco, Son.). This is one of the better-run RV parks in Puerto Peñasco; facilities include a coin laundry, hot showers, recreation room with satellite TV, convenience store, and boat ramp.

Beach camping is permitted at Sandy Beach for a reasonable US$2 per person; showers are available at El Reef/Sandy Beach Club. North of Cholla Bay or southeast of Playa Miramar are more secluded beach areas where camping is free.

Food

Seafood is one of Puerto Peñasco's big draws, especially for landlocked Arizonans. Jumbo shrimp is sold on the streets and at the fish market in the old town for around US$20 per two-kilo (five-pound) bag. At the market you'll also find oysters, clams, snapper, squid, and flounder for sale.

On Blvd. Kino in the commercial district are two gringo favorites, **Restaurante Los Arcos** (tel. 638-3-35-96) and **Restaurante La Curva** (tel. 3-34-70), both of which offer a menu of Mexican standards, steak, and seafood for US$8-12 per entree. La Curva also does burgers, potato skins, and other American food for US$5-8. **Restaurante Puesta del Sol** at Playa Bonita is also popular among gringos for steak, seafood, and Mexican standards.

In the old town, a less gringoized (and somewhat less expensive) alternative to the above is **La Cita Café,** on Paseo V. Estrella near the Hotel Costa Brava. This diner-style place has been in business since 1957 and serves simple Mexican and seafood dishes for breakfast, lunch, and dinner; shrimp dishes are particularly good here. **Restaurante El Delfín** (tel. 3-26-08) nearby on Calle Alcantar is slightly more upscale and is open 7:30 a.m.-9 p.m.

The restaurants at **Hotel Costa Brava** and **Hotel Viña del Mar** in the old town are each highly regarded for seafood. The latter has a particularly good Sea of Cortez view.

For quick burritos or *tacos al carbón,* the **Asadero Sonora** on Calle Constitución (opposite the railway station) is Puerto Peñasco's best bet. **La Flor de Michoacán** at Calle 17 and Av. de la Barrera has good *aguas frescas, licuados,* and *paletas.*

For groceries, the **Jim Bur** supermarket on Blvd. Juárez will take care of most needs. Farther into town is a bakery, **El Buen Gusto** (Calle Bravo and Av. Cuauhtémoc), with a good selection of *pan dulce, birote,* donuts, pies, and

cakes. Fresh fruits, vegetables, and dairy products are available at **Frutería Las Delicias,** Calle 16 (or Blvd. Sonora) and de la Barrera.

In Cholla Bay, **Abarrotes Patricia** is the main outlet for groceries and fishing supplies. As one might expect, prices are a bit higher than in town.

RECREATION

Bars

The relaxed outdoor bar at **Manny's Beach Club,** Playa Miramar, is a popular gathering place for all ages. The sunset view here would be great if it weren't for the foolish placement of a bandstand directly across the sight lines. During the week, the bandstand usually features a lone musician playing honky-tonk keyboard; on weekends a combo plays.

Bar Las Margaritas at Hotel Viña del Mar offers sports betting and large-screen TV; the same hotel has a disco.

J.J.'s Cantina is *the* spot at Cholla Bay for early evening happy hour. Although it has a clubby atmosphere (all the patrons seem to know each other), outsiders are welcome.

Fishing

Puerto Peñasco's main gamefish are black seabass, dorado, pargo, pompano, mackerel, seatrout, shark, and the occasional yellowtail. A fishing tournament is held in June; for information contact **Cholla Bay Sportsmen's Club** (c/o John Fowler, P.O. Box 5, Lukeville, AZ 85341).

Fishing charters are available from **Pasitos Tours** (tel. 638-3-20-83 in Puerto Peñasco; P.O. Box 251, Lukeville, AZ 85341) at Blvd. Juárez near the fish market, as well as from **Rojo's** (tel. 3-39-56) at Cholla Bay near J.J.'s Cantina. Typical per person rates are US$40 all day, US$30 per half day. At the Puerto Peñasco harbor it is also possible to rent *pangas* by the day (around US$50-70 for two to four persons).

Fishing tackle, bait, and boat or motor parts are available at the **Proveedora de Pesca,** Blvd. Kino and Calle Prieto.

Windsurfing

The Puerto Peñasco area has excellent windsurfing, especially during the winter and early spring months. Experienced boardsailors can put in just about anywhere along the coast; novices should stick to Cholla Bay or the estuaries north and south of Puerto Peñasco. Sailboards can be rented at Rojo's in Cholla Bay or from China Sea Sailing and Diving (see below).

Diving

Although not exactly a world-class diving destination, the Puerto Peñasco coastline does provide a few spots of interest to snorkelers and scuba divers. Nearby Isla San Jorge (known among the Cholla Bay crowd as "Bird Island") in particular offers rock reefs with soft corals, plus nearby sea pinnacles amid scenic sand flats. A colony of sea lions at the island adds another dimension to the underwater sightseeing. Rocky areas near the old town as well as at the north end of Sandy Beach are suitable for snorkeling and beach diving.

China Sea Sailing and Diving Co. (tel. 638-3-54-50), next door to La Cita Café on Paseo V. Estrella, sells air; rents snorkels, fins, masks, tanks, regulators, and diving accessories; and can arrange dive trips to Isla San Jorge. Rojo's at Cholla Bay offers similar services.

TRANSPORT

By Bus

From Puerto Peñasco's bus terminal at Blvd. Juárez and Calle Cárdenas, the **TNS** (tel. 638-3-20-19) line runs first- and second-class buses to Sonoita, Hermosillo, San Luis Río Colorado, and other points in northern Sonora.

By Train

Trains to/from Mexicali and Caborca (and as far south as Mazatlán and Guadalajara via a connection with the Pacífico line) stop at the FNM railway station (tel. 638-3-26-10; for reservations in Mexicali call 65-7-23-86) at Calle Serdán and Calle Ferrocarril. If you're heading south by public transport, the train to Benjamin Hill is the best way way to avoid looping north all the way back to Sonoita and Nogales. The first-class Pacífico train No. 2 leaves Puerto Peñasco at 1:20 p.m., arriving in Caborca at 3:37 p.m and Benjamin Hill at 5:10 p.m. It then continues southward at 5:44 p.m. with arrivals in Hermosillo at 7:45 p.m., Ciudad Obregón at 11:24

p.m., and Mazatlán at 8:15 a.m. the following day. You can save time, however, by changing to bus transport in Benjamin Hill.

Driving

The main gateway to Puerto Peñasco is the border town of Sonoita, opposite Lukeville, Arizona, exactly 100 km (62 miles) from Puerto Peñasco via Mexico 8. This road is usually in super condition, partly because the original roadbed was constructed by the U.S. Army Corps of Engineers during WW II to provide defense access to the Sea of Cortez (at the time considered vulnerable to Japanese submarine attack). By private vehicle, the drive takes about an hour and a half if you observe the speed limits.

Fuel: Magna Sin (unleaded gas) is available at the PEMEX station on Blvd. Juárez and in Sonoita.

Puerto Peñasco To Caborca

From the east, Puerto Peñasco can be reached via a 160-km road (Sonora 37 and Sonora 003) from Caborca, a scenic route that parallels the railway much of the way. This two-lane highway is paved *most* of the way; an unpaved, 26.5-km (16.5-mile) stretch between the town of Sahuaro and Puerto Peñasco is sandy and rough in places, and suitable only for vehicles with high road clearance. About two km before the western end of the dirt stretch (around 20 km/12 miles from Puerto Peñasco) is a Mexican customs check where you must present a tourist card and auto permit.

The scenery along this little-used route includes a long section of desertscrub (predominantly ocotillo and cholla) near Bahía San Jorge, and an equally long stretch—toward Caborca between Km 20 and 40—of cultivated fields of grape, olive, and citrus. The entire Puerto Peñasco-Caborca route can be driven in two to three hours, depending on road conditions along the unpaved portion.

INFORMATION AND SERVICES

In Lukeville, Arizona the **Gringo Pass** complex (tel. 602-254-9284) on Arizona Hwy. 85 has a post office, trailer park, coffee shop, grocery store, coin laundry, motel (US$42-58), Mexican insurance, propane, and Puerto Peñasco tourist information—in short, just about everything you'd need for a Puerto Peñasco vacation.

Mail And Phone

In Puerto Peñasco, the Mexican government post office is at Blvd. Fremont and Calle Coahuila. Private mail service is available through **Rocky Point Express Service** (tel. 638-3-39-88). Many seasonal residents shuttle back and forth between Lukeville and Puerto Peñasco at regular intervals for mail service. International calls can be made from the public pay phone next to Restaurante La Curva or from any of the several private long-distance phone offices in town; as with mail, many long-termers use Lukeville for telephone service.

PUERTO PEÑASCO TELEPHONE NUMBERS

Police: 3-26-26
Red Cross: 3-22-66
Immigration: 3-25-26
Customs: 3-26-93
Green Angels: 3-41-29
COTP: 3-30-35
Puerto Peñasco area code: 638

Money

Bancomer, just south of Jim Bur Plaza and Palacio Municipal on Blvd. Juárez, is the best place to change money or open a bank account. Outside of banking hours you can buy pesos at **Video Distribuidora,** Av. 19 and Calle 23.

Insurance

If you've been foolish enough to drive into Mexico without Mexican insurance—or if your current policy is running out—stop in at **Alejandro Portugal M. Insurance** (tel. 638-3-23-90) at Blvd. Juárez and Calle Morua (Calle 20).

Other Information

The *Rocky Point Times,* a free newspaper distributed at all the gringo spots in town, contains a mix of information for tourists and residents—probably the paper's best feature is the monthly tide tables. A *Rocky Point Souvenir Map*

Poster (available at Hotel Playa Bonita and tourist-oriented restaurants) costs US$5 and contains lots of printed information on the opposite side of the cartoonlike, distorted-scale map.

The Sonora state **tourist office** (tel. 638-3-30-01) has a branch in Jim Bur Plaza. In the U.S. you can also dial (800) 4-SONORA for general information on Puerto Peñasco and the state of Sonora.

Street names in Puerto Peñasco can be confusing since many streets have both a name and a number. Calle Constitución and Av. 12 are one and the same, as are Av. Juan de la Barrera and Av. 15; Av. Sinaloa and Av. 18; Calle S. Morua and Calle 20; Av. Campeche and Av. 10.

Official Permits: Neither tourist cards nor temporary vehicle import permits are required for visits to Puerto Peñasco, which is part of the little-publicized Sonoran Free Trade Zone. If you plan to fish here, however, you will need a Mexican fishing permit (see "Fishing" under "Outdoor Recreation," p. 44, for details).

CABORCA TO MAGDALENA

As you move east from Sonoita and the Sea of Cortez, the Sonoran Desert gets increasingly green as it joins the alluvial plains of the Río Sonora system and foothills of the Sierra Madre Occidental. This was one of the earliest areas in northwest Mexico to become missionized as the Spanish Jesuits pushed northward in search of native converts, a legacy which has left behind several historic mission chapels along with a number of nonnative fruit orchards.

The Yaqui and other Amerindian groups originally inhabiting this area have been almost totally displaced by Mexicans, who have used irrigation systems to turn the Caborca area into an agricultural oasis. The most prosperous towns of the region—Caborca, Santa Ana, and Magdalena—serve as trade centers for regional farming, while smaller towns function as their satellites.

The casual visitor interested in mission history will find chapels or other mission architecture in Caborca, Pitiquito, Oquitoa, Tubutama, Magdalena, San Ignacio, and Cocóspera. The scenery

PADRE EUSEBIO FRANCISCO KINO

During his remarkable 24-year missionary career in Northern Mexico, Jesuit priest Eusebio Francisco Kino managed to establish some 30 pueblos in Sonora and Arizona, baptize over 4,000 natives as Roman Catholics, successfully petition the Guadalajara diocese against Indian slavery in the northwest, introduce cattle ranching and the cultivation of fruits and wheat to Sonora, and refute the hypothesis that California was an island.

Born Eusebio Chino in Segno, Italy, in 1645 and educated in German schools, the young Kino became seriously ill at age 18 and made a vow to St. Francis Xavier that he would dedicate his life to religion if saved. Upon his recovery he joined the Society of Jesus and was sent to Nueva España as a Jesuit *misionero* attached to the Guadalajara diocese (which at the time included all Spanish territories to the north and west). After unsuccessful attempts to missionize Baja California, Kino convinced Guadalajara's crown representatives to issue a *cedula* (royal decree) against Amerindian slavery in the mines, then proceeded to Cucurpe, Sonora in 1687 to found the first Jesuit mission in the northwest. From Cucurpe he gradually assembled a mission circuit that extended north to Arizona's Santa Cruz River valley (near Tucson), west to Caborca, south to Magdalena, and east to Cocóspera.

In 1701 Kino accompanied an expedition from northwest Sonora to the mouth of the Río Colorado, thus confirming the claim that Baja California was a peninsula and that Alta California could be reached by land. Along the way he traversed parts of El Desierto de Altar and the Sierra del Pinacate, producing the first historical descriptions of this volcanic terrain. In 1706 he completed the first Spanish survey of Seriland and Isla Tiburón on the Sea of Cortez. Wherever he traveled, Kino produced detailed maps and notes that have become part of a rich Sonora/Arizona legacy frequently tapped by present-day historians. His 1701 map of northwest Mexico was so functionally accurate that it wasn't superseded for 150 years following his death. Ironically, Kino died in 1711 while dedicating a chapel in Magdalena to his patron saint, Francisco Xavier.

PADRE KINO MISSIONS

© MOON PUBLICATIONS, INC.

surrounding these towns is a soothing blend of rolling hills, lush Sonoran Desert, and cultivated fields of grain, grapes, melons, broccoli, peaches, and olives.

Caborca

Once a Papago ranchería (the name is a Spanish corruption of the Papago *kavork,* meaning "rounded hill"), this prosperous agricultural center of 100,000 residents features a tidy, modern downtown along with an older section of pastel-colored adobes. The main attraction here is **La Concepción de Nuestra Señora de Caborca,** a twin-towered neoclassical church completed by the Franciscans in 1809. It's also known as "Misión Padre Kino," although the original 1693 mission built by Kino was destroyed in a 1695 Pima attack.

In 1857 Caborca residents used this church as a fort to defend the surrounding valley against an American freebooter invasion led by Henry Crabb. The invasion was defeated, Crabb and his men were executed, and every year on **April 6** a local festival commemorates the victory. Bullet holes from the battle are still visible on the church's facade.

Other Caborca festivals of note include the **Fiesta de Uva (Grape Festival)** in September and the **Feria del Algodón (Cotton Fest)** in late November.

Accommodations: Few tourists spend the night in Caborca, though the town is well equipped with hotels, among them: **Hotel El Camino** (upscale), Av. Quirón and Mora; **Hotel Rivera** (budget), Calle 5a and Av. B; **Motel Los Arcos** (budget), Calle 8 and Carreta; and **Hotel San Fernando** (moderate), near Hotel El Camino.

Food: The main street through town is lined with small restaurants and cafes serving classic Sonoran cuisine. The **Asadero Bífalo** is known for first-rate *carne asada* from its own *carnecería* across the street, plus quesadillas, *chiles toreados, cebollas asadas,* and fresh guacamole. The casual dining room is very clean and service is excellent.

Nearby Missions: About 11 km (seven miles) southeast of Caborca via Mexico 2 is **Pitiquito,** home of one of the earliest Sonoran mission churches still standing, **Iglesia de San Diego.** Built in 1786 by Franciscan missionaries on a site formerly established by Padre Kino around 1706, the folk baroque-style church is famous for a set of macabre interior murals. Among the subjects depicted are a set of scales, a huge human skeleton, and a bird's head. If you can manage a visit on Nov. 13, the *día de santo* for San Diego, you'll see the little town of Pitiquito at its most animated.

Misión San Pedro y San Pablo Tubutama in Tubutama, 73 km (45 miles) northeast of Caborca via Sonora 64, is another church built on the site of a Kino mission. The original mission chapel was completed in 1691, destroyed by a Pima rebellion in 1695, and again destroyed in 1751. Whitewashed like the Kino missions

Iglesia de San Diego, Pitiquito

JOE CUMMINGS

of southern Arizona, the current Franciscan chapel dates to 1783 and is one of the more impressive missions in northern Sonora, with a cruciform, barrel-vaulted floor plan, a folk baroque facade, and a small collection of religious art. On **June 29,** the church's saint day, a modest festival is held.

At **Oquitoa** (from the Papago *hókito* or "boundary"), between Tubutama and Caborca off Sonora 64, is a relatively minor mission church dating to 1730. In overall layout it's not as grand as Tubutama but the facade shares many of the same design characteristics, including arched ridges and simple, neoclassic niches. Church bells hang from arches surmounting the facade rather than in a separate belltower.

Alternative Route: Tubutama, Oquitoa, and Caborca can be reached by car from the U.S. border via the border towns of Sasabe, Arizona/Sonora. On the U.S. side, Arizona highways 86 and 286 from Tucson lead to Sasabe, meeting Sonora 64 on the Mexican side. The first 45 km of Sonora 64—until Sáric—are unpaved but quite passable by ordinary passenger car.

NOGALES/AGUA PRIETA TO HERMOSILLO

NOGALES, ARIZONA

The twin border towns of Nogales make up the main border entry point for North Americans heading down Mexico's Sea of Cortez/Pacific coast by road. Before leaving Nogales, Arizona, visitors interested in regional history might want to stop in at the **Pimeria Alta Historical Society Museum** (tel. 602-287-4621) at Grand Ave. and Crawford St., just 150 meters north of the border. Many of the exhibits pertain to northern Sonora as well as southern Arizona.

Nogales, Arizona is also a good place to buy pesos, as the **moneychangers** usually offer better rates than on the other side of the border.

Accommodations

If you need to spend the night in Nogales, Arizona, you'll have several places from which to select. **Mission Motel** (tel. 602-287-2472) at 820 Grand Ave. has recently been remodeled and costs US$25-30. Closest to the border is the **Americana Motor Hotel** (tel. 287-7211, 800-974-8079; 639 Grand Ave.) with rooms for US$50 s, US$55 d. The **Best Western Siesta Motel** (tel. 287-4671; 673 Grand Ave.) offers standard motel rooms for US$38.

The nearest campground with full hookups is **Mi Casa RV Park** (tel. 281-115), 4.5 miles north of the border at 2901 N. Grand Avenue. Rates are US$9 for tents and campers, US$16 for trailers/RVs.

Border Transport

Visitors planning to use public transport can reach Nogales from Tucson by air-conditioned bus via **Citizen Auto Stage** (tel. 602-287-5628 in Nogales; 792-0972 in Tucson), which has 10 roundtrip departures daily for US$6.50 each way. From Tucson International·Airport you can get a taxi (US$5) to the highway bus stop at US 89 and Valencia Rd. to meet the Tucson-Nogales bus.

Buses into Mexico can be picked up at the Nogales, Arizona, bus terminal (tel. 287-5628; 35 N. Terrace Avenue). **Tres Estrellas de Oro** offers daily departures to Mexico City, Chihuahua, Hermosillo, Ciudad Obregón, Mazatlán, Culiacán, Navojoa, Cananea, and Los Mochis.

Nogales Taxi (tel. 287-3325) and Carillo's Taxi (tel. 287-3356) provide taxi service to (and across) the border.

Mexican Vehicle Insurance: If you're driving your own vehicle and don't already have a policy valid for Mexico, you can arrange reliable, moderately priced insurance at **Sanborn's** (tel. 281-1873, fax 761-1215; 2921 N. Grand Ave.), just off I-19 at Mi Casa RV Park.

NOGALES, SONORA

One of the oldest border towns in Mexico, Nogales (originally "Los Nogales," in reference to a landmark stand of walnut trees) was founded in 1880 as a customs and trading post at strategic Nogales Pass, a travel conduit previously used by the Hohokams and Pimas for at least 2,000 years. Its importance as a trade route resulted in successive military occupations led by generals Alvaro Obregón, Plutarco Elías Calles, and Pancho Villa in the early 1900s.

Tourism came to Nogales with U.S. Prohibition in the '20s and '30s. Booze has been supplemented by boot shops, handicrafts, Mexican kitsch, and Sonoran restaurants as the major draws for Arizona tourists. A vestige of Prohibition's gambling heyday lives on in the **Nogales Turf and Greyhound Club,** part of the Hotel Fray Marcos de Niza on Av. Obregón. Other contributors to the local economy include over 70 nearby factories, many of them *maquiladoras*.

For visitors from farther afield, Nogales is simply a gateway to northwest Mexico and a place to pick up the proper tourist permits. As a hospitality gesture, the Nogales municipal government allows foreign visitors (except those from adjacent Santa Cruz County, Arizona) to use metered parking spaces without putting money in the meters.

Accommodations

Nogales has nine hotels and motels, but frankly the only reason to spend the night here rather than on the U.S. side is that hotel rooms are generally US$10-25 cheaper. Many of the hotels on this side cater to Mexican business travelers

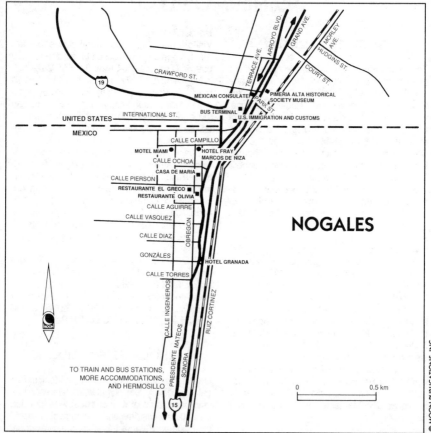

and are in the US$23-25 range; often they are booked up during the week.

Motel Don Luis (tel. 631-2-70-70) at González and Obregón costs US$23 and welcomes gringo traffic. **Hotel Granada** and **Hotel Imperial,** both downtown on Av. L. Mateos, offer more character at about the same rates. Nicer and a bit more expensive (US$30-35 per room) is the high-rise **Hotel Fray Marcos de Niza** (tel. 2-26-51) at Av. Obregón and Calle Campillo downtown; facilities include the Nogales Turf and Greyhound Club (with off-track betting/ sports book), travel agency, coffee shop, and restaurant. **Motel Miami** (tel. 2-54-50), also conveniently located a short walk from the border at calles Ingenieros and Campillo, has adequate but somewhat musty rooms for US$25.

South of town at Km 7.5 on Mexico 15, the modern and efficient **Hotel Plaza Nogales** (tel. 4-15-10) offers rooms from US$45, along with tennis courts, coffee shop, restaurant, pool, cable TV, and gift shop.

Food

The main bar and restaurant areas are along Av. Obregón west of the railway and Av. Ruíz Cortinez on the east side. **Restaurante Olivia,** at Av. Obregón 125, is a local favorite for *chivichangas,* tacos, and tamales. For typical Sonoran cuisine (including *menudo estilo sonorense*), head for **Restaurante Olga** (Calle Juárez 43), which is open 24 hours. Arizonans flock to the well-appointed **Restaurante El Greco** at Av. Obregón 152 for seafood, steaks, and Mexican standards; **El Cid Restaurant** at Av. Obregón 124 Altos is similar. **Restaurante Las Brasas,** Calle Dinamarca 101, specializes in *carnes al carbón.*

Casa de María at Plaza Niños Heroes has a modest range of *platillos típicos* and is a less expensive alternative to the above.

Transportation And Border Formalities

See the "Entry Regulations" section, p. 100, for important information on Mexican immigrations and customs requirements. The Nogales crossing is open 24 hours.

Bus: At the border you can catch a white city bus down Av. Obregón to the Nogales bus terminal, opposite the railway station on Av. L. Mateos; by foot this is roughly a 30-minute walk from the border. Tres Estrellas de Oro, TNS,

and Transportes del Pacífico run first- and second-class buses to Hermosillo, Guaymas, Obregón, Navojoa, Los Mochis, Huatabampo, Tijuana, Mazatlán, Culiacán, Caborca, and Cananea.

Train: The useful Pacífico line runs between Nogales and Guadalajara twice a day in each direction. The second-class train (No. 4) departs at 7 a.m.; the first-class train (No. 2) leaves at 3:30 p.m. Fares are: Hermosillo US$8.30 first class, US$2.50 second class; Guaymas US$12.50/ US$3.60; Ciudad Obregón US$16/US$4.60; Culiacán US$28.53/US$8.20; Mazatlán US$36/ US$10.

Fuel: Magna Sin is available at the Km 5 (Super Servicio Nogales) and Km 20.6 PEMEX stations along Mexico 15.

AGUA PRIETA/DOUGLAS

Agua Prieta (Douglas on the Arizona side) is the second most popular border crossing from Arizona and is a good choice for people arriving by bus, since downtown Douglas is within easy walking or taxi distance of the border. The border offices are open 24 hours here. A clean, whitewashed town surrounded by windswept desert, Agua Prieta has virtually nothing of interest for the average visitor but is a gateway for explorations along Mexico 2 (west to Cananea and Magdalena, east to Janos and Casas Grandes, or south along the Río Sonora) through grassy hills and gorgeous valleys.

Douglas (117 miles southeast of Tucson, Arizona) was founded in 1901 as a copper smelter site; the smelter has since closed and the economy is now dependent on border trade with Agua Prieta and the employment provided by around 30 *maquiladoras* in the area.

Accommodations

In Douglas the top choice is the historic **Gadsden Hotel** (tel. 602-364-4481), which was built in 1907, rebuilt in 1928, and now contains an Italian marble staircase, Victorian chandeliers, and a 42-foot stained-glass mural. It's also remarkably inexpensive, with standard rooms for less than US$30, suites up to US$95. Campers and RVers can check into Douglas's **Double Adobe RV Park and Campground** (tel. 364-4000), 17.5 miles northwest of town on Double Adobe

Rd.; full hookups cost US$11, tent/camper spaces US$8.

On the Mexican side the best place to stay is the efficient **Hotel La Hacienda** (tel. 8-06-21) on Calle 1 and Av. 6. Air-conditioned rooms cost US$40 s, US$44 d, and a good restaurant is attached. Adequate choices in the US$25-30 range include **Hotel Ruíz** (tel. 8-24-99) at Calle 10 and Av. 6, and the **Arizona Motel** (tel. 8-25-33) at Calle 18 and Av. 6 near the bus station.

Border Formalities
See the "Entry Regulations" section, p. 100, for important information on Mexican immigration and customs requirements.

Transport
Douglas is served by **Douglas Municipal Airport** (tel. 602-364-3501) in town and **Bisbee-Doŗ·glas International Airport** (tel. 364-2771) eight miles north of town on US 666. **Bridgewater Transport** (tel. 364-2233) offers bus service from Tucson and Bisbee. For taxi service, call **Gadsden Taxi** (tel. 364-5555).

Agua Prieta's new, high-tech bus terminal is a 25- to 30-minute walk from the border (taxis to the bus terminal cost US$4). TNS and Tres Estrellas de Oro list daily bus departures to Hermosillo, Ciudad Juárez, Chihuahua, Los Mochis, Ciudad Obregón, Guaymas, and Navojoa.

Information
Douglas's friendly **chamber of commerce** (tel. 602-364-2477; 1125 Pan American Ave.) has lots of information on surrounding Cochise County, Arizona as well as Sonora; the office is open Mon.-Fri. 9 a.m.-5 p.m.

Should you need automotive assistance, the local Green Angels unit (tel. 633-8-09-34) is headquartered at the Palacio Municipal.

Alternative Route
Mexico 2 can also be accessed from the small border town of **Naco, Arizona,** 32 miles east of Douglas (11 miles south of Bisbee) via Arizona highways 80 and 92. The border crossing here is open daily 8 a.m.-midnight. A 15-km paved road leads south from Naco, Sonora, to Mexico 2.

MAGDALENA

This important agricultural center about an hour's drive from the border via Mexico 15 has an older side worth exploring for the simple Sonoran bread-loaf architecture, leafy plaza, and **Misión San Francisco Xavier,** site of Padre Kino's death in 1711 at age 66. The padre's remains were discovered in 1966 by archaeologists excavating the town plaza. Kino now shares church space with four other priestly cadavers, and under the church floor are buried 500 pounds each of gold and silver—a typical missionary arrangement in these parts. Only the church foundation and door are original; all else has been rebuilt. The church itself is nothing special although the adjacent plaza is nice. Visit at night when Kino's bones are lit.

A special festival commemorating San Francisco Xavier, centered around the church of the same name, is held each year Sept. 22-Oct. 4. Pilgrims from all over northern Sonora—including Seri, Papago, Yaqui, and Pima—flock to Magdalena to participate.

Accommodations And Food
For visitors just passing through, **Motel La Suite** (tel. 632-2-07-92) at the north end of town has good air-conditioned rooms for US$26-38. **Motel Kino** (tel. 2-09-83) at Magdalena's south end is well-disposed toward road tourists with similarly priced rooms; **RV parking** with full hookups are also available for US$12.

If you want to spend some time exploring the town, your best choice is the humble but very friendly **El Cuervo Hotel** (tel. 2-07-048, Av. 5 de Mayo 316) near the San Francisco Xavier church. Rooms with a/c cost US$20 s, US$24 d; English is spoken and a restaurant and cantina are attached.

Standing out among the numerous standard eateries is the **Home Plate Café** at Calle Allende Ote. 115. The spartan decor is a heartfelt tribute to *el béisbol,* while the food is solid Mexicana (no menu, but the *comida corrida* is good and coffee costs only US$0.30—cheap for Mexico).

Transport And Fuel

TNS has **buses** to Hermosillo, Navojoa, Huatabampo, Chihuahua, Ciudad Obregón, Mazatlán, Guaymas, and Culiacán; smaller bus companies go to Cananea and other nearby towns.

Magna Sin is available from at least three stations in town.

Vicinity Of Magdalena

Mission buffs might consider exploring two nearby Kino sites. **San Ignacio** is about four km north of Magdalena off Mexico 15 and features a whitewashed mission church dating to 1720 on a site founded by Kino in 1693. The religious relics on display inside include an original *retablo;* a spiral staircase of mesquite leading into the bell tower is also original.

A paved road southeast of town ends 48 km (30 miles) from Magdalena at the small mission town of Cucurpe, where a decaying but nonetheless impressive **Misión Cucurpe** rests on a hillside. The dating for this one is uncertain, though it's definitely older than the 1821 bell in the tower might indicate. According to rumor, there's a cache of gold and silver beneath the floor in the rear of the church. If the church is locked, ask around town for a key.

SANTA ANA

Santa Ana is an important road junction where highways Mexico 2 and Mexico 15 meet. In late July, many Yaquis convene in Santa Ana to perform the *danza de venado* or sacred deer dance at a regional fiesta.

Southwest of Magdalena is **Las Trincheras,** a mysterious archaeological site featuring a 120-meter (400-foot) series of overgrown stone terraces along a mountainside. Similar terraces have been found elsewhere in Sonora but this is the largest example. Archaeologists don't know who built them or why, but neither agriculture nor defense seem to be workable explanations. Local residents may be able to direct you to nearby petroglyph sites. To reach Las Trincheras, drive west of town 31 km (19 miles) via Mexico 15, then south 20 km (12 miles) on a signed unpaved road to the town of Trincheras; or take a train between Caborca and Benjamin Hill, getting off at the Trincheras station.

Accommodations And Fuel

Several hotels and motels along the highways intersecting at Santa Ana offer rooms for US$20-35 per night. **Motel San Francisco** at the Mexico 15/2 junction is at the higher end of this range and is probably the best. Next to the bus terminal, **Motel Elba** is at the lower end.

Punta Vista RV Park (tel. 632-4-07-69) at the south end of town on Mexico 15 comes highly recommended for convenience and efficiency. Edgar, the owner, speaks excellent English and can arrange guide service to nearby missions and other attractions.

Fuel: The two PEMEX stations in Santa Ana pump Magna Sin.

Benjamin Hill

Pronounced "Ben-HA-min Heel" and named for a general of British descent who fought on the side of the *constitucionalistas* in the Mexican Revolution, this town south of Santa Ana is little more than a railway junction where the Mexicali-Benjamin Hill line meets the Pacífico. If you're heading south from Puerto Peñasco, the train to Benjamin Hill is quicker than buses via Sonoita and Nogales (see "Puerto Peñasco" for details). From Benjamin Hill onward, however, buses are generally faster.

Several cafes opposite the railway station offer basic Mexican fare. Magna Sin and ice are available at the highway PEMEX station.

RIO SONORA VALLEY

At Cananea, 84 km (52 miles) southeast of Agua Prieta, Mexico 2 meets Sonora 118, a highway south that parallels the scenic Río Sonora for 217 km (134 miles). The same route used by Spanish explorers (including Coronado) and missionaries centuries ago is now lined with picturesque farming towns and villages set amidst rolling hills and along the river. The area is most colorful following the summer rains—when wildflowers are blooming and the trees are in full canopy—or later in the fall as the leaves of the alamos (cottonwood trees) turn copper.

One of the most prominent local agricultural products is chile peppers, including the large, red, dried variety often known as the "New Mexico chile" in the United States. Beginning in October, strings (*ristras*) of chiles hanging out to dry are a common sight. At the south end of the valley, the famous wild *chiltepín* grows in abundance—look for racks of small, berrylike chile pods.

Cananea

Like Douglas, Arizona, and Agua Prieta to the north, this town owes its existence to copper mining. A large deposit known as Cobre Grande still produces a great deal of copper—virtually the entire national output—and its mine works dominate the town physically as well as economically. Locals simply refer to the mine as *la compañía*.

American William Greene started the mine during the Porfiriato around the turn of the century, but by the early 1900s he was faced with a miners' rebellion that became one of the cause célèbres leading to the 1910-20 Mexican Revolution. The jail that Greene used for the incarceration of Mexican strikers has been turned into the **Museo de La Lucha Obrera** (Museum of the Worker's Struggle), located on Calle 3; a sign out front reads "Cárcel de Cananea" (Cananea Jail). Exhibits include old photos of the mine, displays of mine interiors, local Indian artifacts, and various tidbits on the geology and anthropology of the region. Sergio, a 53-year veteran of the mine, is usually around to dispense information. The museum is open Wed.-Sun. 7 a.m.-6:30 p.m.; entry is free.

Practicalities: Hotel Alameda at Av. Sonora 135 (around the corner from the museum) has basic rooms for US$13-16, and a good,

THE CHILTEPINES OF SONORA

One of the most characteristic Sonoran chiles is the *chiltepín* (pronounced "chill-teh-PEEN"), a small spherical chile pepper used as a primary ingredient in Sonoran-style red chile sauces or eaten in its dried form as a condiment. The most prized variety in Mexico measures only five to eight mm in diameter; nonetheless it is one of the hottest chiles in the world, rated at an average 70-100,000 Scoville units by weight. By comparison, a Tabasco chile measures only 30-50,000 units, a jalapeño a mere 2,500-5,000 units.

Bowls of dried *chiltepines* are a common sight on Sonoran tables, and to a lesser extent in Sinaloa and Chihuahua as well. The tradition of using whole *chiltepines* as a condiment dates back to at least the mid-1700s, when German Jesuit priest Ignaz Pfefferkorn noted that "[The *chiltepín*] is placed unpulverized on the table in a salt cellar and each fancier takes as much of it as he believes he can eat. He pulverizes it with his fingers and mixes it with his food." The name may derive from a Nahuatl term meaning "flea chile"—descriptive of size as well as "bite," or perhaps from the Spanish *chile pequín*, meaning "little chile." In some parts of Mexico, like the Región Huasteca, it is in fact known by the latter term.

Whatever it's called (even botanists disagree as to which variety of *Capsicum annuum* it actually is), the *chiltepín* is closely related to the original wild capsicum, thought to have come from Bolivia or Brazil. Jesuit padres described the use of these tiny chiles in Sonora as an indigestion remedy among the Papago Indians in 1794, and until recently the Papagos made annual pilgrimages into the sierra foothills to gather them. Today they are still highly valued among the Tarahumaras, who build stone walls around *chiltepín* bushes to protect them from animals.

Like Brazil nuts, pinenuts, and wild rice, *chiltepines* grow best in the wild—when cultivated they tend to elongate like their domesticated cousins and lose some of their characteristic heat. Wild *chiltepín* bushes flourish in interior chaparral at around 1,500-2,000 meters, often beneath mesquite, shrub live oak, and other thornscrub and desertscrub species. Under optimum conditions, *chiltepín* bushes become trees that may proliferate into small forests. In Sonora the total harvest—most of it from the Río Sonora valley (including tributaries such as Río Moctezuma)—reaches over 20 tons per year, around six tons of which is exported to the United States. Due to the *chiltepín's* recent popularity among chile fanatics, the going price tripled between 1987 and 1990 and quarter-ounce packets now sell for around US$2 each in Tucson, Arizona.

To buy *chiltepines* at their source, or simply to view the colorful fall harvest, visit the south end of the Río Sonora valley (especially the towns of Mazocahui, La Aurora, and Cumpas) beginning in late October.

inexpensive **restaurant** is located next door. Best place to stay in town is **Motel Valle de Cobre,** on Mexico 2 coming in from Nogales/Magdalena—not convenient for town exploration on foot—with rooms for US$28-36.

Regional **buses** leave from the main street through town for Magdalena, Agua Prieta, Arizpe, Ures, and Hermosillo.

Arizpe

The northernmost Río Sonora point of interest is this sleepy town (pop. 3,000) whose colonial character has been preserved by the fact that it lies in a gorge a bit away from the highway. Originally founded in the 1600s, Arizpe rose to a position of importance as an administrative center for all of northwestern colonial Mexico (including Alta and Baja California, Sonora, Arizona, and New Mexico) by 1788. Remnants of this era include the whitewashed, baked-bread style of adobe architecture typical of Sonoran colonial outposts—some examples of which still sport heavy wooden doors—red cobbled streets, a pretty plaza, and a simple, single-towered church. Inside the church **(Nuestra Señora de la Asunción)** are the uniformed remains of Juan Batista de Anza, famous as the founder of Yerba Buena (now San Francisco), California.

Practicalities: Arizpe sometimes charms people into wanting to stay a bit longer than planned. The friendly **Hotel de Anza,** just north of the plaza, has very clean rooms with hot shower and fan for US$23 s/d. **Kankun Kafe** opposite the hotel serves basic *norteña* fare with excellent Sonoran tortillas.

Buses leave from the edge of the plaza for Ures, Hermosillo, and Cananea once or twice a day.

Huepac-Mazocahui

Around 56 km (34 miles) south of Arizpe, Huepac is another fading Sonoran colonial outpost. Founded in 1679, the town features a tidy plaza fronting **Misión San Lorenzo,** a church originally built by Jesuits in the 18th century.

At the foot of the Sierra Aconchi, nine km south of Huepac, is the small town of Aconchi, renowned for its chiles and for a nearby hot springs (tubs on-site). Twin-towered **Misión San Pedro Aconchi** dates to the 18th-century Franciscan presence in the area; a unique black Christ figure surmounts the altar, a pure-

ly Mexican indication that hot springs are in the vicinity.

The hot springs (*agua caliente*) are best reached from the village of San Felipe de Jesús, four km north of Aconchi. Take the "main" dirt road west and northwest from the village (about 9.5 km or six miles) to the hot springs. Pumped by solar panels, the springs feed into a series of pools and tubs of varying temperatures; a German woman manages the complex. A picnic/camping area provides shade, barbecue grills, toilets, and showers; very modest fees are charged for day use and camping.

Toward the junction of Sonora highways 118 and 21 are **Baviácora** and **Mazocahui,** both regional centers for the *chiltepín* trade. Though these towns were founded in the 17th century, neither offers much of obvious historical interest to the potential visitor. **Posada Familiar Baviácora** has six clean rooms (one with a/c) around a courtyard for less than US$20 per night.

Ures

When Cabeza de Vaca and his Amerindian followers from the American Southwest arrived in Ures in 1536, the natives offered 600 deer hearts to the travelers. De Vaca's comment on the local population: "They are a substantial people with a capacity for unlimited development." Under Spanish rule, Ures prospered (on the backs of the natives, whose population today is not so substantial), and in postcolonial Mexico went on to serve as the state capital twice in the 19th century.

A way station between Mazocahui and Hermosillo on Sonora 21, present-day Ures is a town whose natural charm has been partially obscured by Mexican highway culture. A few remainders of the town's glory days are in evidence, chiefly the **Plaza de Armas** and scattered 18th- and 19th-century architecture. The **Misión San Miguel** stands locked and neglected.

Machaca vendors line the highway through town, as Ures is deservedly famous for the Sonoran-style dried and shredded meat. The town is also well known for *panocha,* a candy made from sugarcane—most available following the annual cane harvest each fall. Hermosillo residents often drive up to Ures for the carne asada, *machaca,* and *rajas poblanas* (roasted chile strips) at **Restaurante La Diligencia de Ures.**

Should you decide that Ures is a place where you'd like to spend the night, **Hotel Misión d'Sales,** opposite the bus terminal on the main road, has rooms for around US$23.

HERMOSILLO

Set amidst sweeping plains of golden grasses and green-tufted hills with taller, serrated peaks rising abruptly in the background, this bustling city serves a dual role as Sonora's state capital and major regional center for Sonoran agriculture. Before the *entrada,* Hermosillo was the site of a Pima Indian settlement called Pitic that was centered at the junction of the Sonora and San Miguel rivers, now impounded by Presa Rodríguez at the eastern outskirts of the city. The Spanish superimposed a colony called Santísima Trinidad del Pitic in 1700, but because of confrontations with Pimas and Seris, it was nearly a century before the settlement area was considered "safe" for general habitation.

In 1828 the city's name was changed to Hermosillo in honor of a general from Jalisco who was a hero in the war for independence from Spain. As New Spain became Mexico, and Mexico subdivided its territory into smaller states, Hermosillo became in turn the capital of the state of Occidente, then of Sinaloa y Sonora, and finally of Sonora.

A pleasant mix of modern Mexico and old Sonora, today's Hermosillo is a common stopover for North American visitors heading down the coast because it has all the conveniences of "home," including diverse restaurants, supermarkets, ice-cream parlors, discos, a university of 20,000 students, and an American consulate. A few Americans have chosen to live here for these reasons and for the fact that Hermosillo has the lowest consumer price index of Mexico's 35 largest cities—yet it's less than two hours away from the Sea of Cortez.

Some visitors are put off by the congested traffic, but for a city of over a half million the traffic here actually moves quite well. If you avoid commute hours, you can breeze through town in 10-15 minutes. But Hermosillo is worth a longer stopover for downtown strolls along the laurel-lined avenues and visits to the cathedral, regional museum, and ecological park.

The best time of year for a visit is Oct.-May. During the summer, daytime temperatures in Hermosillo can reach 38° C (100° F). During Semana Santa (the week before Easter), local Yaquis give native dance performances in the city's Barrio del Coloso.

SIGHTS

Many of the city's prominent sights are found along or near a major north-south boulevard variously labeled as Blvd. Kino, Blvd. Rodríguez, and Blvd. Rosales.

Plaza Zaragoza
Hermosillo's city heart since 1865, this spacious downtown plaza features a lofty, Florentine-style *kiosco* (kiosk) built in the early 1900s. At either end of the plaza are the city's two greatest architectural attractions, the Palacio de Gobierno and Catedral de Asunción (see below).

To reach the plaza from the city's northern entrance, drive or catch a city bus south along Blvd. Kino until it becomes Blvd. Rosales. The plaza is bounded at the north and south by Blvd. Hidalgo and Calle Dr. Paliza, both of which run west off Blvd. Rosales.

Palacio De Gobierno
Sonora's seat of government was originally constructed (as a Casa Municipal) of brick and adobe in the neoclassic style in 1859, using Yaqui labor and stone quarried from Cerro de la Campana. Governor Don Carlos Rodríguez had it rebuilt in 1881 to serve as the Instituto Sonorense de Bellas Artes (Sonoran Institute of Fine Arts), a dream never realized as political complexities forced the governor to leave before his term ended.

Converted into the Palacio de Gobierno by the next governor in 1884, the building was almost completely destroyed by fire in 1948. In recent years it has been extensively restored and is now one of the most impressive government buildings in Northern Mexico. An interior courtyard is planted with trees and displays murals with regional themes.

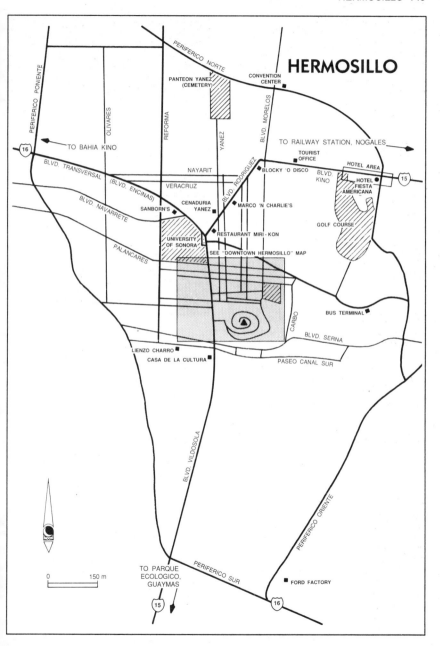

HERMOSILLO

Catedral De La Asunción

This huge, white, twin-towered cathedral with a striking, tiered facade sits opposite the Palacio de Gobierno at the other end of the plaza. The original adobe chapel on this site, completed in 1778, had decayed so much by 1877 that 800 local women petitioned the Catholic diocese to have it replaced. The current neoclassical edifice was constructed in 1908 with a tall, single bell tower; the south tower was added in 1912. Between the two is a huge cupola; with tiered columns, niches, and arches, the whole effect is of a very elaborate wedding cake.

Museo De Sonora
(Museo Regional De Sonora)

Perched just above the foot of Cerro de la Campana, the imposing 19th-century stone building that houses this museum served as a state penitentiary from 1907-1979. In 1985 Mexico's Instituto Nacional de Antropología e Historia (INAH) turned it into a museum devoted to regional research, conservation, and education. The museum's 18 rooms feature comprehensive exhibits on the astronomy, geology, history, natural history, and anthropology of Sonora. Although not part of the regular tour, you can ask the staff to open the underground cells where prisoners were kept in solitary confinement.

Hours are Wed.-Sat. 10 a.m.-4:30 p.m., Sun. 9 a.m.-3:30 p.m; admission is US$0.60. A small public library on-site (tel. 62-12-12-34) is open Mon.-Fri. 8 a.m.-2 p.m.; admission to the library is free.

To reach the museum from downtown Hermosillo, take Blvd. Encinas east to Calle Jesús García, then turn right (south) on Jesús García eight blocks toward Cerro de la Campana until you see the museum on the right.

Museo Regional Uni-Son

This museum, part of the campus of the University of Sonora (Universidad de Sonora) at the intersection of Blvd. Rosales and Blvd. Encinas, opened its doors in 1974 and contains numerous historical and archaeological exhibits from northwestern Mexico. Among them are the 500-year-old mummies of a Pima mother and child from Yécora, a 1900-vintage topographic map of Hermosillo, a deck of cards made of

Catedral de la Asunción

leather by Spanish colonists and decorated with Seri motifs, and original musical scores by composer Silvestre Rodríguez. Open Mon.-Fri. 9 a.m.-1 p.m. and 4-6 p.m., Sat. 9 a.m.-1 p.m.

Parque Ecológico De Sonora

Created in 1984, this part-zoological, part-botanical gardens just south of town exhibits regional flora and fauna on 2,470 acres of desert. A 2.8-km (1.7-mile) asphalt path weaves through the center's various displays, which cover around 300 plant and 200 animal species, many of them indigenous to Sonora.

The park is open Wed.-Sun. 8 a.m.-5 p.m.; admission is US$1.35. The turnoff for the park is three km (1.9 miles) south of town off Mexico 15 (watch for a sign reading "Parque Ecológico"), after which you must follow a two-km access road east to the main entrance and parking lot. Except for city taxi, no public transport to the center is available.

ACCOMMODATIONS

Hermosillo's hotels are concentrated in two separate areas, the *zona hotelera* along Blvd. Kino at the north end of the city (where the higher-end hotels and restaurants tend to be located) and the downtown district close to Plaza Zaragoza and the municipal market (less expensive and better for city explorations on foot). Only one RV park is available, however—more options lie west (details below).

Zona Hotelera (Blvd. Kino)

The city's top hotel property is the very modern and efficient **Hotel Fiesta Americana Hermosillo** (tel. 62-15-11-12; 800-00-999 toll free in Mexico fax 62-15-57-21) at Blvd. Kino 369. A popular choice for visiting business executives, the five-star Fiesta Americana costs US$114 during the week for very comfortable s/d rooms with all the amenities, less on weekends. Facilities include an attractive lobby bar, popular disco, heated pool, restaurants, and security parking.

Coming down to the four-star category in the same vicinity are several *zona hotelera* choices in the US$50-80 range (going east on Blvd. Kino): **Hotel Pitic Valle Grande** (tel. 14-45-70; 800-62-333 toll free in Mexico), Blvd. Kino and Calle R. Corral; **Hotel Bugambilia Valle Grande** (tel.14-50-50, 800-62-333), Blvd. Kino 712; **Hotel Gándara** (tel. 14-44-14), Blvd. Kino; and **Araiza Inn** (tel. 15-82-37) at Blvd. Kino 353. All of these hotels feature pools and security parking; the Araiza Inn also has a lighted tennis court. Room tariffs for each seesaw between US$50 and US$80 depending on whether they're running special rates or not; it's worth calling in advance to see which hotels are offering discounts.

A slightly less expensive alternative also in this area is **Motel La Siesta** (tel. 14-39-89), Blvd. Kino and Calle Carpena, a one-story American-style motel whose comfortable US$45 rooms come with satellite TV, phone, and small refrigerators. Similar in price and comfort but designed in Sonoran colonial style (one-story *portales* surrounding a simple courtyard) is **El Encanto Motel** (tel. 14-47-30) at Blvd. Kino 901 between Hotel Gándara and the Araiza Inn.

DOWNTOWN HERMOSILLO

Downtown

The most easily accessible downtown hotels are those lined up on Blvd. Rosales, which connects with Blvd. Rodríguez and Blvd. Kino to the north. The bland, high-rise **Calinda Comfort Inn** (tel. 62-17-23-96) at Rosales and Calle Morelia costs US$45 s/d per night for standard-looking rooms. The colorful old **Hotel San Alberto** (tel. 12-18-00) at Rosales and Serdán costs US$38 s, US$45 d; these rates include a full breakfast. This hotel has character and ambience, but the somewhat musty rooms are a bit overpriced.

Although it's a bit harder to find, one of the better downtown hotels is **Hotel La Finca** (tel. 17-17-16) at Calle Matamoros and G. Madrid. The clean and efficient La Finca costs US$50 s/d. The three-story hotel surrounds a courtyard with pool and Jacuzzi; a small parking lot is attached.

The best budget choice in the city is the friendly **Hotel Washington** (tel. 13-11-83), very near downtown eating and shopping at Calle Dr. Noriega Pte. 68 (between Guerrero and Matamoros). The simple but clean rooms are very good value at US$16 s, US$17 d. The hotel doesn't have a parking lot but parking can be arranged at one of the nearby security garages at 24-hour rates. A couple of the Hotel Washington staff speak good English.

RV Parks And Campgrounds

Most RVers and campers head straight west for Bahía Kino or south to Bahía San Carlos, where plenty of RV/camping facilities are available. In Hermosillo the only choice is the small **Kino RV Park** (tel. 62-15-31-97) east of the Hotel Fiesta Americana on Blvd. Kino. Full hookups cost US$12 per night, a bargain considering the zona hotelera location.

FOOD

Sonoran cuisine—centered around ranchero-style cooking—is well represented in Hermosillo. The state claims to have the highest quality beef in Mexico; carne asada (grilled beef), served with huge, paper-thin Sonoran flour tortillas and pickled chiles, is a big favorite and is available at virtually every restaurant in town. Smaller, thicker flour tortillas called coyotas, baked in an oven instead of on a comal (griddle), are also common. Coyotas are said to have originated in Hermosillo's Villa de Seris.

Other local specialities to look for include cocido (a stew of garbanzo beans, beef or pork, corn, onions, tomatoes, potatoes, and other vegetables), burros de machaca (burritos made with dried, shredded beef), and chivichangas (similar to a burrito with additional vegetable ingredients, deep-fried whole). These latter dishes aren't always found in the zona hotelera restaurants; check out the taquerías and loncherías downtown. The municipal market's well-worn lunch counters are an inexpensive place to experiment—located on the southern end of Matamoros between calles Morelia and Serdán.

At the most typically Sonoran eateries you'll see bowls of red, berrylike chiltepines on the tables or counters—local customers munch the fiery spheres as a condiment along with their meal. Be sure to have a glass of water on hand before dipping into the bowl. Or a soda, as Sonorans tend to call soft drinks (refresco in most of Mexico).

Also very popular in Hermosillo are tacos de cabeza (literally "head tacos," featuring beef cheek and tongue), commonly sold by street vendors—some of whom take in as much as US$2000 a day. Although some vendors set up for lunchtime, prime taco stand hours are dusk to midnight.

Because Hermosillo is close to the Sea of Cortez coast, seafood restaurants provide alternatives to the typically beef-oriented Sonoran menu.

The following list represents places selected for quality, reliability, and location—you'll find dozens of other restaurants to sample in the city if you have the time and inclination.

Carne Asada And Steak

$$ **Restaurante Xochimilco** (Jardines de Xochimilco, tel. 62-13-34-89), Calle Obregón 51 off Blvd. Rosales, in the Villa de Seris district at the south end of the city. Established in 1949, this is the most famous restaurant in Hermosillo for carne asada, costillas (ribs), and tripitas (tripe, served as an appetizer). Most customers purchase a paquete, which includes carne asada or costillas, tortillas, beans, and tripitas for one price. Trobadores wander from table to table. Open daily 9 a.m.-midnight.

$$-$$$ Xochimilco Steak (tel. 14-59-06), Blvd. Kino 908. Conveniently located in the hotel zone, this is a more "international" version of the original Xochimilco featuring aged steaks. Open daily noon-midnight.

$$ La Carreta (tel. 15-01-30), Periférico Sur (South Loop), 300 meters west of Blvd. Vildósola. In addition to *carne asada,* this buffet-style restaurant offers a wide selection of other Sonoran specialties, including *carne con chile* (beef in a chile sauce), *picadillo* (spicy meat salad), and *tamales de elote* (fresh corn tamales). Open daily noon-5 p.m.

$$ Steak del Herradero (tel. 15-84-06), Blvd. Navarrete, Colonia La Huerta. Rustic ranch-style decor; the specialty is American-style steaks served on hot platters. Open daily noon-midnight.

Mexican

$ Cenaduría Yáñez (tel. 62-14-18-72), Calle Yáñez 7 (off Blvd. Rodríguez). This very simple family-run restaurant is probably the best all-around eatery in the city for value, quality, and selection of *platillos típicos.* Among the menu selections are *tacos, enchiladas, pozole, menudo, machaca, chivichangas, quesadillas,* and *gorditas.* Very inexpensive *comidas corridas* are also available. Service is excellent but restaurant Spanish is a must (see "Spanish Phrasebook"). Open daily 7 a.m.-midnight.

$$ Restaurante Elba (tel. 18-46-22), calles Olivares and de Niza, Colonia Los Arcos. Specialties include Mexican-style *milanesa* (breaded veal), *enchiladas suizas,* and fried shrimp. Open daily 7 a.m.-11 p.m.

$$-$$$ Marco 'n Charlie's Sonora Bar & Grill (tel. 15-30-61), corner of Blvd. Rodríguez and Calle San Luis Potosí. Although it's part of the mostly tourist-oriented Grupo Anderson chain (Señor Frog's, Squid Roe, etc.), this particular permutation has one of the chain's best kitchens (and decors) and caters almost exclusively to Hermosillenses (especially upscale couples). The menu changes periodically, but always features authentic interpretations of regional specialties; tortillas are handmade on the premises. The bar is a good place for evening drinks and *botanas.* Open Mon.-Sat. 1 p.m.-midnight.

$ Taquería Acuarios, Blvd. Rodríguez 136 (between Zacatecas and Tamaulipas). A lively nighttime taco place specializing in *tacos caramelos* (tacos stuffed with beans and cheese). Open Mon.-Thurs. 7 p.m.-2 a.m., Fri.-Sat. 9 p.m.-4 a.m., and Sun. 6 p.m.-1 a.m.

International

$$$ Henry's (tel. 62-14-73-93), Blvd. Kino 904. One of the hotel zone's classiest restaurants; housed in a converted mansion with a menu that includes chateaubriand, filet mignon, and other continental dishes. Open Mon.-Sat. 1-11:30 p.m., Sun. 1-6 p.m.

$$ Sanborn's (tel. 15-75-15), Blvd. Encinas and Navarrete. Truly international, the Sanborn's menu features an ample selection of tasty continental, American, and Mexican dishes at reasonable prices. Breakfasts start at US$2.70 and are particularly good—try the *huevos ahogados con rajas poblanas* (eggs smothered in roasted chile strips).

$$$ Swiss Haus (tel. 17-50-40), Calle Dr. Paliza 62. Pricey but good; specialties include oxtail soup, paté, and fondues.

Seafood

$$ El Corral (tel. 62-12-39-79), Calle Puebla and Garmendia. Lots of informal business transactions take place over El Corral's popular seafood cocktails (scallop, shrimp, octopus, oyster, clam, or squid—depending on the season), *caldo largo* (seafood soup), fish tacos, or *pargo frito* (fried snapper). Open daily 8 a.m.-6 p.m.

$$-$$$ Restaurante Los Arcos (tel. 13-22-20), Calle Ocampo and Michel, Colonia Centenario. Specializes in more unusual seafood dishes such as *caguama* (sea turtle—legally harvested), *filete de mero a la Culichi* (broiled seabass fillet), marlin tacos, and baked crab.

Vegetarian

$-$$ Restaurante Jung (tel. 62-13-28-81), Calle Niños Heroes 75, off Blvd. Encinas near the corner of Calle Matamoros. As is common in Mexico, Jung is actually a combination natural foods and herbal medicine shop, health library, and vegetarian cafe. Many dishes are attempted equivalents of Mexican standards, others are international. You can buy fresh yogurt and whole wheat bread here as well. Open Mon.-Sat. 8 a.m.-8 p.m.

Pizza And Italian

$ **La Fabula** is national chain that has nine locations in town with reliable American-style pizza, spaghetti, and sandwiches.
$$ **Pizzeria La Romana** (tel. 62-13-19-55), calles Yáñez and Morelia. Good all-around pizza, lasagna, and pasta dishes. Open daily noon-11 p.m.

Chinese

Hermosillo has more Chinese restaurants than any other city in Northern Mexico. For the most part they are very similar, specializing in large servings of Cantonese dishes somewhat oriented toward Mexican tastes.
$-$$ **Miri-Kon Comida China** (tel. 13-16-97), Blvd. Rodríguez and Calle G. Madrid. Judging from the crowds, this is one of the most popular Chinese eateries in the city. It is also the only one focusing primarily on Mandarin (or northern Chinese) cuisine. Open noon-midnight daily.
$-$$ **Restaurante Bar Jo-Wah** (tel. 13-13-99), Calle P. Suárez 190. A huge, ornate banquet-style restaurant that specializes in Cantonese seafood. Open noon-midnight daily.
$-$$ **Restaurante Lai-Wah** (tel. 14-55-55), Blvd. Rodríguez 6. Jo-Wah's main competitor features a similar menu with an equally ample seafood section. Open noon-2 a.m. daily.

RECREATION AND ENTERTAINMENT

Cultural

Hermosillo's **Casa de la Cultura** (tel. 62-17-12-63) on Blvd. Vildósola hosts weekly performances of ballet and folkloric dancing, films in the Sala de Cine (Sat.-Sun. noon, 4 p.m., and 6 p.m.), gallery exhibitions, and the occasional outdoor musical or drama event in the central courtyard.

Foreign films are sometimes shown at the University of Sonora's humanities department (*departamento de humanidades*), blvds. Rosales and Encinas.

Discos

Two discos along the city's main artery vie for most of Hermosillo's dance crowd. **Blocky'O** (tel. 62-14-56-02) at Blvd. Rodríguez and Aguascalientes is a middle-class spot popular with visitors as well as locals; it's open daily 9 p.m.-2 a.m. Down the road a bit, **Nova Olimpia** (tel. 17-30-13) at Calle Soria and Fronteras is larger, newer, flashier, and requires semi-formal dress (sports jackets for men). Nova features live music Mon.-Thurs., disco on weekends, and is open 9 p.m-2 a.m.

The **Hotel Fiesta Americana** (see "Accommodations") has a small but popular video disco that's packed on weekends.

Shopping

Hermosillo's traditional shopping district is centered around the 1920-vintage **Mercado Municipal José María Pino Suárez** at Calle Matamoros near calles Serdán, Monterrey, and Morelia. The latter three streets are lined with specialized shops selling leather goods, clothing, Mexican curios, sporting goods, shoes, household goods, and just about anything else you can think of. Street parking is very scarce during the daytime; rather than circle endlessly, park in the inexpensive pay garage next to the market.

Also in the downtown area are several hat and boot shops at the corner of calles Guaymas and Sonora, next to a *zócalo* (town square).

A newer shopping district has grown up around the intersection of Blvd. Encinas and Calle Reforma in the center of the city. Among the several department stores in this area are **Sanborn's** and **Mazón Boulevares,** both at blvds. Encinas and Navarrete. Sanborn's has the best selection of English-language books and magazines in town, as well as a small but high-quality selection of arts and crafts.

Other stores specializing in handicrafts include **Arte Típico** at Calle 12 de Octubre (between Campeche and Quintana Roo) and **Los Tilliches** at the Hotel Fiesta Americana on Blvd. Kino. You'll also find some handicrafts at the *Mercado Municipal*. Among the best local buys are Seri *canastas* (large baskets) made from fibers of the torote prieto, a desert tree. The famous Seri ironwood (*palo fierro*) sculptures are found in a number of stores around town; **Artesanía Sonorense de Palo Fierro** at calles Serdán and P. Suárez has the largest selection.

Charreadas

The Asociación de Charros de Hermosillo (tel. 62-18-60-67) maintains **El Lienzo Charro el Sonorense** at Blvd. Paseo del Vado and

(top, left) *matachine* dancers, Matamoros; (top, right) *rebozo* weavers, Santa María del Río; (bottom) Day of the Dead, Durango (photos by Joe Cummings)

(top) Río Tunal, Durango; (bottom) Cráter El Elegante, El Pinacate National Park (photos by Joe Cummings)

Comonfort. During the Sept.-May season, the association organizes monthly *charreadas* (usually on Sunday) with *charro* associations from other Sonoran towns. If you can't attend a regular *charreada,* you might try observing one of the weekly practice sessions on Tuesdays, Thursdays, and Sundays at 8 p.m. at the *charro* stadium. *Escaramuza* practice for *charras* takes place on Wednesdays and Fridays at 10 a.m.

Fishing And Hunting
Most visiting sportfishers are en route to Bahía Kino or San Carlos (see the appropriate sections).

Freshwater fishing is possible at several northern Sonora lakes. The sportfishing season for lake bass and tilapia is Feb.-May, when anglers hone in on Presa Plutarco Elías Calles (Presa Novillo) in San Pedro de la Cueva, 130 km (80.6 miles) east of Hermosillo. Hermosillo's own lake, Presa Rodríguez, is hardly worth throwing bait or lure into.

Deportes Acampar at calles Dr. Noriega and Garmendia near the municipal market has an extensive selection of sporting goods, including fishing and camping gear. Bird-hunting trips with English-speaking guides can be arranged here.

Muy Grande Outfitter (tel. 62-16-98-32, fax 62-16-38-92), Calle Celeste 6, organizes guided hunts for mule deer, Coues deer, doves, ducks, and geese.

Baseball
When world-famous pitcher Fernando Valenzuela was called up to the Baltimore Orioles in 1993, he had just finished a season playing for the Hermosillo Naranjeros ("Orange-ers"), one of the best teams in Mexico's Pacific Coast League. In 1976 Hermosillo won the Caribbean World Series, which is held here every few years (always in February) on a rotating basis with Mazatlán, Culiacán, and several Caribbean capitals.

The Naranjeros play at Hermosillo's **Estadio Hector Espino** (named for one of Mexico's most famous ballplayers), which is at the intersection of Blvd. Encinas (Blvd. Transversal) and Periférico Poniente. This is one of the nation's nicest ballparks; during the PCL season (Oct.-Jan.), advance tickets can be purchased at the stadium. Ask at the state tourist office (see "Ser-

vices and Information," below) for a current schedule of home games.

TRANSPORT

Air
Aeroméxico (tel. 62-16-82-06, Blvd. Navarrete 165) operates direct flights to Chihuahua, Ciudad Obregón, Guadalajara, Los Angeles, Los Mochis, Mexico City, Monterrey, San Diego, Tijuana, and Tucson.

Regional carrier **Noroeste** (tel. 17-49-88, Blvd. Rodríguez 99) flies to Ciudad Juárez, Ciudad Obregón, Chihuahua, Durango, La Paz, Mexicali, and Monterrey, while newcomer **TAESA** (tel. 17-36-06, Blvd. Rodríguez 99) has daily flights to Mexico City and Mexicali.

Mexicana (tel. 17-11-03, Blvd. Rosales and Palancares) flies to Mexico City daily.

Transport between the airport (15 km) and downtown Hermosillo costs US$12 by taxi, US$5 by *colectivo.*

Taxis
These are plentiful throughout the city, especially in the hotel zone and around the central shopping district. Rates run around US$1.50 per km.

Bus
An extensive system of local buses ply the city streets from dawn to midnight. Fares on most are US$0.20. As elsewhere in Mexico, destinations are displayed on the front of the vehicle. Several small, modern shuttles run the north-south route between the hotel zone along Blvd. Kino and the downtown area along Blvd. Rosales.

Hermosillo's main long-distance bus companies include Transportes Norte de Sonora (TNS), Tres Estrellas de Oro, Transportes del Pacífico, and Autobuses Estrella Blanco, all of which use the **Central de Autobuses de Hermosillo** (tel. 62-17-04-01) on Blvd. Transversal (Encinas). Together these bus lines cover the following destinations: Santa Ana, Magdalena, Nogales, Caborca, Sonoita, San Luis Río Colorado, Mexicali, Tijuana, Guaymas, Ciudad Obregón, Navojoa, Los Mochis, Culiacán, Mazatlán, Tepic, Guadalajara, and Mexico City.

In addition, Transportes Chihuahuenses runs

a daily departure to La Junta, Chih.; Union de Transportes Foraneos de Paisaje has daily buses to Cananea; Estrellas Blancas has one daily bus to Chihuahua; and the new "Blus" line operates a luxury bus to Nogales with onboard video and snacks. For buses to Bahía Kino, use Transportes de la Costa de Hermosillo (tel. 12-21-94) at Av. P.E. Calles 99.

Train

Hermosillo's railway station (tel. 62-14-38-29) sits on the Pacífico line, 2.4 km (1.5 miles) north of downtown, but there is a ticket office (tel. 17-17-11, 13-87-01) at Blvd. Transversal and Calle González.

The Pacífico No. 1 (first class) train to Nogales/Mexicali departs at 7:45 a.m. while the No. 2—the same train in reverse—leaves for points south to Guadalajara at 7:45 p.m.

Driving

With the new four-lane toll highway from Nogales and the new two-lane from La Junta, Chih. (an alternative to taking the Chihuahua al Pacífico train), Hermosillo is easier to reach by road than ever before.

Coming from Nogales/Santa Ana, Mexico 15 links Blvd. Kino at the north end of town with Blvd. Vildósola at the south end, where it continues on to Guaymas and points farther south. The city is bisected in the east-west direction by Blvd. Encinas (also known as Blvd. Transversal west of Mexico 15); if you follow Blvd. Encinas west it joins the highway to Bahía Kino. A periférico joins these two main arteries as a loop or bypass, although first-time visitors to Hermosillo may find the loop's permutations a bit confusing due to the many intersections along the way. If you stick to the main boulevards you'll probably manage better.

Fuel: PEMEX stations are abundant in prosperous Hermosillo and finding Magna Sin is rarely a problem. If you're just passing through, probably the best place to fill up is at the large **El Sahuaro** station 3.2 km (two miles) south of town; besides unleaded fuel, the station has clean restrooms and ice.

Auto Rental

The following agencies rent cars out of Hermosillo: **Avis** (tel. 62-15-99-20; Blvd. Kino and Villareal), **Hertz** (tel. 14-16-95; Blvd. Rodríguez and Guerrero), **National** (tel. 14-09-36; Hermosillo Airport), **Budget** (tel. 14-38-05; Blvd. Rodríguez and Tamaulipas), and **Facil** (tel. 10-18-00; Blvd. Rodríguez and Zacatecas). Cars can also be rented at several hotels and travel agencies in the *zona hotelera*. Rates start at around US$25 per day with added per-km charges.

SERVICES AND INFORMATION

Tourist Offices

The Sonora state tourist office (tel. 62-14-84-07, fax 62-14-63-04) is on the second floor of the Edificio Pitic at Blvd. Kino and Ocupicio. SECTUR (tel. 17-08-57) also has an office on the lower floor of the Palacio Gobierno downtown.

Maps

Topographical maps for Sonora, Chihuahua, and Sinaloa can be purchased at the INEGI office (tel. 62-16-11-03, fax 62-16-07-63) at Edificio Ocotillo Business Park, Periférico Pte. 310, Colonia Las Quintas.

Money

Along with the many banks found throughout the city, Hermosillo also has a number of *casas de cambio*. Two are on Calle Matamoros downtown: **Casa de Cambio Sonora** (open Mon.-Fri. 1-6 p.m.) and **Casa de Cambio Euromex** (open Mon.-Fri. 8:30 a.m.-1 p.m. and 3:30-5:30 p.m.).

U.S. Consulate

Visiting Americans can take care of consular business (reporting lost or stolen passports, voting in absentia, etc.) at the U.S. Consulate (tel. 62-17-23-75, 62-17-25-42) on Calle Morelia.

USEFUL HERMOSILLO TELEPHONE NUMBERS

Police: 18-64-16
Red Cross: 06
Highway Patrol: 18-90-99
Hospital: 13-25-56
Green Angels: 14-63-04, 15-31-97
Cruz de Oro: 13-66-16
Hermosillo Area Code: 62

BAHIA KINO

This eight-km-long, sandy bay opposite Isla Tiburón is 117 km (72.5 miles) from Hermosillo —about an hour and a half drive through Sonoran Desert scenery and small highway towns. Opinions are mixed on how worthwhile a destination Bahía Kino is. The bay itself is beautiful, and the hills rising from the cardón-studded desert to the east add to the setting; sunsets can be spectacular. But the development along the bay is rather haphazard, ranging from a ramshackle collection of block houses in the fishing village of **Kino Viejo** ("Old Kino") to a characterless string of North American beach homes and built-over trailers known collectively as **Kino Nuevo** ("New Kino" or simply "Kino Bay" to most Americans).

The public beach roughly at the middle of Bahía Kino has *palapas*, showers, and stands from which chilled coconuts are sold; on weekends and holidays it is usually crowded with Hermosillo day-trippers. At the north end of Kino Nuevo is **Cerro Prieto,** a spiky desert hill with excellent bay views (the base of the hill can be reached by dirt road from Kino Nuevo).

The **Museo de los Seris** in Kino Nuevo, at the corner of Calle Progreso and Av. Mar de Cortés (the main street paralleling the beach), has good displays of Seri clothing, folk utensils, reed kayaks, and other cultural artifacts, plus historic photos taken earlier this century. The museum is open daily 10 a.m.-1 p.m. and 3-6 p.m.; admission is free but donations are gratefully accepted.

Although about a quarter of the population living in Kino Viejo are Seris, most Seris now live farther north on the coast in Punta Chueca and El Desemboque. Seri ironwood sculptures and torote-fiber baskets can be purchased from vendors in Kino Viejo or at the aforementioned villages.

The area's best coastal features are found north and south of these main settlements, down dirt and gravel roads to deserted coves and beaches, as well as opposite the bay on Isla Tiburón. Unless you've come for the fishing, how much you enjoy a Kino visit may largely depend on whether you have the time and means to explore beyond the main bay developments.

Climate

Bahía Kino's high season for gringos is Dec.-April, when days are generally warm and nights are cool. Summers can be very warm and are a popular time for Hermosillo beach goers, while the only rain to speak of (less than 7.5 cm/three inches) falls July-Sept.

ACCOMMODATIONS

Motels

Bahía Kino's accommodations tend to be weatherworn, musty, and overpriced. **Posada del Mar** (tel. 624-9-16-24) at the bay's south end between old and new Kino, has large air-conditioned rooms with lukewarm showers for US$54 d, US$67 t. The pool and sea-view terrace almost compensate for the lack of upkeep.

Farther north along Av. Mar de Cortés, the **Santa Gemma Hotel** (tel. 2-00-26) is right on the beach and offers 14 bungalows that were under extensive renovation as we went to press. Room rates will probably be in the US$40 range; if the renovations are successful, this could become Kino's top choice.

For now the best motel deal in town is toward the north end of Kino Nuevo at **Kino Bay Motel** (tel. 2-02-16), where clean, well-kept rooms with kitchenettes on Av. Mar de Cortés across from the beach start at US$25.

Saro's is a small place on the beach in the middle of Kino Nuevo with four basic but cozy apartments managed by an Italian immigrant. Rates start at US$40 for one night, negotiable for longer stays.

In Kino Viejo you may be able to stay at **Islandia (Isla) Marina,** featuring a few basic, three- to four-person cabins with kitchens for only US$27 a night. Trailer parking is also available here.

RV Parks

Kino accommodation fares better if you bring your own. **Kino Bay Trailer Park** (tel. 624-2-02-16), across from the beach at Kino Nuevo's north end, has 179 sites, a decent restaurant/bar, coin laundry, boat ramp, propane, and a small general store. Rates are US$12 for two persons, US$2.50 for each additional person.

At the very north end of Av. Mar de Cortés is **Caverna del Seri Trailer Park** (tel. 62-14-71-34 in Hermosillo) with 33 sites, satellite TV, boat launch, and a restaurant/bar for US$12 a day.

Kunkaak Trailer Park (tel. 62-17-44-53 in Hermosillo), near Club Deportivo, has 54 sites and a coin laundry for US$15. Also near the Club Deportivo is the 12-slot **Cesares Trailer Park,** the least expensive place to park at US$10 a day.

El Cactus Trailer Park is on the road to the airfield and costs US$12.

If staying in Kino Viejo appeals, try for a spot at **Islandia Marina** (tel. 2-00-80), right on Kino's main fishing beach. RV/trailer spaces, some with *palapas* or pull-through shelters, cost a bargain US$10.50 per day.

PRACTICALITIES

Food

Several simple restaurants in Kino Viejo offer seafood fresh from local fishing boats. During the Oct.-May shrimping season, fresh shrimp is especially abundant. **La Palapa del Pescador** and **Restaurante Marlín** are old favorites catering to gringos as well as Hermosillenses. **Restaurante Doritas** on the main street in from the highway has good breakfasts and *antojitos*.

More local in ambience are two rustic, *palapa*-style places in Kino Viejo, **Restaurante Las Gaviotas** and **Costa Azul**, adjacent to one another on the south side of the village. In the evenings, live *norteña* bands sometimes play for small groups of fishermen here.

In Kino Nuevo, the **Kino Bay Motel/Trailer Park** has a reliable menu with Mexican standards and seafood specials.

You can buy fresh oysters at the *ostionerías* on the north end of Estero Santa Cruz, southeast of Kino Viejo, for around US$2.30 per dozen.

Fishing

Although Kino sportfishing isn't what it used to be, offshore it's possible to land marlin, sailfish, and dorado during the summer, or tuna, yellowtail, *cochito* (triggerfish), and seabass the remainder of the year. Inshore and onshore brings in *pargo* (dog snapper), surfperch, ladyfish, sand bass, and shark.

MEXICAN LOBSTERS

Of the several species of lobster scooting about in Mexico's seas, the two most numerous are: *Panulirus interruptus* (known as red lobster or *langosta roja*), found as far south as the 25th parallel on both the Pacific and Sea of Cortez sides; and *P. inflatus* (blue lobster or *langosta azul*) in the Pacific and lower Cortez as far south as Tehuantepec, Oaxaca. None of the lobster species found in Mexican waters are related to the cold-water type (genus *Homarus*) found off the coast of the northeastern U.S. and southeastern Canada. Mexico's warm-water lobsters are sometimes referred to as "spiny lobsters" because their shells bear spiny projections (the *Homarus* shell is smooth). Spiny lobsters also have smaller pincers than the cold-water varieties.

Adult spiny lobsters reach up to 61 cm (24 inches) in length and weigh as much as six kilograms (13 pounds). Most varieties are nocturnal and tend to frequent depths of 5-30 meters. During the daytime they stay beneath or between rocks to hide from their natural enemies (sharks, octopi, rays and a few larger finfish). Their diet consists mostly of crustaceans, mollusks, and other small sea organisms.

Lobstering is a major part of the fishing industry in Mexico, the world's eighth largest harvester of lobster. An average 700 metric tons are harvested annually; about half of the total catch is exported, earning around US$9 million in foreign revenues. The official lobstering seasons are: March 16-Sept. 30 (red lobster) and June 1-Sept. 15 (blue lobster). It is illegal to take lobsters out of Mexico unless accompanied by a receipt that shows they were purchased from a store or a *cooperativa de pesca* (fishing cooperative).

Favorite surf casting spots are the beach at Kino Viejo and the rocks next to Caverna del Seri Trailer Park. Onshore fishing is even better if you're willing to head north or south from Bahía Kino, ferreting out sandy roads to deserted rock points. *Pangas* can be rented in Kino Viejo for offshore fishing trips. Larger fishing cruisers are available in Kino Nuevo—check with the Kino Bay Sportsman's Club. Typical rates are US$120 per day or US$300 per three days, but these are sometimes negotiable—some boat pilots will go for US$80 a day if you pay for the gas.

The local headquarters for gringo anglers is the **Club Deportivo Bahía Kino** (tel. 624-2-01-51; A.P. 84, Bahía Kino, Son. 83340), in a large quonset hut decorated with U.S. state flags at the north end of Kino Nuevo. Also known by its English name, Kino Bay Sportsman's Club, this membership organization provides a variety of services for visitors and residents alike, including emergency assistance ("Rescue One") when necessary. Club members monitor CB channel 14 and VHF channel 16; if you leave the name of your boat, number and name of passengers, and time of expected return with the club, they'll keep tabs on you, and will notify the local coast guard if you don't return on time. The club also maintains a community bulletin board with sale notices for boats and local real estate. Open Mon.-Sat. 8 a.m.-noon and 1-5 p.m.

Limited fishing supplies are sold at shops in Kino Viejo. More gear is available at Deportes Acampar in Hermosillo (see "Fishing and Hunting" under "Hermosillo").

Transport And Fuel
Buses run seven times daily between Hermosillo (from the terminal on Av. Serdán, between Jesús García and González) and Bahía Kino. The fare is about US$2. At Bahía Kino the buses usually stop at the PEMEX station at the edge of Kino Viejo and farther on along Av. Mar de Cortés in Kino Nuevo. The Kino Viejo PEMEX station usually carries **Magna Sin.**

Telephone
Telephone service in Kino is a bit spotty—many people use radio phones. The local area code is 624.

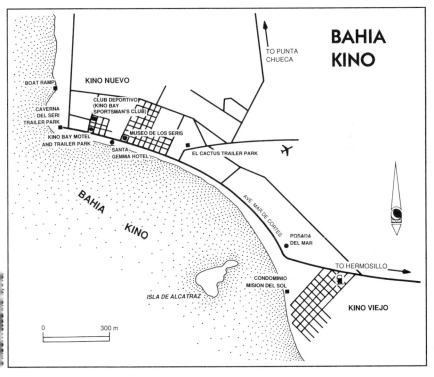

VICINITY OF BAHÍA KINO

Isla Tiburón

Measuring 47 km (29 miles) long and 24 km (15 miles) wide, with a surface area of approximately 1,000 square km, Isla Tiburón (Shark Island) is the largest island in the Sea of Cortez. As a continental island—a chunk of the mainland left behind as San Andreas Fault activity separated Baja California from the rest of Mexico—Tiburón's desert landscape is much like that along the Bahía Kino coast. Among the island's distinguishing geographic features are two small sierras, Menor and Kunkaak, with peaks rising as high as 1,200 meters (4,000 feet).

Once an important Seri Indian homeland, the island is now a national wildlife refuge for bighorn sheep and other Sonoran Desert species extinct or nearly extinct on the mainland. Two springs also support a population of hares, coyotes, bobcats, foxes, deer, pelicans, sea swallows, and petrels. Clams and squid are reportedly plentiful along the rocky shores.

The island can be reached by powerboat from Kino Nuevo in about 45 minutes. Inquire at the Kino Bay Yacht Club (Club de Yates Bahía Kino) for charters, which typically cost US$40 per person for drop-off and pick-up service. The charter includes a SEDESOL permit, required for all non-Seri visitors to the island. Visitors with their own boats should apply to the SEDESOL office in Hermosillo for the necessary permit.

Sometimes a stop at **Isla Pelicano,** a smaller island between Kino and Isla Tiburón, can be arranged.

Playa San Nicolás

This stunning cove south of Bahía Kino is remarkably pristine and unvisited, considering its proximity to Hermosillo and Bahía Kino. For years rumors of an upcoming hotel development have simmered, but for now it's one of the nicest beaches along the Sonora coast, to some extent preserved by bad roads and general anonymity.

You'll need your own transport—rugged transport—to get here. Heading west on Mexico 16 toward Bahía Kino, take the signed turnoff south between Km 94 and 95. The Playa San Nicolás sign reads "12 km" but with detours around recently washed-out sections, it's more like 22.5

km one-way. The first part of the road is wide and graded but eventually the road veers west before the village of Valle Verde and turns into a bumpy, sandy ride all the way to the cove.

The drive, however, is almost as rewarding as the beach itself. Unless it has been a particularly dry year, along the way you'll pass desert basins, including the huge Salinas Santa Cruz, filled with shrimp and frequented by waterfowl. Total required driving time is around 1-1½ hours, depending on road conditions, type of vehicle driven, and off-highway driving skills. Don't attempt this trip without a 4WD vehicle if it has recently rained heavily.

Seri Villages

Around 450 Seris live north of Bahía Kino in the villages of **Punta Chueca** and **El Desemboque** (also known as Desemboque del Seri), which are supported primarily by fishing and the manufacture of baskets and ironwood carvings. These two villages are respectively 29 km (18 miles) and 90 km (56 miles) north of Kino via a coastal dirt road. The first leg to Punta Chueca is passable by ordinary car, while the stretch beyond to Desemboque requires a sturdy vehicle with good road clearance.

In spite of their small numbers, the Seris (who call themselves *konk'aak,* "people") have resisted government efforts to integrate them into Mexican society. About half are bilingual in Spanish and their native tongue; a few have also learned English from the steady trickle of Bahía Kino tourists who manage to find their way north.

History: The intensive occupation of the upper Sonoran coast and Isla Tiburón began when the makers of Tiburón Plain Ware (also known as "eggshell pottery") arrived some 500-1,000 years ago—these were the probable ancestors of the Seri. When the Spanish arrived the Seri still had a very sophisticated pottery technology in which the thinness of the walls in ratio to carrying capacity was the highest in North America. An early anthropologist measured a Seri pot that held 15 liters but weighed less than two kilograms (a comparable Papago pot of four-liter capacity was said to weigh 17 kilograms). Unfortunately, the ceramic techniques that produced such wonderful pots has not survived.

When the first Spanish missionaries settled

among the Seris in the early 18th century, Seri homelands extended well inland from the Río Yaqui into Pimería Alta. They lived in cliff and cave dwellings and relied on hunting and foraging for food. A large number were missionized but in the 1740s and 1750s, after tiring of constant maltreatment by Spanish soldiers and warning their missionary padres to leave, the Seris attacked Spanish settlements throughout the area—killing perhaps hundreds of Spaniards —and retreated to the coast.

Repeated Spanish attempts to attack and exterminate the Seris were unsuccessful, as they turned out to be adversaries as fierce and accomplished as the Yaquis. Among all the Amerindian groups in Mexico, only the Seris used poison-tipped arrows, which they could shoot with such force as to penetrate the eight layers of deerskin the Spanish soldiers wore as frontier armor. German missionary Ignaz Pfefferkorn described the efficacy of the arrows: "The smallest wound inevitably causes quick death. At the most, two days may elapse before the wounded person is a corpse. The flesh becomes coal black and falls from the bones in pieces, as though decayed."

In spite of the military prowess they demonstrated in defense of their coastal homelands, the Seris dwindled in number. In 1844 a Mexican army officer counted 421 Seris on Isla Tiburón and along the nearby coast; no one knows how many may have lived here when the Spanish arrived. Today there are about 500 Seris left, up from a low of 164 in 1934.

Concerned for the Seris' welfare (and perhaps vexed by their insular social habits and perceived rebellious nature), the Mexican government forced them to leave their Isla Tiburón homeland in 1956. Twenty years later they were given permission to return (though the island remains closed to non-Seri overnight visitors), but the Seris have become so accustomed to coastal mainland living that they have yet to move back on a permanent basis.

The early Seris dressed in an odd costume of pelican skins—with feathers intact. Nowadays Seri men wear the same sorts of clothes their Mexican counterparts typically wear; women generally wear long, full skirts and tie their heads in colorful scarves. Ritual face-painting is still practiced during Seri festivals and in association with rites of puberty and spiritual protection. The residents of Punta Chueca and El Desemboque will paint their faces in the traditional way for tourist photos; the going rate is a dollar a shot. The natural pigments are mixed from local ingredients, poured in seashells, and applied to the face with a bird feather.

Whether a Seri is painted or not, you should always ask for permission to take a photo before snapping away; photographers who haven't asked first have on occasion been stoned.

Beliefs and Festivals: Seri worship revolves around sea deities personified by dolphins, whales, and sea turtles, as well as an earth deity who appears in the form of a mole. Their biggest festivals are centered around the arrival of the *caguama* or sea turtle in May and during the fruiting of the pitahaya cactus in July.

Crafts: Basket connoisseurs agree that the Seri produce the finest basketry in Mexico. Before the Río Colorado was dammed, the Seri used to ford the river in huge, watertight baskets made from torote (a desert tree) fiber. Baskets of this caliber and size are still available but may cost hundreds of dollars. Smaller, heart-shaped baskets called *coritas* are more affordable.

A more recent Seri handicraft tradition involves the carving of ironwood (*palo fierro,* another Sonoran Desert tree) into smooth,

Seri woman with huge basket made of torote fiber

graceful figures—often dolphins and manta rays, or abstracts with a marine motif. Because it sinks when tossed into the sea, ironwood is traditionally used as a talisman by Seri fishermen to calm the Sea of Cortez. Thus to avoid spiritual offense, the Seri won't cut a live ironwood tree, preferring instead to work with fallen, dead wood. Many Seris have stopped carving altogether as local Mexicans are now producing figures with power tools; the Mexicans also cut live trees, so the supply of wood is dwindling as well. Along with the modernization of the production process, the souvenir industry has extended the range of ironwood sculptural subjects to include just about anything under the sun.

Also popular with tourists are inexpensive necklaces made from limpet shells and from the vertebrae of sharks and snakes.

GUAYMAS AND VICINITY

As early as 1539, Spanish explorers recognized the strategic and commercial potential of Guaymas's large natural harbor, protected from high winds and swells by Isla Pájaro. Occupied by fierce Guaymenas, the area didn't come under Spanish control until padres Salvatierra and Kino founded a short-lived mission pueblo here in 1701. This was soon destroyed by the natives, but another attempt was made in 1769 with a town called San José de Guaymas; this later became Villa de San Fernando de Guaymas and then Puerto de Altura, but eventually under Mexican independence the name reverted to Guaymas.

The port was thrice occupied by foreign military forces: first by U.S. naval troops during the 1847-48 Mexican-American War, then very briefly by freebooter William Walker in 1853, and again in 1865 by the French under Emperor Maximilian. A major turning point in the area's economic development was achieved when a rail line connecting Guaymas with Nogales on the U.S. border was opened in 1881.

Today Mexico's seventh largest port carries around four percent of the nation's total maritime cargo, most of which is shipped straight across the Sea of Cortez to Santa Rosalía, where it is sent by road to the western United States. Home to a large commercial fishing fleet, Guaymas also services 14% of Mexico's annual fishing take. Shrimp is the biggest earner; during shrimping season vendors stand on street corners and along the Bahía Empalme bridge east of town hawking pink crustaceans by the bucketful. Oysters are another important source of income—the bayfront is even constructed of oystershell landfill.

Busy Bahía de Guaymas is the city's main attraction. Although it's not beautiful in the travel-brochure sense, tours around its perimeter from Plaza del Pescador on the city harbor to Las Playitas opposite leave a different impression with each trip, depending on weather, time of day, and shipping activity. Even the bay islands, bristling with profuse stands of saguaro, seem to change color every few hours. Sunset bay cruises may be arranged through **Gary's Boat Trip** (tel. 622-6-00-49, 622-6-00-74).

The only points of sightseeing interest in the town itself are the **Palacio Municipal,** built in grand 19th-century Romanesque style, and the nearby **Parroquia de San Fernando,** a picturesque church next to the small but verdant Plaza 13 de Julio. The nearest beach is **Playa Miramar** at Bahía Bacochibampo, a palmy stretch of sand around a small bay that almost looks like it could have been lifted from the South Seas. Follow signs to "Colonía Miramar" just six km west of town.

Most visitors to Guaymas are on their way west to Bahía San Carlos or points farther south such as Alamos or Mazatlán. Others are on their way to or from the passenger ferry pier (south of town), with daily service between Guaymas and Santa Rosalía on the Baja California peninsula across the Sea of Cortez.

People driving through town rarely leave the Av. Serdán, the main business street lined with banks, restaurants, dentists, and supermarkets. Off-the-main-drag explorations are easier once you figure out that the **east-west streets** are *avenidas* numbered with Roman numerals, while the **north-south streets** are *calles* numbered with regular Arabic numerals.

One of the best times to visit Guaymas is during Carnaval, held the week before Lent (for a description of Carnaval, see "Festivals and Events," p. 57, in the "Out and About" chapter).

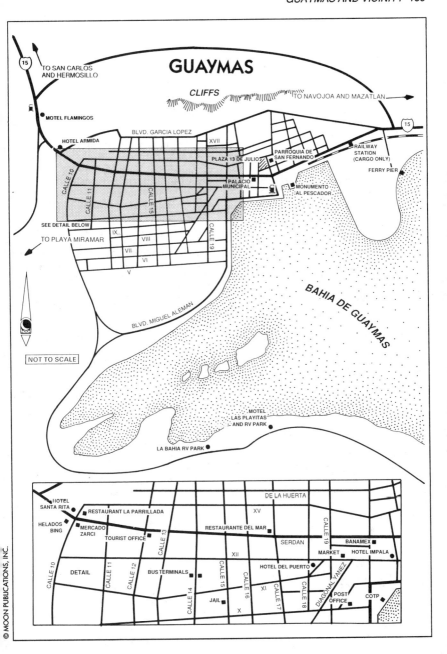

GUAYMAS

CLIFFS

TO SAN CARLOS
AND HERMOSILLO

TO NAVOJOA AND MAZATLAN

MOTEL FLAMINGOS

BLVD. GARCIA LOPEZ

HOTEL ARMIDA

XVII

PLAZA 13 DE JULIO

PARROQUIA DE
SAN FERNANDO

RAILWAY
STATION
(CARGO ONLY)

FERRY PIER

CALLE 10

CALLE 11

CALLE 15

PALACIO
MUNICIPAL

MONUMENTO
AL PESCADOR

SEE DETAIL BELOW

IX

VIII

VII

VI

V

CALLE 19

TO PLAYA MIRAMAR

BAHIA DE GUAYMAS

BLVD. MIGUEL ALEMAN

NOT TO SCALE

MOTEL
LAS PLAYITAS
AND RV PARK

LA BAHIA RV PARK

HOTEL
SANTA RITA

DE LA HUERTA

RESTAURANT LA PARRILLADA

XV

HELADOS
BING

MERCADO
ZARCI

TOURIST OFFICE

CALLE 13

RESTAURANTE DEL MAR

SERDAN

CALLE 19

BANAMEX

MARKET

HOTEL IMPALA

CALLE 10

DETAIL

CALLE 11

CALLE 12

BUS TERMINALS

CALLE 15

XII

CALLE 16

HOTEL DEL PUERTO

DIAGONAL YANEZ

CALLE 14

JAIL

X

XI

CALLE 17

CALLE 18

POST
OFFICE

COTP

© MOON PUBLICATIONS, INC.

Día de la Marina (June 1), when homage is paid to those mariners lost at sea, is another big festival in Guaymas.

Tours

Ecogrupos de Mexico, a new tour company specializing in nature excursions, runs a seven-day trip out of Guaymas to local Seri communities, the little-known Oasis Nacapules, and then by boat to the Sea of Cortez islands of San Pedro Nolasco, San Pedro Mártir, San Esteban, Rasa, Partida, and Angel del la Guarda. Each of these islands is an important habitat for various indigenous and migrating bird species, as well as for rare reptiles and native cacti. While at sea, you can observe dolphins, sea lions and other marine mammals.

During the boating segment of the trip, passengers sleep and eat all meals on board. This very unique trip costs US$1700, including all transport, accommodation, and meals. In Guaymas, you can contact Ecogrupos by phone at (622) 1-01-94 or by fax at (622) 1-20-30. In the U.S., contact Points of Exploration (tel. 212-691-0733, 212-649-3428), 325 W. 16th St., Suite 4W, New York, NY 10011.

This is the first trip of its kind to be offered out of Sonora and the itinerary looks exciting. If you have an opportunity to take the tour, please write the author with your comments. Ecogrupos also offers diving and whalewatching trips aboard their cruiser *Baja Treasure*.

ACCOMMODATIONS

Hotels And Motels

The three-story **Hotel Santa Rita** (tel. 622-4-14-64), at Av. Serdán and Calle Mesa at the west end of downtown, has adequate air-conditioned rooms with TV for US$22 s, US$27 d, or US$32 t. At the other end of town near the harbor, the slightly larger **Hotel Impala** (tel. 4-09-22) offers similar rooms at the same rates. Also in this price range is the well-run **Motel Flamingos** (tel. 4-09-61) west of town on Mexico 15, where rooms surrounding a parking lot cost US$22 s, US$25-30 d, or US$38 d in nicer, recently renovated rooms.

If you're planning to stay awhile, consider moving round the other side of the bay to **Motel Las Playitas** (tel. 2-27-27). Cheaper digs in town are available at **Motel Puerto** next door to the bus terminal on Calle 14 Sur and **Hotel del Puerto** near the municipal market at Diagonal Yáñez 92 and Calle 18. Both offer basic but tidy rooms with private baths for US$17 s/d.

The best highway hotel Guaymas offers is the modern and efficient **Armida Hotel** (tel. 800-6-47-06, 2-53-20 in Mexico; 800-732-0780 in the U.S.) on Mexico 15 at the west entrance into the city. Rated at four stars by the state, the Armida has rooms with phone, TV, and a/c for US$40-51. Hotel facilities include a pool, bar, video disco, and three restaurants.

Also at the upper end of the scale is the 60-year-old **Hotel Playa de Cortés** (tel. 2-02-21) on Playá Miramar, Bahía Bacochibampo. Originally built by the Southern Pacific Railroad, this faded but pleasant resort-style hotel offers a range of room rates depending on which wing you choose: US$58 in the original low rise, US$70 in the oceanview high rise, and US$133 for the new deluxe bungalows. Facilities include spacious grounds, tennis courts, and a pool.

RV Parks

Top choice in Guaymas is the well-kept trailer park at **Motel Las Playitas** (see "Hotels and Motels," above) on the peninsula at the south side of the bay. Spaces with full hookups cost just US$10 per day; monthly discounts are available. If Las Playitas is full, you can try **Bahía Trailer Court** (tel. 622-2-35-45), off the same road to Las Playitas. Spaces here cost US$9 per night or US$190 per month. Although not as cozy as Las Playitas, the Bahía does have a boat ramp. Small houses built over trailer slots sometimes rent by the month independently.

Hotel Playa de Cortés at Playa Miramar (see "Hotels and Motels," above) has a set of new full hookup slots with rates of around US$12 —this includes use of all hotel facilities. Also at Playa Miramar is **Escalante Trailer Park,** which was closed when the author visited—if it reopens, rates should run a bit lower than at the Playa de Cortés.

Empalme Accommodations

If you happen to find yourself stuck in Empalme for the night waiting for (or arriving from) a late train, **Hotel Jardín** (tel. 622-3-02-20) at Av. Reforma and Ocampo has decent rooms for around US$22 a night. **Hotel Baluarte** (tel. 3-23-80) at Av. Revolución and Calle 4 has basic rooms for as low as US$15.

FOOD

As Sonora's primary fishing port, Guaymas takes pride in its fresh seafood—virtually every menu in town features a section devoted to *pescados* or *mariscos*.

Seafood

$$-$$$ **Restaurant Bar Gary's** (tel. 622-2-54-81), Av. V and Calle 10. An old favorite for shrimp dishes, deviled crab, and squid salad. Also serves a range of continental and Mexican dishes. Open daily noon-midnight.

$$-$$$ **Restaurante Del Mar** (tel. 4-02-25) at Av. Serdán and Calle 17. Fresh seafood and steaks. Like Gary's, this restaurant receives regular gringo traffic and is priced accordingly. Open daily 12:30 p.m.-10:30 p.m.

$$-$$$ **Restaurant Bar Mirador** (tel. 2-70-10), on the top floor of the Edificio Vizcaíno Altos on Calle 22 (behind the Palacio Municipal). Fresh seafood with a city and bay view. The Mirador also specializes in Sonoran steaks. Open daily 1 p.m.-midnight.

Carne Asada

$$ **Jardines de Xochimilco** (tel. 4-27-99), on Mexico 15 just east of Motel Flamingos. A branch of the famous Hermosillo restaurant specializing in Sonoran-style *carne asada paquetes.* Open daily noon-midnight.

$$ **La Parrillada,** Av. Serdán near Calle 10. An informal place with good *carne asada* and tacos al carbón. Open daily 11 a.m.-10 p.m.

Chinese

$$ **Restaurante Jo-Wah.** Yet another spinoff from Hermosillo, specializing in Cantonese-style seafood. Huge servings. Open daily noon-11 p.m.

Mexican

$ **Mercado Zarci,** Av. Serdán between Calle 10 and 11. The cafeteria attached to this supermarket has an inexpensive but tasty menu fea-

turing many *platillos típicos,* tacos, burritos, enchiladas, *chiles rellenos,* Mexican soups, and breakfasts. Excellent value.

You can buy fresh tortillas at the supermarket's **Señor Maíz** *tortillería.*

Other

$-$$ **Jax Snax (Jax Pizza),** corner of Av. Serdán and Calle 14. Small, casual spot with decent pizza, spaghetti, salads, and draft beer. Open daily 8 a.m.-11 p.m.

$ **Helados Bing,** Av. Serdán and Calle 10. A branch of Mexico's best ice-cream parlor chain. Open 11 a.m.-11 p.m.

$ **Las 1000 Tortas,** south side of Av. Serdán between Calle 17 and 18. Efficient and clean place featuring inexpensive breakfasts, *tortas,* hamburgers, *antojitos,* and *comida corrida.* Open daily 7 a.m.-9 p.m.

SHOPPING

Guaymas is a good place to put in for supplies if you're heading for a long-term stay in San Carlos or elsewhere in the vicinity. **Mercado Zarci** at Av. Serdán and Calle 10 is a huge grocery/department store with everything from tortillas to cassette tapes, plus a concession that carries camping, fishing, and diving gear.

On the highway just north of town is the newish **Plaza de Vigia,** a huge, modern shopping center with attached Ley supermarket, cinema, and various shops selling shoes, toys, and other mall goods.

The **Mercado Central,** on Av. Rodríguez between Calle de Alemán and Calle 19, has the usual selection of household goods and fresh foodstuffs.

GUAYMAS INFORMATION

The local SECTUR office (tel. 622-4-29-32) is at the corner of Av. Serdán and Calle 12, above an electrical supply store named "La Bombilla." The tourist office has moved several times in recent years—if it has moved again, inquire at the Palacio Municipal for the latest location. Information on both Guaymas and San Carlos is available here.

The local area code is 622.

You'll find several banks in the vicinity of the Palacio Municipal—the Banamex on Av. Serdán west of the Palacio is the best for foreign exchange services.

GUAYMAS TRANSPORT

Air

Guaymas International Airport (tel. 622-2-33-34) is located at Km 2 along the Guaymas-San Carlos highway off Mexico 15. **Aeroméxico** (tel. 2-01-23; city ticket office at Calle 16 and Serdán) fields direct flights to La Paz, Tucson, and Mexico City.

Bus

The main inter-city bus terminals are on Calle 14 Sur between Av. XII Pte. and XIII Pte. (Av. Rodríguez). TNS (tel. 622-2-70-07) and Tres Estrellas de Oro (tel. 2-12-71) share a terminal on one side of the street, while Transportes del Pacífico (tel. 2-05-75) is on the opposite side. Together the three companies run first- and second-class buses to every major town in Sonora and Sinaloa, plus Guadalajara, Mexico City, and Mexicali. Regional bus lines Transportes del Río Sonora and Autobuses de Guaymas serve smaller towns nearby.

Buses to San Carlos (US$1.50) leave frequently from Calle 19 and Calle Yáñez near the municipal market. If you need transport to the Empalme railway station, catch a red bus along Calle 20.

Train

Although Guaymas has no passenger railway station, the Empalme station is only 9.5 km (six miles) east of town across Bahía Empalme. The Pacífico No. 2 train heads for points south (Ciudad Obregón, Culiacán, Mazatlán, Tepic, and Guadalajara), while in the opposite direction the No. 1 train goes to Hermosillo and Nogales. See the railway schedule on pp. 86-87 for departure and arrival times.

Ferry

Tickets for the ferry to Santa Rosalía are sold at the SEMATUR ferry pier (tel. 622-2-23-24, fax 622-2-33-93) east of town off Ave. Serdán—turn right (south) just before the big power plant.

Advance tickets may be purchased here daily 7 a.m.-2 p.m.

Two passenger ferries are currently running out of Guaymas, the 550-passenger *Benito Juárez* and the smaller *Puerto Vallarta*. For fare and schedule information, see the "By Ferry from Baja" section under "Getting There."

Sometimes tickets are sold for a second men-only crossing to La Paz on Tuesdays, a trip referred to as *carga negra* or "black freight" because of the sunburnt faces of the mostly seamen passengers. Presumably women aren't sold tickets for the *carga negra* boats because no separate onboard facilities are available for women.

Auto Rental

Budget (tel. 622-2-55-00, west end of Blvd. García López, or 2-14-50 at the airport) and **Hertz** (tel. 2-10-00, airport) have cars for rent starting at US$28 per day plus kilometer charges.

SAN CARLOS

The names "San Carlos," "Bahía San Carlos," and "San Carlos Bay" generally refer to an area about 11 km (seven miles) northwest of Guaymas that encompasses Playa San Francisco, a long, stony beach parallel to the Guaymas-San Carlos highway; the yacht harbor (Bahía San Carlos proper) formed by two rocky peninsulas that jut into the Sea of Cortez; and the curving, sandy beach of Playa los Algodones on Ensenada los Algodones (also known as "Sonora Bay"). Backed by the 600-meter (2,000-foot) Sierra de Bacochibampo, the area is one of the most scenic coastal areas in Northern Mexico. Several islands in the bay—Venado, San Pedro Mártir, San Nicolás, La Ventana—add to the pleasing topographic variation.

This is also the first coastal area south of the U.S. border where you begin seeing palm trees with regularity. Just offshore, the abundant marinelife produced by the **Guaymas Trench**, a 1,500-meter-deep (5,000-foot-deep) sea canyon, attracts sportfishers from all over Mexico and North America. A well-protected bay with full-service marina has also made San Carlos the pleasure boating capital of the eastern Sea of Cortez.

SAN CARLOS

TO GUAYMAS AND AIRPORT

SOLIMAR HOTEL AND COUNTRY CLUB

TETAKAWI AND TOTONAKA TRAILER PARKS

HOTEL FIESTA SAN CARLOS

MOTEL CRESTON

CLUB MED

COSTA DEL MAR CONDOMINUMUMS

SAN CARLOS GRILL

LA POSADA DE SAN CARLOS

HOWARD JOHNSON PLAZA HOTEL

MARINA SAN CARLOS

RESTAURANTE EL YATE

PLAYA LOS ALGODONES

SHANGRI-LA RV PARK

MARINA REAL

TETAS DE CABRA

BAHIA DE SAN CARLOS

PENINSULA DEL CARACOL

GUAYMAS-SAN CARLOS HWY

SEA OF CORTEZ

0   500 m

© MOON PUBLICATIONS, INC.

Spared from the commercial fishing and shipping industries of Guaymas by government designation as a tourist zone, over the last decade San Carlos has developed into a small but full-blown vacation and retirement colony. Permanent, year-round residents here number around 2,000; in peak tourist seasons the population may swell as high as 6,000. San Carlos has enough markets, hotels, restaurants, and trailer parks—not to mention a country club—to make a visit pleasant, but so far they're few enough in number that the area almost never feels crowded.

The heaviest concentration of retirement/vacation homes blankets hilly **Peninsula del Caracol** at the bay's east end. Many of the Caracol homes are custom designed and have magnificent sea views; the neighborhood even has its own private police patrols. On the bay side of the peninsula is a small, sandy cove with shady coconut palms.

But without a doubt the nicest beach in San Carlos is Playa los Algodones ("Cotton Beach"—a reference to the fine white sand), west of the twin peaks known as Tetas de Cabra or "Goat Teats." Two resort hotels, a condo development, and a marina share the beach that was once used as a location setting for the American films *Catch 22* and *Lucky Lady*. If you're driving here, take the small road between Howard Johnson and Club Med to reach the beach, which is open to all visitors whether or not they're staying at either of the resorts. Another access road is located just beyond the Club Med wall.

Climate And Seasons

Temperatures average a mild 20.9° C (69° F) in the winter, zooming to 35°C (95° F) in summer, with scant rain falling mostly in the late summer. Early fall—when the ocotillo leaves come out following summer rains—is one of the best times to visit. Peak tourist seasons are Dec.-

May (mostly North American snowbirds) and July (Mexicans).

Accommodations

Hotels and Motels: Most of San Carlos's places to stay are strung out along Playa San Francisco. The first on approach from Guaymas at Km 8.5 is the **Hotel Fiesta San Carlos** (tel. 622-8-02-29), which has nice beach grounds, a tiny pool, and clean-appearing but musty-smelling rooms for US$38 s, US$45 d, US$52 t, US$58 q. With kitchen, the rates are US$45 s, US$54 d, US$62 t, US$70 d. All rooms come with complimentary American breakfast.

Next up, across the road from the beach, the **Hacienda Tetakawi Trailer Park** (tel. 6-02-20, fax 6-02-48) and **Totonaka Trailer Park** (tel. 6-03-23, 6-04-81) have basic efficiency apartments that rent for around US$25 a night. Tetakawi is currently building a new suite-style hotel that will probably cost a bit more.

When available, a good choice is the clean and well-run **Motel Creston** (tel. 6-00-20), farther along on the beach side of the road, with rooms for US$27 s/d in the off-season, up to US$55 in high season (Dec. 19-May 1), when it is often full. Facilities at the Creston include a small but well-maintained pool, a few barbecue grills, and a palm-shaded courtyard.

West of Motel Creston on the other side of the road (about 20 minutes' walk from the beach) is **Solimar Hotel and Country Club** (tel. 6-00-07, fax 2-04-48), a newish brick-and-tile con-dotel development where hotel rooms cost

US$37 per night, studio condos US$57, one-bedroom condos US$84, two bedrooms US$124, and three bedrooms US$158. Hotel and condo guests have use of the club's 18-hole golf course, pool, and 14 tennis courts.

On the highway beyond the country club, a turnoff to the left (Km 11.5) leads to a nearly private beach and **La Posada de San Carlos** (tel. 6-00-72 or 706-226-0015 in the U.S.), one of the first San Carlos tourist developments. A variety of rooms is available in different buildings, starting at US$40 for a standard room in the original single-story building or in the back of the newer high rise, US$55 for a high-rise ocean view, US$58 for ocean view and balcony, US$63 for beachfront motel-style units, US$75 for larger beachfront units, and US$100 for a family bungalow. Facilities include an airy restaurant, two pools, a beach *palapa* bar, and two tennis courts.

Up on the Peninsula del Caracol near Restaurante El Yate is the simple **Apartamento Ferrer,** with five apartments with an angled view of the Marina San Carlos area for US$20-25 a night. Farther along, on a section of the peninsula known among gringos as "Pelican Point," the **Shangri-La RV Park** used to rent simple cottages for US$20-32.50. The park has been closed for renovations and at press time the management was uncertain whether the cottages would stay.

Luxury Resorts: Playa los Algodones, San Carlos's prettiest beach, is the site of two hotel resort establishments along with a couple of

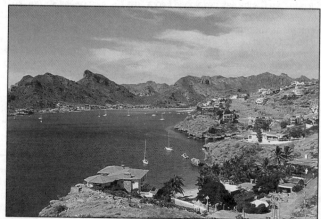

San Carlos

just-getting-off-the-ground condo developments. All rooms at the **Howard Johnson Plaza-Hotel and Resort** (tel. 6-07-77; 800-7-02-04 toll free in Mexico; 800-654-2000 in the U.S.; fax 6-07-78) have sunset and ocean views, satellite TV, phone, servibar, and all the other amenities you'd expect at Sonora's only five-star hotel. The attractive beachfront pool-and-*palapa* design takes maximum advantage of the natural setting; other facilities include tennis courts, outdoor Jacuzzi, restaurant, coffeeshop, lobby bar, and a full range of water-sport equipment rentals. When Ho-Jo first opened, rates started at US$165 but have recently been adjusted to US$119 s, US$129 d for the Dec. 19-June 17 high season; US$99 s, US$109 d the remainder of the year.

Farther on, past the Costa del Mar condo project, **Club Med Sonora Bay** covers an extensive, fenced-in section of the beach (though the beach is open to the public) and offers seven-day packages for US$656 (plus 20% for single rooms), including all meals and recreational activities (boating, diving, windsurfing). Other options include a 24-hour package for US$104; a night without meals for US$59; a half day (2 p.m. till closing) for US$54; a half day (11 a.m.-5 p.m.) with lunch and activities for US$44; and a disco-dinner package for US$25. Club Med's rooms are nowhere near as nice as Howard Johnson's but the all-inclusive rates and exclusive veneer still appeal to some vacationers.

RV Parks: San Carlos has several adequate RV/camping facilities, though none of them really stand out. Since the closing of the Shangri-La, most RVers stay at one of three parks clustered together on the opposite side of the road from the beach near Hotel Fiesta San Carlos, all with Amerindian names. The well-established **Tetakawi Trailer Park** (tel. 6-02-20) has spaces with full hookups and satellite cable for US$12.50 per day, US$78.75 per week, or US$235 per month. **Yori RV Park** (tel. 6-01-50) has some less expensive spaces for US$10 per night, others with shelter for US$12-15 or tents/campers for US$8. **Totonaka Trailer Park** (tel. 6-03-23), between Tetakawi and Yori, is priced similarly to the Tetakawi; the Totonaka has a coin laundry which is open to the public.

The **Shangri-La Trailer Park** (tel. 6-02-35, fax 6-02-63) on the beach at Pelican Point has over 300 spaces with full hookups that are now under renovation. When reopened, they will probably cost US$10-12 per day.

Food

The restaurants in San Carlos are generally casual affairs with good but not outstanding food. The very popular **Rosa's Cantina** on the main road along Playa San Francisco specializes in *tortas,* tacos, enchiladas, *carne asada,* and pecan pie. Rosa's is open daily 7:30 a.m.-10 p.m.; a bulletin board inside carries community announcements and sale notices for boats and real estate. **El Yate,** on a hillside overlooking Marina San Carlos, is equally popular (especially during the 5-7 p.m. happy hour) and offers fresh seafood, Mexican standards, and steak.

Slightly more upscale than any of the above is **San Carlos Grill,** on the road to Playa los Algodones just past the Marina San Carlos turnoff. The menu features all the gringo favorites, including steak, seafood, continental, and toned-down Mexican. For fresh seafood, **La Roca,** overlooking the shore between Hotel Fiesta San Carlos and Motel Creston, is a good choice.

Near Motel Creston, the friendly **Bananas Restaurant Bar** features laid-back, *palapa*-roof ambience, paintings by local artists on the walls, draft beer, and Mexican breakfasts from US$1.

La Michoacán, near the entrance to the Caracol development and El Yate, sells *licuados, aguas frescas, paletas,* and ice cream. Groceries are available from several small markets near El Yate; **Super Frutería** is the best-stocked.

Recreation

Boating: Marina San Carlos (tel. 622-6-02-30) is the main center for boating activities in San Carlos. Several places near the marina offer sales and repair services for boats and outboard motors. Rates for slips or moorings (400 spaces total) at the marina are US$3 per day up to 10 feet, US$11.50 per day 10-50 feet, or US$85 per month. Facilities include showers and a PEMEX station; dry storage is available for US$55 per month.

The newer Marina Real at the east end of Sonora Bay (Playa los Algodones) has 325 slips at similar rates. According to the Sonoran government, more marinas are planned for the area in the future.

During the second week of October, sailors compete in the **Cristóbal Colón (Christopher Columbus) Regatta**.

Fishing: Because of the nearby Guaymas Trench, San Carlos waters offer the best sportfishing along the Sonora coast. Offshore catches include marlin, sailfish, dorado, pargo, cochito, and grouper; inshore there are triggerfish, seabass, seatrout, sierra, and others. The best overall fishing season (especially for billfish) is early summer, although there's something biting all year round. The **Sociedad Cooperativa Tetabampo de Pesca Deportiva** (tel. 6-00-11) near Marina San Carlos organizes sportfishing charters. A deep-sea fishing tournament is held each September.

Diving: The rocky outcroppings at either end of the bays and the offshore islands provide good snorkeling and diving opportunities. **El Mar Diving Center** near Motel Creston and **El Centro de Deportes de Sonora** (tel. 6-09-29) opposite the PEMEX station in town (with a branch on the beach at La Posada de San Carlos) arrange dive trips, air, and equipment rental.

Golf and Tennis: The **San Carlos Country Club** (tel. 6-03-39) has 14 world-class tennis courts and an 18-hole, 6,617-yard golf course with Sea of Cortez views. Public play is permitted upon payment of daily use fees.

Other Sports: The marine and terrestrial environments around San Carlos are perfect for sailing, windsurfing, sea kayaking, and mountain biking; **El Centro de Deportes de Sonora** (tel. 6-09-29) offers instruction and equipment rental for all of these.

Transport

The only regular public transport to San Carlos is the daily red buses from Guaymas (see the "Guaymas Transport" section for details), which stop along the Guaymas-San Carlos highway and terminate near the minimarket district near Marina San Carlos and El Yate. Marina San Carlos has a **PEMEX** station.

Taxis to/from the airport (see "Guaymas Transport" for flight details) cost around US$10 to the Playa San Francisco hotel strip, US$20 to Playa los Algodones.

CIUDAD OBREGON TO LOS MOCHIS

CIUDAD OBREGON

Obregón got its start as a railroad station in 1921, when it was still called "Cajeme" after a Yaqui chieftain who led a revolt against the Mexican authorities in the 1880s. In 1924 the city's name was changed to honor the late revolutionary general and Mexican president Alvaro Obregón. With the damming of the Río Yaqui, a half-million acres of former desert surrounding Ciudad Obregón have become a major agricultural producer, yielding tremendous amounts of wheat and cotton for domestic and international markets. As a result this city of 400,000 has one of the highest per capita incomes in Mexico, as evidenced by the palatial houses and groomed lawns in several residential districts.

Other than the Yaqui Museum, Ciudad Obregón has little of tourist interest. For bass anglers it serves a supply point for trips to nearby Presa Alvaro Obregón. It is also an important transit point for people arriving by air on their way to colonial Alamos. Those interested in Yaqui Indian culture may also use the city as a base for visits to the Río Yaqui valley homelands.

Museo De Los Yaquis

This small museum housed in the public library (Calle Allende and 5 de Febrero) next to the Palacio Municipal contains ethnological exhibits on the Yaquis, including historical photos, costumes, household utensils (among them reed bird cages, "indispensable to the Yaquis"), and a facsimile of a Yaqui dwelling. A few Yaqui crafts, including *pascola* masks, are on sale near the entrance. The museum is open Mon.-Fri. 8 a.m.-6 p.m.; admission is US$0.20.

Zona Indígena Yaqui

Fifteen km southeast of Guaymas begins a Yaqui reservation that extends southward some 80 km (50 miles) to Ciudad Obregón. Much admired and feared for their tenacity, the Yaquis managed to fend off both the Spanish and the Mexicans throughout most of their history, but in the 1900s many Yaqui families were deported to the Yucatán peninsula. The "indigenous zone" is a Mexican gesture toward the restoration of Yaqui homelands. The Yaquis originally occupied a much wider territory.

Most of the Yaquis living in the zone are bilingual in Spanish and their mother tongue. They make their homes in the Río Yaqui valley and support themselves through agriculture, fishing, and the collection of cactus fruit and other edible desert plants. Some settlements still maintain traditional leadership councils consisting of *gobernador, pueblo mayor, capitán,* and *comandante,* all of whom are chosen by the pueblo from persons over 50 years of age who have proven their standing in the community.

The towns of Cruz de Piedra, Pótam, Vícam, and Bácum are worth visiting during Semana Santa or Día de los Muertos to observe native dances such as the famous *danza del venado.* Bácum also has a mission church, *Iglesia de Santa Rosa de Lima,* of minor interest for its modern Yaqui artwork.

LA DANZA DEL VENADO (DEER DANCE)

Dances revolving around deer symbolism are common among the Amerindian tribes of Northern Mexico, but the Yaqui/Mayo version is the most famous. Dancers who portray the deer are trained in the proper movements from a young age and have the title "Maso" (deer) added to their names. The costume and dance ornaments—including deer antlers—must be handled with care and proper etiquette to evoke the spirit of the dance. Musical accompaniment is played on Yaqui flute, harp, violin, and percussion instruments.

Basically the dance is a dramatic representation of life-and-death cycles in which a deer—a revered animal that symbolizes "good" in Yaqui culture—is hunted by coyotes (also sacred but feared). In the drama, the deer kills one of the coyotes in self defense; the coyote is reincarnated as a bow hunter, which in turn kills the deer in a poignant finale.

Presa Alvaro Obregón

This huge impoundment of the Río Yaqui 42 km (26 miles) north of the city is a major bass-fishing destination. The main boating and fishing access is via **Marina del Rey** at the lake's southern end, where you'll find cabins and trailer spaces (with sewer hookups) for rent, plus a small cafe-store where boats and fishing guides may be hired. In season, hunting trips for white-tailed deer, white-winged dove, and quail can also be arranged. From Marina del Rey the lake extends some 48 km (30 miles) northward; the only other access is via the fish camp of Alamos (not to be confused with colonial Alamos farther south) near the northern end, accessible by an unpaved road that curves around the west side of the lake.

Accommodations

Hotels in this city tend to cost more than you might expect, probably because of the steady business traffic. The nicer, and more expensive, hotels are lined up along Blvd. Miguel Alemán, the main avenue through town (linked to Mexico 15). These include **Hotel Nainari** (tel. 641-4-09-40), **Motel Costa de Oro** (tel. 4-17-76), and **Hotel Valle del Yaqui** (tel. 3-39-69), all modern and efficient places on Miguel Alemán with rooms for around US$56 s/d. Because of the competition, one or more of these upscale establishments is usually running "promotional" specials as low as US$43.

At the budget end are three *casas de huéspedes* on Calle Coahuila Sur, not far from the bus terminal: **Yaqui, Rosa,** and **Vallarta.** Accommodations are very basic (no a/c), with *baños colectivos,* and cost US$10-15 (cheaper weekly rates are available).

Cheaper yet is the **Villa Deportiva Juvenile** (tel. 5-15-60), west of the city center at Laguna de Nainari s/n. Dorm beds at the hostel cost just US$1.50 per night, and reservations can be made as many as 15 days in advance. Although the hostel is some distance from the bus terminal and city center, these areas can be reached by city bus in about 15 minutes.

Food

For fresh seafood, try **Mariscos La Palapa** at Blvd. Miguel Alemán 628 or **Merendero Playas de Mazatlán** at Calle Durango and No Reelección. Good *comida sonorense—carne asada,* quesadillas made with huge *tortillas de agua, cocido,* etc.—is available at a number of places in town, including **Restaurante El Bronco** (Calle Sinaloa 219), **Restaurante Los Apaches** (Calle Veracruz Sur 253), yet another branch of Hermosillo's **Restaurante Jardines Xochimilco** (Blvd. Miguel Alemán Sur 660), and **Merendero de José Luis** (Calle Durango and No Reelección). A *combinación* at movie-postered Merendero de José Luis includes *salsa dina* (a spicy soup), beans, Sonoran quesadilla, and *carne asada* for US$8; good seafood here, too.

Shopping

A half dozen leather shops in the vicinity of the bus terminal fashion handmade saddles, bridles, *chaparreras,* and other accoutrements for the working *vaquero.*

Transport

Air: **Noroeste** and **Aeroméxico** have direct flights to Ciudad Obregón airport from Culiacán and Hermosillo. Aeroméxico also has flights from Guadalajara; most people flying in from abroad use this connection, since it provides a wide selection of international flights to Guadalajara. The Aeroméxico office (tel. 641-3-21-90) in Ciudad Obregón is at Calle No Reelección Ote. 509.

The airport is about 13.5 km (eight miles) south of the city off Mexico 15. Taxis to and from town cost US$15, *colectivos* US$6.50.

Bus: **Estrella Blanca, Tres Estrellas de Oro,** and **TNS** operate buses to major towns throughout Sonora and Sinaloa, plus Tepic, Guadalajara, Mexico City, Tijuana, Tecate, and Mexicali, from the huge Central Camionera at the south end of town.

The regional **Autobuses de Los Mochis** has buses to Huatabampo, Nogales, Culiacán, Guasave, and Los Mochis.

Train: Ciudad Obregón's railway station is west of the highway opposite Calle Hidalgo. There are first- and second-class trains north to Hermosillo, Nogales, and Mexicali, and south to Mazatlán, Tepic, and Guadalajara. See the "Railway Schedule," pp. 86-87, for schedule information.

Driving: Several PEMEX stations carry Magna Sin, among them a 24-hour station in the center of town. Another PEMEX at the south end of town on Mexico 15 (near the Juárez statue) has a car wash and oil change service.

Four local agencies offer auto rental services: **Budget** (tel. 4-11-88; Blvd. Miguel Alemán Nte. 669), **Hertz** (tel. 4-71-40; Blvd. Miguel Alemán and Allende), **Avis** (tel. 4-81-44; Calle Hidalgo and 5 de Febrero), and **Facil** (tel. 3-18-32; Calle Hidalgo Ote. 903).

Information

Ciudad Obregón's helpful, English-speaking tourism office (tel. 641-4-01-12) is in Allende Plaza at Calle Allende and Sinaloa (a block and a half west of Blvd. Miguel Alemán).

Telephone: The area code for Ciudad Obregón is 641. For local police, call 3-51-97, Cruz Roja (Red Cross) 5-00-88.

NAVOJOA

Started as a Mayo Indian mission pueblo in the 17th century, Navojoa (pop. 100,000) has grown into an important center for cotton production. The many wheat fields and flour mills in the vicinity have also earned the town its reputation as "Mexico's Breadbasket." Light manufacturing contributes as well to the local economy; American guitar manufacturer C.F. Martin has a plant here which makes its "Backpacker" travel guitar.

Today Navojoa's Mayos, closely related in language and custom to the Yaquis, have for the most part assimilated into mainstream Mexican culture. To supplement incomes earned by farm labor, a few Mayos still produce traditional handicrafts such as sarapes and baskets, which you can find for sale at the municipal market at Calle Morelos and Allende. Mayo dances (including a version of the deer dance almost identical to that of the Yaquis) are performed during festivals, particularly on Día de San Juan (June 24), Día de los Muertos (Nov. 2), Día de la Virgen de Guadalupe (Dec. 12), and Semana Santa (the week before Easter).

Among Mexicans, Navojoa is known as the birthplace of the late president and revolutionary war hero Alvaro Obregón (buried in nearby Huatabampo). For most visitors, Navojoa serves as a launching point for side trips to the little-known beach at **Huatabampito** and the quaint ex-mining town of **Alamos.**

Accommodations

The four-star **Motel Del Río** (tel. 642-2-03-31), north of town next to the Río Mayo on Mexico 15, has comfortable, air-conditioned rooms for US$40-50 a night. The nearby, well-run **Alameda Trailer Park** (tel. 2-14-14) rents RV spaces with full hookups for US$11 a day.

Hotel Belem at Blvd. Pesqueira 411 (Blvd. Pesqueira is the main avenue connecting with Mexico 15) has cheaper rooms in the US$18-24 range. Also on Blvd. Pesqueira, toward the southern edge of town, is the three-star **Hotel Colonial** with decent air-conditioned accommodation for around US$30.

Food

Navojoa is renowned for *pollo asado* (grilled chicken), so you'll find many *tacos de pollo asado* stands and restaurants in town. One of best and most convenient places to eat for folks passing through is **Tip's** on the main highway through town. This clean, efficient, air-conditioned restaurant offers a wide range of *antojitos,* steaks, soups, and salads at reasonable prices. **Restaurante Quinta El Asadero,** near Motel Del Río on Mexico 15, is good for *carne asada.*

Transport

You'll find the terminal for buses to Alamos and Huatabampo at Av. Guerrero and Calle Rincón.

In 1992-93 traffic snarls were common in the city as streets were being extensively repaired. Once the major repairs are complete, the transition from Mexico 15 to Sonora 001 (the two-lane highway to Alamos) should be easier.

ALAMOS

This Sonoran colonial paragon set in the foothills of the Sierra Madre Occidental was visited by Spanish conquistador Coronado in 1531 but didn't take root until silver was discovered in 1683. Originally named "Real de los Frailes" (Mining Camp of the Friars—a reference to two nearby peaks that resemble monkish figures) and later "Real de la Limpia Concepción de los Alamos," the town had reached a population of 30,000 by 1781. At its peak it was the wealthiest town in Sonora and attracted immigrants from all over the Pacific, including a number of Chinese and Japanese (the latter even founded a silk factory) who were expelled in 1916 for wielding too much economic power.

A series of rebellions by Yaqui mine laborers, followed by the 1910-20 revolution, brought all mining to a halt by the 1920s—the town quickly declined. Today only around 6,000 residents remain, many of them expatriate North Americans who have restored the charming Sonoran-style casas wrapped around interior courtyards in the center of town. In a twist on the usual pattern, Alamos has managed to hold onto a traditional feel partially because of (rather than in spite of) the gringo presence. Around 200 Americans and Canadians have houses here but fewer than a dozen live here year-round. North American interest in Alamos has grown following an article that appeared in *Town and Country* magazine in 1991.

The expat group here is a different breed from that found along the coast; although most gringo homeowners—like their San Carlos-Bahía Kino counterparts—are only winter residents, many take the time to learn Spanish and are interested in cultural events. Some visitors might take the cynical view that the casa lords are turning Alamos into a gringo fantasy of what they think Mexico *should* be. Some may find the social atmosphere a bit rich as well; a local English-language publication suggests that Americans come to Alamos because, among other reasons, "Household and garden help is available so that one can live graciously," and "The attitude of the natives...make[s] contact with service people pleasant."

Romanticists, on the other hand, may find Alamos almost a living dream. Declared a National Historic Monument by the Mexican government, the town has no billboards and no neon; every sign or exterior renovation, in fact, must be approved as stylistically compatible before being displayed. The streets are swept cleaner here than anywhere else in Mexico. (For an idea of what Alamos might look like without the expat influence, visit El Fuerte in Sinaloa.)

Because Alamos has been isolated from the rest of the Mexican world for so long, a few of the older native residents still speak a dialect mixed with 17th-century Spanish that has managed to survive over three centuries. Most of the Mexican population now live on the outskirts of town; downtown residences have almost all been purchased by North Americans, several of whom are involved in (or have retired from) the U.S motion picture industry.

There is little to do in Alamos beyond wandering the narrow cobblestoned streets, admiring the stately architecture, and soaking up the atmosphere of Old Mexico. The entire town can easily be seen on foot in less than two hours.

Seasons And Geography

Because of Alamos's western sierra location (elev. 450 meters/1,500 feet) in a rain shadow of the Sonoran Desert as well as in the north-south transition zone between Sonoran thornscrub and Sonoran tropical deciduous forest, five distinct seasons are recognizable. The "foresummer," dry and hot, lasts May through June; trees are leafless and dormant, the cicadas are practically shrieking, and only the toughest gringos hang out in town. During the summer rainy season July-Sept., 13 cm (five inches) of rain can fall in 10 weeks, filling the two arroyos that cradle the town and causing local vegetation to green and flower. In late September and October it's dry and hot again, then in November it cools off for the mild winter season, when gentle rains bring spring blooms.

As the winter months offer the most pleasant weather, the tourist/winter resident season runs Nov.-March, with a definite Dec.-Jan. peak.

Sights

Plazas: The town's visual centerpiece is the tidy **Plaza de Armas,** surrounded by houses that have been converted into inns, restaurants, and a museum. During the winter, music ensembles perform folk music and opera in the plaza's wrought-iron kiosk, which was built in Mazatlán in 1904.

Commercial life revolves around a small municipal market and line of shops adjacent to the **Plaza Alameda**—shaded by large alamos (cottonwood trees)—between calles Rosales and Morelos. The traditional Mexican evening promenade tends to focus on Plaza Alameda (just northwest) rather than Plaza de Armas.

La Parroquia de la Purísima Concepción: This large stone church on the Plaza de Armas was completed in 1786, after the adobe original—built during the mining heyday of the late 17th century—was destroyed in a 1772 Yaqui

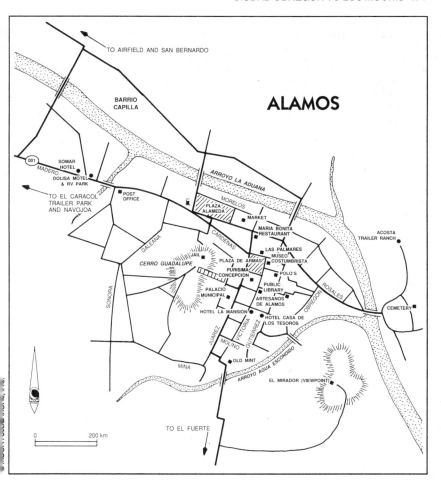

uprising. Of four bells in the single bell tower, one was forged locally while three hail from Spain; the exterior clock came from Rome. Inside the church is a late baroque-style altar. Among other unique features are the porcelain plates set into the belltower exterior; these were supposedly donated by the women of Alamos in 1804. Although many of the plates were shot out during the revolutionary period, a few can still be seen.

Beginning with a church festival on Dec. 8, Purísima Concepción stays very active throughout the Christmas and New Year's season, which coincides with the high tourist season.

Museo Costumbrista de Sonora: This small museum off the Plaza de Armas on Calle Victoria was established in 1984 and contains historical exhibits on Alamos mining (one room is plastered to look like a mine interior), fashion, printing, coin minting (silver coins were once produced here), and the early cultivation of wheat, tobacco, and citrus. Open Wed.-Sun. 9 a.m.-1 p.m. and 3-6 p.m. Admission is free (donations accepted).

Restored Homes: From the outside, the many restored mansions in Alamos appear similar: imposing, blocklike, single-story structures with grand entryways and tall, iron-grilled windows. The most elaborate casas feature *portales,* sheltered walkways characterized by Doric columns topped with Roman arches. Behind the facades, the houses follow a U- or L-shaped plan around a courtyard, where residents have expressed their individual tastes with varied interior design schemes—some traditional and some quite innovative. The least successful renovations mix motifs from all over colonial Mexico instead of sticking with the understated Andalusian style brought to Alamos directly from Spain in 1770.

The best way to view the interior restorations without collecting individual invitations is to join one of the **House & Garden Tours** given each Saturday at 10 a.m. starting from the public library at Calle Comercio 2. The cost is US$7 per person, which includes coffee and cookies served at the library. Weekday tours can sometimes be arranged by stopping in at the library a few days ahead of time.

El Cárcel: Promoted as one of the town's tourist attractions, this ancient-looking stone jail sits on Cerro Guadalupe in the middle of town. Only six inmates at a time can be held here, with maximum sentences of three years—more serious offenders are sent to Ciudad Obregón or Hermosillo. Inmates support themselves by making hatbands, bolos, and belts from horsehair; these can be purchased from the yard in front of the jail. The main reason to visit the jail is to take advantage of city views from the hill. To get there, ascend the stone stairs at the end of the alley next to the Palacio Municipal (off Calle Juárez).

Town Tour: Rotund Alamos native "Candy Joe" (José Trinidar) leads two-hour, English-language walking tours (US$5 per person) that take in historical sights as well as one or two restored casa interiors. You can usually find Joe at his crafts and jumping-bean shop on Calle Rosales near the municipal market.

El Mirador: Drive or walk south on Calle Juárez and follow signs reading "Camino al Mirador" to reach a hill with the best townscape view. Several barbecue grills and a gazebo have recently been built at the summit.

La Aduana: This almost abandoned mining town near Alamos is famous for its simple **Iglesia de Nuestra Señora de la Balvanera.** The church was built at the site where a saint sup-

posedly appeared in a vision atop a cactus; when the vision-seers approached the cactus, the saint vanished but a rich silver vein was suddenly visible nearby. Growing out of the side of the church about three to four meters off the ground is a "miracle" cactus (it appears to be a pitahaya) as if to remind the faithful of the event. Among the Mayos, this church is very holy; Mayos and other believers will walk from Navojoa to this church for the Dec. 12 Festival Guadalupana to repay favors granted by the Virgin of Guadalupe.

A recently opened *artesanía* in the village sells native handicrafts, including small pouches fashioned from goat scrotums.

To reach the village, take the signed dirt road at Minas Nuevas, seven km (4.5 miles) south of Alamos on Sonora 001, and then proceed east about 3.5 km (two miles) to the village. The road is rough, winding, and sandy in spots.

Accommodations

Visitors and seasonal residents start arriving around Thanksgiving; by the end of March most are gone. January is consistently the busiest month when it's really necessary to have advance room reservations.

Hotels and Motels: Most out-of-town visitors choose to stay at one of the restored colonial casas near Plaza de Armas. Two of the nicest share the west end of Calle Obregón, two blocks south of the plaza. **Hotel Casa de los Tesoros** (tel. 642-8-00-10, fax 642-8-04-00, A.P. 12, Alamos, Son. 85760), built as a convent in 1789, has 18 antique-furnished, recently renovated rooms with five-meter-high ceilings, fireplaces, and private baths. The lovely courtyard, surrounded by *portales* set with chairs and low tables beneath lazily spinning ceiling fans, is a favorite meeting place for local gringos during the 6:30-7:30 p.m. cocktail hour, when guitar ensembles play *música romántica* and the occasional Sonoran ballad. Dining tables are placed at one end of the courtyard, a pool at the other, with a bar/kitchen between. The daily tariff at Los Tesoros is US$95 s, US$125 d, which includes breakfast, light lunch, and dinner.

One block west of Los Tesoros on Calle Obregón is the well-restored **Hotel La Mansión de la Contesa Magdalena** (tel./fax 8-02-21), originally built in 1683 as the home of a silver magnate. The 12 large rooms surrounding the courtyard are named instead of numbered and are tastefully furnished with art and antiques—the nicest rooms in Alamos. Each has a fireplace and private bath; rates are a reasonable US$45 s, US$55 d, US$65 t or suite (meals are not included). The courtyard contains a tropical garden of banana trees, fan palms, mango, avocado, bougainvillea, hibiscus, and taro; the dining room has been relegated to a corner room. President Carlos Salinas and former president Miguel de la Madrid have each stayed at La Mansión since its 1986 renovation.

Facing Plaza de Armas are two less expensive old casas. **Hotel Los Portales,** owned by the town's first gringo resident, Levant Alcorn, has eight simply furnished rooms with private baths around an empty courtyard for US$30-35 s/d. In the early evenings, guests, friends, and staff sit in rocking chairs under the exterior portal to watch the passing street show and catch up on town events.

Next door to Los Portales is **Hotel Enriquez** (no sign when I visited, but it was definitely in business), where very basic but livable rooms with shared bath just US$10.

Three more choices are found on the outskirts of town. The friendly **Dolisa Motel & RV Park** (tel. 8-01-31) sits on the road to Navojoa near the town entrance. In true motel style, Dolisa's eight rooms angle around the parking area (at all other places in town you must park on the street outside). All rooms come with a/c, TV, and a fireplace. Rooms with one double bed cost US$26, two beds US$30, and three beds US$31.

Somar Hotel (tel. 8-01-95), almost adjacent to the Dolisa Motel, has 16 quite adequate rooms around a courtyard/parking area for US$13-15 s/d, US$15-18 t, US$17-20 q in basic non-air-conditioned rooms; slightly nicer rooms with a/c cost US$20-23.

Rooms at **Acosta Trailer Rancho** (tel. 8-02-46), on the northeastern outskirts of town about one km from the plaza (bear left at the cemetery, proceed along the cemetery wall, then left again at the little bridge), are often occupied by visiting hunters but nonhunters are welcome. Large, clean, recently refurbished rooms with private bath cost US$33 s/d. From early November to early March, dove- and quail-hunting packages (including room, meals, and guided hunts) can be arranged.

Bed and Breakfast: The recently opened **Casa Encantada** (tel. 8-04-82; 800-422-5485 for reservations in the U.S.) on Calle Juárez offers 10 comfortable rooms decorated with Guatemalan fabrics in a 250-year-old Andalusian-style casa. Although the architecture is similar to that of Alamos's other casa inns, owner-managers Rod and Statia Carey have created a casual, family-style atmosphere that contrasts with the slightly more formal, Mexican ambience of La Mansión and Los Tesoros.

All rooms have fireplaces and private baths; rates include a continental breakfast of homemade breads, juice, and coffee, plus a self-service cocktail hour with *sangría* and *tapas*. The courtyard has a pool and guests may borrow bicycles at no extra charge. June-Sept., courtyard rooms cost US$45 s, US$59 d; add US$10 to these rates for October, April, and May and add US$20 for Nov.-March. Larger deluxe rooms are US$59 s, US$79 d June-Sept., plus US$10 and US$20 more in shoulder and peak months. Luxury suites with separate sitting rooms and private **casitas** run US$105 s, US$115 d in the June-Sept. low season; add US$10 and US$20 respectively for the shoulder and peak periods.

RV Parks and Campgrounds: RVers with large rigs may find the streets of Alamos a bit too narrow for comfortable navigation. If you think your rig might fit this category, consider staying at **El Caracol RV Park** 14.5 km (nine miles) before town on the Navojoa-Alamos highway or at the **Dolisa Motel & RV Park** near the town entrance. Both are friendly, well-run facilities. Buses to Alamos stop at El Caracol, so you won't be stranded; Dolisa is within walking distance of downtown. Trailer slots with full hookups cost US$8.50 at El Caracol, US$12-15 at Dolisa. El Caracol charges US$7.50 for campers or vans, US$6 for tents, while Dolisa asks US$13 for campers, US$10 for vans or tents. These rates are good for two persons per site; add US$1-1.50 for each additional person. Dolisa has a coin laundry and hot showers; El Caracol has a pool, hot showers, restaurant, and laundry. Both places offer weekly and monthly discounts.

The **Acosta Trailer Ranch** (see "Hotels and Motels," above) charges US$10 for full hookups, US$8 for campers or small- to medium-sized trailers, US$5 for van or tent. To reach Acosta you'll have to drive through town—make an exploratory trip by foot or taxi first if you think you might have trouble getting your rig down the narrow streets.

Food

One of the most consistently popular restaurants in town is **Las Palmeras** (tel. 642-8-00-65), a small, family-run place on Calle Cárdenas facing the Plaza de Armas. House specialties include pan-fried *tamales de elote* (corn tamales) and *queso fundido* (melted cheese topped with chorizo), plus daily meal specials that might include *carne asada,* ham, fish, or chicken; prices are reasonable. Las Palmeras is open daily 7 a.m.-10 p.m.

Just west of the plaza in an old, simply decorated casa on Calle Zaragoza, the friendly **Polo's** (tel. 8-00-01) offers delicious Mexican breakfasts (US$2.60-4.30), sandwiches (US$4), and dinners of *carnes* and *antojitos* (US$9-12).

The fanciest eatery in town, **Maria Bonita Restaurant** on the corner of Calle Juárez and Rosales features a nice outdoor seating area with a fountain as well as a semi-formal indoor, air-conditioned dining room. Menu prices—for steaks, seafood, and Mexican specialties—are commensurate with the decor. The funky bar next door, under the same management, has live music—mostly *norteña*—on some evenings.

The courtyard dining area at **Hotel Casa de los Tesoros** is open to the public with lunches and dinner at set times and prices (US$13 and US$16 respectively), while breakfast is *a la carta*. Every Saturday at 6:30 p.m., Mayo dances are performed for diners. For lunches and dinners, outside guests should make advance reservations.

For less formal meals, **Taquería Blanquita** in the municipal market building serves passable *tacos de carne asada, menudo,* and tostadas from dawn to dusk. **Sifecha Jugos Naturales,** in a corner of the market building, offers *licuados, refrescos,* and *tortas.*

Shopping

Every Sunday folks from near and far come to Alamos for an open-air market held at Arroyo La Aduana, north of Plaza Alameda. Everything from fresh chiles to household goods are bought and sold at the market.

At the municipal market adjacent to Plaza Alameda, open daily, vendors sell crafts, foodstuffs, and clothing. **El Vaquero,** a shop on the west side of the market facing the plaza, carries fine, locally made saddles, basketry, belts, chaps, and a good selection of hats made by Guarojillo from the Río Mayo area. An unformed *palma real* costs US$16; take it to a hat shop in Navojoa and have it blocked and formed for another US$6.50-7. Synthetic straw hats are less expensive.

Artesanos de Alamos, on Calle Comercio near the church, is a nonprofit artisan's co-op selling dolls, gourds, masks, toys, rustic furniture, and other regional crafts. Some of the items for sale are made by the Guarojillos (a small tribal group living in southeastern Sonora's Alamos and Quiriego *municipios*), who work mostly in palm, wood, and clay to produce musical instruments and pottery.

Jumping Beans: Just up Calle Rosales from the market, facing Plaza Alameda, is Candy Joe's **Curios Artesanías** shop. In addition to a modest collection of minerals and Mayo crafts (mostly pascola masks, water gourds, and dolls), Joe is the main dealer in town for "Mexican jumping beans." Called *brincadores* locally (*Sapium biloculare* to botanists), these little beans only occur within a 1,000-square-km (400-square-mile) area around Alamos. Oct.-March a species of moth lays eggs on the *Sapium's* flowers, and after the flowers drop the beans (or seeds), the moth eggs hatch inside. The movement of the moth larvae inside the beans makes them hop around. Alamos ships around 22,700 kilograms (50,000 pounds) yearly, most of it to international destinations; local pickers are paid US$6-10 per kilo.

In season, Candy Joe keeps a cardboard box full of jumping beans to show passersby; the movement inside the box sounds like gentle rainfall. You can buy the beans from Candy Joe for US$3 per 15. Once the eggs have hatched, the average bean will hop for around six months. Mexicans will place *brincadores* in a circle and bet which will hop out of the circle first.

Recreation

Opinions differ regarding the bass fishing at **Presa Ruíz Cortines** (Presa Mocuzari), northwest of Alamos. Some say they're still jumping while others say the lake has slowed down considerably. Hunting for quail, dove, duck, and blue pigeon is also popular around the lake.

The signed turnoff for Mocuzari is about halfway between Alamos and Navojoa; from Sonora 001 it's roughly 20 km (12 miles) by gravel road to the south end of the lake. It's possible to camp near the lake, though most sportfishers camp at El Caracol (see "RV Parks and Campgrounds," above) or stay in Alamos. It may also be possible to rent a cabin from someone in Mocuzari, a village near the end of the gravel road by the lake.

At the southeast outskirts of town, near Arroyo Agua Escondida, **Centro Recreativo Camuca** has a public swimming pool that's open May-October. Admission is US$1.60 per person.

Transport

Air: The nearest commercial airport is outside Ciudad Obregón (see "Transport" under "Ciudad Obregón," p. 168), 120 km (74.4 miles) from Alamos. Taxis to/from the Ciudad Obregón airport cost US$80 one-way. Inquire about airport shuttles when making hotel reservations.

Alamos has its own 1,200-meter (4,000-foot) airstrip open to pilots of small planes (unicom 122.8); buzz the town once and a taxi will make a pickup for US$6 (US$9 in the opposite direction).

Taxi: Add to the fares above US$160 to Guaymas, US$150 to Los Mochis, and US$50 to either Navojoa or Presa Mocuzari.

Driving: It takes about an hour to drive 53-km (33-mile), two-lane Sonora 001 from Navojoa to Alamos. Cars can be rented easily in Ciudad Obregón (see "Transport" under "Ciudad Obregón," p. 168, for agency names).

From Alamos it's possible to drive north and east to Bahuichivo in the Copper Canyon area via the tiny lumber and mining towns of San Bernardo, Chínipas, and Témoris. The road alternates between graded gravel and rough dirt surfaces and takes the better part of a day. Don't attempt this trip unless you have a rugged, high-clearance vehicle (and don't attempt it at all during the late summer rainy season); bring spare fuel and water.

An even rougher road heads south approximately 100 km from Alamos to El Fuerte, Sin., a stop on the Chihuahua al Pacífico railway line through the Copper Canyon. Along the way the road passes Presa Miguel Hidalgo (see "El Fuerte," p. 183, for more information).

Fuel: At the time of writing Alamos had one Nova-only PEMEX station, but a new pump with Magna Sin was supposed to be added in 1993. If you fill up in Navojoa you should be okay either way.

Information: A small tourist office (tel. 642-8-02-11) on Calle Juárez next to the plaza dispenses hotel brochures and town maps.

The area code for Alamos is 642. The local police can be reached at tel. 8-02-09, Red Cross tel. 8-02-25.

NAVOJOA TO LOS MOCHIS

Playa Huatabampito

Playa Huatabampito, a 20-km flat beach backed by sand dunes along Bahía Santa Barbara (an estuary where the Río Mayo feeds into the Sea of Cortez), is the nearest beach to Ciudad Obregón and Navojoa. A couple of *palapa* restaurants offer fresh seafood; beach camping is possible, using nearby Huatabampo (pop. 45,000) as a supply point. FONATUR reportedly has development plans for Huatabampito, but for the time being it's just miles of sand and a few *palapas*.

Getting There: Sonora 49 leads 36 km (22 miles) southwest from Navojoa through heavily cultivated farmland to the town of Huatabampo. From here follow another road southeast toward Yavaros, but take the turnoff south signed for Huatabampito after roughly 11 km (6.8 miles). Buses to Huatabampito run from the main drag (Av. Guerrero) in Huatabampo several times daily.

Masiaca And Las Bocas

Forty-four km (27 miles) southeast of Navojoa along Mexico 15 on the way to Los Mochis is a turnoff onto a gravel road that leads in either direction. To the east a few km is **Masiaca**, a Mayo village famous for rug-weaving.

In the opposite direction, the road leads southwest approximately 15 km (9.3 miles) to **Las Bocas**, a fish camp with a long, flat beach similar to Playa Huatabampito. Surf casting and inshore fishing are said to be good here; since Las Bocas is far from any major city, there isn't a lot of competition. *Pangas* can be rented from local fishermen. A sand road paralleling the shore leads a few km south to another fish camp/beach, **Camahuiroa**.

THE STATE OF SINALOA

Coming from an Amerindian word for "round prickly pear," the state's name suggests a desert province, yet this is one of the most fertile and well-watered areas in Mexico. Eleven major rivers drain the western slopes of the Sierra Madre Occidental and traverse Sinaloa en route to the Sea of Cortez. Along the way these waters irrigate vast tracts of land that enable roughly half the state's population to earn their living from agriculture, ranching, forestry, hunting, poultry, and inland fishing.

Sinaloa produced over 75% of the nation's total soy and 33% of its sesame output in 1990. It is a major grower of wheat, sorghum, corn, rice, safflower, sugarcane, tomatoes (over a quarter of Mexico's production), bell peppers, potatoes, garbanzos (chickpeas), and chiles. Bananas, mangoes (the state tops the list for Mexican mango output), avocados (Haas avocados were developed here by Antonio Haas), and other tropical produce are cultivated in the southern end of the state.

With a 656-km (407-mile) shoreline, fishing is also a major source of livelihood, with sardine, tuna, and shrimp leading the offshore catch.

The many bays, estuaries, and marshes where river systems meet the Sea of Cortez produce a combination of inshore saltwater and freshwater fisheries as well.

Not surprisingly, food packing has become the state's primary industry, with manufacturing a very distant second. Although the first Spanish settlers came in search of gold and silver—concentrating on the mountainous, eastern half of the state—later immigration from all over the world focused on the fertile river valleys and coastal plains. Today the state's population is a melting pot of Spanish, French, English, American, Lebanese, Greek, and Chinese ancestries.

Sinaloa's most well-known tourist entities are Mazatlán (the closest major beach resort to the U.S. border) and the western portion of the Chihuahua al Pacífico ("Copper Canyon") railway, but other places worth visiting include the historic Sierra Madre ex-mining towns of El Fuerte, Cosalá, and Copalá, the bustling state capital of Culiacán, and the sleepy *lagunas* in the southern tip of the state.

LOS MOCHIS TO CULIACAN

LOS MOCHIS

This booming agricultural and shipping center (pop. 206,000) at the junction of Mexico 15 and the Chihuahua al Pacífico rail line (and within a half-hour's drive of Mexico's deepest port) was originally founded by American Alfred K. Owens in 1872 as part of a utopian colony along with nearby Topolobampo on the coast. Although Owens's utopian experiment failed, his dream to build a rail line for transshipment to the western U.S. coast was eventually realized by American railroaders who arrived on the scene afterwards.

In 1893 Benjamin Johnston established another American colony at Los Mochis with more capitalist objectives. Johnston succeeded in building a major sugar mill (now owned by Mexico's largest sugar company) and in laying out the American-style town grid still in use. (The main difference between American and Mexican grids is the avoidance of diagonal streets in the former.)

Today Los Mochis is a town whose boxy modern architecture, one-way streets, and businesslike atmosphere aren't particularly endearing to out-of-town visitors. For most tourists it's simply a necessary stopover while waiting for the morning train across the Sierra Madre Occidental to Creel or Chihuahua; others spend a short time here after arriving at nearby Topolobampo by ferry from La Paz, Baja California Sur.

Av. Obregón, the most colorful street in town, is a cut-rate shopping district with mazelike markets and funky downtown cafes. The **Museo Regional del Valle del Fuerte** at Av. Obregón and Rosales (open Tue.-Sun. 10 a.m.-1 p.m. and 4-7 p.m., US$1 admission) has displays on regional history and anthropology as well as rotating art exhibits.

Accommodations
Hotels: Hotel Lorena (tel. 2-02-39, fax 2-45-17), at the corner of Av. Obregón and Calle G. Prieto near the municipal market, provides pleasant, reasonably priced rooms with a/c, cable TV, and private bath for US$25 s, US$37 d, or US$47 t. Nearby **Hotel Beltrán** (tel. 2-07-10) at Calle Hidalgo and Zaragoza is very similar.

The comfortable, popular, and moderately priced **Hotel Santa Anita** (tel. 5-70-46; 800-876-3942 toll free in the U.S.; fax 2-00-46) has recently renovated rooms with cable TV, phone, a/c, and private bath for US$65 s, US$70 d, or US$80 t. Conveniently located at the heart of Los Mochis' downtown, the Santa Anita is part of the Balderrama hotel chain, which operates several properties along the Chihuahua al Pacífico train route. Overflow visitors from the Santa Anita—along with those on hunting packages—are lodged just north of downtown at Balderrama's **Plaza Inn** (tel. 2-00-75) on Calle G. Leyva and Calle Cárdenas. The Plaza Inn is a bit far from the downtown action but has a pool and a very popular disco.

Hotel Florida (tel. 2-12-00) at Calle G. Leyva and Ramírez offers a/c, TV, and private bath for US$40-54 s/d; rooms with kitchenettes are also available for a bit more.

Many road visitors lodge at the **Hotel Colinas** (tel. 2-01-01, fax 2-03-58) just off Mexico 15. Rooms at the Colinas come with a/c, TV, and phone for US$60-70 s, US$70-80 d per night. Facilities include two tennis courts and two pools (one with huge, amusement park-style water slides).

RV Parks: The popular **Hotel Colinas RV Park** has a pleasant *palapa* area for socializing and costs US$12 per night (for two persons, plus US$2 for each additional person) for full hookups. RV guests may use the hotel facilities described above. **Los Mochis Copper Canyon RV Park** (tel. 2-68-17) off Mexico 15 on the northern outskirts of town is similarly priced and perhaps a bit quieter.

Sixteen km (10 miles) north of town on the Río Fuerte, just off Mexico 15 at Km 18, the **Río Fuerte Trailer Park** (tel. 2-00-75) offers full hookups for US$12, electricity and water only for US$9.

Food
What it lacks in charm, Los Mochis makes up for in the restaurant department. At the splurge end, the **Hotel Santa Anita** dining room is

well-known for its delicious shrimp flambé and **sopa de tortillas** (see "Accommodations"). **España** (also known as "Madrid") at Av. Obregón and Calle G. Leyva offers elegant decor, attentive service, and Spanish/international cuisine.

For an extensive yet inexpensive selection of regional Mexican dishes, head for the paragon **El Taquito** on Calle G. Leyva between Independencia and Hidalgo downtown. It's open from early in the morning till late at night, but is especially good for *almuerzo* (late breakfast) with a choice of the "Sonorense" (eggs with

machaca), "Taquito" (with ham), or "Sinaloense" (with *chilorio,* a venison or pork sausage with chiles), each with coffee, fruit, potatoes, toast, and tortillas, for US$5. The specialties of the house—served anytime—are *taquitos* (soft tacos) and *tacos dorados* (fried tacos).

Jugos Chapala, around the corner from El Taquito on Calle Independencia, features a large selection of *licuados* made from fresh Sinaloa fruits.

Restaurante El Farallón at Av. Obregón and Flores and **El Bucanero** at Calle Allende 828 Nte. (at Calle Cano) are highly favored for seafood.

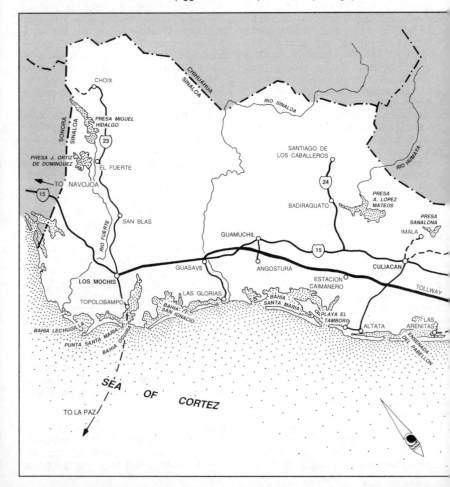

At night you'll find a dozen *tacos de carne asada* vendors along Calle Independencia east of Calle G. Leyva. On weekends *pollo asado* (grilled chicken) and *mariscos* vendors line the canal parallel to the Los Mochis-Topolobampo road a bit south of town.

Entertainment

The most popular discos in town are **Scorpio's** at Hotel Florida and **Fantasy** at the Plaza Inn. For a quiet drink, Hotel Santa Anita's **Closet Bar** or Hotel Florida's **Bar Las Bugambilias** are good choices. The larger **Bar La Hacienda** at the Santa Anita features live music most nights.

Hunting And Fishing

Balderrama Tours (tel. 681-5-70-46, fax 2-00-46) at Hotel Santa Anita can arrange hunting trips for geese, doves, ducks, deer, and wild pigs, as well as fishing trips in nearby lakes or in Topolobampo's Bahía Oguira.

Transport By Air

Los Mochis airport is served by **Aeroméxico** (tel. 681-5-25-70; Calle G. Leyva 168 Nte.), and

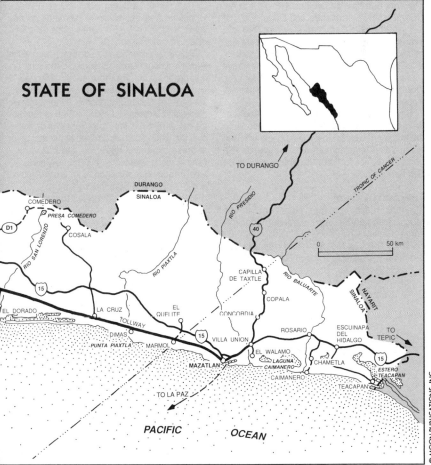

STATE OF SINALOA

© MOON PUBLICATIONS, INC.

by **Aero California** (tel. 5-22-50; Calle Hidalgo 440 Pte.) with nonstop flights to/from Culiacán, Guadalajara, Hermosillo, La Paz, Los Angeles, Mazatlán, Mexico City, and Tijuana.

A smaller operation, **Leo López Airlines** (tel. 2-94-82, Calle G. Prieto 864), runs two daily flights Mon.-Fri. between El Paso and Los Mochis via Chihuahua, using 16-seater Fairchild Metro II or Metro III turboprops.

Transport between the airport (20 km) and downtown Los Mochis costs US$15 by taxi, US$5 by *colectivo*.

Transport By Bus

The **Tres Estrellas de Oro** bus terminal is at Av. Obregón between Allende and Degollado, not far from the municipal market, while **TNS** and **Transportes del Pacífico** have adjacent terminals at Calle Morelos 327 (four blocks north of Av. Obregón). Together the three bus lines have routes all over northwestern Mexico. From Av. Obregón you can catch frequent local buses to Topolobampo and Culiacán.

City buses ply the main avenues—look for the name of the principal road destinations on the bus windshields. Most routes begin and end along Calle Degollado between Independencia and Castro, not far from the Tres Estrellas de Oro terminal.

Transport By Train

The main reason foreign visitors come to Los Mochis is to board or disembark from the 674-km (418-mile) Chihuahua al Pacífico train excursion. The Los Mochis railway station (tel. 681-2-08-53) is around two km (1.2 miles) east of downtown on Av. Onofre Serrano (approximately one km from Blvd. M. Gaxiola).

Special first-class reserved ("Servicio Estrella" or "expresso") seats on train No. 73 to Chihuahua cost US$32 per person, or US$34 with up to two stopovers along the way; this train departs Los Mochis at 6 a.m. daily and usually takes around 13 hours to reach Chihuahua. The second-class No. 75 ("El Tarahumara," or more colloquially *el pollero*) costs just US$6, leaves at 7 a.m., and is supposed to reach Chihuahua in 15 hours (but it often takes up to three hours longer).

Other fares along the Chihuahua al Pacífico route, from Los Mochis, include: Bahuichivo US$12; Posada Barrancas/Divisadero US$14; Creel US$16; La Junta US$22. Add 15% for stopovers (maximum of two permitted on one ticket); children ages 5-11 are eligible for a 50% discount on all fares.

Tickets for either train can be purchased at the station an hour before scheduled departure, but first-class tickets are more easily arranged in advance through **Viajes Paotam** (tel. 5-82-62, fax 5-19-14), Calle S. Rendón 517 Pte. (between Flores and Mateos/G. Leyva) or **Viajes Flamingo** (tel. 2-16-13) in the Hotel Santa Anita. Fares cost the same whether booked at the station or at these two travel agencies, the only authorized ticketing agents for FNM in Los Mochis. Viajes Paotam is open Mon.-Sat. 8 a.m.-1 p.m. and 3-7 p.m., and Sun. 9 a.m.-1 p.m.

Hotel Santa Anita offers van transport from the hotel to the railway station every morning at 5:15 a.m. for US$3.30 per person, including continental breakfast. The Santa Anita can also arrange long-term parking in a security lot behind the hotel for US$4 per day. Other hotels in town may provide similar services.

Since the most scenic sections of the Chihuahua al Pacífico train journey begin east of El Fuerte (over 100 km northeast of Los Mochis), some visitors drive or bus to El Fuerte and board the train there. Because the train leaves El Fuerte around 7:30 a.m. (as opposed to 6 a.m. in Los Mochis), this means rising a bit later in the morning as well. It is also an hour quicker to drive to El Fuerte than to take the train—but you still might want to book your onward ticket at Viajes Paotam or the railway station in Los Mochis rather

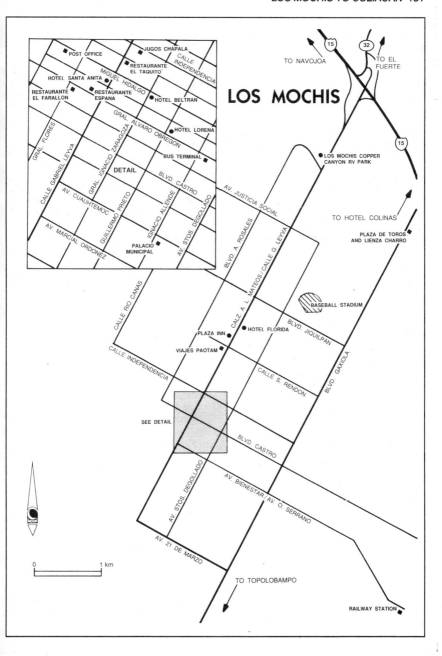

LOS MOCHIS

than in El Fuerte if traveling in the Nov.-March high season. If you're driving, the main drawback to this alternative is the lack of security parking in El Fuerte.

Ferry

Tickets for the SEMATUR ferries between nearby Topolobampo and La Paz, Baja California Sur, can be reserved and purchased at **Viajes Paotam** (see "Transport by Train," above), the only travel agency in Los Mochis authorized to distribute ferry tickets.

See "By Ferry from Baja" under "Getting There" in the "Out and About" chapter, p. 80, for details on the ferry service.

Driving

Hertz (tel. 681-2-11-22), **National** (tel. 2-53-60), and **Budget** (tel. 5-83-00) have offices at Los Mochis International Airport.

Magna Sin is readily available at several Los Mochis PEMEX stations.

Other Practicalities

Several *servicios de cambios* along Av. Obregón near the municipal market offer moneychanging services.

Librolandia, just east of Restaurante El Taquito on Calle G. Leyva, carries a selection of English-language magazines.

The area code for Los Mochis is 681.

TOPOLOBAMPO

This small port town, called "Topo" for short, was Albert Kinsey Owens's first project although today it's little more than a nondescript, somewhat scruffy town spread over hills above Bahí Oguira (also spelled Ohuira). The town's main claim to fame is that its harbor happens to be the world's third deepest (and Mexico's deepest), with a consistent, navigable depth of 12 meters (40 feet).

So far the harbor's potential has yet to be fully tapped. It was opened only recently in 1991 as a cargo port, and shipping volume is far below that of Guaymas or Mazatlán. Fishing is the main local business; at last count 27 fishing cooperatives were in town. PEMEX also has a large storage and shipping facility here. The state hopes to transform the 24-km Los Mochis-Topolobampo corridor into an industrial zone. Already in place are several plants engaged in textile manufacture and food processing.

For the visitor, the main points of interest are offshore. Bay tours arranged in town stop off at **Roca El Farallón,** a breeding ground for various birds and sea lions; bottle-nosed dolphins often frolic around the boats. Fishing *pangas* can be rented at **Club de Náutico** near the ferry terminal for tries at yellowtail, grouper, and roosterfish (year-round) or marlin and dorado (summer). Or hire a *pangero* for drop-off and pickup at the lovely white-sand beaches of **Isla Santa María,** northeast of Bahía Oguira. The humble seafood restaurants on nearby **Playa Maviri**—accessible by road or by boat—are superb. A local cooperative offers *pangas* that can take up to 10 persons on a bay tour for US$16 total, or all the way to Playa Maviri and back for US$33.

Other nearby islands worth exploring include the pristine **Isla San Ignacio** and **Isla Macapule,** both of which are more easily accessible from Bahía San Ignacio, the next bay south (between Los Mochis and Guasave) from Bahía Oguira. Surrounding tidal estuaries are excellent for birding.

Accommodations And Food

Topolobampo has a couple of hotels, including the four-star **Hotel Yacht** (tel. 681-2-38-62) overlooking the bay, but most overnight visitors to the area choose to stay in Los Mochis because it's so much tidier.

Seafood aficionados, on the other hand, will like the simple tables at **Chicho's** and **Grecia,** two rustic seafood places flanking the harbor. Sitting on the top floors of two otherwise undistinguished-looking buildings, these restaurants serve up a variety of fresh shrimp, oyster, crab, and fish platters. The Hotel Yacht restaurant, only slightly more refined than the previous, features fresh seafood platters as well as Mexican and Sinaloan dishes.

Transport By Bus And Taxi

Buses for Topo depart frequently from the municipal market area in downtown Los Mochis during daylight hours. The 24-km trip takes about 45 minutes and costs US$1.60 per person. A taxi between the two towns costs US$20.

A taxi out to Playa Maviri costs US$13-14.

Transport By Train

Although the Chihuahua al Pacífico terminates in Topo, very few people choose to board here rather than Los Mochis, as the scenery between Topo and Los Mochis is not very impressive. See the "Los Mochis" section above for details.

Ferry

Ferries bound for La Paz leave from the **Atracadero de los Transbordadores** (tel. 681-2-03-21) near the PEMEX storage facility. Tickets can be booked at the pier or from Viajes Paotam in Los Mochis. The ferry leaves Sun.-Thurs. at 9 a.m. and takes about 18 hours to reach La Paz. For further details, see "By Ferry from Baja in the "Out and About" chapter, p. 80.

Driving

From Los Mochis, follow Blvd. Gaxiola south until it meets the four-lane highway all the way to Topo. Once you hit the Topo outskirts, follow the Topolobampo Sur signs to get into town, otherwise you'll end up at the pier and PEMEX facility.

Auto Rental: National (tel. 2-53-60) has an office at Calle G. Leyva and Callejón Municipal near Hotel Santa Anita. Rentals tend to be as expensive as US$45-50 a day for a three-year-old VW Jetta.

EL FUERTE

Originally home to the warring Zuaque, Sinaloa, and Tehueco tribes, "The Fort" received its first Spanish settlers in 1564 and a Franciscan mission in 1590. In 1610 the Spanish built a *presidio* here on a bend in El Gran Río Zuaque to subdue the local population. Eventually the river took on the name Río Fuerte for the fort on its banks, although locally many residents still call it the Río Zuaque.

The most important river system in northwestern Mexico, the Río Fuerte irrigates an extensive agricultural zone running through parts of Sinaloa, Chihuahua, Sonora, and Durango. Its major tributaries include the Alamos, de Choix, Septentrión, Batopilas, and Urique rivers, all of which descend from the western slopes of the Sierra Madre Occidental. The Fuerte alone feeds a basin of 33,600 square km, with annual catchment of nearly five million cubic meters. Already partially impounded by Presa Hidalgo, the Fuerte may soon be getting a new dam, Presa Huites, in the state's bid to generate more hydroelectric power and a higher irrigation capacity.

El Fuerte's two known attractions are inland sportfishing at nearby lakes and the Chihuahua al Pacífico railroad, which makes a stop here. Savvy travelers begin their eastbound rail journeys (or end their eastbound journeys) here rather than in Los Mochis simply because the best rail scenery begins east of El Fuerte.

Less known is the fact that El Fuerte is a thriving example of a lower Sierra Madre, ex-colonial Mexican town and a repository for traditional Sinaloan culture. Once an important way station on the Camino Real (and Sinaloa state capital 1824-26), the town served as a banking and supply center for sierra mining towns during the days of massive silver exploitation. Although business has slowed considerably, El Fuerte (pop. 25,000) today performs much the same function for local ranching and agriculture. The *palacio municipal* is still bullet pocked from the Mexican revolution days, and *tamboras sinaloenses*—brass-and-drum bands that perform a lively German-Mexican musical blend peculiar to Sinaloa—practice in the streets.

The downtown architecture is exemplary of provincial colonial construction, with tall, single-story, L- and U-shaped casas with iron-grille windows and *portales* built around tidy courtyards. Don't go expecting another Alamos, Son., however; this is Alamos without the moneyed gringo stewardship. Unlike its staid Sonora counterpart, the markets and cobblestoned streets of El Fuerte are bustling with activity. Paint peels from the old casas, but for the most part they remain authentic and free from San Miguel de Allende or Alamos affectations.

During the day, pedestrian activity is centered around the municipal market; in the evenings the focus shifts to the well-kept, shady plaza. Though somewhat insular in ambience, it's a town that "grows" on those who stay around awhile.

The Río Fuerte riverbank and ruined walls of the Spanish fort are a short walk from Hotel Posada del Hidalgo, and a sunset stroll along the dirt road paralleling the river can lead to some rewarding vistas. The Posada del Hidalgo can arrange one- to two-hour guided walking tours, horseback rides, and river tours.

Hotels

El Fuerte's main tourist center, **Hotel Posada del Hidalgo** (tel. 681-3-02-42 in Los Mochis; 800-876-3942 in the U.S.), has 30 large rooms furnished with antiques (much of it shipped direct from San Francisco in the 19th century) in a huge colonial mansion near the old-town plaza. Originally built in 1895 as the palatial home of grandee Rafael Almada, the inn has a garden courtyard on one level and a pool and dining room on another. The late Pres. Venustiano Carranza spent a night here in 1913. Most rooms are air-conditioned and all come with hot showers; rates are US$65 s, US$70 d, US$80 t. This hotel is part of the Balderrama chain based in Los Mochis; reservations can be made through Los Mochis' Hotel Santa Anita.

Behind the Posado del Hidalgo, the equally historic **Paloma Blanca Lodge** is upgrading its facilities from rustic accommodations for hunters and sportfishers to a full-scale inn. At the moment simply furnished rooms in this old casa, with shared bathroom facilities, cost US$30 s, US$34 d.

For lower budgets, the best deal in town is the friendly **Hotel San Francisco,** a one-story, provincial-style casa around a courtyard on Av. Obregón (the main downtown street) near the municipal market. Clean, simple rooms with private baths cost US$22 s, US$30 d.

Also on Av. Obregón is the quite passable **Hotel Montesclaros,** a newer place without much atmosphere for US$17 s, US$24 d.

Opposite the municipal market, **Hotel San José** is a classic truck-drivers' dive with merchandise piled in the small lobby. Room rates are under US$10 but camping by the river would be a cleaner alternative.

RV Parks And Camping

About 9.6 km (six miles) southwest of El Fuerte, near Presa Dominguez, is a rustic campground run by twin brothers **José and Pepe Castillo** (tel. 681-3-08-36). RV slots with full hookups cost US$10 per night, tent space US$5.

Food

Restaurante Anita, facing the south side of the plaza, is the fanciest dining spot outside the Posada del Hidalgo. Open for dinner only, Anita specializes in delicious fresh bass (*lobina*) prepared in various styles as well as seafood—*rellenos de camarón, abulón,* and *caguama* (sea turtle)—for around US$7 per meal.

The small, clean, air-conditioned **Restaurante Capri,** next door to Hotel San Francisco, has a good selection of Mexican standards at moderate prices. It's open for breakfast, lunch, and dinner.

The dining room at Hotel Posada del Hidalgo is quite good (fresh bass is the specialty) although service can be a little slow—especially if a rail tour group is staying at the hotel.

Taco vendors near the municipal market serve the usual *carne asada.* El Fuerte is famous for *agua de cebada,* a delicious *agua fresca* made with sweetened barley, vanilla, and cinnamon.

Fishing And Hunting

West and northwest of El Fuerte are **Presa Miguel Hidalgo** (an impoundment of the Río Fuerte) and **Presa Josefa Ortíz de Dominguez** (from the Río el Cuchujaqui), both well stocked with largemouth bass and catfish. Except for the Castillos' campground near Presa Dominguez (see "RV Parks and Camping," above), facilities are scarce. Most visiting sportfishers use El Fuerte for a base since the town is only a half-hour drive away from either lake.

The same area is popular for hunting Canadian goose, pintail, widgeon, teal, various duck species (mallard, speckled, tree, redhead, canvasback), quail, and white-winged dove. Waterfowl season runs Nov.-Feb., while quail and dove are in season Oct.-March. Bonded hunting and fishing guides are available for hire through the Posada del Hidalgo.

Transport

Air: The nearest commercial airport is in Los Mochis. A 1,200-meter (4,000-foot) airstrip near town can accommodate small planes; buzz the town once for taxi pickup.

Bus: Buses to El Fuerte (US$3) leave frequently throughout the day from the Los Mochis bus terminal.

Train: The first-class Chihuahua al Pacífico train is scheduled to depart El Fuerte at 7:26 a.m. eastbound, 6:16 p.m. eastbound. The railway station is about six km east of town; taxis to the station cost US$6.60-8.30 (negotiation is necessary). If you're planning on a westbound morning departure, you can arrange a taxi to the station at the taxi stand at Av. Obregón and Calle Juárez (opposite Bancomer) the night before. The Posada del Hidalgo and Hotel San Francisco will also make taxi arrangements on request.

The second-class *pollero* train usually passes through El Fuerte around 9 a.m. eastbound, anytime between 9:30 p.m. and midnight in the reverse direction.

CULIACAN AND VICINITY

Originally founded in 1531 by Nuño Beltrán de Guzmán, one of the most hated and feared of all conquistadores (he was excommunicated from the Catholic Church for his cruelty to Indians), Culiacán served as an important base for early Spanish explorations of northwest Mexico. The city's name means "Where Two Waters Meet," a Nahuatl reference to the junction of the Humaya and Tamazula rivers. In typical Mexican fashion, the river formed by this junction is deemed a third river, in this case the Río Culiacán.

Irrigation has turned the river valleys surrounding Culiacán into a major agricultural zone producing huge crops of tomatoes, eggplants, green peppers, cucumbers, peas, garbanzos (chickpeas), and other vegetables. Bright yellow marigolds, purchased by Purina in the U.S. for addition to chicken feed—in order to make egg yolks more yellow—are another important source of foreign income. The city also has six industrial parks with a total of 78 plants in operation—over half engaged in food and beverage processing or packing.

In addition to being a farming center, Culiacán is the seat of Sinaloa's state government and home to 440,000 residents according to the last official census (unofficial estimates place the population as high as 600,000). As the state's largest and most modern city, sprawling Culiacán radiates commerce, activity, style, and power. Few visitors spend more than a night here, however, and then only when they've underestimated the time it takes to reach Mazatlán farther south. Mexico 15 drivers can circumvent the city via a marked bypass road.

Several city projects underway promise to provide at least a few hours of distraction in the near future. A **Science Center** with planetarium, educational exhibits, auditorium, and meeting facilities is scheduled to open by the time you read this. The more ambitious **Tres Ríos** project aims to build a 46-km riverfront district with promenades, park areas, and floating restaurants by 1997. Also involved in the project is the construction of a new dam (to eliminate recurring problems with flooding), the dredging of the rivers, 10 new bridges, and wider city boulevards. A small riverfront promenade or *malecón* already exists along the Río Tamazula off Paseo Niños Heroes.

SIGHTS

Museo Del Arte De Sinaloa
One local sight worth visiting is this new art museum containing over 300 works by Diego Rivera, Rufino Tamayo, Pedro Coronel, and famous Sinaloan artist López Sanez. The museum is just southwest of the Centro Cultural DIFOCUR between Rosales and Buelna. Open Tues.-Sun. 10 a.m.-1 p.m. and 4-7 p.m.; admission is US$1.30 adults, US$0.30 children under 12. For information call 67-13-99-33.

Cultural Centers
Centro Cultural DIFOCUR (tel. 67-15-03-11), Culiacán's most well-endowed cultural center, hosts foreign cinema, dance, and musical performances; lectures; contemporary art shows; and occasional historical or cultural exhibits. The center is located off Av. Obregón near the Río Tamazula in the northern part of the downtown area.

An older **Casa de Cultura** at Flores and Noris (opposite Plaza Rosales) houses a small gallery with works by local artists.

Parks
Culiacán has several large city parks. **Parque Revolución,** off Av. Obregón between Villa and Leyva Solano, is an amazing amalgam of shade trees, *juegos de video* (video games), food vendors, and sparking lovers, while **Parque Constitución** east of downtown at Buelna and Guerrero even has a zoo (open 9 a.m.-6 p.m.,

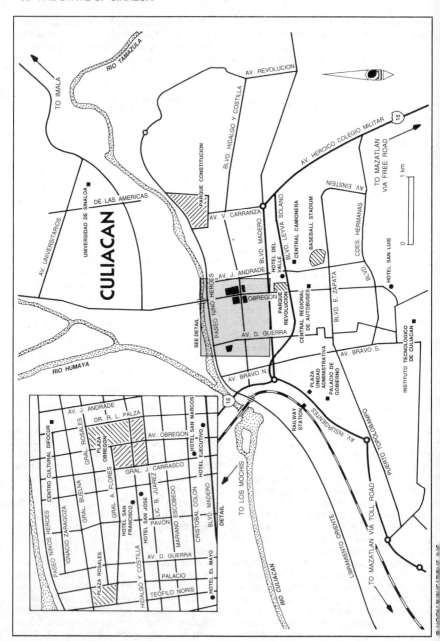

admission US$0.60) with regional fauna. The latter park reportedly contains the second largest meteorite (47 tons) in the world.

ACCOMMODATIONS AND FOOD

Hotels
In the downtown area, the best hotel for location and value is the clean, friendly, and efficient **Hotel San Francisco** (tel. 67-13-58-63) at Blvd. Hidalgo y Costilla 227 Pte. (two blocks west of Av. Obregón). Rooms with a/c, TV, and phone cost US$20 s, US$23.30 d, US$28 t. Another branch with similar rates is the **Hotel Francis** (tel. 12-47-50), nearby at Calle Escobedo 135 Pte.

A number of hotels in the vicinity of the bus station charge about the same rates as the San Francisco but are a poor value and best avoided. The cheapest downtown place, **Hotel San Jose** (Calle Juárez 233 Pte. at Calle Rubi), costs US$8.30 s, US$10 d per night for basic rooms with *baño colectivo.* Far better in the budget range is the **Gran Motel** (tel. 13-57-00) at Calle Salvador and Palma, where simple but clean rooms are US$12 s, US$15 d.

Near the bus terminal but better than the above is **Hotel Del Valle** (tel. 13-90-20) at Blvd. Leyva Solano and Andrade, where rooms with a/c, TV, and phone cost US$37 s/d, US$47 t, US$57 q. **Hotel San Marcos** (tel. 13-78-76), Calle Carrasco 44 Nte., and **Hotel Ejecutivo** (tel. 13-93-00) at Blvd. Madero and Av. Obregón, offer decent facilities for rates on a par with the Del Valle's. The San Marcos is currently undergoing expansion and renovation so rates may increase in a year or so.

Another economic but decent choice is **Hotel El Mayo** (formerly Hotel Colonial, tel. 15-22-30) at Blvd. Madero 730 Pte., where decent air-conditioned rooms with private bath go for US$28 s, US$30 d, US$34 t, and US$37 q.

Moving to the top of the scale, the popular Balderrama-owned **Hotel San Luis Lindavista** (tel. 16-84-90, fax 15-08-15), on Av. Las Palmas, overlooks the city near the Instituto Tecnológico de Culiacán. Rates are US$65 s, US$70 d, US$80 t for rooms with all the amenities, including a swimming pool and security parking. To reach Hotel San Luis by car, drive south on Av. Obregón—follow signs to ITC—

until the institute is on your right; the hotel will be visible on the hill to the left.

Motel Tres Ríos (tel. 15-41-40, fax 13-93-00), on Mexico 15 northwest of the city, is another popular tourist lodge. It is currently under renovation; room rates of US$40-50 may increase once remodeling is complete.

RV Parks And Camping
Motel Tres Ríos has 40 RV spaces with full hookups for US$11 a night, electricity and water only for US$8.

Food
Downtown Culiacán is chockablock with inexpensive *cafeterías* and fast-food eateries. **Panama,** opposite the north end of Parque Revolución on Calle Fco. Villa, has a good selection of Mexican *antojitos* served buffet-style. Another inexpensive, popular buffet-style place is **Chic's,** opposite Hotel Executivo. Both are open for breakfast, lunch, and dinner.

At the casual, very popular **Jugos California** on Calle Flores near the municipal market, the house specialty is a roast chicken (*pollo asado*) platter that comes with tortillas, salad, salsas, and beans for under US$4. As the name suggests, fresh *licuados* (*nopal con naranja* or "prickly pear with orange" is a unique one) and *aguas frescas* are available, along with *comida corrida,* tacos, *tortas,* and tostadas. Jugos California generally is open early to late for breakfast, lunch, and dinner.

Chinese restaurants are well represented in Culiacán due to the relatively high Chinese presence. **Kim Hap,** on the corner of Calle Juárez and Av. Andrade, is one of the better downtown examples.

Steak and seafood are the emphases at **Restaurante Los Arcos** at Blvd. Xicotencatl and Lago de Cuitzeo, two blocks east of Parque Constitución. The restaurants at Motel Tres Ríos and Hotel San Luis are popular among visiting gringos. **La Fabula Pizza** has a branch at Av. Obregón 700 Sur.

SHOPPING AND RECREATION

Nightlife
Disco-going is a popular activity in fashionable Culiacán practically every night of the week.

Most *au courant* are the Hotel San Luis's **Morocco,** Hotel Ejecutivo's **La Cava, MTV** on Calle Buelna, Motel Tres Ríos' **O'lydia** (currently the largest disco in Northwest Mexico), and four along the river on Paseo Niños Heroes: **Chaplin, Hard Rock, Chips and Beer,** and **Chico's.**

Several downtown movie houses show the latest Latin American and North American films: **Multicinemas** (Calle Buelna and Xicotencatl), **Cine Reforma** (Calle Flores and Dr. Paliza), **Cinema Culiacán 70** (Calle Buelna), and **Cine Diana** (Av. Obregón).

Shopping

The main shopping district is centered around Av. Obregón and the municipal market on Blvd. Hidalgo y Costilla. Along neighboring streets you can find a large selection of department stores, shops, and mall vendors selling virtually everything.

Hunting

The Valle de Culiacán swarms with geese, ducks, white-winged doves, quail, and blue pigeons, and local farmers welcome hunters to help keep the population down. Motel Tres Ríos can arrange hunting guides. A list of guides and outfitters is also available from the Culiacán tourist office (see "Information" below).

TRANSPORT AND INFORMATION

Air

At Culiacán International Airport (12 km west of the city center), **Aeroméxico** (tel. 67-15-37-72; Av. Rosales 77 Pte.) and **Aero California** (tel. 16-02-50; Blvd. Madero and Av. Obregón) field nonstop flights to/from Chihuahua, Durango, Guadalajara, Los Angeles, Mexico City, La Paz, Los Mochis, Ciudad Obregón, and Mazatlán. Regional airlines **Noroeste** (tel. 16-88-99) and **SARO** (tel. 13-59-28) add flights to/from Durango, Hermosillo, Mexicali, Monterrey, Tijuana, and Torreón. Tickets and reservations for Noroeste and SARO are available through local travel agencies.

The standard taxi fare to/from the airport is US$10.

Bus

Transportes del Pacífico, Tres Estrellas de Oro, and **TNS** operate from the Central Camionera at Blvd. Leyva Solano and Calle Corona, with buses to virtually all towns and cities in Sinaloa and Sonora plus Mexicali, Tijuana, Tepic, Guadalajara, and Mexico City. Express buses to Los Mochis (leaving every 15 minutes 5 a.m.-7 p.m.), as well as local buses to Altata and El Dorado, leave from just outside the station. The bus terminal cafeteria offers probably the largest selection of American-brand beers in northwestern Mexico.

Train

The FNM station (tel. 67-14-70-59) is on Av. Insurgentes opposite the Plaza Unidad Administrativa and the Palacio de Gobierno. For scheduling information on Del Pacífico train No. 1 (special first class reserved), see the "Railway Schedule," pp. 86-87. Second-class train nos. 3 and 4 pass through at 12:55 a.m. (southbound) and 3:10 a.m. (northbound).

Driving

Traffic in Culiacán is intense, and many downtown streets are one-way. To reach the downtown area coming south via Mexico 15, turn left (east) at the first traffic circle (about two km/1.6 miles south of the Cuauhtémoc Brewery) onto Blvd. Madero.

A trunk highway encircles the city, connecting old Mexico 15 with the new toll highway between Culiacán and Mazatlán. From downtown Culiacán you must drive west on the trunk highway (follow signs to "Costa Rica," a Culiacán suburb) to reach the toll road (US$5 to Mazatlán).

Auto Rental

Avis (tel. 67-14-40-87), **Budget** (tel. 14-77-37), and **National** (tel. 13-68-58) rent cars at the airport. Cars can also be rented through Hotel San Luis Lindavista.

Information

The useful state tourist office (tel. 67-14-06-10) is on the second floor of the Palacio de Gobierno, off Av. Insurgentes near the railway station.

Culiacán's area code is 67.

VICINITY OF CULIACAN

Beaches

Around 60 km west of Culiacán is a system of bays, estuaries, and barrier peninsulas. Sonora 280 leads west to **Altata,** a dingy gray beach on Bahía Altata with a few *palapa* restaurants and beach homes. Better is the sand-and-palm **Playa El Tambor** 15 km north of Altata by gravel and sand road, next to the shrimp camp of Dautillos. Surfers' note: January and February usually bring high, surfable breaks to El Tambor.

Farther south, near the farming/sugar refining community of El Dorado (53 km/33 miles from Culiacán), is **Playa Las Arenitas,** a fair beach on the fishing bay of Ensenada del Pabellón.

Imala

About 24 km (15 miles) east of Culiacán via unpaved road, the village of Imala has a rustic *balneario* (spa) with thermal baths. The first pool is the smallest and hottest, while three other pools become progressively larger and cooler. Palm trees provide shade and you'll find cabañas (for changing) with restrooms for bathers, plus small brick cabins for rent. If you visit midweek you'll probably have the pools to yourself. The gardener may ask for a donation for grounds upkeep (US$1 is standard).

You'll need your own wheels to reach Imala. The road begins next to the monument at the entrance of the Universidad de Sinaloa in northeastern Culiacán—count on a 50- to 60-minute drive at a leisurely pace. Villages passed along the way include Aguamita and Jotagua (if in doubt you're on the right road, stop and ask). The *balneario* gate is directly across the plaza from Imala's 17th-century church.

A few kilometers east of Imala via a rough dirt road is **Presa Sanalona,** a little-known bass-fishing spot.

Presa López Mateo

As Mexico's fifth largest lake, Presa López Mateo is impounded by the nation's third highest dam and is the most popular freshwater fishing locale in the area. Rustic facilities and supplies may be available at the village of El Varejonal at the lake's southern tip. Gringo anglers who have dropped lines here have stayed at Culiacán's Motel Tres Ríos (see "Accommodations and Food" under "Culiacán and Vicinity"), where fishing guides can be arranged.

To reach the lake, take the signed turnoff at La Campana, drive 31 km north of Culiacán on Mexico 15, then proceed northeast 25 km (15.5 miles) to El Varejonal.

Cosalá

Founded in 1562, the Sierra Madre town of Cosalá is the oldest in the state. The name is a Spanish corruption of Quezala, a Sinaloa Indian term for "place of the macaws." Yet another in a succession of mining towns that temporarily served as Sinaloa's state capital (when the population exceeded 20,000 in 1827), Cosalá once boasted silver deposits so rich that the surrounding area was referred to as the "silver mountains." Although it's hard to believe given today's laid-back ambience of benign neglect (*muy tranquilo,* say the locals), the town also published the state's first newspaper in 1826.

Blessed with a moderate year-round climate and reliable water sources, the town has a small but dedicated following among savvy travelers who find Cosalá's steep, cobblestoned streets lined with tile-roofed stucco buildings—many of them over two centuries old—reminiscent of Taxco or a provincial Italian village.

Barrel-vaulted, brick-and-stone **Capilla Cosalá,** founded by Jesuit padres in 1607, is the city's oldest historical structure, though many visitors miss it. On the plaza is the folk baroque **Iglesia de Santa Ursula,** whose interior is decorated with silver ore donated by miners. Opposite the church, the **Museo de Minería e Historia** contains artifacts chronicling the town's 400-year history. Another attraction is the city hall's 200-year-old clock, which uses a rock counterweight, raised by pulleys, to propel the clock hands in 24-hour cycles.

If you're looking for a one-of-a-kind Mexican saddle, check out the shop belonging to renowned saddlemaker **Arcadio García** (on the right as you enter town from below). One of García's saddles was presented to former U.S. president Ronald Reagan by the Mexican government.

Two blocks off the plaza is a small municipal market.

Accommodations and Food: Hotel **Alfredo** and **Hotel Conde** near the plaza offer basic rooms for around US$8-10 per night. Nicer in ambience is the similarly priced **Hotel Colonial,** an 11-room inn with colonial-style courtyard also next to the plaza. For each of these hotels, bathroom facilities are shared.

El Pueblito Café, owned by former Camino Real hotel employee Eduardo Marino, serves the best food in town (several locations—it's a chain). Home-style fare is also available from informal, signless cafes near the plaza; usually these are open for breakfast and lunch (about 8 a.m.-5 p.m.) only.

Getting There: Cosalá is reached via Sinaloa D1, which runs northeast from Mexico 15 beginning exactly halfway between Culiacán and Mazatlán (103 km/64 miles from either city). From the Mexico 15 turnoff, the two-lane, paved road runs 55 km (34 miles) to Cosalá. By car the trip takes no more than 1 1/2 to two hours from Culiacán or Mazatlán.

Buses to Cosalá run from Mazatlán and Culiacán several times daily; the trip takes about three hours.

Presa López Portillo (Comedero)

Only open a little over five years, Presa Comedero, an impoundment of the Río San Lorenzo set in beautiful subtropical mountain scenery, has quickly become one of Mexico's top bass-fishing spots. Hunting for deer, dove, and quail in the area is also highly reputed.

The only facilities on the lake are operated by **Comedero Sportsman's Lodge** in conjunction with fishing or hunting packages. For information, call or write Ron Speed (tel. 214-489-1656, fax 214-489-2856), Malakoff, TX 75148.

The lake can be reached via a 48-km (30-mile) dirt road running north from Cosalá.

MAZATLAN AND VICINITY

From the north, Mazatlán is the first major beach area along mainland Mexico's west coast that is washed by the open Pacific Ocean. With the 1992 completion of the Nogales-Mazatlán tollway, Mazatlán now enjoys the additional distinction of being the only major Mexican beach resort within a day's drive of the U.S. border (1,200 km/744 miles from Nogales, Arizona—about 11½ hours by car).

Whether viewed from land or sea, day or night, Mazatlán's lengthy *malecón*—scalloped by sand-and-palm beaches with green hills and glittering beachfront hotels in the background—is one of the nation's most enduring seaside images. Combining Mexico's longest uninterrupted beach (26 km/16 miles) with a well-preserved historical and cultural heritage, this is a favorite destination for both Mexican and international vacationers, many of whom return year after year.

Depending on the source, estimates of the city's current total population vary wildly from a conservative 260,000 to a high of 500,000. Most likely Mazatlán has no more than 350,000 people within the city limits, though if satellite towns are included in a "metropolitan area," that figure might exceed 400,000. For many visitors and residents, this is a perfect size—large enough that cultural and entertainment venues are numerous, small enough that getting around is convenient. Another secret to Mazatlán's success as a repeat destination: Since tourism still isn't the city's main economic focus, one is less subjected to a "tourist trap" ambience than in Puerto Vallarta, Acapulco, or Cancún. And yet another: Mazatlán is a remarkably tolerant city due to the steady flow of immigrants who have disembarked on its shores from all over the world during the last four centuries.

INTRODUCTION

History

The area wedged between today's Bahía de Puerto Viejo (Old Port Bay) and the natural harbor formed by the Infiernillo, Astillero, and Urias estuaries was once inhabited by the Totorame,

a Mesoamerican Marginal tribal group known for finely crafted, polychromatic ceramics. When Nuño de Guzmán sent 25 Spanish explorers here in 1531 from Culiacán, the Chibcha people they encountered were probably Totorame descendants, although disagreement remains as to whether the Totorame culture still existed at that time.

Guzmán moved on to establish his west coast base in Culiacán, reporting only that the native name for the area was "Place of Deer," or *mazatlán*. Since this is a Nahuatl word, most likely the name actually originated with the Spaniard's Aztec interpreter.

The first colonists to settle here in any numbers were primarily *mulatos* (mixed-race colonists whose physiognomy was predominantly Amerindian or African), and so the settlement was originally called "Pueblo de los Mulatos." After a flood destroyed the town, a new settlement called San Juan Bautista de Mazatlán took its place. In the early 17th century, this became an important Spanish port for exploration of the Baja California peninsula.

As gold and silver were discovered in the nearby Sierra Madre Occidental in the late 18th century, Mazatlán rose to eminence as a supply depot (and bullion shipment point) for mines at Rosario, Copalá, and Pánuco. During the mining era, pirates—including England's Sir Francis Drake and Thomas Cavendish—visited the bay frequently to prey upon gold- and silver-laden Spanish galleons en route to Manila. In the opposite direction, these galleons arrived filled with silks, spices, and gems from the Orient, along with pearls from Baja California (source of Mazatlán's tourist catchphrase, "Pearl of the Pacific").

As the Spanish colonial era wound to a close and Mazatlán's importance as a Spanish port declined, German immigrants moved in and began supplying equipment to local farmers and ranchers. By the time Mexican independence was declared in 1821, the town claimed only 500 residents. Small and relatively remote, Mazatlán managed to avoid many of Mexico's 19th-century conflicts, although the U.S. Navy occupied the town briefly during the Mexican-

American War (1846-48). The French also attacked in 1864, but valiant Mazatlecos managed to defend their town successfully against Napoleon III's imperial forces.

As Sinaloa's mild climate, fertile soils, and stable politics attracted an increasing number of immigrants—including many of Greek, Lebanese, American, Chinese, and Japanese descent—the city grew in importance as a trade center. In 1831 Sinaloa was granted statehood (separating from the former state of Sonora y Sinaloa), and from 1859 to 73 Mazatlán served as the state capital.

The late 19th century brought railroads to Mexico's Pacific coast and the town was transformed almost overnight. With increased access to national and international markets, the local fishing industry flourished, more workers and tradespeople arrived, and the city expanded steadily.

Fishing also lured the first tourists to the area in the '40s and '50s. When sportfishers returned home with reports of Mazatlán's mild tropical climate, picturesque beaches, and tasty seafood, the town's resort status was quietly established. Pleasure visits to Mazatlán have grown steadily since the '50s, and today tourism is second only to fishing as the main source of local income.

Climate And Seasons
One of the reasons for Mazatlán's popularity is the city's near-perfect climate. Located just south of the Tropic of Cancer, the city enjoys warm temperatures year-round, although it's not far enough south to fog your glasses. Pacific Ocean breezes buffet the coastline, moisturizing the dry air that drifts south from the Sonoran Desert and keeping the mercury from rising too high. Water temperatures along the beach hover between 20° C (68° F) and 24° C (76° F) year-round, while air temperatures average 19.4° C (67° F) in January, 27.2° C (81° F) in July.

Another important climatic influence is the Sierra Madre Occidental, which prevents tropical storms off the Gulf of Mexico from reaching this far west while at the same time blocking the Altiplano's desert heat.

Most of the area's annual precipitation falls June-Oct., which leaves mostly clear skies the remainder of the year. For those of us from temperate zones, the only time of year the weather may feel consistently uncomfortable is July-Sept., when frequent rain and summer temperatures combine to produce hot and muggy afternoons (though it's not as bad as, say, southern Texas). As elsewhere in Mexico, room rates and other prices generally drop to their lowest from August to mid-October, so some budget-conscious visitors make a point of vacationing in Mazatlán this time of year.

July is Mazatlán's biggest month in terms of tourist visitation—in July 1992, 132,000 tourist arrivals were recorded, of whom around 110,000 were domestic visitors. The city's second highest tourist month is December, when foreign arrivals outnumber domestic tourists (but don't worry, in Mazatlán the local population always greatly exceeds the tourist population). Except during Carnaval (late February or early March), these are the only two months of the year when advance hotel reservations are absolutely necessary.

SIGHTS

No matter how you choose to transport yourself around the city (see "Getting Around," p. 216), the first thing to get straight is how the 24-km (15-mile) waterfront avenue changes names six times. Starting from the southern tip of the peninsula at the causeway to Cerro del Crestón, **Calz. Crestón Alzada** becomes **Paseo Centenario** at Cerro del Vigia, which turns into **Av. Olas Altas** at Playa Olas Altas and then almost immediately becomes **Paseo Claussen** (some buildings along this stretch will be listed under both street addresses) upon curving around Cerro del Nevería. At Playa Sur the name changes to **Av. del Mar** for a long stretch along this beach and Playa Norte, and finally becomes **Calz. Camarón Sábalo** as it enters the Zona Dorada.

Sometimes the entire non-Zona Dorada stretch is referred to as "Paseo Costero."

Zona Dorada ("Golden Zone")
Much of the city's tourist industry is focused in the "Golden Zone," which runs southward from **Punta Sábalo** (next to the Westin Camino Real) to **Punta Camarón**. Strung out along both sides of Calzada Camarón Sábalo (sometimes called Avenida Camarón Sábalo), the main avenue

DOWNTOWN MAZATLAN AND OLAS ALTAS

PUNTA CHILE
FUERTE CARRANZA
PUNTA TIBURON
ESCUELA DE CIENCIAS DE MAR
(MARINE SCIENCES SCHOOL)
PLAYA SUR
SUITES VIDALMAR
PLAYA LOS PINOS
PASEO CLAUSSEN
JABONERIA
PALMAS
MEXICANA AIRLINES
RESTAURANTE EL MARINERO
16 DE SEPTIEMBRE
AVILES HERMANOS HUNTING OUTFITTERS
SIMON BOLIVAR
MAMUCAS
2D PEÑUELAS
ALEJANDRO QUIJANO
LUIS ZUNIGA
ZARAGOZA
TO MEX 15
JACARANDAS MORELOS
PLAZA ZARAGOZA
POLICE
MONUMENTO A LA MUJER MAZATLECA
GENERO ESTRADA
5 DE MAYO
NELSON
HIDALGO
CERRO DE LA NEVERIA (ICE HOUSE HILL)
MELCHOR OCAMPO
CANIZALES
VALLE
MERCADO
AV. OLAS ALTAS
CENTRO DE IDIOMAS
21 DE MARZO
HOTEL DEL CENTRO
BASILICA DE LA INMACULADA CONCEPCION
LIBRARY
CINEMA ACUARIO
PLACIO DE GOBIERNO
PLAZA REPUBLICANA
HOSPITAL
HOTEL SIESTA
HOTEL CENTRAL
CORREOS Y TELEGRAFOS
AV. FLORES
TOURIST INFORMATION
HOTEL BELMAR
CAFE PACIFICO
RESTAURANTE DONEY
MARIANO ESCOBEDO
LA CASA DE ANA
CONSTITUCION
PLAYA OLAS ALTAS
PLAZUELA MACHADO
MUSEO ARQUEOLOGICO
SIXTO OSUNA
VENUS
NIÑOS HEROES
CALLE BELISARIO DOMINGUEZ
HERIBERTO FRIAS
AV. CARNAVAL
TEATRO ANGELA PERALTA
BENITO JUAREZ
AV. A. SERDAN
TENIENTE JOSE ASUELTA
DR. M. CARVAJAL
PACIFIC OCEAN
HOTEL FREEMAN
ROOSVELT
CABO VIGIA
C. CRUZ
CUSTOMS
AV. MIGUEL ALEMAN
TO MEX 15 SOUTH AND AIRPORT
J. CARRANZA
CERRO DE VIGIA
0   0.2 km

© MOON PUBLICATIONS, INC.

running parallel to the beach, are all of Mazatlán's five-star hotels and restaurants, along with most of the city's tourist-oriented souvenir shops, car rental agencies, and beach recreation facilities. The zone is even patrolled by its own *policía turística.*

Two new marinas currently under construction at the north end of the Zona Dorada (along Laguna del Sábalo) will, when completed, form the largest marina complex in Mexico and one of the largest in all of Latin America. Eventually the complex will include four new five-star hotels along with several condo developments (the first condo phase has sold out in advance of construction).

For most tourists, the Zona Dorada is where the action is. Some may find it a bit too glitzy, preferring the more low-key Playa Norte or Olas Altas areas (see "Beaches" below) farther south. Very few, however, manage to visit Mazatlán without taking a stroll through at least part of the zone; most stroll-worthy is the concentration of hotels, restaurants, bars, and shops found in a loop formed by Av. R.T. Loaiza off Calz. C. Sábalo, between Av. de las Gaviotas and Calz. R. Buelna.

Harbor

Mazatlán's estuarial harbor, which has a navigable depth of 10 meters, is the city's true economic heart. Although it's only ranked 10th among Mexico's ports in terms of total maritime cargo, Mazatlán is the nation's greatest shipper of tuna and shrimp, the bulk of which is exported to the U.S. and Japan via this harbor. Of the nine quays ringing the harbor, four are devoted to receiving and processing tuna, one is for shrimp, and one is used exclusively for freezing and packing.

El Centro (Downtown)

Arguably, three beach resorts in Mexico—Acapulco, Puerto Vallarta, and Mazatlán—can claim colonial histories. Of the three, Mazatlán has the best preserved architecture, some of it within just a few blocks of Playa Olas Altas. The recently formed Old Mazatlán Association—the only such organized effort anywhere along Mexico's Pacific coast—is taking further steps to preserve and promote the 200-year-old downtown.

An interesting walking route through old Mazatlán can be taken from Playa Olas Altas. Starting at Paseo Claussen, walk east along Av. Constitución to **Plazuela Machado** (see description below). A left onto Av. Carnaval at the east end of the plazuela, an immediate right back onto Av. Constitución, and another left on Av. Juárez will take you to **Plaza Republicana.** Two blocks further north on Av. Juárez is the **central market.** If you continue north along Av. Juárez, you'll end up on Av. del Mar at Playa Sur (the south end of Playa Norte). Walk or catch any bus south along Av. del Mar if you need to return to Playa Olas Altas.

Plazuela Machado: At Av. Constitución and Av. Carnaval, this centerpiece of the city's restoration efforts is named for Juan Machado, an early Filipino settler who donated the land for the plaza in the 1900s. A century ago the plaza was the commercial center of the city; now it's making a gradual comeback as a somewhat gentrified entertainment venue, with chic cafes along the north side and the elegantly renovated **Teatro Angela Peralta** around the corner from the west end.

Constructed between 1860-75 as the Teatro Rubio, the theater was restored to its original Italianate Victorian grandeur at a cost of US$5 million and reopened in Oct. 1992 for dance, musical, and theatrical performances. The theater's renovators renamed the former opera venue in honor of famous 19th-century opera diva Angela Peralta (dubbed "the Mexican nightingale" by the press), who died of yellow fever in the Hotel Iturbides next door after giving her first and last Mazatlán performance. An accomplished composer and an opera impresario, Peralta brought Giuseppe Verdi to Mexico City in 1873 to conduct her performance of *Aída.* Her remains are interred at the Rotunda de Hombres Ilustres in Mexico City.

Along the east end of the plaza, the **Portales de Canobbio** provide a good example of the arcade-style architecture once common in urban colonial Mexico.

Plaza Republicana: Two and a half blocks north, bounded by Calle 21 de Marzo, Av. Juárez, Calle Flores, and Calle Nelson, is the city's main, everyday plaza. At the north end of the plaza is the **Basílica de la Inmaculada Concepción,** the city's largest and most important religious edifice. Built between 1875-90 on the site of an Indian shrine, the church was granted *basílica* status in 1935, when the two steeples were added. Architecturally, its lumbering neo-gothic style is unimpressive, but the gilded altar inside is worth a look.

Plaza Republicana is ringed by shoe service stands where the workers don't just shine shoes but will perform repairs and recondition a pair of shoes from soles to uppers; you can leave your shoes here and pick them up a half-hour or so later—looking almost new again. Under the large wrought-iron kiosk in the center of the leafy plaza is **El Jardín,** a simple *cafetería* with *tortas,* hamburgers, breakfasts, and soft drinks; take an outside table to watch the passing show of people.

Mercado José Pino Suárez: Two blocks north of Plaza Republicana off Av. Juárez is Mazatlán's central municipal market. Also known as Mercado Central, the huge complex was originally built in 1895 on the site of a former bullring. This is a very typical, well-stocked Mexican market, with vendors selling a wide variety of fresh produce, meats, cheeses, herbs, flowers, arts and crafts, and household utensils.

Plazuela Zaragoza: This large, busy plaza at Av. Zaragoza, Calle Nelson, and Calle 5 de Mayo is known for its cluster of flower vendors. The day before the Day of the Dead (Nov. 1-2), the plaza is packed with flower wreaths and customers. Four blocks east is the city's oldest church, **Capilla de San José,** constructed by Italian priests between 1831-42.

Museo Arqueológico

This well-run museum at Av. Sixto Osuna 76 (tel. 69-85-35-02) between Playa Olas Altas and Plazuela Machado features exhibits on the pre-Cortesian history and culture of Sinaloa, including collections of petroglyphs, sculpture, and early Totorame pottery. Open Tues.-Sun. 10 a.m.-1 p.m. and 4-6 p.m.

Acuario Mazatlán (Mazatlán Aquarium)

Over 50 saltwater and freshwater tanks (containing a total volume of 123,175 liters/32,500 gallons) display around 250 reef fish species in this modest aquarium. Also on the premises are a marine museum and a small botanical garden, and a new dolphin pool is planned for construction in the near future. The aquarium (tel. 69-81-78-15) is a half block east of Av. del

Mar at Av. de los Deportes 111, behind Motel Del Sol. Open daily 9:30 a.m.-6:30 p.m.; admission is US$2 adults, US$0.75 children.

Beaches

Mazatlán's beaches begin well north of the city and extend southward almost to the tip of the peninsula carved by the Pacific Ocean and the Estero del Astillero. Naming of the beaches can be arbitrary, with each beach sometimes having two or more different names; but generally speaking, what separates one beach from the next is a *punta* or point whose name just about everyone agrees on. As fishing and tourism are Mazatlán's only major industries, the beaches stay fairly clean.

North of the city limits (north of Punta Cerritos) is **Playa Escondida** ("Hidden Beach"), a mixture of rock and sand frequented by local fishermen. Though the rocks prevent it from being the best swimming beach, Escondida's undeveloped remoteness makes it quite suitable for camping. Also known as Playa Brujas ("Witches Beach"), this beach is accessible only by dirt road from the highway bypass that leads from Mexico 15 to Playa Cerritos and the Zona Dorada farther south. During a good summer swell, surfable breaks come off Punta Cerritos at the south end of the beach.

Running south from Punta Cerritos to Punta Sábalo and the Westin Camino Real is **Playa Cerritos** ("Little Hills Beach"), a slowly developing beach with sand dunes that still bear a few indigenous grasses and vines. Probably because the Playa Escondida Trailer Park is located here, the beach is sometimes called Playa Escondida. To really appreciate this beach, you must maneuver around the RV parks and hotels that now block the view from the road.

Next south is Playa Sábalo ("Ladyfish Beach"), a lovely stretch of golden sand extending from craggy Punta Sábalo in the north to

---

SURF FLAG CODES

Color-coded flags on Mazatlán's beaches alternate according to the following surf conditions:

Green: calm   White: jellyfish

Yellow: surf/tide caution   Red: surf/tide danger

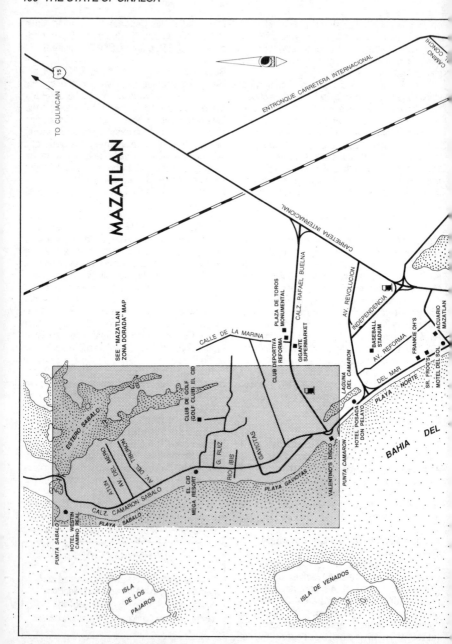

© MOON PUBLICATIONS, INC.

Playa Gaviotas

JOE CUMMINGS

gentle Punta Codo in the south. Under certain weather conditions, hard shore breaks and a stiff undertow make swimming a bit hazardous on this beach. Although part of the Zona Dorada, development along Playa Sábalo isn't quite as end-to-end as farther south.

Below Punta Codo, also in the Zona Dorada, **Playa Gaviotas** ("Sea Gulls Beach") looks much the same as Playa Sábalo except that it's thicker with hotels, condos, and restaurants. Offshore protection offered by Isla de los Venados also keeps the surf gentler and makes the beach less steep. Playa Gaviotas and the Zona Dorada come to a sudden halt at rocky Punta Camarón, topped by the striking white domes and turrets of the Valentino's restaurant-bar-disco complex.

South of Punta Camarón begins the city's original *malecón*, a 9.5-km (six-mile) seawall promenade along **Playa Norte** ("North Beach"). Although not as fine-sanded as beaches farther north, Playa Norte is the city's most popular beach, attracting a friendly mixture of fishermen, local volleyball players, regular strollers, boogie-boarders, and tourists. At night the string of bars and seafood restaurants opposite Playa Norte along Av. del Mar fills with local residents and a few Zona Dorada escapees.

Fishing boats anchor at the south end of Playa Norte (sometimes called Playa Sur or "South Beach") near Punta Tiburón, after which a headland of rocky beaches swells around to cozy Bahía Olas Altas and Mazatlán's south-ernmost beach, **Playa Olas Altas** ("High Waves Beach"). The city's oldest tourist lodge, Hotel Belmar, still stands opposite the middle of the beach. High-divers plunge headlong into the surf from a 13.5-meter (45-foot) platform on **Punta de las Clavadistas** ("Divers Point") on weekends and holidays. Divers must time the tide and swells accurately, as even at high tide the water below the platform measures only two meters (six feet) deep between waves.

Although it's a favored surfing spot, the breakers at Playa Olas Altas are generally a bit too strong for average swimmers.

Las Tres Islas

This cluster of three volcanic islands just offshore offers opportunities for daytime getaways by boat. The clear waters and pristine beaches of **Isla de los Venados** ("Deer Island") and **Isla de los Chivos** ("Goats Island") are popular for swimming, snorkeling, and scuba diving (but no goats in sight). Birders flock to **Isla de los Pájaros** ("Birds Island"), an important nesting ground for around a hundred species, especially the native brown pelican.

Amphibious boat transport to these islands can be arranged from Playa Gaviotas 200 meters north of Hotel Playa Mazatlán or from in front of El Cid Mega Resort. The crossing takes only about 15-20 minutes and costs US$10 roundtrip. If you plan to stay awhile, make an appointment for the return trip—and don't pay till you've been picked up!

Isla De La Piedra

Not really an island at all, "Stone Island" is a peninsula just opposite the harbor canal with 16 km (10 miles) of mostly undeveloped beach (there are a few *palapa* restaurants near the boat landing) and Mexico's third largest coconut grove (about 8,000 acres). Overnight camping is permitted.

Several companies arrange all-inclusive day trips to Piedra. **Viajes El Sábalo** (tel. 69-84-30-09) at Los Sábalos Resort Hotel, for example, has daily departures from a dock off Av. del Puerto at 10 a.m. on its 15-meter (50-foot) motor catamaran *El Sábalo,* which sails by the lighthouse and pelican rookeries before landing at the beach for the afternoon; the boat returns around 4 p.m. The per-person price of US$30 includes lunch, beverages (including beer), and guide services.

Launches can also be arranged on your own from the Av. del Puerto docks for about US$15 roundtrip.

Cerro De La Nevería

Just inland from Punta de Clavadistas on Playa Olas Altas, "Ice House Hill" is named for a tunnel that was used to store ice shipped from San Francisco in the 19th century. During the city's earlier history it served as a lookout point for Spanish sentries guarding against pirates and foreign naval attack.

During the Mexican Revolution, Gen. Venustiano Carranza ordered a biplane to drop a crude, pigskin-wrapped bomb of dynamite and iron onto a munitions dump atop Cerro de la Nevería, a 1914 event that made Mazatlán the second city in world history (after Tripoli, Libya) to be bombed from the air. The airsick bombardier reportedly missed the hill entirely, dropping the bomb on a nearby street and killing two civilians.

Paseo Vistahermosa, off Calle Morelos in Old Mazatlán, leads around the top of the hill to both Pacific Ocean and city views.

At the seaward base of the hill facing the city is the **Monumento a la Mujer Mazatleca** (Monument to Mazatlán Women), a five-meter-high sculpture representing the local feminine ideal.

Cerro De Vigia

This hill south of Playa Olas Altas is surmounted by **Pérgola de Cerro de Vigia,** a garden plaza with an 1875 English cannon and a cityscape view over Old Mazatlán. A little below the plaza, the little-known Café El Mirador offers chairs and refreshment noon-9 p.m. daily. Paseo del Centenario, off Blvd. M. Alemán in the Olas Altas district, winds up the hill to the plaza.

Cerro Del Crestón

A causeway at the southwest end of Av. del Puerto leads to Isla del Crestón, topped by 154-meter (515-foot) El Faro, reportedly the world's tallest lighthouse. A 25-minute hike from the end of the road, along a winding path, leads to the summit.

Other Sightseeing

Built by the Spanish and stocked with an English cannon, the **Fuerte Carranza** (Carranza Fort) at Punta Chile, west of the Playa Sur's southern tip, was used to defend the city against the attempted 1864 French invasion.

Mazatlán's famous Pacífico beer is brewed at the independently owned **Pacífico Brewery** (tel. 69-82-79-00) east of downtown at Calle Ocampo and Av. Leyva; beer aficionados may be able to arrange tours with help from the state tourist office (see "Mazatlán Information," p. 213).

MAZATLAN ACCOMMODATIONS

Mazatlán boasts around 10,000 tourist rooms to choose from. Nearly half are upscale hotels; around 2,000 are condos, apartments, and timeshares; and the remainder are budget-to-moderate accommodations.

Hotel occupancy, especially for less expensive accommodations, remains fairly high throughout Nov.-April—Mazatlán's "high season"—when advance reservations are recommended. Rates are also highest during this period, although shopping for package deals usually brings substantial savings over "rack rates." Two- to seven-night packages taken before Dec. 25 run as low as US$23 per night at midclass places or US$40 per night at luxury properties. Add US$20 to these rates for high-season packages.

Because seasonal, package, and rack rates vary so widely, it's virtually impossible to nail down a single set of rates for Mazatlán's

PUNTA SABALO
WESTIN CAMINO REAL
HOTEL PUEBLO BONITO
PLAYA ESCONDIDA
TRAILER PARK

TO PLAYA CERRITOS, PUNTA CERRITOS, AND MEX 15 NORTH

ESTERO SABALO

RESTAURANT SENOR PEPPER'S

BLVD. DE MARLIN

AV. DEL PULPO

PLAYA SABALO

SAN BARTOLO TRAILER PARK

HOTEL OCEANO PALACE
CARAVELLE BEACH CLUB

AV. DEL ATUN

AV. DEL MERO

RESTAURANTE TRES ISLAS

AV. DEL TIBURON

MAZATLAN ZONA DORADA

MAR ROSA TRAILER PARK

FIESTA AMERCANA MAZATLAN

AV. CIRCUITO DEL CAMPEADOR

EL CID MEGA RESORT

HOTEL PUESTA DEL SOL

CALZ. CAMARON

CLUB DE GOLF EL CID

AV. G. RUIZ

PACIFIC OCEAN

HOTEL INN AT MAZATLAN

HOTEL COSTA DE ORO

HOTEL BALBOA TOWER

RIO IBIS

AV. CIRCUITO DEL CAMPEADOR

RACQUET CLUB

CHICO'S BEACH CLUB

AV. SABALO

APARTAMENTOS FIESTA

APTS. LOS GIRASOLES

AV. DE LAS GAVIOTAS

SIERRA DE VENADOS

BANAMEX

TORTAS HAWAII

LAS PALMAS TRAILER PARK

AV. LOMAS DE MAZATLAN

PUNTA CODO

SUITES LINDA MAR

LA CASA CONTENTA

MOTEL MARLEY

SUITES LAS FLORES

TOURIST POLICE

JUNGLE JUICE

AEROMEXICO

SIERRA NEVADA

TO MEX 15 AND AIRPORT

AV. R.T. LOAIZA

PLAYA GAVIOTAS

HOTEL PLAYA MAZATLAN

CINEMA

LOS SABALOS RESORT HOTEL

SIERRA QUEMADA

CALZ. R. BUELNA

PLAYA CAMARON

LA POSTA TRAILER PARK

MOTEL CAMARON

TO PLAYA NORTE AND DOWNTOWN

VALENTINO'S DISCO

0   1.5 km

© MOON PUBLICATIONS, INC.

hotels. SECTUR's star-rating system, however, has established a standard range for each hotel category specifically for Sinaloa (differs from national rating): US$100-200 per night for five stars or *gran turismo;* US$50-100 for four stars; US$40-65 for three stars; US$20-35 for two stars; under US$20 for one star or *clase económica.*

Budget Hotels And Apartments

Hotels: Mazatlán's first tourist lodgings were built along Playa Olas Altas in the 1940s but are now separated from the beach by Paseo Claussen near Playa los Pinos downtown. The oldest continuously operating beach hotel in the city, **Hotel Belmar** (tel. 69-85-11-11) on Paseo Claussen, is still popular among budget-conscious travelers. Well-worn double rooms—all with a/c—in this six-story hotel cost around US$20 per night (a bit more for ocean views); facilities include a pool and sidewalk restaurant. The Belmar always fills up for Carnaval in late February or early March.

A bit farther north along Paseo Claussen is the equally popular **Hotel La Siesta** (tel. 81-26-40), which is built around the semi-outdoor El Shrimp Bucket, Carlos Anderson's first Mexican chain eatery. Rooms here cost around US$25 a night with a/c and TV. Because of the courtyard restaurant, this hotel can get a bit noisy at times. Like the Belmar, La Siesta books out quickly for Carnaval.

At the southern heart of the Zona Dorada, opposite the huge Hotel Playa Mazatlán, is **Hotel Tropicana** (tel. 83-80-00, fax 83-53-61, Av. R.T. Loaiza 27), perhaps the zone's least expensive hotel accommodations. Large but less-than-clean rooms, many with balconies, cost US$25-35, even less in the off seasons. The Tropicana is very popular with spring-breakers and Carnaval-goers because it's inexpensive and close to the action.

If you're interested in staying in Old Mazatlán downtown rather than at the beach, **Hotel Central** (tel. 82-18-88) at Calle B. Dominguez 2 Sur (between Calle Flores and Mariano Escobedo next to Plaza Hidalgo) offers clean, air-conditioned rooms—some with plaza views—for US$24-28 s/d. The hotel is conveniently located within walking distance of all the major plazas as well as the Centro de Idiomas language school. Even cheaper, and closer to the market and

cathedral, is **Hotel del Centro** (tel. 81-26-73) at Calle Canizales and Av. Juárez. Basic rooms cost US$15-18, plus US$2 extra for a/c, another US$2 for TV.

Apartments: Perhaps the most economical way to vacation in Mazatlán—besides camping—is to rent an apartment where you can cook at least some of your own meals. Rents vary from a low of US$160 per month for a studio, to US$300-350 per month for a one-bedroom apartment, to US$500-750 per month for a two- to three-bedroom place. The main areas for vacation apartments are the Zona Dorada and Playa Olas Altas; apartments in the former district tend to be a bit more expensive than in the latter, though not substantially so.

Suites Vidalmar (tel. 81-21-90) at Calle Las Palmas, opposite Punta Tiburón at the south end of Playa Sur, has simple but well-maintained one-bedroom apartments with bay views and a pool for US$26 d, US$35 q. Other small apartment complexes in this area have similar rates; a few one- or two-bedroom places—usually booked a year in advance—rent for as low as US$300 per month.

Apartamentos Fiesta (tel. 13-53-55, Calle Río Ibís 502 at Calle Río de la Plata), four blocks east from central Playa Sábalo in the Zona Dorada, features ten apartments—some with kitchenettes—around a lush tropical garden. Studio apartments rent for around US$200 per month, one-bedroom apartments with kitchenettes for US$300. Call or write well in advance to reserve a spot in this popular complex.

Medium-priced Hotels And Apartments

Playa Norte: A string of three- and four-star hotels built in the '60s and '70s, all with air-conditioned rooms, swimming pools, restaurants, and security parking, are lined up along busy Av. del Mar, which separates the hotels from the beach between the Zona Dorada and downtown.

Next door to Señor Frog's on Av. del Mar (and only three blocks from the bus terminal) is Playa Norte's best value, the three-star **Hotel Las Arenas (Sands)** (tel. 69-82-00-00, fax 69-82-10-25), where all rooms come with refrigerators, phones, and TVs for US$30 s/d in the low season, US$38-40 Dec. 19-March 15. The Sands advertises occasional specials for US$23 per night. Similar in price (US$25-35 s/d) and facilities are **Motel del Sol** (tel. 85-11-03, fax 85-26-03), Av. del Mar 800; **Hotel Playa Mar Club** (tel. 82-08-33), Av. del Mar 840; and **Hotel Posada de Don Pelayo** (tel. 83-18-88, fax 84-07-99), Av. del Mar 1111.

Nicer and a bit more expensive is Best Western's four-star **Hotel Aguamarina** (tel. 81-70-80, fax 82-46-24) farther south on Av. del Mar. Clean, comfortable rooms with phones and satellite TV, some with balconies, cost US$50-60 s, US$55-65 d.

Hotel de Cima (tel. 82-73-00, fax 82-73-11), just a bit farther south on Av. del Mar, has the usual four-star amenities plus an underground tunnel that links the hotel with Playa Norte (thereby saving guests from having to dash across Av. del Mar). Large standard rooms—some with ocean-view balconies—cost US$50 s/d; four two-bedroom units are available for US$60 each.

Other Playa Norte hotels in the US$50-60 range include: **Hotel Hacienda Mazatlán** (tel. 82-70-00, fax 85-15-79), Av. del Mar and Calle Flamingos; **Hotel Las Jacarandas** (tel. 84-11-77, fax 84-10-77), Av. del Mar 2500; and **Hotel Suites Las Sirenas** (tel. 83-18-88, fax 84-07-99), Av. del Mar 1100.

Zona Dorada: Between the luxury high-rise hotels along Playa Gaviotas and Playa Sábalo are a number of smaller inns and apartment complexes with very reasonable rates. One of the best deals in this area is the quiet, three-star **Hotel Plaza Gaviotas** (tel. 13-43-22, fax 13-66-85) at Calle Bugambilias 100 (on the opposite side of Calz. C. Sábalo from the beach). Spacious, simple but comfortable rooms (most with balconies) built around a pool and shady garden cost US$35 s, US$44 d; off-season specials may dip as low as US$20 a night. All rooms come with a/c and satellite TV.

On Playa Sábalo at the Zona Dorada's quieter north end, **Hotel Océano Palace** (tel. 13-06-66; 800-352-7690 in the U.S./Canada; fax 13-96-66) has rooms—many with ocean views, some with kitchenettes—for a reasonable US$45 s, US$50 d April 12-Dec. 19, US$10 more the remainder of the year. Farther south on Playa Sábalo is the similar **Hotel Costa de Oro** (tel. 13-53-44; 800-876-5278 in the U.S./Canada; fax 14-42-09), where rooms are US$56 s, US$69 d year-round.

On Punta Codo between Playa Gaviotas and Playa Camarón, **Motel Marley** and **Suites Linda Mar** (tel. 13-55-33, Calle R.T. Loaiza 222, A.P. 214) share the same owner and offer similar apartment-style accommodations in a quiet area for US$49 for one bedroom, US$67 for two bedrooms. All apartments comes with kitchenettes and a/c; Motel Marley has a small pool. Favorites among migrating snowbirds who spend their winters surf casting a few yards in front of the apartments, both properties fill up early every year.

Between Motel Marley and Suites Linda Mar is the similar but separately owned **La Casa Contenta** (tel. 13-59-39; Av. R.T. Loaiza s/n), where one-bedroom apartments rent for US$44 per day, larger bungalows for US$130 per day.

Right on Playa Gaviotas, **Suites Las Flores** (tel. 13-50-11, fax 14-34-22) at Av. R.T. Loaiza 212 offers apartments with kitchenettes for US$40-60 in low season, US$60-80 peak season.

Luxury Hotels

All of the city's upscale accommodations (and its one *gran turismo* property) are located along Playa Sábalo and Playa Gaviotas in the Zona Dorada. Each hotel has a distinct high season (Dec. 20-April 11 or thereabouts) and low season (the remainder of the year) rate schedule; the difference between high and low tariffs is often substantial. Some of these hotels also offer "time-share" sales in which you purchase room or apartment space for one, two, or more weeks per year (see special topic "Buying or Leasing Property in Mexico," p. 63, for more information).

Farther north on Punta Sábalo is the nicely landscaped **Westin Camino Real Mazatlán** (tel. 69-13-11-11; 800-228-3000 in the U.S./Canada; fax 14-03-11), where large, luxurious rooms cost US$100-115 per night; all have ocean views. Set on its own private cove, with a pool, tennis courts, and open-air lobby, the Camino Real is Mazatlán's top hotel property at the moment.

The **Fiesta Americana Mazatlán** (tel. 13-57-33; fax 14-12-87), popular among Mexican business travelers and conventioneers in its former incarnation as a Holiday Inn, has the advantage of being located at the quiet northern end of the zone's Playa Sábalo (off Calz. C.

Sábalo), away from the busy Playa Gaviotas tourist ghetto. Recently renovated, the rooms run US$75-90 s/d in the low season, US$90 up in high season. Facilities include two restaurants, pool, and tennis courts.

Showing four stars on some hotel lists, five stars on others, the venerable **Hotel Playa Mazatlán** (tel. 83-48-22; 800-762-5816 in the U.S./Canada; fax 84-03-66) was the first hotel to build on Playa Gaviotas and is still the most successful due to its reputation for good service, reasonable rates, efficient maintenance, and good beach positioning (just a few steps from the sand). It's also popular for its twice-weekly Fiesta Mexicana (see "Entertainment," below) and Sunday evening beach fireworks, as well as for its location in the heart of the Zona Dorada action. Rooms—some with ocean views —cost US$64-73 in the low season, US$75-90 in the high season. Cheaper package deals are available—call and ask.

The infamous **El Cid Mega Resort** (tel. 13-33-33; 800-525-1925 in the U.S./Canada; fax 14-13-11), at the middle of Playa Sábalo, features three hotels with over a thousand rooms, a convention center, 12 restaurants, six palm-shaded swimming pools, an 18-hole golf course, 17 tennis courts, theater, disco, and shopping mall. A veritable town unto itself with as many as 4,000 residents (half employees, half guests) at one time, El Cid is the kind of place you can easily get lost in. A huge marina is currently under construction nearby. Room rates hover around US$100 s/d in the high season, down to US$85 the remainder of the year. Although El Cid has a *gran turismo* rating, it relies heavily on guests supplied by package tours and as such doesn't give you the same sense of luxury as the five-star Camino Real.

Two other five-star luxury properties on the beach (off Calz. C. Sábalo) in the Zona Dorada —all in the US$75-95 range—include **Hotel Pueblo Bonito** (tel. 14-37-00, fax 14-17-23), just south of the Camino Real on Playa Sábalo; and **Los Sábalos Resort Hotel** (tel. 83-53-33; 800-528-8760 in the U.S./Canada; fax 83-81-56), just south of Hotel Playa Mazatlán on Playa Gaviotas. Both are well-run establishments.

On The Highway

Drivers wanting to stay out on the highway or to bypass Mazatlán altogether on their way farther south can stay at the **Motel Oasis** (tel. 69-83-09-89) on Mexico 15 North for around US$35 per night.

There are a couple of basic US$10-15 hotels in the junction town of Villa Unión just south of Mazatlán; **Hotel del Piñon** looks the best.

RV Parks And Camping

At any given time, Mazatlán has seven or eight trailer parks in operation with a total of around 500 spaces, all of them near the northern beach strip. Rates are generally US$10-12 per rig per night for two people, plus US$1-2 for each additional person; monthly rates of US$250-300 (or lower in the off-season) are usually available.

Slots can fill up quickly during the annual Dec.-April snowbird migration—write or call in advance to be sure of a space if you plan to arrive that time of year. Where available, A.P. (post office box) addresses are listed below with phone numbers. Another reason to contact these parks in advance is that some may close down during the June-Oct. off-season.

The huge, 262-space **Playa Escondida (Holiday) Trailer Park** (tel. 69-83-25-78; A.P. 682) on Playa Cerritos costs US$12 per night for full hookups, US$8 for tents/campers. Facilities include hot showers, coin laundry, a saltwater pool, and recreation hall.

On Calz. C. Sábalo opposite Playa Sábalo (near the Hotel Océano Palace) is **San Bartolo Trailer Park** (tel. 83-57-55), a relatively small, 48-space park with full hookups for US$10 a day. San Bartolo is closed June-October.

Mar Rosa Trailer Park (tel. 13-61-87; A.P. 435), next to the Fiesta Americana, has 65 unsheltered beachfront spaces with full hookups for US$11 per day. Besides hot showers and a small store, Mar Rosa has a few apartments for rent—a plus when a long-term RVer decides to invite friends or family for a visit.

The well-kept, shady, secure, and often full **Las Palmas Trailer Park** (tel. 83-64-24) at Calz. C. Sábalo 333, farther south in the Zona Dorada near Fandango Disco and Las Palmas Suites, has 66 spaces with full hookups for US$12 per day. Facilities include a coin laundry and hot showers.

Amidst a tropical setting of mango, papaya, avocado, and banana trees, **La Posta Trailer**

Park (tel. 83-53-10; A.P. 362), at Calz. R. Buelna 7 (near the PEMEX station a couple of blocks east of Calz. C. Sábalo) offers 210 full-hookup slots for a budget US$10 per day, tent/camper spaces for US$6. Because La Posta is so large, this is your best bet when arriving in town unannounced during high season. On the premises are a large pool with sundeck, coin laundry, convenience store, *palapas,* and hot showers.

Motel Camarón, just north of the Valentino's complex on Punta Camarón, has eight slots with full hookups at US$11 per night.

Primitive, free beach camping is possible at Playa Escondida north of Playa Cerritos, at the north end of Cerritos itself, on Isla de la Piedra, and on Isla de los Venados.

FOOD

Culiacán may be Sinaloa's state capital, but Mazatlán is the state's food capital, with more restaurants per capita than anywhere in Northern Mexico outside Monterrey. It would take an entire book just to cover the city's restaurants; the following list represents the best places in each category.

Not described are the chains and fast-food places, many of which are in the Zona Dorada. Burger King and KFC are already in town, while a McDonald's is being built near the Valentino's complex. At the intersection of Calz. C. Sábalo and Av. R.T. Loaiza are several fast-food purveyors, including **Helados Bing** (Mexican ice-cream chain), **Dairy Queen** (burgers and ice cream), **TCBY** (frozen yogurt), **Rin Rin Pizza** (pizza and pasta), and **Tortas Hawaii** (Mexican sandwiches).

Seafood

Seafood is what Mazatlecos do best, and Sinaloan seafood at its best includes *pescado zarandeado* (barbecued fish), *caldo sudador* (red snapper soup), *camarones con mango* (mango shrimp), and *marlín ahumada* (smoked marlin). If you're not sure what to choose, most seafood places offer a mixed seafood grill (*parrillada de mariscos*) that contains a selection of fresh fish and shellfish—oysters, shrimp, crab, swordfish or red snapper, and whatever else might be the catch of the day.

Shrimp is particularly plentiful since no other port in Mexico takes in as many of the pink crustaceans—an average 16.8 million kilograms (37 million pounds) per annum from a fleet of over 800 shrimp boats.

$$-$$$ Chiquita Banana (tel. 69-13-11-11), Westin Camino Real, Zona Dorada. Despite the cutesy name, this is one of Mazatlán's nicest restaurants, with an open-air, *palapa*-style arrangement overlooking the beach. House specialties include oysters and shrimp á la orange. Open daily noon-11 p.m.

$$ Mamucas (tel. 81-34-90), Calle Bolivar 404 Pte. and 5 de Mayo (in back of the Mexicana Airlines office). This very popular, no-nonsense seafood place, in business for 40 years, specializes in fresh snapper served Veracruz style, smoked marlin, and a mixed seafood grill for two. Open daily noon-11 p.m.

$$ El Marinero (tel. 81-76-82), Paseo Claussen at 5 de Mayo, Playa Norte (Sur). Another dependable standby featuring shrimp prepared in a variety of ways, smoked marlin, ceviche, and *pescado zarandeado* cooked on mangrovewood fires. Two menus are available, the regular menu plus a less expensive "Tourist Economical Menu," which features smaller shrimp. Open 11 a.m.-11 p.m. daily.

$$ Puerto Azul (tel. 82-40-31), right on the beach at Playa Norte/Sur (off Av. del Mar and Miramar) near the Monumento al Pescador. A rustic but intimate decor combined with attentive service, great food, and simultaneous sunset and city views make this a personal favorite. Menu highlights include *pescado zarandeado* barbecued over an open wood fire near the entrance, *chinchulines* (marlin tacos), assorted ceviches, and *alambres de camarones* (shrimp kabob). The English menu has some particularly amusing translations. Open daily noon-midnight.

$$ El Shrimp Bucket (tel. 81-63-50), Paseo Claussen 11 (in the courtyard of Hotel La Siesta). A festive, indoor-outdoor restaurant famous for shrimp served in every conceivable fashion, including the ever-popular fried shrimp served in a terra-cotta bucket. Breakfasts are also good here. This was Carlos Anderson's first chain restaurant endeavor (but not his first restaurant, which was Mexico City's Sí Cómo No); Grupo Anderson now has over 50 Mexican restaurants (in four countries), each of them known for their whimsical themes and original recipes. Open daily 6 a.m.-11 p.m.

$$-$$$ Restaurante Tres Islas (tel. 13-59-32), on the beach between the Fiesta Americana and Caravelle Beach Club on Calz. C Sábalo, Zona Dorada. A large, *palapa*-style restaurant esteemed for its mixed seafood grill prepared at tableside. A second branch, **Paraíso Tres Islas**, north of Hotel Playa Mazatlán in Centro Comercial Tres Islas, has a similar menu and a beach view, but is not on the beach. Open daily 7 a.m.-midnight.

Mexican

$$ Restaurante Doney (tel. 69-81-26-51), Calle M. Escobedo 610 at Av. 5 de Mayo downtown. A Mazatlán institution since 1959, Doney offers Mexican home-style cooking in a beautiful old house decorated with historical photos and a brick-domed ceiling. Specialties include (*carne*) *asada al carbón*, traditional Mexican *antojitos* (tacos, enchiladas, etc.), and *chilorio*, a spicy, Sinaloa-style sausage. Doney's *comida corrida* (served weekdays noon to 4 pm), a complete meal of soup, entree, side dishes, and dessert, is an especially good deal. Open daily 8 a.m.-10:30 p.m.

$$-$$$ Señor Frog's Bar & Grill (tel. 82-19-25), Av. del Mar 30, Playa Norte (halfway between Valentino's and the Monumento al Pescador). Carl Anderson's second chain venture is still one of his most popular. In fact it gets downright raucous here most nights, with the waiters and waitresses vying with the patrons to see who can act more outrageously. Specializes in the restaurant's own brand of Mexican food, barbecued ribs, stuffed shrimp, and very potent margaritas. *Bandido*-garbed waiters wearing *bandoleros* stuffed with shot glasses and carrying bottles of tequila roam the restaurant in search of victims. Open daily noon-midnight.

$ Tacos (Señor) Luna, Calz. C. Sábalo, Zona Dorada (there are two branches, one on either side of Sábalo). This indoor-outdoor taco bar, very popular with both locals and gringos, has the best tacos in town—your choice of marlin, shrimp, ceviche, *carne asada, pollo asado, carnasa* (cheek, tongue, or brains), or *carne de puerco adobado* (adobo pork)—plus delicious and inexpensive quesadillas, *queso fundido,*

guacamole, *alambre con queso,* (kabob with cheese), and ice-cold beer.

On every table is a fiery "guacamole" of pounded tomatillos and green serranos (avocado guacamole must be ordered separately), *pico de gallo* (similar to *salsa fresca* or *salsa cruda),* and a pureed red *chile de arbol* sauce. Open Mon.-Thurs. 1 p.m.-midnight and Fri.-Sat. 1 p.m.-1 a.m.

$$ Terraza Playa Mazatlán (tel. 83-44-55), Hotel Playa Mazatlán, Zona Dorada. This casual, popular, open-air restaurant facing the beach offers gut-busting breakfasts and Mexican buffets at moderate prices. The "Fiesta Mexicana" on Tuesdays, Fridays, and Saturdays at 7 p.m. is a one-price deal that includes cocktails, beer, music, dancing, folkloric performances, and a huge buffet with steaks, fried chicken, Mexican standards, and seafood. Open for breakfast 6-11 a.m., lunch noon-4 p.m., and dinner 6-11 p.m.

$$ El Tunel (no phone), Av. Carnaval, opposite the Teatro Angela Peralta. Consisting of a narrow hallway lined with tables and a traditional kitchen in an Old Mazatlán casa, this little hideaway serves authentic Sinaloan and Mexican dishes like *chilorio* (Sinaloan-style sausage made with pork or venison mixed with chiles) and homemade mole, a thick sauce of chocolate, sesame, chiles and spices.

International

$$ Café Pacífico, corner of Av. Constitución and Calle H. Frias on Plazuela Machado. This nicely decorated bar-cafe in a restored turn-of-the-century Victorian features European pub-style food and Spanish specialties. Open daily 10 a.m.-2 a.m.

$$$ Casa de Tony (tel. 85-12-62), Calle M. Escobedo 111. Often cited as the city's "best" (read "expensive") restaurant, Tony's serves gourmet steak, seafood, continental, Mexican, and daily specials in the courtyard of an elegantly restored Old Mazatlán mansion. Open daily 6-11 p.m.

$$-$$$ Hostería Machado, Av. Constitución 519, next to Café Pacífico on Plazuela Machado. This chic, continental-style restaurant is set in a 19th-century Spanish townhouse. Open daily 10 a.m.-midnight.

$-$$ **Lyni's** (tel. 14-07-54), opposite the Aeroméxico office at Calz. C. Sábalo and Av. Lomas de Mazatlán. One of the best values in the Zona Dorada, this super-clean, air-conditioned wonder serves a wide selection of reasonably priced soups, salads, breakfasts, Mexican specialties, and seafood in a coffee shop-style atmosphere. A good choice for those put off by the zone's tourist-oriented restaurants but too timid to eat at funkier places. Open daily 7 a.m.-10 p.m.

$$$ **Señor Pepper Restaurant-Bar** (tel. 14-01-01), opposite the Westin Camino Real on Calz. C. Sábalo. Probably the most elegant restaurant in the Zona Dorada, with polished-brass ambience and tuxedoed waiters. Despite the name, house specialties are prime-grade steak, pork chops, lobster, and shrimp, mostly prepared and served American- or European-style. Open daily 6 p.m.-midnight.

$$$ **Restaurante El Sheik** (tel. 84-44-78), on Punta Camarón, where Calz. C. Sábalo turns into Av. del Mar. The architecture is post-modernist Moor, the decor gleaming silver and white tablecloths, the cuisine international and national with an emphasis on seafood and steak. Flaming coffees and liqueurs are a house specialty. Excellent ocean and coastline views. Open daily 6 p.m.-1 a.m.

Vegetarian

$$ **La Casa de Ana** (tel. 69-85-25-39), Av. Constitución 515, Plazuela Machado (next to Hostería Machado). Simple but pleasantly decorated, with a changing variety of salads, yogurt, vegetarian tamales and *pozole*, and *comida corrida*. A special Sunday vegetarian buffet costs only US$4. Open daily 10 a.m.-10 p.m.

$ **Restaurante Vegetariano**, Calle B. Dominguez, diagonally opposite Centro de Idiomas. A small shop/cafe sells curative herbs, vitamins, yogurt, fruit, teas, and fresh-baked whole wheat bread. The cafe section is open for lunch only, when a *comida corrida* including soup, salad, entree, and fruit or vegetable drink costs US$4. The owner, a Mexican woman of French-Chinese descent, speaks good English. Open daily 1-3 p.m. for lunch, 8 a.m.-5 p.m. for retail.

$-$$ **Tienda Naturalista**, Calle Flores 208 Pte., near Plaza Republicana. Another shop/cafe with imaginative *comidas corridas* and natural food items. Open daily 1-3 p.m. for lunch, 8 a.m.-5 p.m. for retail.

Other

$-$$ **La Copa de Leche** (tel. 69-82-57-53), Av. Olas Altas 33 Sur. Also known as Antojitos El Farol, this casual indoor-outdoor cafe has been a local favorite for sunset- and people-watching for 30 years. Open 7 a.m.-7 p.m.

SIERRA CEVICHE

Ceviche (sometimes spelled "cebiche" or "sibiche") is a seafood appetizer consisting of fish or shellfish marinated in lime juice until "cooked." It's very popular throughout Pacific Mexico, and for every cook, you'll find a different recipe—it can be a wonderful experience in one restaurant and a poor excuse for getting rid of fish scraps in another.

Since it's easy to make even while camping on the beach (no fire necessary), ceviche offers an excellent alternative to the usual fried, baked, or grilled fish dishes with which most Mexico anglers are acquainted. One of the best fishes to use for ceviche is the sierra, a common type of mackerel usually caught inshore-offshore; John Steinbeck, during his 1941 Sea of Cortez expedition, pronounced it "the most delicious fish of all." Other great candidates for ceviche are halibut, shark, shrimp, lobster, or just about any other fish whose flesh is not too "dry" (the oilier the better, since the lime juice counteracts the oil). Always use only the freshest fish available.

Serves four

1/2 pound fresh sierra fillets, thinly sliced

1/4 cup fresh lime juice

one avocado, peeled and cut into half-inch cubes

eight ripe, red cherry tomatoes cut in half (or 1 large ripe tomato)

one serrano chile, minced (or more if you want it *really* hot)

two tbsp. fresh cilantro leaves, minced

one tbsp. olive oil

1/2 tsp. salt (optional)

Put the sliced sierra in a large bowl, mix with the lime juice, and marinate in a cooler for a half-hour. Drain; gently toss with the remaining ingredients. Best served with fresh tortilla chips (or spread over *tostadas*, whole fried corn tortillas) and cold *cerveza*.

$$ Jungle Juice, Calle de las Garzas and Laguna, Zona Dorada, opposite Evolución Bookstore. This funky, tourist-oriented place specializes in fresh tropical fruit smoothies, the namesake for which blends six fruits with ice and orange juice. Another blend, "Moctezuma's Revenge Remedy," mixes guava, rice, water, and lime juice in a tasty but effective concoction. The menu features breakfasts, shrimp, burgers, vegetarian and simple Mexican food. The restaurant downstairs is open 7:30 a.m.-10 p.m., the popular roof bar 9 p.m.-1 a.m.

Groceries
Mazatlán's biggest supermarkets are the **Gigante** at Calz. R. Buelna and Calle la Marina and **Plaza Ley** on the highway. **El Arbol, Sábalo Real,** and **Super Las Palmas** are smaller, more expensive mini-markets for tourists on Calz. C. Sábalo.

The freshest produce is available at the municipal market on Av. Juárez in Old Mazatlán. Ripe Sinaloan mangoes are plentiful in the summer, while Haas avocados (originally cultivated by Mazatlán native Antonio Haas) are available year-round.

ENTERTAINMENT

Nightlife
Discos: Like other Mexican beach resorts, Mazatlán is awash in discos, most of them in the Zona Dorada. Cover charges typically run US$5-10, while hours are roughly 9 p.m.-4 a.m. Not many people arrive before 11 p.m. or midnight.

Currently the hottest nonhotel disco in town is **Frankie Oh's** (tel. 69-82-58-00), next door to Señor Frog's on Av. del Mar. Weekends at Frankie's feature live music; Saturday nights, when an updated *tambora sinaloense* style of music is performed, are very popular with a younger local crowd. **Lion's Salsa and Zafari** (tel. 83-02-00), at the Caravelle Beach Club, Calz. C. Sábalo and Calle Atún, also has live music and dancing.

Walking along Calz. Camarón Sábalo toward Playa Norte, you can't miss **Valentino's** (tel. 83-62-12), a disco with banks of pulsating videos and three dance floors housed in a white edifice that looks like something from the planet Krypton, perched on Punta Camarón at the south

end of Playa Camarón. The clientele here tends to be a mix of upscale Mazatlecos and Zona Dorada tourists.

El Caracol at El Cid Mega Resort captures the El Cid crowd; a unique feature here is a brass firehouse pole used for rapid transits from the upper seating level to the dance floor.

Bars: The Valentino-El Sheik complex also features **Mikonos,** a sedate piano bar popular for cocktails and appetizers on the sea-view terrace. **Bora Bora Beach Club** in the same complex features live pop music in a tropical ambience, along with a bar, several dance floors, two swimming pools, and a volleyball court.

Amadeus Café at Calle Carranza Sur 18, near the Customs House in the Olas Altas district, is a charming, upmarket *peña* with live folk and jazz nightly except Sunday. In spite of the name, there's a full bar as well as a moderately priced menu of Mexican *antojitos*. Service is excellent and credit cards are accepted.

Time Out at Calz. Sábalo 1446, opposite Pueblo Bonito, is an American-style sports bar with big-screen satellite TV. Billed as the "Unofficial Home of the Chicago Cubs," the **No Name Café** (tel. 13-20-31), opposite Suites Las Flores on Av. R.T. Loaiza, is another hangout for armchair jocks.

During the high season, the most popular Zona Dorada bars are the super-casual **Jungle Juice, Gringo Lingo,** and **Joe's Oyster Bar,** all three on the Av. R.T. Loaiza loop.

Theater and Dance: Teatro Angela Peralta, on Av. Carnaval next to Plazuela Machado, hosts ballet, dance, musical, and theater performances year-round. In spring the theater serves as headquarters for the Sinaloa International Cultural Festival, in which some 1,500 performers participate. Tickets for theater performances are available at the theater box office during the day or an hour before curtain time.

Although it's not highbrow entertainment, many tourists enjoy the **Fiesta Mexicana** held Tuesdays, Fridays, and Saturdays at 7 p.m. at the Hotel Playa Mazatlán's Terraza Playa restaurant (tel. 83-53-20 for reservations). A single admission price includes beverages, food, and Mexican dance performances (see the Terraza Playa Mazatlán entry under "Food" for more detail).

Plaza Music: Musical entertainment in Mazatlán that doesn't cost a centavo is occasionally played in the kiosks of Plaza Zaragoza and Plaza Republicana. Many kinds of music are aired but if you're lucky, you'll be able to listen to an ensemble playing local *perrada* or *tambora sinaloense,* a type of brass-and-drum band music originally brought by German immigrants but adopted and adapted by local Mazatlecos. Around the turn of the century, *perrada* became the "music of the people" when string music was still for the elite; during the 1910-20 Mexican revolution it became a rallying soundtrack for the *constitucionalistas.*

Today the usual instrumentation for a *tambora* ensemble is three clarinets, two trumpets, two bass horns, and a sousaphone, which together play a combination of European marches and Mexican tunes—sometimes fused into one composition.

Events

Carnaval: The city's most attended annual event since 1898 officially begins a week before Ash Wednesday (late February to early March), the start of Lent. Attracting as many as 300,000-400,000 participants, Mazatlán's Carnaval is estimated to be the third largest in the world after Río de Janeiro's and New Orleans's.

The primary focus of the street action is the "Carnavaldome" on Av. del Mar on Playa Norte (which is blocked off to vehicular traffic Thurs.-Tues.), a temporary assortment of stages and booths accommodating continuous music (*tropicale,* mariachi, rock, and *norteña*), food vendors, outrageous costume-wearing, and all-night dancing throughout the festival. Av. del Mar is also the site of two pyrotechnics displays, the traditional *castillo* (a castlelike fireworks platform unique to Mexico) on Saturday night, and an offshore fireworks finale representing a mock naval battle (in commemoration of Mazatlán's 1864 victory over the French navy) on Sunday night. Admission to the nightly Carnavaldome street dance is US$1.60.

The main events kick off the Friday evening before Shrove Tuesday ("Mardi Gras" in New Orleans) with the *juegos florales* ("floral games") in the city baseball stadium. During this well-attended event, a Flower Queen is crowned and literary awards are bestowed upon contestants who have written the best "flowery verse." Top prize is the prestigious Clemencia Isaura Poetry

Award, a 68-year tradition that honors the best unpublished work from anywhere in Mexico.

Saturday evening activities begin with the coronation of La Reina de Carnaval ("Carnaval Queen") and El Rey Feo ("Ugly King") at the Estadio Teodoro Mariscal, an event that usually includes concert performances by major Latin artists. This is followed by the Quema de Mal Humor, or "Burning of Bad Humor," in which an effigy (usually modeled after an unpopular politician of the day) is hanged and burned. Sunday is the biggest Carnavaldome night, while the Monday following this weekend is El Día del Marido Oprimido, the "Day of the Oppressed Husband," in which married men are to be allowed 23 1/2 hours of freedom to do whatever they wish.

Two large costume parades, one on Sunday at 6 p.m. and the other on Tuesday at 4 p.m., feature dozens of floats representing various mythological figures from Aladdin to Zeus, plus the newly crowned Carnaval "royalty." *Tambora sinaloense* bands come from all around the state to participate in the parades, which may feature as many as 10 *tambora* ensembles per day. Because of their prime location along the main parade routes, the streetfront rooms at Hotel La Siesta, Hotel Freeman, and Hotel Belmar are booked out months in advance of Carnaval.

At the turn of the century, Plazuela Machado was the central focus of Carnaval. Now that the plaza area has been restored, Carnaval activities have returned with a gastronomic fair held every evening Fri.-Tuesday. Prominent dishes on hand include Mazatlán's famous *pescado zarandeado* and barbecued shrimp.

Several of the events described above, including the Saturday evening coronation ball, require admission tickets that cost US$3-20 each.

Sinaloa Cultural Festival: Since 1987 this yearly event has brought a month-long series of performing arts to the state from late Oct.-late November. Although performances are also held in Los Mochis, Guasave, and Culiacán, the main focus is Mazatlán, and in particular the Teatro Angela Peralta. The variety of performances generally encompasses opera, ballet, symphony, jazz, flamenco, rock, folkloric dance, and drama. Recent headline performers have included Latin greats Lola Beltrán, Willy Colón, and Celia Cruz.

Bullfights And *Charreadas*

Mazatlecos are deeper into baseball than bullfighting, but for the sake of visitors (Mexicans as well as gringos), *corridas de toros* are held Dec.-April at 12,000-seat Plaza de Toros Monumental, located on the north side of Calz. R. Buelna midway between the highway and the beach. Advance tickets can be purchased at the plaza or at the kiosk in front of Valentino's. The program begins promptly at 4 p.m.

During the rest of the year, Plaza Monumental hosts occasional Sunday *charreadas.* For information on scheduled plaza events, call 69-93-35-98 or 84-17-77.

Shopping

Downtown: The city's best bargains are found in the traditional shopping district surrounding the **Mercado Público José Mario Pino Suárez** or Mercado Central, bounded by Juárez, Ocampo, Serdán, and Valle. Amid the usual fresh produce, meats, herbs, and curios are a number of quality handicraft vendors. Just outside the market, **Artesanías Marina Mercante** offers a decent selection of crafts from all over Mexico. Around the corner, **Huarachería Internacional** at Ocampo and Juárez sells a variety of Mexican sandals at reasonable prices.

Merida, near Plaza Republicana at Calle Flores 613 Pte., has an extensive selection of *guayaberas,* the Yucatán-style men's shirt now popularly worn throughout tropical Mexico. Prices start at around US$10.

Also along Calle Flores is a string of photo shops with the city's best prices on film and processing.

Zona Dorada: Packed in among the hotels and restaurants are dozens of shops catering almost exclusively to tourists. Much of what is offered is of the "Mexican vacation" souvenir variety, e.g. T-shirts, beer mugs, and other logo-emblazoned items from branches of Señor Frog's Official Store—which seem to be on every other corner. **Mazatlán Arts and Crafts Center** (tel. 69-13-52-43), opposite Suites Las Flores and next door to the No Name Café, contains a large selection of blankets, rugs, woodcarvings, hats, leather goods, and other crafts from around the country. With some bargaining, prices can be surprisingly good here, although you should probably compare downtown prices before going on a spending spree.

Mazatlán Art Gallery (tel. 84-36-12), at Av. R.T. Loaiza 404 in the Zona Dorada, sells contemporary paintings, lithographs, and sculptures by Mexican artists, some of them quite well known. Another Zona Dorada shop of interest is **Evolución Bookstore** (tel. 16-08-39) at Av. R.T. Loaiza 401-14. Although mostly devoted to New Age, astrology, and occult titles—along with crystals, incense, massage oils and the like—the store carries a good assortment of tourist maps and guidebooks. A small coffee bar in the store sells coffee, tea, and natural food snacks.

Of the several hotel shops selling books and magazines, the best is Hotel Playa Mazatlán's bookstore-pharmacy, which carries *USA Today* and the *Los Angeles Times,* plus an assortment of foreign magazines and English-language best-sellers. A more complete selection of foreign newspapers and magazines is available at **Kioskito de Tin Marín,** a kiosk newsstand opposite the Dairy Queen on Calz. C. Sábalo.

Many shops in the Zona offer beachwear, much of it either cheap/tacky or expensive/tacky; among the most wearable Mexican-made designs are those found at the **Aca Joe** outlet at Calz. C. Sábalo and Paseo Díaz Ordaz.

Pharmacies: Three pharmacies in the city are open 24 hours—**Parque Zaragoza** (tel. 82-83-78), Calle. G. Nelson 2200; **Atlantis** (tel. 81-45-45), 5 de Mayo s/n; and **Cruz Verde** (tel. 81-22-25), Calle. G. Náhera 477.

SPORTS

Baseball

The local pro team, Los Venados, participates in the AAA Pacific Coast League roughly Oct.-April. Check with the tourist office (see "Mazatlán Information," below) for the schedule of home games at the city's Estadio Teodoro Mariscal (on Calle T. Mariscal, about 500 meters east of Playa Norte off Av. Revolución). The hot ticket of the season is the game played with Mazatlán's biggest baseball rival, Culiacán. Call 69-83-30-12 for game information.

EL BEISBOL

by Tom Huhti

While many North American ball fans recognize the Latin Caribbean (Dominican Republic, Puerto Rico, and Cuba) as a baseball powerhouse, Mexico is generally under-appreciated except for a brief episode of "Fernandomania" in the L.A. basin in 1980. Yet the south-of-the-border giant has embraced the Grand Old Game as passionately as—and for as long as—any country outside the United States. And unlike other Latin American or Caribbean lands, which depend on exporting their best talent to the U.S. (and which schedule their own games during the U.S.'s off-season to accommodate migrant players), Mexico has succeeded in remaining independent enough not only to keep many of their hottest players at home, but also to maintain a summer league scheduled head-to-head with the *Yanqui* season up north.

Today Mexico boasts the largest organized baseball system in Latin America, with a 15-team, nationwide Mexican League that plays during the summer and a 10-team Mexican Pacific League centered on the west coast during the winter. Together these leagues maintain the year-round loyalties of millions of fans throughout Mexico; on the amateur level, an estimated four million Mexicans play baseball, third behind only the U.S. and Japan.

The Sierra Transversal belt that separates Northern from Southern Mexico also divides Mexico loosely into baseball and soccer camps. Roll into an otherwise unimpressive Northern Mexican hamlet on any given afternoon and you're likely to see Little-Leaguers shagging flies in pristine stadiums that shame more than a few U.S. minor league AA ball clubs. Of the 49 Mexican players to have played pro ball in the U.S., all but seven were from the North; as might be expected, average player statistics are also slanted in favor of Northern ballplayers.

In part the North's affinity for the grass diamond is due to the obvious proximity to baseball's country of origin. Nuevo Laredo's Tecolotes ("Owls")—a Mexican team that actually plays on both sides of the border—is a good example of what can go right between two contiguous nations. Yet for the most part Mexican baseball has aligned itself with the annual Caribbean World Series rather than looking toward the U.S. minors (and rather than restricting itself to Mexican playoffs), showing a stronger affinity for Caribbean ball in spite of the geographic distance between Northern Mexico and the principal Caribbean ball clubs. Mexican teams have twice won the Caribbean World Series (Hermosillo in 1976, Mexicali in 1986).

To a large degree, the Mexican leagues have been forced to remain aloof from U.S. ball by the pro sports industry on both sides of the border. In the 1940s, a U.S. baseball commissioner instituted a ban on any American player who "defected" to a Mexican team in the off-season. The ban was lifted the following year (during the winter many U.S. minor- and even major-league "scrub" players head south with bat and glove), but Mexican baseball fans haven't totally forgotten the insult.

On the opposite side, if a U.S. ball club desires to woo a Mexican player north, Mexican teams require that the player's contract be purchased outright—for a steep sum meant to compensate for gate revenues lost to migrating talent (one American club owner lamented that you can hire five Dominican players for the price of one Mexican). In a sense it's unfair to compare U.S. and Mexican league politics, since the difference in pay scales means better Mexican players tend to move north while the lesser U.S. talent moves south, putting Mexico at the disadvantage.

Since Sonora's Baldamero Melo Almada became the first Mexican national to play in the U.S. (for the Boston Red Sox in 1933), nearly 50 Mexican players have been drafted by U.S. teams. Of those who have become big-name players—among them Ruben Amaro, Jorge Orta, Cy Acosta, Aurelio "Señor Smoke" López, and Teodoro ("Teddy") Higuera—undoubtedly the brightest star so far has been pudgy screwballer Fernando Valenzuela, who caused a national frenzy in 1980-81 on the way to winning Rookie of the Year, the Cy Young Award, and the pride of the U.S. Hispanic population. In Mexico, a pandemonium approaching presidential occurs every time Valenzuela makes a public appearance. In the U.S. he is one of the few ballplayers to inspire an American pop song (F. Sternwheeler's "Fernando de Sonora" in 1981).

At last count, 13 players from Mexico were on the rosters (11 of them from Northern Mexico)—including Valenzuela, who earned a pitching spot with the Baltimore Orioles in a valiant comeback attempt. Yet the biggest and best of Mexican baseball—Ramón Araño, Angel Castro, Epitacio Torres, and,

EL BEISBOL
(continued)

likely the greatest Mexican player of all time, Hector Espino (who holds the Mexican home-run record)—almost never set foot in the United States due to a combination of national pride and the Mexican leagues' prohibitive price tags.

El Béisbol Talk

base robada—stolen base
blanqueo—shutout
caminar—walk
carrera—run
cuadrangular—home run
entrada—inning
jardín—outfield
lanzador—pitcher
lanzamiento descontrolado—wild pitch
lanzamiento ilegal—balk
paso de conga—"conga step," 1-2-3 inning
poncho—strikeout
torpedero—shortstop
¡Bésela!—Kiss it! (equiv. to "Kiss that baby goodbye!")
el día de los fanáticos—fan appreciation day

Surfing

Mazatlán is really the first place along the Mexican mainland's Pacific coast with steady wave action. Starting in the north, decent beach and reef breaks are sometimes happening at **Punta Cerritos.** Farther south, depending on the season, **Punta Camarón** ("Valentino's") yields left and right point breaks on either side. Boogie-boarders can sometimes catch decent beach breaks toward the north end of **Playa Norte,** though generally the action here is limited.

"The Cannons" at **Punta Chile** near the old fort (also called Playa los Pinos) is one of the best and most challenging summer point breaks in the area. Almost any time of year high surf can also break at the north end of **Playa Olas Altas.**

North of Mazatlán at Punta Piaxtla (see "Vicinity of Mazatlán," p. 217) is a secluded beach area with occasional strong breaks.

The city's main shred-shed is **Rainbow Surf Shop** (tel. 69-81-58-92) at Paseo Claussen 31, Playa Norte, where friendly Salvador Guerrero carries surfing accessories and rents, sells, and repairs new and used boards; Sal is a good source of info on local breaks as well. Surf-boards and boogie boards can also be rented at Aqua Sports Center, Ocean Sports Center, or Chico's Beach Club in the Zona Dorada.

Kayaking

The Mazatlán area offers several kayaking possibilities. Experienced kayakers can easily explore **Las Tres Islas** offshore (see "Las Tres Islas," p. 198, for details on the islands) from Playa Gaviotas. When the Pacific surf is rough, launching is easier at Playa Norte, even though this means a longer paddle. Another good spot for kayaking is the Isla de la Piedra peninsula, which has a number of interesting inlets and islets on the landward side.

Farther south along the coast are two large estuarial systems, **Laguna el Caimanero** (Laguna del Huizache) west of Rosario (put in at Agua Verde or Caimanero) and **Laguna Agua Grande** at Teacapán, with nearly limitless kayaking venues. (See "Vicinity of Mazatlán" for more information on this area.)

Kayaks can be rented at the Ocean Sport Center and Chico's Beach Club.

Windsurfing

The channel between Playa Gaviotas/Playa Sábalo and Las Tres Islas is good for sideshore breezes and is the most popular windsurfing spot. Hotshots can find higher winds and more chop at Playa Cerritos and farther north at Playa Escondida.

Several Zona Dorada hotels offer a limited selection of windsurfing equipment suitable for novices. Experienced boardsailors in need of equipment will find the best selection of rental gear at Chico's Beach Club.

Parasailing

If you take a stroll along Playa Gaviotas, sooner or later you'll be approached by someone offering a parasail experience, in which you're harnessed to a parachute connected by a long line to a motorboat. The boats run parallel to the beach so that—theoretically at least—you can launch and land on the sand.

Opinions are divided as to how safe a sport this is, though vendors claim they haven't lost a customer yet. The winds are usually steadiest (and thus more predictable) in the mornings—if winds are strong you might think twice before strapping in. The ride—and the beach view from the air—is thrilling; vendors typically charge US$20 for a 10- to 15-minute ride.

Diving
Although Mazatlán isn't a great area for snorkeling or scuba diving, the rocky offshore islands provide opportunities for viewing rock corals and tropical fish. Maximum visibility in good conditions is about 10 meters (30 feet).

The best-equipped place for dive equipment is **Aqua Sports Center** (tel. 69-13-33-33, ext. 341) at El Cid Mega Resort. In addition to providing air and equipment rental (snorkel, mask, and fins go for around US$7 a day), the staff at Aqua Sports offers scuba instruction and guided dive trips. Equipment and instruction are also available at Ocean Sports Center and Chico's Beach Club.

Boating
Two huge boating facilities, Marina El Cid (sometimes referred to as Marina del Sábalo) and Marina de Mazatlán, are currently under construction at Estero de Sábalo northeast of Playa Sábalo. Together they are expected to form the largest marina complex (about 561 hectares) in Mexico and one of the largest in all Latin America.

The US$200 million project is being built in six phases, beginning with an outer harbor four meters (12 feet) deep and ending with an inner harbor with navigable canals, four new five-star hotels, and a condominium complex. The first phase, which will include 120 slips accommodating yachts 12-16 meters (41-55 feet) in length, is expected to open by 1995.

In the meantime, boats can be anchored or launched at the **Centro de Ciencias del Mar** at Isla del Crestón for US$17 per day. If you're planning to launch or anchor more than two

---

WATER SPORTS EQUIPMENT

AQUA SPORTS CENTER
El Cid Resort
Calzada Camarón Sábalo
tel. 13-33-33, ext. 341

CHICO'S BEACH CLUB
Hotel Costa de Oro
Calzada Camarón Sábalo
tel. 13-53-44

OCEAN SPORT CENTER
Westin Camino Real
Punto de Sábalo
tel. 13-11-11

RAINBOW SURF SHOP
Paseo Claussen 31
tel. 81-58-92

---

days in a month, a US$34 one-month anchor permit will save money. For trailered boats, another public launch ramp is available at the end of the sportfishing pier at **Club Naútico** (tel. 69-81-51-95), where an all-day launch permit (no anchoring) costs US$20.

Hobie catamarans can be rented for US$20 an hour from the Aqua Sports Center or Chico's Beach Club.

Fishing
Mazatlán rivals Cabo San Lucas as western Mexico's sportfishing capital. Approximately 7,000-9,000 billfish (swordfish and striped marlin Dec.-April, blue and black marlin May-Dec.) are caught offshore each year, along with tuna (year-round), skipjack, Pacific snapper, mackerel, and snook (summer), and dorado (year-round except Jan.-February).

At least 10 sportfishing fleets (*flotas deportivas*) offer guided fishing trips from the city's sportfishing piers on Isla del Crestón (at the west end of Av. del Puerto). **Bill Heimpel's Star Fleet** (tel. 69-82-38-78; 800-426-6890 in the U.S. and Canada; fax 512-377-0454) is the oldest, largest, and best known. Party boats cost US$60 per person including all bait and equipment, while charter

yellowfin tuna

boats taking six to eight anglers cost US$240-300 a day. Several of Star Fleet's clients have set IGFA records; a record-breaking black marlin weighing 619 kilograms (1,362 pounds) was landed in 1990.

Less expensive is **Flota El Dorado** (tel. 81-62-04), which charters 38-foot boats with guide plus bait and tackle for six anglers for just US$175. El Dorado also offers a half-day *lancha* trip for up to four persons for US$70.

Panga Fishing: If billfish aren't your thing or if you simply prefer fishing closer to shore, *pangas* (small fiberglass launches with outboard motors) are a less expensive alternative to party boats and fishing cruisers. From **Playa Norte** local *pangeros* will take one or two sportfishers out to hook dorado or red snapper for around US$50 per boat. You must provide your own bait and tackle; these can be arranged through local fishermen if necessary.

Super Sport Pangas, associated with the Star Fleet, has *pangas* for US$60 per person or US$75 for two persons (only one line each), with a three-person limit.

Hunting
The Presa Comedero area north of Mazatlán is a popular hunting spot for a wide variety of game, including pintail, gadwall, bluebill, widgeon, cinnamon teal, green-winged teal, bluewing, dove, quail, deer, and wild pig. In Mazatlán the **Aviles Brothers** (tel. 69-81-37-28; 800-633-3085 in the U.S. and Canada), at Paseo Claussen and 5 de Mayo, are the most experienced outfitters; English-speaking guides are available. Packages must be booked in advance because of the time needed to arrange permits.

Tennis And Golf
The city's best tennis facility is **The Racquet Club** (tel. 69-83-59-39), Calz. R. Buelna, which has three clay courts and four hard courts. Court time costs US$10 per hour; opening hours are 6 a.m.-10 p.m. **Club Deportiva Reforma** (tel. 83-12-00) is also on Calz. R. Buelna and has eight hard courts with rates and hours similar to those at The Racquet Club. Hotels with tennis courts (usually guests only, but try calling) include Torres Mazatlán, Costa de Oro, Camino Real, and Los Sábalos.

El Cid Mega Resort (tel. 13-33-33) has an 18-hole, par 72 golf course open only to El Cid and Camino Real guests; greens and caddy fees total around US$25. **Club Campestre** (tel. 84-74-94), at Km 1195 on Mexico 15, has a nine-hole course open to the public daily 7 a.m.-6 p.m.; fees cost around US$12 per day.

MAZATLAN INFORMATION

Tourist Offices And Publications
The very efficient **Coordinación General de Turismo del Estado de Sinaloa** (tel. 69-85-18-47, fax 85-12-22), at Av. Olas Altas 1300 between the Belmar and La Siesta hotels, has stacks of printed information on Mazatlán and the surrounding area. The bilingual staff can also answer just about any inquiry.

A privately run consortium, the **Mazatlán Tourism Trust** (tel. 14-19-55, fax 14-19-77) at Calz. C. Sábalo 333, also dispenses tourist information and is more convenient to Zona Dorada visitors. If for no other reason, stop by the office for a free copy of the *Mazatlán Coupon Catalog and Guide,* which contains coupons for room upgrades, restaurant and gift shop discounts, an events calendar, a city map, and a list of hotels, restaurants, shops, and attractions. In the U.S. and Canada, you can call (800) 438-

---

CONSULATES IN MAZATLAN

BELGIUM

Av. Olas Altas 1-Bis.
tel. 85-14-66

CANADA

Calle Albatros 705
tel. 13-73-20
Av. R.T. Loaiza 201
tel. 14-66-55

FINLAND

Calle Venus and Roosevelt 136
tel. 81-39-07

GERMANY

Av. Jacarandas 10
tel. 11-20-77, 12-28-09

ITALY

Av. Olas Altas 66-105
tel. 85-14-78

4825 to have this booklet sent to any address in these two countries.

Another useful publication is *Pacific Pearl,* a giveaway newspaper with short features on local history and culture, plus a listing of current events and restaurant specials. The small, magazinelike *Inside Mazatlán* is similar in content. Both can be picked up at almost any hotel in the Zona Dorada.

Library: The city's main public library, on Plazuela de los Leones at Av. Flores and Niños Héroes, has a large collection of Spanish-language books and periodicals, plus the all-English **Benjamin Franklin Library** upstairs.

Maps: A number of free maps of the city are available in hotel lobbies or from the tourist office; these are usually adequate for most visitors. If you're planning extensive explorations of the city, or if you plan to drive downtown, try to find a copy of the HFET *Culiacán* map, which includes a large, detailed street map of Mazatlán (as well as Los Mochis).

Post And Telegraph

Mazatlán's central post office is at Av. Juárez and Calle 21 de Marzo opposite the Palacio de Gobierno. The telegraph office is next door.

American Express cardholders can receive mail at **American Express Travel Services** (tel. 69-13-06-00), Calz. Sábalo 310. This office is open Mon.-Fri. 9 a.m.-1 p.m. and 4-6 p.m., Sat. 9 a.m.-1 p.m.

Language Study

The **Centro de Idiomas** (tel. 69-82-20-53, fax

MAZATLAN TELEPHONE NUMBERS

Tourist Police: 84-84-44
State Tourist Office: 84-02-22
Red Cross: 82-36-90, 85-14-51
Immigration: 81-38-13
Weather: 81-45-27
Federal police: 82-18-67
Highway Patrol: 1-63-55
SEMATUR (ferry): 81-70-20
Railway Station: 81-58-92
Bus Terminal: 85-17-36
Mazatlán Area Code: 69

69-85-56-06), Calle B. Dominguez 1908 in Old Mazatlán offers a variety of intensive Spanish-language courses in a converted century-old house. Classes run two to four hours per day Mon.-Fri., with special activities every Saturday (e.g., aquarium visits, bay cruises). Courses begin every Monday of the year except Easter Week and Christmas vacation (Dec. 19-Jan. 1).

Group classes cost US$120 per week for the intensive, four-hours-per-day course, US$90 for the two-hours-per-day schedule. Individual one-on-one instruction costs more. Homestays with Mexican families—strongly encouraged—cost US$115-135 (including three meals) per day.

Money

Banks are plentiful in Mazatlán. A few in the Zona Dorada even have extended hours to accommodate tourists, including **Banamex** at Calz. C. Sábalo 434 and **Bancomer** at Av. Juárez and 21 de Marzo, both of which are open Mon.-Fri. 9 a.m.-1:30 p.m. and 3:30-5:30 p.m.

Two reliable moneychangers in the Zona Dorada are **Casa de Cambio Mazatlán** on Av. R.T. Loaiza and **Casa de Cambio Sanchez** at Calz. C. Sábalo 109.

GETTING THERE

Earlier this century Mazatlán was a six-day Pacific steamer trip from San Francisco; nowadays it's a day's drive from the U.S. border or just an hour or two by plane.

By Air

Rafael Buelna Airport, 20 km (12.4 miles) southeast of the city, is served by several international, national, and regional airlines.

Aeroméxico (tel. 69-14-11-11; Calz. C. Sábalo 310) has nonstops to/from Ciudad Juárez, Culiacán, Durango, Guadalajara, Los Cabos, Los Mochis, and Tijuana.

Aero California (tel. 13-20-42; El Cid Mega Resort) flies nonstop to/from La Paz and Mexico City, and direct to/from Tijuana (via La Paz).

Alaska (tel. 85-27-30; airport) flies direct to Mazatlán from Los Angeles (via Puerto Vallarta).

Delta Airlines (tel. 82-41-55; airport) flies nonstop to/from Los Angeles.

Mexicana Airlines (tel. 82-77-22; Paseo Claussen 101-B) flies nonstop to/from Denver,

Guadalajara, Los Cabos, Mexico City, and Puerto Vallarta.

Noroeste (tel. 14-38-33; El Cid Mega Resort) has nonstops to/from Culiacán and Durango.

SARO (tel. 86-14-74; Av. del Mar 1111) has nonstops to/from Torreón and direct flights to/from Monterrey (via Torreón).

Airport Transport: Most of the Zona Dorada hotels operate airport shuttle buses; some collect a US$4-5 fare, while others are free.

A taxi between the Zona Dorada and the airport costs around US$17, *colectivo* (share taxi) US$4 per person. Several times daily, city buses also go to the downtown area for around US$0.60.

By Bus

Mazatlán's Central de Autobuses is off Calle Río Chachalacas and Av. Carrasco (downtown extension of Mexico 15), about three blocks east of Playa Norte.

Estrella Blanca (tel. 69-81-53-81) has buses to/from Durango (12 daily), Torreón (one daily), Ciudad Juárez (one daily), Mexico City (seven daily), Zacatecas (one daily), and San Luis Potosí (one daily).

Del Pacífico (tel. 82-05-77) operates every hour to Tijuana, Mexicali, Nogales, Santa Ana, Hermosillo, Guaymas, Ciudad Obregón, Navojoa, Los Mochis, Culiacán, and Tepic, plus once daily to Guadalajara and Mexico City.

TNS (tel. 81-23-35) goes to Ciudad Juárez (two daily), Chihuahua (two daily), Parral (two daily), Durango (five daily), Torreón (two daily), Monterrey (three daily), Nuevo Laredo (two daily), and Saltillo (five daily).

Tres Estrellas de Oro (tel. 81-36-80) goes every hour to Culiacán and Los Mochis, plus Nogales (two daily), Hermosillo (two daily), Guaymas (two daily), Tijuana (six daily), Guadalajara (four daily), and Mexico City (two daily). Tres Estrellas also has deluxe *Ejecutivo* service once daily to Culiacán, Los Mochis, and Guadalajara. Other luxury bus lines with executive services to major Mexican cities include **Elite, Transpacífico,** and **Plus.**

By Train

El Tren del Pacífico No. 2 leaves Nogales at 2:20 p.m. and arrives in Mazatlán at 6:55 a.m. In the reverse direction, train No. 2 departs Mazatlán at 5:30 p.m., arriving in Nogales at 10:50

a.m. The one-way, first-class fare is US$28.50; this is less than the total cost of vehicle tolls along the newly completed four-lane highway! (For information on scheduling from other cities, including Guadalajara and Hermosillo, see the "Railway Schedule," pp. 86-87.)

The railway station is in the Emiliano Zapata district off Camino al Conchi, not far from the intersection of Av. G. Leyva and the highway bypass (Entronque Carretera Internacional). The station's advance ticket office is open Mon.-Sat. 8 a.m.-12:30 p.m. and 3-5 p.m., Sun. and holidays 8 a.m.-noon.

Ferry

A passenger-vehicle ferry runs between La Paz, B.C.S. and Mazatlán daily except Saturday from the Muelle Transbordador (tel. 69-82-21-59) at the southern end of Av. Carnaval on the Canal de Navegación leading into the main city harbor. SEMATUR (tel. 81-70-20, 84-11-98) has a ticket office at Paseo Claussen 310 in the Olas Altas where advance tickets can be purchased weekdays 8 a.m.-2 p.m.

For complete information on fares and departure times, see "By Ferry from Baja," p. 80.

Driving

The Mazatlán-Culiacán segment of the Nogales-Culiacán Carretera Internacional toll road was finally inaugurated in Nov. 1992, the last link in Mexico's finest highway to date. Mexican engineers reportedly built the highway with reference to specifications used by California and Texas highway departments.

This shortens the old route from Culiacán by 26 km, though some drivers still prefer the old road because it passes through more scenic countryside (and saves the steep Culiacán-Mazatlán toll of US$27.72).

Motorists coming from Durango and other points east will arrive via Mexico 40, one of the most scenic and harrying drives in Northern Mexico. Allow five to six hours to complete the 318-km (197-mile) road trip between the state capital of Durango and Mazatlán; the middle section through the Sierra Madre Occidental is known as Espinazo del Diablo or "Devil's Backbone" because the road is so precipitous and winding. Although most of the highway is paved, wide swaths of mud occasionally wash onto sections of road high in the mountains during the late summer monsoon season (when this road is best avoided). Gasoline—but not necessarily Magna Sin—is available in La Ciudad, 146 km (90.5 miles) west of Durango and again in Concordia just 15 km short of Mazatlán. For more information on this route, see "Durango to Mazatlán" in the Durango chapter.

GETTING AROUND

Bus
Two buses will serve all the needs of the typical visitor. Bus route No. 9 ("Sábalo/Cerritos-El Centro") runs between the northern end of the Zona Dorada and the central market, while the blue beachfront bus ("Sábalo-Paseo Costero") runs only along the waterfront from north to south. Fares are a bargain US$0.30 each way; operating hours are 6 a.m.-11 p.m.

Taxi
Cabs are plentiful in the downtown area and in the Zona Dorada. The standard fare between the middle of the zone and downtown Mazatlán is US$4. Trips within the zone cost around US$2.

More popular than the standard taxicab are three-person, open-air carts called *pulmonías* (literally "pneumonia"), which cost about the same as a regular taxi. Bargaining is permissible, though most drivers will quote the standard fare right off.

Driving
Although gridlock is rare, traffic around the city is fairly turgid. Mid-afternoon is the worst time to be on the road. Make sure you have a good map before attempting downtown forays (see "Mazatlán Information," p. 213).

Vehicle Rental
The following agencies offer auto rental: **Aga** (tel. 69-14-44-05; 13-40-77; Calz. C. Sábalo 316); **Avis** (tel. 83-62-00; Calz. C. Sábalo 314); **Budget** (tel. 13-27-27, 14-32-35; El Cid Mega Resort, Calz. C. Sábalo); **Hertz** (tel. 83-49-55; Av. del Mar 1111); and **National** (tel. 13-60-00, Calz. C. Sábalo 7000; and tel. 83-81-11, Calz. R. Buelna 1000).

Rental rates vary slightly from company to company. The average rate for a no-frills VW bug is US$23 per day plus US$0.18 per km;

for a VW combi (van) US$47 plus US$0.29 per km; and for a Nissan Tsuru II (Sentra) US$34 per day plus US$0.22 per km. With 200 free km, the bug costs US$55 per day, the combi US$99, the Tsuru II US$72. Most companies add charges of US$10.60 per day for a/c and US$8.30 per day for automatic transmission over and above these rates (the VW bug has neither). Weekly rentals usually earn one free day, i.e., you pay for only six days if you keep the car seven days. Rates at Budget and National tend to run 10-15% higher than those at the other companies.

Several agencies in the Zona Dorada rent motorscooters for US$16.50 per day. For getting around town, this is a considerable savings over car rental.

LOCAL TOURS

Harbor Tour
The most popular tour in Mazatlán is the three-hour harbor cruise operated by **Yate Fiesta** from the Isla del Crestón pier daily at 11 a.m.; mid-Dec.-April there's a second departure at 2 p.m. Passengers get a look at the shrimp fleet, packing docks for tuna, shrimp, and sardines, and Isla de la Piedra. The cost is US$13.30 per adult, half that for children ages 5-10. On board is a pay bar.

Jungle Tours
Most tours advertised as "jungle tours" in Mazatlán are boat excursions from the inner bay pier through inland mangrove-lined waterways to Isla de la Piedra. Along the way you'll get a look at the city's shrimp fleet and the seafood packing docks; at Isla de la Piedra you may be able to see iguanas, armadillos, pelicans, and herons. The average jungle tour costs US$35 per person, which includes transport to/from your hotel, the boat ride, a *pescado zarandeado* lunch, and beverages (including beer). **Viajes Attiq** (tel. 69-14-24-00, fax 69-14-24-00; Av. R.T. Loaiza 214) operates such tours each Tuesday, Thursday, and Saturday at 9:30 p.m. (hotel pickup at 9 a.m.).

Marlin Tours (tel. 13-53-01; Privada Laguna 300, Zona Dorada) does a longer "jungle tour" to Teacapán's Laguna Agua Brava for US$45 per person (including continental breakfast, lunch, and drinks) on Tuesday, Friday, and Saturday.

Birds

Xico Tours (tel. 69-85-19-96) leads birding tours of the nearby Sierra Madre Occidental (tufted jay, eared trogon, yellow-eye junco, summer tanager, white-eared hummingbird, tufted flycatcher, black hawk) and Teacapán (ibis, stilt, *jacana,* loggerhead shrike, hooded oriole) for US$45 per person. Viajes Attiq (see "Jungle Tours" above) can take reservations for Xico Tours.

Other

Marlin Tours (see "Jungle Tours," above) also offers tours of the city (daily, US$12), Concordia-Copalá (daily, US$35), and Rosario (Tuesday, Friday, Saturday, US$20).

VICINITY OF MAZATLAN

El Quelite

This small town 39 km (24 miles) north of Mazatlán is famous as one of the last places in Mexico where *ulama,* a pre-Cortesian, Mesoamerican ball game, is still played. Surviving only in Sinaloa, *ulama* is played with a solid, rubber-like ball made from the fiber of a regional plant called *aguama* mixed with the milk of another plant, *machaguana.* This mixture is cooked over a fire until it thickens into a rubbery mass called *hule,* then cooled in a wooden mold until it forms a sphere. Between games, the 4.5-kilogram (10-pound) *hule* must be kept in its wooden mold in order to keep its shape.

Once a religious game (in which the winners were sacrificed) played by priests or the highest warriors, today's secular *ulama* is played on a rectangular sand court called a *tachtli* that measures 50 by 40 meters. *Tahures* (players) wear protective leather pads and can strike the ball using only their elbows, shoulders, hips, and ankles. Other customary playing garb includes cotton shorts, over which is worn a deerskin loincloth (*fajado*) tied with a leather belt. The players' feet are bare.

Two teams of six players each (one of whom serves, but doesn't field the ball) compete in each match, which is refereed by two umpires (*veedores*). A point is scored each time a team brings the ball forward of a designated line, while points are lost each time the ball touches any part of a player's body other than the legal strike areas. The first team to score eight points wins.

El Quelite's court, El Taste, is at the far end of town. Matches are generally played on Sundays, and visitors are welcome to watch. Other towns in southern Sinaloa where *ulama* is still played include Llanitos, Escuinapa, El Chilillo, Villa Unión, Las Moras, and La Savila.

Barras De Piaxtla

Surfers into high waves and serious solitude should seek out Punta Piaxtla near the village of Barras de Piaxtla. The *barras* ("bars") in the name refer to basalt cliffs along the left bank of the Río Piaxtla where it empties into the sea; over a distance of several kilometers these cliffs gradually descend from a height of 47 meters (155 feet) to smooth sand beaches.

To find Piaxtla you must first get to the railway junction town of Dímas, near the coast around 65 km (40 miles) north of Mazatlán via Mexico 15. A dirt road leads southwest from Dímas to Barras de Piaxtla.

Rancho Las Moras

About 30 minutes northeast of the city by car, this exclusive guest ranch offers all-inclusive vacations in a 150-year-old mezcal (cousin to tequila) hacienda set on 3,000 acres. Recreational activities include horseback riding, tennis, nature hikes, and swimming in the ranch pool. Among other ranch facilities are a menagerie of exotic animals (including llamas, miniature ponies, and peacocks) and a whitewashed chapel overlooking the surrounding countryside.

Six guest rooms ("villas") in the main 19th-century building with original carved wooden doors (some salvaged from haciendas elsewhere) cost US$230 s, US$325 d, or US$360 deluxe, including meals served on the hacienda's dining terrace. Five individual *casitas* with full kitchens are US$400 per night.

Transport from Mazatlán International Airport is provided by Rancho Las Moras, or, if you have your own transport, they will send directions upon confirmation of your reservation. For further information or reservations, contact Rancho Las Moras (tel. 69-16-50-44, fax 16-50-45; Av. C. Sábalo 204, Suite 6, Mazatlán, Sin. 82110; or 9297 Siempre Viva Rd., Suite 15-474, San Diego, CA 92173).

Concordia

Founded as a mission pueblo in 1565, later a silver mining center, this mountain hamlet 45 km east of Mazatlán on scenic Mexico 40 boasts the state's oldest standing church, **Iglesia de San Sebastián.** Built in the baroque style between 1705-85, the pink stone portico is the most striking feature. Much of the town looks the same as it did 200 years ago, with cobblestoned streets and tile-roofed stucco homes, though development along the highway is less charming.

The giant rocking chair on the town plaza symbolizes Concordia's major claim to fame, furniture-making, which has been a local industry since the 17th century. The town is also well known for ceramics; both Mexican and gringo tourists flock here to buy pottery and furniture.

Tepuxtla, 24 km (15 miles) northwest of Concordia via paved road, is famous for hand-forged *machetes.*

Practicalities: Accommodations are available along the highway at the adequate **Hotel Rancho Viejo.** A PEMEX on the highway carries Magna Sin.

Mexico 40, the highway between Mazatlán and Durango, becomes increasingly steep and winding beyond Concordia.

Copalá

Copalá, 21 km (13 miles) east of Concordia along Mexico 40, was founded in the same year as neighboring Concordia, but is even more quaint as virtually all of the buildings are in the rustic provincial-colonial style. Built over cliffs, ravines, and steep lower Madrean slopes (elev. 2,300 feet/690 meters), the town's whitewashed houses, tiled roofs, and narrow, cobblestoned streets are vaguely reminiscent of Tuscany.

The baroque **Iglesia de San José** was begun in 1740 and completed in 1775, by which time the town's population had swelled to 10,000 on the success of local silver mines. During the brief 1860s reign of Maximilian, the French kept a garrison here. Current residents number around a thousand; electricity arrived only in the 1970s.

A sketch map of the town from Daniel's Restaurant outlines a walking tour that will take you past the church and plaza, old courthouse, bullring, and jail to a viewpoint over the town.

Practicalities: Posada San José, on the small town plaza opposite the church, houses

Copalá

guests in a 400-year-old building that served as headquarters for the Butter Copalá Mining Company until the early 1940s. Cozy rooms cost US$17 per night. Downstairs is the **Butter Company,** a restaurant serving standard Mexican fare for breakfast, lunch, and dinner.

Daniel's Restaurant (tel. 85-42-25), near the town entrance from Mexico 40, is a rambling eatery that caters to bus tourists. Owned by Daniel Garrison, a booster of local restoration and tourism, the restaurant allows buses to park in the large lot in front since Copalá's streets are too narrow for bus traffic. Besides good Mexican specialities (perhaps over-billed as "the best Mexican food in Mexico"), the restaurant is famous for banana-coconut cream pie. The dining room is open daily 9 a.m.-5 p.m.

Capilla De Taxtle

Shown simply as "El Taxtle" on some maps, this village perched on the mid-level western slopes of the Sierra Madre Occidental has one primary attraction, the anomalous German-style **Motel Villa Blanca** on the west side of Mexico

40, about 18 km north of Copalá. Quaint rooms decorated with German and Mexican antiques cost US$39 per night including three meals (mostly German food), or US$17 s, US$27·d without meals. From the roof of the inn you can see all the way to Mazatlán and the Pacific coast. Parking space is also available for self-contained campers and RVs.

The area around the inn is suitable for long walks with views of surrounding mountains and valleys. Away from the highway, local wildlife includes white-tailed deer, coyote, fox, wild turkey, and jaguarundi.

Rosario

Forty-four km (27 miles) southeast of Mazatlán via Mexico 15 on the way to Teacapán, Rosario is a nondescript town on the banks of the Río Baluarte; like many towns in northwestern Mexico, it went through a boom-and-bust cycle with the discovery and exhaustion of local silver and gold deposits.

The town's 18th-century **Templo de Nuestra Señora del Rosario** contains a large and

Nuestra Señora del Rosario

gilded baroque altar. Opposite the church stands a 1990-vintage statue of Our Lady of Rosario with hand outstretched and mouth open as if singing. An inscription partially translates as "Rosario, you gave birth to us and raised to all the world the song of Mexico."

Three or four decent hotels in the US$15-23 range are available in Rosario.

West of town via a 30-km (18.6-mile) partially paved road is **Laguna el Caimanero,** also known as Laguna del Huizache, an estuarial lagoon formed near the mouth of the Río Baluarte. Along the way are several farms cultivating mangoes, coconuts, and other fruits and vegetables. Shrimp farming is common in the lagoon area. Follow the road beyond Agua Verde to arrive at **Playa Caimanera,** a so-so beach with *palapa* restaurants.

Escuinapa And Teacapán

This off-the-beaten-track destination is slowly gaining in popularity but is still little known—even among people who vacation yearly in Mazatlán, 107 km (66 miles) to the north.

The main attraction here is 80 km (35 miles) of inland mangrove-lined estuarial waterways, including Laguna El Caimanero, Laguna Los Cerritos, Laguna Agua Grande, Estero Teacapán, and Estero Puerto del Río. Snook, mackerel, and bay snapper fishing is said to be excellent in the area; nonanglers like to visit for the natural environment and overall *tranquilidad.*

The 41-km (25.4-mile), two-lane, paved road between Escuinapa del Hidalgo (the junction with Mexico 15) and Teacapán passes between pretty lagunas Grande and Los Canales, both with plenty of waterfowl, as well as through plantations of mango, sugarcane, coconut, and cassava. This road is rough in spots but is currently being repaved and widened by the state government (50% finished as of April 1993).

Several Pacific beaches, including **Playa Las Cabras, Playa Angel, and Playa La Tambora,** can be visited via sandy side roads that branch off the Escuinapa-Teacapán road. La Tambora is the cleanest of the three; the turnoff for this beach is about 35 km from the highway (follow signs to Lupita's).

The town of Teacapán itself offers little more than a collection of boxy stucco buildings clustered around a tiny plaza. A short walk west will take you to the edge of a sand-encircled penin-

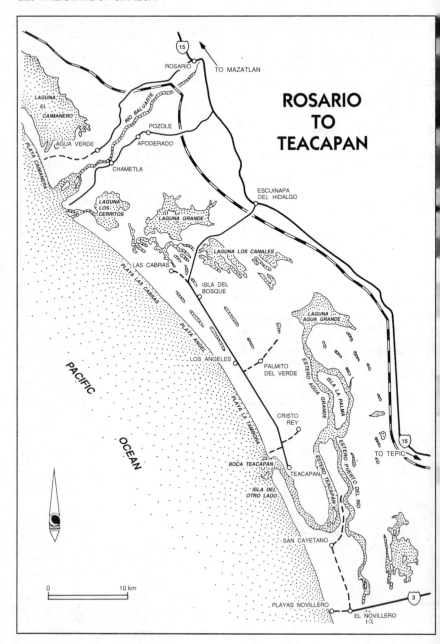

ROSARIO
TO
TEACAPAN

sula that looks like something plucked from the South China Sea, complete with colorful fishing boats and waving coconut palms. *Pangas* can be chartered for cruises around the lagoon in search of tree iguanas, crocodiles, tropical birds (including the flamingolike roseate spoonbill), and dolphins.

Kayaking or canoeing is excellent in these environs. One can put in at Teacapán and follow **Estero Teacapán** south till it curves around the peninsula in the opposite direction and joins **Estero Agua Grande,** which then leads north to **Laguna Agua Grande,** a journey of around 30 km (18.6 miles).

A more ambitious alternative would be to cut east from Estero Teacapán just below **Isla La Palma,** then follow **Estero Puerto del Río** 45 km south until it feeds into massive **Laguna Agua Brava** in the state of Nayarit. Camping is possible on islets and high shores along the way; bring plenty of food, drinking water, and insect repellent.

Accommodations and Food: On the side road to Playa La Tambora, **Lupita's Resort and Motor Park** has full RV/trailer hookups for US$8 per night, tent sites for somewhat less. You can also camp on the beach for free.

Hotel Denisse, built around a small courtyard on the Teacapán plazuela, costs US$16.60 per night—US$12 per night if booked by the week—for clean rooms with ceiling fans (no a/c) and good bathrooms. If the Denisse is booked up, you can stay at **Motel Gratos** or **Motel Santa Cruz** in Escuinapa for around US$10-15 per night.

Simple, fresh seafood meals are available at rustic cafes in Escuinapa and Teacapán. One local specialty is *tamales barbones* or "bearded tamales," in which *masa* (corn dough) flavored with fish broth is folded around garlic, onions, *chiles anchos asados,* cumin, and a peeled and deveined shrimp with the head on so that the "whiskers" poke out. Pineapple tamales are another local delicacy to look for.

Shops around Teacapán's plazuela sell chilled young coconuts, very refreshing in hot weather. *La tuba,* a fiery fermented and distilled palm juice, is available for US$0.20 per *trago.*

Transport: Transportes de Escuinapa runs second-class buses between Mazatlán and Teacapán for US$2.50 each way. Escuinapa has a PEMEX station with Magna Sin, and Teacapán has one with Nova and diesel.

An alternative way to head south from Teacapán without backtracking to Escuinapa and Mexico 15 is to ferry across Estero Teacapán to the Nayarit fishing village of San Cayetano. From here you can catch a bus through El Novillero east to Acaponeta farther south on Mexico 15.

cazonero, *Teacapán*

THE STATE OF CHIHUAHUA

Although Mexico City's *chilangos* might not agree, in many ways the state of Chihuahua has been Mexico's spiritual heartland during the post-Spanish era. As Mexico slowly forged a separate identity for itself, Chihuahua stood by as instigator and protector of Mexican sovereignty, serving variously as refuge for the opposition government during the French occupation, as the last state to recognize Porfirio Díaz's dictatorial rule, and as home to Pancho Villa and his triumphant División del Norte during the Mexican Revolution.

Around 80 separate Amerindian tribes inhabited what is now the state of Chihuahua at one time or another, including the famous Paquimé of Casas Grandes, a ruined city that has been linked to the Anasazi and Pueblo Indian cultures of the U.S. Southwest. Most of Chihuahua's peaceful tribes died out in the face of Spanish conquest or were absorbed by Mexican culture. A major exception are the reclusive Tarahumaras, a substantial number of whom still live in traditional villages in the Sierra Madre Occidental.

In the late 17th century, the more violent Plains Indians began attacking Chihuahuans—natives and immigrants alike—from the Rocky Mountains to the north. For 200 years (roughly 1686 to 1886), Chihuahua bore the brunt of Comanche and Apache raids on Mexico; in the U.S. such attacks occurred over a period less than half as long. According to local mythology, "wild" Apaches ("Apache," incidentally, comes from *apachu,* the Zuni word for "enemy") are still living a clandestine existence in the northwestern Sierra Madre Occidental.

In the imagination of many Mexicans, Chihuahua plays a role similar to that played by Texas in the American psyche: It's huge (12.51% of Mexico's total area); it's perceived as "bold and rugged"; and it's identified with a frontier ethos that is as important a part of modern Mexico's spiritual heritage as the place held by Texas mythology in U.S. culture. The Texas symbol that resonates most in the U.S. is the Alamo; for Chihuahua and Mexico it's Francisco "Pancho" Villa, leader of the only foreign army ever to invade the continental United States.

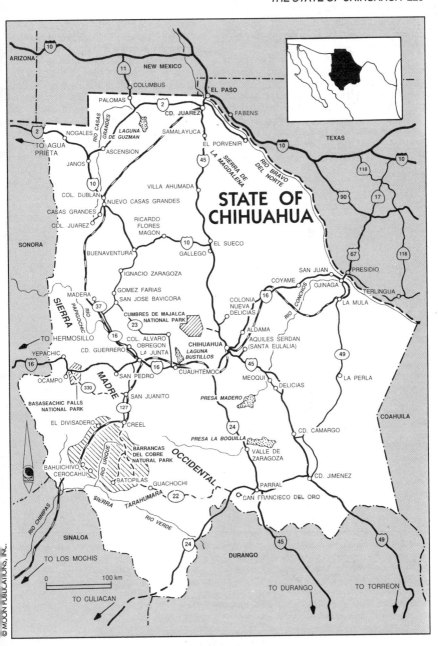

© MOON PUBLICATIONS, INC.

Both symbols are associated with tragic outcomes, all the better to keep the memory alive and poignant.

Like Texas, Chihuahua today is a wealthy state, with the fourth highest per-capita ownership of automobiles in Mexico (after Mexico D.F., Baja California Norte, and Baja California Sur). Around 23% of the nation's *maquiladoras* (twin-plant or in-bond manufacturing facilities) have been established here, although the largest export commodities remain timber and wood products from the Sierra Madre.

The state's second largest occupation is cattle ranching, which produces mostly Angus, Hereford, and Charolais for domestic and U.S. beef markets. Chihuahua and Sonora maintain a constant rivalry over which state produces the best beef. (Sound familiar, Texans and Kansans?) Chihuahua also produces a very tough rodeo steer, a direct descendant of the *criolla* breed brought to the New World by the Spanish four centuries ago. Because it is capable of running for nearly 10 hours straight, it is highly prized by U.S. pro-rodeo associations.

Texans like to brag about how big their ranches are, but historically Chihuahua had even bigger ranches than the infamous King spread. The largest was the Terrazas hacienda, which at its peak encompassed over 20 million acres, an area equal to Switzerland, Belgium, Holland, and Denmark combined. American publishing tycoon William Randolph Hearst owned the 875,000-acre Babícora Ranch, centered around modern-day Gómez Farías, with 20,000 head of Hereford and 22,000 sheep. Following the Mexican Revolution, some of the larger ranches were expropriated by the Mexican government and divided into 30- to 50-acre *ejidos* under the collective ownership of mestizo peasants.

Many powerful ranching families managed to keep parts of their ranches intact, however, and today the state has a more sympathetic outlook on land ownership and free enterprise than most other states in Mexico. While most of the rest of the country has continued to support one-party, PRI rule, rebellious Chihuahuans elected a PAN governor in 1992 for a six-year term (see "Government," p. 31, for more on Mexican politics).

Pancho Villa and his troops, 1914.

Geography

Roughly three times the size of Spain, Mexico's largest state stretches across a remarkably varied terrain of desert, grasslands, chaparral, river valleys, and high mountains.

Towering over the southwestern quarter of the state is the vast Sierra Madre Occidental, a green citadel of 2,700-meter (9,000-foot) peaks, sparkling rivers, and gaping chasms. The desert scrublands, low mountains, alluvial fans, and *bolsones* (salt lakes) of the Chihuahuan Desert —North America's largest desert—cover the northeastern half. Wedged between highlands and desert, occupying about a quarter of the state's center, are the *llanos*—a section of grass basins and low wooded sierras—and the rolling hills of the *lomeríos*.

CIUDAD JUAREZ

From Ciudad Juárez To Chihuahua

Motorists have a choice of two routes between Ciudad Juárez and Chihuahua's state capital.

Mexico 45, modern-day heir to the Camino Real (Oñate's 1598 *entrada*) and the Chihuahua-Santa Fe Trail, takes the more direct southerly angle straight through the Chihuahuan Desert. A four-lane toll road from Villa Ahumada to just north of Chihuahua speeds road progress considerably, while Mexico 45's remaining stretches consist of a two-lane blacktop road that's generally in very good condition. Around 13 km (eight miles) south of the airport is a federal checkpoint; if you don't have a temporary import permit you won't be allowed to drive any farther. The entire Ciudad Juárez-Chihuahua stretch is 354 km (219.5 miles) long and takes most drivers around four hours to complete—not counting rest or lunch stops.

The other route—much more scenic but nearly twice as long—involves driving west on Mexico 2 to Janos (261 km/162 miles from Ciudad Juárez), then south along Chihuahua 10 through the eastern foothills and floodplains of the Sierra Madre Occidental. Along the way are several areas of interest: Casas Grandes (Paquimé ruins, Mormon colonies), Madera on Chihuahua 37 (proto-Anasazi ruins, Madrean woodlands), and Cuauhtémoc at the junction of Chihuahua 16 and 23 (Mennonite camps). The whole route runs 736 km (456 miles) and really should be planned with at least one overnight stay along the way.

Visitors traveling by inter-city bus can choose the quicker Mexico 45 route by taking an express or executive-class bus in Ciudad Juárez. Those with more time may take the longer Mexico 2-Chihuahua 10 route by riding buses bound for Nuevo Casas Grandes, spending a night or two in the Casas Grandes area, then boarding a southward-bound bus from there to Chihuahua or points beyond.

INTRODUCTION

Largest city in the state (1.2 million), the fourth largest in Mexico, and probably the largest border city in the world, Ciudad Juárez is a bursting metropolis that sits 1,128 meters (3,760 feet) above sea level on the Río Bravo (called the Rio Grande in the U.S.), at the edge of the Chihuahuan Desert where the states of Chihuahua, New Mexico, and Texas meet. For most visitors to Mexico it's merely a border crossing—a very large and daunting one with a maze of city streets fanning out in all directions—though for residents of neighboring El Paso it's a destination in its own right for food, nightlife, shopping, and greyhound and horse racing.

When visiting Ciudad Juárez, keep in mind it has the highest consumer price index in Mexico (followed by Veracruz and Puebla). For most North American visitors, shopping remains a bargain but accommodations and food typically cost more than anywhere else in Mexico. Part of the reason for this is the overall affluence of the city, but what really boosts prices is the fact that the city is virtually in the middle of nowhere; transport adds a premium to most costs. Many everyday consumer items are U.S. goods brought in from El Paso. In spite of the relatively high cost of living, the city has Mexico's fifth highest U.S. expatriate population—more than 28,000 at last count (compare with 255,000 in Mexico City, and about 42,000 each in Monterrey and Tijuana).

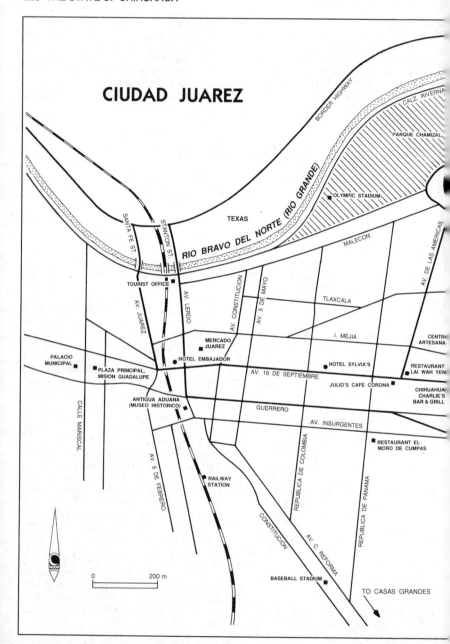

CIUDAD JUAREZ

BORDER HIGHWAY

CALZ. RIVERNA

PARQUE CHAMIZAL

OLYMPIC STADIUM

TEXAS

RIO BRAVO DEL NORTE (RIO GRANDE)

MALECON

SANTA FE ST.

STANTON ST.

AV. DE LAS AMERICAS

TOURIST OFFICE

AV. LERDO

AV. CONSTITUCION

AV. 5 DE MAYO

TLAXCALA

AV. JUAREZ

I. MEJIA

CENTR
ARTESANA

PALACIO
MUNICIPAL

MERCADO
JUAREZ

HOTEL EMBAJADOR

HOTEL SYLVIA'S

RESTAURANT
LAI WAH YEN

PLAZA PRINCIPAL,
MISION GUADALUPE

AV. 16 DE SEPTIEMBRE

JULIO'S CAFE CORONA

CHIHUAHUA
CHARLIE'S
BAR & GRILL

ANTIGUA ADUANA
(MUSEO HISTORICO)

GUERRERO

AV. INSURGENTES

CALLE MARISCAL

REPUBLICA DE COLOMBIA

RESTAURANT EL
MORO DE CUMPAS

AV. 5 DE FEBRERO

RAILWAY
STATION

CONSTITUCION

REPUBLICA DE PANAMA

AV. C. REFORMA

0   200 m

BASEBALL STADIUM

TO CASAS GRANDES

CORDOVA BRIDGE

UNIVERSIDAD
AUTONOMA
DE CHIHUAHUA

BORDER HIGHWAY   TEXAS

COLEGIO MILITAR

RIO BRAVO DEL NORTE (RIO GRANDE)

AV. LINCOLN

U. S. CONSULATE

UNIVERSIDAD AUTONOMA
DE CIUDAD JUAREZ

HOTEL
CALINDA

HNOS. ESCOBAR

HOTEL
PLAZA
JUAREZ

LIENZO CHARRO LOPEZ MATEOS

PLAZA DE LAS AMERICAS,
PUEBLITO MEXICANO

SAN LORENZO CHURCH

PASEO TRIUNFO DE LA REPUBLICA

SANBORN'S

AV. DEL CHARRO

HOTEL
LUCERNA

RIO
GRANDE MALL

PLAZA DE TOROS MONUMENTAL

AV. GUERRERO

AV. LOPEZ MATEOS

P. ELIAS CALLES

AV. DE LA RAZA

AV. TECNOLOGICO

HIPODROMO Y
GALGODROMA
(JUAREZ RACETRACK)

AV. VALENTIN FUENTES

P. S. DE LEON

TO
AIRPORT, MEX 45

TO
ZARAGOZA
BRIDGE

History

Ciudad Juárez (pronounced WHAH-res) is the oldest town along the entire U.S.-Mexico border. New Spain's Rodríguez-Chamuscado expedition mapped a convenient river crossing and mountain pass here in 1581, though Cabeza de Vaca may have stopped here on his epic journey as early as 1527. The crossing was dubbed El Paso del Norte ("Northern Pass") and soon became an important relay point for Spanish colonization northward. Later Anglo-American opportunists coming from the east used the pass to continue westward.

Lured by Indian stories of gold in the mountains of New Mexico and West Texas, Don Juan de Oñate led a group of several hundred Span-

iards across the Chihuahuan Desert to the pass in 1598. De Oñate found no substantial gold or silver deposits in the area (though legend persists he may have stashed a vast treasure in the so-called "Lost Padre Mine" in nearby mountains), but he brought back word that the area was suitable for long-term settlement, with a mild climate and year-round water.

Sixty-one years after de Oñate came north, the first Spanish mission was established at a site that is now downtown Ciudad Juárez. Named Nuestra Señora de Guadalupe, the mission grew into a village that became an important stop on the Camino Real or "Royal Road," which extended between Chihuahua and Santa Fe and became the first road in North America. Later known as the "Chihuahua-Santa Fe Trail" among Anglos, this route is now followed by Mexico 45 (the Pan-American Highway) south of the border and by US Interstate 25 north of the border.

In 1690 another mission, Ysleta del Sur, was founded nearby to receive Tigua and Piro refugees from the Pueblo Indian Revolt in Ysleta, New Mexico. As Villa Paso del Norte's strategic importance increased, the Spanish built a military garrison near Ysleta del Sur to defend the pass against Apache raids.

The first Anglo-Americans began moving into the area in 1827, by the late 1840s, five small Anglo settlements were established north of the Río Bravo. One settlement, Franklin, became the political anchor for what is today El Paso, Texas. Immediately following the loss of New Mexico and Texas to the U.S. via the 1848 Treaty of Guadalupe Hidalgo, the U.S. Army established Fort Bliss on the north side of the Río Bravo, which became the border between the two countries.

The Mexican side of El Paso del Norte continued to grow and prosper until civil war struck both sides of the border. In the U.S., the Confederates briefly occupied Fort Bliss, while on the Mexican side, Benito Juárez and his liberal reformists made El Paso del Norte the provisional capital of Mexico while awaiting the outcome of Mexico's War of Reform. Almost immediately following the reformists' 1861 victory, the French invaded Mexico and the Juárez government remained in exile in El Paso del Norte until they were able to return to Mexico City in 1867. In honor of Benito Juárez's local tenure,

MYSTERY DOG

Typically standing no higher than 13 cm (5.1 inches) at the shoulder and weighing from one-half to three kilograms (one to six pounds), the Chihuahua is the world's smallest dog breed. Though dog fanciers the world over are familiar with its short, pointed ears and large, round eyes, the reasons that the diminutive canine shares the name of the Mexican state and city are lost to history. Legend says the pre-Cortesian natives of Mexico bred the Chihuahua's ancestors, a claim for which there is no archaeological evidence. Another theory says the breed was brought by the conquistadors from Spain, but again, no records have been found to confirm or refute this idea.

Since breeding tiny dogs was popular in imperial China, perhaps the most plausible explanation is that the Chihuahua accompanied the wave of Chinese immigrants who landed on Mexico's Pacific coast in the 19th century. Since many Chinese worked as miners and farmers in the northwestern states of Sonora and Chihuahua, it's possible that, as the breed multiplied, the miniature dogs from this area of Mexico became associated with 19th-century Chihuahua (which to North Americans at the time was much better known than Sonora).

Today the Chihuahua as a "pure" breed has been all but lost in its namesake state. While Chihuahua has plenty of dogs, few can be considered true Chihuahuas, and state residents today show no particular interest in the breed.

the city's name was changed from El Paso del Norte to Ciudad Juárez in 1888.

Today Ciudad Juárez is still capitalizing on its location, now the junction of three major interstate highways (Mexico 45, I-25, and I-10) and several railways. Rail and truck shipping are a major source of income, along with revenue from 13 industrial parks skirting the city's perimeters. The city also serves as an important regional education center, with four major colleges and universities: Universidad Autónoma de Ciudad Juárez, Instituto Tecnológico de Ciudad Juárez, Instituto Tecnológico de Monterrey (a branch of the original ITM), and Universidad Autónoma de Chihuahua.

SIGHTS

Ciudad Juárez doesn't have a lot to see in terms of traditional "tourist attractions," but if you find yourself stuck here for the day you'll have more than a few ways to pass the time. The city's parks, museums, and markets make it a fairly pleasant city to visit once you have your bearings.

Misión Nuestra Señora De Guadalupe

Facing the west side of Plaza Principal (also called Plaza de Armas) between the Palacio Municipal and Mercado Cuauhtémoc, off Calle Mariscal downtown, this humble stone church is dwarfed by the modern cathedral next door.

To appreciate Guadalupe's historic charm, you must enter the church, walk halfway down the center aisle, and look up to see the superb hand-carved *vigas* (wooden roof beams) and *coro* (choir mezzanine). The church was built between 1668-70 but has been restored numerous times.

Museo Histórico De Ciudad Juárez

This INAH-sponsored museum in the recently restored Antigua Aduana (Old Customs) building, on Av. 16 de Septiembre between Av. Juárez and Av. Lerdo, is perhaps the city's most important cultural center. The building's central hall hosts temporary, rotating exhibits on history, archaeology, or anthropology, while rooms surrounding the hall contain the museum's permanent collection.

The first room (Sala 1) begins with Chi-

huahuan prehistory, including displays on the Conchos, Tobosos, Tepehuanes, Sumas, and Jumanos, while the second room (Sala 2) is entirely devoted to the Paquimé culture. Rooms three and four (Salas 3 and 4) continue with the Spanish conquest, Mexican independence, and the Virreinato; followed by the Epoca Nacional and the history of the Chamizal (Sala 5); La Apachería and the Porfiriato (Salas 6, 7, and 8); and the Mexican Revolution (Salas 8 and 9).

American and European film programs are presented twice a week in the museum's auditorium. The museum is open Tues.-Sun. 10-6; admission is free.

Museo De Arte

Sponsored by the Instituto Nacional de Bellas Artes, this small museum in the former PRONAF center (now called Plaza de las Americas) houses rotating contemporary art exhibits of varying quality. Museum hours are Tues.-Sun. 10-6; free admission.

The Cine Club Francés screens French films for the public (free admission) at the Museo de Arte every Sunday evening at 7:30 p.m.

Museo De La Revolución

On the second floor of Pueblito Mexicano in Plaza de las Americas, this small commercial operation is devoted to the 1910-20 Mexican Revolution, with a heavy emphasis on local hero Francisco Villa. Displays include weaponry, period clothing, historic photos (many of them taken by foreign journalists), and newspapers from the era. Open Tues.-Sun. 10-10; admission US$0.50.

Parque Conmemorativo Chamizal

The flood plains encompassed by this 700-acre park were once a serious bone of contention between the U.S. and Mexican governments. Because the Río Bravo-Rio Grande—the natural border between the two countries—occasionally changed course (thus taking huge chunks of land away from one country or the other), neither side was able to establish a mutually agreeable border until 1963, when the two governments agreed to build a concrete channel from which the river could not stray.

At the time of the agreement this meant an 823-acre gain for Mexico, most of which was converted into a national park. Chamizal is a local favorite for long-distance walkers and joggers who savor its shady trees, neat landscaping, and overall tranquility. Other assets include a huge field of basketball courts near Av. Malecón, a swimming pool, an exposition center, and a soccer stadium used by the Cobras, a first-division pro team since 1987.

The park's **Museo de Antropología e História**, open Tues.-Sun. 9 a.m.-7 p.m. (free admission) contains a small collection of artifacts and the usual revolution-era photos, but the museum's real attraction is behind the building itself—a garden with ponds, flowers, trees, and large-scale reproductions of sculpture from ancient Mayan, Aztec, Toltec, Zapotec, Mixtec, Teotihuacán, Olmec, Tarascan, Totonac, and Huastec cultures. Although some of the reproductions are unfortunately deteriorating, a tour of the garden makes a nice stroll.

The park is closed to outside traffic in July, when it's used for Formula 3 racing. Horse cart rides are available in the park year-round for US$1.60 per person.

According to the tourist office, a US$110-million theme park—complete with replicas of Mexico's historical attractions (perhaps similar to Tijuana's Mexitlán)—is planned for some portion of Chamizal in the near future.

ACCOMMODATIONS

Although Ciudad Juárez's hotels (all 77 of them) are a bit pricier than hotels elsewhere in Mexico, quality is generally higher than average as well. Efficient service is the norm, and much of the plumbing and fixtures used in hotel construction comes from north of the border.

Budget

Visitors who want to be within walking distance of the Av. Juárez tourist strip, both municipal markets, and the Plaza Principal might consider the **Hotel Embajador** at the corner of Av. F. Villa and Av. 16 de Septiembre. Once among the fanciest hotels in the city, the seven-story Embajador is faded a bit now—but at US$25 s, US$28 d for a room with TV, a/c, and phone, it's a good value.

Of several other hotels in the same category (US$25-29 per night), another good buy is the clean and efficient **Motel Chula Vista** (tel. 16-17-14-68, fax 16-18-62-88) at the corner of Av. del Charro and Paseo Triunfo de la República on the east side of town—a good location for road departures south out of the city while still within easy driving or city bus distance of the downtown area.

On Av. Lerdo, near the Stanton Street Bridge to El Paso on the northwestern edge of town, are two aging places, **Hotel Santa Fe** (tel. 14-02-70) and **Hotel Impala** (tel. 12-04-31). Both feature a/c and TV and cost around US$21 s, US$30 d; the Impala is the nicer of the two and has a few rooms with kitchenettes. In the center of Av. Lerdo, not far from Mercado Juárez, is the similarly priced **Hotel Continental** (tel. 15-00-84). Two other hotels toward this end of Av. Lerdo, **Hotel Juárez** (tel. 12-99-85; Av. Lerdo 143 Nte.) and **Hotel Correo** (tel. 15-08-75; Av. Lerdo 250 Sur) offer basic but adequate rooms for US$11-12 s, US$12-16 d.

Racetrack enthusiasts or those needing to make a quick highway getaway might choose the tidy, motel-style **Hotel Villa del Sol** (tel. 17-24-24) at Paseo Triunfo de la República 339 Sur near the Juárez Racetrack, the airport, and Mexico 45 South. Rooms cost US$27 s, US$33 d; this is one of the only hotels in this price range in town with a swimming pool. Farther west toward town on Paseo Triunfo de la República are two motels good for a cheap night's sleep (US$11-16): **Motel Mi Ranchito** (tel. 13-20-29; Paseo Triunfo de la República 5825) and **Motel La Hacienda** (tel. 16-10-36; Paseo Triunfo de la República 3208).

Medium-priced And Luxury

A favorite among tourists and visiting businesspeople alike is the modern, well-run **Hotel Sylvia's** (tel. 16-15-04-42, fax 16-15-25-11) at Av. 16 de Septiembre 1977 Ote. between República de Colombia and República de Panama. Its location is more or less equidistant between the Av. de las Americas shopping and restaurant area, downtown Ciudad Juárez, and access to Mexico 45 South. All rooms come with a/c, satellite TV, heating, and telephones. Room rates are US$60 s, US$66 d; the hotel also has a few singles without balconies for US$55. Other facilities include a pool, Jacuzzi, bar with live music, and restaurant. **Hotel Calin-**

da Juárez (tel. 16-34-21, fax 13-72-50) at Calle H. Escobar 3515 near Av. Lincoln has similar rates and facilities.

The popular **Hotel Plaza Juárez** (tel. 13-13-10, fax 13-00-84) at Av. Lincoln and Coyocan has the advantage of being located within walking distance of Plaza de las Americas; for this privilege you pay US$70 s, US$80 d. **Hotel Colonial Las Fuentes** (tel. 3-50-50, fax 13-40-81), nearby at Av. Lincoln and Av. de las Americas, is equally well located but costs only US$54 s, US$58 d.

The city's top-deck cruise is the **Hotel Lucerna** (tel. 13-32-32; 800-LUCERNA in the U.S./Canada; fax 13-37-78) at Paseo Triunfo de la República 3976 (at the corner of Av. López Mateos), with 140 fully equipped rooms, a heated pool, two bars, and a gourmet French restaurant. The Lucerna is part of an independent, three-hotel chain whose other properties are in Mexicali and Tijuana. Rates are US$71 s, US$74 d. A new **Holiday Inn** under construction next to Sanborn's Department Store on Paseo Triunfo de la República nearby promises to give the Lucerna a run for its money when opened (probably by the time you read this).

FOOD

Ciudad Juárez has hundreds of places to eat, from sidewalk taco stands to elegant dining rooms in restored Porfiriato mansions. In spite of the city's location adjacent to El Paso, its first McDonald's (at Av. López Mateos and Paseo Triunfo de la República) only opened in 1992.

Mexican

$$-$$$ **Chihuahua Charlie's Bar & Grill** (tel. 16-13-99-40), Paseo Triunfo de la República 2525. The northernmost outpost (in Mexico, that is) of the famed Grupo Anderson chain, Charlie's features a menu of original recipes based on such familiar Chihuahua standards as *carne asada* and *queso fundido,* along with fresh seafood (tequila shrimp and *huachinango veracruzano* are specialties) and homemade tortillas. Open daily 8 a.m.-1 a.m.; live music Wednesdays and Sundays.

$$-$$$ **Degá Restaurant Bar** (tel. 14-64-90), Av. 16 de Septiembre 1559. Housed in a large,

turn-of-the-century casa with a pleasant, understated decor, Degá offers a number of standard Mexican *platillos,* plus several daily specials. Very attentive service. Open daily for lunch and dinner.

$ **El Burrito Crisóstomo** (no phone), corner of Av. V. Guerrero and Av. de la Huerta, opposite Río Grande Mall. A simple but very popular stand-up diner with some of the best burritos and quesadillas in the city. Open 24 hours.

$$ **Julio's Café Corona** (tel. 13-33-97), Av. 16 de Septiembre near Av. de las Americas. This large restaurant with old-fashioned, white-coat service was very popular with visiting El Pasoans until an El Paso branch was established. Specialties include *caldo tlapeño* (a spicy chicken-avocado soup) and *lobina veracruzana* (Veracruz-style bass). Other offerings are very similar to dishes in the El Paso/New Mexico style of cooking, with lots of deep-red chile sauces. Open daily 10 a.m.-1 a.m.

$ **Mercado Cuauhtémoc,** off Calle Mariscal south of the Palacio Municipal. The bottom floor of this everyday-style market houses several inexpensive *loncherías,* the most popular of which are **Doña Chole** and **Cafetería Chavez.** A good spot for breakfast, lunch, or snacks; strolling *trovadores* entertain. Open daily 7-7.

$$ **Restaurant El Moro de Cumpas** (tel. 13-87-78), Av. Insurgentes and Calle de la Raza. Specializes in *comida norteña,* including *cabrito, carne asada, pollo asado,* and *barbacoa.* Open daily 11 a.m.-midnight.

$ **Restaurant El Norteño** (tel. 12-55-45), Av. Juárez 129. This large, inexpensive eatery next door to the infamous El Sinaloense nightclub serves *comida norteña,* with *pollo al carbón* a house specialty. Open daily 11 a.m.-2 a.m.

$ **Pueblito Mexicano** (no phone) in Plaza de las Americas. The second floor of this newer shopping plaza offers a number of clean, inexpensive snack bars serving tasty tacos, *tortas,* and other *antojitos,* along with *licuados* and *dulces.* Open daily 10 a.m.-9 p.m.

$$ **Restaurant Viva México** (tel. 29-01-56), first floor, Pueblito Mexicano. The walls of the large, circular dining room are painted to look like a colonial cityscape in silhouette—kind of corny —but the food is very dependable and very Mexican, and the clientele is more local than gringo. The attached Cantina El Atorón serves

"Pancho Villas" and *vampiros*, two typical Chihuahuan cocktails. Open Mon.-Thurs. 8 a.m.-2 a.m., Fri.-Sat. 8 a.m.-3 a.m.

Steak

$$-$$$ **Las Brasas Restaurant Bar** Specializes in USDA prime beef and seafood. Two locations: Av. 16 de Septiembre and Anahuac (tel. 16-12-86-81), and Av. de las Americas and Mejía (tel. 13-68-48). Open daily 11 a.m.-11 p.m.

$$-$$$ **Restaurant Nuevo Martino** (tel. 12-33-70), Av. Juárez 643. In the heart of the Av. Juárez bar-restaurant-disco strip, this venerable establishment is known for steak Milanesa (Mexico's version of chicken-fried steak) and Spanish brochette—skewered chunks of beef, onions, tomatoes, and green peppers served over Spanish rice. Open daily 11 a.m.-midnight.

$$-$$$ **Restaurant Parilla del Río** (tel. 13-06-42), Av. Lincoln 1194, opposite Pueblito Mexicano. Generally considered to have the best Chihuahua-style steaks in town. Open daily noon-11 p.m.

Miscellaneous

$-$$ **Café de Europa.** With at least eight branches throughout the city, Europa's wonderful pastries, ice cream, pizza, and espresso are never very far away. A convenient branch for most tourists is the one on Av. 16 de Septiembre near the intersection with Av. Juárez. Open daily 7 a.m.-11 p.m.

$$ **Restaurant Lai Wah Yen** (tel. 16-13-12-91), Av. de las Americas 276 (at Av. 16 de Septiembre). This restaurant and the Shangri-La across the street try to outdo each other in opulent, Chinese banquet-style ambience; LWY has the edge. Open daily noon-1 a.m.

$$ **Restaurante Paco Figaro** (tel. 13-23-92), Paseo Triunfo de la República 2525, opposite Plaza de Toros Monumental. Advertising itself as a Mexican-Texan-Italian restaurant, this unique spot specializes in mesquite-grilled meats and pasta. Open daily noon-midnight.

$-$$ **Sanborn's** (tel. 16-92-03), Paseo Triunfo de la República and Av. López Mateos, opposite Hotel Lucerna. An old standby that serves a reliable menu of Mexican, American, and continental dishes at reasonable prices. Open daily 7:30 a.m.-10 p.m.; special *almuerzo* buffet served 7:30 a.m.-1 p.m.

SHOPPING

Ciudad Juárez has two main shopping districts: the traditional area surrounding the cathedral and municipal markets near the intersection of Av. 16 de Septiembre and Av. Juárez; and the newer, flashier strip along Av. de las Americas, which caters to day-trippers from El Paso.

The government-sponsored **Centro Artesanal**, on Av. Lincoln opposite the Plaza de las Americas (formerly PRONAF), carries an extensive selection of quality ceramics—including some one-of-a-kind pieces—plus clothes, woodcarvings, masks, basketry, and other craft media, all of it handmade. Ample parking is available at Plaza de Americas opposite; several other upscale handicraft shops are also located in the vicinity.

In the Plaza de las Americas itself, the newish **Pueblito Mexicano** features a collection of small shops—a *farmacía, dulcería* (with sweets from all over Mexico), duty-free *perfumería*, photo studio where you can pose in old-fashioned Mexican clothing, and dozens more that haven't opened yet—around a simulated, enclosed town plaza, all in air-conditioned comfort. More shops are planned for the future. This is a major stop for the daily Border Jumper trolley-bus from El Paso.

Farther south in the same general area, **Sanborn's** (Paseo Triunfo de la República and Av. López Mateos) carries a small but high-quality selection of Mexican crafts as well as English-language books and magazines, maps, and pharmaceuticals. Sanborn's *cafetería* is quite popular (see "Food," above).

Closer to the real thing is the **Mercado Juárez** at Av. 16 de Septiembre and Av. Melgar in the city's older shopping district. This funky, two-story market building is filled with vendors selling handicrafts, fruits, piñatas, clothes, foodstuffs, silver, Mexican curios (my favorite, chess sets in which the opposing sides represent *federales* vs. revolutionaries, or *conquistadores* vs. Indians), and leather—some of it at good prices. Outside along one side of the building is a half-gentrified section with open-air cafes, restaurants, and ice-cream parlors.

More traditional yet is the three-floor **Mercado Cuauhtémoc**, off Calle Mariscal south of the cathedral. The ground floor is taken up with cheap *loncherías* (see "Food," above), fresh meats, and *queso asadero* from Villa Ahumada. On the upper floors you'll find an assortment of live chickens, doves, parrots, fruits, flowers, medicinal herbs, and lucky buddhas (with crosses and other charms inside). East of the market, extending three or four blocks, is an outdoor market consisting mostly of fruit and vegetable vendors, while Calle Minas behind the market is lined with *carnicerías* (butcher shops) and various other *tiendas*.

A more mixed shopping venue, popular among tourists as well as locals, is **Av. Juárez,** which runs from the Puente Santa Fé border crossing south to Av. 16 de Septiembre. Small shops along the avenue offer Mexican-made boots, untaxed liquors, Cuban cigars, kitschy souvenirs, clothing, and a myriad of other items meant to please everyone, from the *campesino* with only a few pesos to spend, to first-time North American visitors bent on emptying their pockets.

Ciudad Juárez has several modern shopping malls, the largest of which is **Río Grande Mall** at Paseo Triunfo de la República and Av. López Mateos. Shoes are among the best mall buys.

Many El Paso residents visit Ciudad Juárez regularly to take advantage of lower prices on pharmaceuticals. **Farmacías Catedral de Juárez** has three branches open 24 hours, the most conveniently located of which is at Av. López Mateos 372 Nte. (tel. 16-13-89-88).

RECREATION

Bullfights

Although Ciudad Juárez has two bullrings, only one holds regular corridas—**Plaza de Toros Monumental** on Paseo Triunfo de la República. Seating up to 17,000, Monumental is the world's fourth largest bullring. The annual season runs April-Sept.; admission is US$9-18 depending on the seat, while parking costs US$1 and cushions can be rented for US$0.40. The city's older ring, Plaza Balderas (downtown at Calle F. Villa), is now used only for concerts and other events.

Charreadas

Two *charro* rings, **Lienzo Charro López Mateos** (Av. del Charro between Av. Hnos. Escobar and Paseo Triunfo de la República) and

Lienzo Charro Baca Gallardo (Carretera Panamericana Km 13) host Mexican rodeo events off and on year-round—usually on Sundays and national festivals. Inquire at the SECTUR office (see "Information," below for address and phone).

Racing And Off-Track Betting

The **Hipodromo y Galgodromo de Ciudad Juárez** (Juárez Racetrack), at the easternmost extension of Av. Guerrero, features greyhound racing Wed.-Sun. at 8 p.m. year-round, and horse racing Wed.-Sun. at noon from June-August. Seats in the air-conditioned general admission section cost US$0.50, while the Jockey Club section upstairs costs US$3. The advantages to Jockey Club seating are giant-screen replay and table service for food and beverages. A bar downstairs offers off-track betting and sports book, TV tables at which to watch several races and sports events, and full food-and-beverage service. The racetrack operates shuttle buses to and from several of the city's major hotels.

The **Juárez Turf Club,** downtown just a block south of the Santa Fe Bridge on the east side of Av. Juárez, allows El Pasoans to walk over Santa Fe Bridge and wager on live greyhound horse races without going all the way out to the track. Facilities include a full bar, multiscreen TV for off-track betting and sports, and betting counters. Open daily 10 a.m.-midnight.

Bars And Discos

For locals as well as tourists, Av. Juárez is the city's major entertainment center, a place where you can wander past an assortment of night spots designed for every budget and proclivity. At the southern end of the avenue is a cluster of ranchero bars that feature dancing to live *norteña* music. Although this end of the avenue has a rough reputation, the clubs with cover charges (usually around US$2.50) are generally pretty safe. **El Sinaloense,** on Av. Juárez just north of 16 de Septiembre, usually has the best bands.

Another bar rich in local tradition is the 1920s-vintage **El Kentucky Club** at Av. Juárez 629. Housed in a building that has been a cantina or bar for nearly 150 years, El Kentucky's wood-paneled ambience still attracts a few regulars.

North of Calle Mejía on Av. Juárez are the more "modern" bars and discos. Of the many discos, the most popular are **Noa Noa Disco** (owned by famous romantic singer Juan Gabriel), at Av. Juárez and Calle M. Martínez near the Woolworth store; **Sarawak Disco** at Av. Juárez 645; and **Cosmos Discotheque,** 1½ blocks from the Santa Fe Bridge. **Crazy Town Bar,** opposite Cosmos, is popular with visiting weekend gringos. **Bar Mariachi,** two blocks from the bridge, has live mariachi music and no cover charge.

Just opposite the bridge is a cluster of other bars and discos that cater almost exclusively to an El Paso crowd, including **XO Laser, Fantasy, Spanky's, Cheers Video Bar,** and **Tequila Derby.** The next couple of streets west of Av. Juárez, particularly Calle Mariscal, are devoted to go-go bars—which do not, as promised by street touts, feature topless or nude dancers, but young women dressed in bikinis. (Topless dancing is illegal in Ciudad Juárez.)

Away from Av. Juárez entirely, the most popular disco in the city is **Electric Q,** on Av. Lincoln near Pueblito Mexicano. On the west side of the loop around Plaza de las Americas is **El Angel Azul,** a video bar where art films (including films by Pedro Almodavar and other Latin filmmakers) are free for the price of drinks.

Radio

For the best of border radio, tune in 105.1 FM, a bilingual station that plays a vigorous mix of *norteña*-style *cumbias, rancheras,* and *boleros.*

INFORMATION

Tourist Office

SECTUR (tel. 16-14-01-23) has a large, informative office in the Unidad Administrativa Municipal (UAM) just across the border from the U.S. on Av. Colegio Militar between Av. Juárez and Av. Lerdo. It's open Mon.-Fri. 8-8, Sat.-Sun. 8-noon.

Consulates

Ciudad Juárez has a U.S. consulate (tel. 16-13-40-48, after hours 915-525-6066 in El Paso) at Av. López Mateos 924, just north of the Universidad Autónoma de Ciudad Juárez.

El Paso has a Mexican consulate (tel. 915-533-3644) at 910 E. San Antonio Street.

Telephone

Ciudad Juárez has the usual telephone offices and hotel phone systems, but if you need to make an international call, it's much less expensive to walk across the Santa Fe Bridge to downtown El Paso and use the U.S. system. Many Juárez residents take advantage of phone booths only a few meters beyond the U.S. customs station.

The **area code** for Ciudad Juárez is 16.

Green Angels

The local Green Angels unit (tel. 16-14-66-92, 14-06-70) is based at the tourism office.

GETTING THERE

Air

Regional carrier **TAESA** (tel. 16-11-35-35; Calle I. Mejía and PRONAF 369) fields flights to/from Chicago, Durango, Mexico City, Tijuana, and Zacatecas.

Aero California (tel. 18-33-99; Av. de la Raza 6108-2) has nonstop flights to/from Torreón, plus connecting flights to/from Culiacán, Durango, Guadalajara, La Paz, and Mexico City.

Aeroméxico (tel. 13-87-19; Av. Lincoln 759) offers nonstop flights between Ciudad Juárez and Chihuahua, Mazatlán, and Mexico City.

The airport is 18.5 km (11.5 miles) from the city center—about a half-hour by car or taxi. The standard taxi fare is US$13; a *colectivo* costs US$5 per person. Or you can hop a blue-and-white bus marked "Aeropuerto" on the sides for US$0.30.

Bus

Built in 1991, the city's impressive Central de Autobuses, at the intersection of Paseo Triunfo de la República and Av. López Mateos (near the Plaza Río Grande shopping center and Plaza de Toros Monumental), features a left-luggage service, moneychanger, post office, long-distance telephone counter, customs check (for buses arriving from the U.S.), and sparkling clean *cafetería* serving pizzas, burgers, *tortas,* and *flautas.*

Because Ciudad Juárez is a major transport junction, buses depart to virtually anywhere in Mexico from this station. **Tres Estrellas de Oro** and **TNS** offer once-daily first-class departures to Hermosillo (US$27) and Guaymas (US$31).

Turistar has higher-class *ejecutivo* service to Chihuahua (US$25, seven daily departures), Torreón (US$50, three daily departures), Guadalajara (US$75, two daily departures), Monterrey (US$76, one daily departure), and Durango (US$49, one daily departure).

The less expensive **Omnibus de Mexico** operates first-class buses to/from Nuevo Casas Grandes (US$9, three daily departures), Chihuahua (US$13, every hour 6 a.m.-9 p.m.), Cuauhtémoc (US$19, three daily departures), San Luis Potosí (US$45, four daily departures), and Zacatecas (US$39, four daily departures).

Chihuahuenses has hourly departures to Chihuahua (US$13) and El Paso (US$5), plus twice-daily buses to Mazatlán (US$45); **Estrella Blanca** runs similar routes for slightly lower fares.

Other stateside departures are provided by **Transportes del Norte,** which operates daily buses to/from Los Angeles (US$35), Albuquerque (US$15), and Denver (US$69).

Several smaller, regional companies offer regular second-class bus service from the Central de Autobuses to towns within the state of Chihuahua; a typical second-class fare to Chihuahua is around US$6.

Border Jumper

The El Paso-Juárez Trolley Co. (tel. 915-544-0061 in El Paso) operates a bus called the "Border Jumper" every hour Wed.-Sun. 10 a.m.-6 p.m. A US$5 ticket is good for unlimited stops along the bus route, which starts at the El Paso Civic Center, crosses the border via the Cordova Bridge and Av. de las Americas, and stops at Plaza de las Americas (Pueblito Mexicano), Chihuahua Charlie's, Mercado Juárez, and the Museo Histórico de Ciudad Juárez on Av. 16 de Septiembre before returning to El Paso via Av. Juárez.

The Chihuahua Charlie's stop is only about two blocks west of the Central de Autobuses, so the Border Jumper is a viable alternative to the Chihuahuenses bus (which costs the same but

leaves from El Paso's downtown bus terminal). The main clientele for the Border Jumper, however, are El Pasoans on daytime shopping excursions.

Border Taxis

A number of taxicab companies on the El Paso side specialize in quick trips across the border, including **Texas Cab** (tel. 915-562-0033), **Border Taxi** (tel. 565-1440), and **Yellow Cab** (tel. 533-3433). A short trip between downtown El Paso and downtown Ciudad Juárez costs around US$10. The fare from the Mexican side is about the same; a taxi stand is located near the Stanton Street Bridge.

Train

The División del Norte train No. 8 offers second-class seats to Mexico City with stops in Chihuahua, Jimenez, Torreón, Zacatecas, Aguascalientes, and Querétaro. Between Zacatecas and Mexico City, special first-class reserved is also available.

Although the fare between Ciudad Juárez and Chihuahua is only US$3, few people choose to take the División del Norte between the two cities since it involves a 10 p.m. departure from Juárez with a 3:15 a.m. arrival in Chihuahua (for a comfortable 9:30 a.m. arrival in Mexico City). A second-class bus between the two cities costs around US$6 and takes about the same amount of time, but you have the choice of several daily departures—all at more reasonable hours.

The Tren Mixto, Región Norte, offers mixed passenger-cargo service between Ciudad Juárez and La Junta, with stops in Nuevo Casas Grandes and Madera. Passenger space is inconsistent, however, and you can't count on getting a ticket unless you inquire at least four days ahead of your intended departure. The train leaves Ciudad Juárez daily except Sunday at 7:45 a.m., arriving in La Junta between 10 p.m. and midnight depending on the cargo. In the reverse direction the train leaves La Junta at 10:30 a.m. and arrives in Ciudad Juárez around 1 a.m. In either direction, arrival times in Nuevo Casas Grandes and Madera are in the mid-afternoon. Fares are under US$10 for any destination along the line.

Border Formalities

Mexico's customs and immigration station at Ciudad Juárez is large and efficient. If you're planning to stay more than 72 hours you'll need a tourist card. If you plan to drive beyond the federal checkpoint 13 km (eight miles) south of the airport, you'd better stop for a temporary auto-import permit.

GETTING AROUND

Taxi

Ciudad Juárez taxis operate from *sitios* or stands throughout the city; they can also be flagged down on the street. Typical fares include: Hotel Sylvia's to Av. Juárez US$8; Av. Juárez to downtown El Paso US$10; downtown Ciudad Juárez to Central de Autobuses US$8.80.

Bus

City buses cost US$0.20. As elsewhere in Mexico, the terminating destination is marked over the windshield. Any bus taken west along Av. 16 de Septiembre ends up downtown on either Av. Juárez or Av. Lerdo; any bus taken east on Av. Malecón ends up going south on Av. Lincoln or Av. de las Americas. Utilizing these two routes—which together form a circuit around the city's commercial heart—you can get to most areas of historical or shopping interest.

Driving

The most heavily used bridge crossing is the Santa Fe Bridge (called both Puente Juárez and Puente Santa Fé on the Mexican side), which costs US$1.95 for vehicles, US$0.50 for pedestrians. This bridge allows one-way vehicular traffic into Ciudad Juárez; in the reverse direction motorists use the parallel Stanton Bridge.

The traffic along the Santa Fe and Stanton Street bridges is intense; a better alternative for motorists visiting Ciudad Juárez is the Cordova Bridge (called Puente de las Americas on the Mexican side), which has an exit directly off highway I-10 east on the U.S. side. This bridge takes you through Parque Chamizal to the junction of Av. de las Americas, Av. Lincoln, and Av. Malecón, three streets that will take you almost anywhere in the city.

If your goal is to reach Mexico 45 as quickly

and easily as possible, your best bet is to use the new Santa Teresa border crossing, which puts you west of Ciudad Juárez on Mexico 2 between Km 22 and 23. Mexico 2 links with Mexico 45 just southeast of the city. Coming from I-10 east, you can also cross at the Zaragoza Road Bridge (near Ysleta del Sur), about 16 km (10 miles) east of downtown Ciudad Juárez. This crossing, too, connects with Mexico 45 via Mexico 2.

Fuel

PEMEX stations with Magna Sin are plentiful throughout the city as well as along the city outskirts at Mexico 2 and Mexico 45.

Auto Rental

At last count Ciudad Juárez had 10 car rental agencies, several of which were located along Paseo Triunfo de la República. Avis, Budget, and National also have counters at Juárez International Airport. Rates are a uniform US$30 per day plus US$0.23 per km for standard VW bugs; US$45 per day plus US$0.30 per km for a Nissan Tsuru II (Sentra); US$56 per day plus US$0.33 per km for a Mercury Topaz.

Flat-fee, unlimited-km rentals are sometimes available by the week; Avis International (tel. 800-331-1212) in the U.S. often has the best weekly deals on Mexico rentals.

VICINITY OF CIUDAD JUAREZ

Villa Ahumada

About a third of the way between Ciudad Juárez and Chihuahua, Villa Ahumada is famous throughout the state for *queso asadero* ("grillman's cheese"), *crema* (a thick cream somewhat similar to American sour cream), and chorizo (Mexican sausage). Shops selling these foodstuffs line the highway through town.

Because several good restaurants are also found along the highway, Villa Ahumada is a popular lunch stop for travelers coming from the south. The better ones are **Restaurant Oscar's, Restaurant El Paisano,** and **Restaurant El Oasis.** The latter restaurant is open 24 hours and is attached to a 24-hour PEMEX with Magna Sin. Between here and Chihuahua, 241 km (149.5 miles) to the south (or, heading north, before Ciudad Juárez), there are no reliable

AUTO RENTAL AGENCIES IN CIUDAD JUAREZ

ALPRI RENT-A-CAR

Av. Lincoln and Calle Coyocan
tel. 13-85-23

AUTO RENT FRONTERA

Paseo Triunfo de la República 1198
tel. 16-74-90

AVIS

Av. 16 de Septiembre 999 Ote.
tel. 14-00-19

BUDGET

Av. de las Americas 545 Nte.
tel. 16-42-59

DOLLAR RENT-A-CAR

Paseo Triunfo de la República 3976
tel. 13-32-32

FAST AUTO RENTA

Calle Hermanos Escobar 2751-4
tel. 13-69-40

HERTZ

Paseo Triunfo de la República 2408-2
tel. 14-00-19

MONACO RENT-A-CAR

Paseo Triunfo de la República 4404-2
tel. 13-27-79

NATIONAL

Av. 16 de Septiembre and Calle Venezuela
tel. 15-04-42

QUICK RENT-A-CAR

Calle Hermanos Escobar 3513
tel. 13-17-32

sources of Magna Sin, so be sure to top off if you're down a half tank or more.

Villa Ahumada is also the junction for the toll (*cuota*) and free (*libre*) highways southward to El Sueco. The free road is roughly 65 km (40 miles) longer than the toll highway.

Palomas (Rodrigo M. Quevedo) And Columbus

This little town opposite Columbus, New Mexico is the only official border crossing between Mexico and New Mexico. Known variously as Palomas, Puerto Palomas, and Rodrigo M. Quevedo (its official name), the town is little more than a relay point for agricultural goods produced in the Ascensión *municipio,* the preponderance of which are chile products. Nearly six million kilograms of chile have crossed the border here in just one year, including cayennes (about a quarter of the crop), jalapeños, long greens, fresh reds, yellow hots, and serranos.

Like every town along the U.S.-Mexico border, Palomas is larger than its U.S. counterpart, though in this case that's not saying much. Palomas does have a tidy little *placita* with an attractive, twin-towered stone church, **Nuestra Señora de Guadalupe,** alongside. *Las Fronteras,* a bilingual newspaper representing Palomas and Columbus, is circulated in both towns.

Across the border, the near-ghost town of **Columbus** is known among U.S.-Mexico history buffs as the only place in the continental U.S. to be invaded by foreign troops, thanks to Pancho Villa.

Pancho and Blackjack: After U.S. President Woodrow Wilson declared U.S. support for the Carranza presidential candidacy in Mexico, Francisco "Pancho" Villa (Carranza's sworn enemy) retaliated by attacking the 13th U.S. Cavalry at Camp Furlong near Columbus on March 9, 1916.

U.S. forces at Camp Furlong were able to repel Villa's troops (killing 250 of an estimated 500-1,000 Villistas in the process), but during their retreat the Mexicans stopped in Columbus for a looting and window-shooting spree that left several U.S. civilians dead. President Wilson ordered a "punitive expedition" into Mexico the next day.

Led by General John "Blackjack" Pershing, the expedition entered Mexico on March 15, 1916 with 4,800 troops, plus airplanes and motorized military vehicles (the first time either were used in U.S. warfare) and extended through Feb. 5, 1917, when Pershing left with 10,690 troops. Although Pershing and company got as far south as Parral, Chih., they never captured Villa. It was the last U.S. Cavalry expedition in U.S. military history.

Practicalities: Though few travelers choose to spend the night in either Columbus or Palomas, the latter has one moderately priced hotel —**Hotel San Francisco** (Av. 5 de Mayo 910), US$29-32 per night—and three *clase económi-*

ca places that run about US$15-20 a night. A couple of decent places to eat in Palomas are **Bruno's** (open Tues.-Sun. 7 a.m.-10 p.m.) and **Tillie's** (open daily 11 a.m.-midnight), both just a stone's throw from the border crossing.

Mexico 23 leads south 35 km (21.7 miles) from Palomas to a junction with Mexico 2 called **Tres Caminos,** where there's a PEMEX station with Magna Sin (between Km 112 and 113) and several cafes.

CASAS GRANDES TO CUAUHTEMOC

PAQUIMÉ ARCHAEOLOGICAL ZONE

Long before Mormons or Mexicans arrived in the Río Casas Grandes area, an ancient, little-understood Amerindian culture built a large adobe city called Paquimé on the banks of the river. The ruins of their multistory pueblo so impressed later visitors that the area became known as "Casas Grandes" or "Big Houses" throughout Mexico. Architecture and artifacts at Paquimé suggest the culture lasted nearly 800 years and exhibited a unique blend of Anasazi-Pueblo Indian and Mesoamerican characteristics. The citizens of Paquimé are also thought to have practiced the first agriculture in Northwest Mexico.

Although the ruins were briefly explored by Swiss-American ethnologist Adolph Bandelier in the 1890s (on the basis of a comparative study of Hohokam, Mogollon, and Casas Grandes archaeology, Bandelier concluded that the Casas Grandes and Anasazi cultures were part of the same regional diaspora), Paquimé remained relatively neglected until Sept. 1958 when Arizona's Amerindian Foundation received authorization from Mexico's INAH to carry out a three-year research project. Continuing research is currently being conducted by resident archaeologist R.B. Brown.

History
Centered in a 221,000-square-km area covering northwestern Chihuahua and northeastern Sonora, the Casas Grandes culture (which included Paquimé as its focal point) is known to have existed as early as A.D. 700, reaching its apex during the 11th-14th centuries. In addition to being Northern Mexico's first agriculturists, the citizens of Paquimé traded in obsidian, turquoise, shells, quetzal feathers, and peyote with Anasazi and Mesoamerican groups—thus developing a crossroads between the cultures of the American Southwest and those of Southern Mexico. Archaeological evidence shows Mesoamerican influence in the city's ball-court games, copper ornamentation, and Quetzalcoatl cult, while the general architecture is obviously related to Anasazi-Pueblo Indian styles (in which direction the architectural influence flowed has yet to be determined), though somewhat more advanced. The presence of seashells also indicates contact with communities living along the Sea of Cortez coast.

At its peak, Paquimé may have been linked to hundreds of satellite villages extending from Mesa Verde, Colorado, to Mexico City, a vast area known as "Oasis America" among Mexican anthropologists. The culture is thought to have begun stagnating by the late 13th century, and evidence suggests that Paquimé proper was razed by marauding tribes from the north around 1340 (an alternate theory blames an accidental but all-consuming fire). Mass migrations away from the city, similar to those among the Anasazis of Arizona and New Mexico, may also have occurred—although where these people may have gone is a complete mystery. The uncanny parallels between the Anasazi and Casas Grandes cultures is fertile research territory as yet relatively unexplored.

Architecture And City Planning
The archaeological zone, seven km southwest of Nuevo Casas Grandes via Chihuahua 18, currently extends 123 acres from the banks of the Río Casas Grandes southward, about two-thirds of which have been excavated. Outlines of Paquimé structures occur over 88 acres and are thought to have encompassed 1,780 rooms that were inhabited by as many as 2,200 people. Unexcavated sites outside the zone continue as far south as Laguna Babícora (near Madera), as far north as Janos, and as far west as Nacori Chico, Sonora, with the Río Casas Grandes as the eastern boundary.

Early Paquimé houses were round and semi-subterranean (similar to the "kivas" of the U.S. Southwest), but designs later evolved into rectangular structures with two to four floors, complete with sewage, water systems, and kitchens. As indicated by the construction of the bottom floors (in most instances the only floors visible today), some buildings may originally have contained up to five floors. The partial remains of fourth floors can be seen in places. Walls of rammed earth (adobe) are 1-1 1/2 meters (3-4 1/2 feet) thick.

Rooms were fitted together with complex, right-angled, jigsaw-puzzlelike precision, with as many as 16 interior walls per room. Every doorway is shaped like a thick "T," with a maximum height of 1.3 meters (4.3 feet) so that it was necessary for the inhabitants to pass slowly, one person at a time, through them. The top crossbar of the T-door was narrower than the bottom vertical so that residents could carry things in their arms from room to room. Most likely this door design was a means of defense, preventing invading enemies from moving quickly through the buildings; the complex, mazelike room layout may also have been defense related.

The majority of rooms had heating stoves and windows for ventilation, and many also show wall niches where religious idols may have been placed. Some of the community's dead—possibly family heads—were buried (usually in the fetal or flexed position common to burial customs in all Mesoamerican cultures) in corners of bottom-floor rooms along with offerings of turquoise adornments, pottery, and obsidian points.

Unique interior stairways of cedar and adobe differentiate Paquimé architecture from that of the Anasazis, who used movable ladders rather than permanent stairways. Another major difference between Anasazi and Paquimé building design is that the bottom floors of Anasazi-Pueblo structures were solid bodies that served solely as a base for upper floors, while the bottom floors of Paquimé houses had functional rooms with exterior doors.

The comparative sophistication of Paquimé architecture to Anasazi-Pueblo may be explained by the fact that for most of its history the Casas Grandes culture lived in less defensive, more secure circumstances. Because they

Paquimé

JOE CUMMINGS

needed to be able to retract their simple ladders from the ground when under attack, the Anasazis never developed stairs or ground-floor rooms.

Water in Paquimé was directed from a spring eight km northwest of the city via open pipes or aqueducts made of stone slabs and was stored in 10-meter-deep stone wells. From the wells the water could be directed at will from house to house via another set of stone pipes or used to irrigate nearby fields.

That the Paquimé culture developed a highly efficient social organization in which everyone worked for the community is demonstrated by evidence of labor specialization. Sotol (a liquor made from a type of agave), for example, was produced in a special section of the city where large ovens were used to bake the agave hearts. Another section was used for the raising of the resplendent quetzal (*Pharomachrus mocinno*), whose long, iridescent plumage was highly revered in Mesoamerican cultures.

Other specialized city structures included ball courts, ceremonial plazas, and military emplacements. The city's primary ceremonial monument is a stone cross with five-meter arms lying flat on the ground and surrounded by four circular platforms, each seven meters in diameter and one meter high. The arms of the cross are aligned with the points of the compass, suggesting it was used by Paquimé shamans for astronomic or agricultural-cycle predictions.

An excavated ball court in the shape of a double "T" or capital "I" lies 70 meters west of the cross and is similar to those found farther south during the Toltec period. A highly ornate copper pendant, molded by the lost-wax process into the shape of a turtle with rattlesnake motifs on the reverse, was found on this court. A second, smaller ball court can be seen in another part of the ruins. Other monuments include an offering platform and various other platforms of unknown function.

Pottery

A major hallmark of Casas Grandes culture was a sophisticated ceramics tradition that produced delicate, multicolored pots made without a potter's wheel. Highly prized for their mazelike decorations, agate-polished surfaces, and smooth-curved bottoms that miraculously keep the pots upright, Paquimé pots were traded throughout pre-Cortesian Mexico and the U.S. Southwest. Some of the more elaborate pieces were fashioned in human or animal figures, yet still functioned as pots. (Hopi ceramics bear a certain resemblance, though the Casas Grandes tradition is older.) Original Paquimé pots (also called "Casas Grandes" pottery) are priceless collector's items; a revived Casas Grandes style emanating from the nearby village of Mata Ortíz is also very collectable (see "Mata Ortíz and Hacienda San Diego," below for more information).

Visiting The Ruins

To reach the main archaeological zone, drive six km from Nuevo Casas Grandes' Av. Juárez to Casas Grandes, then turn left onto a one-km dirt road signed "Ruinas Paquimé." The ruins are open to the public daily 10 a.m.-5 p.m.; admission is US$2.60 except Sunday, when it's free. A small shop next to the entrance sells updated Casas Grandes-style pottery.

From the entrance road the ruins look more diminutive than might be expected, so you really have to wander through them to gain a full ap-

preciation for their size and complexity. Because of the mazelike layout, visitors sometimes become temporarily lost in the larger structures, even though they don't appear very large from the outside.

Other Sites

Trips to other nearby sites, such as the secluded cave dwellings at **Valle de las Cuevas** (including "Cueva de la Olla," a cave with a huge, floor-to-ceiling corn urn made of mud-coated, coiled grass, first noted by Norwegian explorer Carl Lumholtz) along Río Piedras Verdes, can be arranged through local guides. Some sites can only be reached by hikes lasting from a half day to four days. Ask at the home studio of potter Manuel Olivas, who lives at the southern edge of "old" Casas Grandes just before Km 9 on the left side of Chihuahua 71 en route to Colonia Juárez. Señor Olivas is very knowledgeable about local Paquimé sites and petroglyphs; the back wall of his workshop is painted with a large map showing many of the principal spots.

Hotel Paquimé or Motel Piñon in Nuevo Casas Grandes can also arrange archaeological tours of the area.

CASAS GRANDES-NUEVOS CASAS GRANDES

These twin towns at the confluence of the Casas Grandes and Piedras Verdes rivers are supported by extensive agriculture in the surrounding river plains. Both rivers originate in the Sierra Madre Occidental; the Río Casas Grandes is the largest of all waterways flowing eastward from the sierra. From here it flows northward into the Chihuahuan Desert, divides into several channels, reunites, and empties into Laguna de Guzmán, a *bolsón* that averages around a meter deep year-round.

Casas Grandes' 1,463-meter (4,845-foot) altitude, gently sloping hills, and plentiful water sources make it very well-suited to farming. Groups of Mormon immigrants settled the area in 1885-1912 to avoid a U.S. ban on polygamy (see "Colonia Juárez," below, for more information on the Mormon colonies). Though many Mormons returned to the U.S. during the Mexican Revolution years, a number stayed behind

and introduced modern farming techniques to the region—including the cultivation of slopes, hitherto not practiced in Northern Mexico—that have contributed much to local prosperity.

Apples and peaches are the principal local cash crops (U.S. pie-maker Sara Lee is a major purchaser), sustaining five major fruit packers (*empacadoras*) and employing hundreds of residents. Casas Grandes is also known for producing the best turkey in the nation; over a half million are produced yearly and distributed throughout the republic.

The main commercial center for the area is prosperous **Nuevo Casas Grandes,** which started as a railway station on the La Junta rail line in 1898 (constructed by the U.S.-based Rio Grande, Sierra Madre, and Pacific Railway Company) and today is a collection of agricultural supply stores, modest hotels for business travelers and the occasional tourist, banks, restaurants, PEMEX stations, and other sundries needed to support a town of 85,000 people. Though surrounded by rolling, grassy hills, the town itself—with its wide avenues spread over a flat plain—gives the impression of a town in the American Southwest more than a typical Mexican town.

Set amidst rolling hills and fruit orchards six km southwest of Nuevo Casas Grandes is "Old" **Casas Grandes,** a quaint, shady farming community of 6,000 that has been quietly neglected since being bypassed first by the rail line and more recently by the national highway. With the slowly increasing notoriety of the nearby Paquimé ruins—the most important archaeological site in all of Northern Mexico—the town obviously hopes to benefit from the trickle of tourists driving through town on their way to see the archaeological zone. A school on the plaza is being converted into a museum that will contain local antiquities.

Dividing the two towns is the lovely Río Casas Grandes, lined with alamo (cottonwood) trees whose leaves alternate between a deep green in spring and summer and bright copper in fall and winter.

Accommodations

Most of Nuevo Casas Grandes' hotels (there are no tourist accommodations available in Casas Grandes, nearby Colonia Juárez, or Mata Ortíz) are lined up along Av. Juárez, which is parallel to Chihuahua 10. **Hotel Paquimé** (tel. 169-4-13-20, fax 169-4-06-58), Av. Juárez 401, is a good choice if you plan to stop over for sightseeing, as the staff is very knowledgeable about the area. Recently renovated rooms cost US$26-31 s, US$30-35 d, US$35-44 t, and US$47 q; all come with phones, satellite TV, a/c, and heating. Security parking is provided below the building.

Motel Piñon (tel. 4-01-66, fax 4-08-47), nearby at Av. Juárez 605, is very similar but has a small pool and courtyard parking. Rooms are US$27 s/d. A small collection of Paquimé artifacts is on display in the lobby; information on local sightseeing is readily dispensed.

If you're just passing through, the simple but clean **Motel Los Arcos** (tel. 4-42-60) is right on the highway south of town and costs US$23 s, US$28 d. Los Arcos also has a few RV/trailer spaces with full hookups for US$10 per night.

The cheapest place to stay at US$22 per night is **Hotel California** (tel. 4-11-10), on Calle Constitución 209 opposite the railway line. Considering how much better the Paquimé and Piñon are for only a few dollars more, it's no particular bargain.

Top of the heap is the modern, 124-room **Motel Hacienda** (tel. 4-10-46, fax 4-48-18), Av. Juárez 2603 toward the north end of town. The clientele here are mostly businesspeople, and many of the staff are bilingual. Rooms with all the amenities cost US$43.30 s, US$46.60 d. The motel has a pool.

Just north of Motel Los Arcos on the highway (called Av. Colón here) is **Motel Las Fuentes** (tel. 4-54-02), where rooms around a courtyard cost US$43.30 s/d. It also has a pool.

Food

Several modest restaurants are located along Av. Juárez in the vicinity of Hotel Paquimé, Motel Piñon, and Motel Hacienda (each of these hotels have their own restaurants as well). Several on Av. Juárez are of the fast-food variety, such as **Pecos Pizza** and **El Bandido,** both popular with a younger crowd. **Restaurant Constantino,** at Av. Juárez 400, has been serving Mexican and regional cuisine in a casual coffee shop-style ambience for over 35 years.

The most notable eating spot in town is **Restaurant Malmedy** (tel. 169-4-10-25), a unique Belgian-Mexican restaurant housed in a turn-of-the-century, Mormon-built wooden house at the north end of Av. Juárez. Belgian-born chef Philippe Gentges has worked in Mexico for nearly a decade. Married to a local woman, he now prepares a toothsome selection of continental-style beef, chicken, and fish dishes, all from original recipes. During warmer weather a few outside tables make for pleasant dining. Malmedy is open daily for lunch and dinner.

Restaurant Dinno's, Calle Constitución (paralleling Av. Juárez to the east) and Minerva, serves pizza and Mexican dishes but is especially popular for breakfast. For steak, town opinion is split between Restaurant Malmedy and **Restaurant El Herradero** at Av. Juárez 2610.

When you're in the mood for ice cream, go straight to **Helados Bing** on Av. Juárez near the corner of Av. 6 de Marzo. Road warriors can chow down day or night at 24-hour **Restaurant El Parador** on Chihuahua 10 south, near Motel Los Arcos.

Shopping

Casas Grandes-style pottery can be perused or purchased at **Pueblo Viejo** (tel. 169-4-43-26), a small shop at Av. 16 de Septiembre 304 in Nuevo Casas Grandes. Casas Grandes Viejo

CASAS GRANDES POTTERY

Juan Quezada, who started the renaissance of the Casas Grandes or Paquimé-style ceramic pottery in Mata Ortíz, is known throughout the international art world for his exquisite ceramic work. Rather than resort to mere reproduction, Quezada accomplished a rare indigenous art revival in which the resulting pots are deemed an authentic, artistic step forward in a style that lay dormant for at least 600 years.

Although his mother was an active potter, Quezada's interest in Casas Grandes pottery began when he found original Paquimé shards in the surrounding valley as a child. After collecting and studying Casas Grandes form and design for over 20 years, he started making pots of his own design—using the originals as stylistic points of departure.

One of the more remarkable aspects of Casas Grandes pottery is the abstract "maze" design painted on the outside, wherein an unpainted area ("negative space" in art terms) can follow an uninterrupted path along the vessel's exterior. Original Paquimé pottery left the lower portion of the vessels unpainted, while the typical Quezada design does away with the circular band that terminated designs along the lower area of the vessel, thus allowing the design to move across the entire surface. For the viewer, tracing the mazes from beginning to end is a hypnotic exercise.

Collectors now recognize four basic types of Casas Grandes/Paquimé pottery. The Ramos Poly design—for which Juan Quezada is famous—involves design repetition, positive-negative color reversal, the outlining of brighter colors with black lines, and the incorporation of abstract mazes over the entire vessel. In Ramos Negra (also called *barro negra),* the entire vessel has a polished black surface. Carretas Poly—the most common original style—is similar to Ramos Poly except that it has a lower border and less design repetition. Villa Ahumada Poly is a name given to taller pots with lower borders.

Pottery has become an important cottage industry in Mata Ortíz. Potters still work entirely without the use of wheels or kilns. To fire the pots, they place the raw vessels on an inverted bucket, bury the whole thing in dried cow chips, and set the chips aflame. The better potters are very picky about the cow chips they use, choosing only black, grain-free manure in order to attain the correct temperature.

Quezada produces seven or eight pots a month, each one a masterpiece that can fetch from several hundred dollars for a smaller piece to as much as US$4000 for a large piece on the international market. A few years ago, Japan's Fuji Corporation had a contract to buy everything Quezada produced within a circumscribed period. Other skilled potters in Mata Ortíz tend to produce work in the US$30-200 range.

also has several small shops selling local works, or you can go straight to the source and try your luck at Mata Ortíz. The selection isn't necessarily any greater in Mata Ortíz, as most potters complete only a few pieces per month; many are bought by dealers as soon as they're finished.

Transport
Most people visit Casas Grandes as part of the Ciudad Juárez-Chihuahua loop, some combining this leg with an extended trip from Chihuahua into the Barranca del Cobre (Copper Canyon) area.

If seeing the state capital isn't an important part of your itinerary, a more original plan would be to bypass Chihuahua by heading straight south from Casas Grandes to Cuauhtémoc—where the Chihuahua al Pacífico train can be met for the rail journey to the coast. Or you can head directly west from Cuauhtémoc to Basaseachic Falls via Mexico 16.

Buses: Caballero Azteca, Estrella Blanca, Omnibus de Mexico, TNS, and **Transportes Rivera** operate from the bus terminal in the center of town. Most buses run along a north-south route; typical fares to Ciudad Juárez or Agua Prieta are US$9.30, to Chihuahua US$11.60. TNS operates buses to Hermosillo and other points west.

Train: You can catch a train from Nuevo Casas Grandes to Madera and La Junta (a junction for the Chihuahua al Pacífico train) every other day, but it's mostly for cargo. If you're bent on taking this ride, show up at the station a couple of days ahead of time and make a few inquiries as to how the load looks.

Taxis: Fares in Nuevo Casas Grandes are reasonable. A taxi from the bus terminal to the Av. Juárez hotel area costs about US$2.30.

Driving: Nuevo Casas Grandes is 315 km (195 miles) from El Paso/Ciudad Juárez; the average drive time is three to four hours. From Douglas/Agua Prieta it's just 211 km (131 miles), but since Mexico 2 is in fairly poor condition between Agua Prieta and Janos, the trip takes about three hours. If road conditions improve, this could be a two-hour trip.

Nuevo Casas Grandes has four PEMEX stations with Magna Sin. The Barrio PEMEX at Av. Juárez and Jimenez offers car washes and oil changes. Heading out of town, you'll find Magna Sin at a PEMEX station 52 km south of Nuevo Casas Grandes on Chihuahua 10—seemingly in the middle of nowhere—on the way to Buenaventura.

Between Nuevo Casas Grandes and Ciudad Juárez, both Janos and Ascensión have stations with Magna Sin.

IN THE VICINITY

Colonia Juárez
This small farming community set in the verdant Río Piedras Negras valley, 27 km (16.7 miles) southwest of Nuevo Casas Grandes via Chihuahua 18 (17 km/10.6 miles from the Paquimé ruins turnoff), is one of two Mormon colonies in Mexico.

American members of the Church of Jesus Christ of Latter-Day Saints (or the Mormon Church) originally founded eight colonies in Chihuahua and Sonora following the 1880s passage of the Edmunds-Tucker Act prohibiting polygamy (plural marriage) in the United States. Although not all of the original colonists were members of polygamous marriages, as one Mormon sister said in 1885, "We came willingly because we had to, for Uncle Sam got cross because there were so many of us women." By the turn of the century 5,000 Mormon colonists were living in Chihuahua and Sonora.

Founded in 1886 on the birthday of Benito Juárez (hence the town's name), Colonia Juárez was the Mormons' second Mexican colony; Colonia Díaz, Chih., founded the year before, was abandoned in 1912 and burned to the ground shortly thereafter. All eight colonies were eventually abandoned during the Mexican Revolution; five were resettled by less than a quarter of the original numbers, and of these only two colonies have survived to this day. The other, Colonia Dublán, has become a virtual northern suburb of Nuevo Casas Grandes.

Fruit farming has been the economic mainstay of Colonia Juárez; the colony operates its own fruit-packing cooperative, Empacadora Paquimé. The Mormons introduced cheese-making to Northern Mexico at least 20 years before Chihuahua's Mennonites, although over the years dairy production has taken a back seat to agriculture.

Hacienda San Diego

The town's charming, Mormon-built brick homes feature sloped roofs—distinguishing them immediately from the flat-roofed homes of their Mexican neighbors—and are surrounded by plentiful shade trees and flower gardens. Besides a Mormon temple and a few small stores, the town boasts the **Academía Juárez,** a K-12 school founded by the Mormons in 1904. The school's English-Spanish bilingual curriculum fulfills requirements for U.S. as well as Mexican high-school diplomas and is probably one of the most successful bilingual programs in the U.S., Canada, or Mexico.

An annual average of over 80% of the Academy's students go on to college or university, many of them at UNAM and ITM. School facilities include a main classroom building of brick, a well-equipped high-school gym (several of Mexico's Olympic basketball players have been A.J. grads), and a soccer field.

Mata Ortíz And Hacienda San Diego

Mata Ortíz, a unique village of dirt streets and dark brown adobe buildings, originally grew up around a prospering U.S.-owned lumber mill placed next to the Ciudad Juárez-La Junta rail line in the late 1800s. Raw timber from Madera was shipped here, milled, and then sent on by rail to Ciudad Juárez for transshipment throughout the United States. North American interests fled during the 1910-20 revolution and the mill closed, but the little antique train station still services trains along the Ciudad Juárez-La Junta line.

Virtually every Mata Ortíz resident today—about 300 in all—is involved in the Casas Grandes-style pottery renaissance. A smaller number dabble in cattle ranching and farming, and several picturesque *ranchitos* are located along the Río Piedras Verdes, which runs alongside the village. Pottery can be bought at the source from many of the households in Mata Ortíz—look for people firing pots behind their homes. Even if you're not looking to buy any pottery, Mata Ortíz is an interesting place to wander around.

About 11 km from Colonia Juárez along the road to Mata Ortíz are the ruins of **Hacienda San Diego,** once part of the vast Luis Terrazas estate. Built 1902-04, the main building dominates the surrounding valley and features a sandstone facade with an iron-pillared terrace and engraving ("LT"). Terrazas's San Diego holdings are now *ejido* lands; the former grain storage buildings and workers quarters are inhabited by *ejidatarios*. The main building is under INAH stewardship but is decaying badly.

Getting There

To reach Hacienda San Diego or Mata Ortíz by car, follow the dirt road heading southeast from Colonia Juárez between the narrow bridge and the Juárez Academy. Mata Ortíz is 19.8 km (12.3 miles) from the Academy via this road. Hacienda San Diego is reached 8.8 km (5.5 miles) before Mata Ortíz.

MADERA

Founded in 1906 by the Sierra Madre Land and Lumber Co. as a lumber transshipment point along the Chihuahua-La Junta railway, Madera ("Wood") still bases much of its livelihood on the timber industry. The town sits above the pine belt, just west of the Continental Divide, on the lower slopes of the Sierra Madre Occidental at an elevation of almost 2,000 meters (6,500 feet). The area enjoys mild summers and crisp winters—perfect for year-round hiking.

A substantial number of ancient, pre-Paquimé cave and cliff dwellings, many of which have barely been explored, are found within a 100-km (62-mile) radius of the town. Most are difficult to find without the services of a guide, which can be arranged in Madera through Motel Real del Bosque or possibly one of the other motels in town. All sites require some mountain hiking to reach—anywhere from a half-hour's walk over fairly level cliff rock to three hours' up-and-down slogging across ravines, slippery scree, and steep slopes. A few sites can be reached only by rock climbers.

Arroyo Sirupa

The main concentration of cave and cliff dwellings is west and southwest of Madera along a tremendous gorge (arroyo or *barranca*) formed by the Río Sirupa. From here north, for a distance of around 60 km along the river, are scattered adobe remains tucked away in rock clefts; some seem virtually unreachable, so precarious are their positions relative to terra firma. Whether the original inhabitants used ladders to reach these homes isn't known—but no evidence of ladders has so far been found.

One of the easiest sites to find (though a guide is still recommended) is the **Complejo Anasazi** or Anasazi Complex, 46 km west of Madera via a gravel-and-dirt logging road. After 11 km this road meets Campo 3, a logging settlement, then jogs south for 35 km before reaching the Complejo Anasazi area (if you come to El Paraje, you've gone too far on the first road). The ruins here are some of the best-preserved cliff dwelling sites in Northern Mexico—far better than the more accessible Cuarenta Casas site north of Madera. Archaeologists have dated the ruins to around 800 A.D., a bit older than the ruins today visible at Paquimé (earlier structures at Paquimé were presumably built over). The name is speculative; informed guesses as to the identity of the original Río Sirupa inhabitants vary from Mogollon to Anasazi to early Paquimé.

Wedged into the upper portion of a sheer cliff, suspended in time and space over the river gorge, is the most impressive site at Complejo Anasazi, **El Nido de las Aguilas** ("Eagle's Nest"). A few paintings remain on the adobe interior, along with broken manos and metates, potsherds, original roof beams, and storage urns for corn. The cliff itself forms the eastern face of a huge rock point jutting out into the gorge; around on the western side is the long **Cueva de la**

El Nido de las Aguilas

Serpiente, which contains 14 well-preserved dwellings, some with two stories.

Reaching either of these sites requires a strenuous hike of about an hour from the logging road. A passage supposedly links the two sides of the bluff; the author, not knowing of such a passage, had to hike around the yoke of the cliff to reach both sides—probably the most difficult and dangerous part of the venture. If the passage exists and if you can find it, use it.

Another 16 km southwest via the same road (66 km from Madera) is **Cueva Grande,** a cave of 50 meters (164 feet) depth with a small waterfall near the entrance. The adobe dwellings inside this cave are numerous but little explored since the site requires a long hike across the Barranca Sirupa.

The area west of Madera toward the Sonora state border is one of the last habitats of the *carpintero grande* (*Campephilus imperialis*) the world's largest woodpecker—whose continued existence is endangered by heavy logging. Other rare and endangered species thought to live in the area include Mexican wolf, black bear, puma, and possibly jaguar.

A useful topographic map for negotiating Arroyo Sirupa—as well as Valle de las Cuevas farther north—is the INEGI 1:250,000 Madera H12-9. While none of the ruins described above are marked on the map, the Sirupa and Piedras Verdes rivers are clearly marked, as are the gravel and dirt roads.

Cuarenta Casas

Less famous than Paquimé but more well known than the Arroyo Sirupa sites is the Cuarenta Casas ("Forty Houses") complex in **Arroyo del Garabato,** northwest of Gómez Farías off Chihuahua 23 and just north of the village of El Vallecillo.

The numerous cave dwellings (around 40, hence the name) are similar in style to the ground dwellings at Paquimé. As these ruins are frequently visited by area residents, virtually nothing remains in terms of projectiles, potsherds, or other artifacts, and the ruins themselves are not very well preserved since they have been inhabited by various nomadic groups since their initial construction a thousand or more years ago.

To reach Cuarenta Casas, take the only paved road northwest out of Gómez Farías to Las Varas, then an unpaved road northwest to just beyond El Vallecillo—ask someone in the village for directions to the ruins if you're traveling on your own. A one-km, unpaved access road leads to a parking lot, from where a footpath descends into Arroyo del Garabato to the caves.

The dirt road continues northwest over the Continental Divide to Nacori Chico, Son., via Tres Ríos—an interesting off-highway route between Chihuahua and Sonora. Four-wheel drive isn't necessary but a vehicle with high road clearance is recommended.

Accommodations And Food

Hotel Real del Bosque (tel. 157-2-05-38, fax 157-2-00-66), just off Chihuahua 37 at the south entrance to Madera, has large, comfortable, heated rooms with TV for US$50 s/d. The bilingual manager is very helpful and can arrange guided visits to nearby archaeological sites as well as Sierra Madre hunting trips for goose, duck, wild turkey, white-tailed deer, and mule deer.

In the center of town **Hotel San Pedro** (tel. 2-03-84; Calle 5a 2001), **Hotel Alpino** (tel. 2-03-84; Calle 3a and Ojinaga), and **Hotel Mirmay** (tel. 2-02-77; Calle 3a and Guerrero) offer basic two-star accommodation for US$25-30 s/d.

A notch or two lower in quality, **Motel Maras** (no phone) at Calle 5a and Juárez has plain rooms catering to transient loggers for around US$10-15 a night. **Cabañas El Prado** (no phone), Calle 3a 2006, has seven rustic rooms with kitchenettes for US$21 s/d, US$24 t per night.

The restaurant at Hotel Real del Bosque is very good for Mexican food, steaks, and the local specialty, fresh rainbow trout from nearby Presa Piñitas. If you're doing your own cooking, you can buy fresh trout from truck vendors along Calle 3a in town for US$5 per kilo.

Ostionería y Pescadería Boquilla, at Calle 3a and 5 de Mayo, is a fair choice for inexpensive *antojitos,* breakfasts, and seafood. Along Calle 1a, in the vicinity of the plaza and post office, are several *taquerías.*

Basic hotels and restaurants are also available in nearby Gómez Farías.

Transport

Bus: Direct buses are available between Madera and Chihuahua, Cuauhtémoc, and Gómez

Farías. From Ciudad Juárez your best bet is to take a bus to Gómez Farías and switch to a Madera-bound bus there.

Train: See the "Casas Grandes-Nuevo Casas Grandes" Transport section, above, for rail information.

Driving: From the north, Madera is reached via Chihuahua 10 and Chihuahua 65. The turnoff for the latter is at San José Bavícora just south of Gómez Farías. From Cuauhtémoc to the south, Mexico 16/Chihuahua 16 is the shortest route (and has the least traffic), although many people take the longer and more heavily traveled Chihuahua 23 route through Colonia Alvaro Obregón because the road surface is a bit better.

Gómez Farías, around 95 km northeast of Madera, has the nearest PEMEX station with Magna Sin.

CUAUHTEMOC AND THE MENNONITE CAMPS

Cuauhtémoc sits in the center of Chihuahua's scenic *llanos,* an area of plains and rolling hills. Surrounded by flourishing farmlands (the local apples are said to be Mexico's best), this town of 150,000 inhabitants has prospered from supplying its hard-working Mennonite neighbors with farm machinery and everyday consumer goods. At the Ananuac industrial park, cellulose is produced from Sierra Madre timber. It's also an important transport junction where highways Mexico 23 and Mexico 16 meet the Chihuahua al Pacífico rail line.

Although there is little of tourist interest to see in the town, the Mennonite *campos* north of Cuauhtémoc are easily reached by road, and Basaseachic Falls is within an short day's drive (see "Basaseachic Falls National Park," p. 297, for details). Visitors traveling the Barranca del Cobre-Casas Grandes loop can also use Cuauhtémoc to bypass the city of Chihuahua, proceeding directly north to Madera and/or Casas Grandes or westward to the Barranca del Cobre.

Mennonite Camps

Chihuahua's famous *campos menonitas* are mostly concentrated to the north and south of Cuauhtémoc, although there are communities as far north as Madera and as far west as La Junta.

Altogether the Mennonites number around 15,000, most of whom speak a Low German dialect and maintain a strict adherence to the Mennonite faith.

The most accessible camps are strung out along the 42-km (26-mile) section of Chihuahua 23 between Cuauhtémoc and Alvaro Obregón to the north. This stretch features around 20 Mennonite communities, each one numbered rather than named (e.g., Campo 3, Campo 5, etc.). Surrounded by cultivated fields, each community consists of around 20 families (not untypically with nine or 10 children each) whose peaked-roof, wood-frame-and-adobe houses line one long, usually unpaved, street parallel to the highway, which is accessed from the *campo* by two long dirt roads at either end.

Don't visit the *campos* expecting to see buggies and black suits like those seen among Pennsylvania's Mennonites. Except for their red cheeks and blond hair, most Chihuahua Mennonites look very much like any other Mexican farmers. Men typically wear jeans, boots, and cowboy hats or John Deere gimme caps. Some of the women wear distinctive, colorful print dresses, and most cover their heads with scarves topped by straw hats. The rare business sign appears in German. Gleaming farm machinery in the fields and Ford pickups parked next to tidy white houses give the impression of a rural farming community in the U.S. Midwest.

History: Around 9,000 Mennonites first arrived in Mexico in 1921-22 from Canada, but the sect got its start in 15th-century Friesland (an island district of northern Holland) as pacifistic "Silent Communities" or "Communities of the Cross" led by ex-Catholic priest Simons Menno (1492-1559). Constantly persecuted for their ascetic socio-religious practices and refusal to volunteer for military service, the group moved from Friesland to Prussia, Russia, and Canada before they were forced to leave Canada for declining to serve in the Canadian army during WW I.

In 1921 Canadian leaders of the sect met with President Obregón, who allowed them to immigrate to Mexico with exemptions from military duty and the swearing of allegiance, while giving them the right to enter and leave the country at will and the authority to establish and administer their own schools without government interference. Many Mexican citizens protested that this allowed them all the benefits of citizenship with few of the corresponding responsibilities, but Obregón wisely saw the Mennonite immigration as an opportunity to upgrade Mexican farming techniques and raise the standard of living in Chihuahua. Unquestionably, the Mennonites have been more of an asset than a liability to Mexico.

Cheese: The Mennonites' most famous product is *queso menonita* or Mennonite cheese, known as *queso chihuahuense* or Chihuahua cheese outside the state. Although the Mennonites weren't the first to produce cheese in Mexico (the Mormons of Colonia Juárez began production in the 1890s), they've been curding it since the 1920s and their cheese is widely considered the nation's best.

Hence no visit to the *campos* is complete without a visit to a *quesería*. The typical Mennonite cheese is a type of mild white cheddar; altogether around 200 cooperative members deliver 22,500 liters of milk daily to two major *queserías* which produce about two tons of cheese per day. The cheese factory in Campo 6½ is open to the public for tours every day except Sunday. Another cheese factory in Campo 2B is also open to the public.

Practicalities: Virtually everything in the *campos*, including the cheese factories and restaurants, is closed on Sundays, when many of the residents are cloistered in church or at their homes. For more activity, it's best to visit Mon.-Saturday.

Hotel Rancho La Estancia, 10 km (6.2 miles) from Chihuahua 65 via a turnoff between Km 20 and 21 (near Campo 6), has the only tourist accommodations in the area, save for hotels and motels in Cuauhtémoc (see "Cuauhtémoc Accommodations and Food," below).

Peter's, 12.8 km (eight miles) north of Cuauhtémoc on Mexico 23, is a Mennonite-run trailer park with full hookups for US$12 per night, tent camping for less. You can reserve a space in advance by writing A.P. 401, Cuauhtémoc, Chihuahua.

Restaurant El Duff, on the west side of the highway near Campo 22, serves Mexican and Mennonite food for breakfast, lunch, and dinner daily except Sunday. **Doña María's,** opposite the cheese factory in Campo 2B, can prepare home-cooked Mennonite meals with a day

or two's advance notice. Mennonite cooking is similar to Dutch or West German cuisine.

Cuauhtémoc Accommodations And Food

Few travelers choose to overnight in Cuauhtémoc unless they're waiting for the train or have simply run out of daylight en route to Chihuahua.

The place most geared toward tourists—with maps and information—is the **Motel Tarahumara Inn** (tel. 141-1-19-19, fax 141-2-48-65), at Av. Allende and Calle 5a, where pleasant rooms with a/c, heating, and satellite TV start at US$28 s, US$33 d. The Tarahumara Inn can arrange tours to nearby attractions, including the Mennonite camps, the Barranca del Cobre, and Basaseachic Falls. Car rentals are also possible through the hotel. On the opposite corner of Av. Allende and 5a, the similarly priced and slightly older **Hotel Union** (tel. 2-11-14) has more character but fewer services.

At Km 3 of Mexico 23, just north of the Mexico 16 junction along the northwestern outskirts of town, is the modern and efficient **Motel del Camino** (tel. 1-00-88, fax 1-01-46), a steal at only US$25 per night for clean, fairly new s/d rooms. This is probably the best choice for the motorist passing through on the way north to Madera or Casas Grandes, or southeast to Chihuahua. The motel also has a good coffee shop.

Less expensive *clase económica* hotels in town include **Hotel Cuauhtémoc** (Av. Morelos 306) and **Hotel del Norte** (Calle Reforma 302), where rooms cost US$15-18 a night.

Hotel Rancho La Estancia (tel. 12-22-82, fax 5-52-97, A.P. 986, Chihuahua, Chih.) is 20 km north of Cuauhtémoc via Mexico 23, then 12 km west on a gravel road into the Sierra Madre foothills at 2,160 meters (7,200 feet). Operating primarily as a resort, Rancho La Estancia offers a private landing strip, heated pool and sauna, horseback riding, and guided hunting/fishing trips to nearby Laguna Bustillos. Rooms cost US$50 s/d per night.

Two of the nicest restaurants in town are **Equs Restaurant-Bar** at Av. Allende 1310 and **Restaurant La Cueva** at Av. Guerrero 423, both of which serve Mexican and international cuisine. Near La Cueva at Av. Guerrero 317, **Restaurant Rancho Viejo** is locally renowned for steaks. The popular **La Fama** near the plaza serves tasty and inexpensive Mexican *antojitos*.

Transport

The westbound **Chihuahua al Pacífico** departs Cuauhtémoc at 9:15 a.m.; eastbound, the train departs at 6:25 p.m.

Motorists have a choice of two highways between Cuauhtémoc and Chihuahua: the free road through the small towns of Trias, Riva Palacio, and Bustillos; and the faster, more direct toll road. The free road winds around sharp but well-marked curves through scenic rolling hills and apple orchards.

Although most maps mark the road between Cuauhtémoc and Colonia Alvaro Obregón as Mexico 23, signs along the highway read Chihuahua 65. This highway joins Mexico 16 west of Cuauhtémoc.

Several PEMEX stations in Cuauhtémoc pump Magna Sin.

La Junta

Officially named Adolfo López Mateos, this important rail and highway junction—where the state's oldest railway, the Ciudad Juárez-La Junta line, meets the Chihuahua al Pacífico—is little more than a large holding place for rail cargo and tractor trailers. The Ciudad Juárez-La Junta line was constructed in two stages: the Ciudad Juárez-Casas Grandes section by the Rio Grande, Sierra Madre, and Pacific Railway Company in 1898; and the Casas Grandes-La Junta section by Enrique Creel and his Kansas City, Mexico, and Orient Railroad between 1910-14.

Practicalities: If you must overnight here, **Hotel Pie de la Sierra** off Mexico 16 has clean rooms with private hot-water bath, heating and a/c, and three-channel TV (d and t rooms only) for US$10 s, US$13.30 d, US$18.30 t. Although the hotel is readily visible from the highway, finding the right dirt streets to the hotel is a trial-and-error undertaking.

The **Posada del Camino** is closer to the highway and a bit more expensive—but not as quiet because of the passing truck traffic.

A truckers' favorite, **Restaurant Winn's** (next to the PEMEX station on Mexico 16 west) serves decent Mexican food for breakfast, lunch, and dinner.

If you're heading for Madera from points south, La Junta is where you pick up highway Chihuahua 16 north, the most direct route to Madera.

OJINAGA TO CHIHUAHUA

For travelers heading for Chihuahua from points east of El Paso, Ojinaga provides a convenient Mexico gateway as it avoids the hassles of crossing at El Paso/Ciudad Juárez—it's a much more direct route. Highway US 67 leads directly to Presidio, the Texas side of the border, from US 90 (which in turn links San Antonio, Del Rio, Marathon, Alpine, Marfa, and El Paso). Out-of-state visitors sometimes combine a trip to Texas's Big Bend National Park with a visit to Chihuahua.

Ojinaga

Named in honor of Manuel Ojinaga, former governor of Chihuahua and military commander who was killed while defending western Chihuahua against the French, this border town of 45,000 is primarily an agricultural center for the fertile flood plains of the Río Conchos and Río Bravo (Rio Grande). Over 300 years old, it was originally founded as a Spanish *presidio* or garrison—hence the name of the Texas town on the opposite river bank—with the ungainly moniker Nuevo Real Presidio de Nuestra Señora de Betleña y Santiago de Las Amarillas de La Junta de los Ríos Norte y Conchos ("New Royal Garrison of Our Lady of Bethlehem and St. James on the Banks of the Junction of the Ríos Grande and Conchos"), later shortened to Presidio del Norte.

The surrounding river plains are the oldest continually cultivated farmlands in North America. When the Spanish arrived in the 16th century, they were astonished to find "advanced" Amerindians living in adobe houses and cultivating their own food. The Patarabueyes, about whom little is known except that they seem to have been a Pueblo Indian group, had apparently been farming this land since at least A.D. 1200. By the late 1600s the Patarabueyes had been missionized and, due to Spanish mistreatment and Mescalero Apache pressure, they disappeared by the 19th century.

Today, principal crops include cotton, wheat, and beans. The Chihuahuan Desert also provides material for local cottage industries inherited from the former native inhabitants—rope and twine called *istle* made from lechugilla (*Agave lechugilla*), bootleg liquor from sotol (*Da-*

sylirion wheeleri), wax from candelilla (*Euphorbia antisyphilitica*), and herbal remedies from a number of other desert plants. Local *botánicas* still trade in these herbs. The bilingual *Presidio Paper,* published across the river but available on both sides, is priced in both U.S. and Mexican currency.

Ojinaga was once notorious as a conduit for contraband drugs coming from the interior of Mexico, but state and local police have largely wiped out the drug trade in recent years and the town is now very safe for foreign visitors. The local *tránsitos* (traffic police) are very helpful to visiting motorists and will even provide free escort services for lost drivers as well as emergency automotive repairs.

The town also provides short- or long-term security parking in a large, fenced lot in the middle of town (at Calle Hidalgo and Calle de la Paz) for motorists wishing to take the bus to Chihuahua or beyond.

Midsummer, Presidio/Ojinaga is one of the hottest areas in either Texas or Mexico. In July or August it's not unusual for afternoon temperatures to reach or exceed 40° C (104° F).

Accommodations and Food: Hotel y Motel Rohana (tel. 145-3-00-78), downtown at Calle Juárez Trasviña y Retes, is a quaint three-star hotel with high ceilings and tiled floors for around US$28 per night. The attached restaurant is popular among border-hoppers for quail and other border specialties. **Motel Armendariz** (tel. 3-11-98), Calle Zaragoza 713, has adequate rooms for around US$20. **Restaurant Los Comales,** opposite city hall at Calle Zaragoza 106, serves Mexican platters and steak. **Chuco's,** at Av. Trasviña y Retes and Calle 13a, is a popular gringo stop for beer and Mexican food and claims to stay open 365 days a year!

On the Presidio (Texas) side, **Three Palms Inn** (tel. 915-229-3611), US 67, has clean, basic rooms for US$22, plus a popular coffee shop with steaks and good Tex-Mex food.

Border Formalities: The Presidio-Ojinaga border crossing is open Mon.-Fri. 7:30 a.m.-9 p.m., Sat.-Sun. 8 a.m.-4 p.m. If you're planning to stay more than 72 hours you'll need a tourist card, and if you're planning to drive to Chihuahua you'll need a temporary auto-import permit—both are available at the border station.

Transport: Ojinaga-Chihuahua passenger rail service was discontinued some years ago, but Transportes Chihuahuenses operates eight buses per day to Chihuahua (US$7.30).

Driving time to Chihuahua is around three hours (238 km/147.5 miles). Magna Sin gasoline is available in town; if you're heading west toward Chihuahua, be sure to top up here (or in Presidio), as the next PEMEX station is 209 km (129.5 miles) away in Aldama.

A group of Texas investors recently purchased the rights to a railway route that runs from Dallas's Union Station to Presidio. They've also bought several Pullman cars and reportedly have plans to launch a regular passenger service within the next year or two. Without a corresponding rail link with the Chihuahua al Pacífico on the Mexican side, however, it remains to be seen whether this project will succeed.

Coyame

This small town 87 km (54 miles) west of Ojinaga is most known for its mineral springs and for one of the last sotol distilleries in Chihuahua. A kilometer south of town by dirt road are the little-visited **Grutas de Coyame** or Coyame Grottoes, which contain 15 limestone caverns with plenty of stalactite/stalagmite and crystal formations.

Cañon de Peguis, 31 km (19 miles) northeast of town off Mexico 16, provides a scenic *mirador* (lookout point) over the Río Conchos.

Villa De Aldama

Most often known simply as Aldama, this farming center 22 km (13.6 miles) northeast of Chihuahua was originally founded as Misión Santa Ana de Chinarras by Jesuit padres in 1717. The mission church's two-story baroque facade is being restored, and other historic provincial-colonial architecture is under renovation as well —with the intention of attracting weekend and holiday visitors from the state capital.

Hotel Los Pedales offers two-star accommodations for US$14-18. Aldama's PEMEX station is usually stocked with Magna Sin.

CHIHUAHUA (CITY) AND VICINITY

Capital of Mexico's largest state, Chihuahua (pop. 515,000) serves a dual role as state administrative center and commercial hub for timber, cattle ranching, and mining. Set near the junction of the Chuvíscar and Sacramento rivers, on a high desert plain ringed by mountains, the urban landscape blends ordinary-looking Mexican commercial districts with a stately Porfiriato downtown and a wealthy residential quarter of renovated Victorian mansions at the southwest edge of the city.

Most foreign visitors to the city come either to conduct business with the industrious Chihuahuans or to embark on (or disembark from) the Chihuahua al Pacífico rail journey across the Sierra Madre Occidental. Although not usually considered a tourist destination per se, the city has a number of historical sights worth seeing, including the Pancho Villa museum (Quinta Luz), the regional museum (Quinta Gameros), and the Centro Cultural Chihuahua.

Climate And Seasons

At an elevation of 1,410 meters (4,700 feet) and surrounded by desert, Chihuahua has a very dry climate with the only precipitation of note—less than 10 cm (3.9 inches) per month—falling July-September.

June, when daytime highs average 30.5° C (87° F), is generally the warmest month of the year, while January is the coolest month with evening lows of around 1-4° C (34-40° F). Occasional northern winds in the winter will force the thermometer below freezing and add a windchill factor (light snow isn't unknown); hence the best overall time to visit Chihuahua is March-November.

HISTORY

In 1707 Spaniard Juan Holguín registered a claim on a silver mine at Santa Eulalia (present-day Aquiles Serdán) on the banks of the Río Chuvíscar, 18 km southeast of the current state capital. Other rich silver veins were discovered in the area and several small mining settlements soon sprouted in the vicinity of Santa Eulalia, including one near the confluence of the Chuvíscar and Sacramento rivers that was made a *cabecera* (district seat) of Nueva Vizcaya. The local Tarahumaras called the site *"chihuahuara,"* meaning "place where sacks are made." Under Spanish control the town was named San Francisco de Cuellar.

The Jesuits soon arrived and established San Francisco de Cuellar as a religious center, building a Colegio de la Compañía de Jesús in 1718 and the Templo de San Francisco in 1724. Apache raids held back further development in the area until the late 1800s. Along with Indian attacks, Chihuahua had to contend with the Mexican independence struggle, during much of which Chihuahua remained loyal to the Spanish crown. Padre Miguel Hidalgo y Costilla, the father of Mexican independence, was captured by Royalist forces, convicted of treason and heresy by the Holy Office of the Inquisition, and executed in Chihuahua in July 1811. Following independence the government chose to replace the Spanish name for the city with the original "Chihuahua."

During the 1840s Mexican-American War the city was briefly occupied by U.S. troops, an event described as "pallid compared to the terror inspired by an Apache raid." With the capture of Apache chief Victoria in the 1880s, Chihuahua enjoyed a brief period of relative peace until the 1910-20 Mexican Revolution. In 1910 Pancho Villa and his División del Norte army took the city and based themselves there for the duration of the revolution (Villa's *quinta* or manor is now a museum).

Chihuahua's prosperity peaked in the 1920s, after which the economy weathered decades of nationalization and misgovernment to become a major Northern Mexico capital. Manufacturing has recently begun supplementing Chihuahua's traditional dependence on timber, mining, and cattle. Ford Motors has a plant (not a *maquila* since it produces for both national and international markets) which turns out around 4,000 autos per year at the city's Complejo Industrial; Zenith and Data General also have manufacturing facilities in the area.

SIGHTS

Catedral De San Francisco

Also known as Catedral Metropolitana de Chihuahua, this important religious edifice on the city's Plaza de Armas (Calle 2 and Libertad) was begun in 1724 as the "Parroquía de Nuestra Señora de la Regla de San Francisco de Asís" and built in stages through 1826. In 1891 the church attained cathedral status with the creation of a separate Chihuahua Diocese.

The twin-towered facade, sculpted in quarried pink stone, features the 12 apostles in late baroque style—complete with a profusion of foliage, flowers, and fruit. Inside is a large 1920-vintage altar of Carrara marble beneath three naves arranged in typical cruciform fashion. A side chapel contains the **Museo de Arte Sacro** (Museum of Sacred Art), dedicated in 1984 and featuring Mexican religious paintings (including works by Cabrera, Páez, Alcíbar, and Antonio de Torres) from the 18th century.

Centro Cultural Chihuahua

Cattle baron and ex-governor of Chihuahua Don Luis Terrazas had this palatial mansion at Calle Aldama and Ocampo (a brief walk from Plaza de Armas) built in 1889 as his home. In typical Spanish style, the two-story stone building forms a rectangle of huge rooms around a central patio finished with fine tile flooring, ironwork bannisters, and a stone fountain.

Since Terrazas's death, the building has been used as a monastic cell, boardinghouse, IMSS (Mexican social security) state headquarters, and now as a cultural and educational institution owned by Grupo Chihuahua, an association dedicated to maintaining regional identity through the support of Chihuahuan art and culture. All the stonework, woodwork, and ironwork have been beautifully restored and reconstructed to original specifications.

In addition to the grand fin-de-siècle architecture—an attraction in itself—the second floor of the Centro Cultural houses a high-quality, permanent collection of Paquimé pottery. Other rooms in the building contain rotating displays on the art, anthropology, and archaeology of the region. A noticeboard on the ground floor posts information on cultural events to be held at the center and elsewhere in the city. Entry to the building—and all exhibits—is free.

Museo De La Revolución (Quinta Luz)

Of the several small museums dedicated to Francisco "Pancho" Villa throughout the state of Chihuahua, this is the most complete. During the Mexican Revolution, this 50-room *quinta* (manor) served as Villa's home and headquarters for his revolutionary army, the División del Norte. After the revolution Villa retired to the Parral area farther south, but following his 1923 assassination, the government awarded the mansion to his only legal wife, Luz Corral de Villa (Pancho was known to have had at least 22 common-law wives or mistresses).

Señora Luz restored several rooms to their original 1910 decor and allowed visitors in for brief tours before she passed away in 1981. Since then the Mexican army has taken possession of the building and turned it into a full-scale museum displaying an array of Villa's personal effects, historical photographs, revolutionary weaponry, and the bullet-riddled black Dodge in which Villa was assassinated.

The museum, located at Calle 10 and Méndez on the southeastern side of town, is open daily 9 a.m.-1 p.m. and 3-7 p.m.; admission is US$0.65. Although it's a 13- to 14-block walk, the museum can be reached on foot from the downtown Plaza de Armas area in about 30 minutes. You could stop at the Museo Regional along the way, breaking the trip into two neat halves.

Museo Regional (Quinta Gameros)

Built in 1907-11 by wealthy miner Manuel Gameros, this is one of the preeminent examples of French art nouveau—complete with fin-de-siècle stained glass and skylights—in Mexico or North America. Several of the rooms contain authentic, original art-nouveau furnishings (including a dining room decorated completely in this style), a living room that's basically Louis XV with art-nouveau influences, and an impressive, art-nouveau bathroom.

A second-story room displays exquisite Paquimé ceramics, including rare vessels with humanlike faces and limbs, along with the implements used for making the pottery and for grinding and mixing pigments. Other galleries in the museum house traveling exhibits of modern art and photography.

The museum is at Paseo Bolívar and Calle 4. Hours are daily 9 a.m.-1 p.m. and 4-7 p.m., admission US$0.65. From the downtown area, Calle 4 leads directly to the museum—follow this street southeast from behind the cathedral if you feel like the 20-minute walk.

FRANCISCO "PANCHO" VILLA

Born Doroteo Arango in San Juan del Río, Dur., in 1877 (1879 according to some sources), the man most of the world knew as Pancho Villa spent much of his life in Durango until, at age 16, he killed a man who had molested his younger sister. Little record exists of the next four or five years of his life, during which time he changed his name to Francisco Villa to evade the law.

By the time he was 20, Villa had moved northward to Chihuahua, working on and off as a miner in Parral while selling stolen cattle in Chihuahua (official government biographies list his occupation then as "wholesale meat-seller"). In 1899 he returned to mining, this time in Santa Eulalia near Chihuahua, but he soon tired of the laborer's life and added bank robbery to cattle rustling and murder on the list of crimes for which he was wanted by the Díaz government.

Villa's Robin Hood story began after he established himself and his bandit followers in the sierras in 1900 (officially, the years 1900-09 are "unaccounted for") and became a legendary hero to the poor for skillfully evading the Porfiriato's oppressive *rurales* for nearly a decade. In 1910 Villa and his men came down from the hills to join Francisco I. Madero's revolutionary forces, thereby making a historical transition from *bandidos* to *revolucionarios*.

Following Madero's short-lived victory and assassination, Villa remained in command of his División del Norte army in resistance—along with Coahuila's Venustiano Carranza and Sonora's Alvaro Obregón—against the 1913-14 Victoriano Huerta dictatorship. Around this time Villa also became something of a folk hero in the U.S, and Hollywood filmmakers as well as U.S. newspaper photographers flocked to Northern Mexico to record his battle exploits—many of which were staged for the benefit of the cameras.

A split among the revolutionary leaders soon pitted Villa against Obregón and Carranza. When the U.S. government came out openly in support of the Carranza presidency, Villa retaliated by raiding U.S border towns, most notably Columbus, New Mexico. On the U.S. side of the border, Villa's image plummeted while many in Mexico saw Villa as an avenger

Villa crying at the grave of President Guerrero

COURTESY MUSEO DE LA REVOLUCIÓN, CHIHUAHUA

of decades of *Yanqui* oppression. After two U.S. Army "punitive expeditions" into Mexico in 1916 and 1919 failed to route Villa, the Mexican government retired Villa on a general's salary to Canutillo, Durango. In 1923 he was assassinated while returning from bank business in Parral, Chihuahua (see "Hidalgo de Parral," p. 264, for more on his death and burial).

Today Villa is remembered with pride by most Mexicans for having led the most important military campaigns of the constitutionalist revolution, in which his troops were victorious as far south as Zacatecas and Mexico City, east as far as Tampico, and west as far as Casas Grandes. Because of Villa's Columbus escapade and subsequent evasion of U.S. troops, he is also often cited as the only foreign military personage ever to have "successfully" invaded continental U.S. territory. When speaking with Mexicans—especially *norteños*—about Villa, don't underestimate the respect his name still garners in Mexico.

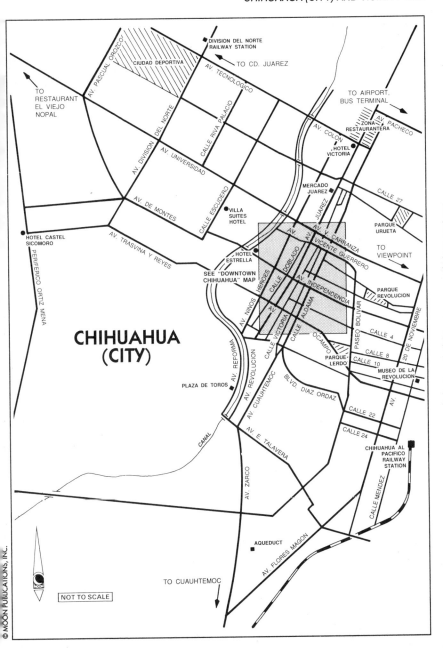

CHIHUAHUA (CITY)

Aqueduct (Acueducto)

This impressive, five-km-long, 15-meter-high structure of stone arches was built by the Spanish between 1751-86 to carry water from nearby Presa Chuvíscar to the city. Until 1969 it served as the main water supply to the city.

The best-preserved section of the *acueducto* is found between Calle 32 and Av. Zarco.

Government Buildings

Chihuahua has several turn-of-the-century buildings used by the government in the downtown area. The three-story, rectangular **Palacio de Gobierno** on Calle Aldama (facing diminutive Plaza Hidalgo) was built toward the end of the 19th century; in the central courtyard is the Altar de la Patria (Fatherland Altar), on which burns a perpetual flame in honor of Padre Miguel Hidalgo y Costilla—who met his death in front of a firing squad on this very spot. The interior walls feature murals depicting the history of Chihuahua, as painted by muralist Aarón Piña Mora.

Before he was executed, Padre Hidalgo was kept prisoner in a *calabozo* or "dungeon" (actually a tower room) in the **Palacio Federal** at Av. Juárez and Av. Carranza. A verse of compassionate thanks written in charcoal by Hidalgo to his jailers is preserved in bronze and displayed. The Palacio Federal was originally built as the Colegio de Loreto de la Compañía de Jesús in the 18th century.

The **Palacio Municipal**, facing the Plaza de Armas, was designed by English architect Alfred Giles and erected in 1906 to house the Casa de Cabildo or town council; the Sala de Cabildos contains what is reportedly one of the largest conference tables in the world.

CHIHUAHUA ACCOMMODATIONS

Two gold points for Chihuahua's hotels: one for having a good selection of places to stay in all budget categories, another for the fact that so many hotel staffers are Spanish-English bilingual.

Budget Hotels

A perennial favorite with folks watching their pesos is **Hotel San Juan** (tel. 14-10-00-35), an older hotel with 61 rooms around a courtyard at Calle Victoria 823 (a couple of blocks south-

west of Plaza de Armas). Plain rooms come with heating and private bathroom and cost just US$11 s, US$14 d. The San Juan is the only two-star in the city with its own restaurant and bar. Similar in price but with less character (and no restaurant/bar) are **Hotel María Dolores** (tel. 10-47-70; Calle 9 917 at Av. Niños Heroes) and **Hotel Carmen** (tel. 15-70-96; Av. Juárez and Calle 10).

If a/c and parking are considerations, the well-worn but efficient **Hotel Apolo** (tel. 16-11-00) at Av. V. Carranza 102 (at Av. Juárez) has its own parking lot, a restaurant-bar, and basic but comfortable rooms with heating and a/c for US$23 s, US$30 d. Also good is **Hotel Campanario** (tel. 15-45-45) at Blvd. Díaz Ordaz and Privada de Libertad, where clean, comfortable rooms go for US$30; a decent *cafetería* is attached.

One-star wonder **Hotel Reforma** (tel. 10-58-00), at Calle Victoria 809 near the San Juan, has basic rooms for US$9 s, US$11 d. For US$5 s, US$10 d you can get a room with *baño colectivo* at the even more spartan **Hotel Estrella** (tel. 10-54-18), Av. Revolución and Bolívar.

Medium-priced Hotels

Room rates really jump once you move from two-star to three-star ratings (for Mexico's SEC-TUR rating system, see "Rates," p. 62). **Hotel Avenida** (tel. 14-15-28-91) at Av. V. Carranza 1101 (opposite Hotel Apolo mentioned above) is popular with middle-class Mexican businesspeople and costs US$38 s/d for rooms with TV, a/c, and heating. The hotel doesn't have its own parking lot, but parking can usually be arranged nearby.

Grand old dame **Hotel Victoria** (tel. 10-05-48), Av. Juárez and Colón in the city's "Zona Rosa," was at one time the biggest and most popular hotel in Chihuahua. Other hotels have since eclipsed the Victoria's four stars, but it still has a regular clientele. Its 120 rooms ramble through a large postcolonial-style complex with charming pool, bar, and lobby areas, and lots of tilework throughout. Depending on their location in the building, standard rooms cost US$46-56. The owners have placed the "Vic" on the market (without closing it), so it could change names/owners/rates any time.

Another four-star, downtown favorite is the friendly and efficient 106-room **Motel Posada Tierra Blanca** (tel. 15-00-00) at Av. Niños He-

NOT TO SCALE

© MOON PUBLICATIONS, INC.

roes 100, opposite the more expensive Hotel Palacio del Sol. Rooms surround a secure parking lot and swimming pool and cost US$55 s, US$57 d.

For those preferring to stay close to the highway rather than downtown, the best mid-priced choice may be the almost new **Hotel Parador San Miguel** (tel. 17-03-03), at Av. Tecnológico 7901—on the way into Chihuahua from Ciudad Juárez via Mexico 45 (south of the Ford plant, north of Av. Vallarta). Though it looks fairly ordinary from the outside, this very clean, well-run, motel-style place features nice touches such as arched brick ceilings in the rooms and local folk art in the coffee shop and other public rooms. Rates are US$42 s, US$45 d; all rooms have satellite TV, heating and a/c, and phones. Two more pluses: You can leave your vehicle and store your luggage here at no charge while taking the Chihuahua al Pacífico train ride; and it's next door to Chihuahua's SECTUR tourist office.

A bit lower in cost, and popular with North Americans because it's on the highway and has parking space for RVs/trailers, is **Motel Nieves** (tel. 13-25-16) at Av. Tecnológico and Ahuehuete. Simple rooms around a pool and parking lot go for US$33 s, US$36 d.

Deluxe Hotels

Five hotels compete for business travelers and better-heeled tourists. Heating, a/c, multichannel satellite TV, telephones, and security parking are standard. A good choice for downtown location is the efficient and comfortable, 132-room **Hotel San Francisco** (tel. 14-16-77-70, 800-14-107 in Mexico; 800-847-2546 in the U.S./Canada; fax 14-15-35-38), at Victoria 409 close to the Plaza de Armas. Room rates are US$72 s, US$74 d.

For quick access to Mexico 45, another good choice is the new motel-style **Hotel Casa Grande** (tel. 19-66-33, 91-800-14-222 in Mexico; 800-343-6344 in the U.S./Canada; fax 19-32-35), at Av. Tecnológico 4702. Spacious rooms with IDD phones and all the amenities cost US$72 s/d. Hotel facilities include a tennis court, pool, travel agency, and business center with fax, copy, and secretarial services.

Hotel Castel Sicomoro (tel. 13-54-45, fax 13-14-11) is on the extreme west side of town at Perif. Ortíz Mena 411; rooms cost US$80-100

s/d. This modern five-star hotel has a pool and disco but little else to recommend except for its location toward the Complejo Industrial (hence its popularity with visiting *maquila* execs).

If the Hotel San Francisco is full, a second downtown choice is the high-rise, 190-room **Hotel Palacio del Sol** (tel. 15-50-00, fax 15-99-42), two blocks north of the Plaza de Armas at Av. Independencia and Av. Niños Heroes. Because of its size, many tour groups use this hotel; tariffs are US$91 s/d.

The **Villa Suites Hotel** (tel. 14-33-13, fax 14-33-50), at Calle Escudero 702 between Av. Independencia and Av. Universidad (northwest of downtown), gets high marks for its suites with refrigerators, VCRs, and complimentary continental breakfast. The hotel also has two heated pools, sauna, and Jacuzzi. Rates are US$108 s/d.

RV Parks

Motel Nieves (see "Medium-priced Hotels," above) has around 30 spaces with full hookups for US$12 per night. Showers and LP (liquefied petroleum or propane) gas are available; some of the electrical outlets are 220V—ask before plugging in. **Chemaju Trailer Park** (tel. 13-25-16), at Av. Tecnológico 6505, has 23 spaces with electricity and water for US$10 per night.

FOOD

Inexpensive restaurants are abundant in the vicinity of Plaza de Armas, along Calle Aldama, along Av. Niños Heroes, and in Plaza Libertad, a pedestrian mall created by closing off Calle Libertad (from Av. Independencia to Av. J.N. Santos) to vehicular traffic.

In Mercado Reforma (off Av. Niños Heroes west of the Plaza de Armas) are several inexpensive *loncherías* open for breakfast and lunch. The area around Mercado Reforma is also dotted with inexpensive *taquerías* and street vendors, especially at night when the daytime markets close and the streets are packed with snackers. Chihuahua's most popular street food is *barbacoa,* pit-cooked head of sheep or cow.

Mexican
$$ **Cafetería Dega,** ground floor, Hotel San Francisco. This is a very clean and efficient cof-

fee shop with an extensive menu of Mexican and regional specialties (plus a few North American dishes) at moderate prices. Open daily 7 a.m.-11 p.m.

$$ Chihuahua Charlie's Bar And Grill (tel. 15-75-89), Av. Juárez 3329. Although it's part of the Grupo Anderson chain, the locals usually outnumber the tourists at this low-key outpost, and the bar often fills with young Chihuahuans in their twenties. The menu features a number of regional dishes made from original recipes. Open daily 11 a.m.-1 a.m.

$$ Mi Café (tel. 10-12-38), Calle Victoria 1000. This is a modern, coffee shop-style place specializing in *pollo o lengua en mole,* and *machaca en chile colorado,* as well as moderately priced breakfasts and *comida corrida.* Open daily 7 a.m.-11 p.m.

$-$$ La Parilla (tel. 15-59-53), Calle Victoria 420, opposite Hotel San Francisco. The house specialty is Chihuahuan-style *carne al carbón* (charcoal-grilled steak), along with a splendid array of Northern-style tacos and *antojitos,* including *cebolletas* (grilled spring onions) and *frijoles norteños.*

$$ El Viejo Nopal (tel. 14-34-51), Calle Universidad and Ingeniería. A place for large Mexican appetites, with all manner of breakfasts and *platillos mexicanos* with tacos, enchiladas, *pollo en mole, asado de puerco, chiles rellenos,* and more. Open Mon.-Sat. 7:30 a.m.-midnight.

International

The city's compact "Zona Restaurantera" at the north end of Av. Juárez is lined end-to-end with upscale restaurants specializing in steak, seafood, and continental: La Calesa, Los Vitrales, Salignac, Chihuahua Charlie's, Los Parados de Tony Vega, El Galeón, La Olla, La Vianda, and Club de los Parados. The coming and going of chefs and local trends make it difficult to single out the "best," but the following tend to be the most consistent.

$$-$$$ La Calesa (tel. 10-10-38), Av. Juárez and Av. Colón. Good selection of steaks and international and Mexican food. Open daily 1 p.m.-midnight.

$$-$$$ La Olla (tel. 14-78-94), Av. Juárez 331. Steaks, seafood, and continental food served in a converted 19th-century brewery. Open daily 1 p.m.-1 a.m.

$$$ Salignac Restaurant (tel. 15-86-16), Av. Juárez 3215. Semi-formal atmosphere, continental food, attentive service. Open daily noon-midnight.

$$-$$$ Los Vitrales Restaurant-Bar (tel. 15-06-76), Av. Juárez and Av. Colón. Cantonese and international cuisine served in a converted mansion.

Vegetarian

$-$$ El Bocado del Sol, Calle Libertad 1910. Typical combination of natural food/herb shop with vegetarian lunch fare.

$$ Los Olivos Restaurant Vegetariano, Calle de la Llave 202, between Calle 2 and 4 near the Museo Regional. A charming, casual spot with a varied vegetarian menu of Mexican and international dishes. Open for breakfast and lunch.

Other

Visitors staying on the northern outskirts of the city at one of the hotels or motels along Av. Tecnológico will find several fast-food places in the **Plaza Vallarta** shopping center (near Hotel Casa Grande), including Pizza del Rey, Ricky's Tacos, KFC, and Burger King.

$$ Chalet Italiano, Calle 13 and Escorza. Large menu of Italian specialties and pizza. Open daily noon-midnight.

$$-$$$ Reggé Restaurant Bar (tel. 15-47-55), Perif. Ortíz Mena and Bosque de la Reina. An upscale Cajun (yes, you read that right) restaurant with live music nightly.

$-$$ Woolworth Cafetería, Plaza Libertad (Calle Libertad pedestrian mall) opposite the cathedral. Reliable, popular, and inexpensive, with a mix of Mexican standards and North American coffee shop fare; open daily 7:30 a.m.-8 p.m.

Groceries

In downtown Chihuahua the best area for grocery shopping is a complex of small streets (generally referred to as **Mercado Reforma,** the name of the largest open-air market here) between Av. Juárez and Av. Niños Heroes, where a number of open-air markets and grocery stores can be found. This area has superseded the much-touted Mercado Juárez on Av. Juárez and Calle 25, which isn't as busy as it used to be.

Mercado Reforma itself has every foodstuff imaginable. The smaller **Mercado Combate,** between Calle Doblado and Niños Heroes around the corner from Mercado Reforma, has beautiful vegetables and a good assortment of Mennonite cheeses. Nearby are two well-stocked grocery stores, **Soriana** on Av. Juárez and **Super Grande** on Av. Niños Heroes.

On the city bypasses, **Plaza Vallarta** on Av. Tecnológico and **Futurama Leones** on Perif. Ortíz Mena have supermarkets.

RECREATION

Entertainment
Industrious Chihuahua seems to go to bed earlier than other Mexican cities of similar size, so you won't find much to do after dark. Following, however, are a few suggestions.

Behind Club de los Parados on Av. Juárez is a popular outdoor bar called **Alameda Corona** (don't look for a sign; you won't find one). It's known locally as "La Cervecería" ("The Brewery"). Inexpensive beer and cocktails (including *vampiros*) are served in what looks like an American-style drive-in; *trobadores*—both mariachi and *norteña*—provide the music. A similar place, **Los Alamos Tecate,** can be found at Av. Colón and Canal.

Several of the city's five-star hotels have bars and discos. One of the most lively is the Hotel San Francisco's **Bar Los Primos,** which features live music nightly.

Several modern **cinemas** showing first-run European and North American films are located downtown near the Palacio de Gobierno around Av. V. Carranza. The **Alliance Française Mexique (Alianza Francesa de Chihuahua),** tel. 14-16-14-91, at Calle Aldama 430, occasionally screens French films.

Also check the Centro Cultural Chihuahua (see "Sights," above for location) for occasional art and music events.

Bullfights
The 8,000-seat **Plaza de Toros Esperanza,** off Av. Reforma next to the western end of the canal, holds *corridas de toros* on Sundays at 4 p.m. during the summer. For the latest schedule, contact the state tourist office (see "Chihuahua Information," below).

Shopping
Plaza Libertad, the pedestrian mall along Calle Libertad opposite the cathedral and Plaza de Armas, is flanked by watch and jewelry shops, booteries, Mexican versions of Sears and Woolworth, and various other specialty shops and department stores.

For a greater selection of Mexican boots, cruise the back-to-back **boot shops** along Av. Ocampo between Aldama and Juárez.

Mercado de Artesanías, at Calle Victoria 506, is a large and rather touristy curios store. Some good buys can be found if you take time to wade through the kitsch.

Toto, a small *librería* at Av. V. Guerrero and Calle Aldama opposite small Plaza Hidalgo, carries a selection of English-language magazines.

CHIHUAHUA INFORMATION

Tourist Offices
For highway travelers arriving from the north, the most convenient information stop is the SECTUR office (tel. 14-17-89-72) at Av. Tecnológico 7901, which is open daily 8 a.m.-1 p.m.

Downtown, the most convenient source of information is the state tourism office (tel. 16-24-36) in the Edificio Agustín Melgar at Calle Libertad and Calle 13. Hours are Mon.-Fri. 8 a.m.-7 p.m.

Post And Telephone
Chihuahua's central post office is in a huge turn-of-the-century building at the corner of Calle Libertad and Av. V. Carranza. Hours are Mon.-Fri. 9 a.m.-6 p.m. and Sat.-Sun. 9 a.m.-noon.

Operator-staffed long-distance TelMex offices at Av. V. Carranza 1403 and the Central Camionera are open daily 9 a.m.-9 p.m.

USEFUL CHIHUAHUA TELEPHONE NUMBERS

State Tourist Office: 16-24-36
Red Cross: 11-22-11, 12-15-58
State Hospital: 15-90-00
Federal Highway Police: 17-95-13
Green Angels: 17-89-72
Chihuahua al Pacífico Station: 10-37-51, 10-56-43
Chihuahua Area Code: 14

TRANSPORT

Air
Aeroméxico (tel. 14-15-63-03, Calle Victoria 106) operates regular nonstop flights between Chihuahua and Ciudad Juárez, Culiacán, Hermosillo, Los Angeles, Mexico City, Monterrey, and Torreón.

Regional carrier **Leo López Airlines** at Calle Coronado 421 (tel. 16-28-28; 915-778-1022 in El Paso, Texas) has daily flights to/from El Paso aboard 16-seater Fairchild Metros. Mon.-Fri., a second El Paso-Chihuahua flight continues on to Los Mochis, Sinaloa. These flights are popular for North Americans who take one-way rides on the Chihuahua al Pacífico and fly back to El Paso.

TAESA (tel. 16-51-46, Av. Jimenez 1204) flies daily to/from Ciudad Juárez and Mexico City.

Bus
Chihuahua's cavernous new Terminal de Autobuses or Central Camionera (the old name, but still in use) is at the southeastern outskirts of the city on Av. Juan Pablo II, the road to the airport. This ultra-modern edifice has all kinds of services, including a pharmacy and telecommunications center. City buses (US$0.25) from Av. Niños Heroes downtown (marked "C. Camionera") go to the bus terminal; in the reverse direction they end up along Av. Juárez. Some Chihuahua city maps still mark the old downtown location of the Central Camionera.

The main bus line for the state is **Estrella Blanca** (tel. 14-12-49-87), which runs buses to Creel (US$8.60, eight times daily), Madera (US$8.60, hourly 6 a.m.-6:30 p.m.), Cuauhtémoc (US$4.50, every half-hour 6 a.m.-6:30 p.m.), and La Junta (US$4.80, every half-hour 6 a.m.-6:30 p.m.). Tickets for Estrella Blanca buses can be purchased at the line's city ticket office (tel. 18-86-59; Av. R.F. Magón and Calle 44).

Transportes Chihuahuenses (tel. 12-01-01) has similar routes, along with Ojinaga (US$7.30, eight times daily), Ciudad Juárez (US$13.60, every half-hour 6-6), Parral (US$7.50, five times daily), Durango (US$25, eight times daily), Torreón (US$17, 12 times daily), San Luis Potosí (US$30, four times daily), Zacatecas (US$31, 11 times daily), and Mexico City (US$43, five times daily).

Moving to the larger first-class lines, **Tres Estrellas de Oro** (tel. 16-14-08) and **TNS** (tel. 12-47-73) have buses to Sonora's Agua Prieta (US$18.30, six times daily), Nogales (US$27, twice daily), Hermosillo (US$31, twice daily), as well as Tijuana (US$49, three times daily).

Omnibus de México (tel. 15-06-65) operates first-class buses to/from Ciudad Juárez (US$21, three times daily), Durango (US$37, once daily), Monterrey (US$45, once daily), San Luis Potosí ((US$61, once daily), and Mexico City (US$82, once daily).

Turistar (tel. 15-62-82) specializes in *ejecutivo* service to/from Ciudad Juárez (US$25, three times daily), El Paso (US$25, twice daily), Torreón (US$29, once daily), Monterrey (US$52, once daily), Aguascalientes (US$53, once daily), Cuauhtémoc (US$6, once daily), and Parral (US$12.60, once daily).

Train
One thing to get straight from the start—Chihuahua has two separate railway stations, one each for the Chihuahua al Pacífico (tel. 14-12-31-57, Calle Méndez and Calle 24) and División

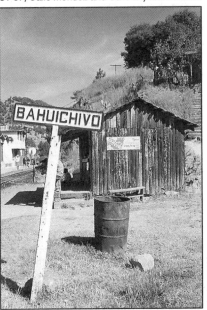

Bahuichivo train station

del Norte (tel. 13-00-93, Av. División del Norte) trains.

The División del Norte train has only second-class, unreserved seating between Ciudad Juárez and Chihuahua (and as far south as Zacatecas, where first-class seats to Mexico City become available). For details on this leg, see "Getting There" in the Ciudad Juárez section.

The División del Norte line continues on to Mexico City via Torreón, Zacatecas, Aguascalientes, and Querétaro. See the "Railway Schedule," pp. 86-87, for departure and arrival times.

The Chihuahua al Pacífico train, one of the main tourist objectives for visitors to the city of Chihuahua, runs between Chihuahua and Los Mochis, Sin., on the Sea of Cortéz coast. Since the entire trip takes around 13 hours and the best scenery occurs between Cuauhtémoc and El Fuerte, travelers taking the train for sight-seeing purposes should consider breaking the trip into shorter segments. This can be done by spending the night somewhere along the line, or by taking the train only as far as El Fuerte (or vice versa)—a rail journey of around 11 hours.

First-class (only) Chihuahua al Pacífico fares out of Chihuahua include Creel US$12, Divisadero US$15, Posada Barrancas US$15.30, Bahuichivo US$16.50, El Fuerte US$23.50, and Los Mochis US$32. Add 15% for stopovers (maximum of two permitted on one ticket); children ages 5-11 are eligible for a 50% discount on all fares. Fares are of course subject to change.

Scheduling and conditions for the Chihuahua al Pacífico are discussed in more detail in the Sierra Tarahumara "Copper Canyon" section; see also the "Railway Schedule," pp. 86-87.

The second-class Tarahumara line departs Chihuahua daily at 8 a.m., arriving in Los Mochis sometime before midnight. Fares are less than a third of the ordinary Chihuahua al Pacífico fares but the Tarahumara (nicknamed the *pollero*) is crowded and slow.

Train tickets can be purchased at the station an hour before scheduled departure, but tickets for the Chihuahua al Pacífico are more easily booked in advance through a travel agency authorized to sell FNM tickets. In Chihuahua two agencies have this authorization: **Quezada Tours** (tel. 15-71-41, fax 15-76-06, Calle Aldama 316-4) and **Viajes Línea Nueva** (tel. 15-

84-16, fax 15-89-30, Centro Commercial Plaza Campestre, Perif. Ortíz Mena 211; a second branch is in the Hotel Castel Sicomoro).

Getting Around

Bus: Chihuahua has a comprehensive city bus system that costs US$0.25 for one-way rides anywhere in the city. You can catch city buses to the airport (marked "Aeropuerto") and bus terminal (marked "C. Camionera") along Av. Niños Heroes.

Taxi: Major taxi stands are found next to the Plaza de Armas on Av. Juárez and near the Mercado Reforma on Av. Niños Heroes. Taxis also hang around all the larger hotels. Fares within the downtown area are around US$3, between the downtown and the Terminal de

---

AUTO RENTAL AGENCIES IN CHIHUAHUA

ALPRI RENT-A-CAR

Hotel Victoria
tel. 10-60-83, 10-05-47

ANSA RENTA DE AUTOS

Hotel Castel Sicimoro
tel. 14-21-71

AVIS

Av. Universidad 2749
tel. 13-17-82, 14-19-99

BUDGET

Av. Independencia 1205
tel. 16-09-09, 16-04-04

CONTINENTAL

Av. Reforma 601-B
tel. 16-99-95

DOLLAR RENT-A-CAR

Av. Colón and Av. Reforma
tel. 14-39-07, 14-42-28

HERTZ

Aeropuerto Internacional
tel. 16-64-73, 15-78-18

NUMERO UNO AUTORENTAS

Blvd. Díaz Ordaz 222
tel. 13-88-33
and Hotel Palacio del Sol
tel. 20-55-55

Autobuses US$5, and to the airport US$8.60.

Driving: Chihuahua is 374 km (232 miles) from Ciudad Juárez via Mexico 45, typically 3 1/2 to four hours by car (not allowing time for getting lost in Ciudad Juárez).

If you're driving south toward Durango, Zacatecas, and Mexico City, and don't plan to stop over in Chihuahua, stick to Av. Tecnológico and follow signs for Mexico 45. Several motels and PEMEX stations are available along this road. If you're coming from Ciudad Juárez and plan to bypass the city on your way to Cuauhtémoc or Creel, turn west (right) on Periférico de la Juventud, a loop that leads around the western outskirts of Chihuahua to Mexico 16.

If you're driving in from Ojinaga (238 km/147.5 miles/three hours) on Mexico 16, you'll enter the city limits near the airport and inter-city bus terminal; to get downtown, take a right on Av. Pacheco, which heads north and intersects with Av. 20 de Noviembre and Av. Juárez in the city.

Fuel: You'll find PEMEX stations with Magna Sin throughout Chihuahua, especially along the various bypass roads encircling the city.

VICINITY OF CHIHUAHUA

Santa Eulalia (Aquiles Serdán)

Although it's only 15-20 minutes by car from the capital, the state's second mining settlement (founded 1707) retains the charm of "old Chihuahua." Some parts of town have been restored; some parts are still in ruins. Street lights have recently been put in around the plaza.

The town is seven km (4.3 miles) from Mexico 45 via Chihuahua 245, 18 km (11 miles) total from Chihuahua. At the town entrance, follow the road along the arroyo to the left and park a few blocks ahead. Then wander the narrow cobblestoned streets to view pastel-colored, one-story colonials, an old church, and village-style shops. Local bands play live music in the plaza on Sundays.

Chihuahuan visitors almost always eat at **El Mesón de Santa Eulalia** (tel. 14-16-60-89) near the plaza, especially on Sundays when the restaurant features a large Mexican buffet. Open Tues.-Sun. 1-10 p.m.

RVs: The streets aren't wide enough for most RVs, so park your rigs near the town entrance and walk in.

Cumbres De Majalca National Park

This oasis northwest of Chihuahua protects 11,790 acres of stony peaks, rock formations, oak and evergreen forests, and canyons cut by streams feeding into the Chuvíscar and Sacramento rivers. Opportunities for hiking, canyoneering, or rock-climbing are plentiful, and wilderness camping is permitted. Summer, when natural sources of water are most abundant and the canyons are most attractive, is the best time for backpacking the park. The contrast between the cool greenness of the *cumbres* (peaks) and the surrounding Chihuahuan Desert can be striking.

Basic lodging is available in park cabins or in motels on Mexico 45 nearby. The turnoff for the park is 30 km (19 miles) north of Chihuahua via Mexico 45; then it's 40 km northwest on a gravel road.

CHIHUAHUA TO PARRAL

Motorists have a choice of two routes to Parral (Hidalgo del Parral) from Chihuahua. The first is Mexico 45, which now features a 113-km (70-mile) section of four-lane tollway as well as the original 301-km (187-mile) two-lane free road that zigzags to Parral via ciudades Camargo and Jimenez. The quicker and more direct route is Mexico 24, which meets Mexico 16 about 30 km southwest of Chihuahua and descends 182 km (112 miles) almost straight south (via Valle de Zaragoza) to Parral, a distance savings of 119 km (75 miles). The longer Mexico 45 route allows stopovers in ciudades Delicias, Camargo, or Jimenez, while Mexico 24 runs through mostly unpopulated *lomeríos*.

Ciudad Delicias

This prosperous town halfway between Chihuahua (84 km/52 miles northwest) and Ciudad Camargo on Mexico 45 benefits from nearby **Presa Francisco I. Madero,** a Río San Pedro/Conchos impoundment that irrigates surrounding fields of vinifera, watermelon, corn, wheat, peanuts, and cotton. The sizable lake at Presa Madero is reportedly a productive bass fishery as well as a site for duck, goose, and dove hunting.

The area competes with Cuauhtémoc for the "best Mexican apple" title; earlier this century the Hacienda de las Delicias developed the Red and Golden Delicious apples now famous in North America. Wineries in the area produce wines that, while not as famous as those from Zacatecas or Baja California, are nonetheless quite drinkable.

Meoqui, nine km north on Mexico 45, is a historic mining settlement of the same era as Santa Eulalia and Aldama. A hot springs nearby is channeled into two rustic *balnearios* (spas), **El Delfín** and **Junta de los Ríos.**

Ciudad Camargo

Another prosperous little Camino Real town, Camargo is supported by a mix of farming, cattle ranching, and textiles; much of the wheat grown in the Delicias-Camargo area is also milled here. The **Iglesia de San Francisco de los Conchos,** 21 km southeast of town via the paved road to Presa La Boquilla, is a 17th-century mission church with a two-story, folk-baroque facade.

Although it's in the middle of the Chihuahuan Desert, rivers and springs keep the area sufficiently watered and provide residents and visitors with a variety of recreational possibilities. And at an altitude of 1,632 meters (5,440 feet), Camargo's summer climate is milder than that of the surrounding plains. **Ojo Caliente Pascualeño,** a *balneario* 20 km (12.5 miles) southwest of town, offers hot mineral baths and swimming. Other *balnearios* nearby include **Los Filtros** at San Francisco de Conchos and **Ojos Calientes de Santa Rosalía,** nine km northeast.

Presa La Boquilla (Lago Toronto), a huge lake formed by the impoundment of the Río Conchos 29 km (18 miles) southwest of Camargo, is stocked with catfish, black bass, perch, and bluefish and is popular for swimming, boating and fishing. The dam is also an important source of hydroelectric power for much of Chihuahua.

Accommodations: The new **Hotel Casa Grande** (tel. 148-2-02-00, 91-800-14-222 in Mexico; 800-343-6344 in the U.S./Canada) at Av. 6 Ote. 601 offers spacious, modern rooms with all the amenities starting at US$55. The less expensive **Motel El Dorado** (tel. 2-13-77) has clean rooms for around US$30.

RVs: The well-run **Villa del Charro Motel y Trailer Park** (tel. 148-2-22-21), 5.3 km (3.3 miles) south of town, has 45 spaces with full

hookups, plus showers, a convenience store, and propane. The attached motel has eight basic rooms.

Ciudad Jimenez

At the junction of highways Mexico 45 and 49, Ciudad Jimenez is a regional transport hub, as well as a center for cattle, cotton, and wheat production. Historical attractions include the 18th-century **Parroquia de Santo Cristo de Burgos** and a turn-of-the-century municipal market constructed of iron.

Motel Las Pampas (tel. 154-2-10-41), on Mexico 45, has four-star accommodation and a restaurant, while **Motel Florido** (tel. 2-01-86), Av. Juárez and 20 de Noviembre, is rated at three stars (for Mexico's SECTUR rating system, see "Rates," p. 62). For a quick bite to eat, **Pollos Guamuchil** on the highway is a good choice.

Valle De Allende

Twenty-five km east of Parral on Mexico 25, then south six km, this beautiful area of fruit and nut orchards is a favorite weekend spot for Parral residents, who come to bathe at the *balnearios* near the entrance to town. The older haciendas along the river are attractive, as is the 17th-century **Iglesia de Nuestra Señora del Rosario** with its arches and octagonal window.

HIDALGO DE PARRAL

One of the oldest towns in Chihuahua, Parral owes its existence to the founding of La Negrita mine in 1631 and nearly 200 mines founded since then. Now called La Prieta, the founder mine as well as several others were working until the mid-'80s, when the ratio of precious metal prices to local ore supplies was no longer profitable. Since then Parral's economy has had a tough go of it, though the 1991 establishment of a General Motors automotive plant has sounded a hopeful note.

Farming and ranching contribute to the economy, though the town is too high and dry for intensive agriculture. The area reportedly produces some of the best pecans in the world—according to locals, something about the angle of the sun results in nuts with thin, easy-to-crack shells and plump, orange meat.

Residents are very proud not only of their pecans but of the town's distinctive history. Wedged in a valley between the Sierra Madre Occidental foothills and the high central Chihuahuan Desert, in a relatively isolated part of Mexico, Parral has also developed its own distinctive culture and accent. In fact, the particularly thick version of Chihuahuan Spanish spoken here can lead to minor communication difficulties even for those who know Mexican Spanish well.

Once you're off the highways (Mexico 45 and 24, which intersect here), the funky, hidden charms of downtown Parral become apparent. Crossed by nine small bridges, the crooked Río Parral snakes through a collection of shops and hotels that look like they've been kept in a glass case since the 1940s or '50s. Tourists are relatively rare, and the townspeople are happy to give directions (often necessary as the streets seem to follow a particularly distorted pattern) or to hold forth on a little town history.

All of the town sights can be explored on foot in a single afternoon. In addition to several historic churches, Parral is host to a small museum dedicated to Pancho Villa, who spent the final chapter of his life here.

As in the city of Chihuahua, the climate in Parral is mild most of the year. The occasional north wind can bring near-freezing temperatures to the valley Dec.-March.

Sights

Virtually everything of any size or beauty in Parral was built with mining money. The **Catedral de San José** is renowned for the diamond-shaped masonry motif on its walls and for a striking interior containing a large baroque altar of pink marble with gilt edges. Interred in the altar are the remains of Don Juan Rangel de Viesma, Parral's founder. Miners began constructing the church in 1846 and completed it in 1854; pillars supporting the roof are decorated with chunks of ore from nearby mines. Formerly a *parroquía*, the church attained cathedral status in 1992 with the assignment of a bishop to the area.

The building opposite the cathedral was built as a hotel in 1906 by a French architect for the wealthy Alvarado family, who later presented it to Pancho Villa. Villa's body was brought here immediately following his 1923 assassination.

The building is mostly empty now, save for a store selling decorative items in one of the large ground-floor rooms; inside, the original pressed-tin ceiling can be seen.

Nearby at the corner of Calle P. de Verdad and Riva Palacio is **Palacio Alvarado**, an 1899-1903 mansion constructed in Byzantine-baroque style. A tortured-looking face sculpted over the door is said to represent an Indian miner at work. Founder of the Mina La Palmilla, one of the world's richest silver mines, Don Alvarado was so wealthy he offered to pay off Mexico's national debt—but Díaz refused. Scions of the Alvarado family still live in the building.

The **Templo de la Virgen de Fátima,** on a hill overlooking the city near Mina La Prieta, was built almost entirely of metals taken from local mines. Instead of pews, the church features short, square pillar-stools fashioned in the shape of claim boundary markers; the walls and pillar sides show tiny ore chunks from area mines, including gold, silver, zinc, and lead. Finished in 1956, the interior of the church is said to look similar to those of chapels built into caverns in some of the larger mines.

The town's oldest continually functioning church, the **Templo del Rayo,** was built in the 17th to 18th centuries and is unremarkable except for its extremely tall and narrow profile. Older but abandoned is the tiny and plain 17th-century **Templo de San Tomás** at the south edge of the city.

To commemorate the town's 350th anniversary in 1980, Parral residents erected a bronze statue of founder Don Juan Rangel de Viesma in the town plaza. A colonial-style *kiosko* is also a rather recent addition to the plaza.

Villa Memorials

In 1920, after 10 years of fighting in the Mexican Revolution, Francisco "Pancho" Villa retired (with a lifetime general's pay) to a ranch in Canutillo, 80 km southeast of Parral. Accompanied by his entourage of Dorados ("Golden Ones"), Villa frequently made trips to Parral for banking and other errands. On July 20, 1923, the last day of his life, Villa had picked up a consignment of gold with which to pay his Canutillo ranch staff and was driving through the city in his black Dodge roadster when a group of seven riflemen fired 150 shots (in just two minutes) into his car.

To this day it's not known for certain who ordered the killing. The assassins were given light prison sentences, leading many people to believe that someone in the Mexican government gave the order simply because ex-*bandido* Villa had become an embarrassment to post-revolutionary Mexico.

The **Museo de General Francisco Villa,** upstairs in the local library, contains colorful murals depicting battle scenes, old photos, old newspaper cuttings, pieces of Villa's coffin, weapons, and a death mask of Villa that was found in Redford College in El Paso (a German furniture-maker is said to have made the mold of Villa's face from which the bronze death mask was cast and then smuggled it out of Mexico). Outside on the sidewalk is a starburst-shaped bronze plaque where Villa's car ran into a tree after being riddled with bullets; it is the last in a series of bronze historical plaques marking Villa's last-day route through the city. The fusillade was fired from the building directly opposite the library-museum. The museum is open Mon.-Fri. 9 a.m.-8 p.m., Sat. 9-1; admission is free.

Villa's grave in the Cemeterio Municipal is a source of mystery nearly as piquant as that shrouding his assassination. Three years after Villa's burial, someone exhumed the body and removed Villa's head. Most Mexicans believe a long-time rumor that says the decapitation was performed by an American adventurer on behalf of an eccentric Chicago millionaire who collected the skulls of historic figures. As if this weren't bizarre enough, three years following the decapitation the federal government ordered Villa's body moved to Mexico City so that it could be interred in the Tomb of Illustrious Men.

Local residents, however, will tell you that their mayor had the body shifted in the graveyard a meter or so to the right of the marked grave and replaced with another body to prevent any more of Villa's body parts from being taken. It was this decoy body, they insist, that was later taken to Mexico City! Whether Villa's headless body is still in the ground or not, his tall, stately tombstone remains in place and people still lay flowers on the grave. To the right of Villa's headstone is the grave of his son Miguel, who died in a Mexican Air Force crash in 1950 at age 30.

Accommodations

Parral has a number of very similar, older downtown hotels in the US$16-25 range that are perfectly adequate for a night or two. Each has an attached restaurant.

Best value of the lot is **Hotel Acosta** (tel. 152-30-09-51), just off the downtown square at Calle Barbachano 3. Rooms with TV, a/c (but no heat), and private bath cost US$16.60 s, US$20.60 d, US$25 t, and US$26.60 q.

Another fair one is the friendly and efficient **Hotel Turista** (tel. 2-44-89) at Plazuela Independencia 12. Well-worn but clean rooms with TV, a/c, heat, and phone cost US$25 s, US$30 d, US$35 t. The manager and staff are very knowledgeable about local sights; some English is spoken. **Hotel San José** (tel. 2-24-53) at Calle S. Méndez 5 is similar, perhaps a bit spiffier.

The newish **Miller Inn** at the intersection of Mexico 24 and Mexico 45, is convenient for motorists and costs US$44 s, US$47 d, US$48 t, US$50 q, for modern rooms with a/c, heat, and satellite TV.

Toward the downtown area from the Miller Inn along Av. Independencia, the main access road, is **Motel Las Nogales,** with basic but clean rooms for US$15 s, US$17 d.

A bit farther along the same road, next to the PEMEX station, the American-style **Motel El Camino Real** has rooms with TV, a/c, and heat in the US$30-40 range, plus a swimming pool. **Motel Villa Cariño,** at the south edge of town on Mexico 45, costs US$20-28 for rooms with a/c (no heat).

Food

Your best bets in Parral are the traditional restaurants attached to the older downtown hotels. One of the nicer ones is the **Restaurant La Parroquía,** attached to the Hotel San José.

The breakfast and lunch specials at the restaurant attached to the Hotel Turista are tasty and inexpensive. A well-prepared, complete *comida corrida* at the Turista costs US$5 and is better than the usual US$5 *comida corrida* in other Mexican cities.

Cabrito al Pastor El Asadero, on the road into town from Mexico 24, has very good *pollo asado,* roasted over a wood fire, as well as *cabrito.*

Transport

Buses: Several lines operate buses between Parral and towns in Chihuahua and Durango. Between the city of Chihuahua and Parral, a variety of classes is available: second class for US$4.60-$6 (depending on the bus line); first class for US$8.30; and US$12.60 for *ejecutivo*.

Driving: Via Mexico 24, the Chihuahua-Parral drive takes around two to three hours. At the junction for Valle Zaragoza, 62 km (38.4 miles) north of Parral, you'll find a couple of basic hotels and restaurants as well as a PEMEX station (Nova only). Magna Sin is available in Parral.

Sierra Tarahumara/Barranca de Batopilas: Parral offers a nifty back-door entrance into Sierra Tarahumara country for motorists with rugged vehicles. Follow Mexico 24 west from Parral 32 km (19.8 miles), then bear right onto gravel-surface Chihuahua 22 and follow signs to Samachic (Samachique), about 270 km (167 miles) from this junction. Nova gasoline is available along the way in Guachochi and other villages. Samachic is on the Batopilas-Creel road. For more detail see "Batopilas," p. 282, or "Creel," p. 278.

Pacific Coast: It is also possible to drive from Parral across the Sierra Madre to the Pacific coast near Culiacán via Mexico 24. The road is paved for 140 km (86.8 miles) only as far west as Guadalupe y Calvo. Following Guadalupe y Calvo is an unpaved, partially graded section for 85 km (52.7 miles) until Santiago de los Caballeros, after which it's another 75 km (46.5 miles) to Mexico 15. Nova is available at a couple of towns along the way. Stick to the main road all the way—some of the side tracks lead to areas where opium and marijuana are grown illegally.

To/From Durango: See "Durango to Parral" in the Durango chapter for details on the Mexico 45 route between Parral and Durango.

emerald toucanet

SIERRA TARAHUMARA
("COPPER CANYON")

The Sierra Tarahumara, one of the highest and most rugged sections of the Sierra Madre Occidental, is also one of Mexico's premier attractions, yet remarkably few North Americans seem to have heard of it. Few maps of the area, in fact, even include the name "Sierra Tarahumara," a term used to designate a 64,000-square-km (25,000-square-mile) zone that is the traditional (though not the original) homeland of Mexico's 50,000 Tarahumaras. Although the Tarahumaras are by far the most numerous Amerindians in the sierra, the region is also inhabited by Pimas (northwest), Guarojillos (west), and Tepehuanes (south).

The Canyons

People who know of the area may be more familiar with the term "Copper Canyon," which is often loosely applied to one of the sierra's most salient geographical features, its vast network of canyons. Cut into the sierra by the Chínipas, Candameña, Urique, Tararécua, Septentrión, Batopilas, and Verdes rivers (among others), these canyons represent North America's largest canyon system, with at least four canyons (each over 1,800 meters/5,900 feet deep) that are deeper than Arizona's Grand Canyon (1,425 meters/4,654 feet at Hopi Point) according to standard canyoneering measures. Not to put too fine a point on it; none of the Sierra Tarahumara canyons are as wide as the Grand Canyon—most are deep and relatively narrow by comparison (though wide enough that you can't see rim to rim in the larger ones). Together they have nearly four times the volume of the Grand Canyon.

"Copper Canyon," a translation of the Spanish "Barranca de Cobre," refers to a section formed by the Río Urique that extends eastward from the Río Urique/Río Tararécua junction as far south as Puente Humirá, where the Creel-Batopilas road crosses the Río Urique. It's a bit confusing since the section of the Río Urique southward from the Urique/Tararécua junction is termed "Barranca de Urique" or "Urique Canyon" even though it's basically a continuation of the

same canyon. Although most of the individual canyons have their own names (usually named after the rivers that form them), locals often refer to the entire canyon system as "las Barrancas del Cobre." The Mexican government has designated the entire region as "Parque Natural Barrancas del Cobre" or "Copper Canyons Natural Park," an honorary appellation that has bestowed no public facilities (and no special protection) on the area except for one campground near Creel.

"Cobre," incidentally, refers to the color of the canyon walls more than to the fact that copper may have been mined here. Gold and silver, however, have been mined in vast quantities over the centuries. Although there's insufficient ore left to interest large mining concerns, perhaps hundreds of small-time gold prospectors still manage to eke out a living in the canyons.

Most North American visitors to the Sierra Tarahumara traverse the area by train, catching glimpses of three magnificent canyons along the way: Septentrión (Témoris area), Urique (Bahuichivo to El Divisadero), and Tararécua (El Divisadero to Creel, with glimpses of Barranca del Cobre in the distance). Of those who take the time to descend into the canyons—whether on foot or by motor vehicle—most end up in the Cobre, Tararécua, Batopilas, and Urique, each one a world unto itself. A hardy few make it as far as the Barranca de Sinforosa in the extreme southeast portion of the sierra.

Climate And Seasons

The Sierra Tarahumara region harbors two distinct climatic zones, one in the highlands and another at the canyon bottoms, with various gradations between. In the highlands the weather is mild April-Oct., with warm but not hot days (18° C/65° F to 24° C/75° F) and cool, crisp nights. From mid-November to April, nighttime temperatures drop considerably, often hitting the freezing point (or lower) in the early morning hours. Winter snowfalls in the highlands are not uncommon, though they don't usually cover the ground for very long. Occasional heavy rains

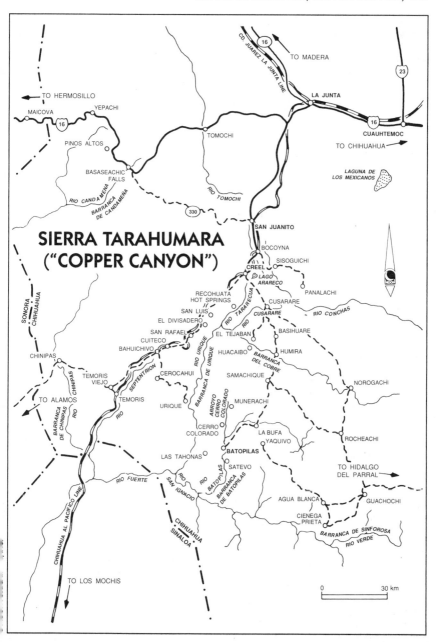

TO HERMOSILLO

MAICOVA
YEPACHI
16
PINOS ALTOS

BASASEACHIC FALLS
RIO CANDAMEÑA
BARRANCA DE CANDAMEÑA

TOMOCHI

RIO TOMOCHI

330

CD. JUAREZ LA JUNTA LINE
16
TO MADERA
LA JUNTA
23
16
CUAUHTEMOC
TO CHIHUAHUA

LAGUNA DE LOS MEXICANOS

SIERRA TARAHUMARA ("COPPER CANYON")

SAN JUANITO
BOCOYNA
CREEL
LAGO ARARECO
SISOGUICHI
PANALACHI

RECOHUATA HOT SPRINGS
SAN LUIS
EL DIVISADERO
SAN RAFAEL
CUITECO
BAHUICHIVO

RIO TARARECUA
CUSARARE
RIO CUSARARE
RIO CONCHAS
EL TEJABAN
BASIHUARE
HUACAIBO
BARRANCA DEL COBRE
HUMIRA

RIO URIQUE
BARRANCA DE URIQUE

SONORA
CHIHUAHUA

CHINIPAS

TEMORIS VIEJO
SEPTENTRION
CEROCAHUI
SAMACHIQUE
NOROGACHI

TO ALAMOS
BARRANCA DE CHINIPAS
RIO CHINIPAS
TEMORIS
RIO
URIQUE
ARROYO CERRO COLORADO
MUNERACHI

CERRO COLORADO
LA BUFA
YAQUIVO
ROCHEACHI

BATOPILAS
LAS TAHONAS
SATEVO
TO HIDALGO DEL PARRAL

RIO FUERTE
RIO SAN IGNACIO
RIO BATOPILAS
BARRANCA DE BATOPILAS

CHIHUAHUA AL PACIFICO LINE

CHIHUAHUA SINALOA

AGUA BLANCA
CIENEGA PRIETA
GUACHOCHI
BARRANCA DE SINFOROSA
RIO VERDE

TO LOS MOCHIS

0   30 km

mid-July to mid-September are normal, sometimes to the extent that unpaved roads become impassable. The average monthly precipitation during these months is 13.5 cm (5.3 inches), with a total year-round average of around 63 cm (25 inches).

Down at the canyon bottoms temperatures are subtropical year-round. The hottest time of year is May-July, before the summer monsoon arrives; afternoon temperatures frequently break 40° C (104° F). Once the rains begin, daytime maximums drop several degrees but afternoons can still be almost intolerable for some visitors. The rivers and streams reach their highest levels this time of year, hence you can't count on crossing them whether hiking or driving. Monthly and yearly averages for precipitation are around 20% lower than in the highlands.

Timing Your Visit: If you're only planning to stay in the highlands or along canyon rims, any time of year is good for a visit, though you run the greatest risk of rain and cloudy skies July-September. Whatever the time of year, come prepared for warm days and cold nights.

For canyoneers, the optimum time to visit is immediately after the monsoon, i.e., late Sept.-Oct., when water is plentiful and the canyons are greenest. Winters are also very pleasant, though the vegetation is more bare and brown, and water can be scarce. The one time of year that canyon-bottom trips should be avoided is during the May-June peak hot season, when water scarcity and high temperatures combine to sap the will of all but the most masochistic.

FLORA AND FAUNA

Plants

Unlike the canyonlands of the U.S. Southwest, which are mostly desertic, the Barrancas del Cobre are typically green and wooded. Mixed evergreen forests of ponderosa pine and Douglas fir are generally found along the upland areas and highest canyon rims (over 2,000 meters), with piñon-live oak-juniper woodlands at slightly lower mountain/rim elevations (500-1,500 meters). Sierra Tarahumara forests are superlative on two counts: They contain the largest stands of old-growth forest in the Americas; and they produce more pine and oak than any other area in the world.

The undergrowth of the lower piñon-oak woodlands (or "Madrean evergreen" woodlands) also includes a number of scrub, succulents, and short cacti such as hedgehog, catclaw, cane cholla, prickly pear, agave, and yucca.

Just below the rims on canyon slopes, arid-tropical deciduous thorn forests begin appearing, with scrub oaks, mesquite, agave, bromeliads, bursera, and various large and columnar cacti. Most of the trees are short and drought-deciduous, dropping their leaves during long deciduous periods between rains. For this reason the canyons generally appear most lush in October, following the late summer rains.

Down on the canyon floors bordering the rivers are sections of tropical-subtropical riparian forests showing a mix of both deciduous and evergreen vegetation, including wild figs, liana, orchid, palm, bamboo, sycamores, river cane, and various grasses and thornscrub species.

Mammals

Mexican wolf, black bear, and puma (mountain lion) live in the highlands of the Sierra Tarahumara but are rarely sighted by visitors. Unconfirmed sightings of the Mexican grizzly bear (*Ursus horribilis mexicanus*), thought to be extinct, have also been reported. Along the canyon bottoms jaguar and jaguarundi have been reported. More common and wide-ranging mammals include white-tailed deer, coati, bobcat,

---

SAVE THE SIERRA TARAHUMARA

The World Bank recently approved a US$45 million loan to develop logging in the Sierra Tarahumara through the construction of pulp mills and the upgrading of roads. To go through, the loan must receive matching funds from the Mexican government. Although the loan would undoubtedly help Mexican and North American investors in the area, the living Tarahumara culture would be sieged by an intrusion greater than anything since the Spanish *entrada* (not to mention the potential effects on wildlife). If you would like to express an opinion regarding the project, write to the World Bank, 1818 H St., Washington, DC 20433. For a policy paper on the project, call the Texas Center for Policy Studies at (512) 474-0811.

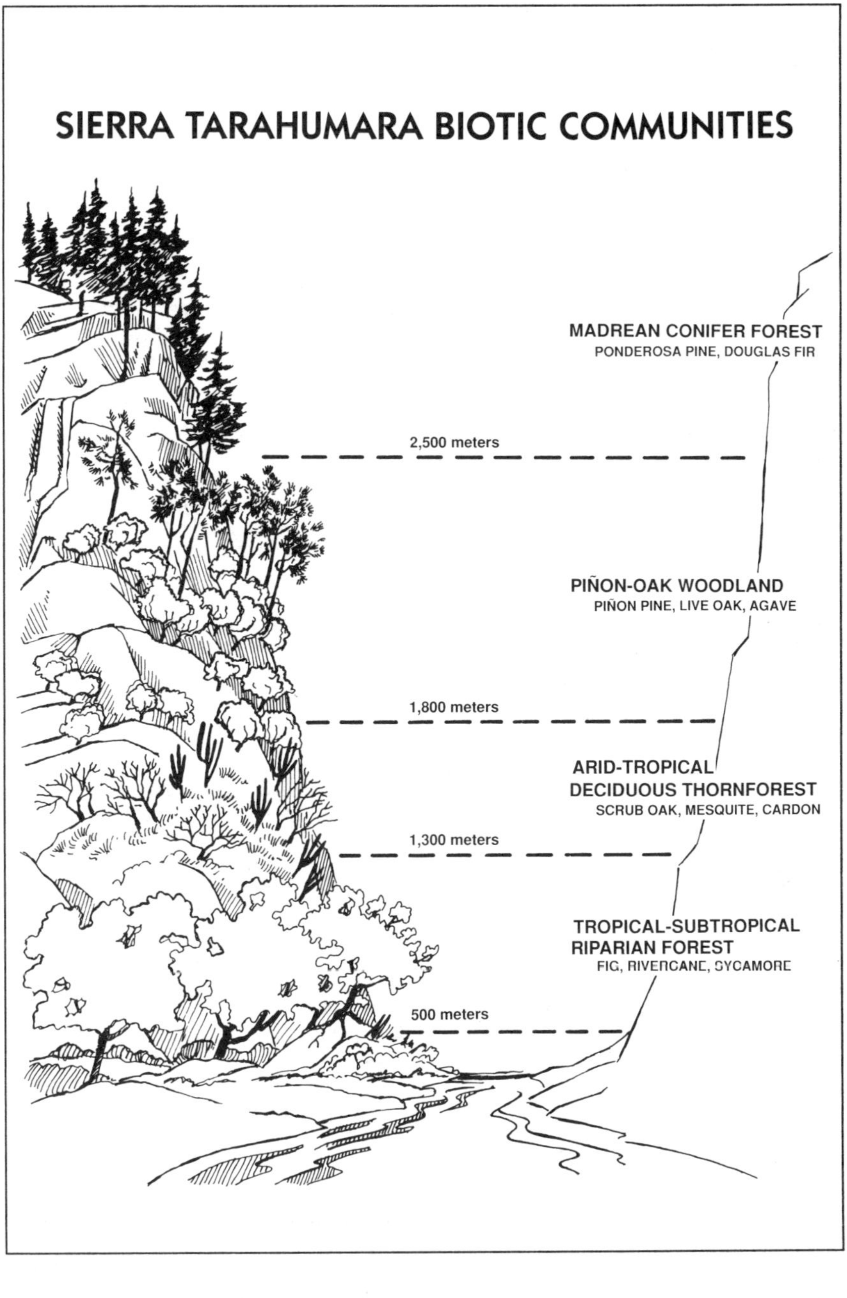

SIERRA TARAHUMARA BIOTIC COMMUNITIES

MADREAN CONIFER FOREST
PONDEROSA PINE, DOUGLAS FIR

2,500 meters

PIÑON-OAK WOODLAND
PIÑON PINE, LIVE OAK, AGAVE

1,800 meters

**ARID-TROPICAL
DECIDUOUS THORNFOREST**
SCRUB OAK, MESQUITE, CARDON

1,300 meters

**TROPICAL-SUBTROPICAL
RIPARIAN FOREST**
FIG, RIVERCANE, SYCAMORE

500 meters

BOB RACE

javelina (collared peccary), ringtail, coyote, gray fox, river otter, and various squirrels and skunks. You will also see wandering domestics—goats, sheep, cattle, burros, and pigs.

Birds

Over 200 migratory and indigenous bird species have been spotted in the sierra, including eared trogon, elegant (coppery-tailed) trogon, bald eagle, red-tailed and white-tailed hawk, crested caracara, Aplomado falcon, Inca dove, green parakeet, canyon wren, great blue heron, roadrunner, and—perhaps the most impressive bird for visiting North Americans—the military macaw, a large green, red, and blue parrot seen at lower elevations.

Reptiles

Notable indigenous species include Arizona and canyon tree frogs in the higher woodlands; Tarahumara frog, Ditmar's horned lizard, and alligator lizard in the piñon-oak woodlands; beaded lizard and coral snake (both venomous) in the arid-tropical evergreen/deciduous forest; and leopard frog and boa constrictor along the canyon rivers.

Rattlesnakes—predominantly the relatively small rock and twin-spotted varieties—are more common in the highlands than in the canyons.

Fish

The Tarahumara build stone chutes in canyon streams to catch channel and flathead catfish and freshwater eel for food. Among other common fish species found in the sierra are carp, mullet, tilapia, Mexican stoneroller, molly, and shiner.

TRAVELING IN THE CANYONS

The most popular and romantic way to reach the Sierra Tarahumara is via the Chihuahua al Pacífico train; this mode of transport is a tourist attraction in itself and is discussed in detail elsewhere in this section under "Chihuahua Al Pacífico Rail Journey." Travel by rail gives you a choice of the following jumping-off points for more extensive excursions into the canyons: Creel, Posada Barrancas, Bahuichivo, and Témoris.

A second way of getting into the eastern end of the sierra (as far as Creel) is by daily public bus from La Junta, Cuauhtémoc, or Chihuahua. From Creel thrice-weekly buses also go to the town of Batopilas at the bottom of Barranca de Batopilas. This mode of transport limits you to the Barranca del Cobre and Barranca de Batopilas, unless of course you strike out on foot for other canyons.

Driving your own (or a rented) vehicle offers the most flexibility and the widest range of potential destinations. Inherent problems are the scarcity of fuel (and complete nonavailability of unleaded gas) in the Sierra Tarahumara, the overall lack of mechanical assistance, and the rough road conditions. (See "Fuel, Parts, and Repairs," p. 97, for information on using leaded fuel in unleaded cars.)

Roads are gradually improving in the area; ordinary sedans with a full tank of gas (when unleaded is necessary, fill up with Magna Sin in La Junta) can now get as far as Creel and Cusárare. For other destinations, vehicles best suited for Sierra Tarahumara road travel will have high road clearance, rugged chassis, heavy-duty tires, and either the capacity to burn leaded gas or a spare fuel tank (see "Driving in Northern Mexico," p. 90, for more information). Four-wheel drive would be a definite plus, especially for crossing sandy, muddy, or stream-filled arroyos.

With an off-highway vehicle you can reach all of the same towns accessible by rail (since a dirt road roughly parallels the track as far south as Témoris), as well as the Batopilas, Urique, Septentrión, and Sinforosa canyons (not to mention dozens of villages along a fairly extensive network of unpaved roads southeast of the rail line).

Hiking

The Chihuahua al Pacífico train journey through the Sierra Tarahumara canyons is spectacular, but to really experience this great wilderness you've got to get out and walk in it. The variety of terrains is simply astounding, from cool, resin-scented pine forests to sand-fringed, bamboo-curtained rock pools filled with turquoise spring water.

As the entire canyon region is crisscrossed with footpaths created by the Tarahumaras for walking (or running) from one ranchería to another, the Sierra Tarahumara's hiking potential is limited only by your hiking stamina and your capacity to carry provisions. This latter concern is the most important, as outside of the canyon-bottom towns of Urique and Batopilas, and the few towns along the canyon rims, no provisioning sources are available along the way. Tarahumara settlements almost invariably operate at a subsistence level, hence to attempt to rely on Tarahumara pueblos for food and water (except in emergencies) would place an unreasonable burden on their livelihoods.

You can avoid loading yourself down with food and water by using larger canyon or mountain towns as bases for day-hikes, by hiring a guide with pack burros, or by signing up with an organized backpacking tour. It is not advisable to consider setting off on a multiday backpacking trip on your own, unless you're going with someone who knows the area very well. Even with Mexican topo maps, people tend to get lost on long hikes because of the many intersecting trails. Another danger is running across a clandestine marijuana field whose tenders may be less than happy to see you.

Guides And Outfitters

Many Sierra Tarahumara trails link canyon rims with canyon rivers below. These rim-to-river hikes typically take one easy day to descend and one strenuous day—or an easier day and a half—back up. For a typical three- or four-day, rim-to-river roundtrip, a local guide is usually sufficient.

The better, more experienced guides—whether Tarahumara or mestizo—charge US$15-25 a day, plus the cost of food. More casual guides, i.e., someone who knows the territory but hasn't necessarily led many (or any) backpacking trips before, charge as little as US$10 a day. Pack burros cost an extra US$5-10 per day and each can carry around 45 kilos (100 pounds); riding horses may be available for certain segments on an hourly basis (figure around US$3-4 per hour). Make sure you get some kind of recommendation from other local residents for whomever you're considering. Guides can often be contacted through hotels or guesthouses in Creel, Cerocahui, Bahuichivo, Batopilas, and Urique. The larger, package-tour-oriented hotels charge the most for guide

road to Batopilas

JOE CUMMINGS

services—US$50 or more per day, of which the guide may receive only a small percentage.

For longer, more extensive backpacking trips, an organized group trek is recommended. Typically these involve 5-10 paying customers along with an experienced guide and a small local staff who take care of portage and cooking. One of the most reputable standard trips is the six-night/seven-day "Great Canyon Crossing Adventure," operated roughly eight times per year, Nov.-March, by **Copper Canyon Lodges** (tel. 313-689-2444; 800-776-3942 in the U.S./Canada; fax 313-689-9119) and led by canyons expert Jesús Olivas. This trip used to go all the way from Cusárare to El Divisadero, where hikers caught the train, but the current route goes from Cusárare to El Tejabán on the north rim of the Barranca del Cobre, then crosses the canyon to the village of Huacaibo, where the trip reverses itself (hikers are picked up by van or truck in El Tejabán for the return to Cusárare). The cost is currently US$694 per person, but call to be sure.

Wilderness Expeditions (tel. 602-882-5341; P.O. Box 40092, Tucson, AZ 85717) offers a variety of more specialized trekking tours to the Sierra Tarahumara, including six-day Christmas and Easter trips for US$650-760 per person and a rugged "Unknown Tarahumara" trip to a non-Christian Tarahumara area (US$750 per person). Customized itineraries are also available.

Two other reputable companies that can arrange organized and customized treks of almost any length and in any direction are **Columbus Tours** and **Adobe Tours** (see "Train Tours," p. 275, for contact information).

For those with more time than money, a good approach is simply to turn up in Creel or Cerocahui and ask around. Weeklong trips are sometimes thrown together on the spur of the moment—when enough visitors express an interest—through New Pensión Creel and Casa de Margarita's in Creel. These are generally the most inexpensive organized treks in the region and since they can be customized according to the tastes and hiking skills of the participants, they often result in the best wilderness experiences the Sierra Tarahumara has to offer.

Maps

In the INEGI-distributed topo series, the 1:250,000-scale "San Juanito" map covers most of the upper Sierra Tarahumara (as far south as Batopilas and Urique) and is good for general trip planning and off-highway driving. For serious hikers, more detail is available in eight different 1:50,000 maps which, put together, cover approximately the same territory as the San Juanito map with a bit extra on the southern end. These maps are *usually* available for purchase at the Tarahumara mission store (Artesanías Misión) in Creel (sometimes one or more of them may be out of stock), but to be on the safe side, check with the INEGI office in Hermosillo, Son. (see "Services and Information" under "Hermosillo" for the address), if you have a chance on your way to the Sierra Tarahumara. Buy whatever maps you need there. These maps are not infallibly accurate, and in fact some of the trail and village placement is obviously quite off. Nonetheless, they're the best cartographic sources available; it would be crazy to take more than a day's hike without the appropriate map.

Another very useful map to have for general orientation is the "Sierra Tarahumara-Barrancas del Cobre" map issued by the International Map Co. (University of Texas at El Paso, Box 400, El Paso, TX 79968-0400). This simple but accurate map shows most towns and major villages, major rivers, many roads (some with kilometer distances), and the Chihuahua al Pacífico railway. It can be ordered by mail or purchased at the mission store in Creel. I've also seen it for sale in the Terlingua Trading Co. bookstore/gift shop (tel. 915-371-2234) in Terlingua, Texas (on the outskirts of Big Bend National Park).

Other Considerations

Accommodations: Although the Chihuahua state tourist office doesn't list them, every town that has a train station has at least one place to stay, often a rustic hotel or guesthouse that costs US$7-10 per night for a spartan room with *baño colectivo*. Simple meals can usually be ordered with a couple of hours' advance notice. It isn't necessary to stay in the highly visible, US$80-plus-per-night, all-inclusive tourist hotels, though they are definitely more comfortable. Specific hotels and guesthouses in all price categories are cited under the appropriate destination sections below.

Camping: Although most of the sierra's annual precipitation falls in the late summer, a danger of flash floods in arroyos (streambeds or gullies) is present year-round. *Never* camp in an arroyo. Almost any flat area on high ground will make a suitable campsite. Shallow caves and rock overhangs are common along some trails, though you may find yourself sharing space with Tarahumaras on the move from one part of the sierra to another. Wilderness etiquette demands you offer something to eat or drink to camp companions as a gesture of courtesy.

Except in the early summer, when a two-season or even summer-weight sleeping bag will suffice from rim to river, you'll need a good three-season bag rated to around -4° C (25° F)—possibly with an insulating liner for cold nights—to cover all elevations.

For a more general discussion of hiking and backpacking in Northern Mexico, read "Hiking and Backpacking," p. 41. Also see "Climate and Seasons," above, for important weather concerns.

Getting Around: Local buses are available between the larger towns and villages, but usually run only once a day or perhaps no more than two or three times per week. If you're driving your own vehicle, note that the nearest gas station with Magna Sin (unleaded) is in La Junta, 102 km from Creel. Creel is supposedly getting a Magna Sin pump. At the moment only Nova (leaded) is available.

Nonhikers

If for some reason you're not able to hike in the canyons, and you don't have your own vehicle, you can still enjoy the scenery by arranging for day or overnight visits by vehicle from most of the highland hotels in Creel or Posada Barrancas, or by taking a train tour.

Train Tours

For those with more money than time, several U.S. and Mexican tour operators organize package tours in conjunction with the Chihuahua al Pacífico railway. One company that continually receives the best reports and has the most flexible itineraries is **Columbus Travel** (tel. 800-843-1060, fax 210-885-2010; Rt. 12, Box 382-B, New Braunfels, TX 78132-9701). Columbus operates basic trips of three, four, seven, and 10 nights, in addition to customized trips of virtually any length for individuals or small groups. Most tours allow the option of choosing Los Mochis, Chihuahua, El Paso, or Presidio (Texas) as gateways.

Currently, Columbus's basic trips out of Chihuahua or Los Mochis cost about US$469 (three nights/four days) to US$1,359 (10 nights/11

CHIHUAHUA AL PACÍFICO RAIL JOURNEY

Known as the "Q" line among FNM officials or the "Copper Canyon train" among tourists, Mexico's Chihuahua al Pacífico is the most spectacular train ride in North America in terms of both scenery and sheer engineering marvels. Some railroad buffs have gone so far as to claim it the world's most scenic railroad line under 1,000 km.

What makes this 674-km (418-mile) rail line between Mexico's Altiplano and the Sea of Cortez coast so awe-inspiring is the way it winds through a conifer-forested Sierra Madre canyon complex four times larger than the Grand Canyon, then drops 2,400 meters (8,000 feet) onto the tropical-arid coastal plains. Along the way the railway passes over 37 bridges, threads 86 tunnels, and crosses the Continental Divide three times.

The most sensational section is around Témoris (Km 707), where three levels of bridges, tunnels, and viaducts all converge into a canyon formed by the Río Septontrión. Looking over this scene from one of the rail cars is like finding yourself miniaturized and magically transported into an elaborate toy train setup. Between Km 688 and 708 the railway threads 16 tunnels carved into the edge of the canyon.

History

The mountains and canyons of the Sierra Madre Occidental have been a major transportation challenge ever since the mid-19th century, when road and rail engineers began seeking a way to link the

fertile Chihuahua plains (and the American Midwest) with a west-coast shipping route. The Chihuahua-Topolobampo route was first conceived by American railway engineer and utopian impresario Albert Kinsey Owens when he arrived in Mexico in 1861. After choosing Bahía Oguira (Topolobampo) as the western rail terminus, Owens formed a Mexican-American company in 1863 to design the project and was granted a contract by the Mexican government to build a railway between Piedras Negras and Topolobampo, with branch lines to Mazatlán, Alamos, and Ojinaga.

After Owens failed to produce sufficient funds to begin construction, his contracts were taken over by Foster Higgins and his Rio Grande, Sierra Madre, and Pacific Railway Company. Higgins and company were able to complete a 259-km railway between Ciudad Juárez and Casas Grandes in the state of Chihuahua in 1898 before throwing in the towel.

Along came entrepreneur Enrique Creel and his Kansas City, Mexico, and Orient Railroad, who completed a Casas Grandes-La Junta line between 1910 and 1914. Creel also started the Ojinaga-Chihuahua-Creel section of the railroad but left it unfinished in 1914 due to revolutionary attacks along the route. Although Creel is often given credit for the entire Chihuahua al Pacífico line, the truth is that he only established the least challenging sections at the line's eastern end.

continued

In the early years the Chihuahua-Creel stretch took two or three days (four hours today); the train would stop anywhere along the line for passengers and it is said that 90% of the trains derailed at least once per journey. Passengers helped lever the cars back onto the tracks and stopped to chop wood along steeper grades to fire up enough steam to get the train over the top.

By the turn of the century various small American and Mexican companies had extended a rail line east from Topolobampo to El Fuerte and in 1927-28 the Mexican government finished the Chihuahua-Ojinaga section begun by Creel. This left a gap of around 260 km (161 miles) in the most difficult Sierra Tarahumara terrain, with an elevation change of roughly 2,100 meters (7,000 feet). In 1940 the government nationalized the railway companies at both ends of the line and in 1953 announced plans to complete the route.

After 18 years of tunneling and laying track, the gap was finally closed in Nov. 1961, almost exactly 100 years after Albert Owens had pronounced his vision. The final construction tab was over US$100 million. The Chihuahua al Pacífico train became part of the Ferrocarriles Nacional de México system in 1987.

Until the 1992 paving of the Chihuahua-Hermosillo highway, the Chihuahua al Pacífico line was the only commercially viable land route across the Sierra Madre Occidental. The train remains the most direct route from central and northeastern Mexico to the nation's deepest port, Topolobampo.

Train Highlights
From Los Mochis, the Chihuahua al Pacífico moves from sugarcane fields and truck farms along the coastal plains to the chaparral of the Sierra Madre Occidental foothills near El Fuerte. East of Loreto (Km 791), lower mountain valleys cloaked in oak, juniper, piñon, and agave rise along either side of the line.

As the elevation increases, ponderosa pine and Douglas fir begin appearing as the line moves from Madrean evergreen woodland to montane conifer forest. With increasing elevation, scenic tributary canyons or arroyos break into the main canyons cut by the Fuerte and Septentrión rivers as mean annual precipitation rises to as high as 114 cm (45 inches) in the upper heights. About 75% of this rain falls between July and September, making late September or early October an especially beautiful time of year to make the trip.

Other landmarks and points of interest along the way include:

*Km 942 **Topolobampo,** western terminus of the line

*Km 921 **Los Mochis,** bustling commercial center where most train tourists board or disembark

*Km 882 **Sufragio,** rail junction with FNM's Del Pacífico line (north-south service between Nogales/Mexicali and Guadalajara)

*Km 805 **Puente del Río Fuerte,** at 491 meters (1,637 feet), the longest bridge along the line

*Km 748 **Puente de Chínipas,** the highest rail bridge (106 meters/355 feet above the Río Chínipas) along the route

*Km 707-8 **Témoris,** three parallel levels of track curving around one another

*Km 703 **Placa Conmemorativa,** marking the spot where crews working from both ends of the line finally met in 1961

*Km 665 **Bahuichivo,** jumping-off point for road trips to Cerocahui and Urique

*Km 662 **Cuiteco.** Between here and Km 647 are nine tunnels totaling 1,504 meters (4,933 feet) and five bridges totaling 641 meters (2,103 feet)

*Km 639 **Puente de la Laja** (212 meters long, 65 meters high), the first bridge in Mexico built with reinforced concrete beams

*Km 622 **Divisadero,** a major sightseeing stop for sweeping views over the Barranca del Cobre (Copper Canyon), one of six major canyons in the Sierra Tarahumara

*Km 592 **El Lazo,** where the line makes a 360° loop over itself, first over and then under a rail bridge

*Km 583 **Los Ojitos,** the highest point (2,421 meters/8,071 feet) along the line

*Km 564 **Creel,** Barranca del Cobre's tourist headquarters and starting point for trips to Cusárare and Batopilas

*Km 562 **Continental Tunnel** (1,260 meters/4,133 feet long), so named because it pierces the Continental Divide

*Km 531 **San Juanito,** a lumber town (elev. 2,400 meters/8,000 feet) that typically registers the coldest annual temperatures in Mexico

*Km 451 **La Junta,** where the Chihuahua al Pacífico is joined by the Bosques de Chihuahua freight line, a major carrier of timber from the northern Sierra Madre Occidental; a major rail workshop for the Q line is located here

*Km 401 **Cuauhtémoc,** agricultural trade center for Chihuahua's Mennonite colonies

*Km 268 **Chihuahua,** capital of the state of Chihuahua and a rail junction where separate lines (carrying mostly freight) continue to Ojinaga (connecting with the Atchison, Topeka, and Santa Fe railroad in Presidio, Texas) and Ciudad Juárez (connecting with the Southern Pacific, Union Pacific, and Atchison, Topeka, and Santa Fe railways in El Paso, Texas)

Train Riding Tips

When the trains run on time, it really doesn't matter whether you travel westbound or eastbound, as the most spectacular points (Divisadero, Témoris) are reached in mid-afternoon in either direction. If the westbound train (No. 74) is running late, however, you risk not seeing Témoris—which is scheduled for a 4:30 p.m. arrival going west, 11:11 a.m. going east—in the winter when the sun sets early. Hence if your main objective is the train ride itself (as opposed to stopping over in the Sierra Tarahumara for a few days), the journey is best taken from the western end. Although many people start the trip in Los Mochis, it is just as well begun in El Fuerte since the scenery isn't that spectacular until well east of El Fuerte.

Overall, the best views are seen from the south side of the train, i.e., the left side westbound or the right side eastbound. Since the train windows are rarely kept clean enough for an unobstructed view, passengers often crowd onto the small platforms between cars for a look at the passing scenery. Wear clothes you don't mind getting dirty if you anticipate standing between cars—the dust and diesel soot outside may not be noticeable at first but they have a definite cumulative effect.

There is no checked baggage for personal items (unless you're dealing with FNM's cargo department), but overhead space is ample for most bags. Seats—arranged four across in pairs—usually recline in first-class cars and there's plenty of leg room. If the train isn't full, you can easily change cars when necessary (e.g., when the a/c or heating system in your car isn't working properly).

Food service is available but you'll do better to bring your own snacks along. A styrofoam-boxed (and unrefrigerated) sandwich with Coke costs around US$4.75. Beer and soft-drink service is more dependable.

For details on Chihuahua al Pacífico fares, see the "Transport by Train" section under "Los Mochis," p. 180; for departure and arrival times, see the "Railway Schedule," pp. 86-87. Advance train reservations can be made by writing to the Jefe, Depto. Reg. Pasajeros, Ferrocarriles Nacional de Mexico, P.O. Box 46, Chihuahua, Chihuahua. Tickets are also available at each train station along the line an hour before departure.

days) per person; El Paso or Presidio departures cost roughly US$80-100 more. The company can also arrange hiking, burro, and backpacking trips in the Barranca del Cobre area.

Another reputable stateside company that sometimes works in conjunction with Columbus is **Adobe Tours** (contact through Columbus Travel above). Of particular interest is Adobe's yearly 11-day Semana Santa trip, which includes tours of Chihuahua, Los Mochis, and Topolobampo along with visits to Tarahumara villages in the Barranca de Urique for the climax of Holy Week (see the special topic "The Tarahumaras," pp. 290-293, for details on Semana Santa traditions in the Sierra Tarahumara).

Balderrama Tours at Hotel Santa Anita in Los Mochis offers two economical, no-frills package trips. A two-night/three-day package includes roundtrip rail tickets between Los Mochis

and Creel, overnight stops in Cuiteco and Creel, and all meals (except lunch in Creel) and transfers for US$135 per person. A two-day package only goes as far as Divisadero, with one overnight stop in Cuiteco, plus all meals and transfers, for US$100.

Hotel Colinas in Los Mochis advertises mid-price packages of US$365 s, US$512 d for four nights/five days; or US$418 s, US$575 d for five nights/six days. The price includes rail transport, tours, hotel, and some meals.

Finally, **Tauck Tours** (tel. 800-468-2825; P.O. Box 5027, Westport, CT 06881) offers a deluxe eight-day rail package aboard the privately owned Sierra Madre Express from Nogales, Son. to Creel, Chih. and back, with side trips by bus to Alamos and Tucson. The Sierra Madre Express consists of five Pullman cars, including a dining car, lounge car, two sleeping cars and an observation dome car. Departures are scheduled during the periods of Feb. 18-May 20 and Sept. 30-Nov. 18 only; the cost is US$2235-2325 per double stateroom and includes all transport from Tucson, two nights of onboard train accommodations, two nights of hotel accommodations in the Barranca del Cobre, one night's hotel each in Tucson and El Fuerte, all meals, and guided excursions.

Arizona AAA Travel Agency (tel. 800-352-5382 in Arizona) offers a similar itineray, but uses bus transport between Phoenix/Tucson and El Fuerte (with side trips to Guaymas and Alamos), then the Chihuahua al Pacífico train to Cuauhtémoc, then a bus to Casas Grandes and back to Tucson/Phoenix via Palomas. The cost is US$789 per person, including roundtrip motorcoach, rail transport, five nights' hotel, eight meals, and guide service.

CREEL

Named for railroad tycoon Enrique Creel, this overgrown logging village of around 3,000 residents is the most popular base for extended Sierra Tarahumara explorations. It's at Km 564 (counting from Chihuahua) along the Chihuahua al Pacífico rail line at an altitude of 2,338 meters (7,668 feet), the second-highest stop along the line (San Juanito to the north is 10 meters higher).

Spreading across a wide, gentle-sloped arroyo, Creel is a strange mix of frontier town and tourist haven, a place where *vaqueros* riding horses meet gringos in Ford Broncos at the same intersection. Although wags may say it's getting too touristed for its own good, the truth is that most of the time Creel's attention remains focused on logging. And the town does make a good base for excursions in the surrounding forests as well as to three nearby canyons: Barranca de Tararécua, Barranca del Cobre, and Barranca de Batopilas.

For vistas of the town, climb the hill (elev. 2,410 meters/7,905 feet, about 72 meters/236 feet above Creel) west of the rail station to the cement Cristo Rey statue. The lower Cerro Chapultepec, east of Av. López Mateos, offers a view that requires less legwork.

Surrounding Creel are several Tarahumara settlements and mission villages consisting of timber houses, cave dwellings, and small corn and vegetable plots. Other attractions include **Valle de los Hongos** ("Valley of Mushrooms"), an area of mushroom-shaped rock formations about three km south of Creel, and **Lago Arareco,** a scenic, horseshoe-shaped lake ringed by huge boulders and pine woodlands seven km south of Creel off the road to Cusárare.

Accommodations

Creel basically offers three types of accommodations: small, traditional hotels oriented toward Mexican visitors or small-timers in the logging business; guesthouses for hikers and backpackers on shoestring budgets; and a couple of motels for package tourists and travelers seeking Creel's most comfortable rooms.

Next door to the small bus terminal, above the railroad tracks, is the fairly clean and adequate **Hotel Korachi,** which has simple rooms with shared bath for US$8.30 s, US$10-13.30 d, US$16.60 t, and US$20 q. Only the hallways are heated, so in peak cold weather you might suffer a bit if you don't have a warm sleeping bag to throw over the bed. In back of the hotel are a few cabins with private baths and small woodstoves for US$16.60 s, US$23.30 d, US$33.30 t, US$40 q.

A couple of doors down from the Korachi is the similar **Hotel Nuevo,** which costs US$23.30 s/d. Non-functioning baths and toilets are attached to the rooms; a better *baño colectivo* is located down the hall. Nearby, the **Posada** (formerly the Hotel Chavez) has very bare rooms with outhouse-style bathrooms and indifferent service for US$10 per person.

The relatively new **Pensión Creel** (tel. 145-6-00-71, fax 145-6-02-00) offers eleven well-maintained rooms in a rustic stone building at the south end of Av. López Mateos (No. 61) about 800 meters (a half mile) from the plaza and train station. Some rooms sleep two persons while a few sleep up to four. Rates are US$10 per person and include breakfast; a kitchen is also available where guests may cook for themselves. A large dining/sitting room with a fireplace contains an information board with bus and train schedules, local maps, and information on nearby hikes. Mountain bikes and some camping equipment are available for rent. The *pensión* is within hiking distance of several local attractions (see "Excursions From Creel," below) and also offers reasonably priced trips to Lago Arareco, Cusárare Falls; the *aguas calientes* at Recohuata; El Tejabán; and the Urique, Batopilas, and Cobre canyons. All things considered, this is the most convenient backpacker's center in town.

The old backpacker's standby, **Casa de Margarita's,** seems like a rabbit warren by comparison, though if you enjoy a lively atmosphere (it's on the plaza and is near all the bars and restaurants) you may find Margarita's to your liking. Rates vary from US$6 per person in a dorm to US$10-20 for tiny rooms (s/d/t) with private bath; rates include breakfast and dinner. Margarita's has added a newer, upscale section in a separate building down by the river; these rooms cost US$40 (including breakfast at the main lodge) for comfortable accommodations and private bath.

Motel Cascada Inn (tel./fax 145-6-01-51), down the street at Av. López Mateos 49, has comfortable rooms with private bath and heating for US$42.60 s, US$46 d, US$60 t, US$69 (add US$27 per person for three meals per day). The motel also has a parking lot and a restaurant/bar.

Next door to the Cascada Inn is the **Motel Parador de la Montaña** (tel. 145-6-00-75, fax 145-15-34-68 in Chihuahua) at Av. López Mateos 41, where spacious rooms with private bath and heat (but cold tile floors) cost US$60 s/d, US$63 t. Add another US$28 per person for full board. Both the Cascada Inn and Margarita's upscale rooms are better value than the Parador, whose standards have fallen over the years.

Opposite the Parador and Cascada Inn, **Casa de Valenzuela** and **Hotel Tarahumara** have basic rooms for rent for US$10-15. A few other on-again, off-again *casas de huéspedes* in the area also rent rooms in this price range.

The owners of Pensión Creel plan to build a new hotel called Sierra Madre Lodge on a slope behind town. Rates are projected to be US$60-80 a night for first-class accommodations.

Camping

About three km (two miles) south of Creel on the way to Cusárare (near the lake) is a posted public camping area where you can pitch tents for free. Water and trash service are available. Creel has no RV parks, but self-contained rigs

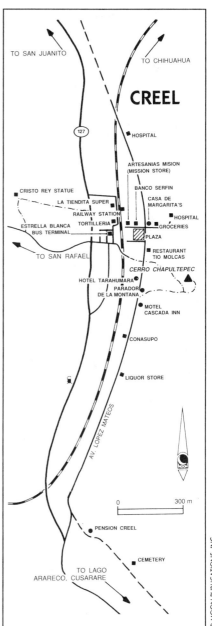

CREEL

TO SAN JUANITO
TO CHIHUAHUA
HOSPITAL
ARTESANIAS MISION (MISSION STORE)
CRISTO REY STATUE
BANCO SERFIN
LA TIENDITA SUPER
CASA DE MARGARITA'S
RAILWAY STATION
HOSPITAL
ESTRELLA BLANCA BUS TERMINAL
TORTILLERIA
GROCERIES
PLAZA
TO SAN RAFAEL
RESTAURANT TIO MOLCAS
CERRO CHAPULTEPEC
HOTEL TARAHUMARA
PARADOR DE LA MONTANA
MOTEL CASCADA INN
CONASUPO
LIQUOR STORE
AV. LOPEZ MATEOS
0   300 m
PENSION CREEL
CEMETERY
TO LAGO ARARECO, CUSARARE

can park in the Parador or Cascada Inn lots for a nominal fee.

Food

Creel's simple eateries are concentrated along Av. López Mateos between the plaza and the Parador de la Montaña. **Restaurant Veronica** serves good *pollo asado* as well as a decent *comida corrida*. Popular among hikers and backpackers is the funky **Restaurant Tío Molcas,** which does a small range of *antojitos.* Similar restaurants along the "strip" are the **Restaurant Cabaña** and **Restaurant Lupita.**

For North American food and steak, **The Steakhouse** at Motel Cascada Inn is somewhat popular. The clean **Taco Creel Pub Grill** opposite the Parador has good tacos.

A couple of small grocery stores can also be found along Av. López Mateos.

Bus

Estrella Blanca operates the main inter-city bus service in Creel; the small terminal is next to Hotel Korachi above the train tracks. To or from Chihuahua, the four-hour bus trip costs US$8.60, with seven to eight departures per day.

Train

The first-class Chihuahua al Pacífico train (US$13) arrives from Chihuahua around 12:30 p.m. daily; from Los Mochis (US$15) it arrives at 3:15 p.m. The slower and more crowded Tarahumara or *pollero,* over two-thirds less expensive than the Chihuahua al Pacífico, is scheduled to arrive at 2 a.m. from Chihuahua or 5:05 p.m. from Los Mochis, but it isn't unusual for the train to run up to two hours late.

Driving

The drive to Creel along Mexico 16 from La Junta, Cuauhtémoc, or Chihuahua is fairly smooth all the way. At this writing, the Creel PEMEX station pumps only Nova, so be sure to top off with Magna Sin in La Junta on the way if your vehicle takes unleaded fuel. Creel will supposedly be getting a Magna Sin pump in the near future. Beyond Creel the road is good as far as Lago Arareco and Cusárare, after which only rugged vehicles with off-highway capacities should continue.

Money

Despite what other guidebooks might say, traveler's checks can easily be cashed at Banco Serfin.

Post And Telephone

The town post office is on the plaza, opposite the Tarahumara mission store. The local area code is 145.

EXCURSIONS FROM CREEL

For hikers the topo map to have is the Creel G13A22 1:50,000-scale quadrangle, usually available at the Tarahumara mission store on the plaza (or from the INEGI office in Hermosillo, Sonora).

Good destinations for day-trips include placid Lago Arareco (five km from the south edge of town) and **San Ignacio de Arareco,** a Tarahumara mission village only two km east of Pensión Creel. Valle de los Hongos ("Valley of Mushrooms") and **Cueva de Sebastián** are short walks from the mission. A further 3.5 km northeast of San Ignacio is **Valle de los Monjes** ("Valley of Monks"), a set of peculiar rock formations that look vaguely like hooded, robed monks. A dirt road continues on from San Ignacio 16 km (10 miles) via the tiny hamlet of Gonogochi to the rim of a medium-sized canyon formed by the Río Conchos.

Longer, multiday trips can be arranged either on your own, using other Sierra Tarahumara towns (such as Cusárare, Batopilas, Cerocahui, or Urique) as springboards, or through local hotels and guesthouses. Pensión Creel, for example, offers a two-day car trip to Batopilas, at the bottom of Barranca de Batopilas, for US$35 per person; they also offer a hiking trip to **El Tejabán** on the edge of the Barranca del Cobre, with a descent to the Río Urique at the canyon bottom and back, for US$80-98 per person depending on mode of transport chosen. If you want to do the El Tejabán trip on your own, however, it's better to use Cusárare as a base.

A more challenging trip from Creel would be the trek to the **Recohuata Hot Springs** in Barranca de Tararécua, about 10 km south of Lago Arareco via logging roads—study a topographic map before setting out and don't go without a compass. You may also be able to reach the springs by following the river all the way from the lake through the canyon, but for this you will definitely need a guide who knows the arroyo. The canyon rim near the hot springs (about a 45-minute walk) can be reached by off-highway vehicle from Creel or Cusárare if you prefer doing it the easy way.

Before deciding on which hikes or day-trips to take, it's a good idea to talk to other travelers who have been in the sierra awhile for personal recommendations—Margarita's and Pensión Creel are good places to get this kind of word-of-mouth information. After talking to a few people, you may be able to customize your own trips, hiring burros, guides, and cooks as needed. The standard fee at Pensión Creel for each of these is US$15 per day.

San Juanito

From the smell of wood smoke to the stacks of timber in all directions, you'll know this small town 30 km north of Creel is almost totally dedicated to the lumber business. Few visitors stop here except for fuel (PEMEX with Nova only) or groceries. In addition to a Banamex, the town has several grocery stores and *cafeterías,* an Estrella Blanca bus terminal, and the rustic **Motel Posada del Cobre,** where rooms are available for US$16-18 per night.

A gravel road leads 70 km northwest from San Juanito to Basaseachic Falls (see "Basaseachic Falls National Park," p. 297). For anyone wishing to visit the falls by vehicle from Creel, this is a quicker route than doubling back all the way to Mexico 16 near La Junta, in spite of the fact that Mexico 16 is a paved highway.

Cusárare

A Tarahumara name meaning "Place of Eagles," Cusárare is a collection of native *ranchitos* fanning out from a scenic gorge formed by the Arroyo de Cusárare. The main village of the same name is centered around an 18th-century mission church of minor interest.

One of the most popular day hikes in the region is to **Cusárare Falls** via a trail from the Copper Canyon Sierra Lodge, the only tourist accommodations in the area. From the lodge parking lot, the trail heads west parallel to a

stream, about an hour's leisurely walk each way. The trail crosses the stream three times but is fairly easy to follow. Along the way are several sandy "beaches" (the water is cold but swimmable in the summer), huge boulders, and shady idylls. Local Tarahumaras use the same trail and you're likely to come across a few basket-and-trinket vendors. Keep an eye out also for the eared trogon, a small, iridescent, orange-feathered bird related to the sacred quetzal of the Aztecs.

The falls themselves are 30 meters (98 feet) high and very broad, but not thundering; when the water is low you can walk across the top of the falls and peer into the stream below. For the best view of the falls, look for a path that leads past the falls on your left. Sometimes a park entry fee of US$1 is collected by a local Tarahumara *ejidatario* standing on the trail with a book of tickets.

Other short hikes in the area can be made to the **Cueva Pintada** (a rock shelter with polychromatic pictographs of undetermined age)—a 40-minute roundtrip walk that passes Tarahumara *ranchitos*—and to **Cusárare village,** about an hour roundtrip on foot (2.5 km/1.5 miles upstream if you follow the stream in the opposite direction from the falls). Ask at the lodge for a key to the mission church before setting off for the latter. Beyond Cusárare the trail continues east for three to four km to the bucolic Tarahumara hamlets of Gomírachi and Chochípachi. Tarahumara children will sometimes volunteer to serve as guides for these short hikes for an expected tip of around US$0.40 per visitor.

Guides for longer hikes to **Recohuata Hot Springs** can be arranged through the Copper Canyon Sierra Lodge at a cost of US$10-13 per day per guide. Horseback trail rides can also be arranged for US$3.50 per hour per horse plus an additional US$3.50 per hour per guide. The trek to Recohuata takes three to five hours each way, which includes a 300-meter (thousand-foot) descent into the Tararécua Canyon. Geothermals exit the north wall of the canyon near the headwaters of the Río Tararécua and are piped into a primitive concrete bathhouse smelling of sulfur and mineral salts and just a bit warmer than the average air temperature. According to John Fayhee's whimsical Tararécua Canyon chronicle, a better, lesser-known hot spring is only a half day's hike downstream. Beyond this point the canyon is filled with boulders that are very difficult to negotiate.

Trips to **El Tejabán,** a ranchería overlooking the Barranca del Cobre, usually involve a four-hour drive along logging roads, then an hour's hike into the canyon. Although the view over the canyon from El Tejabán is one of the sierra's most beautiful, it's probably not worth the eight-hour roundtrip drive unless you plan to make it an overnight camping trip.

Accommodations: The **Copper Canyon Sierra Lodge** (formerly the Sierra Madre Lodge, and known locally as Cabañas Cañon del Cobre) is the only place to stay in Cusárare. Built of logs and other native materials, the 23-room lodge is delightfully quiet and rustic, and is staffed by Tarahumaras from the local *ejido* (the lodge sits on *ejido* lands). Each room has a small woodstove (and supply of wood), a couple of kerosene lanterns, a private bathroom with hot shower, and comfortable furnishings.

Rooms are offered only as part of an eight-day trip that starts with one night in Chihuahua at Hotel Palacio del Sol, then two nights at the Sierra Lodge, three nights at the Riverside Lodge in Batopilas, another night at the Sierra Lodge, and the final night in Chihuahua again. During high season (mid-December to mid-January and mid-March to mid-May) the cost is US$1300 per person double occupancy or US$1400 single, rates which include all ground transport (including Chihuahua-Creel-Chihuahua train tickets), all meals, guided excursions, and lodging. Regular season rates are US$250-300 less. These trips run every Saturday and Monday year-round except for two weeks in June.

For information or reservations, contact **Copper Canyon Lodges** (in Mexico tel. 145-6-01-79, fax 145-6-00-36; in the U.S./Canada tel. 313-689-2444 or 800-776-3942, fax 313-689-9119) 1100 Owendale Dr., Suite G, Troy, MI 48083.

Camping: There are no campgrounds in the area, but you might try asking for permission to camp in the *ejido* near the Cueva Pintada, or else simply pitch a tent in the woods along the trail to the falls.

Transport: Ay, there's the rub. Unless you have reservations to stay at the Copper Canyon Sierra Lodge (in which case you'll be met at the train station and driven to the lodge), you'll have to arrange your own transport. Cusárare is 23 km from Creel via the road to Batopilas, though the lodge (and trailhead for the Cusárare Falls hike) is beyond the turnoff for Cusárare off the main road. It's possible to hitchhike but you can't count on catching rides in both directions on the same day. A taxi from Creel costs US$25 one way.

BATOPILAS

In a turn of phrase more suitable for a travel brochure than a realistic appraisal, a 1992 issue of *National Geographic Traveler* attempted to evoke Batopilas with "Imagine Tahiti, Treasure Island, hidden away in the bottom of the Grand Canyon . . ." You'll be hard pressed to find anything obviously reminiscent of Tahiti or Treasure Island in Batopilas, although there's probably more potential for adventure here than anywhere in Tahiti or the Society Islands. Perhaps it was the tropical fruit—mangoes, papayas, oranges, bananas, avocados—growing here that infected the writer's imagination. Gold is mined in the Batopilas area, but it's mostly of the "green" variety, the cultivation and trade of which is a source of local cash (though this doesn't mean that Batopilas is an unsafe place to visit as long as you stay aloof from the trade). About half the population is of Tarahumara descent.

The first vehicle road to Batopilas was constructed only around 15 years ago, but the town chronology goes back over 350 years. Spanish *adelantados* (advance guard) arrived in 1632 and found pure silver on the river banks. Because river currents polished it to a smooth white finish, the Spaniards called it *plata nevada* ("snowy silver") and soon established a mine called Mina Nevada and a town called San Pedro de Batopilas (the latter a corruption of the Tarahumara description *bachotigori,* meaning "near the river"). Native silver masses weighing up to 200 kilos apiece weren't unusual in the early years. After the Spanish left, Mexicans and Americans took over the mines and added many more, the biggest of which were the turn-of-the-century holdings of Alexander Shepherd's Batopilas Mining Company.

Batopilas's historical legacy shows in the town's late 19th-century architecture, but the ambience is much sleepier than it must have been during the silver mining heyday. Mule trains with dubious cargo from nearby villages put in for supplies, and a few prospectors still pay with gold or silver nuggets from clandestine mines. Horses are as common as cars or trucks. Travelers with flexible schedules often find themselves lingering in Batopilas for longer than originally planned in order to savor the history and atmosphere, and to explore the many trails fanning out from the town.

A carpenter next to Plaza Constitución at the south end of town makes custom Tarahumara-style sandals—tire strips laminated with leather and tied to the ankle with a long leather thong.

Hacienda San Miguel

Alexander Shepherd administered his silver empire from this site on the east side of the Río Batopilas, about a kilometer northeast of the town center. His Hacienda San Miguel lies in brick ruins, among which are the remains of an assay office, refectory, boardinghouse, corral and stables, machine shop, iron foundry, ingot mill, and amalgamation sheds. At one time an 800-meter aerial tram linked canyon slopes on both sides of the river. Much of the current attraction is botanic and exploring the ruins is a bit of a jungle walk; several large fig trees grow on the compound walls and the tallest building is overgrown with a huge bougainvillea plant, while shorter trees and plants occupy the remainder of the grounds. When I last visited, someone was reconstructing one of the smaller buildings on the property for use as a living space.

You must cross the bridge (originally built by Shepherd and company) at the north entrance of town to reach the ruins. The front gate to the hacienda is usually open during the day—ask in town first to make sure.

Church

In the middle of town is an older church with ore fragments studding the lower interior walls, a telltale sign that it was built by miners. Along one wall is a Christ-in-a-box used annually for Easter processions, and in a niche on the opposite wall is a black saint.

Aqueduct And Dam

This functioning stone marvel was built by Shepherd and company nearly a hundred years ago to provide a constant water supply for the town and to generate hydroelectric power. Batopilas

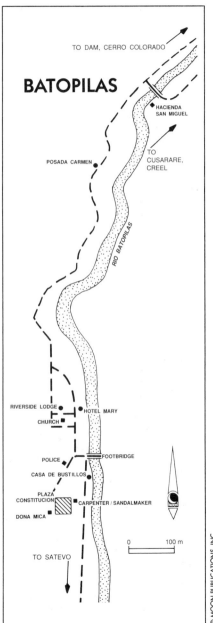

BATOPILAS

TO DAM, CERRO COLORADO

HACIENDA SAN MIGUEL

POSADA CARMEN

TO CUSARARE, CREEL

RÍO BATOPILAS

RIVERSIDE LODGE

HOTEL MARY

CHURCH

POLICE

FOOTBRIDGE

CASA DE BUSTILLOS

PLAZA CONSTITUCIÓN

CARPENTER / SANDALMAKER

DONA MICA

TO SATEVO

0   100 m

© MOON PUBLICATIONS, INC.

still relies on the structure for its main water supply (several *ranchitos* north of town irrigate their crops via the aqueduct) and in 1988 hydroelectric capabilities were reinstalled. A walk north along the trail below the aqueduct leads to the simple stone dam across the Río Batopilas, a great spot for cooling off on a hot day. For more detail on this outing, see "Hikes from Batopilas," below.

THE BATOPILAS MINING COMPANY

Since 1632 more than 300 mines, claims, and veins have been worked in the Batopilas district, most of which were established at an elevation of 700-1,200 meters. The Nuestra Señora del Pilar mine, founded around 1730, yielded 40,000 pesos a week for nearly 30 years. Mining subsided immediately after the Spanish expulsion in 1820, but new mines were started by Mexicans in 1842. In 1861 American John Robinson bought an older property of two mines thought to be worked out.

Robinson was completing a tunnel between the two mines when he came upon a blind vein that came to be known as La Veta Grande or "Great Vein," a major source of native silver. Transport of the raw ore to Chihuahua for processing seemed prohibitively expensive, however, and Robinson sold the so-called San Miguel Tunnel to Alexander Robey Shepherd for US$600,000 in 1880.

Shepherd had been the last governor of Washington, D.C. before the U.S. government removed him from office (and banished the D.C. governorship altogether) in the 1870s for alleged corruption in public works. (The accusations were never proven, and, due to Shepherd's efforts to upgrade Washington's public works, the U.S. government canceled its plans to move the U.S. capital to St. Louis.) Following the purchase of the tunnel, Shepherd moved to Batopilas with his family and soon filed over 350 other claims in a 31-square-km area, with total underground workings encompassing 120 km. His holdings were consolidated as the Batopilas Mining Company, and this town at the bottom of a deep canyon soon became one of the wealthiest spots in Mexico.

Shepherd wisely constructed his own amalgamating/retorting facility and foundry at his Hacienda San Miguel on the river, and between 1880 and 1906 approximately 20 million ounces of silver were extracted from the company mines. At the 1893 Chicago World's Fair, silver ore from his mines took first place in the competition with a solid silver mass weighing 172 kilograms (380 pounds). Shepherd's company cast the processed silver into bars weighing 30 kilograms each, then loaded them two per mule into monthly bullion trains that transported at least 50 and often 100-200 silver bars on the backs of 30-100 mules to the Banco Minero in Chihuahua. Pancho Villa once stole US$38,000 in silver bars from one of the company's mule trains, a deed that forever tainted Villa's reputation among gringo miners.

Most of the buildings standing in Batopilas today were constructed during the 1890s heyday of the Batopilas Mining Company. At the time, it took eight days to reach the town from Chihuahua—three days by rail and five on muleback—but Shepherd and company managed to ship in an incredible variety of cultural and technological accoutrements in spite of the town's remoteness. Hence Batopilas became one of the first places in North America (the second in Mexico) to have electricity. A local "Ladies Society" also restored the old church and hosted concerts, theater, dances, and even occasional operas.

By the time Shepherd died in 1902, the town's population had grown from 400 to around 5,000 (it is now around 600). The hydroelectric facility he installed on the river was restored in 1988 and once again powers the town, and his original aqueduct still provides the local water supply.

Shepherd's sons ceased operations in 1920, by which time the lion's share of the ore had already been extracted. At their peak, Shepherd's mines were the wealthiest in the world, paying around US$1 million in dividends per year. Other miners made unsuccessful attempts to get the mines going again as late as the 1940s.

Grant Shepherd, one of Alexander Shepherd's sons, has written *The Silver Magnet* (New York: E.P. Dutton, 1938), a detailed account of the Shepherd mining business and town history. Though a number of common Spanish words are strangely misspelled (e.g., chile and tequila), the book gives a good idea of what life in Batopilas must have been like at the turn of the century. Photos in the book show Batopilas hasn't changed much—at least physically—since 1895.

Satevó

One of the premier local attractions is this impressive, triple-domed mission church 6.5 km (four miles) south of Batopilas in the heart of Barranca de Batopilas, an easy half-day hike now that the road—part of the Camino Real—has been graded. Along the way you'll pass a quaint footbridge across the river as well as impressive views of the church and canyon in the distance.

The church itself is about 14 meters (48 feet) high from its base to the top of the naves, with a single bell tower extending another four meters or so which contains bells dated 1801, 1720, and 1630, plus others on which the dates are obscured. A long, shaky ladder inside the church leads to a *coro* overlooking the interior, and another ladder—short and shaky—leads into the bell tower. Climb with extreme caution. Still in use by the small Satevó community, the church also features whitewashed walls stained with berry juice to signify Christ's blood. Crypts beneath the flagstone floor reportedly hold the remains of Jesuit padres. The church is often locked on weekdays—you'll have to ask someone at the nearby general store to unlock it.

A few years ago an over-imaginative writer (Batopilas tends to get the pens working overtime) dubbed the Satevó church the "Lost Cathedral," but evidence suggests the church was never a cathedral (which requires the presence of an archbishop) and it was certainly never "lost" in the sense that locals and visitors didn't know of its existence—especially since it's on a branch of the Camino Real, Mexico's most well-known historical thoroughfare. The date of construction is indeed a mystery, but architectural styles suggest it was probably erected in the 17th century and may have been the original site of San Pedro de Batopilas. Since Jesuit records were often destroyed by the Franciscans when they took over church administration in the 18th century, the exact dating of the church will probably never be known (though if it had been a cathedral, not even the jealous Franciscans could have kept this secret from present-day historians).

The graded road to Satevó makes a hot and dusty walk—if you plan to walk, best go in the morning before it heats up. Traffic along the road to Satevó is almost nil, but you can hire a truck to drop you off at the church for around US$6 if you prefer not to walk both ways. Cold soft drinks are available at a small store near the church.

Semana Santa

As Barranca de Batopilas is a stronghold for less-assimilated Tarahumaras, the nearby villages are good places to observe Semana Santa celebrations (see special topic "The Tarahumaras," pp. 290-293, for detail on this festival and for visiting guidelines).

Accommodations

Little Batopilas has six places to spend the night, five of them quite basic but adequate for most hikers. **Posada Carmen,** near the bridge and north entrance to town, has the cheapest rooms at US$5-7 per night with a cold-water *baño colectivo*. The main drawback to staying here is that it's a fairly long walk to/from the center of town.

On the east side of the plaza that doubles as a basketball court, **Casa de Bustillos** is a favorite backpackers' hangout mainly because the owner-manager, Monse Bustillos, speaks English. Rooms cost US$7-10; guests share a cold-water bath or bathe in the river behind the house. The proprietor also sells Tarahumara artifacts and can arrange meals (including vegetarian) for US$5-6.60 per meal.

The nearby **Hotel Mary** (also known as Hotel Parador) opposite the town church costs US$8.30 for clean, simple rooms; the collective bathrooms sometimes have hot water. This is the most livable of the town's small hotels. **Hotel Batopilas,** three blocks north of the plaza opposite the massive Riverside Lodge, has small, plain rooms for US$5 per person with cold-water shared bath.

Occupying a huge block in the center of town is the two-story **Copper Canyon Riverside Lodge** (also known locally as Hotel Hacienda Batopilas), originally built around 1890 as a hacienda for a wealthy Mexican family and now a pet project of tour impresario Skip McWilliams. Batopilas has been called "wonderfully weird" and this hotel fits that description perfectly, a time-warp oasis in a remote corner of Mexico, inspired perhaps by A.R. Shepherd's Hacienda San Miguel. Mozart and Patsy Cline, emanating from a tape system in the parlor, drift across interior courtyards planted with kumquat and avocado trees. The parlor itself is furnished with Porfiriato antiques and sports a ceiling fresco depicting a whimsical history of Batopilas.

Other public areas include a Mexican-style prayer room, roof terrace, open-air dining room, and library containing historical literature and maps. Guest rooms, most of them with small colonial-style terraces overlooking the streets below, are large, comfortable, and well-furnished, with attached hot-water bathrooms. Although the kitchen, dining rooms, and parlor are electrified, the guest rooms are lamp-lit. The hotel does not take walk-in guests and only books rooms in conjunction with an eight-day package that includes accommodations in Cusárare and Chihuahua (see "Cusárare," above, for details on the package). Once you've sprung for the package deal, it's possible to book extra nights in Batopilas.

Food

Except for the well-prepared meals at the Riverside Lodge, food is not the town's strong suit. Though usually empty, **Restaurant Quinta Patio** at Hotel Mary is the town's most organized eatery, with a simple menu of *antojitos* that cost US$3-4 per person. Local legend **Doña Mica** serves home-cooked, ranchero-style meals on the front porch of her house (also known as Michaela's) south of the town's smaller plaza on a winding side street. It's best to let her know a few hours in advance if you want to dine on her front porch—sometimes you'll be offered a choice, but most often it's potluck. Señora Bustillos can arrange meals at her guesthouse as well.

Other than the above, your best bets are the local grocery stores, of which there are few. Locally grown fruits and vegetables are reasonably priced, while just about everything else is costly due to the long distances supplies must travel. (A horse that costs US$300 in Creel goes for US$1000 in Batopilas.)

Batopilas is a dry town, so alcoholic beverages can't legally be consumed, bought, or sold (the Riverside Lodge is an exception). A bootleg can of Tecate—the only beer available, under the table at certain stores—costs US$1.60. Lechugilla, a strong contraband liquor made from the succulent of the same name, is surprisingly expensive at nearly US$17 per liter.

Transport

Half the attraction in coming to Batopilas is the scenic road trip from Creel. Before this 135-km (84-mile) road was completed 15 years ago, a branch of the Camino Real—little more than a steep, winding path—was the only way in and out. The road is paved to a point just beyond Cusárare and then goes to gravel, winding down across the canyons of Basíhuare (40 km/25 miles from Creel) and Humirá (60 km/37 miles) before continuing to **Samachique,** a lumber settlement roughly halfway to Batopilas. Just before Samachique is a junction for another gravel road that heads southeast to Guachochi (90 km/56 miles from the junction) and onward to Mexico 24, which leads to Hidalgo del Parral. Past Samachique, the Creel-Batopilas road worsens considerably but the canyon scenery becomes very dramatic.

Descending into Barranca de Batopilas, the road then passes two small villages, the all-Tarahumara **Basigochi** and the mixed Tarahumara and mestizo **Quírare** (Kirare). The best view along the road comes after Quírare, where you can see deep into the canyon as the vegetation passes from alamillos (cottonwood) to oak to mesquite. Look for **Cerro El Pastel** ("Cake Hill"), named for its alternating layers of pink and white volcanic rock, on the left. A few kilometers beyond Quírare the road arrives at **La Bufa,** a scenic Río Batopilas crossing and site of a former silver mine, made obvious by the mounds of slag covering a nearby cliff. On your right you should be able to make out the Camino Real winding along the side of the canyon; this path is still used by Tarahumaras and prospectors, since for travel by foot or mule train it reaches the top more quickly than the newer vehicle road.

By car or truck, the road takes about five hours from Creel to Batopilas or vice versa. Needless to say, neither fuel nor mechanical assistance are available along the way (although you can buy Nova from barrels—at an elevated price—in Batopilas). Many of the curves along the way are blind and feature steep, unguarded drops; this is not a road for squeamish drivers.

Buses to Batopilas leave from Creel Tuesdays, Thursdays, and Saturdays at 4 a.m., usually arriving around noon (or later—depending on the passenger load and number of stops); the fare is less than US$8. The return bus to Creel leaves on Mondays, Wednesdays, and Fridays at the same hour but arrives in Creel at 9 or 10 a.m.; the ride uphill is faster than downhill because the driver doesn't have to pamper the brakes as much. The bus can be crowded and slow but is quite a cultural experience.

Hitchhiking can be very difficult along this road; if you're going to try it, early morning (5-7 a.m.) is the best time to start at either end. After 8 or 9 in the morning you can forget it.

Information

Batopilas has no banks or moneychangers, so bring plenty of cash; U.S. dollars are negotiable at most stores and hotels.

The ancient post office gets very little business and most people take their own mail to Creel or give it to friends or relatives going there. The town has a small clinic that can handle minor medical problems but not much else.

You may occasionally see armed soldiers in town when the Mexican army sweeps through Batopilas and the surrounding area to make a show of marijuana trade suppression. Although searches of gringos are rare these days, if you cheerfully cooperate with the search things will go smoothly and quickly.

HIKES FROM BATOPILAS

The INEGI topographic map to have for extensive canyon forays in the area is the Batopilas 1:50,000 quadrangle (G13A41).

Several moderate hikes north of town can be taken nearby without a guide. If you've just arrived, consider warming up to the territory with the relatively easy walks to Hacienda San Miguel and Satevó described above.

Aqueduct Trail

A pleasant half-day's outing can be made along the aqueduct north of town to the old dam. Actually there are two trails, one that runs below the aqueduct most of the way, another along the top of the aqueduct itself. The lower trail—a much-used section of the Camino Real—is shadier and more scenic, and it crosses a couple of small waterfalls formed by runoff from the aqueduct into the Río Batopilas. Walking across

or through these falls isn't a problem most of the year, but if the flow is heavy (usually during the July-Sept. rainy season), the trail over the top of the aqueduct will have to be used.

Along the way you'll pass nearby the Porfirio Díaz Mine (2,340 meters/7,800 feet long), above the aqueduct near the bridge—be sure to bring a flashlight along if you plan to explore this or other tunnels on the way. You'll also pass a few *ranchitos* that irrigate their fruit orchards directly from the aqueduct—farmers will sometimes offer oranges, avocados, or papayas for sale to passing hikers. Swimming is possible in places where the aqueduct meets the river.

The lower trail parallels the aqueduct most of the way, then rises gently over it at a place where the stone structure pierces a large boulder—an amazing engineering feat. At this point the lower trail is still paved with large stones left over from the days when the Camino Real was a major thoroughfare. Occasionally you'll meet mule trains, men on horseback, or Tarahumaras on foot carrying cargo in or out of the canyon.

At a leisurely pace it's about an hour's walk from the Río Batopilas bridge to the dam at the mouth of the aqueduct. Some of the best swimming spots in the river are found here. Beyond the dam, the trail turns westward from the river into the Arroyo Cerro Colorado and then continues northward to the villages of Cerro Colorado and Munérachi and eventually across the Barranca del Cobre to El Tejabán, where it meets a logging road to Cusárare.

Cerro Colorado-Munérachi

The Camino Real-aqueduct trail described above can be continued through the lovely Arroyo Cerro Colorado to the Mexican village of Cerro Colorado and Tarahumara village of Munérachi. Bring plenty of drinking water along, as this can be a hot day's slog.

From the dam the trail hooks left to the tiny village of Las Juntas (it's hard to miss, but you can use the village of Casas Colorados on the opposite side of the river as a landmark) and climbs along the left side of the canyon. From Las Juntas, follow the trail parallel to the canyon stream for about three hours to reach Cerro Colorado (a total of four hours from Batopilas). The trail crosses the stream several times along the way, providing opportunities to soak tired feet; in times of high water it may be necessary to detour to a higher trail parallel to the stream (there's one on each side of the stream). Along the way you'll pass a couple of smaller Mexican villages settled by small-time prospectors who practice placer mining. Keep an eye out for *tahonas,* rustic hand- or river-powered mills used to grind gold ore. In Cerro Colorado is a small store with beverages and a few groceries for sale.

Munérachi is another two to three hours upstream along Arroyo Cerro Colorado and Arroyo Munérachi (which branches northeast from Arroyo Cerro Colorado about an hour's walk from Cerro Colorado). Very little in the way of supplies is available in Munérachi, so don't come this far unless you're self-contained.

If you decide to make this an overnight hike from Batopilas, you can camp on the outskirts of Cerro Colorado or ask at the store about a room to rent in the village.

Beyond Munérachi it isn't advisable to continue without a guide because of the rugged terrain, number of intersecting trails, and relative lack of village life. With a guide, it's possible to reach El Tejabán to the north with another three days' hike through canyon and high forest country, or you can head west (via Cerro Colorado) to the town of Urique at the bottom of the Barranca de Urique in one day. Another option is to hike back to Cerro Colorado via Santa Rita, a small village below a mesa that reportedly affords outstanding views of Barranca de Batopilas.

Other Trails

The Batopilas area is honeycombed with footpaths through shady arroyos clouded with parrots and butterflies, along precipitous canyon walls, to crystal, sand-fringed springs, and over mountain peaks. **Arroyo las Minas** (north of town) and **Arroyo Huinolito** (just south) are two of the more challenging all-day hikes.

A popular two- to three-day hike (depending on which of at least three routes you choose) crosses the **Barranca de Urique** from Batopilas to the town of Urique. Twelve km northeast of Batopilas is the logging settlement of **Yaquivo,** where you can pick up a logging road to **Guachochi** (via Agua Blanca), a junction town for "back door" exits from the Sierra Tarahumara to Parral. **Agua Blanca** can also be used as a

gateway for backpacking trips into the deep, little-explored **Barranca de Sinforosa.**

But aside from the well-traveled Cerro Colorado routes described above, these trips really shouldn't be attempted without the guidance of someone who knows the territory. Besides the danger of getting lost or injured in a remote spot, there's the added risk of stumbling onto a pot or poppy patch, which can get you in trouble with either the growers or the *federales* if your timing is bad.

Ask at Casa de Bustillos in Batopilas for guide services. Bob Francis, who sometimes works as a guide for the Copper Canyon Riverside Lodge and who usually keeps a room at Bustillos's, knows the area well and will lead hikes for very modest fees—if he's not off on a San Blas surfing trip.

Guachochi

This large Tarahumara mission pueblo in the eastern sierra is sometimes visited by road travelers using the "back door" route in or out of the Sierra Tarahumara via Parral. It's also at the northern outskirts of the Barranca de Sinforosa, one of the deepest canyons in North America and relatively unexplored. Local guides may be available for canyon descents; you can drive as far as Ciénega Prieta at the canyon's edge via a dry-weather road.

Practicalities: Basic rooms are available at the **Hotel Los Piños** and **Hotel Chaparro** for US$6-10 per night.

A gravel road northwest out of Guachochi leads to the Napuchi/Samachique junction (90 km/55.8 miles), about midway between Batopilas and Creel. A dry-weather road also heads west to Agua Blanca, than northwest to Yaquivo, which is about a 12-km hike from Batopilas.

A PEMEX station in Guachochi carries Nova only.

EL DIVISADERO TO CHINIPAS

El Divisadero-Posada Barrancas

These two stations just minutes apart on the Chihuahua al Pacífico rail line are major stopovers for tour groups doing the rail circuit. The train always stops at El Divisadero ("The Viewpoint") for 15 minutes to allow passengers to look over the rim into the "eye" of the Barranca del Cobre. Souvenir and food vendors crowd the platform at El Divisadero whenever a train arrives.

Unless you're staying at one of the hotels here, hiking in the area is limited by the unavailability of provisions, as this area is geared more toward hotel tourists than backpackers. Guides can be contacted through local hotels for trips down to the Río Urique and/or across to the Tarahumara settlement of Pamachi on the other side, a vigorous day's hike along a good trail. Short day-hikes can also be taken along and below the rim here to a heavily touristed Tarahumara cave dwelling. From here the trail continues to the bottom of the canyon. Guides can be contacted at the Hotel Mansión Tarahumara nearby, though they're not absolutely necessary for a one-day descent and return. The hotel offers two-hour horseback tours along the rim for US$10 per person. A guided trip to the river at the bottom of the canyon by horse or on foot costs US$20.

Hotels: Accommodations at both stations are a bit pricey, no doubt due to the "priceless" canyon views and lack of competition as well as the fact that rooms are available on the all-inclusive American plan only.

On the canyon rim near the Posada Barrancas station is **Hotel Posada Barrancas,** part of the Balderrama chain based in Los Mochis. Large rooms with tile floors, wood beam ceilings, fireplaces, and private baths cost US$90 s, US$140 d, and US$165 t per day including three meals. Balderrama is completing a new 27-room hotel, tentatively called **Posada Barrancas Mirador,** just below the rim near the original hotel; the five-star rates are projected to be 20% higher than at Hotel Posada Barrancas. For information or reservations at either hotel, contact the Hotel Santa Anita, A.P. 159, Los Mochis, Sln. 81200 (tel. 681-5-70-46 in Los Mochis; 800-876-3942 in the U.S./Canada).

A bit farther away from the station hustle-bustle is the 46-room, medieval castle-style **Mansión Tarahumara** (tel. 14-16-26-72, fax 14-16-54-44 in Chihuahua). Although this hotel isn't built directly on the rim like its rivals, panoramas of the canyon are a short walk away. Rates, including three meals a day, are US$80 s, US$120 d, US$165 t, and US$200 for a private

cabin with Jacuzzi. Guide services and horseback trail rides are available at nominal cost. The Mansión Tarahumara will also store excess luggage if guests decide to go on overnight hiking excursions.

Five minutes south by train at El Divisadero station is the well-designed **Hotel (Cabañas) Divisadero Barrancas** (tel. 14-12-33-62, 14-15-11-99 in Chihuahua; A.P. 661, Chihuahua, Chih. 31238), where rooms with private bath and fireplace plus three meals a day cost US$94 s, US$140 d, US$187 t, and US$233 q, with a three-day minimum stay. The tastefully decorated lobby-bar has large, picture-window canyon views.

The only places serving food in the area are the four hotels and the collection of daytime food vendors at El Divisadero station. The latter serve tacos, quesadillas, and other snacks to locals as well as tourists who disembark from the train every day, hence they generally set up around scheduled train arrival times, then pack up after the trains have left.

These station villages are sorely lacking in budget accommodations for hikers or backpackers of modest means. Camping is certainly possible, though you'll have to search a bit to find spots that won't be trammeled by sightseers.

Transport: For railway departure and arrival times, see the "Railway Schedule," pp. 86-87.

An unpaved road south from Creel crisscrosses the railway all the way to both station settlements. This road is in fairly good condition, the main hazards being the sometimes blind railroad crossings (switch off your engine to listen for oncoming trains) and the occasional stream crossing.

Cuiteco

Only 12 minutes north of the Bahuichivo station by train, Cuiteco offers a rail stopover that's less frequented than Bahuichivo, El Divisadero, Posada Barrancas, or Creel. The village itself has little to see other than a small, 300-year-old mission chapel. The area from here south (Cuiteco, Bahuichivo, Cerocahui, Urique, Témoris, Chínipas) is sometimes called "Baja (Lower) Sierra Tarahumara."

continued on p. 294

THE TARAHUMARAS

The semi-native inhabitants for whom the Sierra Tarahumara is named have been the subject of heavy doses of myth and romanticization ever since Norwegian explorer Carl Lumholz, in 1902, pronounced the Tarahumara "many times better off, morally, mentally, and economically, than his civilised brother." More recent writings have described the Tarahumaras as "Neolithic noblemen" or "selfless and innocent people" living a Walden Pond sort of existence.

The truth is that very, very few non-Tarahumara can claim any sort of in-depth knowledge of these people or their culture. Modern-day Jesuit missionaries, who have found their way back into the mountains where the Tarahumara originally fled to avoid missionization and Spanish slavery, probably know them best. But even the missionaries associate only with "baptized" Tarahumaras or those amenable to conversion and assimilation into the Mexican mestizo culture; the more culturally resistant "gentiles" have retreated ever more deeply into the mountains and canyons of the Sierra Tarahumara, holding off dire predictions of cultural extinction that have been repeated with increasing frequency over the last hundred years. Fame-seeking anthropologists have also found an ever-tightening cult of secrecy which the Tarahumaras have developed in reaction to keen outside interest.

The latest threat to the Tarahumara culture is a proposed US$45.5 million World Bank loan to expand logging in the western Sierra Tarahumara. (To find out more—or to file a protest—contact loan manager William Beattie at World Bank, 1818 H St. NW, Washington, D.C. 20433.)

Naming And Language

The Tarahumara have always called themselves Rarámuri, "The Runners," to differentiate themselves from sedentary Amerindian groups; "Tarahumara" is actually a Spanish corruption of the native term. Mestizo locals sometimes call Tarahumaras *"tohuises,"* while the Tarahumara in return call Mexicans *"chabochis;"* both terms carry pejorative connotations (thumbing their noses at the mestizo epithet, a Tarahumara musical group from Batopilas calls itself "Los Tohuises del Norte").

Their language, Rarámuri, belongs to the Uto-Aztecan linguistic family and can be divided into three main dialects roughly corresponding to the deeper canyons and mountain ridges between Bahuichivo and Batopilas (sometimes referred to as the Baja Sierra Tarahumara), the area northeast of Río Batopilas, and the area north of Río Urique. The standard reference work on the language is *Diccionario Rarámuri-Castellano* by D. Brambila (published by Mexico City's Obra Nacional de la Buena Pensa), usually available at Creel's Mission Store.

Abodes And Way Of Life

When the Spanish arrived in the early 1500s, the Tarahumaras occupied the fertile *llanos* and *llomerías* of central Chihuahua. To evade Jesuit missionaries and Spanish exploitation, they gradually abandoned their homelands and moved west into the Sierra Madre Occidental's rugged mountains and canyons, where they have remained for 400 years, preferring to maintain an aloof subsistence rather than integrate into the Spanish or Mexican economies.

Today around 62,000 Tarahumaras (Northern Mexico's second largest native tribe after San Luis Potosí's Huastecas) are scattered within a 67,000-square-km (26,000-square-mile) section of the Sierra Madre Occidental—an area often referred to as the Sierra Tarahumara—in 25 of Chihuahua's 67 *municipios*. They tend to live apart from Mexicans in out-of-the-way places, including caves, cliffsides, or small wood-and-stone houses in secluded meadows. Jesuit padres divide their communities into "pueblos," those settlements with churches, and "ranchos," those without churches. To the Tarahumara, all ranch and farm groupings are simply *betechi* or *beterachi,* "places to live" in Rarámuri.

Except where Tarahumaras are working for timber or mineral concerns, their settlements tend to be quite small, usually a loose collection of only a few households. Many settlements are seasonal, since traditionally the Tarahumaras live in highland caves or cabins along the canyon rims during the summer, and move to lowland houses and canyon bottoms in the winter.

Self-sufficient farming and ranching have allowed at least some portion of Tarahumara society to survive without assimilation into the local timber and mineral industries. Tarahumara agriculture is said to be one of the most complex and productive systems of native agriculture anywhere in the world. Their crops may be raised anywhere between 300 and 2,700 meters (1,000 and 9,000 feet), from canyon bottoms to mountain peaks.

Fields along river plains are fertilized with manure in the *barbecho* or "moving corral" rotation method, while on steep canyon slopes the Tarahumaras employ swidden ("slash-and-burn") methods. The latter involves cutting Madrean woodlands in Nov.-Dec., setting aside the timber to dry for fuel, burning the brush in late spring, and then planting crops in the ashen, nitrogen-rich soil as the rains arrive in June. Land processed thus is fertile for two or three years, after which it is unfarmable for the next 5-10 years; hence new plots must be sought out, cut, burned, and planted in serial fashion. A third technique, *trinchera* ("trench") farming, uses stone walls arranged stepwise along steep slopes to form terraces where crops can be planted along flat planes.

Corn is the Tarahumaras' major crop and the major constituent of the Tarahumara diet. Just about every household maintains at least one *milpa* or cornfield, where they plant up to six principal strains, including blue, yellow, red, and white corn. Many local corn varieties are said to come from rare pre-Cortesian, nonhybrid strains. Other important crops are beans, squash, peaches, apples, and potatoes.

Tarahumaras supplement their mostly vegetable-legume-grain diet by raising cattle, pigs, goats, and sheep, all of which are kept as much for their fertilizing manure as for their hides, wool, or meat. In some traditional cave dwellings these animals may be kept in "basements" created by inserting simple timber floors between the human and animal living spaces. Other sources of protein include freshwater fish trapped in streams and rivers, deer and small game, and—in hard times—lizards, toads, insects, berries, and fungi. The Tarahumaras' vast knowledge of herbs, roots, and other medicinal/culinary plants has hardly been cataloged.

Traditional dress for Tarahumara men includes a short, white muslin skirt, a billowy, white or flower-print shirt *(zaraza)* with huge sleeves, and a long red cotton headband. Some men walk (and run) barefoot while others wear sandals with a single leather thong that passes between the toes from the sole and wraps around the ankle. In or near mestizo villages and towns, many Tarahumara men dress in the typical ranchero fashion with boots, jeans, plaid shirt, and straw cowboy hat. Women wear long dresses, long-sleeved blouses, and head scarves—all made from colorful print material.

Running

One aspect of the Tarahumara way of life that eas-

ily lends itself to myth and lionization is the tradition of long-distance running. Walking and running are still the main modes of transport among the Tarahumara, whose resting heart rates and blood pressure reportedly run around 20% below "normal." When running for sport, a Tarahumara can cover 65 km (40 miles) of rough canyon and mountain terrain (up to 97 km/60 miles on flat terrain) in six to eight hours; when hunting, good runners are supposedly capable of chasing deer to the point where the animals collapse of exhaustion.

It is common knowledge (confirmed by the writings of Carl Lumholz) that before the Creel-Batopilas road was built, Tarahumara men carried the mail on foot between Chihuahua and Batopilas at the bottom of the Barranca Batopilas, a journey of 300 miles each way. The mail carrier took six days to complete the route in one direction, rested for just one day, and started back the other way.

Another oft-repeated story describes how in the 1968 Mexico City Olympics the Mexican government fielded two Tarahumara men in the marathon (41.8 km/26 miles) competition. The Tarahumaras didn't even place, however, as they reportedly complained about being made to run in shoes and for having to run a distance so short it was hardly worthy of real runners.

The Tarahumaras have their own homegrown running event beside which the modern marathon pales. In *rarjíparo* (or *rarahipa*), teams of 2-12 male runners kick a 10-cm (four-inch) ball made of solid wood up and down boulder-studded slopes, through thick pine forests, across streams and gullies, and over fences for up to two days without stopping—all this at altitudes of up to 2,400 meters (8,000 feet). When stuck in a crevice or stream, the ball may be dislodged using a stick the players' companions carry for this purpose; otherwise the ball cannot be moved forward except with the feet. (Tarahumara women have their own version called *dowérami* in which two interlocked hoops of lechuguilla fiber are flipped along a course with sticks.) Spectators bet on which team will kick the ball across the finish line first. Physicians who have examined the runners immediately following the end of the race have found diastolic blood pressure readings of zero, rising to 60-80 after a few minutes of rest.

Although visitors to the Sierra Tarahumara will rarely have the opportunity (or the stamina) to observe one of these races, it's not uncommon to see individual Tarahumaras trotting up or down narrow, steep mountain paths and carrying loads—some-

continued

times as large as the carriers—slung from the forehead by a tumpline.

Beliefs And Rites

As is common among traditional societies throughout world history, shamans and priests are the highest authorities and source of political power in the community; in post-Cortesian times this power has come to focus on the Jesuit padre. But like native peoples throughout the Americas, the Tarahumaras have woven strands of their pre-Christian belief systems into the missionary religions, creating a hybrid that is neither one nor the other (or both, depending on your viewpoint). Most Tarahumaras identify Tata Dios (God the Father, also called Onorúame) with the sun and the Virgin Mary with the moon; both are often the objects of food and *tesgüino* (a thick, fermented corn beverage) offerings.

The *tesgüinada*, or *tesgüino* drinking session, is an integral part of all religious celebrations. *Tesgüino* (called *suguiki* in Rarámuri) is made by soaking dried corn kernels in water and leaving them to sprout in a dark place, then hand-grinding the sprouted corn until it forms a paste, which is then boiled with a local grass seed (*basiáwi* or brome grass) and fermented for a day or so. The resulting low-alcohol beverage must be drunk within two to three days (after which it will spoil), which perhaps has something to do with how so much *tesgüino* is consumed in so short an interval at the typical *tesgüinada*. Gourd cups called *hueja* are dipped into pots (*ollas*) of *tesgüino* day and night until the brew is finished and virtually everyone participating has passed out from drunkenness.

Another psychoactive substance used far less frequently and less extensively by the Tarahumaras is peyote, a Chihuahuan Desert cactus known as híkuli among the Tarahumaras, *Lophophora williamsii* to Western botanists. A complex set of ritual taboos restrict its ingestion to Tarahumara shamans and pickers of the cactus, although it may also be applied externally for various afflictions, including snakebite and rheumatism, and may in rare cases be administered internally as a last resort for seemingly incurable diseases. According to anthropologist John G. Kennedy, peyote is widely feared by Tarahumaras as a substance with an independent soul which can "see." Among those remote villages that still count peyote as an important religious sacrament, a yearly journey is made to certain desert ridges between Ojinaga and La Perla in eastern Chihuahua to gather the cactus.

Semana Santa: The most important religious ceremony of the Tarahumara calendar is Semana Santa ("Holy Week"), the week leading to and including Easter Sunday. Much has been written about the "standard" Tarahumara customs and ceremonies during Semana Santa, but the truth is that every part of the Sierra Tarahumara seems to celebrate the week differently. What they all have in common is music, dance, and *tesgüino*; where they differ most is in costuming and roles assigned during the religious dramas enacted on the Friday and Saturday before Easter Sunday.

This differentiation must have come about because Spanish padres originally taught Christianity to the Indians by acting out religious dramas based on biblical stories; since the Tarahumaras passed on their own myths this way, they quickly adopted and adapted the new Christian myths. But after the Jesuits were expelled from Mexico in 1767, the dance-dramas continued to evolve in relative isolation from Catholic influences, hence each village was able to develop its own style.

In spite of all the North American attention directed toward the ritual battles (described below), the true religious heart of Semana Santa is probably the Holy

CHRIS HUMPHREY

raising the Judas effigy, Semana Santa

Thursday enactment of the Passion along the *via dolorosa* or "sorrowful way" beneath temporary arches—made from tree branches and saplings in mountain pueblos or simply represented by three wooden crosses in canyon pueblos—to the village church. A framed picture of the Virgin of Guadalupe, accompanied by a woman carrying a censer filled with burning copal (Mexican incense), may also be carried in the procession to the accompaniment of violins, flutes, guitars, drums, and whirl rattles (*matracas*).

The social side of the celebrations begins in earnest on Friday. In many canyon areas the common dramatic thread is a ritual battle between evil and good, as represented by the Pharisees (*fariseos*), often daubed with white clay paint and carrying wooden swords or guns and a white flag, and the soldiers (*soldados*), who may be dressed in traditional Tarahumara garb or in ordinary Mexican clothes and carrying wooden spears and a red flag to protect the Virgin of Guadalupe from the mocking Pharisees. The Pharisees, some wearing head feathers or diabolic horns, come running into the village on Friday afternoon, get drunk, scare young children, laugh inside the church, and in general create mayhem. Chasing them around the village—between *tesgüino* bouts—are the soldiers.

This continues until the middle of the night, when the two sides join in drunken wrestling matches (in some villages wrestling has been banned due to the high number of past injuries), all the while accompanied by live music. The wrestling and drinking continue all night; late Saturday morning, the ritual chase-dancing becomes more organized and culminates in the appearance of a straw Judas effigy displaying a huge wooden phallus. The Pharisees parade the Judas around the church environs until the soldiers capture the effigy, lash it to a stake, spear the figure into a pile of straw, and then set fire to it.

This is but one way in which the Friday-Saturday drama may be celebrated. Instead of *fariseos*, other villages may role-play *pintos* (Norogachi), *mulatos* (Tónachi), or *moros* (Samachique) in opposition to the *soldados*. An interesting confusion of didactic myths seems to be taking place here, mixing representations of the struggle between Pharisees and Christians in the Bible, Moors and Christians in Spain, and mestizos and Amerindians in Mexico. On top of everything else, in biblical literature the soldiers and Pharisees are on the same (evil) side, yet somehow they've become opposed in Tarahumara mythology.

In other areas no struggle between good and evil is enacted, although participants may costume themselves similarly. In Cerocahui the celebration focuses on *matachine* dancers, and the whole affair is more like that of an all-night country dance. In Creel and other logging towns, local mestizos participate together with the Tarahumaras, and the fiesta is more reminiscent of an ordinary Mexican Semana Santa. In some places—Divisadero-Posada Barrancas, for example—Semana Santa activities are organized expressly for visiting tourist groups.

Another important festival for the Tarahumaras is Fiesta Guadalupana, held on Dec. 12 in honor of the Virgin of Guadalupe. Characterized by all-night *matachine* dances inside pueblo churches, this celebration is less touristed than Semana Santa (though most Tarahumara Semana Santa celebrations are relatively unexploited compared to Patzcuaro's Day of the Dead, for example).

When you are traveling in the Sierra Tarahumara, remember you are a guest in a region to which the Tarahumaras moved hundreds of years ago first and foremost because they wanted to be left alone. Above all, be sure to respect their sense of privacy, which extends to their simple dwellings and to any fenced areas nearby. Never attempt to enter a Tarahumara home or cross a fence around a home without asking permission first. The same goes for photos of the people or their homes—always ask permission first and if refused, move on.

The Coordinación Estatal de la Tarahumara, a state office that oversees Tarahumara affairs, offers these guidelines for visitors attending Semana Santa or Fiesta Guadalupana celebrations:

Do:
• Act with the same respect you'd like other people to show toward your own religious celebrations.
• Obey all indications from the Tarahumaras or their authorities about taking photos, trespassing in reserved places, time to stay or leave, etc.
• Keep a discreet distance at every moment during the celebration of "La Fiesta."

Don't:
• Participate in processions, dances, or rites. Keep apart.
• Take places inside the churches assigned to the authorities or to the Tarahumaras themselves.
• Make any comments, play music, or take photos which would distract or interrupt the celebration.
• Go dressed as if you were going on a picnic. This religious celebration, although different, is holy.

canyon rim, El Divisadero

Hotel Cuiteco (Cuiteco Casitas Hotel) has basic accommodations for US$40 per night, reasonable considering this rate includes four meals. Unconfirmed rumors say the hotel also has dormitory beds for US$10 per night—this is where college students from Sinaloa come for a Sierra Tarahumara experience. Reservations can be made through the Hotel Santa Anita in Los Mochis (see "El Divisadero-Posada Barrancas," above for contact information). A small village store carries a limited selection of food-stuffs.

When you're driving to Cuiteco or beyond from the north, the river crossing here can be particularly tricky since you must drive upstream for about 180 meters (600 feet) before completing the crossing. It's best to get out of your vehicle and scout the stream first to find the route with the least rocks and shallowest water. From here southward the road is very rugged; fuel, even Nova, is scarce.

For railway departure and arrival times, see the "Railway Schedule," pp. 86-87.

Bahuichivo

The next station south on the Chihuahua al Pacífico line, Bahuichivo, is a good jumping-off point for longer excursions into the Barranca de Urique since food supplies are available along the way in Bahuichivo, Cerocahui, and Urique.

Accommodations and Food: A ramshackle lumber village extends eastward from the Bahuichivo station. Several nondescript buildings, including the funky **Hotel Camino Real,** have spartan rooms for rent for around US$7 a night. Three or four cafes serve basic potluck fare; a couple of stores stock canned food, *pinole* (ground roasted corn that can be mixed with water to form an edible gruel), and a few fresh fruits and vegetables brought up from the canyon floors.

Transport: There is a daily bus to Cerocahui, 1½ hours away, for US$2.50 per person.

According to rumor, Bahuichivo will soon be getting a PEMEX station. For the time being, Nova is available from barrels at a shop along the main street.

Cerocahui

This highland Tarahumara pueblo (elev. 1,500 meters/5,000 feet) of around 800 inhabitants was founded as a Jesuit mission in 1680 by Padre Juan María de Salvatierra—the same priest who 17 years later founded Baja California's first mission in Loreto. The sandstone mission church is one of the most attractive in the Sierra Tarahumara. A small plant powers the town 8-11 p.m. only.

Several small-scale gold mines are still functioning in the area, including the Mina Sangre de Cristo an hour away. One of the easiest and most scenic hikes from Paraíso del Oso Lodge (see "Accommodations," below) is to nearby **Cueva de las Cruces,** a Tarahumara burial cave painted with 51 crosses. The cave itself is little more than a large, curved depression in the side of a cliff, but the trail to the cave passes through a fertile valley where *trinchera* ("trench" or terrace) farming was practiced centuries ago, then follows a beautiful stream flanked by grass that looks as if it were manicured by fairy-tale illustrators. On the way back you can hike over a plateau with views of the valley instead of backtracking along the stream. A half-dozen other canyon and cave hikes are available in the vicinity of the Paraíso del Oso.

Accommodations: On the pueblo's small plaza is a *casa de huéspedes* (no sign) with very basic rooms for US$7 per night. Next to the mission church, the 30-room, Balderrama-owned **Hotel Misión** has pleasant lodge-style rooms for US$90 s, US$140 d, US$165 t including three meals. Some rooms have fireplaces or wood stoves. The hotel provides free transport from the train station. Make reservations through Hotel Santa Anita in Los Mochis (see "El Divisadero-Posada Barrancas," p. 288, for contact information).

North of town on the way to Bahuichivo (12 km/7.4 miles from the railway station) is the **Paraíso del Oso Lodge,** a top choice among hikers and backpackers who have come to explore Barranca de Urique and the highlands near Cerocahui. Comfortable, lamp-lit rooms with wood stoves and hot showers cost US$85 s, US$110 d, US$135 t, US$160 q per night, including three meals and roundtrip transport from the railway station. The lodge has a large dining room with fireplace and a small library of classic literature on the Sierra Madre; hiking maps and a detailed bird list are available on request.

Behind the main lodge is a relatively new addition, **Rancho del Oso,** where tent sites cost US$3-4, dorm rooms with breakfast just US$7 (no transport included). Guided trips to the bottom of the canyon, Cerro Gallegos on the canyon rim, Témoris (timed so that rail buffs can observe trains passing through the most spectacular portion of the Chihuahua al Pacífico line), or the mining town of Piedras Verdes are available from the lodge for modest fees, as are local horseback trail rides. Several other hikes can easily be taken in the area without a guide. For more reservations or information, contact Paraíso del Oso (c/o Columbus Travel, tel. 800-843-1060, fax 210-885-2010; Rt. 12, Box 382-B, New Braunfels, TX 78132-9701).

Transport: Both Hotel Misión and Paraíso del Oso provide van transport from the railway station for guests with reservations. Public buses bound for Piedras Verdes or Urique meet the trains as well, and these will take you to Cerocahui and Paraíso del Oso Lodge for around US$2.50.

If you're driving to Cerocahui from the north, you'll find an all-weather dirt road roughly parallel to the railway as far as San Rafael (about 1 1/2 hours from Creel), after which the road deteriorates for the stretch through Cuiteco, then looks a bit better as it heads south from Bahuichivo to Cerocahui. Over the next couple of years the San Rafael-Cerocahui portion of the road will be upgraded. Barrel Nova is available in Bahuichivo and Cerocahui.

Urique

At the bottom of the Barranca de Urique on the banks of Río Urique, this town was the first place in the Sierra Tarahumara officially named by the Spanish, who somehow found their way here toward the end of the 16th century. One of the larger *municipios* in Chihuahua, Urique covers 3,968 square km and has a population that is 75% Tarahumara, 25% Mexican.

The town itself is mostly adobe buildings with tin roofs and dirt floors (Batopilas is a metropolis by comparison), many of which grow oranges, mangoes, avocados, and guavas in small orchards out back. As in Batopilas, a more clandestine crop is rumored to be under cultivation farther away from town. Burros and horses are a common sight on the main street. Like Cerocahui, the town has electric power 8-11 p.m. only.

Several gold mines, some dating to the Spanish colonial period, are still in operation in the area, but people are very close-mouthed about their location since many are worked without claims. One old fellow I met near Cerocahui takes around 45 kilos of ore per day from an abandoned mine, packs it by burro to his *tahona* (ore mill) on the river, and extracts US$2-3 in gold for each day's labor.

Several places are suitable for swimming in the Río Urique near town, as well as for pleasant day-hikes along the river in either direction.

Accommodations and Food: Three small, rustic hotels offer basic rooms along the town's main drag. The best is **Hotel Cañon de Urique,** US$6.60-8.30 single, US$11.60 d, or US$16.60 t with *baño colectivo* (rates may be negotiable if the hotel is empty). Of the town's three rather unimpressive cafes, the friendly **Restaurant Plaza** is marginally better. A meal—whatever's on the hearth that day—costs around US$3.

A new gringo-run spot, upstream from town about 750 meters, supposedly rents rooms by the week and also offers campsites.

Hikes from Urique: A number of one- to three-day hikes can be taken out of Urique either along nearby arroyos (Mezcalerita, Hacienda, Cañitas, Camuchines, and La Higuera to name a few) or along the river itself. If you follow the river a few kilometers in either direction you'll come to Tarahumara villages. Particularly scenic is the walk north along the river and across a suspended footbridge to Guadalupe Coronado.

The popular Urique-Batopilas hike can be easily accomplished in two days. Several routes are possible, the easiest being the southern route via Guapalaina. Because of all the intersecting trails and the possibility of inadvertently running across a pot patch, it's best to engage the services of a guide for the crossing. The typical cost for a guided Guapalaina-Batopilas trip, including a pack burro, is US$50 for two persons; food costs extra, and can be bought in several *tiendas* in town or brought with you. Inquire at Hotel Cañon de Urique, at Restaurant

tahona

Plaza, or in Guapalaina.

In years past, Guadalupe Coronado (north of town across the river) and Guapalaina (south of town on the same side of the river) have hosted well-attended Semana Santa fiestas.

For hikes in the Urique area you should use the Batopilas 1:50,000 topo map (G13A41).

Transport: The same padre (Salvatierra's successor) who built the Cerocahui mission church also had a tunnel cut through canyon rock to connect Cerocahui and Urique by road. The result is a trip with spectacular views, equal or superior to anything seen on the Creel-Batopilas road.

The Bahuichivo-Urique bus costs US$5 per person and meets the Chihuahua al Pacífico train (Chihuahua-bound No. 73) at around 12:15 p.m. each day. If the train is late, the bus usually waits. In the opposite direction the bus leaves Urique at 7 a.m. The second train of the day is met by a bus going to Piedras Verdes rather than Urique—be sure to ask before boarding (this bus leaves Piedras Verdes at 7 a.m.). The Bahuichivo-Urique bus trip takes five to six hours.

Témoris And Chínipas

These two mining towns at the southwestern edge of the Sierra Tarahumara are on the unpaved road to Alamos, Sonora. Témoris is also a station on the Chihuahua al Pacífico rail line and is a favorite spot for rail buffs who come to marvel at the design and construction of three levels of railway bridges, tunnels, and viaducts, all converging into the Barranca de Septentrión. The original town a few kilometers northwest is sometimes called "Témoris Viejo" or "Old Témoris."

Before the railway was built, Chínipas was the main staging point for traversing the canyon country for nearly 400 years; along the Río Chínipas is one of the largest Spanish aqueducts (around 48 km long) in Mexico. Downstream from Chínipas along the river is the little-explored Barranca de Chínipas, one of the sierra's deeper canyons.

Practicalities: Basic hotel accommodations are available in Témoris. If you plan to hike in the area, you'll need the INEGI topo map Témoris G12B39.

The road from Bahuichivo to the northeast continues as far as Témoris, where another

JOE CUMMINGS

road heads northwest to Chínipas (2½ hours from Témoris) and from there all the way to Alamos (six hours from Chínipas under good conditions). This road is often impassable during the July-Sept. monsoon season. Nova gasoline is available in both Chínipas and Témoris.

For railway departure and arrival times for Témoris, see the "Railway Schedule," pp. 86-87.

BASASEACHIC FALLS
NATIONAL PARK

This rugged, 14,300-acre area along the northern edge of the Sierra Tarahumara achieved national park status in 1981, making it the only part of the sierra thus protected. An accident of topography in which the Arroyo Basaseachic meets the Barranca de Candameña, cut by the Río Candameña, has created the park's centerpiece, the Cascada de Basaseachic (also spelled Basaseachi). The third highest waterfall in North America, Basaseachic drops 246 meters (806 feet) according to the most conservative measurement (Mexico's national park service says 299 meters/980 feet, while AAA and the state of Chihuahua claim 310 meters/1,020 feet). While the canyon itself is pristine by most standards, logging and overgrazing threaten areas along the fringes of the park.

The average elevation along the canyon rim is 2,000 meters (6,560 feet) and yearly rainfall averages around 650 cm (25 inches), most of it occurring during late summer. The best time to see the falls is at the end of the rainy season (late September, early October) when the water volume is greatest. For hiking, winter is best since the areas surrounding the top and base of the falls are safer and more accessible.

At least five other cascades are within the park boundaries as well as several trails in and out of Barranca de Candameña. The main trails are marked—a bit of a shock if you've just been hiking in the Urique, Cobre, or Batopilas canyons. A trail that descends from near the top of the falls to the base takes about 45 minutes down, 1½ hours up. Although the falls are impressive from the lookout points opposite, you really need to hike down to the base to appreciate the scale and to revel in the misty pine forests along the way.

The park has two main entrances: one at the southeast end of the park off Chihuahua 330 (the road from San Juanito) and one at the northern end off Mexico 16 (the Chihuahua-Hermosillo highway). Near the southeast entrance are two marked *divisaderos* or viewpoints with cross-canyon vistas of the waterfall. Divisadero I is a short walk from the parking lot while Divisadero II is a 20-minute, winding descent (a stiff 30 minutes coming back up) below Divisadero I. From the north entrance parking lot, a 1.6-km trail leads to La Ventana, another canyon-breach view of the falls.

Other highlights include fascinating rock formations and an abundance of birdlife.

Motels And Lodges
At Km 278 on Mexico 16 (1.3 km/0.8 mile from the park access road) in the highway hamlet of Alma Rosa, **Motel Alma Rosa** has small rooms facing the highway with private showers and small fireplaces for US$24 per night. Behind the motel are larger, more modern rooms for US$50-56—a bit overpriced for what are essentially simple rooms. Only two of the latter rooms have fireplaces, albeit large ones. The Alma Rosa has an attached cafe with decent Mexican fare.

Hotel Nena, also in Alma Rosa, has stark cement cells with low ceilings for US$8.30 per person—definitely a last resort.

Between Km 262 and 263 on Mexico 16 (7.2 km/4.5 miles east of the San Juanito road junction), **Villa Alpiña** rents A-frame cabins for US$35-40, a better bargain than Motel Alma Rosa's more expensive rooms.

A large, privately run visitors lodge has recently been constructed near the south entrance to the park; check with the state or federal tourist offices in Chihuahua to find out whether it's open yet.

Camping
Basaseachic Falls National Park has perhaps the best public campgrounds in Northern Mexico. A well-maintained, no-fee Zona de Camping near the two *divisaderos* features tent sites, barbecue pits, trash barrels, water spigots, and outhouses set amid small pines and junipers. This camping area is reached via Chihuahua 330, the 107-km road linking San Juanito and Mexico 16. The turnoff is 93 km/58 miles from

San Juanito; the 1.4-km (0.9-mile) access road is paved.

Another camping area off Mexico 16 near the main north entrance to the park has similar facilities, but is slightly less private due to the heavier visitor traffic from this end of the park. Next to the parking lot, several food vendors sell *antojitos* during the day. At least one vendor here rents a small two-bed room in back of his shop for US$10 per night (this would be preferable to the Hotel Nena in nearby Alma Rosa); simple evening meals can be arranged.

Transport

Mexico 16—now paved all the way from Chihuahua or Hermosillo—is the main access route for the park, which is 200 km (124 miles) west of Cuauhtémoc, 305 km (189 miles) west of Chihuahua, and 372 km (230.6 miles) east of Hermosillo. The highway section between Basaseachic and La Junta follows a very scenic arroyo, with especially beautiful rock formations in the Km 200s.

Magna Sin gasoline is available in La Junta. About halfway between La Junta and Basaseachic, at around Km 217, the lumber town of Tomochi offers a small hotel, groceries, and a PEMEX with Nova only.

For visitors coming from Creel or elsewhere in the heart of the Sierra Tarahumara, the most convenient access is via 107-km (66-mile) Chihuahua 330—most of which is gravel-surfaced—from San Juanito. The latter town is 30 km (18.6 miles) north of Creel via Chihuahua 127; the total 137-km (85-mile) trip from Creel to Basaseachic takes three to four hours. This road cuts off at least an hour from the longer Creel-La Junta-Basaseachic route.

THE STATE OF DURANGO

Though only the fourth largest state in Mexico (behind Chihuahua, Sonora, and Coahuila), Durango provides an even deeper study in contrast than its neighbors to the north because it contains both the heavily forested mountains of the Sierra Madre Occidental to the west and the Bolsón de Mapimí—the starkest section of the Chihuahuan Desert—to the east. Between the two are sections of plains and valleys irrigated by the Colorado, Tamazula, Los Remedios, Aguanaval, Tunal, Mezquital, and Nazas rivers where cotton, pecans, grapes, oregano, wheat, chile, and safflower are cultivated in abundance.

Durango's portion of the Sierra Madre Occidental (here called the Sierra Tepehuanes) produces some 2.5 million cubic meters of timber each year, nearly twice Chihuahua's output and over a quarter of the national production. Cattle ranching is also an important means of livelihood for Durangueños, who specialize in raising hardy rodeo steers.

The entire state population totals only 1.6 million, nearly half of whom live in the capital. Although the population is predominantly mestizo, a small colony of Mennonites living near Santiago Papasquiaro in the north produce renowned apples, cheese, and cured meats. The southern corner of the state, where the Sierra los Huicholes spread across the junction between Durango, Nayarit, and Jalisco, is inhabited by some 4,000 Huichol, along with several thousand Coras and Tepehuanes.

In Mexico the state has a reputation for rough living and still has relatively few paved highways. Notorious revolutionary hero Pancho Villa was born in San Juan del Río in central Durango (110 km/68 miles northwest of the capital) in 1877. As in Chihuahua, Villa is a potent regional symbol and one does not speak disapprovingly of the man. According to Mexican legend, Villa once made a pact with the Devil in a cave north of the city of Durango to relinquish his soul in return for "mastery over men."

Climate

Durango has a climate similar to that of western Chihuahua, except that temperatures tend to be a bit cooler due to the gradual ascension of the Altiplano from north to south. Along the central plains May is the hottest month, with temperatures in the 30s C (90s F). In this area the monsoon season extends June-Sept., during which time an average 56 cm (23 inches) of precipitation falls on the plains; in the mountains rainfall reaches as high as 100 cm (40 inches) per annum. Scant precipitation also occurs in January and February.

The eastern, desertic third of the state bordering Coahuila and Zacatecas is much drier, with annual rainfall of less than 25 cm (10 inches) and temperatures exceeding 38° C (101° F) in the summer.

Much as in Chihuahua's Sierra Tarahumara, the climate of the western sierra varies tremendously from canyon bottom to mountain peak.

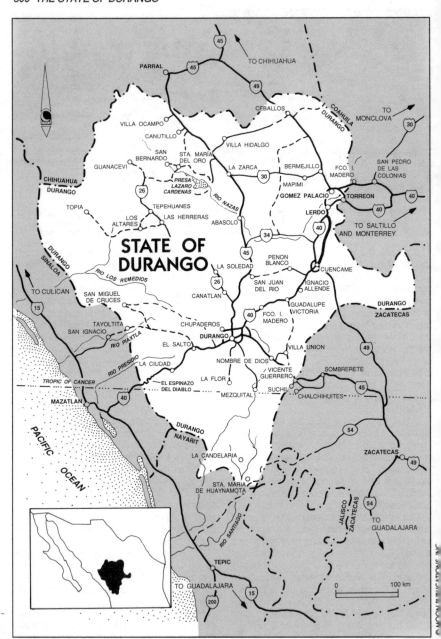

Overall the best time for mountain visits is fall or early spring. Light snow in the mountains isn't uncommon in January and February.

DURANGO (CITY) AND VICINITY

Francisco de Ibarra founded the settlement of Guadiana (named for a river that flowed from Spain's central plateau to the Atlantic coast) in 1563 but later that year changed the name to Durango in honor of his home village in the Spanish province of Vizcaya. Durango became an important outpost of Nueva Vizcaya, the largest province in Nueva España (covering what is now Durango, Sinaloa, Sonora, and Chihuahua), but friction between the Spanish settlers and local Tepehuanes and Acaxes restricted early development of the area.

A particularly bloody confrontation on the plains of Cacaria in 1616 resulted in the deaths of 15,000 natives. Because of local hostilities, between 1679 and 1738 each Durango governor carried out his term in Parral, Chihuahua, some 411 km to the north. By the mid-18th century, when the Indian "threat" was deemed manageable, colonial construction in Durango continued in earnest.

A substantial boost in Durango's fortunes occurred after English timbermen founded the lumber and mining camp of El Salto on the nearby slopes of the Sierra Madre Occidental around the turn of the century. The English built a railway between El Salto and Mexico City and by the early 1900s Durango had become an important transshipment point for lumber and minerals taken from the sierra.

Now officially named Victoria de Durango, the city has grown to a population of 600,000 and sits 1,893 meters (6,209 feet) above sea level in the Valle del Guadiana. Looming over the city is the Cerro de Mercado, a mountain of iron ore first discovered by Vázquez de Mercado in 1532 but "forgotten" until 1828, when iron production first began. Considered one of the largest iron deposits in the world, the mountain produces over 300 tons of iron daily and is estimated to continue production at this rate for at least a century.

The city serves as an important transport junction since it sits at the crossroads of Mexico 40 (connecting the Pacific port of Mazatlán with Torreón, Saltillo, and Monterrey) and Mexico

45 (Durango to Mexico City). Because of the city's historic architecture, most of which dates to the 17th and 18th centuries (including around a dozen historic churches spanning gothic to neoclassic styles), the Mexican government has declared Durango a national monument. It is a city best seen on foot, since its moderate charms tend to be missed when driving through on the main boulevards linking Mexico 40 and 45.

Among film buffs, Durango is famous as a location setting for over a hundred motion pictures, most of them in the "western" genre (see special topic "Durango on Film," pp. 304-305).

SIGHTS

Catedral Basílica Menor (Catedral De Durango)
The city's premier *virreinato* architecture is actually the third religious structure to have been built on this site, the first being a 1571 parish church that was destroyed by fire in 1631, the second being an ill-conceived twin-towered church that had to be demolished because it was in danger of toppling.

Construction on the current edifice—on Av. 20 de Noviembre facing the Plaza de Armas—began in 1691 and was augmented step by step through 1770. Reflecting the evolution of Mexico's grand baroque period, the principal facade has four columns in the Tuscan style on the lower *portada*, six on the upper *portada* in Solomonic style, and bas relief surrounding the pillars that prefigure the ultra-baroque style seen in the Catedral de Zacatecas. The building plan originally followed classic cathedral design with five naves in a cruciform with a dome in the center. Two more domes were later added in front.

The cathedral's interior was altered from the neoclassical style so that the choir—which originally was located in the center of the church like the *coros* of cathedrals in Mexico City and Puebla—has been moved to the back. On display is a rare gilded *sillería* (clerical pew) dating to 1737, the only other example of which can be

Catedral de Durango

ERIN DWYER

found at Mexico City's San Ildefonso. A collection of paintings chronicling Durango's bishops dates from the 17th century.

Legends: Almost hidden in shadow at the back of the eastern nave is a heavy wooden confessional that is the subject of a chilling local legend. According to most versions of the story, Spaniard Juan Pérez de Toledo made a pact with a satanic emissary for his soul in exchange for money and women. Later, as his resultant excesses almost wore him out, he decided to renounce the pact before he died. Just as he was about to receive pardon for his sins from a priest at the confessional, Satan appeared and pinned the priest to the wall. At the same moment Pérez was reportedly struck down by a beam of light that left a strange odor of sulfur. The community has abandoned the confessional since 1738, the year of the reported incident.

Another legend associated with the cathedral is that of *la monja de la catedral*. In the mid-18th century a French soldier sought asylum in the cathedral after deserting the Napoleonic army, which at the time had invaded Mexico. A nun (*monja*) stationed at the church fell in love with the Frenchman and the two made plans to marry. Before celebrating their nuptials, however, they decided that the soldier should return to France and seek pardon for his crime of desertion; when he came back to Durango the nun would leave the nunhood and the two would marry. On his way back to France the soldier was captured by his countrymen in Mexico and executed.

Not knowing of his fate, the nun climbed to the tower balcony nightly to await her lover's return until she finally died of heartbreak. To this day, Duranguéños swear that an apparition of the nun can be seen in the middle balcony of the west tower each night at sunset. If you want to see for yourself, the best vantage point is a spot next to the entrance of the Hotel Plaza Catedral on Calle Constitución, along the west side of the cathedral. Gaze at the middle balcony of the nearest tower and you should be able to make out the apparition—or trick of the light, or whatever it is.

Casa Del Conde Suchil
Built between 1760-70 in the typical Spanish style by a Spanish count, this large colonial jewel features a Churrigueresque facade, along with magnificent tiled flooring and wooden paneling in the interior. The building, at Calle 5 de Febrero and Madero near the plaza, now contains a bank (the best place to see the restored interior) and several shops.

Templo Del Sagrado Corazón
This 19th-century church on Calle 5 de Febrero between Progreso and Saucos is a well-preserved example of the Mexican gothic style. The fortresslike structure is enlivened by its arched windows, stained glass, and a *rosetón* carved of native stone over the main entrance.

Edificio Central De La Universidad Juárez
Originally a Jesuit convent dating to the 16th century, this two-story colonial building of native stone at Calle Constitución and Pino Suárez (near the plaza) was transformed into the Insti-

tuto Juárez in 1856. In 1956 it became the Universidad Juárez del Estado de Durango (Juárez State University) with a variety of academic departments, including law, medicine, accounting, business administration, art, music, sociology, and others. Murals with contemporary social themes are painted over stairway landings.

Teatro Ricardo Castro

Constructed in 1901 as Teatro Principal and renamed for a Durango native who was an illustrious pianist and composer, this neoclassical-style theater was renovated in 1990 to prepare for a visit by Pope John Paul II. The interior, which features beautiful tile and marble flooring, is used for visiting theatrical, music, and dance performances as well as ongoing film programs. The theater is located at the corner of Av 20 de Noviembre and Bruno Martínez.

Santuario De Los Remedios

On the summit of a hill of the same name, this is the oldest surviving church in Durango. Established in 1640, the austere stone edifice built in the style of a fortress served not only as a place of worship but also as protection against Apache and other Indian raids.

A legend attributes the building of the church to a miraculous apparition. According to the legend, a shepherd caring for his animals on the hill spied a tiny woman carrying some mud on a tray toward the summit. When asked what she was doing, the woman replied that she wanted to build a church at the top of the hill. The shepherd pointed out that she would need a large quantity of mud to build a church, far more than she was carrying. Her response was, "If you don't believe I can do it, go tell the *cura* (parish priest) that the Virgen de los Remedios would like him to build a church atop the hill."

Convinced by her words and manner, the shepherd paid a visit to the priest, who dismissed the old man as crazy. Some weeks later the shepherd returned to the hill and saw the Virgin carrying small stones up the hill with the intention of building the church from small stones. The shepherd tried once again to convince the parish priest of the existence of the Virgin and was again rebuffed. Returning a third time to the hill, the shepherd found the Virgin binding the small stones one on top of another with the mud. This time, after some pleading, the

sacerdote and his entourage visited the hill, immediately recognized the Virgin as genuine, and set about building a church in her honor.

Today few visit the Santuario de los Remedios except to take advantage of the sweeping city views. The hill is southwest of the town center, across Blvd. Dolores del Río from the end of Av. 20 de Noviembre.

Movie Sets

Villa del Oeste: One of the oldest movie sets (*escenario*) still visible is the Villa del Oeste (also known as Rancho Howard) near Km 10 north of Durango on Mexico 45. Originally built from scratch as a "typical" Old West town, the town was later occupied by squatters until bit by bit it became an actual village. Access to Villa del Oeste is privately owned; sometimes it's open, sometimes not, and you might have to pay an entrance fee.

Chupaderos: Just a bit farther north along Mexico 45 at Km 14 is the more accessible Chupaderos, an actual Mexican village "discovered" by John Wayne. It was turned into a movie set and used for more Hollywood westerns than any other Durango location. Driving through Chupaderos, one is struck by the juxtaposition of Mexican peasants sitting on the porches of Old-West style buildings that have been added to the village over the years. A couple of kilometers south of Chupaderos is an uninhabited film set often referred to as "Chavez County" with a set of decaying Old-West structures. This latter set is protected by a locked gate; usually someone at the gate will let you in for a look around, perhaps for a tip of N$2 or N$3.

Los Alamos: Currently the most intact local set is one constructed to represent the town of Los Alamos, New Mexico, for the filming of *Fat Man and Little Boy,* a 1989 motion picture about the development of the atom bomb starring Paul Newman. The large set includes several wooden military-style barracks, a water tower, and a log cabin where Newman stayed during the location shooting. To find the latter you must walk along a short trail from the set's center to a bluff overlooking a canyon cut by the ríos Chico, Los Arcos, and Tunal. It's an easy hike to the bottom of the canyon a hundred meters or so below for a swim.

The *Fat Man* set is 29 km south of Durango on the road to La Flor (follow Blvd. Domingo

DURANGO ON FILM

Durango's heyday as a location setting for Hollywood westerns began in the '50s when producer/director Robert Jacks (of later *Zorba the Greek* fame) found the terrain perfect for his 1955 *White Feather,* a film starring Robert Wagner, Hugh O'Brien, and Debra Paget about gold prospectors encroaching on Indian territory. This film and the following year's *The Tall Men* (featuring Clark Gable, Robert Ryan, and Jane Russell) put Durango on movie screens for the next 30 years; the trend slowed in the 1980s following the decline of the western film genre. Relatively recent major productions in the Durango area have included *Romancing the Stone, Power, The Old Gringo, Revenge,* and *Fat Man and Little Boy.*

In the U.S., the late John Wayne was the actor (and director) most associated with films shot in Durango, though Burt Lancaster and Robert Ryan turned up almost as often. Sam Peckinpah directed two groundbreaking films in Durango, *The Wild Bunch* and *Pat Garrett and Billy the Kid.* Many Mexican-produced films have also used Durango for location shooting; in Mexico, it's Rodolfo de Anda whom viewers most associate with the state.

Directors from both countries favor Durango for three reasons. First, it's sparsely populated, with few paved roads or power lines in sight, making it especially suitable for movies with pre-20th century themes. Second, the weather is consistently sunny most of the year and the quality of the light is said to be especially photogenic. Finally, wages are low in this state because of the lack of other industries, so labor—and acting extras—are inexpensive even by Mexican standards.

More than 116 motion pictures—around 60% of them by North American directors—have used Durango for location shooting. Of the many Mexican productions, several used B-grade U.S. actors (e.g., *El Mal,* made in 1965 with Glenn Ford and Stella Stevens) but were released only in the Spanish-speaking world. Others, such as *Guns for San Sebastian* (a 1967 Mexico/Italy/France co-production starring Anthony Quinn and Charles Bronson) were produced for international release.

Some of the more notable North American films shot partially or entirely in Durango are (dates reflect shooting schedules rather than year of release):

White Feather (1954, Robert Wagner, Hugh O'Brien, Debra Paget)
The Tall Men (1955, Clark Gable, Robert Ryan, Jane Russell)
Comanche (1955, Dana Andrews, Linda Cristal)
The Wonderful Country (1958, Robert Mitchum, Julie London)
The Unforgiven (1959, Burt Lancaster, Audrey Hepburn, Audie Murphy)
Geronimo (1961, Chuck Connors, Kamala Devi)
Major Dundee (1964, Charlton Heston, Richard Harris, James Coburn)
The Sons of Katie Elder (1965, John Wayne, Dean Martin)
The War Wagon (1966, John Wayne, Kirk Douglas)
Hour of the Gun (1966, James Garner, Robert Ryan, Jason Robards)
The Scalphunters (1967, Burt Lancaster, Shelley Winters, Telly Savalas)
Day of the Evil Gun (1967, Glenn Ford, Arthur Kennedy)
Five Card Stud (1968, Robert Mitchum, Dean Martin, Inger Stevens)
The Wild Bunch (1968, William Holden, Ernest Borgnine, Robert Ryan)
A Man Called Horse (1968-69, Richard Harris, Dame Judith Anderson)
The Undefeated (1969, John Wayne, Rock Hudson)
Chisum (1969, John Wayne, Bruce Cabot, Forrest Tucker)
Lawman (1970, Burt Lancaster, Lee J. Cobb, Robert Duvall)
Big Jake (1970, John Wayne, Maureen O'Hara, Richard Boone)
Buck and the Preacher (1971, Sidney Poitier, Harry Belafonte, Ruby Dee)
Something Big (1971, Dean Martin, Brian Keith, Honor Blackman)

still from The Sons of Katie Elder

Kid Blue (1971-72, Dennis Hopper, Warren Oates, Peter Boyle)
The Wrath of God (1972, Robert Mitchum, Frank Langella, Rita Hayworth)
Pat Garrett and Billy the Kid (1972-73, Kris Kristofferson, Bob Dylan, James Coburn)
Cahill, U.S. Marshal (1972-73, John Wayne, George Kennedy)
The Deadly Trackers (1973, Richard Harris, Rod Taylor)
The Devil's Rain (1975, Ernest Borgnine, Eddie Albert, Ida Lupino)
The Return of a Man Called Horse (1975, Richard Harris, Gale Sondergaard)
The Great Scout and Cathouse Thursday (1975-76, Oliver Reed, Lee Marvin, Kay Lenz)
Who'll Stop the Rain (1977, Nick Nolte, Michael Moriarty, Tuesday Weld)
Goin' South (1977, Jack Nicholson, Mary Steenburgen)
Eagle's Wing (1978, Martin Sheen, Harvey Keitel)
Cattle Annie and Little Britches (1979, Burt Lancaster, Rod Steiger, Amanda Plummer)
Caveman (1980, Ringo Starr, Barbara Bach, Dennis Quaid)
Romancing the Stone (1983, Michael Douglas, Kathleen Turner, Danny DeVito)
Power (1985, Richard Gere, Julie Christie, Gene Hackman)
The Old Gringo (1988, Jane Fonda, Gregory Peck)
Revenge (1988, Kevin Costner, Anthony Quinn, Sally Kirkland)
Fat Man and Little Boy (1988, Paul Newman, John Cusack)

Arrieta south out of town). It's well worth the short trip just for the canyon views, though there has been some talk of turning the set into a police training center.

Film Office: The state has its own office dedicated to assisting filmmakers in Durango, the **Dirección Estatal de Cinematografía** (tel. 181-1-21-39, 1-11-07; Calle Hidalgo 408 Sur) in the same building as the state tourism office. This office also organizes group tours of local film sets.

DURANGO ACCOMMODATIONS

Durango has a good variety of places to stay in all price ranges, including several in historic colonial buildings. Occasionally when a movie production is in town the better rooms may be booked up by film crew and actors, but this is a much less common occurrence than it was during the '50s to '70s heyday of Durango westerns.

Hostels And Budget Hotels
Durango has a **Villa Deportiva Juvenil** (tel. 181-8-70-71, 8-70-11) at Av. Heróico Colegio Militar s/n with 80 beds for US$1.50 per night per bed. Unlike hostels in many Mexican cities, this one is conveniently located just a few blocks from the main bus terminal and a short bus ride from the city center. An inexpensive *cafetería* is on-site.

One of the best deals in town is the 100-year-old, colonial-style **Posada Duran** (tel. 1-24-12), near the Plaza de Armas at Av. 20 de Noviembre 506 Poniente. Spacious rooms surrounding an interior courtyard with spartan furnishings and private bath cost US$14.60 s, US$18.30 d, US$22 t.

Nearby at Calle Constitución 102 Sur, **Hotel Posada San Jorge** (tel. 3-25-57) offers economic rooms in a two-story colonial building for US$16.60 s, US$20 d, US$24 t, US$27.60 q. **Hotel Roma** (tel. 2-01-2) at Av. 20 de Noviembre 705 Pte. near the cathedral has rooms in a similar two-story colonial for US$17 s, US$20 d, US$24, US$28.60 q.

Also known as the Durango Hotel, the four-story **Hotel Suites Durango** (tel. 1-55-80) at Av. 5 de Febrero 103 Ote. has large a/c rooms with private bath for US$18 s, US$22 d, US$26 t, plus suites for US$26-30.

Basic but adequate rooms with private bath cost US$10 s, US$12 d, or US$18 t at the one-star **Hotel Prince** (tel. 1-92-58), Calle Juárez 502 Sur.

Medium-priced Hotels
Around the corner from the Posada Duran at Calle Constitución 216 Sur is the similarly historic but better furnished **Hotel Plaza Catedral** (tel. 181-3-24-80), where rooms cost US$24 s, US$27 d, US$34 t.

The two-story, semi-modern **Hotel Reforma** (tel. 3-16-22) at Av. 5 de Febrero and Madero lacks charm but has fairly comfortable rooms with private bath and phones for US$24 s, US$26 d, US$29 t.

Located in the restored colonial section of Calle Negrete near the cathedral and several good restaurants, **Hotel Posada Santa Elena** (tel. 2-78-18) offers surprisingly economic rooms with TV and telephone at US$23 s, US$26.60 d, or US$43 for a three-person suite.

The six-story **Hotel Casablanca** (tel. 1-35-95, fax 1-47-04) at Av. 20 de Noviembre 811 Pte. also has a convenient downtown location with a parking garage (a block from the hotel) and a/c rooms for US$28 s, US$33 d.

Farther east downtown, the smaller **Motel Arvel** (tel. 2-53-33) at Calle Progreso 104 Sur has decent rooms for US$22 s, US$22-26 d, US$26 t, US$29 q.

Motel Campo Mexico Courts (tel. 8-77-44, fax 8-30-15) at Av. 20 de Noviembre and Colegio Militar is a favorite overnight stop for gringos because it's close to Mexico 40, the highway northeast to/from Torreón and Monterrey. Rooms cost from US$35 for a standard single with satellite TV, a/c, and phone to US$50 for a superior double. Facilities include a swimming pool; many of the rooms have refrigerators. The main sign out front reads "Mexico Motel."

Deluxe Hotels
The top choice for business travelers, filmmakers, and upscale tourists is the efficient **Hotel Gobernador** (tel. 181-3-19-19, fax 1-14-22) at Av. 20 de Noviembre 257 Oriente. Housed in a former prison that has been completely made over into a modern yet atmospheric four-star hotel, the Gobernador offers all the amenities, including a/c, heat, satellite TV, direct-dial phones, and the city's nicest coffee shop and best hotel

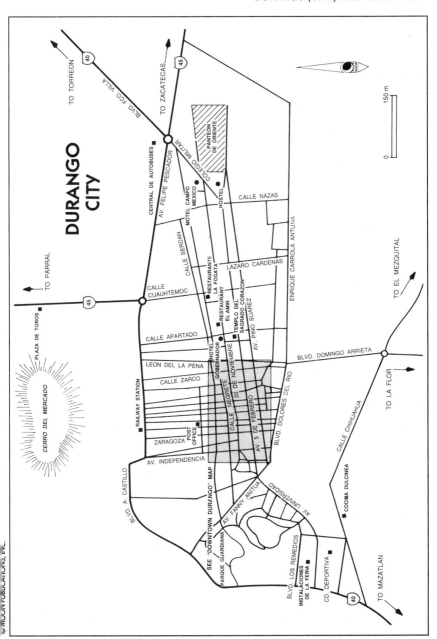

pool. Including tax, rooms cost US$64-92 s/d depending on size and location.

The recently opened four-star **Hotel Fiesta Mexicana** (tel. 1-98-80), at Av. 20 de Noviembre and Independencia downtown, is completely decorated in traditional but elegant Mexican style. Rooms with a/c, heat, TV, and phone cost US$62 s/d, quite reasonable considering the facilities and central location.

Motel Los Arcos (tel. 8-77-77), near the Motel Campo Mexico Courts at Av. Colegio Militar 2204 Ote., has large rooms surrounding a secure parking lot for US$53 s/d, US$64 t, US$79 t.

RV Parks

The **Motel Campo Mexico Courts** (see "Medium-priced Hotels" for address) has around a dozen RV spaces with full hookups (some outlets are 220V, so check before plugging in) for US$10 a night. **Motel Los Arcos** will allow RVers to park in the motel lot and use bath facilities for a nominal fee.

FOOD

Durangueños take pride and pleasure in eating, and the city's restaurants offers some of the best and most *típico* food in Northern Mexico. A famous local specialty is *caldillo durangueño,* a thick soup made with small pieces of dried venison (or beef) and chile strips. *Gorditas,* thick corn tortillas stuffed with a choice of beans, cheese, *picadillo* (chopped meat-and-chile salad), egg, potatoes, and other fillings are also quite popular. Other local delicacies include *asado de puerco* (pork in a sauce of tomatillo and *chile verde*), *quesadilla durangueña* (flour tortillas filled with melted cheese and chorizo), *calabaza/biznaga cubierto* (crystallized squash or barrel cactus—eaten as sweets), and *dulces de almendra* (almond sweets).

Mescal, a potent liquor made from hearts of maguey in the mountains of southern Durango, is available for around US$8 per liter in the city or US$4 in mountain villages where it's distilled. The smoothest distillate is a variety locally known as *mescal tepemete.*

If you're not sure exactly where you want to eat, take a stroll down Calle Negrete near the cathedral; on and off this street are a number of restaurants and cafes in restored colonial buildings.

Mexican And Regional

$ **Cocina Dulcinea** (tel. 181-3-23-16), Calle Río Yaqui near the Ciudad Deportiva at the southwest edge of the city. One of the most authentic eateries in Durango, this small, family-run spot is said to prepare the city's best *caldillo durangueño* and *gorditas.* A delicious *comida corrida* in the afternoon sells for US$4.60. Local mescal is available on request. Open daily 1-9 p.m.

$$ **La Fonda de la Tía Chona** (tel. 1-77-48), Calle de Nogal 110 near the Hotel Fiesta Mexicana. A slightly upscale restaurant in a restored colonial mansion decorated with traditional Mexican art and artifacts. The unwritten menu—a mix of regional dishes as well as Mexican standards—changes periodically and is recited by the waiters, so you'll need to use your best restaurant Spanish to feed well. Prices are moderate and the food is very good. Tía Chona's original, less fancy location at Calle Florida 1121 nearby is still in operation. Open daily 11 a.m.-11 p.m.

$$ **Restaurant El Kilo** (tel. 8-19-92), Km 7, Mexico 40. Specializes in *birria, barbacoa,* and *carnitas* sold by the kilo, accompanied by fresh tortillas. Open daily 8 a.m.-11 p.m.

$ **Ultramarinos Finos** (tel. 7-18-43), Calle Libertad and Fpe. Pescador. A good spot for quick and cheap *tortas, burritos, molletes, quesadillas, taquitos,* and *hamburguesas,* plus delicious juices and *licuados.* Open daily 8 a.m.-8 p.m.

Steak

$$-$$$ **Far West** (tel. 181-2-30-73), Av. 20 de Noviembre and Independencia. This popular restaurant serves Durango and American-style steaks, *chilorio* (venison-and-chile sausage), *carne adobada* (beef in adobo sauce), and *caldillo durangueño* in a tastefully done saloon atmosphere. Photographs from films shot in Durango decorate the walls. Open daily 11 a.m.-11 p.m.

$$ **Restaurante La Fogata** (tel. 7-03-47) at Calle Cuauhtémoc and Negrete. Offers Durango-style *carne asada* and *arracheras* (known farther north as *fajitas*) by the kilo, plus domestic and imported wines. Open daily noon-11 p.m.

International

$$$ Restaurante El Amir, Av. 20 de Noviembre 510 Oriente. A short walk from the Hotel Gobernador, this immaculate, air-conditioned restaurant specializes in Lebanese, Mexican, and continental dishes. It's a bit overpriced in general, with a small bowl of rather ordinary *caldillo durangueño* going for US$7.60. Open Tues.-Sat. noon-9 p.m.

$$ Corleone Pizza (tel. 181-3-31-28), Calle Constitución 114 Nte., a few blocks north of Calle Negrete. Corleone's funky wine-cellar decor is popular with the local university crowd. The menu offers a wide variety of pizza in two basic sizes, plus cocktails, beer, wine, pasta, and salads. Open daily noon-midnight.

$$$ Sloan's Restaurant Bar (tel. 2-21-99), Calle Negrete 1003 Pte., just west of Calle Hidalgo (a few doors from Hotel Posada Santa Elena). Housed in a huge restored colonial, Durango's most upscale restaurant serves steaks and continental and Mexican food. Open daily 1 p.m.-midnight.

Seafood

$$-$$$ Fiesta del Mar y Su Palapa (tel. 181-2-76-57), Calle Cuauhtémoc 315 Norte. House specialties include *pescado zarandeado* (an imported Mazatlán favorite), *caldo de caguama* (turtle soup), and *marlín entomatado* (marlin in tomato sauce); plus shrimp, oysters, scallops, and lobster prepared in various ways. Open Tues.-Sun. 11 a.m.-11 p.m.

$$ Playa Azul Restaurant-Bar is a less expensive seafood chain with branches at Av. Colegio Militar 312, Calle Chihuahua 1450, Calle Constitución 241, and Calle Madero 508 Sur. Open daily 10 a.m.-9 p.m.

Coffee Shops

$ La Zocabón and **El Esfuerzo,** on Av. 5 de Febrero Pte. near the southeast corner of the Plaza de Armas. These two cafes offer inexpensive breakfasts for around US$1.60-2.30. El Esfuerzo is the nicer of the two; both are open 7 a.m. till late.

$$ Hotel Gobernador, Av. 20 de Noviembre 257 Oriente. The moderately priced restaurant/coffee shop at the Gobernador is very popular for business breakfasts and lunches. Breakfasts here—whether American, Mexican, or continental—are the best in Durango. *Pan dulce* is

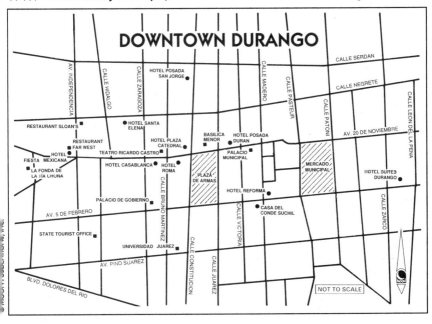

available from 7 a.m. till they run out (usually around 8:30 a.m.). Open daily 7 a.m.-midnight.

Vegetarian
$$ Antojitos El Buen Comer (tel. 181-1-13-47), Calle Zaragoza 213 Sur. Features vegetarian versions of typical Mexican dishes, including *gorditas, tostadas de ceviche,* and *mole verde,* plus "hamburgers" and sandwiches, all made with soy or gluten meat substitutes. The attached store sells whole wheat bread, yogurt, and other natural foods. Open Mon.-Sat. 8 a.m.-6 p.m.

$$ Samadhi Comida Vegetariana (tel. 1-62-27), Calle Negrete 403 Pte. at Calle Madero. Similar to El Buen Comer, with gluten and soy-based Mexican dishes, breads, yogurt, etc. Open Wed.-Mon. 8 a.m.-7 p.m.

RECREATION

Entertainment
The bars at Sloan's, Corleone Pizza, and other restaurants in the area of Calle Negrete and Calle Constitución are popular with *durangueños* of all ages. Hoping for pickup gigs, mariachi and *norteña* musicians hang out along Av. 20 de Noviembre between the Hotel Reforma and the Posada Duran. *Norteña* music is very big in Durango; the Mexican disco scene really hasn't hit the city (yet).

Shopping
Durango is known for its wool sarapes, leather boots, *charro* clothing, and Tepehuán crafts, all of which can be found inside or near the **Mercado Municipal** (Mercado Gómez Palacio) between avenidas 20 de Noviembre and 5 de Febrero (with main entrances on calles Patoni and Pasteur).

Fancier boutiques near the Plaza de Armas and on the lower floor of the plaza's grand *kiosco* carry consumer goods from all over Mexico and abroad.

Charreada
Durango is big on Mexican rodeo, with no less than five *charro* rings in town. *Charreadas* are held year-round, usually on alternating Saturdays. Check with the tourist office for the latest schedule.

Festivals
The **Feria de la Fundación de la Ciudad de Durango** (the Founding of Durango Fair) takes place annually during the second week of July, preceded the previous week by—and merging with—the **Feria Agricola, Ganadera, Forestal, Industrial y Comercial** (Agricultural, Ranching, Forestry, Industrial, and Commercial Fair).

Together the two fairs produce a number of expositions and activities revolving around the display of regional skills in ranching, farming, technical/trade affairs, and sports. Many live musical performances, folkloric dancing, and regional handicraft exhibits are also held, making this one of the largest urban festivals in Mexico. Fair events are centered at the Instalaciones de la Feria and in the adjacent sports arena in Durango's southwest corner, though many activities are scattered throughout the city. If you would like to attend the festivities, be sure to book a hotel room at least two months in advance. The state tourist office (see "Durango Information," below) can provide an up-to-date schedule of events and venues.

During the **Days of the Dead** (Días de los Muertos, Nov. 1-2), the huge Panteón de Oriente off Av. Colegio Militar at the east end of the city is resplendent with flowers and other offerings to the deceased.

DURANGO INFORMATION

Tourist Offices
The **Dirección Estatal de Turismo** (tel. 181-1-21-39) at Calle Hidalgo 408 Sur distributes information on hotels and tourist attractions in the state of Durango. Some of the staff speak good English. Also in this building are the state cinematography office and the **Centro de Amistad Durango** (Durango Friendship Center), which assists visitors with consumer complaints, accidents, theft, and other mishaps.

SECTUR (tel. 2-76-44) has an office at Calle Bruno Martínez 403 Sur with similar information, although the state office is better staffed.

Maps
Topographic maps of Durango, Zacatecas, and Chihuahua are available at the **INEGI office** (tel. 181-2-82-30, fax 2-82-28) at Calle Madero 107 Sur.

TRANSPORT

Air
Aeroméxico (tel. 181-1-26-52; Calle Juárez 201 Sur) has direct flights between Durango and Culiacán, Guadalajara, Mazatlán, Mexico City, Monterrey, and Torreón.

Aero California (tel. 7-71-77; Av. 20 de Noviembre 1410) flies to Durango direct from Guadalajara and Torreón, as well as from Ciudad Juárez and Tijuana via Torreón.

TAESA (tel. 3-66-81; Durango Airport) fields daily flights from Ciudad Juárez and Mexico City.

Airport Transport: The airport is 26 km northeast of downtown Durango off Mexico 40; a *colectivo* costs US$5, a taxi US$13 for the half-hour trip.

Bus
Durango has a huge bus station with many *loncherías* at the junction of Av. Colegio Militar and Av. Felipe Pescador near Mexico 40. **Omnibus de México** (tel. 181-8-33-61) has buses daily to/from Ciudad Juárez (US$37), Chihuahua (US$37, *ejecutivo*), Mexico City (US$30), and Guadalajara (US$34, *ejecutivo*).

Transportes Chihuahuenses (tel. 181-8-37-81) and **Transportes del Norte** (tel. 8-30-61) combine services for first-class buses to/from Nuevo Laredo (US$39), Monterrey (US$41), Chihuahua (US$32), Ciudad Juárez (US$50, *ejecutivo*), and Mexico City (US$60, *ejecutivo*).

Less expensive first- and second-class buses on smaller lines such as **Estrellas Blanca** (tel.

8-32-41) and **Transportes Frontera** (tel. 8-34-99) offer once-daily services to/from Mazatlán (US$12), Torreón (US$7), Chihuahua (US$24), Monterrey (US$20), Saltillo (US$17), San Luis Potosí (US$15), and Zacatecas (US$10).

Getting Around
Bus: A good city bus system circulates Durango's main streets for US$0.30 per trip. Perhaps the most useful is the line that runs between the Central de Autobuses and El Centro (downtown) along Av. 20 de Noviembre, the city's main east-west artery. Most hotels and sights worth visiting are within easy walking distance of this line.

Taxi: Taxi stands are concentrated in the downtown area and at the larger hotels. A taxi anywhere in the downtown area costs US$3.50-4, to the outer fringes of the city US$5. Taxis can be hired on a time basis for US$10 an hour. Beyond five hours, it might be more economical to rent a car (it's US$50 per day; see the "Auto Rental Agencies in Durango" chart, below).

Driving: The traffic in Durango moves fairly well and most streets are well marked. Parking in the downtown area near the cathedral can be a problem (though nothing like in Zacatecas or Guanajuato), especially during the daytime, so you may want to consider leaving your vehicle at your hotel and getting around town by bus or taxi.

Fuel: PEMEX stations with Magna Sin are numerous, especially along the bypass roads such as Av. Felipe Pescador (north edge of town), Av. Colegio Militar (east), and Calle Chihuahua (southwest).

TOURS

For visitors interested in wilderness travel, Durango is a state well worth considering. The state's wilderness areas have been so little explored that basic travel infrastructure—roads, hotels, camping areas—is rather limited. An experienced guide can take you to places in the Sierra Madre Occidental, for example, that you would never find on your own (unlike in western Chihuahua, where the sierra is fairly well traveled).

At the moment the widest variety of itineraries is available from **Pantera Excursiones** (tel. 181-2-21-64; 800-487-4783 in the U.S./Canada; A.P. 670, Durango, Dgo. 34001) at Calle Constitución 216 Sur. Operated by Walter Bishop, the bilingual, bicultural son of a former British consul to Durango, Pantera Excursiones leads tours all over the state, including trips to the Zona de Silencio, Mapimí, the Sierra Madre, Huichol territory on the Durango-Nayarit border, and the Sierra Tarahumara in Chihuahua. Some itineraries focus on mountain biking, others on trekking or camping; groups are kept to a maximum number of 15. Rates are very reasonable and include the leadership of experienced, ecologically sensitive guides, support vehicles, food, and all land transport.

Another agency, **Viajes Anamar** (tel. 1-42-71, fax 2-50-80) at Calle Negrete 1204 Pte., specializes in trips to the Zona de Silencio (see "El Bolsón de Mapimí and La Zona de Silencio," p. 317).

DURANGO TO MAZATLAN

The 318-km section of Mexico 40 that extends between Durango and Mazatlán (in Sinaloa) through the Sierra Madre Occidental is one of the most scenic drives in all of Mexico. It is not a drive to take lightly, however, and motorists should carry all the spare parts, including tires and belts, that might be needed to remedy automotive problems along the way, as no repair facilities are available between the two cities. (See "Driving in Northern Mexico," p. 90, for more information.)

Mexico 40 begins climbing into the sierra around 40 km east of Durango. **Cabañas El Soldado** at Km 43 near Agua Blanca offers cabins for rent as well as horseback rides in the surrounding forest. **Parque Nacional El Tecuán** at Km 57 is a public parkland set amid mountain pines and meadows with picnic tables and grills. Moderately priced cabins with fireplaces, gas stoves, and hot water can also be rented here; for information or reservations, contact the Dirección Estatal de Turismo (tel. 1-21-39, 1-96-77; Calle Hidalgo 408 Sur, Durango, Dgo. 34000).

Private cabins oriented toward hunting vacations are available for rent further on near Km 105 at **Cabañas Mil Diez** near the village of Mil Diez.

Región De Las Quebradas

Four-wheelers can use a logging road running north off Mexico 40 around 15 km before El Salto (about 85 km/53 miles west of Durango) to explore an area of the Sierra Madre Occidental called "Las Quebradas" ("The Breaks"); the name derives from the huge canyons slashed into the mountains by the Quebrada del Salto, El Varal, Tabillas, Miravalles, and Las Paridas rivers. The road is fairly good as far as the village of Unidos Venceremos, after which it is generally traversable only in dry weather and in high-clearance (preferably 4WD) vehicles. A hundred km (62 miles) north is the former mining town of **San Miguel de Cruces**, a good jumping-off point for canyon-sierra explorations. Las Quebradas is so steep and rugged that, unlike in the so-called Copper Canyon country farther north in Chihuahua's Sierra Tarahumara, not a single Spanish mission was ever established in the area.

A turnoff at Las Flechas, about halfway between Mexico 40 and San Miguel de Cruces, leads west to 17th-century, stucco-and-tile **Tayoltita,** the earliest mining site in the state and one of the most remote and quaint towns in the sierra. The road from San Miguel is very bad, however, and Tayoltita can be reached more easily from the state of Sinaloa via a gravel road from San Ignacio, which is 33 km northeast of Mexico 15 between Culiacán and Mazatlán. From San Ignacio it's a 70-km, six-hour drive to Tayoltita along the scenic Río Piaxtla. This latter road, though slow, can be traversed by any high-clearance vehicle Dec.-April. During periods of rain, *vados* are often too deep to cross.

B. TRAVEN, MYSTERY AUTHOR

No literary work is more identified with the Mother Range than *The Treasure of the Sierra Madre*, B. Traven's novel of greed and betrayal set in 1920s Northern Mexico. Although Traven published over a dozen novels and short story collections around the world before his death in 1969, *Treasure* has survived the vagaries of literary fashion via John Huston's brilliant 1948 motion picture version, which featured a grizzled Humphrey Bogart in the starring role (along with Walter Huston and Tim Holt). Huston won an Oscar for his direction of the film, which featured the often misquoted line "I don't have to show you any stinking badges!" spoken by a Mexican *bandido* leader—yet another of Hollywood's many contributions to the *bandido* stereotype.

Like the novel, the film tracks a trio of down-on-their-luck Americans from Tampico's waterfront boardinghouses to a moral (and politically allegorical) denouement somewhere in Durango's Sierra Madre Occidental. So real were Traven's geographical descriptions (and Huston's film, which was shot on location in Northern Mexico) that fans of the novel continue to debate the location of the fictional mine.

No less mysterious was Traven's past, a story he concealed from his American publishers while he was alive and writing novels, short stories, essays, and movie scripts in English, German, and Spanish. His first novel, *The Death Ship*, appeared in Germany in 1926, and it wasn't until 1933—by which time his books were selling millions in Europe—that Alfred Knopf offered to publish a few titles in the United States. Called "one of the neglected geniuses of 20th-century American literature," Traven assiduously avoided all contact with the press and lived a secluded life in Mexico until his death in 1969.

A 1966 dust-jacket biography claimed that B. Traven had been born Traven Torsvan in Chicago in 1890, had shipped out of San Francisco as a cabin boy on a tramp freighter around 1900, and then had jumped ashore in Mazatlán in the 1920s. Following Traven's death, however, a carefully researched BBC documentary revealed a more intriguing past. According to information obtained from Scotland Yard and F.B.I files, Berick Traven Torsvan was born in a Polish district of Germany, where he spent part of his later youth as an actor. During WW I he wrote revolutionary literature under the pen name

"midget card" for Treasure of the Sierra Madre

"Ret Marut"; when the war ended he accepted a government office in the short-lived Bavarian Socialist Republic.

After the BSR was overthrown, Traven was sentenced to death but managed to escape a roomful of condemned prisoners and join the disaffected legions drifting through postwar Europe. Somewhere in Europe he boarded a Norwegian freighter that ended up in 1920s Tampico. Traven spent the remaining decades of his life in Mexico, mostly in the state of Tamaulipas, where he took up his literary career.

Among Traven's other novels, *The White Rose* is perhaps the most ambitious. Set in turn-of-the-century Northern Mexico, the compelling story follows the rise and decline of the hacienda system. It is especially notable for its clear-eyed interpretation of pre-WW II U.S.-Mexican relations, wherein both sides made long-range political errors that are only now beginning to be rectified.

El Salto

This rough-and-tumble timber town 95 km west of Durango has little to recommend a stop unless your vehicle can take Nova gasoline. The surrounding area, however, is beautiful and at 2,610 meters (8,230 feet) above sea level, summers are mild and winters crisp. Hiking along the nearby Río Quebrada del Salto might be a rewarding pastime, and longer hikes into the sierra and nearby *barrancas* (deep canyons) can be taken with local guides.

Basic, inexpensive accommodations are available near the rustic bus terminal in El Salto at **Hotel Meza** or farther off the highway at **Hotel Zamora.**

Huichol yarn painting

BOB RACE

West Of El Salto

Around 26 km west of El Salto is an area known as **Mexiquillo** that is famous for unusual mushroom-shaped rock formations similar to those found near Creel in the Sierra Tarahumara. After another 20 km or so begins **El Espinazo del Diablo** ("The Devil's Backbone"), a winding, nine-km stretch of road along a narrow mountain ridge. Heavy rains have been known to turn the road in this area into barely passable mud, but the vistas are unsurpassed. Basic services are available in nearby **La Ciudad.**

Beyond El Espinazo del Diablo the sierra begins its descent toward the Pacific coast. Two historic towns worth visiting along the western slopes of the sierra are **Copalá** and **Concordia** (see the relevant entries in the Sinaloa chapter).

SOUTHERN DURANGO

Nombre De Dios

"Name of God," 52 km southeast of Durango via Mexico 45, was one of the first Spanish settlements in Nueva Vizcaya. Durango's first religious edifice, the Templo de San Francisco, was built here in 1557 although the structure itself was long ago destroyed by fire.

The town's main claim to fame these days is the production of mescal, a high-proof liquor distilled from the boiled and mashed hearts of the maguey (agave) plant. You can see mescal being made at the edge of town.

West of town about four km via Mexico 45 is a scenic, sabino-lined stretch of the Río Mezquital known as **Los Salones,** a favorite local picnicking and swimming spot. On a nearby tributary of the river is **El Saltito,** a 20-meter waterfall and spring.

Suchil And Chalchihuites

On the Durango-Zacatecas border 40 km southeast of Nombre de Dios, the tiny town of Suchil was once a mining center now notable for its abandoned haciendas and the nearby ruins at Chalchihuites.

Positioned almost precisely on the Tropic of Cancer, where the sun turns around at equinox, the ruins of Chalchihuites are thought to have been an astro-religious observatory built by the Teotihuacán culture. Now little more than a row of stone columns, Chalchihuites was the northernmost outpost of Mesoamerica and a major trade center and military outpost.

Although the ruins themselves aren't that impressive to the casual visitor, the volcanic scenery of the surrounding Sierra Sombrerete may enchant.

Mezquital

On the banks of the scenic Río Mezquital, this town 82 km southeast of Durango at the southernmost extreme of the Sierra Madre Occidental is even more famed than Nombre de Dios for mescal production. Most of the distilling actually takes place in nearby Tepehuán villages in the canyon formed by the Río Mezquital; there are also a few villages on the lower slopes of the sierra.

According to local legend, little-studied Amerindian cliff dwellings nearby were once inhabited by a race of pygmies. A more likely explanation is that the low-ceilinged structures were used for grain storage, but so far they haven't been properly excavated.

Thermal springs at nearby **La Joya** are the site of a *balneario* with three pools, a restaurant, and inexpensive cabins. As there are no hotels or guesthouses in Mezquital, this might be the best staging point for hiking and backpacking into what is probably the most unexplored section of the Sierra Madre Occidental.

Huichol Country (Huicholitos)

South of Mezquital, the mountains become steeper and less accessible. The major Huichol settlement in the state of Durango, **Santa María de Huaynamota,** is best reached by private plane, although it may also be possible to hike there from La Candelaría, around 60 km southwest of Mezquital via a network of gravel roads and dirt tracks. From La Candelaría, accomplished backpackers with a local guide could make their way south another 20 km or so along the Río Santiago (also known as Río Jesús María) to Huaynamota.

For guide services from the city of Durango, inquire at Pantera Excursiones (see "Tours" in the Durango section below for details).

DURANGO TO PARRAL

Mexico 45 runs more or less straight north from Durango to Parral (in Chihuahua) for 412 km (256 miles). High desert scenery and light traffic make this a pleasant drive; this is also the route most buses between Durango and Chihuahua use (from Parral, Mexico 24 continues north to Mexico 16, less than 50 km west of Chihuahua).

El Palmito

Along the way motorists can turn west at La Zarca (about halfway between Durango and Parral on Mexico 45) to reach **Presa Lázaro Cárdenas** at the top of Río Nazas (better known to many gringo anglers as Lake Palmito), a good fishing spot for black bass, carp, crappie, mojarra, catfish, and tilapia amidst mountain scenery at 1,500 meters (4,900 feet). "Pancho's" has a few rustic cabins at the lake for rent, plus plenty of space for camping. El Palmito, the village at the east end of the lake, has a small hotel, a PEMEX station, and a couple of *tiendas* (but no ice). Local wildlife includes puma, deer,

HUICOT CULTURES

The southern end of the Sierra Madre Occidental, near the junction of the states of Durango, Nayarit, Jalisco, and Zacatecas, is the northernmost limit of Mexico's remnant Mesoamerican cultures as principally represented by the Tepehuán (numbering 17,600), Huichol (14,800), and Cora (10,200), as well as smaller groups such as the Tepecano of Azqueltán and the Nahua of San Pedro Jícora, Durango. All belong to the Uto-Aztecan ethnolinguistic family and share a common mythology based on key legends concerning the sun, fire, flood, and corn.

The Huicholes have stimulated the most outside interest because of their strong ritual traditions. Although they are to a large degree a Christianized group, the Huichol *mara'akames* or shamans are careful to keep Christian rites separate from Huichol rites so as not to contaminate them. Oddly enough, there is no single word for "tradition" in the Huichol language, the closest being the Huichol word for "journey" or "trip," since for the Huicholes tradition involves a series of offerings made at various sacred sites near and far. Water is one of the most important ritual components, and hence caves containing springs are particularly revered.

Corn, deer, and peyote (a hallucinogenic cactus) form a mystic trinity in the Huichol tradition. The first two components of the trinity are available in their Sierra Madre mountain homelands, but for peyote the Huicholes must make annual pilgrimages to Real de Catorce, San Luis Potosí, in order to gather the cactus tops; the pilgrimage is usually performed between October and January (when there is no corn to tend) by individual groups from each of the five major rancherías in the Sierra los Huicholes. A sacred deer hunt is held in May, followed by the *maíz tostado* ("toasted corn") ceremony in June.

Mexico's Instituto Nacional Indigenista identifies the Huichol/Cora/Tepehuán cultural network by the acronym Huicot, using parts of the names of these three principal tribes. The Mexican government's Proyecto Huicot, created for the development of these communities, focuses on training and assistance in agriculture, education, sanitation, and communications.

bighorn sheep, gray fox, coyote, wild turkey, quail, and various waterfowl.

Northwestern Sierra

Sixty-nine km (43 miles) north of Durango, Mexico 26 splits northwest from Mexico 45 to **Canatlán** and **Santiago Papasquiaro,** two towns noted for apple cultivation, a tradition started by Mennonite colonists early this century. A small museum in Canatlán's Escuela Mariano Valleza exhibits Amerindian artifacts, including arrow points and ceramics found in the area. The community of **Guatimape,** 49 km (30.4 miles) northwest of Canatlán via Mexico 26, is a center for local Mennonite *campos.* Several small hotels in Canatlán and Santiago Papasquiaro offer adequate, inexpensive rooms.

Twenty-two km (13.6 miles) northwest of Santiago Papasquiaro a paved road heads west from Mexico 26 into the Sierra Tepehuanes. Average sedans can make it as far as **Los Altares,** 45 km (30 miles) west of Mexico 26, a scenic drive that passes a couple of thermal springs. Beyond Los Altares the road deteriorates to gravel and then to dirt; 4WD vehicles can make it all the way to the end of the road at **Topía,** a possible staging point for hikes into canyons formed by the Tamazula and Sianori rivers. An adventurous east-to-west sierra-and-canyon crossing from Topía to **Coloma,** a village near the Sinaloa state border, would take about a week of serious up-and-down hiking; guides may be available in Topía.

Mexico 26 continues 52 km north of Santiago Papasquiaro to the sierra town of **Tepehuanes,** once a center for Tepehuanes but now a timber center inhabited mainly by mestizos. Tepehuanes has a PEMEX station (Nova only) and three small, basic hotels.

Canutillo

Francisco "Pancho" Villa chose this small town (pop. 2,090) at 1,890 meters (6,199 feet) in the sierra foothills for his retirement following an illustrious career of banditry and revolution. His retirement was cut short by a fusillade of bullets fired into his car in nearby Parral in 1923 (see "Hidalgo de Parral" in the Chihuahua chapter for details).

A small museum in Villa's retirement hacienda displays photos and memorabilia from his life. Canutillo is just off Mexico 45, 131 km north of Presa Lázaro Cárdenas, or about 85 km south of Parral.

NORTHEASTERN DURANGO

Gómez Palacio

Founded in 1898, this commercial center forms a corner of the Región Lagunera urban triangle that includes larger Torreón and smaller Lerdo. Bringing cotton to market from surrounding farms is the town's main life support; Levi Strauss and Co. has a large plant here, as does Renault, the French automobile manufacturer.

For culture as well as superior hotel selection, most visitors passing through the region opt for neighboring Torreón, just across the border in Coahuila (see the Coahuila chapter for information). If you stop in Gómez Palacio, the only sight of mild interest is the **Casa de Cultura** at calles Berlín and Rosas in Colonía Campestre. Included in the complex are a contemporary art museum with rotating exhibits and a small history museum, both open Tues.-Sun. 9 a.m.-1 p.m. and 4-7 p.m.

Accommodations and Food: The best hotel in town is the four-star **Hotel Posada del Río** (tel. 17-14-33-99, fax 17-14-74-83), at Av. Fco. Madero Sur and Juárez downtown. Rooms with a/c, satellite TV, phones, and private bath cost US$58 s/d.

Several smaller hotels along Av. Fco. Madero in the US$18-25 range include **Motel La Siesta** (tel. 14-28-40; Av. Madero 320 Nte.), **Motel La Cabaña** (tel. 14-16-78; Av. Madero 1630 Nte.), and **Hotel Monarrez** (tel. 14-11-99; Av. Madero and Centenario).

The **Quinta Colima Trailer Park,** three blocks east of the Renault plant, has RV slots with full hookups.

Clean and efficient **Restaurant Martin's** (tel. 17-14-75-41) at Blvd. Alemán and Victoria offers a good menu of Mexican standards as well as breakfasts and a few North American selections. Open daily 7 a.m.-midnight.

Mapimí

The Misión de Mapimí ("rock on the hill") was founded in 1598 by Jesuit padres but the surrounding territory was so inhospitable that development in the surrounding area gradually shifted toward the Región Lagunera (Gómez Palacio, Lerdo, and Torreón), where irrigation was possible.

Today the town of Mapimí, 64 km northwest of Gómez Palacio on Mexico 30, isn't a worthwhile stop in itself except to see the nearby 320-meter (1,050-foot) suspended bridge, **Puente Colgante de Ojuela.** Said to be the longest such span in the Americas, the bridge was built of iron and wood in 1892 on the west side of the Sierra de la Bufa to allow mining trains to ford a deep gorge. Most mining in the area was suspended by the 1920s; now a few Japanese firms maintain chicken farms in the area.

Ask in Mapimí for a local guide who can arrange day trips to the bridge and to the **Grutas de La Lágrima,** a set of picturesque caverns in the nearby Sierra del Rosario. Pantera Excursiones in Durango (see "Tours" under "Durango (City) and Vicinity") also offers small group tours to the Mapimí region.

El Bolsón De Mapimí
And La Zona De Silencio
Roughly centered on an area straddling meridian 104 and parallel 27 near the heart of the arid Bolsón de Mapimí (at the three-way intersection of the Chihuahua, Durango, and Coahuila state borders), the so-called "Zone of Silence" is one of the most remote desert areas in all of Mexico. The name derives from the common assumption (though never thoroughly tested) that radio signals can neither be sent nor received within the zone. Whether this phenomenon is due to a local electromagnetic disturbance or occurs for some more mysterious reason is a matter of ongoing debate.

According to a growing number of occult groups and mystics, the Zona de Silencio forms part of the Earth's "belly-button chakra," a powerful energy source traced by the planet's 27th parallel. Believers in this "Mystery Parallel" point out that it intersects the Caribbean's Bermuda Triangle, Egypt's Great Pyramids, and Tibet's mythical Shambhala in the Himalayan cordillera.

UFOs and Missiles: A smaller following of UFO cultists claim that the *zona* is a landing site used as a "safe haven," free from radar detection or other terrestrial interference, for extraterrestrial spaceship repairs or other necessary ground contact. According to both groups, the unexplained 1970 crash here of an Athena missile fired from Green River, Utah (with an intended White Sands Missile Range, New Mexico, touchdown nearly a thousand miles

north)—as well as the perennial landing of an unusually high number of meteorites in the zone—is an indication that something out of the ordinary is going on in the Zona de Silencio.

The Athena missile crash is particularly perplexing because the 70-ton projectile totally disappeared from U.S. radar screens before leaving Utah airspace. Reports of a strange ball of fire in the sky from a nearby ranch resident led authorities to the vicinity of the crash site, but it took nearly three weeks for scientists in jeeps and helicopters to find the exact location, a large crater (formed by the missile's nose cone, which was carrying radioactive cobalt) in a sand dune just 600 meters from the Chihuahua-Durango line. One of many unanswered questions about the crash is why a missile (and its associated launch mechanisms) with lunar target capabilities could veer from such a short course as the Utah-New Mexico route without detection. Mexican sources have suggested that the Athena crash was engineered by NASA to give U.S. scientists an excuse to scrutinize the mysterious Zona de Silencio more closely.

So otherworldly is the zone that NASA officials had previously considered training American astronauts here to simulate lunar landings. (A training site in Mexico's Desierto del Pinacate in Sonora was later selected instead.) Rocket scientist Werner Von Braun supposedly flew a private plane here several times in 1969-70 with the idea of locating a radio-telescope in the zone because of the lack of radio interference.

Minerals and Meteors: The area surrounding the zone is a favorite destination for mineral collectors due to the abundance of exceptional samples of agate, selenite, calcite, and meteorite chunks. Meteorites are said to fall here almost every day of the year. Whether this is true or not, the zone's exceptionally clear air makes it an excellent place to observe nighttime meteor showers.

Two of the largest ferrous (iron-containing) meteorites ever discovered fell to earth in the zone. But the most notorious meteorite landing here was 1969's "Allende meteorite" (named for a nearby ranch) said to be the most thoroughly investigated piece of cosmic debris in the history of extraterrestrial geology. German and American researchers dated this chunk of carbonaceous material—which entered the earth's atmosphere with a supersonic thunderclap and greenish glow—at over five billion years old, more ancient than anything in our own solar system. *Scientific American* (August 1971) concluded that the meteorite consisted of "virgin planetary material" dating to the primordial cosmic explosion that created the universe. These and subsequent findings forced scientists to alter then-current "big bang" theories which had dated the origin of the physical universe at least a half-billion years later.

Biosphere Reserve: A few kilometers east of the Zona de Silencio is something of more tangible value—the best preserved section of Chihuahuan Desert *bolsón* in Mexico. *Gopherus flavomarginatus,* the largest land turtle in North America, is native to the area and is said to have descended from a species of sea turtle that lived here a hundred million years ago when the region was under a vast Cretaceous Period sea that geologists call the Mare of Tethys. *Flavomarginatus* lives up to 200 years and may weigh as much as 20 kilograms (44 pounds). To protect this exceptional (and endangered) tortoise as well as a number of other endemic fauna and flora, the United Nations—in coop- eration with the Mexican government—declared 160,000 hectares of the Bolsón de Mapimí as a Biosphere Reserve in 1976 as part of its "Man and Biosphere" (MAB) program. To date, the program encompasses around 280 reserves in 70 countries worldwide.

A UNESCO-funded research station, the **Laboratorio del Desierto del Instituto de Ecología,** has been established in the Mapimí *ejido* of San Ignacio to study *bolsón* ecology. For a brief description of *bolsón* environments, see "Geography" in the Introduction chapter.

Getting There: The best way to reach the Zona de Silencio and Biosphere Reserve is by vehicle. Drive north from Gómez Palacio about 120 km (or south 110 km from Jimenez) along Mexico 49 to a gravel road heading east from the highway just south of the small town of Ceballos. This road passes through the heart of the Reserve and leads to the "Punta de Triño" ("Triad Point") where the states of Durango, Chihuahua, and Coahuila meet—the center of the Zona de Silencio—about 55 km from Mexico 49. If you see any little green men or such, please send detailed descriptions!

THE STATE OF ZACATECAS

An inland state in north-central Mexico, Zacatecas sits high on the Altiplano, the central plateau between the Sierra Madres Occidental and Oriental, at an average elevation of around 2,400 meters (7,800 feet). Long before the Spanish entered the region in the 1530s, the Aztecs and other Amerindian cultures had been extracting silver (which they valued over gold) in the area.

Today the state's sparse population depends on the mining of gold, silver, and other minerals at higher elevations, along with ranching (statewide) and limited agriculture in the southern and central regions of the state. Many of Mexico's best fighting bulls are bred and raised at the haciendas of San Mateo, Malpaso, and Trancoso.

The *vaquero* (cowboy) tradition in Zacatecas has a stronger Mexican flavor than farther north, as indicated by the change of hat style from the curly-brimmed, Texas-style Stetson to the broader- and flatter-brimmed *sombrero* with tassels dangling from the back of the crown. *Charrería,* which is said to have originated in the state, is particularly robust in Zacatecas, which means that opportunities to attend *charreadas* or to purchase saddlery and *trajes de charros* (*charro* suits) are plentiful.

ZACATECAS (CITY) AND VICINITY

Perched in a high river gorge between two arid peaks, at an altitude of 2,496 meters (8,200 feet), the state capital is Mexico's second highest city and one of its major cultural treasures. Its steep, cobbled streets lined with colonial architecture constructed of *cantera rosa* (pink sandstone)—including the single best example of Churrigueresque cathedral architecture in all of Mexico—along with museums endowed with some of the best collections of both colonial and modern art in the country, attract a steady stream of Mexican visitors.

Yet the city has remained oddly anonymous among international tourists. Of the republic's 31 states, Zacatecas, with its museums, archeological zones, and historical monuments (*ex-conventos, casas históricas, capillas,* and *templos*), ranked ninth in national tourist visitation according to the 1990 census (drawing 166,000, only 7,800 of whom were non-Mexicans), exceeding figures for Chiapas (164,000), Guanajuato (120,000), and Jalisco (22,000). Another census will not be taken until the year 2000.

Because of its authentically pre-modern cityscape, Zacatecas was chosen as one of the location settings for U.S.-produced *The Old Gringo,* a film starring Gregory Peck and Jane Fonda that speculated about San Francisco journalist Ambrose Bierce's disappearance in Mexico during the 1910-20 revolution. Along

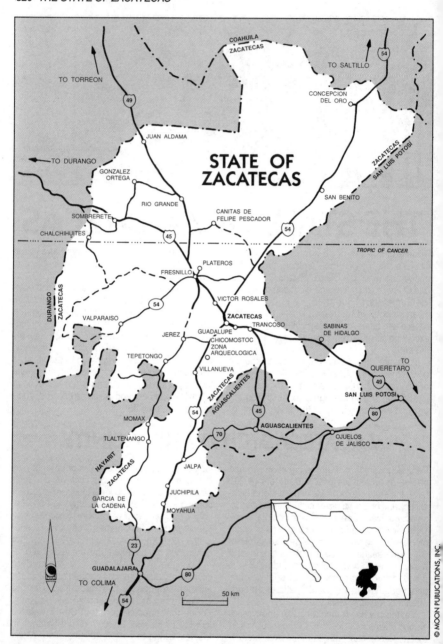

STATE OF ZACATECAS

TO TORREON

TO DURANGO

COAHUILA
ZACATECAS

TO SALTILLO

CONCEPCION
DEL ORO

JUAN ALDAMA

GONZALEZ
ORTEGA

RIO GRANDE

SOMBRERETE

CHALCHIHUITES

ZACATECAS
SAN LUIS POTOSI

SAN BENITO

CANITAS DE
FELIPE PESCADOR

TROPIC OF CANCER

PLATEROS

FRESNILLO

VICTOR ROSALES

DURANGO
ZACATECAS

VALPARAISO

ZACATECAS

TRANCOSO

SABINAS
DE HIDALGO

JEREZ

GUADALUPE
CHICOMOSTOC
ZONA
ARQUEOLOGICA

TO
QUERETARO

TEPETONGO

VILLANUEVA

ZACATECAS
AGUASCALIENTES

SAN LUIS POTOSI

MOMAX

AGUASCALIENTES

TLALTENANGO

NAYARIT
ZACATECAS

OJUELOS
DE JALISCO

JALPA

JUCHIPILA

GARCIA DE
LA CADENA

MOYAHUA

GUADALAJARA

TO COLIMA

0   50 km

© MOON PUBLICATIONS, INC.

with a strong respect for tradition, however, Zacatecans display a definite taste for chic in their fashionable dress and tony downtown shops.

HISTORY

Before the *entrada,* Amerindian groups living in what is now the state of Zacatecas included the Zacatecos (from *zacatl* or "grass," and *tecatl* or "people"), Guachichiles, Pames, and Tepehuanes. Although missionaries were mining for souls in Zacatecas as early as the 1530s, silver drew the Spanish to the area in considerable numbers after Juan de Tolosa found a rich vein at the foot of Cerro de la Bufa in 1546. Initially called "Las Minas de Nuestra Señora de los Zacatecas," the city became the third richest in Nueva España by the mid-17th century, when it was supplying at least 20% of Spain's mineral wealth from the Americas.

A social hierarchy of *criolla* mine owners living in the city, cattle ranchers in surrounding haciendas, military officers in nearby *presidios,* and Indian workers literally at the bottom—extracting silver ore in deep mine shafts day and night—developed early in the city's evolution. The overall prosperity also provided an infrastructure for the establishment of Zacatecas as an important spiritual headquarters for the Catholic missionization of all Spanish-held areas to the north. Most religious architecture in the city dates to the Seraphic Order's founding of the influential Propaganda Fide de Nuestra Señora de Guadalupe during the 18th century; other Catholic sects that based their northern missionary efforts in Zacatecas included the Franciscans, Jesuits, Dominicans, and Augustines.

Silver mining remained strong throughout the 19th and early 20th centuries, interrupted only by the civil wars of the mid-19th century and the 1910-20 Mexican Revolution. On June 23, 1914, Pancho Villa and his División del Norte liberated the city from Huerta's troops in a famous revolutionary battle known as "La Toma de Zacatecas."

Silver from the nearby Mina El Bote continues to be one of the city's major sources of income, supplemented by ranching, viticulture, the arts, and tourism.

CLIMATE

Because of the city's high elevation, temperatures tend to be milder than elsewhere in Northern Mexico. April-Aug. are the warmest months, although daytime temperatures rarely rise beyond 26° C (80° F). Any time of year evenings can be chilly, so be sure to bring a jacket òr sweater.

Rain is negligible Oct.-May, while even during the June-Sept. rainy season monthly precipitation seldom exceeds 8.9 cm (3.5 inches).

SIGHTS

Walking is the best way to see the city, as the narrow streets and switchback curves may be confounding to motorists who don't know the city well. When Spanish architects designed the layout in the 17th and 18th centuries, they couldn't follow the typical grid pattern and instead allowed the Arroyo de la Plata's steep and angled topography to create a city full of twists, turns, and uneven planes—imagine an M.S. Escher drawing brought to life. Sudden ascents and descents of the cobbled street and walkway surfaces, sharp bends, and narrow, steep alleys are commonplace, providing a visual surprise at almost every corner and an overall surrealist perspective to the city. Bring sturdy walking shoes.

In the older part of the city, wedged into the space between Cerro de la Bufa and Cerro del Grillo, the architecture consists of broad planes of stone assembled in cubistic forms with baroque ornamentation. Development moved down the valley from Cerro de la Bufa in a southwesterly direction from here, so that the buildings become more modern in style from east to west. Early Tlaxcalteca masonry skills have been inherited by today's Zacatecan stonemasons, who are among the most talented in Mexico.

As in San Luis Potosí, many buildings originally built in the 18th-century, neo-Hispanic baroque style had their facades remodeled in the neoclassical style during the late 19th and early 20th centuries.

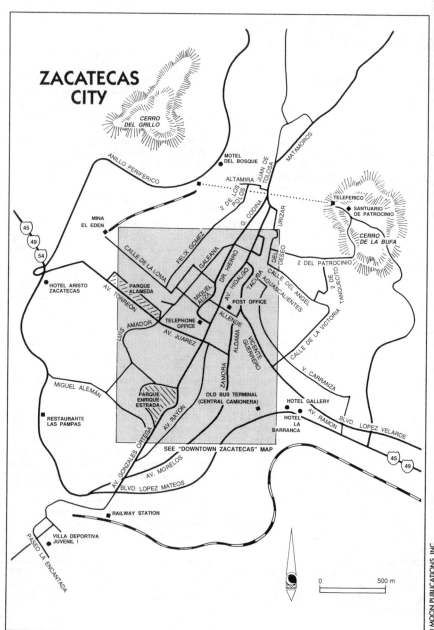

ZACATECAS CITY

SEE "DOWNTOWN ZACATECAS" MAP

© MOON PUBLICATIONS, INC.

Catedral De Zacatecas

Originally constructed as Capilla de Santo Cristo in 1707, then redone as a *parroquía* in 1718, the current cathedral began construction in 1729 and was finally consecrated in 1752. Cathedral status was bestowed in 1859 with the creation of a Zacatecas diocese. The entire construction was carried out in pink sandstone, a typical medium for Zacatecan architecture ever since.

The three-tiered main facade is considered a masterpiece of baroque design, with its intensive floral ornamentation resembling cake frosting artfully squeezed from a *pastelero's* tube onto 18 Solomonic columns. A huge *rosetta* over the heavy wooden doors contains stained glass. Surmounting the facade is a Christ figure presiding over six apostles and six church fathers on baroque pedestals.

A large, classical stone crucifix dominates the north facade, while the south facade features the richly carved Virgen de los Zacatecas, both impressive works of stonemasonry. Symmetrical, tile-domed towers—each containing 16 belfries—are identical in design and coloring even though they're a hundred years apart in construction (north tower 1785, south tower 1904).

The stone interior of the cathedral—worked over during the Reform—is relatively bare.

The cathedral faces Av. Hidalgo, between the Plaza de Armas and the Mercado González Ortega.

Templo De Santo Domingo

Next door to the Pedro Coronel museum, at the junction of calles Villalpando and Dr. Hierro, is the city's most well-endowed church. Built by the Jesuits in 1746-49 and modified by the Dominicans after the Jesuit expulsion in 1767, Santo Domingo has a more impressive interior than the Catedral de Zacatecas, with eight gilded baroque *retablos,* original wooden-plank flooring, and religious paintings by Francisco Martínez (hung in the sacristy).

Ex-Templo De San Agustín

At the southern end of Calle Miguel Auza at Callejón del Lazo, this former Augustinian church and convent is thought to have been designed by Andrés Manuel de la Riva, the architect of Guanajuato's La Valenciana. One of the oldest religious structures in the state, the church was begun in 1590, consecrated in 1617, and renovated in 1782 to produce a unique octagonal, neo-Hispanic baroque cupola over the nave. Following the Reform, the property was sold first for use as a gaming house and hotel in 1863 and then again to the U.S. Presbyterian Society of Missions in 1882. Later the structure was used as a community hall, again as a hotel, then as a warehouse, and finally as a bishopry, its main function today.

The Presbyterians destroyed the beautiful baroque facade in front and replaced it with a plain white wall. Fortunately, a striking Churrigueresque side facade remains intact; it depicts St. Augustine in the garden of his house during his conversion, flanked by six empty or partially empty niches. The restored interior courtyard is decorated with stone masonry of note and contains a few historical exhibits, including sketches of the original facade.

The building is open Mon.-Fri. 10 a.m.-2 p.m. and 4-7 p.m., Sat. 10 a.m.-4 p.m. Admission is free.

Teatro Calderón

This huge, three-story theater (each story four meters/13 feet tall), opposite Mercado González Ortega on Av. Hidalgo, opened in 1832 and remains one of the city's most important cultural centers. Extensive reconstruction in 1891 gave the building a neoclassical style with art nouveau and beaux arts undertones. The authentically restored interior remains faithful to 19th-century theater design.

Operated today by the Universidad Autónoma de Zacatecas (U.A.Z.), the theater regularly hosts drama, music, and dance performances in its main hall, as well as lectures, round-table discussions, readings, theater workshops, and dance classes in smaller ancillary rooms.

Plaza De Armas

The large, empty plaza is more notable for the buildings that surround it than for the flagstone space itself. Facing the west side of the plaza (adjacent to the Hotel Paraíso Radisson) is the neoclassical **Palacio de Justicia,** originally the mansion of a Basque mine owner named Manuel de Rétegui. It's more commonly known as the "Palacio de la Mala Noche" ("Palace of the Bad Night"), named after Rétegui's Mala Noche mine. According to local legend, the mine received its name because its principal lode was unearthed one night while Rétegui sat in his mansion contemplating suicide after having exhausted all his funds on mineral exploration. A side door to the mansion opens onto Callejón de Veyna—a level above the plaza—supposedly put in place to allow Don Manuel to come and go unnoticed from the mansion's second floor. Actually this pedestrian alley is typical of callejones that connect upper and lower street levels throughout the city. The building's large interior courtyard is open to the public.

On the east side of the plaza, the sober, 18th-century **Palacio de Gobierno** has been remodeled to exhibit the flattened window pilasters typical of the post-neoclassical or republican style. In the interior courtyard is a mural by Antonio Pinto Rodríguez depicting the history of the city.

Mercado González Ortega ("El Mercado")

Opposite the south side of the cathedral, this 1886-vintage municipal market is one of the most splendid of its type in Mexico. The beaux-arts-style building was designed so that the upper level, opening onto Av. Hidalgo, was to be used as the main sales area while the lower level, opening onto Calle Tacuba on the opposite side, could be used as a warehouse. Large-scale, wrought-iron columns serve as portales along the upper level, which is now filled with posh boutique-style shops. The Tacuba level is occupied by two restaurants specializing in regional cuisine.

Adjacent to the market building is a widened callejón known as **Plaza Goitia**, where outdoor musical performances are frequently held.

Museo Pedro Coronel

The former Jesuit Colegio y Seminario de San Luis Gonzaga (established 1616) two blocks northwest of El Mercado on Plaza de Santo Domingo (adjacent to Templo de Santo Domingo) houses one of the best private art collections in the country. All are works accumulated by Zacatecas painter and sculptor Pedro Coronel (1922-85), who, before his death, bequeathed his estate to the city. Most of the collection is on display here, while a smaller portion is exhibited at the Museo Francisco Goitia (see entry below).

Opened to the public in 1983, this well-curated, not-to-be-missed museum contains hundreds of works—many of them gifts of the artists—by Pablo Picasso, Salvador Dali, Marc Chagall, Georges Braque, Jean Cocteau, Henry Moore, Victor Branner, Joan Miró, Antonio Saura, Alexander Calder, Robert Motherwell, Josef Albers, and George Segal, as well as paintings and sculptures by Coronel himself. Highlights include a large series of works by Goya (including La Tauromaquía and Los Proverbios), exquisite 18th-century architectural prints by Venetian architect Gian Battista Piranesi, and a roomful of William Hogart etchings.

Separate rooms off the main upper colonnade contain displays of Greek and Roman sculpture dating 200 B.C.-A.D. 200; traditional art from Thailand, Burma, Cambodia, China, Japan, Tibet, Sri Lanka, India, Persia, and Egypt; a small African mask collection; excellent pre-Cortesian sculpture from the culturas de occidente (Colima, Jalisco, Nayarit, and Michoacán); lesser Mayan art from the Yucatán peninsula; Mexican and Guatemalan masks; and 18th-century Mexican religious art.

Students of Spanish literature may be interested in the **Biblioteca Elías Amador** on the ground floor near the entrance. The valuable, 25,000-volume book collection contains the bulk of the city's historical literary sources, including writings from most of the original convents dating from the 16th-19th centuries.

The museum is open Mon.-Wed. and Fri.-Sat. 10-2 and 4-7, Sun. 10-5; closed Thursday. Admission is US$0.60.

Antiguo Templo Y Convento De San Francisco And Museo Rafael Coronel

In 1593 the Franciscans established a convent on this site, from which they sent missionary expeditions to New Mexico, Arizona, Colorado, and Texas. The adjacent church, the oldest in the city, was completed at the end of the 17th century and features a baroque facade with triple-tiered Solomonic columns. The Jesuits eventually took over church and convent until the Jesuit expulsion in 1767, after which the property was abandoned. Mostly roofless, the ruins of the former Templo de San Francisco have been landscaped to create a pleasant, parklike atmosphere, which makes exploring the ruins especially enjoyable.

Opened to the public in 1990 after years of neglect, the convent today contains a collection of over 3,000 Mexican masks that belonged to Zacatecan painter Rafael Coronel (brother of Pedro Coronel). A plaque near the entrance carries a quotation from Mexican writer Miguel Covarubias that summarizes the organizing principles for the curatorship of the masks: "The mask poses strange powers of suggestion over the imagination. It represents the synthesis and essence of deity, diabolism, death, and heroism." The well-labeled (in Spanish) exhibits provide a good overall introduction to basic Mexican mask types.

The main galleries on the convent's second floor display masks used to represent demons, *pascolas* (deer hunts), *moros y cristianos* (Moors and Christians), animals, death, and *pastorales* (the suffering on the journey to Bethlehem in order to view the infant Christ) in traditional ritual and dance. A smaller gallery on the ground floor houses a collection of pre-Hispanic ceramics, and another houses marionettes from Mexico, Indonesia, India, Burma, and China.

The museum and church are about a kilometer northeast of the Plaza de Armas; follow Av. Hidalgo till it becomes Calle Juan de Tolosa; once past the Fuente de los Conquistadores, bear right at the fork, and the church-convent complex will soon appear on the left. Also on the premises are a museum-operated cafe and gift shop. The museum and facilities are open Mon.-Tues. and Thurs.-Sat. 10-2 and 4-7 p.m., Sun. 10-5; closed Wednesdays. Admission is US$1.65.

Museo Francisco Goitia (Goytia)

In an ex-governor's mansion encircled by rose gardens at Calle Gral. E. Estrada 102 (on the west side of Parque Enrique Estrada), this museum houses nearly a hundred years' worth of paintings, silk screens, and sculptures by six Zacatecan artists who lived and worked in the 19th and 20th centuries: Francisco Goitia, Pedro Coronel, Rafael Coronel, Manuel Felguérez, Julio Ruelas, and José Kuri Breña.

The museum is open Tues.-Sun. 10 a.m.-2 p.m., 5-8 p.m.; there is a small admission fee.

Gardens

Jardín Juárez, a leafy and quiet garden plaza tucked away at the southern end of Calle Miguel Auza, just beyond the U.A.Z. rectory, was fashioned in 1857 and offers a nearly hidden refuge from the city's stony streets. A passageway off the garden through the neoclassic, 19th-century **Mesón de Jovito** leads to another small garden, **Jardín de la Madre** (more commonly known as Jardín Morelos).

Farther northwest in the same direction is the considerably larger **Alameda** (full name "Alameda Trinidad García de la Cadena"), Zacatecas's counterpart to New York's Central Park. During spring, this long, rectangular expanse of trees and monuments dedicated to illustrious local figures becomes a daily venue for *trobadores* performing *mañanitas* or morning songs.

The **Parque Enrique Estrada** (also known as the Parque González Ortega because a statue of the Zacatecan hero stands in the park), off Av. González Ortega between the Museo Goitia and the aqueduct, is even larger and more wooded.

Acueducto Del Cubo

At the east edge of Parque Enrique Estrada, across Av. González Ortega, is an impressive stone aqueduct with flying buttresses begun by the Spanish and finished during the early years of the independent republic. The aqueduct continued to carry water from the Arroyo de la Plata until early this century.

Cerro De La Bufa

La Bufa (named for its nearly vertical shape, thought to resemble a *bufa,* the lower visor of a 16th-century Spanish helmet) towers over Zacatecas and provides the widest possible view of the city. It can be reached on foot via Calle del Angel (east of the Mercado González Ortega), by car via a road that winds around to the summit, or by *teleférico* (cable car) from the lower Cerro del Grillo on the northwest side of town.

Several bloody battles were fought on the hill, including confrontations between the Royalists and *insurgentes* during the struggle for Mexican independence, between conservatives and liberals during the War of Reform, and between the Villistas and Huertistas during the Mexican Revolution.

Scattered monuments on the summit bear witness to these and other historical events. The **Santuario del Patrocinio** (also known as the Capilla de Nuestra Señora de los Zacatecas), was built in 1728 to honor the city's patron saint, embodied in a highly venerated image known as the Virgen del Patrocinio. The Virgen dates to the first La Bufa chapel, which was built in 1548; the chapel has been restored many times, most recently in 1967. Every year between Sept. 3-15, thousands of worshipers and *matachine* dancers climb La Bufa in pilgrimage to the sanctuary. The climax of the celebration occurs on Sept. 8, when the Virgen is carried from the sanctuary to the Catedral de Zacatecas below.

In front (west) of the sanctuary, the **Museo de la Toma de Zacatecas** chronicles Pancho Villa's victory over Huerta's forces, a decisive battle in the Mexican revolutionary campaign. Inaugurated in 1984 in commemoration of the battle's 70th anniversary, the simple museum contains weapons, uniforms, newspaper clippings, photos, and a miniature model of the battle. The **Plaza de la Revolución,** on the other side of the sanctuary, commemorates the same event in a larger context. Nearby are equestrian statues of the three *caudillos* who led the revolutionary division: Francisco "Pancho" Villa, Felipe Angeles, and Pánfilo Natera.

Farther east on the road to the summit is the **Mausoleo de los Hombres Ilustres,** a collection of tombs where famous Zacatecans are interred. The **Observatorio Meteorológico,** a functioning weather observatory, sits on the edge of the summit facing town.

Teleférico Zacatecas And Mina El Edén

A Swiss-built *teleférico* (cable car) system carries passengers between the two hills on either side of the city in about eight minutes, a trip that affords panoramic views of the cityscape below.

The main cable car station is on the Cerro del Grillo side off Paseo Díaz Ordaz, a short but steep walk from the Plaza de Armas area.

The station is linked via a two-car tramway with the **Mina El Edén,** a former silver mine which began operations in 1583 and closed in the 1960s. Most of the silver that built the city came from El Edén, an ironic name given the severe working conditions. When the tram is running, visitors can ride to the end of the tracks (1.6 km/one mile), then walk about 400 meters through the mine shafts with a tour guide to view rickety wooden ladders, rope bridges, and a subterranean chapel. The mine shafts are lit with bare light bulbs 12:30-7:30 p.m.; when the tram isn't running you can walk in on your own. A discotheque built into the mine is open at night.

Tickets for both the tramway and cable car cost US$2.60 roundtrip; both run daily 12:30-7:30 p.m.

ZACATECAS ACCOMMODATIONS

Zacatecas doesn't have a huge variety of accommodations, but the selection is more than adequate.

Budget Hotels And Hostels

Zacatecas has two youth hostels (all ages welcome) where beds are only US$2 per person per night. **Villa Deportiva Juvenil I** is a 70-bed facility at Parque del Encantado 103 (tel. 492-2-18-01; A.P. 159), five minutes south of the train station, around 10 minutes from the city bus terminal. **Villa Deportiva Juvenil II** (tel. 2-93-77) has 100 beds at Av. de los Deportes 100, adjacent to the west side of Estadio Francisco Villa—quite a distance east from the city center.

Near the aqueduct and former bullring, **Hotel del Parque** (tel. 2-04-79), at Av. González Ortega 302, has simple, quiet rooms for US$12 s, US$15 d. There is no sign out front—look for the gold letters "HP" on the glass door of a modern building south of Hotel Quinta Real and Parque Enrique Estrada on the right (west) side of the road.

A couple of hotels in the vicinity of the city bus terminal offer basic rooms in the US$10-12 range, including **Hotel Río Grande** (tel. 2-53-49) at Calz. de la Paz 503. The **Hotel La Barranca** (tel. 2-14-94), at Av. López Mateos 401 a bit east of the city bus terminal, has better rooms for US$15 s, US$19 d.

Out on Mexico 45 east of the city, **Motel El Convento** (tel. 2-08-49) is convenient for highway travelers and costs US$18 s, US$22 d; a restaurant is attached.

Medium-priced Hotels

Several historic buildings downtown contain simply furnished, reasonably priced hotels. Rooms tend to be drafty in the cooler months and heating may not be adequate; ask the management for the loan of a space heater (*calen-*

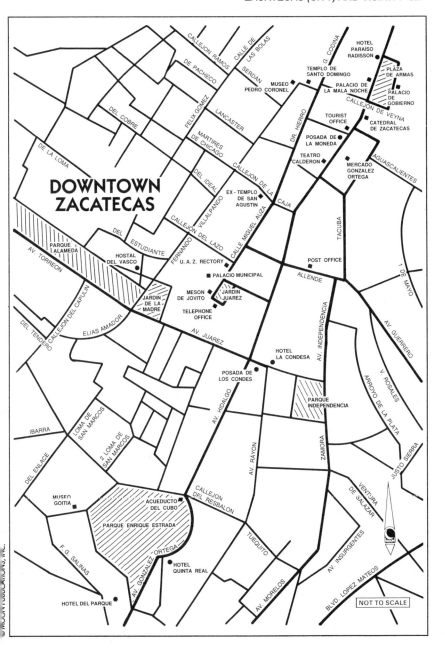

DOWNTOWN ZACATECAS

tador) if your room is uncomfortably cold. Or wear more clothes! These places are built around courtyards; for maximum quiet, request a room off the street.

The 19th-century **Hotel Condesa** (tel. 492-2-11-60), at Av. Juárez 5 (downtown off Av. Hidalgo), looks impressively historic on the outside, less than inspiring but livable inside. Rooms with private bath cost US$22 s, US$29 d.

Housed in an 18th-century mansion on the opposite side of Av. Juárez from Hotel Condesa is **Posada de los Condes** (tel. 2-14-12, 2-10-93), where better rooms go for US$28 s, US$33 d. The moderately priced cafe here receives high marks.

In the 19th-century building next door to the Teatro Calderón on Av. Hidalgo, **Posada de la Moneda** (tel. 2-08-81) has decent rooms with carpeting, TV, and phones for US$30 s, US$37 d. Because of its location near the cathedral, this hotel is often full.

In a quiet corner of the historical district, just off the east end of the Alameda, **Hostal del Vasco** (tel. 2-04-28) provides nine spacious rooms (some with kitchenettes) in a restored 17th-century house for US$46 s, US$56 d. The courtyard contains a small but charming dining area.

Motel Del Bosque (tel. 2-10-34, 2-07-45), on Paseo Díaz Ordaz, Cerro del Grillo (near the tramway and cable car lines), offers aerial views of the city and three-star rooms for US$28 s, US$33 d. The road to the motel is quite steep.

East of the city at Km 120 on Mexico 45, beyond Motel El Convento, **Motel Hacienda Real** (tel. 3-37-45) has decent rooms with TV and phones for US$25 s, US$31 d.

Also east of the city on Mexico 45, beyond Motel El Convento on the right, **Hotel Parador Misión del Real** (tel. 3-26-61, fax 3-42-82) has good rooms with heating, a/c, phones, and satellite TV for US$55 s, US$62 d. Free shuttle service is provided to and from the airport; car rental is also available on the premises.

Luxury Hotels

The modern, five-story **Hotel Gallery Best Western** (tel. 492-2-33-11; 91-800-9-00-13 toll free; fax 492-2-34-15), on Blvd. López Mateos at Callejón del Barro (east of the old bus termi-

nal), has clean, well-maintained rooms with satellite TV, a/c, and individually controlled heating for US$60-65 s/d, US$65-70 t Jan. 1-April 30, plus US$10 on all rates May 1-Dec. 31. Facilities include a coffee shop, two squash courts, an indoor pool, and travel agency with car rental.

Opposite the Plaza de Armas on Av. Hidalgo in the heart of the historical district, **Hotel Paraíso Radisson** (tel. 2-61-83; 91-800-9-00-90 toll free in Mexico; 800-333-3333 outside Mexico; fax 2-62-45) is housed in an 18th-century baroque-neoclassical building that has been restored inside and out to offer 116 five-star rooms. On the premises are two restaurants (one overlooking the plaza), a bar, gift shop, beauty salon, and underground valet parking garage. Rack rates start at US$83 s/d, though room specials as low as US$57 are sometimes available.

A former bullring near the Acueducto del Cubo is now one of Mexico's most interesting hotel experiments, **Hotel Quinta Real** (tel. 2-91-04; 91-800-2-60-15 toll free in Mexico; 800-445-4565 in U.S./Canada; fax 2-84-40), Calle Rayón 434. The 46 suites (10 with Jacuzzis) and public areas have been built into and onto the Antiguo Plaza de Toros de San Pedro, reportedly the second oldest bullring in the western hemisphere (first opened in 1866). Rates are US$172-197 s/d.

Hotel Aristos Zacatecas (tel. 2-17-88), on Loma de la Soledad off Mexico 45 west of (and overlooking) the city, has rooms with all the amenities for US$75 up. Each room has a private terrace with a city view. Facilities include a heated pool, sauna, restaurant, and convention rooms.

A new entry in the luxury market, **Hotel Don Miguel** (tel. 4-10-02, fax 2-08-41), at Blvd. López Portillo and Calle del Plomo on the way to Guadalupe, has 84 rooms with all the international amenities for US$65-75 s/d.

RV Parks And Camping

Tent camping is permitted at the Villa Deportiva Juvenil I (see "Budget Hotels And Hostels," above) at no charge. **Motel Del Bosque** has six RV spaces with full hookups for US$10 a night, but bigger rigs might have trouble making the steep grade and tight turns on the Paseo Díaz Ordaz.

Morelos RV Park, 6.5 km (four miles) northwest of the city at the junction of Mexico 45 and Mexico 49, has 40 spaces with full hookups for US$9-12 per night. The adjacent restaurant is a popular road stop.

FOOD

Although local restaurants don't offer the range of cuisines found in San Luis Potosí, Zacatecans take gastronomy seriously and are keen to recommend places to eat. Common local specialties include *sopa de tortilla, carne adobada, enchiladas zacatecanas, pipián ranchero* (rich, pumpkin-seed sauce served over chicken), and *asado de boda* (a kind of pork mole). As in San Luis Potosí, *colonche,* an alcoholic beverage distilled from fermented cardón fruit juice, is occasionally seen. Zacatecan mezcal, however, is more popular. Zacatecan wines—especially those made from a vinifera hybrid of Carignan and cabernet sauvignon varietals—are among the best in Mexico.

Men riding burros slung with large terra-cotta jars sell *aguamiel,* a refreshing blend of water and honey, in the *centro histórico*.

Regional

$$ La Cantera Musical Fonda y Bar (tel. 492-2-99-28) is on the bottom floor of the Mercado González Ortega facing Tacuba. Housed in the market's former warehouse area, La Cantera features a casual, festive atmosphere and a large menu of regional dishes for around US$6-7 per entree. Among the house specialties are *mole rojo a la zacatecana, asado de boda,* and, on Sundays, a delicious *pipián ranchero* with chicken. *Menudo, pozole,* and *atole* are always available; tortillas are handmade on the premises. Open daily 9 a.m.-midnight.

$$ Restaurant Bar La Cuija (tel. 2-82-75) is on the bottom floor of the Mercado González Ortega facing Tacuba. A bit more formal, but only a little more expensive than La Cantera, La Cuija is associated with the Cacholá winery and features an extensive menu of fish, beef, and chicken dishes, along with a selection of Zacatecan wines. Open daily 8 a.m.-midnight.

National

$$-$$$ Los Candiles Restaurant, Hotel Paraíso Radisson, Av. Hidalgo. The light and airy at-mosphere here is a nice change from the typically dark interiors of many Zacatecas restaurants. The food—Mexican standards, *carne asada,* seafood, and continental—and service are very good. The Sunday buffet, held 1-6 p.m., is a good value. Open daily 7 a.m.-midnight.

$ Las Comales is opposite the cathedral on Av. Hidalgo. This unpretentious little restaurant serves inexpensive *antojitos* and *comidas corridas*. Open Mon.-Sat. 9 a.m.-10 p.m.

$$ La Villita Conjunto Gastronómico (tel. 492-2-62-22), Mesón de Jovito, facing Jardín de la Madre (Jardín Morelos). Divided into restaurant, *cafetería,* and patio sections, this unique spot offers Mexican standards in a colonial atmosphere. Open daily for lunch and dinner.

International

$$-$$$ Estanzzia Restaurant Bar (tel. 492-2-07-24), Av. González Ortega 349. A moderate-to-upscale spot with a Mexican, regional, and international menu. Open daily 1 p.m.-1 a.m.

$$$ Restaurante Las Pampas (tel. 2-30-09), Colegio Militar and Av. López Mateos 123. Specializes in charcoal-broiled steaks and chicken. Open daily noon-midnight.

$$$ Restaurant La Plaza (tel. 2-91-04), Hotel Quinta Real. Built into the former Plaza de Toros de San Pedro, this very elegant restaurant features a menu of original recipes based on Mexican and international standards. Open daily for breakfast, lunch, and dinner.

$$-$$$ Zacatecas Grill (tel. 3-30-39), on Blvd. López Portillo in Colonia Florida, east of city center. This relatively new spot is known for its Pacific seafood and fresh cuts of beef from local *ganaderías*. Open daily noon-midnight.

Other

$$ Café y Nevería Acrópolis (tel. 492-2-12-84), northwest corner of the Mercado González Ortega facing Av. Hidalgo. This coffee shop is popular for breakfasts, sandwiches, Mexican *antojitos,* pastries, ice cream, and 12 kinds of espresso, cappuccino, and other coffee drinks. Open daily 8:30 a.m.-11 p.m.

$$ La Terraza, upper floor of Mercado González Ortega facing east. This location has great potential, but the uninspired menu of burgers, sandwiches, and malts wouldn't attract a soul if it weren't for the view of the Calle Tacuba below. Open daily 11 a.m.-8 p.m.

$$ **Hostería de Santos** (tel. 4-05-61), Callejón del Santero 109, near the Mercado González Ortega. A casual spot with inexpensive *almuerzo,* free *botanas* with beverage orders in the afternoon, and *antojitos* in the evening. Open daily 9 a.m.-11 p.m.

$ Off Calle Allende at No. 116 is a corridor lined with inexpensive *loncherías* mixed in with beauty salons and luggage vendors. Near the old bus terminal are several more *loncherías.*

RECREATION

Bullfights And *Charreadas*

In Zacatecas the first *fiestas bravas* were recorded in 1593, making the city one of the oldest taurine venues in the country. Several bullrings have come and gone in the interim, including the stately Plaza de Toros de San Pedro, recently transformed into the Hotel Quinta Real.

The main stadium is now contained in the **Instalaciones de la Feria,** midway between Zacatecas and Guadalupe off Av. López Portillo. Adjacent to the Instalaciones is a large *charro* ring (*lienzo charro*) where *charreadas* are held regularly throughout the year. For a current schedule of corridas, inquire at the tourist office on Av. Hidalgo.

Bars And Discos

The **Bar Pirame** and **Bar El Botarel,** in the Paraíso Radisson and Quinta Real hotels respectively, are good places for a quiet drink. The **Centro Nocturno Los Granates** in the Hotel Gallery Best Western features live dance music Wed.-Sat. nights.

At the summit of Cerro del Grillo, on Paseo Díaz Ordaz next to the cable car station, the popular **Discoteque de Elefante Blanco** (tel. 492-3-02-02) is open for dancing Thurs.-Sat. 9 p.m.-2 a.m. The defunct **Mina El Edén,** a short distance southwest on Paseo Díaz Ordaz, contains a disco open the same days and hours as the Elefante Blanco.

Callejonadas

Zacatecas has a tradition of small fiestas held in pedestrian alleys (*callejones*), most often taking place on Saturdays. The typical *callejonada* features music (especially brass-band *conjuntos*), folkloric dancing, food, and speeches evoking civic pride. Inquire at the tourist office on Av. Hidalgo to learn of any upcoming alley parties. Plaza Goitia, the enlarged *callejón* next to El Mercado, is a frequent venue.

Shopping

Zacatecas is famous for its silver crafts fashioned from ore extracted from nearby Mina El Bote, and the downtown areas are dotted with silver shops. **Artesanías y Platería Real de Angeles,** near the cathedral at Callejón de G. Farias 97, has a good selection and good prices.

The **Centro Platero Zacatecano** (tel. 492-3-10-07, in the Ex-hacienda de Bernández, 20 minutes east of the city by car, is a silversmithing school where you can observe artisans at work and also buy silver pieces. The Centro maintains a storefront in the Mercado González Ortega downtown as well. To find the school, follow Av. López Mateos (Mexico 45/49) east until it becomes Blvd. México, then continue along this avenida until it ends at a T-intersection. Turn left on Restauradores and continue north along Mina la Cantera till you see signs for the Centro Platero Zacatecano.

Zacatecas is also known for its distinctive sarapes, which feature bold black-and-red stripes trimmed with black-and-white, geometric-patterned borders. Leatherwork—belts, saddles, boots, etc.—is another regional specialty. In the Mercado González Ortega, **La Espuela de Oro** sells *piteado* saddles (embroidered with *pita,* a hemplike succulent fiber), *charro* suits, hats, sarapes, silver *espuelas* (spurs), leather jackets, and other items associated with the state's *vaquero* tradition.

Wine is another good buy in Zacatecas. The *Cacholá* label is quite drinkable, especially the ruby cabernet (made from a grape that's a cross between cabernet sauvignon and Carignan). Other local labels include *Solera del Bodequiero, Puerta de Hierro, Los Pioneros,* and *Flor del Altiplano.* A typical bottle of Zacatecan wine costs just US$5 at one of the wine shops in the Mercado González Ortega. By prior arrangement, you can also visit the Cacholá winery in Valle de las Arsinas, Guadalupe, at Km 634 Mexico 45 (at the junction of Mexico 45 and Mexico 49, about 27 km/16.5 miles east of Zacatecas). Inquire at Restaurant La Cuija, which is partially owned by the Cacholá winery, about a visit; or contact Cacholá Wines (tel. 492-2-

77-30, fax 492-2-72-56), Carretera Panamericana Km 634, Valle de las Arsinas, Guadalupe.

Events
August: For three days each August Zacatecanos celebrate **La Morisma,** a richly costumed reenactment of the defeat of the *moros* (Moors) by the *cristianos* (Christians). Originally the ritual was developed by Spanish missionaries to inspire faith among Mexico's indigenous peoples, but it's now a Mexican tradition in the states of Puebla, Michoacán, Tlaxcala, Mexico D.F., and Zacatecas. The strongest and most elaborate Morisma tradition, however, is practiced in Zacatecas.

The annual venue for the event is El Bracho, a large field in the northeast section of the city where the turbaned Moors meet the helmeted Christians in a mock battle. Before being given lead roles in the performance, participants must train for years at the Cofradía de San Juan Bautista, a Zacatecas association devoted to the preservation of La Morisma. The battle ends with the capture and beheading of the Moorish king and is followed by musical performances and merrymaking.

September: Two weeks in September are devoted to the **Feria de Zacatecas,** which celebrates the founding of the city and pays homage to the city's patron saint, the Virgen del Patrocinio. Ranching, farming, and handicraft exhibitions are held at various places around the city, and the Teatro Calderón hosts a special series of musical and theatrical performances. For out-of-town visitors, the most colorful aspect of the annual *feria* is the *matachine* processions to the Santuario del Patrocinio on Cerro de la Bufa (see the "Cerro de la Bufa" entry above for details).

ZACATECAS INFORMATION

Tourist Offices
The **Dirección Estatal de Turismo** (tel. 492-2-66-83) operates a small information office opposite the cathedral at Av. Hidalgo 606, where sketch maps and brochures are available. Someone usually is on hand who speaks English.

The federal SECTUR delegation (tel. 2-67-50) is at Blvd. López Mateos 923-A.

ZACATECAS TELEPHONE NUMBERS

Local Police: 2-01-80
Highway Patrol: 2-20-39, 2-36-70
Green Angels: 2-40-08, 2-68-24
State Tourist Office: 2-66-83
Red Cross: 2-30-05
Emergencies: 06
Zacatecas Area Code: 492

Books And Maps
The City of Zacatecas, published by the state in 1991, is a glossy 150-page book with high-quality color photos and good background and sightseeing information. Available either in Spanish or English at various gift shops and museums, the book is rather expensive at US$30-40 (depending on where you purchase it).

The bilingual Zacatecas map issued by Centro Regional Zacatecas (Blvd. López Mateos 504) is the best of the locally available maps for sightseeing.

Post Office
The *correo* on the north side of Calle Allende between Hidalgo and Tacuba is a convenient location for visitors staying in or visiting the historical district.

GETTING THERE

Air
Mexicana (tel. 492-2-74-70, 2-32-48; Mercado González Ortega, Av. Hidalgo) flies nonstop to Zacatecas from Chicago, Los Angeles, Mexico City, San Francisco, and Tijuana. Services from L.A. and San Francisco are a bargain at only US$299 per roundtrip ticket.

TAESA (tel. 2-00-50; Av. Hidalgo 305) operates direct flights to/from Ciudad Juárez, Chicago, and Morelia, with connections to Los Angeles, Mexico City, and Tijuana.

Aero Guadalajara (tel. 2-71-94; Calle F. Villalpando 512) has nonstops to/from Guadalajara and Monterrey.

Zacatecas's airport is 25 km (15.5 miles) southwest of the city, a US$10 taxi ride, or US$3 in a *colectivo*.

Bus

Most interstate buses arrive at and depart from the Central Camionera on Terrenos de la Isabelica, off the *anillo periférico* (ring road). **Transportes Chihuahuenses** and **Transportes del Norte** operate first-class buses to/from Ciudad Juárez (US$39, four times daily), Chihuahua (US$31, 11 times daily), Durango (US$10, 10 times daily), Guadalajara (US$12, 12 times daily), Matamoros (US$35, once daily), Mexico City (US$28, four times daily), Monterrey (US$15, four times daily), Nuevo Laredo (US$35, once daily), Saltillo (US$15, four times daily), San Luis Potosí (US$8-10, six times daily) and Torreón (US$11, five times daily).

Estrella Blanca has less expensive second-class buses to many of the same cities as the above companies—including Ciudad Juárez, Chihuahua, Durango, Guadalajara, Monterrey, Nuevo Laredo, Saltillo, and San Luis Potosí—plus Fresnillo (US$5) and Mazatlán (US$15).

Omnibus de México operates from the old bus terminal at Blvd. López Mateo 719 and serves San Luis Potosí, Durango, Guadalajara, and Torreón with fares similar to those posted by Transportes del Norte.

Train

The city railway station is just south of the junction of Av. González Ortega and Blvd. López Mateos. *El División de Norte* stops in Zacatecas on its daily run between Mexico City and Ciudad Juárez. Between Zacatecas and the border, only second-class coaches are available, while between Zacatecas and Mexico City first-class reserved seats can also be selected. Sample fares to/from Zacatecas are Ciudad Juárez US$12, Chihuahua US$8, Torreón US$4.50, Mexico City US$6.60 (or US$24 first class reserved). See the "Railway Schedule," pp. 86-87, for arrival and departure times.

Driving

A four-lane tollway, Mexico 49D, links León Guzman (just south of Torreón) and Zacatecas in three separate sections, each with its own toll gate; the total toll for the entire 386-km (239-mile) route is around US$13. The original free road runs parallel to the tollway much of the way and is not much slower.

Drive cautiously along the stretch of Mexico 49 through Fresnillo (61 km/37.8 miles north-

west of Zacatecas), as the federal highway police are very vigilant in enforcing the 30 kph (18.6 mph) speed limit through town.

Southeast of Zacatecas on Mexico 49 between Guadalupe and Trancoso (about 14 km east of Guadalupe), the 24-hour **Santa Monica Centro de Descanso** offers Magna Sin, ice, a restaurant, clean restrooms, and an auto parts shop. Beyond Trancoso the Altiplano grasslands along Mexico 49 are studded with robust yucca trees, prickly pear, and agave—an area where Mexico's strongest fighting bulls are bred and raised.

GETTING AROUND

Bus

Zacatecas's *centro histórico* can easily be navigated on foot. Of the several city bus lines, most useful are the Ruta 7 between the central district and Blvd. López Mateos and the Ruta 8 bus between downtown and the Central Camionera.

Taxi

Taxicabs around town cost US$3-4 in the central district, US$6-7 for destinations along the Zacatecas-Guadalupe strip.

Driving

With its winding, steep, one-way streets, Zacatecas is not the easiest city to drive in. Fortunately, most streets are marked with names and one-way arrows, so with a little fortitude (and a map), you should be able to find your way around without too much aggravation. If sightseeing is your main objective, however, you'd do best to park your vehicle and see the city on foot.

Auto Rental: Two agencies rent cars in Zacatecas, **Budget** (tel. 492-2-94-58; Blvd. López Mateos 104, or at the airport) and **Arrendadora Número Uno** (tel. 2-09-74; Blvd. López Mateos 305).

VICINITY OF ZACATECAS

Guadalupe

If you have a spare half day to spend while in Zacatecas, don't miss the opportunity to visit this colonial town only five km (three miles) east of the state capital.

Adjacent to the main plaza is the **Ex-Convento de Guadalupe,** originally founded in 1707 by Franciscan friar Antonio Margil de Jesús as a center for the propagation of Catholicism in northern Nueva España. Restored and maintained by Mexico's INAH, the former convent now contains the **Museo de Arte Virreinal de Guadalupe,** a repository for some of Mexico's most outstanding viceregal art. Among the paintings on display are works by Ibarra, Antonio de Torres, Miguel Cabrera, and Andrés López. In the convent's upper cloister is a striking series of 14 oval-framed Cabrera paintings depicting scenes from the life of the Virgin Mary.

The baroque facade of the attached **Templo de Guadalupe** is in good condition and features a unique set of tripartite columns known as *tritósilas.* The choir contains heavy, opulently carved wooden chairs backed with holy portraits. Even more impressive is the convent's 19th-century **Capilla de Nápoles,** with its gilded dome and plasterwork and wood-parquet floor. On the main altar a figure of the Virgin Mary sculpted in Naples sits on an ornate domed pedestal.

The **Museo Regional de História,** in a former orphanage annexed to the convent, contains Huichol artifacts and a collection of horse carriages, antique cars, railway cars, and other transport-related exhibits.

Getting There: Guadalupe is linked to Zacatecas by Calz. López Portillo (Mexico 45/49); the five-km stretch between the two towns has developed so that they have really become part of one metropolitan unit. **Transportes de Guadalupe** runs frequent red-and-white buses from the Alameda in Zacatecas to central Guadalupe for US$0.21 each way.

Jérez De García Salinas

More commonly known simply as Jérez, the town was originally established in 1565 as a military post along the Camino Real and is today known for its authentic provincial-colonial architecture. Horse-mounted *vaqueros* are a common sight in the clean, cobbled streets lined with simple one-story colonials. In the evening the main plaza becomes a venue for a traditional Mexican courtship ritual wherein single men sitting on benches flirt with young women circumambulating the plaza.

Sights: Antique churches include the 18th-

century **Vieja Parroquia de la Inmaculada Concepción** and the 19th-century **Santuario de la Soledad.** The restored **Teatro Hinojosa,** facing the south side of the main plaza, is reportedly an exact replica of Washington, D.C.'s Ford Theater, where U.S. President Abraham Lincoln was assassinated. Both structures were inspired by the Paris Opera.

Jérez was the home of renowned poet Ramón López Velarde, whose house is now a museum containing memorabilia from Velarde's life and career.

Lodging and Food: Three small hotels on the Plaza Principal offer rooms in the US$18-24 range: **Hotel Jardín** (tel. 494-5-20-26; Plaza Principal 5 Pte.), **Hotel Plaza** (tel. 5-20-63; Plaza Principal 9 Sur), and **Hotel Central** (tel. 5-24-83; Plaza Principal 10 Sur). The Hotel Jardín has an attached restaurant and bar.

Seven-story **Leo Hotel** (tel. 5-20-01, fax 5-44-15), on the road in from Mexico 54, has modern rooms with a/c, heating, satellite TV, and phones for US$45 s/d. On the premises are a restaurant, bar, coffee shop, disco, car rental, and pool.

A number of decent restaurants are strung out along Av. E. Carranza-Suave Patria (a broad avenue that crosses the north side of Plaza Principal), including **Restaurant La Luz, Pollos Roca, El Bohemio Hostería,** and **El Patio Jarezano.**

Shopping: Jérez is well known for the cultivation of roses and for *cuero piteado,* leather embroidered with a cactus fiber. Several shops carry embroidered saddles, lariats, bridles, *chaparreras,* and boots—hand-crafted ranching accoutrements collectively known as *talabartería.*

Events: Beginning on Holy Friday in April, the town celebrates the 10-day **Fiesta de la Primavera** with bullfights, cockfights, flower shows, agricultural and ranching expositions, and other diversions.

Getting There: Línea Zacatecas Jérez operates second-class buses between Zacatecas and Jérez several times daily.

If you're driving from Zacatecas, take Mexico 54 south for 23 km (14 miles), then turn west at Malpaso and follow the signed, paved road 26 km (16 miles) to Jérez.

Chicomóstoc Ruins (La Quemada)

These enigmatic ruins south of the capital off Mexico 54 represent the northernmost outpost of

Mesoamerican culture. Archaeological evidence suggests the site was inhabited A.D. 350-1000, either by Toltecs or Náhuatlacs. The site may have been linked to Chalchihuites farther north near the Durango state line.

The ruins consist of several sets of circular, cylindrical, and rectangular monuments made of brick and stone, all perched on a barren hill overlooking the Valle de Villanueva. One of the more remarkable designs is the so-called **Salón de las Columnas** (Room of Columns), a set of 11 two-meter-high (6.5-feet-high) brick columns. The Huicholes of Zacatecas hold a highly secret peyote ceremony here a few days prior to the spring equinox each year, during which time the site is closed to the public.

Another set of stone structures is known as the **Juego de Pelota** ("Ball Court") and was used for the famous Mesoamerican ritual ball game known as far north as Casas Grandes in Chihuahua and as far south as Honduras. The function of the **Pirámide Votiva** ("Votive Pyramid"), at the northern edge of the site, remains a puzzle.

The ruins are open to the public daily except Monday 9 a.m.-5 p.m.

Getting There: There is no public transport to the ruins. A nine-km (5.6-mile) paved access road runs east off Mexico 54, 47 km (29 miles) south of Zacatecas.

Plateros

Seven km (4.3 miles) northeast of the silver-mining center of Fresnillo, at about 2,225 meters (7,300 feet), this small town revolves around pilgrimages to its **Santuario de Plateros.** The 18th-century church contains two highly revered images, El Señor de los Plateros (the patron saint of silversmiths) and El Santo Niño de Atocha (the Christ child as a pilgrim), which are the objects of pilgrimages throughout the year.

The Santo Niño in particular is thought to have the power to grant requests and perform miracles. Written on walls next to native paintings are personal testimonials such as, "I give thanks to El Santo Niño de Atocha for having miraculously opened the doors of work after I was out of a job for eight months."

Sombrerete

Midway between Durango and Fresnillo on Mexico 45, Sombrerete has the state's second largest collection of colonial architecture. Founded in 1155 and named for a nearby hill that resembled a type of Spanish hat worn in the 16th century, the town's main attractions include the 18th-century baroque **Parroquia de San Juan Bautista,** the 17th-century **Templo de Santo Domingo,** and the 16th-century Franciscan **Convento de San Mateo.**

The **Sierra los Organos,** 12 km (7.4 miles) northwest of town via Mexico 45, then five km (three miles) by dirt road, is a half-circle of monolithic rock formations named for their resemblance to organ pipes. John Wayne used the sierra as a backdrop in some of his films; in return for the cooperation of villagers in nearby San Francisco de los Organos, Wayne donated a picnic site with grills and tables near the formations.

Chicomóstoc

THE STATE OF SAN LUIS POTOSI

San Luis Potosí hovers over the hazy cultural and geographic border between Northern and Southern Mexico. Encompassing full measures of the dry, windswept plains of the Altiplano, the mist-encircled mountains of the Sierra Madre Oriental, and the moist, tropical valleys of the Región Huasteca (most of the state lies below the Tropic of Cancer), the state comes close to providing a microcosm of everything—except beaches—that Mexico has to offer: modest pre-Cortesian ruins, jungles, high desert, indigenous arts and culture, an exceptionally varied cuisine, colonial architecture, and a genuine hospitality that comes from having been virtually ignored by mainstream tourists.

The state has also been largely isolated from the rest of Mexico. Despite heavy Spanish activity along the Gulf of Mexico coast, a road to the state capital from Tampico was only completed in 1854, followed by a railroad spur from Mexico City in 1890, then virtually nothing in the way of long-distance transport before highway Mexico 57 (from Piedras Negras) was inaugurated in 1930.

Today the state provides a sometimes startling contrast between modern (the capital) and traditional (the rest of the state). Even the highway into the capital from the airport is paralleled by cart tracks. On a per capita basis, the state has the third lowest number of households with electricity in the country (after Oaxaca and Chiapas).

Mountainous and landlocked, but centrally located, the state serves as an important transport hub for rail and road connections between North and South Mexico. Mining—principally for silver, gold, copper, lead, zinc, antimony, arsenic, and quicksilver—is still a significant source of local income, along with petroleum from the Ebano and Limón oil fields. Other key industries include beer, furniture, textile, flour, and leather production.

SAN LUIS POTOSI (CITY)

One of the most pleasant state capitals in Mexico, San Luis Potosí offers a moderate year-round climate, plenty of historic architecture, and a spate of great restaurants. Few foreigners seem to know that San Luis is an excellent choice for those looking to explore urban Mexico—both modern and historic—at its best; the historical district is small enough to cover on foot and most of it is conveniently closed to vehicular traffic, making it even easier for pedestrians to get around.

Nicknamed "The City of Gardens," San Luis has at least one *jardín* or garden plaza in each of its seven original districts (*los siete barrios*). Although most famous for its outstanding examples of neo-Hispanic baroque churches, the city's architecture is predominantly neoclassical and republican, much like that of older Mexico City districts. According to the 1990 national census (another won't be taken until 2000), the city's current population is estimated to be around 550,000. In the political arena, San Luis Potosí is a key stronghold for PAN opposition to Mexico City rule.

HISTORY

Before the Spanish *entrada,* the present city site in the Valle de San Luis was thought to have been an Amerindian settlement called Tangamanga, inhabited by the seminomadic Guachichiles (an Aztec name meaning "red-painted," describing the way the Guachichiles—possibly related to the Huastecs—painted their hair red). Franciscan missionaries under Fray Diego de la Magdalena passed through in the mid-1500s and established a small Guachachil pueblo in 1583. The community was supple-

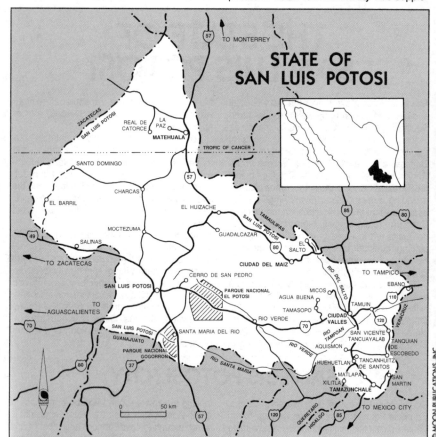

STATE OF
SAN LUIS POTOSI

mented by the 1590 import of Tlaxcalteca settlers—a pattern followed throughout Northern Mexico in which the cooperative Tlaxcaltecas served as model *indígenas* for less docile Amerindian groups.

The pueblo might have faded into obscurity if a large silver vein hadn't been discovered at nearby Cerro de San Pedro in 1592. More Spanish immediately moved in and expanded the town, designing the basic city plan as seen in downtown San Luis Potosí today. The city took the grand title Real San Luis Minas de Potosí; "San Luis" in honor of then-Viceroy of Mexico Luis de Velasco, "Minas de Potosí" for a rich mine in Bolivia. The vein failed to produce as prodigiously as its Bolivian namesake, but ranching and trade filled the gap and prosperous San Luis received official *ciudad* status in 1656. By the 18th century, the city had been declared a regional capital for northeastern Nueva España, with jurisdiction over Coahuila, Nuevo León, Tamaulipas, Louisiana, and Texas. During this era, when San Luis was considered the third most important city in Mexico, many of the city's historic baroque churches were built.

Immediately following independence from Spain in 1824, the city was named capital of the new state of San Luis Potosí. Under Mexican president Benito Juárez, it also twice served as the provisional capital of Mexico, once in 1863 as Juárez was fleeing French forces in Mexico City, and again in 1867 when Juárez returned to San Luis to sign an execution order for Emperor Maximillian.

Under Porfirio Díaz, San Luis Potosí was linked to the national railway network and became the richest city in Northern Mexico. Liberals opposed to the Díaz regime held a seminal meeting here in 1901, and in 1910 revolutionary Francisco I. Madero devised his Plan de San Luis while incarcerated in San Luis's municipal prison. Upon his release from jail, Madero headed to San Antonio, Texas, where his revolutionary plan was unveiled. The plan stated that Díaz had been illegally elected and that Madero was the rightful president of the republic, thus sparking the 1910-20 Mexican Revolution.

Although San Luis Potosí's stature as an economic powerhouse has been somewhat eclipsed by the rise of Monterrey in Nuevo León to the north, perhaps the city's major achievement has been its capacity to modernize while maintaining a strong sense of culture and tradition.

CLIMATE

Just about any time of year is good for a visit to San Luis Potosí. At 1,880 meters (6,170 feet) above sea level, the city has been compared to Jerusalem or Athens for its typically clear, blue skies. Average annual precipitation is just 36 cm (14 inches), with most rain falling between May and October.

The average monthly temperature from hottest to coolest months varies by less than eight degrees Centigrade (15 degrees Fahrenheit), from 20.6° C (69° F) in April to 12.8° C (55° F) in January. The occasional northern wind sends temperatures toward freezing for a few days here and there in December and January, though minimum temperatures seldom drop below 2.4° C (36° F). April and May—before the rains start—are the warmest months, but temperatures rarely exceed 29° C (85° F).

SIGHTS

Although colonial-era architecture can be seen in several quarters throughout the city, San Luis Potosí's main **historical district** is concentrated in the center of the city, in an area bounded by Calle Independencia to the west, Av. Obregón to the north, Av. Constitución to the east, and Calle Abasolo to the south. Several of the streets in this district have been closed to vehicular traffic, making it an especially pleasant and safe area to explore on foot. For people-watching, the best time is early evening when antique street lamps are lit (electrically) and the plazas and narrow streets are full of Potosinos out for an evening stroll.

Plazas, Parks, And *Jardines*
San Luis Potosí is blessed with a large number of plazas, many of which are called *jardines* (gardens) because they are so heavily planted. Because of the city's benevolent climate, they are all well visited and are an excellent place to observe Mexican public life.

Jardín Hidalgo (Plaza de Armas), the city's premier plaza, is in the center of the historical district at calles Los Bravo, Zaragoza, Madero/M.J. Othón, and 5 de Mayo. A large *kiosko* in the center shelters live musical performances on weekends and holidays. The plaza is flanked on the east by the Santa Iglesia Catedral (see "Churches," below) and by the republican-style **Palacio Municipal,** which was built in 1838 and once served as a bishop's residence. The Salón de Cabildos, on the second floor, is decorated with mytho-religious paintings by Italian artist Erulo Eroli.

The **Casa de la Virreina,** built in 1736 but extensively remodeled in the 19th century, faces the north side of the plaza. Originally this building must have been done in the neo-Hispanic baroque style but it is now thoroughly neoclassic/republican. Once a residence for the uncle of Mexico's only *virreina* (or vicereine, the female equivalent to viceroy), it is now occupied on the ground floor by a popular cafe.

On the west side of Jardín Hidalgo stands the imposing, full-block-square **Palacio de Gobierno,** which was constructed in the neoclassic style between 1798 and 1816 to serve as the seat of government for all of northeastern Mexico (it now serves as the state capitol). In the Sala Juárez on the second floor are wax figures of President Juárez refusing Princess Salm Salm's request for a stay of execution for deposed Emperor Maximilian.

The **Plaza de los Fundadores** ("Founders Plaza") at Obregón, D. Carmona, V. Carranza, and Aldama, commemorates the spot where the original city was established. It is flanked by the Capilla de Loreto (see "Churches," below) and several other historic buildings but is otherwise lacking in character or ambience. This is a favorite venue for local political demonstrations.

Fronting the Templo de San Francisco between calles Guerrero, Galeana, and Vallejo is the **Plaza de San Francisco,** a long, narrow, and shady plaza that's a favorite with bench-sitters. Largest of all the central downtown plazas is the **Alameda Juan Sarabia,** a large rectangular park between Av. Universidad and Calle M.J. Othón that has the same dimensions

---

SEVEN GARDENS FOR SEVEN BARRIOS

Each of the seven traditional neighborhoods in San Luis Potosí has its own *jardín* or garden plaza around which local festival life revolves.

Jardín de Tequisquiapan: Av. V. Carranza
Jardín de Santiago: Av. de la Paz
Jardín de San Miguelito: Vallejo amd Gral. Fuero
Jardín de Tlaxcala: Cición and Eje. Vial
Jardín de San Sebastián: Av. Constitución and Sevilla
Jardín de San Juan de Guadalupe: Calle S.J. de Dios Peza
Jardín del Montecillo: Azteca and M.J. Othón

---

as Mexico City's Alameda. Criss-crossed with diagonal paths, it's a popular jogging venue.

Parque Tangamanga: The patriarch of parks in San Luis Potosí, this 411-hectare (1,015-acre) section of greenery is southwest of the city center, off Diagonal Sur and Av. Tatanacho. Its wooded grounds feature walking paths, benches, playgrounds, small-scale carnival-style rides, a 4,000-seat amphitheater, two lakes, a planetarium, a convention center, two museums, and various athletic courts. On weekends and holidays food vendors set up along some of the paths. The park has proved so popular that a Parque Tangamanga II has been built on the north side of the city off Mexico 49.

Churches

Just as each of the city's traditional seven *barrios* is associated with a garden plaza of its own, each has its own major church as well. The impressive variety of styles can be attributed to the fact that, as a regional capital for northern expansion in the 17th-19th centuries, the city hosted almost every conceivable Christian sect—including Augustines, Carmelites, Johnists, and Jesuits—each of which built its own churches and convents. Only Mexico City and Guadalajara compare.

Santa Iglesia Catedral: Most often known simply as *la catedral,* this most important of churches stands on the east side of Jardín Hidalgo. Constructed as a *parroquía* between 1670 and 1730, the cathedral's most outstanding feature is its neo-Hispanic baroque facade, which features four Carrera-marble apostles (replicas of Roman originals) along with Solomonic columns and twin bell towers.

Around the time that cathedral status was bestowed on the church (1866), the interior was entirely redone in a blend of Byzantine and neoclassical styles. Italian artisans carved the wooden *coro* and the San Sebastian statue, which, like the apostle sculptures on the facade, is a replica of Bernini's original at the Basilica of St. John Lateran in Rome. Original vice-regal paintings hang on the walls. In recognition of its historical value, the cathedral was declared a National Monument in 1935.

Templo del Carmen: This church at Av. Constitución and Calle M.J. Othón began construction in 1749 and was consecrated in 1764 by the Carmelites, an ascetic monastic sect most known for their vow not to wear shoes. An atrium, designed to accommodate large numbers of Amerindian worshipers in the open air, once extended from the facade into present-day Plaza del Carmen. The single tower, forbidden in Carmelite churches, was built with the palms-up complicity of local clerical authorities. Most impressive is the central portion of the facade, which represents *churrigueresco* detail rivaled in the north only by the cathedral in Zacatecas. A side entrance, dedicated to San José (St. Joseph), employs the shell motif common to late baroque.

As in the Catedral Santa Iglesia, gilded altars inside are done in neoclassical style. The *altar mayor* or main altar was designed by Francisco Eduardo Tresguerras (1759-1833), an architect, painter, sculptor, poet, and musician who was the most influential Mexican artist of his era. Paintings in the sacristy include works by Francisco Antonio Vallejo (1713-56).

Templo de San Francisco: Facing leafy Plaza de San Francisco, this 1680s-vintage church dedicated to St. Francis has a rather simple baroque facade and asymmetric towers built of pink sandstone. Inside, the sacristy is considered one of the best surviving examples of interior baroque architecture in San Luis Potosí. Several examples of 18th-century art, including paintings by renowned artists Miguel Cabrera and Antonio de Torres, are on display in the sacristy. A ship-inspired crystal chandelier hanging from the dome above the nave was a donation from a parishioner who survived a shipwreck. The rest of the interior, as in most

JOE CUMMINGS

Templo del Carmen

baroque churches in the city, was remodeled in the neoclassic style during the Reform. The original convent and cloister—which once extended into Calle Galeana—also fell victim to the Reform.

Capilla de Loreto: Built in 1700 by the Jesuits, this chapel next to the Edificio de la Universidad on the northwest end of Plaza de los Fundadores (Av. Obregón and Av. D. Carmona) contains one of the few surviving Jesuit *retablos* (altar pieces) in Mexico (most were destroyed following Jesuit expulsion from the New World in 1767). Though rather simple (only two Solomonic columns, one tower), the facade is considered the best of all those executed by the Jesuits in Mexico.

Behind the Capilla de Loreto is another Jesuit chapel, Capilla del Sagraria, which dates to 1675 but is of less architectural interest. A large stone cross between the two chapels commemorates the founding of the city.

Templo de San Agustín: The Augustines established themselves at the current city site in 1599 and built a convent and church on this

SAN LUIS POTOSI CITY

80 57
TO AIRPORT, MOTEL EL MESQUITE,
PARADOR TURISTICO EL POTOSI,
MATEHUALA, AND SALTILLO

AV. 20 DE NOVIEMBRE
BLVD. RIO SANTIAGO
AV. LA PAZ
LA PAZ
EJE VIAL
MERCADO 16 DE SEPTIEMBRE
AV. MEXICO
MERCADO REPUBLICA
MERCADO HIDALGO
"HISTORICAL DISTRICT DOWNTOWN)" MAP
RAILWAY STATION
MANUEL JOSÉ OTHON
70
ALAMEDA
CENTRO TAURINO POTOSINO
AV. UNIVERSIDAD
TO CD. VALLES AND TAMPICO
PLAZA DE TOROS FERMIN RIVERA
VILLA DEPORTIVA JUVENIL (HOSTEL)
CACTUS MOTEL
HOTEL CENTRAL
HOTEL ARIZONA
CAJA DEL AGUA
CENTRAL CAMIONERA
HOTEL REAL DE MINAS
HOTEL MARIA DOLORES
TEMPLO DE SAN SEBASTIAN
TEMPLO DE SAN MIGUELITO
MOTEL SANDS
MOTEL LA POSADA
AV. JUAREZ
CONSTITUCION
5 DE MAYO
RANCHO DEL CHARRO
SANTUARIO DE GUADALUPE
HOSTAL DEL QUIJOTE
57
TEMPLO DE SAN JUAN DE GUADALUPE
TO SANTA MARIA DEL RIO,
CENTRO VACACIONAL GOGORRON,
QUERETARO, AND MEXICO CITY
BLVD. DIAGONAL SUR

0   1 km

© MOON PUBLICATIONS, INC.

spot in 1615. The current church, near the intersection of calles Morelos and Abasolo, was erected in the mid-18th century; the Churrigueresque tower is the exterior's most striking feature. Inside, the main altar dates to the same period but is neoclassical in style. Older, baroque religious paintings hang in the sacristy.

Templo de San Sebastian: Originally founded by the Augustines in 1603, the current church was rebuilt between 1708-75. The baroque facade features Solomonic columns between two simple, asymmetric towers. The pink limestone arches and pilasters in the interior were installed earlier this century.

Santuario de Nuestra Señora de Guadalupe: South of the main historical district on Av. Juárez, Colonia Guadalupe, the city's principal Guadalupana church was consecrated in 1772 on a spot where Spanish captain Francisco de Castro y Mampaso had built a small Virgen de Guadalupe shrine in 1656. During the French era, troops occupied the church and the image of the Virgen de Guadalupe was taken to the cathedral for safe-keeping. The much-revered image was destroyed in a fire and replaced by a new image in 1838 (though many locals maintain the original is still kept in the sacristy), and it wasn't until 1871 that the church itself was restored. The sanctuary's twin towers are the tallest in San Luis Potosí and are thus visible from almost anywhere in the city. The facade exhibits an interesting mix of baroque and neoclassical elements.

Other Historic Architecture

Most of the older buildings in downtown San Luis Potosí date to the late 18th and 19th centuries and represent the neoclassical and republican styles. The earlier neoclassical (late 18th or early 19th century) commercial or governmental architecture typically features two stories of arch-topped windows with iron-grille balconies on elaborately carved pedestals. Windows on both floors are flanked by prominent, rounded columns. The next stage in Potosino architecture (mid-19th century) retained the second-floor window pedestals and grillwork but flattened the tops of the windows.

By the end of the 19th and beginning of the 20th centuries, all curves—including window pedestals and columns—were replaced by rectangles in the "republican" style. Facing the west side of Plaza de los Fundadores, the **Edificio Ipiña** represents the late neoclassic/early republican style, with arched *portales* along the ground floor and rectangular windows on the second.

One of the only secular baroque-style buildings in the city is the **Caja Real** (also rendered "Real Caja"), on the corner of calles Madero and Aldama in the heart of the historic district. Built in the late 18th century as the treasury for the Spanish Crown's *quinto* (the fifth of all mining profits owed to the Crown), it features a truncated corner entrance with massive carved wooden doors, Potosino-style window pedestals, and an interior patio with fountain. The large doorway and spacious interior were designed to allow mules or other pack animals to enter with their cargo of ore. Caja Real is used today as an adjunct building for the Universidad Autónoma de San Luis Potosí.

The unique **Caja del Agua** ("Water Case"), whose rotund, cone-tipped profile appears on official stationery as the symbol of San Luis Potosí's state government, sits in a small park at the northern end of Av. Juárez (at Calle Miguel Barragán), six blocks south of Calle Galeana in the historical district. Originally built in 1832, the elaborate structure stored water piped from the Cañada del Lobo via an aqueduct. The huge "lid" is made of glass tiles and topped by a sculpted pinecone. When the Caja was functional, Potosinos drew water from the eight ornate ducts around the Caja's lower circumference.

The late 19th-century **Teatro de la Paz,** beside the Templo del Carmen and opposite the Museo de la Máscara, features a classical Greek facade (complete with columns and a peaked roof) and wall mosaics by artist Fernando Leal. Modeled after the Paris Opera, the U-shaped interior holds 1,450 seats. The attached Sala German Gedovious contains rotating visual art exhibits.

Museo Regional Potosino

Established in 1952 in a 16th-century former Franciscan convent, this regional museum contains a good collection of pieces outlining the archaeology, anthropology, and history of the state. One of the museum's better exhibits fea-

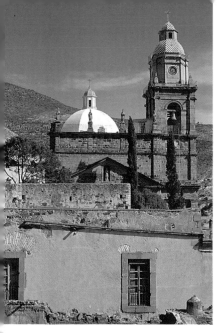

(top, left) Real de Catorce; (top, right) Batopilas rooftops; (bottom, left) Paquimé ruins, Casas Grandes; (bottom, right) mission church, Cerocahui (photos by Joe Cummings)

(top) Plaza 13 de Julio, Guaymas; (bottom) Ex-convento de San Agustín, Xilitla (photos by Joe Cummings)

tures ceramics from the Zapotec, Mixtec, Huastec, Totonac, and Mexica cultures. The Huastecs, like the Olmecs and Mayas, practiced cranial deformation, binding the skull so that it projected upwards, and two such skulls are displayed.

In the room dedicated to the Huastec culture, the most intriguing item is the 1.5-meter tall "El Adolescente," found at El Consuelo (Tamuín). Dated to the Huastec postclassic era (A.D. 900-1500), the figure is carved in sandstone with a network of glyphs engraved on the shoulders, wrists, right lower torso, and right leg. One of the shoulder glyphs represents Quetzalcóatl, the sacred plumed serpent. Another figure on display stands around 1.75 meters and features a two-sided design with the likeness of a shaman or priest on one side and a skeleton on other. The piece is unlabeled, but perhaps represents the shaman's ritual control of life and death.

Other rooms contain viceregal artifacts, the most impressive of which can be found upstairs in the attached **Capilla de Aranzazu.** Constructed in the mid-18th century as a private Franciscan chapel, the chapel is dedicated to the Virgin of Aranzazu. The latter word is reportedly Basque for "among thorns"; according to legend, a priest found a figure of the virgin among *zazus* or thorns. The chapel architecture is typical late baroque on a small scale; particularly notable is the plasterwork along the inside of the cupola. Religious paintings from the 18th and 19th centuries adorn the walls.

The museum is at Calle Galeana 450, around the corner from the Templo de San Francisco. It's open Tues.-Fri. 10 a.m.-1 p.m. and 3-8 p.m., Sat. 10 a.m.-noon, and Sun. 10 a.m.-1 p.m. Admission is free.

Museo Nacional De La Máscara (National Museum Of Masks)
Housed in a beautiful, neoclassical 19th-century building with late baroque undertones, this museum is devoted to the history, description, and display of Mexican masks. Though not as well labeled as its counterpart in Zacatecas, the collection here is quite good and represents virtually all aspects of mask typology. Classrooms in the building are also used to teach mask-making and other arts.

At Calle Villerías 2 (on the opposite side of the same building that contains the main post office), the museum is open Tues.-Fri. 10-2 and 4-6 p.m., Sat.-Sun. 10 a.m.-2 p.m.

Museo Othoniano (Casa Othón)
One of Mexico's foremost poets and dramatists, Manuel José Othón (1858-1906) was born and schooled in San Luis Potosí. His literary work is today considered among the best ever to have appeared in the Spanish language. *Norteños* consider Othón one of their own since he spent most of his life living and working in San Luis Potosí, Tamaulipas, Coahuila, Durango, and Nuevo León.

Othón's birth house at Calle M.J. Othón 225 (two blocks east of the Jardí Hidalgo) has been made into a museum containing a simple collection of furnishings, letters, and mementos of the Othón family. Occasional readings, lectures, and literary events are held in the house. The house is open to the public Mon.-Fri. 10 a.m.-2 p.m. and 4-6 p.m. Small admission fee.

Centro Taurino Potosino

Known in English as the Bullfighting Center of San Luis Potosí, the Centro Taurino is housed in a two-story, whitewashed building adjacent to the Plaza de Toros Fermín Rivera at the corner of Av. Universidad and Calle Triano. San Luis Potosí is one of Mexico's premier *fiesta brava* venues, and a small museum inside the Centro Taurino contains one of the most complete collections of *tauromaquía* memorabilia in the country, including *banderillas, trajes de luces, capotes,* famous bulls' heads, poster art, and historical photographs. The museum has posted hours of Tues.-Sat. 11 a.m.-1:30 p.m. and 5:30-7:30 p.m., but in reality it only seems to be open on bullfight days and during the annual Feria Taurino in November.

The adjacent **Plaza de España** displays bronze sculptures of famous matadors, including one of Manolete donated by a Spanish sculptor. The most prominent space in the plaza, however, is given to a figure of hometown hero Fermín Rivera. The fountain in the middle is a replica of Seville's Fuente de los Fardes.

Casa De La Cultura

Built as a republican-style mansion at the beginning of this century, the large, two-story casa is situated on spacious, landscaped grounds away from *el centro.* A setting for various cultural events held throughout the year, the building also contains a number of exhibit rooms with permanent displays of regional art and archaeology. Highlights include the Huastec exhibit on the ground floor and the Potosino handicrafts exhibit (including *rebozos* and *cajas de rebozos*) on the second floor. The galleries are open Tues.-Fri. 10 a.m.-2 p.m. and 4-6 p.m., Sat. 10 a.m.-2 p.m. and 6-9 p.m., Sun. 10 a.m.-2 p.m.; there is a small admission fee.

Museo Regional De Arte
Popular And Casa De Artesanías

These two museums were recently moved from the historical district to new, joined quarters in the Parque Tangamanga (see "Plazas, Parks, and *Jardines,"* above). Although the new facility hadn't yet opened as we went to press, the exhibits will reportedly include regional ceramics, *rebozos* and *chales* (handwoven shawls), woodcarvings, textiles, and other handicrafts from the state of San Luis Potosí and beyond. Proposed hours of operation are Tues.-Fri. 10 a.m.-2 p.m. and 4-6 p.m., Sat.-Sun. 10 a.m.-2:30 p.m.

Cerro De San Pedro

Eight km (five miles) east of the city via Mexico 70, then 19 km (12 miles) north, this large hill was the source of the area's original wealth—silver. A virtual ghost town was left behind when various mining companies, including the American Smelting and Refining Co., abandoned the mines earlier this century. A couple of small chapels of some historic interest can be seen.

SAN LUIS POTOSI ACCOMMODATIONS

The city has a very good variety of places to stay, most of which represent good values by both Mexican and international standards.

Budget Hotels And Hostels

Bus Station/Glorieta Juárez: The **Villa Deportiva Juvenil** (tel. 48-18-16-17), in the CREA complex just southwest of Glorieta Juárez on Diagonal Sur, has 72 beds with lockers that cost US$4 per night, plus a *cafetería*. It's conveniently located within walking distance of the Central de Autobuses and is a short bus or taxi ride (about two km) from the railway station via Av. Universidad. Reservations are taken up to 15 days in advance.

Railway Station: Next up in price are the *clase económica* hotels in the vicinity of the railway station. Best of the bunch is the clean **Hotel Guadalajara** (tel. 12-46-12) at Calle Jiménez 253, only a couple hundred meters from the station. Rooms with private bath cost US$18 s/d. Around the corner at Calle Xochitl 140 is

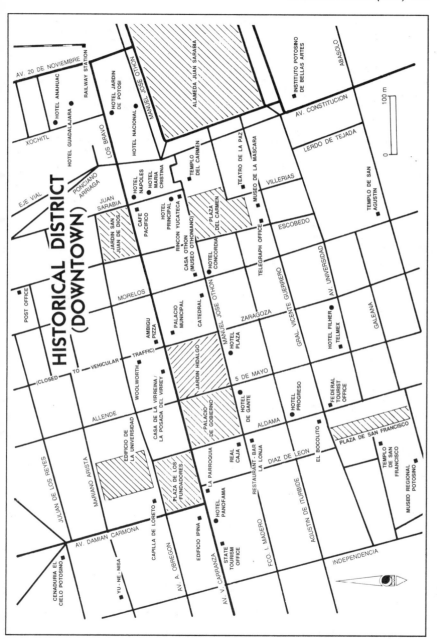

the **Hotel Anáhuac** (tel. 12-65-05), with similar rooms for US$17.

Across the narrow Jardín Escontria from the Hotel Guadalajara, on Calle Los Bravo, is the grungier but adequate **Hotel Jardín de Potosí** for just US$14. Also in this area are the similarly priced **Hotel La Terminal** and **Hotel María Elena**, all within easy walking distance of the railway station and historical district. **Hotel Nacional** (tel. 12-25-50), at Calle M.J. Othón 425 (a block south of the Hotel Jardín Potosí) has rock-bottom rooms with *baño colectivo* for just US$7.

Downtown: In the historical district are several inexpensive hotels in quaint 19th-century buildings. In addition to providing atmosphere coupled with considerable savings on accommodations, these locations allow budget-conscious visitors to explore the city's museums and architecture on foot, thus saving money on buses and taxis. **Hotel Progreso** (tel. 12-03-67), at Calle Aldama 415 diagonally opposite the Plaza de San Francisco, is among the least expensive at just US$15 s, US$17 d, and is housed in a handsome building. **Hotel Principal** (tel. 12-07-84) at Calle J. Sarabia 145, just north of the Templo del Carmen, is neither handsome nor historic; spartan but adequate rooms cost US$12-15.

The 48-room **Hotel Filher** (tel. 12-15-62), at Av. Universidad and Zaragoza, has a historic facade and fairly well-kept if small rooms for US$21 s, US$24 d; a restaurant is attached and overnight parking may be arranged. **Hotel De Gante** (tel. 12-14-92), at Calle 5 de Mayo 140 (a block south of the Jardín Hidalgo) is similar but costs US$20 s, US$22 d. In this same range is **Hotel Plaza** (tel. 12-40-31), facing the south side of Jardín Hidalgo, a two-star bargain at US$13 s, US$20 d. Neither the Plaza nor the De Gante offer parking.

Medium-priced Hotels
Downtown: In the historical district at calles Morelos and M.J. Othón, the quaint **Hotel Concordia** (tel. 48-12-06-66) offers 96 rooms with satellite TV in an older building for US$28 s, US$30 d. Downstairs is a cozy bar-restaurant decorated with art prints; free parking is available in a garage across the street.

The more modern, six-story **Hotel Nápoles** (tel. 12-84-19), at Calle J. Sarabia 120 (near the fabulous Café Pacífico), costs about the same as the Concordia and features a restaurant, bar, car rental, and parking. Just south of the Nápoles at Calle J. Sarabia 110, the similarly modern and 11-story **Hotel María Cristina** is also in the US$30 range but rooms come with a/c; hotel facilities include a pool, parking, and rooftop restaurant.

The efficient, 10-story **Hotel Panorama** (tel. 12-17-77; 800-4-80-01 toll free, fax 2-45-91) is one of the easier downtown places to reach by car from the north since it's near the end of the wide, two-way Av. D. Carmona. Spacious rooms cost US$35-45 and come with a/c, carpeting, satellite TV, and mini-bar; rooms on the upper floors have good views of the city skyline. Facilities include a parking lot, travel agency, car rental, coffee shop, restaurant, and pool.

West of the historical district, in the city's small *zona rosa* on Av. V. Carranza (at Calle Tresguerras), the super-modern, 12-story **Hotel Real Plaza** (tel. 14-69-69, fax 14-66-39) has rooms with a/c, satellite TV, and heavily tinted windows for US$38-46 s, US$46 d.

Glorieta Juárez/Mexico 57 South: Several hotels and motels are strung out along Mexico 57 near the huge traffic circle known as Glorieta Juárez, at the east edge of the city. For the past year or two the Glorieta has been undergoing heavy reconstruction, which has meant very slow traffic and low occupancy. By the time you read this, traffic should be flowing again and this area will be a good choice for motorists on their way to Santa María del Río, Querétaro, or Mexico City. On the other hand, there's absolutely nothing of interest within walking distance of the area (except for auto dealerships), so this is a bad choice if you've come to see the city. Rumor has it that hotel rates here will increase once the area is free of road construction.

Least expensive is the imitation colonial-style **Motel Sands** (tel. 12-74-87), a kilometer southeast of the circle. Rooms with phones, TV, and private bath (but no a/c) cost US$21 s, US$29 d. Similar in price and conditions are two places closer to the Glorieta and bus terminal on Av. Torres, **Hotel Arizona** (tel. 18-19-93; Torres 158) and **Hotel Central** (tel. 22-14-44; Torres 290); the Arizona is the nicer of the two.

The better-kept **Motel La Posada** (tel. 14-40-40), just a bit farther southeast on the highway, has rooms for US$27-32 a night. Facilities include a restaurant and pool.

A gringo favorite on the east side of the highway closer to the circle is the **Cactus Motel** (tel. 12-18-71), where rooms with a/c, satellite TV (with video), and phones cost US$36-43 s, US$39-49 d. A big plus for later arrivals or early departures is the motel's 24-hour restaurant. A trailer park is also on the premises.

North Mexico 57: At Km 13 on Mexico 57, at the northeastern edge of town on the way to/from the airport, Matehuala, and Saltillo, **Hotel El Mesquite** (tel. 12-03-65) has fair rooms for US$20-24 plus a restaurant, pool, and trailer park.

Diagonal Sur: At the south end of town on the loop that links Mexico 80 South and Mexico 57 South, **Motel Colonial** (tel. 15-22-06), Diagonal Sur 340, has three-star rooms in the US$28-32 range.

Luxury Hotels

Glorieta Juárez/Mexico 57 South: Most of the city's upper-end hotels are clustered south of the Glorieta. The **Hotel María Dolores** (tel. 48-22-18-82, 800-4-80-16 toll free; fax 22-06-02) has 213 rooms with all the modern amenities, plus 16 master suites with Jacuzzis, starting at US$60 per night. On the premises are two swimming pools, a restaurant, coffee shop, bar, nightclub, and disco.

Five km southeast of the circle (Km 420) is the top-rank **Hostal del Quijote** (tel. 18-14-11, fax 18-61-05), where nicely furnished rooms with a/c, satellite TV, video, phones, and refrigerators have rack rates of US$81-85. While the nearby *glorieta* was under reconstruction, rooms were readily available for US$45-75. On the well-landscaped grounds are a heated pool, lighted tennis court, restaurant, and coffee shop.

Hotel Real de Minas (tel. 18-26-16, fax 18-69-15), about a kilometer south of the traffic circle, had rooms with all the amenities for US$35-48 during the construction period since this was the most heavily affected of the highway motels. Expect rates of around US$50-60 when access has improved.

The city has a new *gran turismo* hotel, the **Hotel Quinta Real** (tel. 25-01-25) at Real de Lomas 100, off Mexico 80 South at the southwestern edge of the city. Very well-appointed rooms, spacious public areas, a pool, a fitness center, and a long list of other amenities make this a top choice among visiting business executives. Rack rates start at US$85 per night.

A new **Holiday Inn,** under construction on the highway near the Hostal de Quijote, is due to open in late 1993 or early 1994. It will probably be San Luis Potosí's most luxurious—and most expensive—hotel to date.

Mexico 70/80 South: At the extreme west end of the city, between the Glorieta González Bocanegra (near the university) and the highway to Aguascalientes and Guadalajara, is the older but popular **Hotel Tuna Best Western** (tel. 13-12-60, fax 11-14-15, Calle Dr. M. Nava 200, eight km from downtown). Rooms with satellite TV and ceiling fans cost US$45-55 s, US$50-60 d, US$60-70 t. A few rooms come with kitchenettes; other facilities include a pool and parking lot.

RV Parks

Motel El Mesquite (see "Medium-priced Hotels") offers 200 RV spaces with full hookups for US$12 a night. Eighty unkempt spaces at the **Cactus Motel** come with electrical/water hookups only and cost US$14, hence they're usually empty.

FOOD

If one of your objectives in visiting Mexico is to sample authentic regional cuisines, you could hardly find a better place than San Luis Potosí's state capital. Potosinas are extremely proud of their local cooking, whether waxing eloquent over the roast corn or fresh *papitas* (potato chips) sold at every other street corner in pedestrian areas, or praising an elaborate dish of *fiambre potosino* (chicken, beef tongue, and pig's feet, marinated in vinaigrette and served cold on a platter of vegetables).

Typical *cocina potosina* is delicately spiced and features lots of vegetables. The state's most famous dish is *enchiladas potosinas,* in which the tortilla *masa* is mixed with *chile colorado* to form small, delicate, reddish tortillas which are then folded over a ricottalike cheese with a strip of chile or *salsa jitomate* and garnished with chopped onion. In another popular dish, *tacos Camila* (named for the famous *fritanguera* or "fryer" who popularized it), corn tortillas are rolled in tomato sauce, stuffed with cheese, then lightly fried and served under a mound of lettuce, cooked potatoes, carrots, green beans, and crumbled cheese. You may also see *tacos po-*

tosinos, which are similar to *tacos Camila*—small corn tortillas rolled into loose, flattened tubes filled with the same ricottalike cheese (or occasionally chicken), then lightly fried in a chile-tomato salsa and covered with cooked green beans, potatoes, and carrots, and sometimes a little chorizo and extra *queso fresco.*

Another typical Potosino dish is *asado de boda,* a "wedding stew" made with a *chile ancho* base in which bits of pork and various spices are simmered together and served with rice. *Nopalitos*—strips of prickly pear pads (spines removed) pickled with salt, onion, and garlic—make a tasty *ensalada potosina* when tossed with sliced tomato, oregano, cilantro, vinegar, and oil. The typical Potosino meal begins with a complimentary *botana* of pickled tripe (or pork skin) and vegetables. Many Potosino dishes are served with a thin, red, heated table salsa.

The Altiplano's abundant cactus is also employed in *queso de tuna,* a very common sweet in which cardón fruit juice is boiled to a syrup, then heated directly over a fire to form a dense, caramel-like mass the color of *café con leche.* Once you aquire a taste, *queso de tuna* can be quite addictive (fortunately it's a very inexpensive habit). Yet another use for cactus is the equally addictive *colonche,* cardón fruit juice fermented until it produces its own alcohol.

The Huastec influence on the city has made tamales of all kinds very popular, especially in the winter months when many restaurants serve them with hot *atole.*

Cocina Potosina

While in many cities it can be a struggle to find authentic regional cuisine, in San Luis Potosí you'll likely find more *potosina*-oriented restaurants than anything else.

$ El Bocolito, corner of calles Guerrero and Aldama, opposite the Hotel Progreso downtown. This small, student cooperative-run diner with cheap and filling regional specialties is open Mon.-Sat. 11 a.m.-11 p.m.

$ Cenaduría El Cielo Potosino (tel. 48-14-24-28), Calle J. de los Reyes 400-A. This casual diner-style eatery (also downtown) is often cited as the most "typical" of the city's *cocinas.* In addition to the Potosino *antojitos* described above, El Cielo specializes in savory *pozole* and *menudo.* Open 11 a.m.-midnight daily.

$-$$ La Cabaña Huasteca (tel. 12-29-90), Av.

Cuauhtémoc 276 southwest of downtown, focuses on Huastec dishes, including *enchiladas huastecas* (similar to *potosinas* but served with black beans), *zacahuiles* (huge, Huastec-style tamales), *bocoles* (a vegetarian *gordita*), and *guiso borracho* ("drunken stew"). Open daily noon-11 p.m.

$-$$ Café Pacífico, corner of Calle Los Bravo and Av. Constitución, next to Hotel Nápoles downtown. This 24-hour cafe, with its high ceiling supported by iron pillars and hung with ceiling fans, is a very popular local venue for people from nearly all social strata. The dining room is clean, service is fast and efficient, the food is good, and prices are low (most *antojitos* cost US$3-4). *Cocina huasteca con enchiladas* is a house specialty, along with *enchiladas potosinas, tacos potosinos, tacos Camila, atole, pozole, cabrito adobado,* and all manner of regional and national breakfasts (served anytime). Don't confuse the Café Pacífico with the Restaurant Mariscos Pacífico opposite.

$$ La Parroquía (tel. 12-66-82), Av. Carranza 303, next to the Hotel Panorama. More upmarket than the Café Pacífico but just as popular, this 17-year veteran specializes in regional cooking along with a wide range of other Mexican cuisines. The *café con leche* is excellent, and can be ordered with fresh *pan dulce* in the morning (better order before 8:15 a.m. or so, when they usually sell out). Open daily 7:30 a.m.-11 p.m.

Other Regional And National

$$-$$$ Comida del Rancho, Av. V. Carranza 700, just east of Av. de la Reforma and just west of downtown. One of several restaurants housed in restored colonial-era casas in the city's modest *zona rosa,* this one employs a rustic, hacienda-style ambience. As the name suggests, ranchero cookery, particularly *carne asada,* is the central focus. Other *norteña* and Potosino dishes, along with Mexican standards, are on the menu. Open daily 11 a.m.-1 a.m.

$$$ Restaurant Bar La Lonja (tel. 48-12-81-19), calles Madero and Aldama downtown. An elegant, old-fashioned, "club-style" restaurant with a gourmet Mexican and international menu. Specialties include salads made with *cabuches* (barrel cactus buds), *flor de palma* (yucca flowers), *palmitos* (hearts of palm), shrimp, and avocado and *sopa de elote con huitlacoche,* a delicious soup made with fresh corn and blue corn fungus. Open Tues.-Sun. for dinner only.

$$ La Posada del Virrey (tel. 12-70-55), north side of Jardín Hidalgo in the Casa de la Virreina. At this cafe/bar/restaurant, regular patrons linger long over coffee to discuss the issues of the day. The menu is a Mexican/Potosino blend; the *botanas* section is very popular. Open daily 7:30 a.m.-midnight.

$ Rincón Yucateca, opposite the north side of Templo del Carmen, next to Hotel Principal downtown. The small, plain diner features such Yucatecan standards as *cochinita* and *chile habanero*. Open daily 11 a.m.-9 p.m.

$$ Restaurant La Silla (tel. 18-56-68), Km 402, Mexico 57 South (near the hotel-motel cluster). La Silla specializes in *norteña* cuisine, particularly *carnes al carbón*. Open daily noon-midnight.

International

$$$ La Gran Vía (tel. 48-12-28-99), Av. V. Carranza 560, Zona Rosa. This very elegant restaurant, in a restored colonial (Maximilian-era) mansion with courtyard, serves highly rated Spanish and international cuisine. Open daily 1 p.m.-1 a.m. (last order taken at 7:30 p.m.).

$$$ La Virreina (tel. 12-37-50), Av. V. Carranza 830. A bit farther west along the same avenue as La Gran Vía, this restaurant is also housed in a restored mansion. The menu is mostly continental but includes a few regional dishes. Open Mon.-Sat. 1 p.m.-11 p.m.

Vegetarian

$-$$ El Manantial (tel. 48-12-80-99), calles Bolivar and Madero just west of downtown. At this combination of natural foods shop and vegetarian food bar, you'll find yogurt, whole-grain breads, soy products, and so on. Open Mon.-Sat. 10 a.m.-7 p.m.

$$ Los Vitrales (tel. 12-98-82), calles 5 de Mayo and Guerrero downtown. This pleasant vegetarian restaurant is located in a renovated colonial house. Open Mon.-Sat. 1 p.m.-midnight, Sun. 1-8 p.m.

$-$$ Yu-ne-nisa (tel. 14-36-31), calles Arista and Independencia in the northwestern corner of downtown. Similar to El Manantial, Yu-ne-nisa has a small eating area within a natural foods store. Open daily 9 a.m.-6 p.m.

Other

$ Pastelería La Noria, two doors west of the Hotel Panorama on Av. V. Carranza. The large bakery is well stocked with many kinds of *pan dulce* and *pasteles*. Open Mon.-Sat. 7 a.m.-6 p.m.

$-$$ Woolworth, corner of Hidalgo and Obregón in the historical district. As always, Woolworth has good bargains in breakfasts, Mexican standards, soups, and *tortas*. Open daily 8 a.m.-9:30 p.m.

Fast-Food: Opposite the Hotel Real Plaza on Av. V. Carranza is a **Burger King**. Other burger and sandwich joints can be found along Av. V. Carranza west of Hotel Real Plaza. Branches of **Helados Tucky-Tucky,** an ice-cream chain, are all over town. San Luis Potosí has several good pizza/pasta places, including **Ambigu Pizza** (on the corner of Hidalgo and Los Bravo in the historical district), **Pizzería Nápoles** (Av. V. Carranza 775C), and **Tiberius** (Av. Carranza 1047).

RECREATION

Bullfights

Along with Mexico City and Aguascalientes, San Luis Potosí is one of Mexico's bullfighting capitals and hence is one of the best places in the country to view the *sombra y sol* spectacle. The main *corridas de toros* venue is the large and well-designed **Plaza de Toros Fermín Rivera** (named for a famous Potosino matador) on Av. Universidad approximately a kilometer east of the historical district (a kilometer west of Glorieta Juárez). Adjacent to the bullring in the Centro Taurino Potosino is an exhibit of historic artifacts connected with regional *tauromaquía* (see "Sights" earlier in this section for details). Tickets, ranging in cost from US$8.30 for general admission to US$25 for reserved *sombra* (shade), can be purchased at the bullring ticket office or through the state tourist office on Av. V. Carranza.

The main bullfighting season runs May-Sept., although bullfights are also held in association with several of the city's larger festivals year-round. Most notable of these is **La Feria Taurino,** a festival devoted to bullfighting held the third week of November. During the festival *lidias de toros* are held daily and the city fills with bullfight fans from all over Mexico and abroad.

Charreadas

Local *charro* associations practice and compete in three *charro* rings in or near the city. **Cortijo Charro Cinco Hermanos** is in the northwest section of the city, off Av. Muñoz between Blvd. Río Santiago and Av. Ferrocarril; while **Rancho del Charro** is off Av. Juárez near the Santuario de Guadalupe, south of downtown. The third ring, **Lienzo Charro La Pila,** is south of town a few kilometers on Mexico 57 (on the way to Santa María del Río). You can usually count on finding a *charreada* at one of these venues at least every other Sunday year-round. Ask at the tourist office for the latest schedule.

Entertainment

Discos and Bars: While the early part of the week is usually quiet, the city's discotheques fill up Thurs.-Sun., beginning around 11 p.m. The main dance clubs are **Arusha** (tel. 48-17-42-30, Prol. Muñoz 105), **Dulcinea** (tel. 18-13-12; Hostal del Quijote, Mexico 57 South), and **Oasis** (tel. 12-52-43; Hotel María Dolores, Mexico 57 South).

Local bands play live *norteña* and Mexican pop at **Centro Nocturno El Jardín** (Calle Pedro Moreno 833), **Goremoto Club** (tel. 12-18-71; Motel Cactus, Mexico 57 South), and **Bar Jaguar** (tel. 12-17-77; Hotel Panorama, Av. V. Carranza 315).

For a quiet drink, try the atmospheric **Bar Pinín** on Calle de A. Iturbide east of Calle Aldama in the historical district. The piano bar **El Malandante** at the Hostal de Quijote is also suitably mellow.

Cinemas: Along Av. V Carranza are three movie houses, from east to west **Cine Othón** (No. 140), **Cine Avenida Vistarama** (No. 790), and **Cine Las Americas** (No. 1055); the standard bill features a combination of Latin American and North American movies. First-run American movies are also frequently shown at the new **Multicinemas Tangamanga** in the Plaza Tangamanga mall.

Shopping

Callejón Hidalgo is a section of Calle Hidalgo, north of Calle Los Bravo in the historical district, that has been turned into a pedestrian walkway lined with upscale shops selling watches, jewelry, shoes, and clothes. Almost every evening, especially on weekends, the *callejón* is packed with shoppers and window-shoppers. Once you pass Calle Guajardo, walking north, the fancy stores give way to vendors with more inexpensive, everyday wares. Smaller streets off Hidalgo are also jammed with interesting shops; **Abarrotes Uruapan,** at Calle Salazar 125 (a block east of Hidalgo beside the post office), sells fresh-roasted, fresh-ground coffee.

Eventually Hidalgo leads to the **Mercado Hidalgo,** a traditional municipal market with clothes, fruits, and vegetables downstairs, *comedores* upstairs. Surrounding the market is an array of vendors, cobblers, and taco stands. The best time for a stroll through the market area is just after sunset, when downtown residents do their daily shopping. Opposite the south entrance of the market, on Calle M. Mier y Terán, are several shops that sell Potosino handicrafts. Among these, **La Estrella** has the best selection of *chales* and *rebozos;* a good-quality, everyday *rebozo* here costs US$48-54. This shop accepts major credit cards.

If you turn right on Av. Reforma north of Mercado Hidalgo, you'll come to Av. 16 de Septiembre, which leads farther north to **Mercado República** (Reforma and 16 de Septiembre) and **Mercado 16 de Septiembre** (16 de Septiembre and Serdán). Both are typical municipal markets.

Another good place for regional as well as national handicrafts is **Tlaxcalilla Artesanías,** at Plaza del Carmen 325 (opposite the Templo del Carmen) in the historical district. In business since 1973, Tlaxcalilla offers a broad range of curios, carpets, *rebozos,* Huastec musical instruments, and clothing.

For modern consumer goods, one of the best venues is the large **Plaza Tangamanga,** opposite the park of the same name (off Diagonal Sur). The mall has nearly 200 store sites (though not all have been leased yet), including a **Sears, Comercial Mexicana supermarket,** and **Sanborn's department store.** The latter has a small but high-quality arts and crafts department, plus a section with English-language books and magazines.

Events

April: Semana Santa (the week before Easter) is celebrated with much style in San Luis Potosí. Good Friday is the climax of the week when an elaborate reenactment of the Passion of Christ is performed in the Barrio de San Juan de Guadalupe in the early morning. Later that same day, hooded celebrants walk through the downtown streets carrying important holy images from local churches in a silent, torchlit procession known as the Procesión del Silencio. Held annually since 1954, this procession is famous throughout Mexico and abroad for its solemn beauty.

May: The **Festival de Arte Primavera Potosina** runs for 10 days in the middle of the month and involves the whole city in a celebration of art and culture. Local, national, and international artists participate in symphony concerts, live theater, and folkloric and contemporary dance performances around the city. Expositions of visual arts, cinema, and handicrafts are also organized.

August: In the latter part of the month, the **Feria Nacional Potosina** (FENAP) is organized around a series of bullfights, *charreadas,* cockfights, and other sporting and cultural events. The highlight of the festival is the **Maraton Internacional Tangamanga** (International Tangamanga Marathon), which has been held yearly since 1983 and attracts athletes from all over Mexico as well as abroad. The 42-km (26-mile) footrace begins in Parque Tangamanga, with the first 10 km within the park itself, then circles through the streets and gardens of the Siete Barrios, ending near the starting point in Parque Tangamanga. Contact the tourist office (see "San Luis Potosí Information," below) for more information.

October: Performers from the Región Huasteca, along with music and dance scholars from around the country, gather for the **Festival de Música y Danza de la Huasteca** during the

Francisco Gonzales Bocanegra

first half of the month.

In 1854 San Luis native Francisco González Bocanegra composed the Mexican national anthem, which was selected from a nationwide competition sponsored by the Santa Anna government. To encourage other local composers to follow Bocanegra's example, the **Homenaje a Compositores Potosinos,** held during the first half of December, celebrates Potosino composers and their compositions with a series of musical performances centered at the Teatro de la Paz.

SAN LUIS POTOSI INFORMATION

Tourist Offices

The **Dirección Estatal de Turismo** (tel. 48-12-62-03), at Av. V. Carranza 325 (near the Hotel Panorama) has a good selection of maps and brochures containing tourist information for city and state. The **SECTUR** office (tel. 14-09-06) at Calle Guerrero 14 has some of the same information but it is less staffed.

Maps

The state tourist office (see above), in conjunction with the local hotel association, produces useful Spanish-language tourist maps for the city, the Región Huasteca, and the Altiplano sections of the state.

Detailed topographic maps for the state of San Luis Potosí and adjacent states may be obtained at the **INEGI** office (tel. 48-12-30-72, fax 48-13-07-48) at Calle Independencia 1025.

U.S. Consulate And Cultural Center

A U.S. consulate (tel. 48-17-25-01, 17-25-57) is located at Calle Fco. de P. Mariel 103 (off Av. V. Carranza southwest of the Hotel Real Plaza). The office is open Mon.-Fri. 9 a.m.-1 p.m. and 4-7 p.m.

ERIN DWYER

A good place to meet local North American residents is the **Instituto Franklin** (Mexican-North American Cultural Institute) at Av. V. Carranza 1430. The Institute's modest Benjamin Franklin Library is a source of English-language reading material.

SAN LUIS POTOSI TELEPHONE NUMBERS

Local Police: 12-55-83, 12-53-24
Highway Patrol: 12-61-28, 18-29-61
Green Angels: 14-09-06, 12-21-78
State Tourist Office: 12-62-03
Red Cross: 15-33-22
U.S. Consulate: 17-25-01, 17-25-57
San Luis Potosí Area Code: 48

Post Office
The main downtown post office is at calles Salazar and Escobedo, a short walk north from the historical district but very difficult to reach by vehicle since the streets around the post office are narrow and congested.

GETTING THERE

Air
San Luis Potosí is well connected by air via Guadalajara, Monterrey, and Mexico City. One of the main commercial routes—convenient for Texans—runs along a Mexico City-San Luis Potosí-Monterrey-San Antonio axis. Since Mexico City is less than an hour away by plane, flight connections through Mexico City are significantly shorter than for many other Northern Mexican cities.

Aeroméxico (tel. 48-17-79-36), at Av. V. Carranza 1160-2, operates daily nonstop flights to/from Guadalajara, Mexico City, and Monterrey, with connections via Mexico City to/from many other cities in the U.S. and Mexico. Aeroméxico flies nonstop daily between Monterrey and San Antonio, hence San Antonio-Monterrey-San Luis Potosí flights are easily arranged.

Mexicana (tel. 14-11-19), on Calle Madero at Uresti, fields direct flights to/from Mexico City, Monterrey (with connections to San Antonio), and Chicago, plus the usual array of connections through Mexico City.

Airport Transport: The airport is 20 km northeast of city center via Mexico 57. Taxis to/from the airport usually cost around US$13-15 while a *colectivo* is US$6 per person.

Bus
The Central Camionera, south of Glorieta Juárez on Diagonal Sur (about two km east of the city center), has a post office, *cafetería,* and two separate departure/arrival sections for first- and second-class buses.

San Luis Potosí is a major transport junction, so there are buses to nearly every corner of Mexico leaving round the clock. **Transportes Chihuahenses** and **Omnibus de México** operate to Monterrey (US$18, 12 daily departures), Matehuala (US$6, four daily departures), Ciudad Victoria (US$8-10, five daily departures), Reynosa (US$25, two nightly departures), Matamoros (US$30, three daily departures), Mexico City (US$18-20, eight daily departures), Tampico (US$10, one nightly departure), Ciudad Valles (US$6, one nightly departure).

Turistar has first-class/*ejecutivo* buses to Chihuahua (US$54, seven daily departures), Torreón (US$48, seven daily departures), Zacatecas (US$15, five daily departures), Mexico City (US$45, nine daily departures or *ejecutivo* US$60, one daily departure), and Monterrey (*ejecutivo* US$34, one daily departure). **ETN** (Enlaces Terrestres Nacionales) runs similar services to Guadalajara and Mexico City. **Transportes Elite** has first-class but less inexpensive buses to/from Monterrey, Matamoros, Reynosa, and Ciudad Victoria, plus Nuevo Laredo (US$48, one daily departure).

Flecha Amarilla serves points south to Querétaro and Mexico City with inexpensive, second-class buses. **Estrella Blanca** has cheaper fares west to Zacatecas (US$9, two daily departures), Durango (US$18, one daily departure), Mazatlán (US$45, one daily departure), and Chihuahua (US$45, one daily departure). **Omnibus de Oriente** goes to Río Verde (US$15, two daily departures), Ciudad Victoria, Tamuín, Ciudad Valles, and smaller towns in the Región Huasteca.

Autobuses Roja and **Autobuses Potosinos** operate buses to Centro Vacacional Gogorrón and Santa María del Río (both hourly, 6:45 a.m.-11:15 p.m.) for a few dollars each.

Train

A major railway junction, San Luis Potosí has separate stations for passengers and cargo, plus a number of sidings and workshops for the servicing of trains. The west-east Aguascalientes-Tampico line meets the north-south Nuevo Laredo-Mexico City and Monterrey-Mexico City lines at the main railway station just north of Alameda Juan Sarabia, Av. 20 de Noviembre and Calle M.J. Othón. This station is notable for its murals by Mexican artist Fernando Leal.

On the *Mexico City-Monterrey-Nuevo Laredo* line, second-class cars (only) are available between the border and San Luis Potosí, then both first- and second-class cars between San Luis Potosí and Mexico City. A second-class ticket to/from Nuevo Laredo costs US$7, Monterrey US$4.50, and Saltillo US$3.50. Advance tickets can be purchased at the station daily 4:30-6 p.m., or one hour in advance of departure. The complete Nuevo Laredo-San Luis Potosí trip takes roughly 15 hours (see the "Railway Schedule," pp. 86-87, for arrival and departure times), an overnight trip.

El Regiomontano runs between Mexico City and Monterrey, with a connection to Piedras Negras via Saltillo. Although other arrival/departure times for other cities along this line are fairly convenient, the northbound train stops in San Luis Potosí at 12:10 a.m., the southbound at 3:55 p.m. First-class reserved fares (not including extra sleeper charges) are: Monterrey US$16; Saltillo US$12; Piedras Negras US$27; Mexico City US$14. Advance tickets may be purchased at the San Luis Potosí railway station daily 11 a.m.-12:30 p.m. We've heard a rumor that FCN may be discontinuing the *Regiomontano* line—check with the tourist office for the latest.

The second-class *El Huasteco* operates between San Luis Potosí, Ciudad Valles, and Tampico. Number 353 departs San Luis Potosí at 7 p.m., arriving in Tampico 11-12 hours later. In the reverse direction, No. 354 runs on the same schedule. Tickets cost US$5 through to Tampico, about half for Ciudad Valles, and may be purchased an hour before departure. Remember, all this is subject to change according to the whims of FCN.

Driving

If you're heading south to Mexico City on Mexico 57 and don't wish to stop over in San Luis Potosí, take the *libramiento oriente* turnoff near San Elias (northeast of San Luis Potosí). This bypass saves at least 45 minutes of driving time over the old route through the eastern edge of the city.

GETTING AROUND

Bus

San Luis Potosí has a very well-designed and well-maintained city bus system. (*AIM* newsletter—produced by Americans living in Mexico—recently pronounced it "the cleanest and brightest we have ever seen.") Small, modern buses that run up and down Av. V. Carranza (particularly Ruta 11 and 27) are very useful for east-west trips across towns.

To get from the railway station to Glorieta Juárez, take a Ruta 9, 10, or 11; these three numbers are also good for trips between the historical district (catch the bus at the western edge of the Alameda on Calle M.J. Othón) and the bullring. Ruta 9 also stops at the main bus terminal, so this is the bus to take from the terminal to reach the historical district.

Taxi

Taxis in San Luis Potosí are reasonably priced. A cab between the Central Camionera and *el centro,* for example, costs around US$2.30.

Driving

For the most part, city streets are well marked. The east end of the city, near Glorieta Juárez was a mess when this was written, but by the time you read this the situation should have improved.

Driving in the historical district can be a bit harrowing, since some streets are blocked off to vehicular traffic while many others allow traffic in one direction only. For drivers unfamiliar with the territory, this can mean a lot of time spent driving in circles. Visiting motorists would do well to leave their vehicles at their hotels and explore this district on foot. RVers should forget about trying to navigate the historical district in their rigs; the charming streets are simply too narrow for large wheelbases.

NORTH OF SAN LUIS POTOSI

Northern Mexico's Altiplano reaches its highest elevations in the northern quadrant of the state, known as the Altiplano Potosino. Though arid and desertic, the region is high enough that milder temperatures prevail. The desert flora, with yuccas predominating, can be quite impressive.

Outside the state capital, the Altiplano's main attractions are clustered to the north in the mining area around Matehuala.

MATEHUALA

The third largest city in the state is merely a quick gas or motel stop for most visitors on their way to the state capital or heading west to the historic mining town of Real de Catorce. Travelers going to Real de Catorce by public transport have no choice but to break their journey in Matehuala, since no direct buses travel from San Luis Potosí to Real.

The town's name comes from a Guachichil phrase meaning "Don't come." (One can imagine the conquistadors interrogating the locals in Spanish or Náhuatl: "What's this place called?" "Don't come.") Spanish conquistadors ignored the warning and exploited gold and silver ore found in the area. Mining is still an important part of the local economy, although the largest mines quit producing earlier this century. **La Paz** gold and silver mines, about 10 km (six miles) southwest of town, were founded in 1864 and are still being worked. The production of *ixtle,* a hemplike fiber used to make rope, baskets, shoes, and various other household goods, is another means of livelihood in Matehuala.

Street life in Matehuala revolves around the **Plaza Principal,** which is flanked by 19th-century architecture such as the Templo de San Salvador.

Several motels in town (including the Capri, Oasis, and Las Palmas) can arrange six-hour sightseeing trips to Real de Catorce.

Accommodations
Most of Matehuala's hotels and motels are strung along Mexico 57 east of town. From the north, the first you'll see on the highway is the three-star **Motel Hacienda** (tel. 488-2-00-65), at Km 620, which has very comfortable, modern rooms that range in price from US$30-40 depending on amenities. Just south of the Hacienda are the less expensive **Motel El Pedregal** (tel. 2-00-54), **Motel La Mansión** (tel. 2-07-04), and **Motel El Parador de San Miguel** (tel. 2-01-74), all of which offer adequate rooms for US$18-22.

The next batch of motels south along the highway near Km 617 are in the US$28-38 range, including **Motel Oasis** (tel. 488-2-07-42), **Motel Parador Misión del Real** (tel. 2-06-71) and **Motel El Dorado** (tel. 2-10-74). All offer decent a/c rooms; El Dorado also has a pool.

Pick of the pack at this end of town is the **Motel Las Palmas** (tel. 2-00-01), a bit north of El Dorado at Km 617. Las Palmas is very oriented toward Real de Catorce visitors and has a pool, RV spaces with full hookups, and a good restaurant. Rooms with a/c and TV cost US$30-40 s/d; RV spots are US$6-8.

Downtown is a set of smaller, older, and cheaper hotels. Though very plain, the most atmospheric is the *clase económica* **Hotel Matehuala** (tel. 2-06-80), at Calle Bustamante 134 Ote., a colonial-style place with rooms around a courtyard. Upstairs rooms with private bath cost US$12 per night; downstairs rooms share common bathrooms and are only US$10 per night. Similarly priced rooms are available at the **Hotel Monterrey** (tel. 2-07-96; Calle Hidalgo 212 Sur) and **Hotel María Esther** (tel. 2-07-14; Calle Madero 111).

Food
On the highway, the **Oasis** and **Las Palmas** motels have good, reasonably priced restaurants open 7:30 a.m. till late. **Restaurant El Mesquite** and **Restaurant Verona,** on the highway near Motel Las Palmas, specialize in *cabrito asado,* which is a local favorite. **Restaurant Santa Fé,** on the Parque Vicente Guerrero in town, serves inexpensive Mexican standards. Many shops sell *natillas, cajetas,* and other goat-milk sweets.

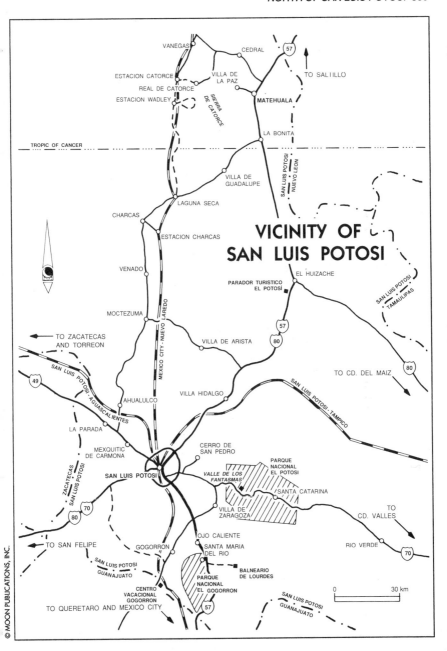

VANEGAS

CEDRAL

57

TO SALTILLO

ESTACION CATORCE

VILLA DE LA PAZ

REAL DE CATORCE

ESTACION WADLEY

SIERRA DE CATORCE

MATEHUALA

LA BONITA

TROPIC OF CANCER

VILLA DE GUADALUPE

SAN LUIS POTOSI / NUEVO LEON

LAGUNA SECA

CHARCAS

VICINITY OF
SAN LUIS POTOSI

ESTACION CHARCAS

VENADO

EL HUIZACHE

PARADOR TURISTICO EL POTOSI

SAN LUIS POTOSI / TAMAULIPAS

MOCTEZUMA

TO ZACATECAS AND TORREON

MEXICO CITY - NUEVO LAREDO

VILLA DE ARISTA

57

80

TO CD. DEL MAIZ

80

49

SAN LUIS POTOSI - AGUASCALIENTES

VILLA HIDALGO

SAN LUIS POTOSI - TAMPICO

AHUALULCO

LA PARADA

MEXQUITIC DE CARMONA

CERRO DE SAN PEDRO

PARQUE NACIONAL EL POTOSI

ZACATECAS / SAN LUIS POTOSI

SAN LUIS POTOSI

VALLE DE LOS FANTASMAS

SANTA CATARINA

TO CD. VALLES

70

80

VILLA DE ZARAGOZA

OJO CALIENTE

TO SAN FELIPE

GOGORRON

SANTA MARIA DEL RIO

BALNEARIO DE LOURDES

RIO VERDE

70

SAN LUIS POTOSI / GUANAJUATO

CENTRO VACACIONAL GOGORRON

PARQUE NACIONAL EL GOGORRON

57

SAN LUIS POTOSI / GUANAJUATO

0   30 km

TO QUERETARO AND MEXICO CITY

© MOON PUBLICATIONS, INC.

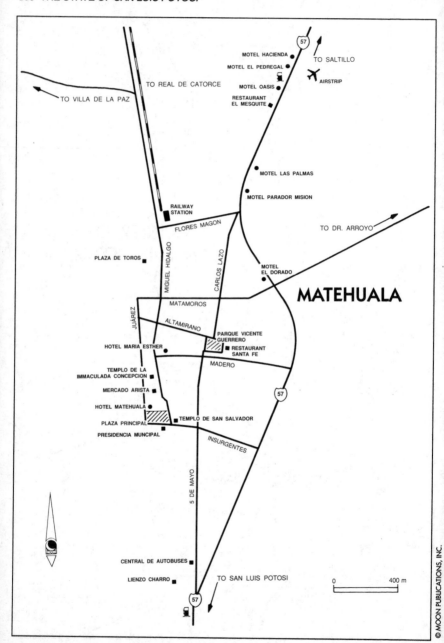

MATEHUALA

Transport

Matehuala's Central de Autobuses is at the south end of town, where Av. 5 de Mayo meets Mexico 57 (about 1.5 km from town center). Only three or four departures leave daily for Real de Catorce, so you may find yourself waiting several hours there. Buses to San Luis Potosí leave every half-hour from early in the morning till around 8 p.m.

A **Green Angels** station (tel. 488-2-08-58) at Blvd. Carlos Lazo 101 is just off the highway.

The PEMEX station on the highway bypass sells Magna Sin. Farther south toward San Luis Potosí, at Km 100, is a large PEMEX with Magna Sin and a **Restaurant Parador.**

MATEHUALA TO REAL DE CATORCE

It takes about 1 1/2 hours to drive from Matehuala to Real (or 2 1/2-3 hours by bus), first 27 km (16 miles) northwest through Cedral via a paved two-lane road and then 25 km (15.5 miles) southwest along a wide, bumpy, cobblestoned road—almost a work of art in itself—into the Sierra de Catorce. This latter road skirts several abandoned mines and semi-abandoned villages, and passes a *mirador* with wide-ranging views of the plains below.

Cedral

Between Matehuala and Real de Catorce (19 km/12 miles west of Mexico 57), this friendly little town is supported by spring-irrigated agriculture and locally quarried onyx. Founded in the 18th century, Cedral has a pleasant plaza surrounded by ash and walnut trees, a parish church, and several *tiendas* where groceries, ice, and beer are available. Local culinary specialties include chorizo and *cabrito guisado de Cedral* (kid goat stuffed with olives and cracklings, covered with **chile ancho** paste, and stewed in its own blood).

Practicalities: Hotel Plaza, on the plaza, has spartan rooms for around US$10 per night. The nearest PEMEX station is in Matehuala.

Transportes Altiplanos buses from Matehuala stop in Cedral briefly on the way to Real de Catorce.

REAL DE CATORCE

Surrounded by rolling hills and desert valleys, this historic ex-mining town sits at a cool 2,756 meters (9,039 feet) above sea level. In its semi-ghost town state, Real's windswept, cobble-stoned streets and stone-block buildings would make the perfect set for a Sergio Leone western, and has in fact appeared in several Mexican cowboy films. Gabriele Salvatores, director of the Oscar-winning *Mediterraneo,* recently used Real de Catorce for location shooting on his latest film, *Puerto Escondido.*

Today the town has less than a thousand full-time residents, most of whom make their living as independent prospectors working the abandoned mines for a few pesos a week or by catering to the tens of thousands of pilgrims who come yearly to worship at the Parroquía de la Purísima Concepción, which contains a highly revered St. Francis shrine. The town's remoteness has kept it in a uniquely preserved state that attracts a trickle of tourists, mostly Potosinos visiting on weekends and holidays. A

Real de Catorce

very small—and fluctuating—artists' colony is located here.

Real is also a traditional pilgrim center for the Huichol rancherías of Nayarit, Durango, Jalisco, and Zacatecas, which visit the area every spring to gather *Lophophora williamsii,* the hallucinogenic cactus more commonly known in Mexico as peyote (or híkuri among the Huicholes). Although peyote is available in other parts of Northern Mexico, for the Huicholes only plants collected from sacred Wírikuta (the Huichol name for the Catorce plateau) are considered appropriate for their rituals. Some say the Huichol peyote cult and San Francisco pilgrims are proof that Real de Catorce is one of the earth's "power spots."

Except during the first week of October, when St. Francis pilgrims throng the streets, Real saturates the visitor with a tranquil, lost-world feeling. Star-gazers will find very clear skies virtually year-round. Visit during the week and you'll have practically the whole town to yourself. Be sure to bring warm clothes if you plan to visit Nov.-March, when evenings can be quite cold. Any time of year, the steep, cobblestoned streets will be easier to negotiate if you wear sturdy shoes or boots.

History

Several legends regarding the origin of the town's name ("Kingdom of the Fourteen") circulate. The most repeated story claims that 14 bandits once headquartered themselves here, while another says 14 soldiers died defending a Spanish encampment from Amerindian attacks. Yet another recounts that 14 travelers discovered silver while spending the night here.

It isn't known precisely when the first silver lode was discovered, though Spanish records indicate that ore was extracted here in 1773 by *afro-mestizo* Ventura Ruíz. In 1779 the town was officially established under the name "Real de Minas de Nuestra Señora de la Limpia Concepción de Guadalupe de los Alamos de Catorce" ("Mining Kingdom of Our Lady of the Immaculate Conception of Guadalupe from the Cottonwoods of Catorce"). By the end of the 18th century it was one of the most prosperous Reales de Minas in Nueva España, with 15,000 inhabitants working the mines or servicing the miners. In 1822 an Englishman brought the first steam boiler ever used in Mexican mines to pump water from flooded shafts. This same joint Mexican-British venture was later the first in Mexico to use dynamite to blast tunnels, the most famous of which is the Túnel de Ogarrio, which provides the main access to the town from the north.

By the late 19th century Real de Catorce had paved streets, electric lights, a municipal water system, a bullring, a cockfighting *palenque,* and its own silver-coin mint. At their peak the local mines produced US$3 million of high-grade silver per year. Around the turn of the century—by which time the richest veins had been used up—the price of silver dropped precipitously. At the lower prices, the smaller, harder-to-work lodes weren't worth mining on a large scale, resulting in a general cutback in production. Mineral exploration stopped completely with the outbreak of the Mexican Revolution in 1910, after which the town slipped into near oblivion.

Sights

Parroquia de la Purísima Concepción: The simple neoclassical exterior of this church in the center of town belies its sumptuous, late baroque interior. Constructed in 1814 by French architect Jean Crusot, the typical Latin cross floor plan features a unique mesquite-wood floor made from coffin lids. The principal object of interest of most *peregrinos,* however, is the small San Francisco image in one of the side altars.

Devotees of Purísima Concepción's San Francisco cult believe that the image has the power to answer prayer requests and to cleanse believers of sin. The origin of the cult is uncertain but it dates to at least as far back as Real's abandonment, 1905-10, when former residents of the town began making annual pilgrimages to "pay" for fulfilled requests. Locks of hair cut from the heads of pilgrims in penance, or in return for the granting of a request, are attached to tin *retablos* in the bell tower. Pilgrims numbering in the tens of thousands arrive during the week of Oct. 4, the feast day for St. Francis.

Casa de la Moneda: The old mint, opposite the church, dates to the early 1860s. To conform to the sloping terrain, the neoclassical structure features three floors on one side, two on another.

Other Historic Structures: A native-stone *palenque de gallos,* built in 1789 for cockfighting matches, still stands on the west side of town.

REAL DE CATORCE

It's occasionally used for outdoor musical and theatrical performances by artists from the state capital. About a kilometer north of the main plaza, beyond the Hotel Puesta del Sol on the left-hand side of the road, is a stone **bullring** from the same era.

On the other side of the road more or less opposite the old bullring is the town *panteón* or walled cemetery. The small Guadalupe chapel on the cemetery grounds was built in 1775.

Museo Parroquial: On the street leading into town from the tunnel, a one-room museum houses a small collection of dusty historical mementos. Admission is US$0.15; hours are erratic.

Túnel de Ogarrio: Real de Catorce is accessed from the east via an impressive 2.3-km tunnel through solid rock; the tunnel was started in 1897 and finished in 1901.

Mountains: Three peaks standing taller than 3,000 meters (9,840 feet)—**El Lucero, El Barco,** and **La Leona**—border the Real de Catorce plateau.

Accommodations And Food

Real de Catorce has three reliable places to stay in town, plus a bed-and-breakfast that's sometimes open on weekends. During festival times several homes open as temporary *casas de huéspedes* with rooms for as little as US$5 per night. With a little asking around, you should be able to find simple rooms for rent by the week or month.

On Calle Lanzagorta, the road leading from the tunnel into town, you might easily miss seeing the **Casa de Huéspedes La Providencia** on the left before the museum. Depending on size and number of beds, rooms range from US$10 s to US$33 t; all are quite basically furnished but clean, with private hot-water showers. Meals can be ordered in the cozy kitchen-dining room at the front of the house.

In the center of town east of Jardín Hidalgo, in a nicely restored colonial mansion on Calle Morelos, is the simple but atmospheric **Hotel El Real** (tel. 488-2-25-93 in Matehuala). High-ceilinged rooms furnished with rustic antiques and attached bathrooms cost US$20 with one bed, US$24 for two beds. A room without bath is also available for US$14. The hotel's roof terrace affords terrific views of the surrounding town. The only drawback to this hotel is that the unheated rooms can get very chilly during cold-weather months. A small dining room downstairs offers à la carte Mexican and Italian meals. As in many out-of-the-way destinations in Mexico, food service can be quite slow.

North of town toward the bullring and cemetery, **Hotel La Quinta Puesta del Sol** (tel. 488-7-02-81 in Matehuala), on Calle del Cemeterio, sits on a hillside overlooking the scenic valley of Barranca El Voladero. The hotel offers 20 rooms with private bathrooms that cost US$21 s, US$27 d. New, more expensive rooms are being built in a wing separate from the original rooms. Fixed-price meals in the hotel dining room cost US$3-3.50 for breakfast, US$4.60-5.30 lunch, US$3.30-4.50 dinner.

Around the corner from the Hotel El Real is a recently established bed-and-breakfast called **El Coral de Conde.** Unless prior arrangements are made, the nicely furnished rooms are only available on weekends. Rates start at US$40 d. For reservations or further information, contact the state tourist office in San Luis Potosí.

The **Art Café,** a tiny place on Calle Morelos north of the Hotel El Real, serves simple meals but is generally open on weekends only.

Recreation

Hotel El Real and Hotel La Quinta Puesta del Sol can arrange horseback riding for US$5 per person per hour or US$30 per half day for up to four persons.

Trails radiating from town in several directions could lead to some interesting hikes.

Transport

Bus: From Matehuala, **Transportes Altiplanos** operates three or four buses per day to Real de Catorce for US$1.50 per person. These buses stop in Cedral, so if you miss a Matehuala departure you may be able to get another bus on to Cedral in time for the Cedral-Real departure.

Mini-van: Several of the motels in Matehuala can arrange for mini-van transport (or six-hour tours) to Real de Catorce. Prices are negotiable depending on the number of passengers and how long the driver is needed in Real de Catorce; it's possible to arrange pickup on another day.

Driving: Negotiating the cobblestoned road between Cedral and Real de Catorce is like riding on a continuous carpet of *topes* (Mexican speed bumps)—but the scenery makes up for the rather slow pace. Toll-takers at the entrance to the Ogarrio tunnel collect a US$1 toll. Since the tunnel can only accommodate traffic in one direction, a radio telephone system—staffed at each end of the tunnel—is used to regulate the change of direction at regular intervals. Hence arriving motorists may have to wait at one end for 20 minutes or so until the direction is reversed.

Motorists with sturdy, high-clearance, 4WD vehicles can also arrive or depart via a dirt track that runs 10 km (6.2 miles) west from Real de Catorce to the Estación Catorce railway depot, then roughly 50 km (31 miles) south, parallel to the railway, to a paved road that continues southwest 19 km (11.7 miles) to Charcas. From Charcas it's 101 km (62.6 miles) south to Mexico 49, the highway between Zacatecas and San Luis Potosí.

Charcas

Few tourists, whether Mexican or foreign, ever make it to Charcas, the oldest town in the Altiplano Potosino. Founded as a Franciscan mission in 1574, it soon developed into one of Northern Mexico's "Reales de Minas." Like Real de Catorce, it was a town built of native rock, with twisted cobblestoned streets and a stone church, the difference being that Charcas is still an important mining center. An 18th-century convent and *parroquía*—containing the patroness of miners, the Virgen de Charcas—stand near the plaza; a festival held at the beginning of September honors the Virgin. The townspeople have converted a 16th-century *alhódiga* or granary into a school.

Four km (2.5 miles) south of town via a gravel road are the **Grutas de la Cueva Azul** ("Blue Cave Grottoes"), a series of caverns with bluish stalagmite/stalactite formations.

Practicalities: The **Roma, Paris,** and **Rosas** hotels offer simple lodging for under US$15.

Charcas is 63 km (39 miles) southwest of Mexico 57 (at La Bonita, which is 19 km/11.7 miles south of Matehuala), or 101 km (62.6 miles) north of Mexico 49. Magna Sin isn't available anywhere along this entire 164-km (101.6-mile) stretch, so be sure to fill up in San Luis Potosí or Matehuala. Buses to Charcas are available in Matehuala and San Luis Potosí.

SOUTH OF SAN LUIS POTOSI

The Altiplano Potosino continues southeast beyond the state capital as far as the Río Santa María Valley, where it begins to merge with the more lush and tropical Región Huasteca.

Along the river itself, within 60 km of the capital, are several *balnearios* and the renowned handicraft center of Santa María del Río. Mexico 57D, the new 45-km tollway through the valley, offers a smooth, divided surface until just past Santa María del Río, where it merges with the old two-lane Mexico 57 to Mexico City. Within the next few years the tollway will extend another 35 km to the San Luis Potosí-Guanajuato state line.

PARQUE NACIONAL EL GOGORRON

Covering 25,000 hectares of the Valle de Gogorrón, this recently established national park is embraced by two mountains: the taller, rockier Bernalejo; and the smaller Cuesta. Both are blanketed with an intriguing floral mix of pines and cactus. Camping is permitted, although outside the Gogorrón *balneario* no public facilities are available.

The **Centro Vacacional Gogorrón** (tel. 48-12-36-36, Calle M.J. Othón 100 in San Luis Potosí) is a large *balneario* at the western edge of the park. Facilities include thermal baths, cabins, restaurant, swimming pools, and landscaped gardens. Rates start at US$28 s/d.

Getting There
Access to the Centro Vacacional Gogorrón is 55 km (34 miles) south of San Luis Potosí—25 km south via Mexico 57 and then 30 km on the road to Villa de Reyes.

The national park extends westward from the town of Santa María del Río. Trails can be accessed from either this town or from the village of Gogorrón on the other side. Guided burro trips may be available in Santa María del Río—check with the Motel Puesta del Sol.

SANTA MARIA DEL RIO

San Luis Potosí's most famous handicraft product, the *rebozo,* hails from this charming town 45 km south of the state capital. One of the most typical of all Mexican clothing accessories, these delicately woven shawls adorn the shoulders of aristocrats and peasants alike throughout the country and are a *de rigueur* part of every Potosina's wardrobe.

Although several regions in Mexico have their own *rebozo* styles, colors, and weaving techniques, those made in Santa María del Río are the most coveted. The state government considers the preservation of this *artesanía* so important to regional culture that since 1953 it has sponsored the **Escuela de Artesanías,** which is housed in a section of the Gobierno Constitucional del Estado off the larger of the town's two plazas. Visitors are welcome to observe the artisans as they work at traditional *telares de cintura* or "belt looms," in which the loom is tied to a post or wall hook and stretched around the backs of the weavers with a wide belt. Other handicrafts, particularly marquetry (wood inlay) and basketry, are also taught at the school.

Santa María del Río, founded in 1589 as a Franciscan mission, has a number of modest but historic structures, including the **Templo de Carmen** (dedicated in 1764). Colonial-era stone houses with wooden door and window frames are common. The town has two plazas, the large **Plaza Principal** in front of the Gobierno Constitucional del Estado, and a smaller one that's diagonally linked with the first. **El Arquillo,** an old aqueduct bordered by walnut trees, can

THE REBOZO

Originating in Persia and India, the *rebozo* or Mexican shawl was introduced to the Spanish during the Moorish conquest of Spain, then brought to Mexico by the Spanish. While the garment was called a *chal* in Spain (*shal* in the Orient, "shawl" in the Anglo world), Mexicans invented their own word, *rebozo*, from the verb *arrebozarse*, "to cover oneself with a cape or coat." Over the years the Mexican shawl lengthened, narrowed, and borrowed influences—including ikat or tie-dye weaving techniques—from shawls brought from China, the Philippines, and India aboard Mexico's Manila galleons in the 16th and 17th centuries. A 1582 royal decree forbidding the wearing of indigenous clothing by *mestizas*, *mulatas*, and *negras* furthered quickened the *rebozo's* rate of adoption among non-Amerindian, non-Spanish women.

Rebozo weaving

It takes one to two months to complete a top-quality silk *rebozo* measuring approximately one meter wide and 2.5 meters long (3.3 feet x 8 feet). The best *rebozos* are so fine that they can be pulled through a wedding ring. Such quality typically costs over US$300. Less expensive silk or cotton *rebozos*—still of high quality—go for around US$100. In Santa María del Río, *rebozos* are often presented inside handmade, inlaid cedar boxes as wedding gifts. The *chal*, a thicker, more utilitarian shawl made of wool or synthetic materials, is typically less expensive than a *rebozo*.

JOE CUMMINGS

be followed to a 15-meter (45-foot) waterfall along the Río Santa María, a favorite local picnic spot.

Farther west, the low Sierra Bernalejo is the beginning of Parque Nacional Gogorrón, an area suitable for camping and hiking.

Accommodations And Food
At the north end of town near the highway, **Motel Puesta del Sol** (tel. 485-3-00-59) has comfortable a/c rooms for US$35 per night. In town, the much more basic **Hotel Jardín** (Calle Jardín Unión 7) and **Hotel Santa María** (Calle Bautista 24) offer simple lodging for US$10-12.

Motel Puesta del Sol has a fair restaurant that's usually empty except on weekends and holidays. Around the smaller of the town's two plazas are a number of restaurants and cafes.

One of the local specialties is *campechana*, a sweet, crispy pastry.

Shopping
Near the main square are several shops selling *rebozos*—for cash only. They can also be purchased at the Escuela de Artesanías, although the school sometimes has a short supply. A fine-quality *rebozo* costs around US$100, though versions made of synthetic materials are priced as low as US$30-40, while a top-drawer shawl may cost as much as US$300. Traditionally speaking, bright colors are considered more suitable for younger women, muted colors for older. Ask at the school or at one of the shops for a demonstration of the many ways to wear the *rebozo*.

Santa María del Río is also known for wood furniture, inlaid cedar boxes (*cajas de rebozo*) used to store Mexican shawls, reed baskets, and *ixtle* bags, all of which can be found in shops around town.

Events
During the first half of August Santa María del Río celebrates the **Feria del Rebozo** along with the feast day of the Virgen de la Asunción.

Transport By Bus
The **Potosinos** bus line operates second-class buses hourly between San Luis Potosí and Santa María del Río for less than US$3. In Santa María del Río these buses arrive and depart alongside the town's smaller plaza.

Driving
A four-lane tollway speeds motorists 45 km south from San Luis Potosí to Santa María del Río in half an hour. Near the town entrance off the highway is a PEMEX station with Magna Sin.

OTHER BALNEARIOS

Approximately 48 km (30 miles) south off San Luis Potosí on Mexico 57, then 11 km (6.5 miles) east on a partially paved road, is the **Balneario de Lourdes** (tel. 48-17-14-04 in San Luis Potosí) on the Río Santa María. Formerly the Hacienda La Labor del Río, this resort features hotel accommodations, a restaurant, mineral baths, a swimming pool, squash courts, horseback riding, and a restaurant. Beyond the resort is a plant where mineral water is bottled. Rates start at US$32 s/d; Lourdes is closed Jan.-Feb. each year.

The **Balneario Ojo Caliente,** a resort with a rustic motel, thermal-fed baths, and three swimming pools, is accessed by a dirt road approximately 30 km south of San Luis Potosí via Mexico 57 on the way to Santa María del Río. The village of Ojo Caliente is regionally famous for *gorditas* and, on weekends, *carnitas.*

REGION HUASTECA

Covering parts of Tamaulipas, San Luis Potosí, Veracruz, and Hidalgo, the Región Huasteca encompasses a lush area of mountains, valleys, and coastal plains that are the ancestral homelands of the Huastecs. The Huastecs inhabited this part of Mexico long before the *entrada* and have imbued the region with a unique culture that is a hybrid of *mestizo* and *indio* ways.

Abundant rivers and streams along with fertile soils produce a bounty of fruits (particularly citrus), vegetables, coffee, sugarcane, and dairy cattle. For the visitor, a combination of natural scenery—waterfalls, lakes, cloud forests, mountains—and indigenous culture makes the region one of Mexico's most attractive destinations. Adding to the allure is the fact that few foreigners—aside from a handful of North American art students who make pilgrimages to Sir Edward James's surrealist retreat—seem to know of the region's existence.

The regional weather is most pleasant in the fall, winter, and early spring when temperatures are very moderate. At lower altitudes the weather in late spring and early summer can be quite hot, as the humid valleys tend to hold in the tropical heat. Cane fields are also put to the torch during this season, an activity that adds a smoky haze to the landscape. Although it can rain any time of year, the rains are heaviest in late summer.

Parque Nacional El Potosí
Roughly 70 km (43.5 miles) east of San Luis Potosí via Mexico 70, surrounding the small town of Santa Catarina, this national park incorporates 2,000 hectares (4,940 acres) of the wooded Valle de los Fantasmas ("Valley of the Ghosts"), including a major portion of the Cañada Grande watershed, the origin of numerous streams that feed into the Río Verde.

The very diverse forest, in which pine and live oak dominate, can be seen from the highway; at its highest points the highway passes through sections of cloud forest where even the mesquite trees are draped with ball moss. The vegetation becomes lusher as you move east. In the highlands you can sometimes spot the bright green plumage and yellow-and-black, canoe-

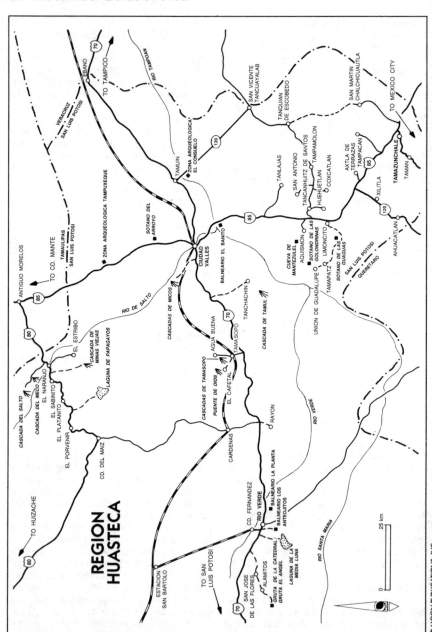

© MOON PUBLICATIONS, INC.

shaped bill of the **emerald toucan.** Even if you don't see one, you might be able to hear its low, nasal barking.

Public facilities and access to the park are virtually nil. To explore the area, try taking the dirt roads north from Mexico 70 toward the villages of Armadillo de los Infante (west of Santa Catarina) and Portrero de Santa Gertrudis (east of Santa Catarina).

Take care if you're driving; in some stretches the winding mountain roads can become obscured by fog without warning.

RIO VERDE

Situated 135 km (83.7 miles) east of the state capital on the banks of the river of the same name, Río Verde has a very agreeable climate and is a center for the cultivation of corn, beans, avocado, and especially oranges. Dairy cattle are also raised in the area. The town is considered part of "La Zona Media," the gateway to the Región Huasteca, and as you're driving through, your car radio may begin picking up radio stations with broadcasts in Huastec dialect instead of Spanish.

Founded in 1617, Río Verde sports an assortment of colonial-era buildings, including the 1761-vintage **Templo de Santa Catarina Mártir** next to Plaza Constitución in the town center. Two-wheeled *solkis* (horse carts) provide transport around town, enhancing the bygone-era atmosphere.

On weekends the **Mercado Colón,** three blocks south of the plaza, bustles with shoppers filling string bags with fresh produce and local cheeses.

Several rustic *balnearios* with thermal spas are near town, including Los Anteojitos, La Planta, San Diego, and Palma Larga.

Train Trip To San Bartolo

From Río Verde one can take a short but scenic train trip 45 km (28 miles) north to San Bartolo. The train leaves Río Verde each day at 9 a.m., arriving in San Bartolo about an hour later, then returns to Río Verde at 1 p.m. The Río Verde railway station is a little over a kilometer west of Plaza Constitución; take Calle Potosinos west to the railbed, then follow the tracks north to the station.

Laguna De La Media Luna

This half-moon-shaped lake, fed by thermal springs and encircled by pines, has very clear water at a constant 20° C (84 ° F), and hence is a favorite local destination for snorkelers and scuba divers. The lake measures 300 meters (980 feet) long and 70 meters (230 feet) wide at its widest point; near the major spring source the depth reaches around 36 meters (118 feet), though the average depth elsewhere is 25 meters (82 feet).

During the week the lake is virtually deserted; camping is permitted. The turnoff for the lake is three km (1.8 miles) west of Río Verde on Mexico 70, after which an 11-km (6.8-mile) dirt road paralleling an irrigation canal leads southwest to the lake. If you would like to dive and need equipment, there is a small *tienda de buceo* (dive shop) on Blvd. Río Verde-Valles (Mexico 70) in Río Verde.

Gruta De La Catedral/Gruta El Angel

To reach these caves you must drive 11 km (6.8 miles) west of Río Verde on Mexico 70, then southwest 15 km (9.3 miles) to the village of Alamitos. In Alamitos you can arrange for a guide to lead you for an hour on foot to the Gruta de la Catedral, named for a large cavern with formations said to resemble a pulpit, altar, and pews; a hole in the ceiling sprays light onto the scene. Seventy meters beyond is the Gruta del Angel, where stalagmite formations in five chambers resemble angels.

Accommodations And Food

Río Verde has four modest hotels in town, plus one very comfortable one, **Motel María Dolores** (tel. 487-2-05-16) at Km 127.5 on Mexico 70, not far from the town entrance. Rooms at the María Dolores come with all the amenities and cost US$30-35. In town your best is either **Hotel Plaza** (tel. 2-01-00) next to Plaza Constitución, at US$15, or the slightly nicer **Hotel Río** (tel. 2-04-58), at Calle Hidalgo 700 toward the town's south entrance, at US$21-24.

Near the Mercado Colón are several restaurants of varying quality. *Enchiladas rioverdenses,* a variation on the *potosina* and *huasteca* styles, are a local specialty. Fresh-squeezed orange juice is very inexpensive.

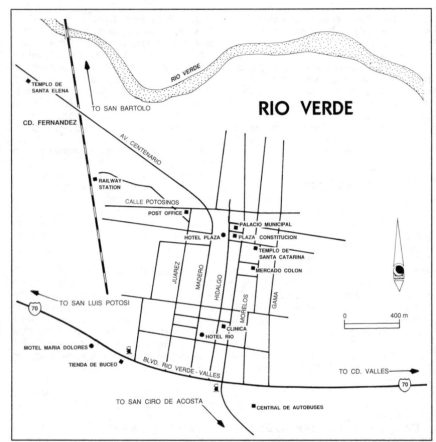

RIO VERDE

RIO VERDE TO CIUDAD VALLES

Tamasopo Waterfalls
Near the village of Tamasopo between Río Verde and Ciudad Valles is a number of *cascadas* or waterfalls that can be reached by car. For **Cascadas de Tamasopo,** take the road north marked for Tamasopo and Agua Buena off Mexico 70, 77 km (47.7 miles) east of Río Verde. Two km north of the village of Tamasopo are the falls, three 20-meter cascades that tumble into a five-meter-deep pool suitable for swimming.

Follow the river in either direction to find other pools. Two km farther north, for example, a side road leads to **El Trampolín** ("The Diving Board"), a wooded area with small cascades and idyllic springs. At the bottom of a gorge that's a 15-minute walk from the El Cafetal railway station (three km by dirt road from Tamasopo) is **Puente de Dios** ("Bridge of God"), where the river has carved a rock bridge between two rock hills. Turquoise-blue waters sparkle in rounded pools to either side of the bridge, with a short waterfall between them and several small cascades that trickle down surrounding rock walls.

Practicalities: The very basic **Hotel Cosmos** in Tamasopo has rooms for US$10-12.

The falls are least crowded during the week. If you like crowds, visit Tamasopo during the colorful sugarcane festival, held in mid-March each year.

Cascadas De Micos

Named for the monkeys (*micos*) once seen frequently in the area, this series of five falls feed into a deep pool in the Río El Salto. To get there, go seven km (4.3 miles) west of Ciudad Valles on Mexico 70 and then take a posted dirt road north for 18 km (11 miles). The last couple of kilometers require vehicles with high road clearance; otherwise you'll have to walk.

Cascada De Tamul

The largest and most impressive waterfall in the state, Tamul is fed by the Río Gallinas and plummets 105 meters (344 feet) into the Río Tampoán, a wide river in a lush *cañada*. During rainy periods the Tampoán spreads up to 300 meters (980 feet) wide.

The only safe way to approach the falls is by boat along the Río Tampoán from Tanchachín. An unpaved road to the latter village starts 25 km (15.5 miles) west of Ciudad Valles on Mexico 70, then proceeds south for 18 km (11 miles) to the village. Ask around for someone who will pilot a *lancha* up the river to the falls, a journey of two hours. The return, downriver trip takes only 45 minutes. The best time to visit the magnificent Cascada de Tamul is during the drier months (Oct.-June).

CIUDAD VALLES

The second most populated city in the state, Valles was founded on the banks of the Río Valles in 1533 by Nuño de Guzmán under the name Villa de Santiago de los Valles de Oxitipa. Little of historical note remains and today the town is a center for ranching, light manufacturing, and the processing and shipping of coffee, sugar, and oranges.

Although there isn't much to see or do in the town itself, Valles makes a convenient headquarters for visits to nearby waterfalls, *balnearios*, ruins, and Huastec villages.

The main business and shopping district is along calles Abasolo and Hidalgo west of the highway through town. Here you'll find the small

Mercado Municipal and a few handicraft vendors. Classier shops are found along Calle Hidalgo, the more straightforward places along calles Independencia and Hidalgo.

Visits to two sugar mills (*azucareros*) outside of town, **Plan de Ayala** and **Plan de San Luis,** can be arranged through the larger hotels.

Museo Regional Huasteca

This small museum off Blvd. Sur (Mexico 70/85 in town) near the Glorieta Hidalgo contains exhibits of ceramics and other Huastec artifacts. Although the posted hours are Mon.-Fri. 9 a.m.-1 p.m., 4-8 p.m., the actual opening times are somewhat more erratic. Admission is free.

Puente Tampoán

Built 1936-39, this steel bridge over the wide Río Tampoán south of Ciudad Valles is an engineering marvel in itself, but the main reason to stop here is to watch the ongoing excavation of river sand. In the shallow waters below the bridge, workers shovel accumulated sand into canoes, then paddle the sand to shore where it's loaded into trucks. This keeps the river flowing while providing a cheap source of material for local cement factories.

Accommodations

Hotel Quintamar (tel. 138-2-32-24), on Mexico 70 on the way into town from San Luis Potosí, is a small, modern, three-story place where rooms with a/c, carpeting, and TV cost around US$40 per night. A restaurant-bar is on the premises.

Continuing east along Mexico 70 and then south on Mexico 85 (Blvd. México-Laredo) into the heart of town, the next hotel on the main road is the delightful **Hotel Valles** (tel. 2-00-50), a worn but clean and friendly place with 10 acres of tropical landscaping and a pool. Cozy rooms cost US$30-50 depending on the size; all come with a/c and private bath.

Farther south along the same road is **Posada Don Antonio** (tel. 2-00-44, fax 2-30-48), a renovated, colonial-style hotel with a variety of a/c rooms in the same price range as Hotel Valles, US$30-50, plus a pool and two restaurant-bars.

Very near the Posada Don Antonio on the same side of Blvd. México-Laredo is the less expensive **Hotel San Fernando** (tel. 2-01-84). Plain but adequate rooms with a/c and satellite

TV are US$18-24. A 24-hour restaurant and parking lot are attached.

Downtown near the plaza and Mercado Municipal, the one-star **Hotel Rex** (tel. 2-03-45), at Calle Hidalgo 418, has rooms for around US$20. Cheaper still are the *clase económica* **Hotel Piña** (tel. 2-01-83), at Calle Juárez 210; and the **Hotel Jardín** (tel. 2-00-92), on the Jardín Hidalgo. Basic rooms at either run US$12-15.

Fifteen km (11 miles) east of town on Mexico 70 (on the way to Tampico), the sugar-cooperative-owned **Hotel Balneario Taninul** (tel. 2-00-00, 2-44-14) offers quiet landscaped grounds, a terrace with rocking chairs, a good restaurant, a tennis court, and a pool fed by hot mineral springs. You'll find hiking trails nearby, including one to the source of the Río Coy. This is a good place to get away and relax for a reasonable US$35 per night.

Just south of town off Mexico 85 (the road to Tamazunchale) is the **Motel Bambu,** a basic US$15 place with security parking.

RV Parks

El Bañito Trailer Park (tel. 138-2-06-08), 9.6 km (six miles) south of town on Mexico 85, offers 60 slots with full hookups (most also have patios) for US$7-12. On the spacious grounds are two thermal-fed pools, a recreation room, mini-mar-

ket, restaurant, and coin laundry. Weekly and monthly rates are available.

Hotel Valles also has 25 RV slots with full hookups for US$8-10 per night.

Food

Several small eateries are located in the shopping area downtown, including Calle Hidalgo's **Bonanza, Principal,** and **Guerra,** all of which serve Mexican standards. **Yoki's,** at Calle Hidalgo 534, is a simple spot with Huastecan specialties. *Enchiladas huastecas* are very similar to *enchiladas potosinas* except that they come with a piece of fried chicken (or a pork chop) and black beans instead of pinto beans.

Larger restaurants are found along the Mexico 70/85 boulevard through town, such as the newish **El Asadero,** a specialist in *carnes al carbón.* The quick and easy **Pollo Loco,** between the Mexico 70 and 85 junction and the traffic circle (Glorieta Hidalgo), has chicken-beans-tortillas combos.

Restaurant Del Bosque, attached to the Hotel Valles, has good food and service, and is one of the only places in town that accepts credit cards.

A coffee shop attached to the Posada Don Antonio serves reasonably priced Mexican, Lebanese, and Huastecan food, including tasty *bocoles* (*gorditas* filled with cheese) with *nopalitos* (strips of cooked or pickled prickly pear cactus) and *jamón* (ham).

Events

During the third week of March, Valles sponsors the **Feria Nacional de la Huasteca Potosina** (FENAHUAP), a big fair with ranching, agricultural, and cultural expositions.

Friendly town residents open their homes to outsiders during the **Days of the Dead,** Nov. 1-2, inviting visitors as well as neighbors in to see their home altars, and to share tamales and tea. Street processions feature altars festooned with hundreds of orange or yellow marigolds; the best receive awards.

Transport

Bus: Valle's main bus terminal is at the southern edge of town (around three km from the town center) off Mexico 85. **Omnibus de México** operates one first-class bus daily to/from San Luis Potosí for US$6; **Transportes del Norte** has a similar San Luis Potosí service plus buses to/from Ciudad Victoria for US$8. The **Potosinos** and **Huasteco** lines handle second-class buses all over the state as well as to Tampico, Guanajuato, and Veracruz.

Train: The San Luis Potosí-Tampico *El Huasteco* stops in Ciudad Valles between midnight and 1 a.m. nightly. Second-class (only) seats cost just US$2.50 one way.

EL CONSUELO (TAMUÍN)

Of the 527 Huastec archaeological sites in the region, the **Zona Arqueológica El Consuelo** is the most well known and the most accessible; many other sites are on private lands. Excavated in 1946, El Consuelo ("The Consolation") covers 17 hectares and features a number of stepped ceremonial platforms. When first discovered, the stucco walls of the platforms featured ancient paintings that have since worn away. Tombs in which corpses in fetal positions faced east were also discovered on the grounds. One of the more remarkable discoveries here was the sculpted figure known as "El Adolescente," now in Mexico City's National Museum of Anthropology (a replica can be seen in San Luis Potosí's Potosino Regional Museum). The iconography and dating of the figure suggests that the Huastecs formed a Quetzalcóatl cult before the Aztecs.

The entire complex faces more or less east, so for photography it's best to arrive in the morning. From the top of the largest platform you can just make out two mounds to the west about three km (two miles) in the distance. On private lands, these mounds are actually two large, overgrown pyramids, the larger of which, known as Cantóc, may be the largest unexplored pyramid in the western hemisphere. Neither has ever been open to the public or excavated.

Getting There: The ruins are six km (3.7 miles) south of Tamuín, which is 28 km (17 miles) east of Ciudad Valles (or 51 km/31.6 miles west of Ebano) via Mexico 70. It is also possible to reach El Consuelo from Tancanhuitz de Santos via Tanquián de Escobedo and San Vicente Tancyayalab, but this southern route is very rough. Even though most maps show a paved road along this route, the road is riddled with huge potholes every hundred meters or so, forcing motorists to drive quite slowly most of the way. If you're driving from Mexico 85 south, it's much quicker to drive all the way north to Ciudad Valles and then proceed east on Mexico 70 to Tamuín, then south to the ruins.

SOUTH OF CIUDAD VALLES

Mexico 85 heads south from Ciudad Valles into the cultural heart of the Región Huasteca. The scenery is lush, with wooded valleys interspersed with sugarcane fields and orange orchards, plus smaller farms of avocado, papaya, or guava. High on the slopes west of the road are a number of small coffee plantations.

Fresh-roasted coffee—whole bean or ground in hand mills on the spot—can be purchased in local markets for only US$2.60 per kilo. Unfortunately, soft world coffee prices (along with three uncharacteristic winter freezes during the last 15 years) have discouraged coffee production in recent years and have wiped out several of the more financially vulnerable operations.

Practicalities: For local color, market days are the best time to visit Huastec towns and villages. Most take place on Fridays, Saturdays, or Sundays; thus weekends are generally the best time to explore the area.

Transportes Vencedor is the main bus line for the region, with routes between Ciudad Valles (also, in some cases, San Luis Potosí) and every town in the area.

South of Ciudad Valles as far as Tamazunchale, no Magna Sin (unleaded) gasoline is available. Each of the larger towns, however, has a PEMEX station with Nova (leaded gas).

Tancanhuitz De Santos
Also known simply as Tancanhuitz ("Place of the Flower of Love") or Ciudad Santos, this is one of the larger Huastec centers in the region. Four km (2.5 miles) east of Mexico 85, the town straddles a *cañada* formed by the Arroyo Huehuetlán, which divides the population into a Náhua section on the north side of the stream, Huastec on south. It is the second most developed Huastec town (after Tamazunchale) in the area, with lots of satellite dishes attached to the largely Mexican-style houses.

Public life revolves around the 18th-century **Parroquia de San Miguel Arcángel** (feast day

Sept. 29). A *tianguis* or open-air market is held every Sunday; here you'll find *quechquémetls,* shoulder bags, baskets, and other handicrafts.

Surrounding villages with more traditional Huastec lifestyles include Huehuetlán, Coxcatlán, and San Antonio. Twenty-five km (15.5 miles) east of Mexico 85 on the main road is the smaller Huastec town of **Tampamalón,** a quaint sugarcane center with thatched-roof homes and an old church.

Accommodations: Although Tancanhuitz can easily be visited from Ciudad Valles as a day-trip, modest lodging is available in town at **Hotel Casa Colorado,** not far from the main bus stop.

Transport: Vencedor operates buses between Tancanhuitz, Ciudad Valles, and San Luis Potosí.

Aquismón
More interesting and slightly more off the beaten track than Tancanhuitz, Aquismón is almost entirely Huastec. A tidy new plaza planted with almond trees and Indian laurels is the site for a weekly *tianguis* held on Saturdays. *Pilón,* blocks of raw sugar wrapped in cane bundles, is a good buy. As in Tancanhuitz, the town's *fiesta patronal* takes place annually on Sept. 29.

Several all-Huastec villages near Aquismón can be visited, including the nearby **Tanquimé** (Tancuimé)—follow the dirt road just north of the plaza about 2.5 km (1.5 miles) until you reach an area of traditional thatched-roof homes. Other villages on the mountain slopes to the west of Aquismón are harder to reach but worth seeking out. A dirt road leads west a few km to the **Cueva de Mantezulel,** a seldom-visited limestone cave.

Accommodations: The small **Hotel San Cosme,** at Calle Juárez 7, offers simple rooms with *baño colectivo.*

Transport: Vencedor operates buses between Ciudad Valles and Aquismón.

Sótano De Las Golondrinas
Seven km southwest of Aquismón on foot or about 30 km (18.6 miles) by road (23 km/14 miles of unpaved road from Mexico 85), this huge pit cave is one of Mexico's major spelunking challenges. Named for the thousands of swifts (*golondrinas*) that inhabit the *sótano* (literally "cellar"), the cave has a mouth measuring

60 meters (197 feet) in diameter, plunges to over 300 meters (1,090 feet) in depth, and has a floor that covers six acres. A tunnel off the floor has been explored to a length of four km (2.5 miles). Special equipment and careful preparation are necessary to even begin to explore Las Golondrinas. The state tourist office in San Luis Potosí may be able to recommend local guides and caving associations that can arrange a descent.

In addition to the swifts commonly seen flying from the cave at sunset, the cave also hosts a large number of colorful parakeets. The Huastecs believe that the "Earth Owner" lives in the cave.

Nearby is the smaller **Sótano de las Guaguas.**

Las Pozas (La Casa De Inglés)

Bizarre metal and reinforced concrete sculptures rising out of the jungle near Xilitla—visible only to those willing to leave the highway—are the Región Huasteca legacy of a visionary Englishman who, in the 1930s and '40s, mingled with Salvador Dali, Aldous Huxley, Picasso, Magritte, Max Ernst, and others involved in the early surrealist movement. Born in Scotland in 1907 as the grandson of King Edward VII, Sir Edward James studied literature in a university and published a number of poems, plays, and short stories before embarking on world travel. While exploring Mexico in 1945, James found the retreat he was looking for in Xilitla and began building this forest idyll next to a spring and waterfall in 1949.

Later, while living at his Xilitla estate, James erected a number of linked pavilions, walls, walkways, and steps leading nowhere, surrealistic sculptures (a set of oversized sculpted hands supposedly represent Dali's right hand, front and back), and other "constructions." James passed away in the 1984 and his works are now decaying and somewhat overgrown; some are also obviously unfinished.

The complex has a sort of hideous beauty, but the best part of visiting Las Pozas is simply walking through the lush grounds, viewing the orchids and other tropical vegetation, and sitting beside the cool falls that run along one side of the estate; these falls were channeled by James into a series of clean pools suitable for swimming. They can be approached from the bottom near the entrance to the estate or via a set of steps that loops through the estate to the top of the falls.

The part of the James estate that contains the falls represents about half the original property and is open to the public daily. A small entry fee is collected at a kiosk near the entrance, where you'll find a small snack bar with a few tables. Another section of the estate has been purchased by an American and is closed to the public.

Getting There: To reach Las Pozas, take Mexico 120 west off Mexico 85 (26 km/16 miles south of the turnoff for Tancanhuitz) and head southwest 12.5 km (7.8 miles) to a graded dirt road on the right, just before a small bridge. Follow this road about a kilometer to a fork in the road and bear left; this branch leads to Las Pozas.

Xilitla

The name of this town means "place of *cozole*" (a type of local freshwater crab) in Náhuatl. One of the earliest settlements in the Región Huasteca, Xilitla was founded in the 1550s by the Augustine sect, who in 1557 constructed the convent of **San Agustín de la Gran Xilitla.** The convent's high, thick, flagstone walls didn't deter local native attacks, and the convent was completely sacked in 1585. Today the convent chapel serves a population of 14,000 and the ancillary rooms are used for community services.

Perched on a precipitous hill at 1,050 meters (3,440 feet) above sea level, the town's steep, narrow streets lead you into what seems like a tiny mountain kingdom. One sizable house on the edge of town was obviously designed by Sir Edward James (see above). The climate is quite temperate and rains tend to fall year-round.

On Sundays a *tianguis* or open-air market behind the chapel offers coffee, copal (a type of incense), *piloncillo* (cones of raw sugar), tobacco, and *zacahuil* (huge Huastecan tamales), among the usual inexpensive consumer goods. Many vendors also set up on the sidewalks on weekends, the better to catch all the visitors from surrounding villages who come to browse and shop.

Eighteen km (9.3 miles) farther along Mexico 120 is the smaller Huastec village of **Ahua-catlán.** Back on Mexico 85, a few km south of the Mexico 120 junction, **Axtla de Terrazas** is well known for its Nov. 24-25 **Fiesta Huasteca** each year, a celebration of Huastec culture through music, dance, and food.

Accommodations and Food: Several small hotels in town offer rooms for US$6-10. The best-looking place is the **Hotel Ziyaquetzas** on the plaza. Around the plaza you'll also find many

LA CULTURA HUASTECA

History

The Huastec civilization developed along the Gulf of Mexico coast over a period of 6,000 years and flourished along river systems west of Tampico for some 2,500 years (1000 B.C.-A.D. 1500) before being suppressed by the Spanish conquest. The Huastecs may have been the first hunters and gatherers in Mexico, and developed "culture" (as defined by the emergence of art, religion, and social organization) contemporaneously with Mesoamerican cultures as far south as Guatemala and Honduras.

Today visible Huastec archaeological sites are found as far north as Río Soto la Marina, as far west as Tamuín and Aquizmón, and as far south as El Tajín. According to historians, Huastec art and social organization reached its apex between 300 B.C. and A.D. 900 A.D., an era anthropologists call the "classic period" or "Pánuco III." Following the scheme generally used to classify pre-Cortesian cultures in Mexico, the years 1000-300 B.C. are deemed preclassic Huastec, 900-1500 A.D. postclassic Huastec. Archaeological excavation and restoration have been scant, as usual, because Mexico City-based authorities have given higher priority to Aztec and Mayan sites in Central and Southern Mexico.

Linguistically related to the Mayans and Toltecs, the Huastecs nonetheless developed along a separate track. During the classic period, Huastec influence in Mesoamerica was so great that several other indigenous groups adopted Huastec deities. Unlike other Mesoamerican groups, the Huastecs originally erected circular buildings of worship, which were usually dedicated to Quetzalcóatl, the Plumed Serpent—later co-opted by the Aztecs, who also took Tlazoltéotl (the goddess of love) and Xochiquetzal (the god of flowers). It has been theorized that the Huastecs may have founded the great citystate of Teotihuacán in Central Mexico, later taken over by the Aztecs.

The Aztec name for the Región Huasteca was Cueztlán ("place of platforms"). Huastec temples were painted with murals in black, ocher, coffeebrown, red, and white, and adorned with sandstone sculptures—predominantly masculine and feminine figures, birds, and serpents. During the postclassic period, Huastec religious architecture converted to rectangular plans similar to those customary among the Mayans and Aztecs.

The Huastecs preferred brightly colored clothes and jewelry, and painted their coiffures red and yellow; according to records compiled by the Spanish, the Aztecs considered them sexually promiscuous. In the 15th century the Aztecs began a 60-year military campaign against the region in an attempt to conquer these peace-loving people.

When the Spanish arrived in the 16th century, the million-strong Huastecs entered into an alliance with them in hopes that the new arrivals would help them defend their homelands against Aztec conquest. Unfortunately, the cruel Nuño de Guzmán was put in charge of the Región Huasteca, and the "alliance" led to the almost complete destruction of the Huastec culture via Guzmán's introduction of the slave trade. By the end of the 16th century only about 100,000 Huastecs remained in the region.

Today approximately 91,000 Huastecs live in southeast San Luis Potosí, northern Veracruz, northeastern Hidalgo, and southern Tamaulipas. In their own language they call themselves Tenec and their traditional homelands Tenec-Bichou. Although their days of building ritual platforms are long gone, the Huastecs still hold fast to tradition, preferring to live in simple thatched-roof homes in isolated rural communities where they can farm, hunt, and practice their own customs. Due to the historical and continuing influence of missionaries, they are largely Christianized, but like indigenous peoples elsewhere in Mexico they've blended Christian and Amerindian elements into a syncretic belief system.

Arts And Crafts

The Huastecs once made beautiful ceramics. Exquisite pots dating to around 1000 B.C. feature tripod feet and incised eyes and mouths, and by 50 B.C, the Huastecs were making polychromatic (orange, red, and brown) animal shapes. Huastec handicrafts today are limited to basketry, reed mats, functional pottery, traditional clothing, and other items sometimes seen in local markets, along with a variety of harder-to-find folk and ritual utensils that aren't usually offered for sale.

Modern Huastec men cut their hair and dress much like the average rural Mexican. As is common with ethnic minorities around the world, it is inexpensive cafes and restaurants.

Transport: Xilitla is 15 km (9.3 miles) southwest of Mexico 85 via Mexico 120. **Vencedor** handles second-class buses between here and other towns in the Región Huasteca, including Ciudad Valles.

the women who tend to wear the most traditional clothing. Most striking is the *petob,* an arrangement of their own hair interwoven with thick skeins of wool in green, orange, pink, and cherry-red, sometimes with a cloth pinned behind the head. A skirt of solid white or black fabric is held in place with a striped red-and-blue fabric belt.

A diamond-shaped tunic, called a *quechquémal* (*quisquem* or *cayem* in the Huastec language), made of white cotton embroidered with flowers (*canhuitz* or *flor de amor*), double crosses, animals (especially ducks, chickens, rabbits), and other figures from nature is worn over the shoulders and torso. Persons knowledgeable about *quechquémal* patterns can identify their village of provenance. In the pre-missionary days, the skirt and tunic would have been the full costume, but puritanical *misioneros* have influenced the Huastec women to wear solid or floral-print blouses beneath the *quechquémal.*

A bag embroidered with similar patterns is often worn over the shoulder. Known as a *talega,* this bag is used to carry a baby's gourd bottle, combs, and other personal items. Among Huastecs it's a common wedding gift offered by *madrinas* (godmothers).

Music And Dance

The Huapango or *son huasteco potosino,* popular well beyond the Región Huasteca itself, cannot be considered a 100% Huastec musical form but is nonetheless a traditional part of modern culture in the Región Huasteca. Afro-Cuban rhythms have joined Huastec melodic motifs to become part of the general folkloric repertoire of Mexico. Marked by fast rhythms and high singing with prolonged falsettos, the typical Huapango is played by two standard violins, a *jarana* (a small, five-stringed guitar), a wooden flute, a small, indigenous three-stringed violin, a 29-string harp, and *maracas, casacabeles,* and other rhythm instruments. The term "Huapango" comes either from the Spanish "fandango" or the Náhuatl *huapantlico* ("on the platform").

Other popular song/dance forms include the *valona* and *décima,* both of which are typically performed by urbanized Huastecs at private functions (weddings, christenings, birthdays, patron saint days) using violins and guitars. More folk than folkloric, *valones* and *décimas* are quite danceable and incorporate a type of improvisational poetry that involves verbal jousting on stage. Musicians who play this type of music call themselves *poesilleros* rather than *músicos.*

Another traditional but more rural dance, *las varitas,* ("the twigs," a reference to sacro-medicinal botanicals used by Huastec shamans) is commonly performed during the feast of San Miguel Arcángel, the Huastecs' main patron saint. In this dance, Huastec men dressed in white hold knives in one hand, bells and ribbons in the other, while performing movements and gestures in imitation of various forest creatures; the dance is accompanied by violin and flute music. In Aquismón, a similar dance called *zacamsón* is performed to the accompaniment of violin, harp, and guitar.

Food

While Huastecan culinary influences have reached restaurants in the state capitals of San Luis Potosí and Tamaulipas, in the Región Huasteca itself the best place to try local specialties is among the vendor stands set up at the weekly *tianguis* or at festivals. Corn is an important local crop and thus a major ingredient in local cuisine. Sugarcane extract—cheap and abundant—is fermented and distilled to produce a fiery contraband *aguardiente,* which is drunk in copious amounts during important religious festivals.

One of the most famous Huastecan foods is the *zacahuil,* a huge tamal made with corn dough soaked in a deep red *chile chino* or *chile pequín* sauce, stuffed with pork or chicken, wrapped in banana leaves, and baked in a wood-fired oven. *Zacahuiles* can reach up to two meters (six feet) long and are especially available during festivals. A similar snack food, the *bolim,* looks a bit like a *zacahuil* but is much smaller and is always stuffed with either chicken or turkey. Another local source of protein is *acamayas* or freshwater shrimp. *Palmito,* or heart of palm, is cooked to a smooth consistency and served as a snack or appetizer with tostadas.

Other popular fiesta foods include the *bocol,* a *gordita de maíz* (thick corn tortilla) filled with cheese, beans or potatoes. Cafes (especially in Río Verde and Ciudad del Maíz) sometimes serve *guiso borracho* ("drunken stew"), a sumptuous stew made with a variety of meats, fruits, and vegetables marinated beforehand in *pulque* (fermented maguey extract), and served in bowls or on crisp tostadas.

Take care on the steep, narrow streets if you're driving. The best strategy is to park as soon as you're at or near the top of the hill and finish exploring the town on foot. RVers with rigs over 20 feet long may want to park at the bottom of the hill.

Tamazunchale

A municipal *cabecera* (capital) and fairly major trade center for the region, this town on the Río Moctezuma is not that interesting except on Sundays, when a large market convenes. Getting here is more than half the fun, as the mountain scenery is impressive. The **Fiesta de Todos los Santos** (All Saints Fiesta, Day of the Dead), Nov. 1-2, is particularly well celebrated here.

The many rivers and streams in the area add increased lushness to an already green area; in several mountainous spots the streams form pools deep enough for swimming. Two km outside town is the *balneario* of **Poxtapa,** in a wooded area with showers, changing rooms, grills, and a snack bar. Entrance is by donation.

Accommodations: Tamazunchale has almost as many hotels as Ciudad Valles, although the standards are by and large a bit lower. Several *clase económica* places in the US$15 range are found along Av. 20 de Noviembre, the main commercial strip, including **Hotel González** (No. 301), **Hotel Mirador** (No. 62), **Hotel Palacio Tropical** (No. 404), and **Hotel Tamazunchale** (No. 122). Cheaper still is the basic **Casa de Huéspedes Lorenzo Sandoval** (Calle Hidalgo 413).

Transport: Several bus companies with San Luis Potosí, Hidalgo, and Veracruz routes serve the town.

Huastec woman

ERIN DWYER

(top) Bahía Kino, Sonora; (bottom) Playa Gaviotas, Mazatlán (photos by Joe Cummings)

(top, left) suspension bridge, Barranca de Urique; (top, right) Cusarare Falls, Chihuahua; (bottom, left) Cascada de Basaseachic; (bottom, right) corn fields, San Luis Potosí (photos by Joe Cummings)

THE STATE OF COAHUILA

Officially named Coahuila de Zaragoza, Mexico's third largest state—after Chihuahua and Sonora—shares borders with Texas, Chihuahua, Durango, Nuevo León, Zacatecas, San Luis Potosí (just a pinch, squeezed between Zacatecas and Nuevo León), and Tamaulipas. The Spanish first explored the area in 1570 and established a colonial settlement at Saltillo in 1577, although early expansion was severely limited by natives whom the Spanish described as "bellicose and indomitable." The Coahuilteca tribes—who have left behind considerable rock art in the state—were later dominated by Lipan Apaches who raided the region from the north. Throughout the 17th century constant friction flared between the Coahulltecas, Apaches, and Spanish, but by the early 19th century the area had been "tamed" and colonization continued in earnest.

Despite large tracts of land classified as desert because of scant rainfall, Coahuila has an extensive river system that allows for year-round cultivation of vinifera, olives, cotton, and other agricultural products. As elsewhere in northeastern Mexico, cattle ranching is also a major economic activity.

Travel highlights include the lofty, forested Sierra del Carmen in the northwest, colonial Saltillo in the southeast, and the pristine *bolsón* environments near Cuatrociénegas in the center. Because they're among the least busy along the U.S.-Mexico frontier, Coahuila's well-equipped border crossings at Piedras Negras and Ciudad Acuña are favorite Mexico gateways for repeat visitors from the U.S. and Canada.

Information
The current state governor is very pro-tourism and has overseen the production of five excellent map guides covering six regions (Frontera, Sureste, Laguna, Centro, Desierto, and Carbonífera); these are available at tourist offices in Saltillo, Arteaga, Parras de la Fuente, Ciudad Acuña, Piedras Negras, Monclova, Nueva Rosita, and Torreón. Each map guide contains a state highway map, a regional map, and a number of city maps with descriptions of tourist attractions.

The state has also posted tourist information map-boards in major cities. These enlightened steps, as well as the overall fine maintenance of state highways, go a long way toward making out-of-state visitors feel welcome.

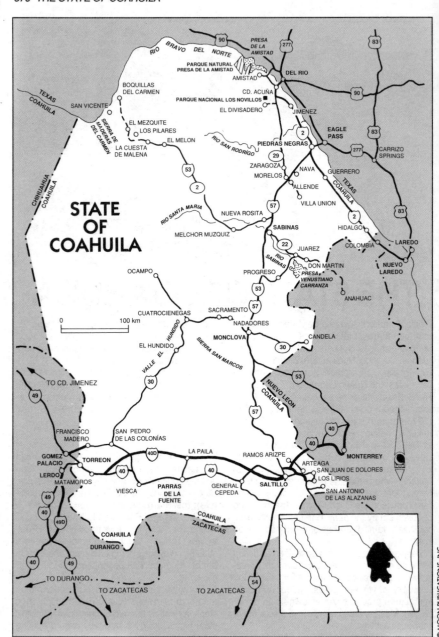

CIUDAD ACUÑA TO SALTILLO

CIUDAD ACUÑA

The smaller of the state's two border gateways, Ciudad Acuña (pop. 56,000) was founded as a military encampment on the Río Bravo (Rio Grande) in 1877. By the 1880s the military were replaced by ranchers who ignobly named the spot Congregación Las Vacas ("Cow Congregation"). In 1912 the town was renamed for noted Saltillo poet Manuel Acuña, although locally some people still refer to the town by the nickname "Las Vacas."

Today, though still a farming and ranching center, Acuña has also taken on a few *maquila* (in-bond plant) facilities which have managed not to disrupt the town's quiet nature too much. It's just large enough to be of varied interest to the casual border-hopper, yet small enough (and remote enough) to have escaped the sleaze of transborder metropolises like Ciudad Juárez and Nuevo Laredo. The town enjoys a particularly amiable relationship with Del Rio, its U.S. twin across the border.

The town's social center is Plaza Canales near the International Bridge; on warm evenings, the streets come alive with food vendors and evening strollers. Though not especially geared toward gringo shoppers, several *artesanías* and liquor stores can be found along Av. Hidalgo near the bridge.

Accommodations
Hotel San Jorge (tel. 877-2-20-70) is conveniently located downtown at Calle M. Hidalgo 165 (at Av. V. Guerrero, two blocks from Plaza Canales). Rooms with carpet, phones, and private baths cost US$18-20 s/d. In the same price range are **Hotel Cristal** (tel. 2-11-94) at Calle Madero and Morelos downtown, and **Motel Plaza** (tel. 2-28-69) at Av. V. Guerrero 2010, on the way out of town toward Saltillo and Piedras Negras.

Moving up a notch, the friendly **Motel Los Alpes** (tel. 2-44-71) on Av. V. Guerrero southeast of the Motel Cristal has clean, well-maintained rooms with a/c, satellite TV, and pool for US$25-38 s/d. Similar rooms are available at

Hotel San Antonio (tel. 2-01-08), Calle Hidalgo and Lerdo downtown; and **Motel Las Vegas** (tel. 2-04-23), Av. V. Guerrero and Villaldama.

Food
The favorite hangout for gringo border-hoppers is **Crosby's Restaurant & Bar** (tel. 877-2-20-20) at Av. Hidalgo 195, just a few blocks from the International Bridge. Since the 1930s, Crosby's has drawn a curious mix of Coahuilan cowboys, Texas ranchers, and tourists, and it's still going strong. House specialties include *cabrito,* Portuguese-style chicken, frogs' legs, roast quail, and the usual border platters. It's open daily 9 a.m.-midnight.

Another outstanding choice is **Asadero La Posta** at Calle Allende 350 (south off Hidalgo eight blocks from the bridge). La Posta specializes in *fajitas, queso fundido, queso con chile,* and *carne asada.* On weekends the upstairs room occasionally hosts live *norteña* music. Open daily 8 a.m.-11 p.m.

Recreation
Lake Amistad: Nineteen km northwest of Acuña, **Presa de la Amistad** ("Friendship Dam") came about after the governments in the U.S. and Mexico, through the International Boundary and Water Commission (IBWC), agreed to build a dam across the Río Bravo (Rio Grande). This site was chosen since it's just below the confluence of the Río Bravo/Rio Grande, Pecos River, and Devils River—giving humans control over three rivers at once and providing water conservation, flood control, hydroelectric power, and recreation.

With a surface area that varies between 65,000 and 89,000 acres and a shoreline of 1,200-1,600 km (744-990 miles), the Amistad is a favorite spot for swimming, boating, and fishing, although the facilities on the Mexican side of this huge lake can't compete with those on the Texas side, which is managed by the U.S National Park Service. To fish on either side, you'll need a valid fishing permit.

Bulls and Horses: Acuña has a bullring, **Plaza de Toros La Macarena,** on Libramiento Oriente (West Bypass), not far from the Inter-

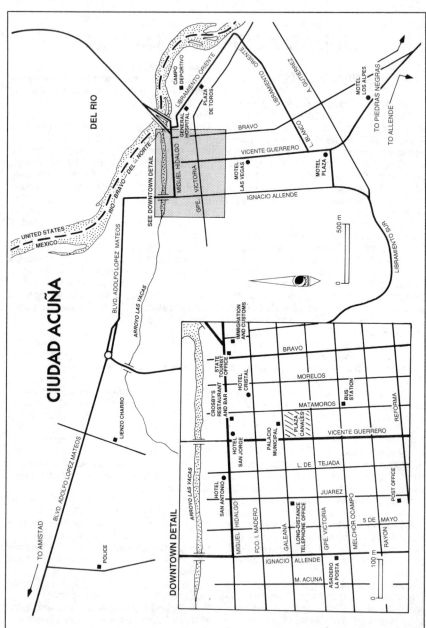

CIUDAD ACUÑA

DEL RIO

UNITED STATES
MEXICO

RIO BRAVO DEL NORTE

SEE DOWNTOWN DETAIL

CAMPO DEPORTIVO

LIBRAMIENTO ORIENTE

PLAZA DE TOROS

GENERAL HOSPITAL

MIGUEL HIDALGO

GPE. VICTORIA

BRAVO

VICENTE GUERRERO

MOTEL LAS VEGAS

IGNACIO ALLENDE

LIBRAMIENTO ORIENTE

A. GUTIERREZ

L. BLANCO

MOTEL LOS ALPES

TO PIEDRAS NEGRAS

TO ALLENDE

MOTEL PLAZA

LIBRAMIENTO SUR

BLVD. ADOLFO LOPEZ MATEOS

ARROYO LAS VACAS

500 m

LIENZO CHARRO

BLVD. ADOLFO LOPEZ MATEOS

TO AMISTAD

POLICE

DOWNTOWN DETAIL

ARROYO LAS VACAS

IMMIGRATION AND CUSTOMS

STATE TOURIST OFFICE

HOTEL CRISTAL

CROSBY'S RESTAURANT AND BAR

HOTEL SAN JORGE

PALACIO MUNICIPAL

PLAZA CANALES

HOTEL SAN ANTONIO

MIGUEL HIDALGO

FCO. I. MADERO

GALEANA

LONG-DISTANCE TELEPHONE OFFICE

GPE. VICTORIA

ASADERO LA POSTA

IGNACIO ALLENDE

M. ACUNA

BRAVO

MORELOS

MATAMOROS

BUS STATION

VICENTE GUERRERO

L. DE TEJADA

JUAREZ

5 DE MAYO

MELCHOR OCAMPO

RAYON

POST OFFICE

REFORMA

100 m

© MOON PUBLICATIONS, INC.

national Bridge, as well as a *charro* ring, **Lienzo Charro El Potrero,** in the northwest corner of town on Calle California off Blvd. López Mateos. Check with the tourist office for a current schedule of *charreadas* and *corridas de toros.*

Parque Nacional de los Novillos: One of Mexico's smallest (42 hectares) and oldest national parks (established in 1940), Los Novillos is centered around a cool arroyo resplendent with prickly pear, oaks, cottonwoods, and willows. A small **balneario,** fed by the Río San Diego (a tributary of the Río Bravo) is popular in summer. The park has day-use facilities only (no overnight camping permitted). Park access is 45 km south of Acuña off Mexico 29.

Festivals: Every Oct. 25 the twin cities of Del Rio (Texas) and Ciudad Acuña celebrate the **Fiesta de la Amistad** or Friendship Festival, with parades, games, music, dancing, and speechmaking.

Carnaval is typically celebrated only in seacoast towns, but Ciudad Acuña uses the proximity of Presa de la Amistad as an excuse to celebrate pre-Lenten **Carnaval** in Feb.-March (one of the few border towns—perhaps the only —to do so). See the "Mazatlán" section in the Sinaloa chapter for a general idea of what goes on during Carnaval; Acuña's is of course a much smaller affair.

Transport

Unlike at some border towns, it's not as easy to walk across from the U.S. to Acuña (from city limit to city limit it's 4.8 km/three miles), which is another reason the town isn't inundated with tourists. Instead, visitors can drive, catch public buses, or take taxis from downtown Del Rio. Las Vacas St. in Del Rio has parking lots where you can park a car all day for US$2.

Bus: Buses pass along Del Rios's Las Vacas St. regularly on the way to Ciudad Acuña and cost US$0.40 each way. In Acuña the **Terminal de Autobuses** is at the corner of Calle Matamoros and Ocampo, three blocks west and four blocks south of the bridge. Passenger buses leave frequently for Saltillo, Monterrey, and Piedras Negras.

Taxi: A taxi from Del Rio (Las Vacas St.) costs US$7 one way. Cab companies on the Del Rio side provide free parking if you hire one of their taxis. Around Del Rio, taxis cost about US$4 a trip.

Driving: Acuña is a fairly easy town to drive in. If you need Mexican insurance, **Arreola's Insurance** (tel. 512-775-3252), near the bridge on Spur 239 in Del Rio, can arrange auto policies for longer journeys south.

Information

The state tourist office (tel. 877-2-40-70) at the border station (opposite the offices of immigration and customs) has informative, annotated maps of the region and state.

Border Formalities: See the "Entry Regulations" section, p. 100, for important information on Mexican immigration and customs requirements. The Ciudad Acuña crossing is open 24 hours.

PIEDRAS NEGRAS

Nearly double the size of Ciudad Acuña, with a population of around 100,000, Piedras Negras (the name, "Black Rocks," refers to a stratum of coal exposed by erosion in the area) is Coahuila's main border crossing. The local economy is supported by cattle ranching and twin-plant manufacturing. It's also an important transport junction because of the railway that runs south to Saltillo.

Although Piedras Negras is the closest border town to San Antonio, Texas (142 miles via US 57/I-35), the town gets far fewer tourists than Nuevo Laredo. The many shops in the plaza area near the bridge are not particularly tourist-oriented so bargains are plentiful. The **Mercado Municipal** on Calle Zaragoza (one block west and two blocks south of the bridge) is full of handicrafts as well as housewares.

Across the Río Bravo is Eagle Pass, Texas (pop. 24,000), virtually a suburb of Piedras Negras. The Mexican newspaper *Zócalo* serves both towns.

Based on a novel by Laura Esquivel and directed by her husband Alfonso Arau, the 1992 Mexican film *Like Water For Chocolate* (*Como Agua Para Chocolate*) was shot on location in Piedras Negras and Eagle Pass.

Small-game hunting (rabbit, hare, quail, dove, duck, goose, javelina) and fishing are very popular pastimes in the area. Sports enthusiasts congregate at the local **Club de Caza, Tiro y Pesca** ("Hunting, Shooting, and Fishing Club") on Calle Ocampo between calles Mina and Dr. Coss.

Accommodations

Hotels and motels in Piedras Negras are geared toward motorists; all have ample parking, usually in a motel-style courtyard.

Along Mexico 57 (Av. Lázaro Cárdenas) on the southern fringes of town are several motels with a/c, heat, and television, including the decent **Motel Casa Blanca** (tel. 878-2-46-46) with rates of around US$28 s, US$32 d.

Autel Río (tel. 1-01-80), an American-style motel at Calle Padre de las Casas 121 in the heart of town (only two blocks from the bus terminal and within walking distance of Restaurant-Bar Moderno and the border), has clean, secure rooms with a/c, heat, TV, and phones for US$28 s, US$30 d.

A cheaper downtown place is the basic but adequate **Hotel Santos** (tel. 2-03-64) at Calle Allende and Hidalgo (a block south of the market), where rooms cost US$21 s/d.

Cheaper still is **Hotel Miranda,** a small, two-story inn on Av. E. Carranza near Calle Veracruz just outside the town center. Tidy but simple rooms start at US$15. Also in this vicinity are **Motel 57** (tel. 2-12-20) and **Motel California** (tel. 2-24-53) on either side of Av. E. Carranza near Veracruz; rates at each are around US$25-30.

Top of the heap is **Hotel Posada Rosa** (tel. 2-50-11, fax 2-37-19) at Calle San Luis and Sinaloa (two blocks northwest of Av. E. Carranza). Well-kept, modern rooms with a/c, heat, TV, and phones surround a clean swimming pool and tennis court. Other facilities include a nightclub, restaurant, and coffee shop. Rates are US$40-45 s/d.

On the Texas side of the river, **Eagle Pass Inn** (tel. 210-773-9531), four miles north of town on US 277, has decent rooms in the US$28-35 range. **La Quinta Motor Inn** (tel. 773-7000), 2525 Main St., has larger, nicer rooms for US$45-60.

Food

Piedras Negras's most famous institution is the **Restaurant Bar Moderno,** three blocks west and two blocks south of the International Bridge on Calle Morelos between Calle Terán and Allende (the old entrance, now closed, faces Allende). Established in 1934 (and originally called the Victory Club), the Moderno is supposedly the spot where cook Ignacio "Nacho" Anaya searched a near-empty pantry for something to feed a late-night party of hunters and came up with tortilla chips topped with melted cheese and sliced jalapeños—the birth of nachos.

You know you're in for something different when you walk in and find a large green Buddha statue at the end of the entrance hallway. Though the Moderno remains a citadel of Tex-Mex cuisine, the dining room and adjacent bar are quite elegant, with uniformed, starched-shirt waiters and clean white tablecloths. Nachos and other border dishes, including frog legs, *chalupas,* and *arracheras* (*fajitas*), are prominently featured, along with steak, Mexican standards, and seafood. The waiters all speak English but at least half the clientele on any given night is Mexican. If nothing else, stop in for a drink; you haven't done the Tex-Mex border if you haven't been to the Moderno. Open Mon.-Fri. 11 a.m.-midnight, Sat. till 1 a.m.; live music and dancing most nights after 9 p.m.

Yes, there are other places to eat in town besides the Moderno. **Sam's,** at the corner of Calle Terán and Padre de las Casas a half block north of Autel Río, is a clean and efficient 24-hour coffee shop with a good selection of Mexican and North American standards. **Donas y Pasteles Posada,** at Calle Matamoros 303 just east of Calle Padre de las Casas on the north side of the street, is a good spot for donuts and pastries.

The reasonably clean **Restaurant Los Arcos,** on the southwest corner of Calle Morelos and Matamoros, offers cheap Mexican breakfasts plus an extensive selection of *antojitos.* Along the north side of Plaza Principal next to the International Bridge is a row of snack booths that are open only in the daytime during cool weather; later during summer months. Next to the plaza is the clean and inexpensive **El Oscar Drive Inn,** a classic takeout (or eat-in) joint with burgers and *antojitos.*

Recreation

Plaza de Toros Monumental Arizpe on the north side of Av. López Mateos between calles Mexicali and Tepic (about two km from the bridge); and **Lienzo Charro Oscar González Ramos,** off Calle V. Suárez in Colonia Tecnológico (about 5.5 km from the bridge), hold bullfights and Mexican rodeos periodically—usually during the summer. Check with the state tourist office in town for the latest schedules.

Local residents picnic, hunt, and fish at the nearby San Diego, Santo Domingo, San Rodrigo, San Antonio, and Escondido rivers. **Rio Grande Rancho Hunting Resort** (tel. 210-773-4444; P.O. Box 1143, Eagle Pass, TX 78853), off Mexico 2 between Piedras Negras and Nuevo Laredo, offers hunting vacations for dove, quail, duck, goose, sandhill crane, and Rio Grande wild turkey.

Information

Tourist Office: The state tourist office (tel. 878-2-08-76) at Calle Hidalgo and Abasolo can answer questions about travel in Piedras Negras and Coahuila. They can also summon the local **Green Angels** unit (tel. 3-01-37), which is based at Calle Guadalupe 307.

Maps: The Piedras Negras **INEGI office,** on Calle Cuauhtémoc between calles Matamoros and Juárez, carries topographic maps for Coahuila, Tamaulipas, and Nuevo León. For excursions into northwestern Coahuila (the Sierra del Carmen area), ask for the 1:250,000 maps H13-9, H14-7, and H13-12 (1:50,000 scale maps are also available but the larger-scale maps are sufficient for most purposes).

Telephone: A **TelMex** long-distance telephone office is on Calle Matamoros between calles Xicoténcatl and Cuauhtémoc. The area code for Piedras Negras is 878.

Transport

Bus: The town's small bus terminal, at Calle Allende and Cuauhtémoc, is used more for cargo than for passenger services. **Autobuses Blancos** and **Autobuses El Aguila** handle all passenger services, with buses to Monterrey (10 daily departures), Saltillo (12 daily departures), and Torreón (two daily departures).

Train: The **Regiomontano** train No. 182 leaves Piedras Negras at 9:15 a.m. and arrives in Saltillo at 6:55 p.m.; in the reverse direction, No. 181 leaves Saltillo at 8:15 a.m. and arrives in Piedras Negras at 5:35 p.m. The fare is US$15 for a reserved seat. The train has not been very popular since it's three hours slower than the bus (nine hours versus six hours), and rumors say the passenger service may be discontinued. The trip is quite scenic, however, and for those with time to spare the train might be preferable to the bus.

Driving: Traffic at the border is usually light, and driving through Piedras Negras is a fairly straightforward undertaking. Av. Lázaro Cárdenas leads southwest to the junction of Mexico 2 (for Nuevo Laredo or Ciudad Acuña) and Mexico 57 (for Saltillo and Monterrey).

Mexican vehicle insurance can be arranged in Eagle Pass, Texas, at **Capitol Insurance** (tel. 210-773-2341; 1115 Main).

Border Formalities: The bridge toll is US$2 for vehicles, US$0.50 for pedestrians. See the "Entry Regulations" section, p. 100, for important information on Mexican immigration and customs requirements. The Piedras Negras crossing is open 24 hours.

PIEDRAS NEGRAS TO SALTILLO

Mexico 57, the highway between Piedras Negras and Saltillo, was almost entirely resurfaced in 1992, so it's fairly smooth going all the way for the moment. Traffic is usually light, and the scenery is classic Altiplano terrain, marked by mesquite, yucca, sotol, maguey, and cholla amid rolling hills and valleys. Fuel is available along the way in Nueva Rosita, Sabinas, and Monclova; the longest stretch without Magna Sin is Monclova-Saltillo (192 km/119 miles).

Sabinas

At the heart of the Región Carbonífera, the municipality of Sabinas (138 km/85.5 miles south of Piedras Negras) is the third largest coal producer in the nation. The town also serves as a supply center for nearby vegetable, wheat, corn, and barley farms irrigated by the Río Sabinas.

Because it offers an adequate array of fuel, food, and lodging, Sabinas is the best place along the highway to break a journey between the border and Saltillo.

Practicalities: Motel Tres Caminos (tel. 861-3-03-89), just off Mexico 57 near the north end of town, has clean, reasonably priced a/c rooms and a pool. Inexpensive rooms are available near the plaza downtown at **Hotel Santa Clara** (tel. 2-12-31, Av. Independencia near Calle Lamadrid). Good food is available at **Restaurant La Carreta** and **Restaurant Guadalajara,** both on the highway in the vicinity of Motel Tres Caminos.

The state maintains an **Infotur** office with material on Coahuila at Km 122, about 20 km north of Sabinas on Mexico 57.

One PEMEX station with Magna Sin is located on the highway section running through the north end of town as well as several stations in the town itself.

Presa Venustiano Carranza

Also known as Lake Don Martín, this 180-square-km impoundment of the Río Sabinas is 70 km (44 miles) east of Sabinas via Coahuila 22. The take here includes trophy-sized striped bass, robalo, catfish, and carp. At **Campo Rumanía** at the northwest end of the lake, you'll find a few rustic cabins for rent, a restaurant, and camping space. Similar facilities are available along the north-east shore of the lake at **Don Martín.** Boats can be launched in several places around the lake's perimeter.

To get to the lake from Sabinas, take the left fork at Motel Tres Caminos and look for the sign marked "Don Martín." Follow the sign to a church on the right, turn left, and then it's about 60 km to the lake via a paved road.

The lake can also be reached from the east by following highway Nuevo León 1 southwest out of Nuevo Laredo 67 km (41.5 miles) to Anahuac, then heading 62 km west on the only paved road in that direction.

Melchor Múzquiz

Thirty-five km (21 miles) west of Nueva Rosita via Coahuila 2, Melchor Múzquiz is the center of Mexico's largest coal-producing region with an output equal to half the nation's coal reserves. Ensconced at the edge of Sierra Hermosa de Santa Rosa, the area is also rich in silver, zinc, lead, and fluorite, and is a center for cattle ranching. In spite of local industry, Múzquiz is a fairly traditional Northern Mexican town.

The Spanish established a military garrison called Santa Rosa here as early as 1735, the only legacy of which is the 18th-century baroque **Templo de Santa Rosa de Lima** at the north-east corner of the main square (Plaza de Armas).

Nearby attractions include the scenic **Balneario La Cascada,** fed by the Río Santa María, and the Kikapú ("Kickapoo") settlement at **El Nacimiento.** In August each year the Kikapú display their handicrafts (including leather and suede garments) at the **Feria Oasis del Norte** in Melchor Múzquiz. If you plan to visit El Nacimiento (37 km/23 miles west of Múzquiz via Coahuila 2), note that although "El Nacimiento" is the official state government name for the village, the Kikapú settlement is usually called "La Ranchería" by local mestizo Mexicans, who generally reserve the name "El Nacimiento" for another village settled by Seminoles eight km south. The Kikapú themselves refer to their village as "Colonia de los Kikapú." About 500 individuals live in the village most of the year; during the summer they move to a ramshackle settlement eight miles south of Eagle Pass, Texas, off FM 1021.

Accommodations: Two hotels on the eastern outskirts of town off Coahuila 2, **Hotel Los Angeles** (tel. 861-6-03-00) and **Motel La Mina** (tel. 6-12-12), offer decent rooms for around US$20 per night; the Los Angeles has a small swimming pool. In the center of town, 2 1/2 blocks northwest of the plaza, the **Hotel María Isabel** (tel. 6-03-68) has simple rooms for US$15-18.

Sierra Del Carmen

This beautiful but little-known, little-explored limestone and volcanic mountain range in Coahuila's northwest corner spills over the U.S.-Mexico border into Texas's Big Bend National Park, where it is known as the "Dead Horse Mountains." On the Mexican side, the highest and most pristine section of the mountain range, an area known as the **Sierra de Maderas del Carmen** (also called Sierra las Maderas or simply "Las Maderas") is entirely volcanic, with two peaks over 2,900 meters (9,500 feet), at least seven peaks over 2,500 meters (8,200 feet), and ten times as much terrain over 1,500 meters (5,000 feet) as Big Bend's Chisos Mountains.

Although the area was heavily logged in the late '40s and early '50s, dense groves of Douglas fir, ponderosa pine, aspen, and Arizona cypress can still be seen at higher elevations, along with grassy, flowered meadows and clear streams similar to those found in Big Bend's Chisos Mountains. Some of the prettiest meadows are found in the Maderas's high *cañones,* including Cañon Cinco and Cañon del Oso. The area is home to hundreds of animal species, many of which are considered rare. The Sierra del Carmen white-tailed deer, for example, lives only in the Sierra del Carmen and Chisos Mountains.

Park Status: Since the 1930s, Mexican and U.S. government officials have been talking about establishing an international park that would encompass Big Bend and parts of the Sierra del Carmen, thus protecting over 1.5 million acres of pristine "mountain islands in a desert sea." Recent meetings between U.S. National Park Service directors and their Mexican counterparts in Mexico City have been more fruitful than in the past, mainly because proposals on Mexican lands are finally proceeding according to Mexican terms. Participants are hopeful that the recent passage of NAFTA will provide a boost for the development of the proposed international park.

Coahuila's state government was so confident that the international park would become a reality in 1990 that "Parque Internacional del Río Bravo" appeared on 1990 state maps (the label has been deleted from the map's most re-

cent version). Weary of waiting for international authorities to come to an agreement, the Coahuila state government is already working toward the establishment of a state park and has set aside 37,000 acres of the Sierra del Carmen as a natural sanctuary.

Practicalities: Coahuila 2 extends 120 km (74.5 miles) northwest from Nueva Rosita (15 km/nine miles north of Sabinas) as far as the mining village of **La Cuesta de Malena** at the foot of the great Sierra de Maderas del Carmen. The Maderas del Carmen can be reached by continuing west about 22 km beyond La Cuesta via a gravel road, then turning northeast onto a dirt road that leads to the ranchería of **Los Pilares.** From Los Pilares you will have to continue on foot to reach the heart of the Maderas del Carmen.

The terrain in this area is very rugged and remote and shouldn't be undertaken without a guide; it may be possible to hire a guide and pack burros in La Cuesta or Boquillas del Car-

THE KIKAPU OF EL NACIMIENTO

Originally hailing from Wisconsin and Michigan, the Kikapú ("Kickapoo") were driven south in the 18th and 19th centuries by westward-moving Europeans. In 1775, Spain's Charles III gave them permission to settle in the colonial province of Coahuila y Texas in return for defending the area against Comanche and Apache raids. By the late 1800s, many of those on the Texas side were banished to Oklahoma reservations. Some were able to flee to Northern Mexico and were given land by the Mexican government (like the Seminoles, a number of Kikapús came north again to serve as scouts with the U.S. Cavalry in Texas).

Today a core of around 500 Kikapú choose to live together and follow a semitraditional lifestyle at two seasonal settlements on either side of the Texas-Coahuila border. They speak an Algonquin dialect as their first language, pidgin (or "broken") Spanish as a second. Those who read and write Kikapú use a syllabary devised by the Cherokee Sequoyah. Their oval-shaped, windowless winter homes in Mexico are built of hackberry, bald cypress, or sycamore wood, with low, dome-shaped roofs. Summer houses feature a rectangular plan with wooden posts supporting airy walls of sotol, a desert succulent.

For the most part the Kikapú dress in a style similar to that of other Mexican peasants. The main difference is in the way females wear their hair; young girls plait their hair in three braids, often joined on top of the head in a topknot. After puberty, women switch to one long braid.

The Kikapú belief system revolves around nature spirits presided over by Kitzihiat, the "Great Spirit." Subordinate to Kitzihiat is Wisaka, the creator of the cosmos. The most common regular religious practice among the Kikapú is the preparation and possession of *misami* or medicine bundles which serve as sacred talismans for warding off evil. *Misami* contents are closely guarded secrets; they usually include a variety of dried plants, roots, and herbs, plus occasional human and animal parts. Wrapped in white cloth and covered by the skin of a two-point buck, the bundles are usually around 60 cm (two feet) long and 15 cm (six inches) wide.

Although the Kikapú employ peyote for medicinal, nonritual purposes only, they sometimes gather a surplus of the cactus to sell to the Oklahoma Kikapú and other Amerindians who use the hallucinogenic substance ritually, since northwestern Coahuila is a primary source of the plant.

PROPOSED PARQUE INTERNACIONAL DEL RIO BRAVO

···· = BOUNDARY OF PROPOSED PARQUE INTERNACIONAL DE RIO BRAVO

NOT TO SCALE

men. Because no camping facilities or marked trails exist, skills in wilderness camping and orienteering are a minimum requirement. INEGI topographic maps H13-9 (Manuel Benavides) and H13-12 (San Miguel) would be very useful for general navigation.

Beyond La Cuesta, a 55-km (34-mile) gravel road leads all the way to **Boquillas del Carmen** on the Río Bravo opposite Big Bend National Park. Boquillas is a popular destination for Big Bend visitors who cross by ferry for the day. The nondescript village has a souvenir shop/cafe known as **Falcón's** with a few tables and a kitchen offering burritos and cold beer. A real bar up the street has a pool table and is well-stocked with tequila and other liquors—including fiery sotol (US$1 per *probita*). Although as yet no hotels or inns have been built in Boquillas, it's not difficult to find rooms for rent by

the night or by the week. Ask at Falcon's for possibilities.

Fuel: Gasoline (Nova only) is available from barrels in La Cuesta and Boquillas at elevated prices. The best approach is to top off in Nueva Rosita and carry enough extra fuel so that you can make it all the way to Los Pilares and back without depending on local supplies.

Rumored changes in the area include the proposed extension of power lines across the river from Texas to supply Boquillas with electricity, a public car ferry across the river, and/or a bridge between Big Bend's Rio Grande Village campgrounds and Boquillas del Carmen. For now, simple rowboat ferries are the only means of communication and transport between the two sides of the river.

Tours From Big Bend: The easiest and safest way to experience the grandeur of the

Sierra del Carmen is to hire a guide on the Texas side. Marcos Paredes, a Big Bend park ranger, leads occasional four- or five-day treks into the mountains on horseback and foot; contact **Far Flung Adventures** (tel. 915-371-2489; P.O. Box 31, Terlingua, TX 79852) for information. The Panther Junction Information Center at **Big Bend National Park** (tel. 915-477-2251) can also provide information on exploring the sierra.

Monclova

Few motorists stop in Monclova since the Coahuila 50 loop enables drivers following Mexico 57 to Saltillo or Piedras Negras to skirt the town entirely.

The town served as the provincial capital of Coahuila y Texas from 1811-24, when Saltillo assumed capitalhood. American Harold R. Pape established the local steel industry and Monclova now supports what is reportedly the largest steel foundry on the North American continent. The **Harold R. Pape Museum-Library** (on the highway through town just south of the IMSS hospital) contains a permanent exhibit of works by Dali, Picasso, Orozco, and Cuevas.

Accommodations: Though tourism in Monclova is practically nil, business travelers support around a dozen hotels. The place of choice among such visitors is the **Hotel Chula Vista** (tel. 863-1-02-11), which sits on a hill overlooking Monclova on Calle Valparaíso, just off the highway through town. Rooms with all the amenities start at US$40 per night. Several hotels on or just off Av. V. Carranza in the center of town near the Plaza Principal and Plaza Alonso de León offer rooms in the US$18-25 range: **Hotel Ilbac, Hotel Viena, Hotel San Cristobal, Hotel Olimpia,** and **Hotel Noruega.**

Information: A state tourist office (tel. 863-5-32-90), next to the firehouse at Blvd. Harold R. Pape (Mexico 57 in town) and Calle Madero, distributes information on state and local attractions as well as tips on food and lodging.

Driving: Motorists heading to Torreón, Durango, or Mazatlán will save time and distance by taking Mexico 30 southwest from Monclova. Although not in the best condition, this route is more direct than hooking through Saltillo. Traffic is light all the way to San Pedro de las Colonías, 65 km (40 miles) northeast of Torreón, where the highway connects with Mexico 40 onward to Durango and Mazatlán.

Vicinity Of Monclova

Around 30 km south of Monclova, Mexico 57 cuts through **Cima de la Muralla** ("Top of the Wall"), a scenic mountain pass in the Sierra San Marcos halfway between Guadalupe and Monclova.

West of Monclova, Mexico 30 threads 140 km (87 miles) through the scenic Sierra La Gloria and Sierra Pájaros Azules to meet Nuevo León 1, the toll-free highway between Nuevo Laredo and Monterrey.

Cuatrociénegas

Founded in 1800, the small town of Cuatrociénegas (pop. 8,500) is famous as the birthplace of Venustiano Carranza, who initiated the Plan de Guadalupe, thus terminating the dictatorial rule of Victoriano Huerta. The house where Carranza was born is now the **Museo Casa de Carranza** (on Calle Zaragoza facing Plaza Zaragoza), with six rooms of exhibits chronicling his life.

The town's name means "four marshes" and refers to a series of gypsum flats or *bolsones,* a common desert feature west of the Sierra Madre Oriental, at the edge of town. The principal water source for the marshes is a series of thermal springs in the Sierra San Marcos, a spur of the northern Sierra Madre Oriental that bisects this particular basin area.

During the rainy season spring water mixes with rain water to form shallow lakes, of which the largest is **Laguna Grande.** Another interesting *bolsón* feature here is the presence of extensive gypsum dunes. Gypsum is dissolved in the spring waters, and as the water evaporates and the lakes shrink, crystallized gypsum is left behind. At the edges of the basin this powdered gypsum is blown into dazzling white dunes 6-10 meters (18-30 feet) above the desert floor.

The desert marshes support a surprising variety of plants and creatures, including bullrushes, cattails, and the world's only aquatic terrapin, *Terrapene coahuila* (*tortuga de bisagra* or "hinge turtle" in Spanish) a box turtle that swims (*Terrapenes* are normally a land-bound species). In spite of its aquatic abilities, the *coahuila* is very sedentary, carrying out all its daily activities within an average 12.4-square-meter area. Though it's mainly nocturnal, the turtle may occasionally be seen in daylight after

Sierra Pájaros Azules at Canela

a hard rain. Another species endemic to Cuatrociénegas is the *cichlid,* a perchlike freshwater fish that feeds on snails and organic bottom debris.

Among the marshes are splendid examples of such Chihuahuan Desert standards as mesquite, yucca, ocotillo, saltbush, lechugilla, creosote bush, and desert Christmas cactus (tasajillo rojo in Mexico).

The same springs that feed the marshes have also been impounded for use by *balnearios* at nearby **El Mojarral, Pozas de Becerra,** and **Pozas de Escobedo** to name but a few (April-June is the *balneario* "season"). Southwest of Cuatrociénegas via Mexico 30 in **Valle El Hundido** are several rock-art sites thought to have been painted by Coahuiltecas, the original inhabitants of the area.

Practicalities: Two very basic places, **Hotel Ibarra** (Calle Zaragoza) and **Hotel Santa Fe** (Av. Juárez), offer simple lodging for under US$20 per night. **Restaurant El Doc,** on Plaza Zaragoza in the center of town, serves standard Mexican fare. The town is famous for sweets made from nuts and honey, which can be bought in local shops.

Cuatrociénegas is 83 km (51.5 miles) northwest of Monclova via Mexico 30, a two-lane paved highway. Magna Sin is available at one PEMEX station in town or from the PEMEX station 43 km (26.6 miles) north of Monclova on Mexico 57.

SALTILLO

For visitors approaching from the north via Mexico 57, Saltillo seems to rise out of nowhere—a Mexican combo plate ringed by desert mountains. Pastel-colored, 18th- and 19th-century stone buildings with arched doorways and iron grillwork are typical of the slightly hilly downtown area and make Coahuila's oldest city the strongest example of colonial Mexico in the northeast.

Though Saltillo is only an hour or so by car from Monterrey, N.L., to the east, its pace of life is much slower and more traditional. The city's 400-year history is preserved in its central Spanish-style grid layout, with modern districts well away from the center along Blvd. Carranza to the north and Blvd. Fundadores to the east. For border-hoppers not inclined to spend their time among the high rises of Monterrey or the kitsch of border towns, Saltillo is a good place to find "Old Mexico" within a half day's drive of the Rio Grande.

History

Once densely populated by Guachichil and Borrado Indians, the Valle de Saltillo saw its first Spaniards in 1577 when the governor of Nueva Vizcaya established a supply point here for *conquista* expeditions along the road from Zacatecas to Texas and Louisiana. The settlement was originally called Santiago del Saltillo del Ojo de Agua, and its first residents dedicated themselves to the capture and sale of Amerindian slaves for use in Spanish mines, a practice then condoned by the mission system. The natives responded with rebellions and attacks, destroying the first Franciscan mission in 1582 and forcing Spanish colonists to flee south.

At the beginning of the 17th century, the viceroy sent a group of "civilized" Tlaxcaltecas to found San Esteban de Nueva Tlaxcala as an example to local natives. By this time European diseases and Apache attacks had weakened native resistance to outsiders, and the Tlaxcaltecas were able to grow wheat, build flour mills, and establish vineyards and cattle ranches. Eventually San Esteban expanded east to include the old settlement at nearby Saltillo. In 1824 Saltillo was made the capital of the state of

Coahuila y Texas, which included the present-day states of Texas, Coahuila, Tamaulipas, and Nuevo León.

In 1847 a decisive battle in the Mexican-American War occurred 10 km south of Saltillo at Buena Vista, where a U.S. force of 4,500 led by Gen. Zachary Taylor defeated Santa Anna's battalion of over 20,000. Saltillo remained the capital of Coahuila but declined in importance as Mexico lost many of its northern territories to the United States. Saltillo slumbered through the remainder of the 19th century until a railway from the border transformed the city into an important transport junction. The economy's traditional ranching and farming base has more recently been supplemented by Chrysler and General Motors automotive plants just east of the city.

Climate

At 1,590 meters (5,216 feet) above sea level, Saltillo enjoys a dry but mild year-round climate where the highest average daily temperature, 22.5° C (72.5° F), occurs in June and July; and the lowest, 12° C (53.6° F), in January. The occasional winter north wind will drop temperatures to near freezing for a day or two, but sunny days are the norm even then.

August and September are the wettest months, with an average monthly precipitation of 4 cm (1.5 inches) and 4.5 cm (1.75 inches) respectively—hardly enough to impinge on a vacation.

SIGHTS

The charms of the city's narrow, colonial-style streets are best seen on foot. A convenient downtown parking lot is located off Calle G. Victoria near the intersection with Calle Xicoténcatl. One of the best streets for native turn-of-the-century architecture—some of it restored and some in an advanced state of decay—is Calle General Cepeda.

Catedral De Santiago De Saltillo

Construction on Mexico's northernmost example of Churrigueresque (or "ultra-baroque") archi-

SALTILLO

TO MONCLOVA

40

40

TO MONTERREY

TO TORREON

40

PERIF. LUIS ECHEVERRIA

BLVD. VITO ALESSIO ROBLES

BLVD. ISIDRO LOPEZ

BLVD. NAZARIO S. ORTIZ GARZA

BLVD. CARRANZA

PERIF. LUIS ECHEVERRIA

■ LIENZO CHARRO PROF. ENRIQUE GONZALEZ

■ RESTAURANT LA MAJADA

■ RESTAURANT PRINCIPAL

● EUROTEL PLAZA BEST WESTERN

■ RESTAURANT - BAR LAS VIGAS

■ IMPERIAL DEL NORTE MOTOR HOTEL

■ LIENZO CHARRO EL RAYITO

TO PLAZA DE TOROS →

JESUS VALDES SANCHEZ

■ INSTITUTO TECNOLOGICO DE SALTILLO

■ UNIVERSIDAD AUTONOMA DE COAHUILA

AV. UNIVERSIDAD

SALVADOR GONZALEZ LOBO

● MOTEL HUIZACHE

● CIUDAD DEPORTIVA

PALACIO MUNICIPAL

BLVD. FCO. COSS

HOTEL CAMINO REAL ●

BLVD. DE LOS FUNDADORES

57

HOTEL LA TORRE ●

MOTEL LA FUENTE

MADERO

JUAN ALDAMA

CRUZ ROJA ●

CARDENAS

PASEO DE LA REFORMA

PARQUE ALAMEDA ZARAGOZA

MUNICIPAL LIBRARY

RAILWAY STATION ■

R. ARIZPE

CASTELAR

CARLOS SALAZAR

SEE "DOWNTOWN SALTILLO" MAP

TO CENTRO DE CONVENCIONES AND MATEHUALA →

BASEBALL FIELD ◆

SAN LORENZO

CALZ. A. NARRO

PEDRO ARANDA

MARIANO ABASOLO

DE LA FUENTE

FELIPE J. MERY

POLICE ◆

PERIF. LUIS ECHEVERRIA

● HOTEL RANCHO EL MORILLO

■ BUS STATION

PERIF. LUIS ECHEVERRIA

■ BASEBALL FIELD

0   1 km

54

tecture began in 1745 and continued through 1800, with the addition of the tower in 1893-97. Originally built as a parochial church dedicated to the city's patron saint (Santiago or St. James), the structure was criticized as being "of a size that exceeds the necessities of a population as small as Saltillo's." The archdiocese disagreed, and the establishment of a bishop's office here in 1891 conferred cathedral status. Now a focus of city and state pride, the cathedral has been restored, preserved, and documented as thoroughly as any church in Mexico.

The ornate baroque facade, elaborate porticos, and wooden doors (carved in the late 1700s and featuring images of saints Peter and Paul) are the most striking exterior features. A shell motif, symbolic of St. James the Elder (Santiago), is reproduced several times in the exterior decoration, predominantly over doorways. Inside, the neoclassical main altar features a statue of Santiago flanked by smaller statues of Christ and the Virgin Mary. More impressive baroque side altars, built between 1745 and 1800 and dedicated to the Sacred Heart and San José respectively, are at opposite ends of the lateral arms of the cathedral's cruciform floor plan. The engraved silver front on the San José altar has been exhibited at New York's Metropolitan Museum of Art. Several viceregal-style sacred paintings by Don José de Alcíbar are hung on the cathedral walls.

Attached to the cathedral is the **Capilla del Santo Cristo,** which contains a highly revered wooden crucifix carved in Spain and brought to Saltillo in 1608.

Two festivals associated with the cathedral include Saltillo's patron saint day on July 25, and the even bigger **Novenario de Santo Cristo** on Aug. 6, when pilgrims from all over the state come to pay homage to the Spanish crucifixion in the *capilla.* Semana Santa and Christmas are also impressively celebrated here.

The cathedral faces the Plaza de Armas at Calle Hidalgo and Juárez.

Parque Alameda Zaragoza

This large and very nicely landscaped park covering eight blocks at the west end of Calle G. Victoria is a good spot to while away an hour or two. An equestrian statue of the park's namesake, Ignacio Zaragoza, stands in the Alameda's

center. Zaragoza was a hero at the Battle of Puebla of May 5, 1862 (celebrated annually in the Fiesta del Cinco de Mayo), in which Mexican troops repulsed French naval invaders.

Museums

Housed in a stately 19th-century colonial at the corner of Calle Juárez and Hidalgo (diagonally opposite the cathedral), **Museo CAVIE** (Centro de Artes Visuales e Investigaciones Estéticas) hosts rotating exhibits by local and regional artists.

The **Ateneo Fuentes** (Fuentes Athenaeum), on Calle E. Carranza on the Universidad Autónoma de Coahuila campus, displays a permanent collection of works by accomplished Mexican and international painters in a Mexican art deco building.

Both museums are open daily 9-6; admission is free.

Plazas

Plaza de Armas and **Plaza de Nueva Tlaxcala,** separated by the Palacio de Gobierno west of the cathedral, are large squares empty except for the occasional stroller or shutterbug trying for an angle on the cathedral.

The real action is at **Plaza Acuña** (two blocks north of Plaza de Armas via Calle Allende), a small, leafy square with benches and food vendors next to bustling Mercado Juárez. The plaza is named for Manuel Acuña, a famous Saltillo poet who killed himself at age 23.

ACCOMMODATIONS

Saltillo has a good selection of hotels both downtown and on the periphery. Generally speaking, rates here are similar to those in Monterrey, i.e., high by Mexican standards.

Budget Hotels

Probably the best deal in town is the colonial-style **Hotel Urdiñola** (tel. 84-14-09-40) at Calle Victoria 211 not far from the Plaza de Armas and convenient to downtown shopping and eating. Tidy, recently renovated rooms around an interior courtyard cost a very reasonable US$25 s, US$27 d.

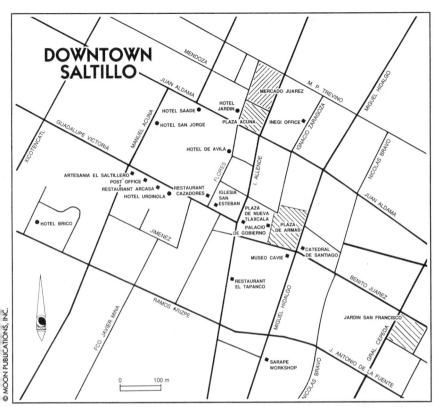

DOWNTOWN SALTILLO

The least inexpensive hotels are found downtown along Calle Flores in the vicinity of Plaza Acuña. The twin **Hotel Jardín** (tel. 12-59-16) and **Hotel De Avila** (same telephone and ownership) near the west side of Plaza Acuña on Flores offer very basic rooms for around US$20 s/d per night. Farther south along Calle Flores is the similar **Hotel Hidalgo.**

A bit farther south at Calle Ramos Arizpe 552 is another US$20 place, **Hotel Brico** (tel. 12-51-46).

Medium-priced Hotels
Hotel La Torre Los Magueyes (tel. 84-15-33-33, fax 16-05-12), six km southeast of town on Mexico 57, has modern rooms in a tower complex with good mountain views for US$34 s, US$42-50 d. On the premises are a swimming pool and tennis courts.

Hotel Premier (tel. 12-10-50), at Calle Allende 508 Nte., is a cheaper downtown place with a three-star rating; rooms come with a/c and TV for US$32 s, US$35 d. Similar rates and rooms are available at the well-located **Hotel Saade** (tel. 12-92-20, fax 12-91-29), on Calle Aldama between calles Acuña and Flores.

North of downtown at Blvd. V. Carranza 1746, **Motel Huizache** (tel. 16-10-00, fax 16-26-62) has rooms with a/c, heat, TV, and kitchenettes for US$30-38 s/d.

Farther north, the two-story **Imperial del Norte Motor Hotel (formerly Motel Estrella)** (tel. 5-00-11), at Blvd. V. Carranza 3747, is a friendly spot with quick Mexico 40 access and renovated rooms for US$32-40 s/d.

Hotel Rancho El Morillo (tel. 17-40-78, fax 14-19-75; A.P. 304, Saltillo, Coah.) is a restored hacienda on wooded grounds with 14 spacious rooms that cost US$28.30 s, US$32 d, US$37 t, and US$40 q per night. Also on the premises are a pool, chapel, Ping-Pong tables, tennis court, volleyball court, and dining room with *comida casera* ("home cooking"). El Morillo is off Periférico Luis Echeverría Sur at Calle Obregón, about three km (two miles) southwest of downtown Saltillo.

Luxury Hotels

Most of Saltillo's top hotels are found along Blvd. V. Carranza (Mexico 40 North) and Blvd. Fundadores (Mexico 57 South). To find the latter boulevard from the city (or from Mexico 40), follow signs reading "Matehuala."

A top choice among visiting North American business travelers is the relaxed but efficient, five-star **Hotel Camino Real** (tel. 84-5-25-25, fax 84-15-38-13), situated on quiet, nicely landscaped grounds on Blvd. Fundadores six km southeast of town. Facilities include a cozy bar, restaurant, coffee shop, putting green, two tennis courts, and a well-maintained, heated pool. Rooms, arranged in separated ranch-style buildings, come with refrigerator/bar, satellite TV, a/c, and telephone; rates are US$64 s, US$88-108 d.

Farther west along Blvd. Fundadores toward town, **Motel La Fuente** (tel. 15-25-99, fax 15-87-19) is a well-kept, one-story courtyard motel (no a/c) with a pool and tennis court. Room rates are in the US$50-60 range.

Hotel San Jorge (tel. 3-06-00), at Calle Aldama and Acuña downtown, charges US$50 s on weekends, US$55 s, US$62 d weekdays for large rooms (no a/c) and a heated pool.

Moving toward the north end of town, the **Eurotel Plaza Best Western** (tel. 15-10-00, 91-800-84-44 toll free in Mexico), at Blvd. V. Carranza 4100 (about 4.8 km/three miles from downtown Saltillo), offers modern rooms with satellite TV, a/c, and heating for US$80-90 s, US$90-100 d. Other facilities include a travel agency, restaurant, car rental, and indoor pool.

RV Parks

The **Imperial del Norte Motor Hotel** and **Hotel Camino Real** each maintain a number of RV and trailer spaces with full hookups. Rates vary with the season but are generally in the US$10-15 range. For addresses and telephone numbers, see "Medium-priced Hotels" and "Luxury Hotels," above.

Self-contained RVs and campers are also permitted to park—for no charge—at the Centro de Convenciones parking lot on Blvd. Fundadores (Mexico 57).

FOOD

Saltillo cuisine is very much in the *norteña* style, with an emphasis on *carnes al carbón* (charcoal-grilled steaks), *cabrito, guisada, machaca,* flour tortillas, and milk-based pastries and sweets. Among Mexicans the city is perhaps most famous for *pan de pulque,* bread made with fermented maguey extract. This delicacy can be hard to find outside people's homes, since the best *pulque* (known as *pulque casera* or "house pulque") is circulated privately. If you're interested in tasting some, ask at a local *panadería*—try **Panadería La Crema,** just south of Hotel San Jorge on Calle Acuña—or take a day trip to Ramos Arizpe, where it's most common (see "Around Saltillo," below).

Restaurant Principal specializes in *carne asada* and *cabrito* at three locations: Calle Allende 702 Nte. (tel. 84-14-33-84), Blvd. V. Carranza (tel. 15-00-15), and opposite the Central de Autobuses.

In the vicinity of the cathedral and Plaza de Armas, **Restaurant Arcasa** next door to Hotel Urdiñola on Calle G. Victoria serves a tasty and inexpensive *comida corrida,* plus a variety of tacos and *tortas.*

Around the corner on Calle Flores (between Victoria and Ocampo), the air-conditioned **Restaurant Cazadores** specializes in moderately priced Mexican standards, cheap breakfasts, burgers, and sandwiches. **Restaurant Victoria,** a bit farther north on the same street, has a similar menu but is cheaper than the Cazadores and isn't air-conditioned.

The outdoor tables in front of **Mercado Juárez** facing Plaza Acuña are pleasant and vendors serve inexpensive *antojitos;* if nothing else, it's a good spot to watch plaza life while sipping a *refresca* or beer.

For something more elegant, try **El Tapanco,** in a converted 17th-century house a block and a half south of the Plaza de Armas at Calle Allende 225 Sur. The varied menu offers both international and Mexican standards for lunch and dinner Mon.-Saturday.

Another dependable eatery with something for everyone is the **Restaurant-Bar Las Vigas** (tel. 15-79-22) at Blvd. V. Carranza 3984 at the north end of town. Las Vigas specializes in steak, *arracheras* (*fajitas*), *platillos típicos*, and breakfasts. It's open daily 7 a.m.-midnight.

Homesick Americans can stop in at **Church's Fried Chicken** opposite Restaurant Arcasa on Calle G. Victoria. A string of other American-style fast-food places (including **Wendy's**) can be found along Blvd. Carranza northeast of Blvd. Fco. Coss.

RECREATION

Bullfights And *Charreadas*
Saltillo's **Plaza de Toros Armillita** is on Av. Jesús Valdés Sánchez (Coahuila 10), the old road to Arteaga, about four km (2.5 miles) east of the Ciudad Deportiva.

The local *charro* association holds *charreadas* in two different rings, the **Lienzo Charro El Rayito (Dr. Carlos Cárdenas V.)** off Blvd. Ortiz Garza in the northeastern section of the city, and the easier-to-find **Lienzo Charro Prof. Enrique González,** on Mexico 40, three km (two miles) north of Periférico Luis Echeverría Nte. The tourist offices (see "Saltillo Information," below) in town should be able to provide current corrida and *charreada* schedules.

Shopping
When the Tlaxcaltecas established the colony of San Esteban de Nueva Tlaxcala in the early 1600s, they brought with them the art of weaving sarapes, multihued, multipurpose blankets associated with the stereotypical campesino or Mexican peasant style. One of the best places to shop for sarapes, rugs, and handwoven wool or cotton items is **El Saltillero** at Calle G. Victoria 469 Pte. just two blocks west of the Plaza de Armas. Sarapes here start at US$8 for a basic souvenir model and reach over US$100 for top-quality, all-wool original designs; a fairly nice one costs about US$27. The traditional Saltillo sarape is a bright, rainbow-colored pattern with a diamond in the center—usually the one that looks most "touristy" to the untrained eye. Sarapes and *jorongos* (a sarape with a hole in the middle for the head) in muted earth tones are a more recent development.

El Saltillero carries a broad range of other regional and Mexican crafts—several curios shops are located along calles Victoria and Ocampo. You can also visit a **sarape workshop** on the east side of Calle Hidalgo just south of Calle Ramos Arizpe downtown.

At **Mercado Juárez** (north end of Plaza Acuña) you'll find many of the same crafts as at the curios shops but at lower prices.

SALTILLO INFORMATION

Tourist Offices
Coahuila's main tourist office is on the second floor of the **Centro de Convenciones** (tel. 84-15-45-04, 30-03-10, fax 30-07-23) at Km 6, Blvd. Los Fundadores (Mexico 57). There is a small branch office called **Caseta Coss** (tel. 12-40-50) at Blvd. Fco. Coss and Acuña, a block west of Blvd. V. Carranza. Both offices distribute high-quality info on Saltillo and the surrounding state; several of the staff speak English.

Post Offices
Saltillo's post offices seem to be better located and easier to find than in most Mexican cities of comparable size; hence if you have mail business to take care of, this is a good city to get it accomplished. Perhaps the most convenient branch is the small post office in a building next door to the Caseta Coss tourist office at Blvd. Fco. Coss and Acuña.

In the center of town another convenient post office branch is on Calle G. Victoria near Hotel Urdiñola.

Maps
Saltillo's INEGI office, conveniently located

SALTILLO TELEPHONE NUMBERS

Local Police: 15-56-61
Highway Patrol: 15-51-22
Green Angels: 14-31-75, 15-41-29
State Tourist Office: 15-45-04, 12-40-50
Red Cross: 14-33-33, 14-81-70
University Hospital: 12-30-00
Saltillo Area Code: 84

downtown on Calle Zaragoza (two blocks north of the cathedral), carries topography maps for Coahuila, Nuevo León, and Zacatecas.

TRANSPORT

Getting There

Air: With the Monterrey behemoth so close, few airlines serve Saltillo directly. In fact the only regularly scheduled commercial passenger service to Saltillo is a daily flight from Mexico City operated by **TAESA** (tel. 84-6-37-32), Periférico Luis Echeverría 361.

Aeropuerto Plan de Guadalupe is 13 km north of Saltillo (via Mexico 40) in Ramos Arizpe.

Bus: The **Central Camionera Saltillo** is on Periférico Luis Echeverría Sur at Calle Libertad, about two km south of the city center. **Transportes Monterrey-Saltillo** (tel. 17-02-43) has a monopoly on buses to/from Saltillo, with departures every 15 minutes between 5 a.m. and 9 p.m. for US$3 ordinary class, US$6 *ejecutivo.* **Omnibus de México** (tel. 17-03-15) and **Transportes del Norte** (tel. 17-09-02) dominate the departure boards. **Transportes Frontera** (tel. 17-01-95) and **Autobuses El Aguila** (tel. 17-01-35) specialize in service to border towns, including Piedras Negras and Nuevo Laredo.

Driving: Savvy motorists heading for the interior of Mexico from the Texas border use Saltillo as a gateway rather than Monterrey since traffic tie-ups are fewer and there are no toll charges along the way (so far). The Mexico 40-D toll from Monterrey alone is US$7, while the Nuevo Laredo-Monterrey toll for Mexico 85-D is US$22.

Getting Around

Bus: Buses marked "Camionera-Centro" ply back and forth between the bus terminal and downtown Saltillo; there are also buses that connect the *centro* with Blvd. Fundadores (for the convention center and La Fuente, La Torre, and Camino Real hotels) and Blvd. V. Carranza (Hotel Huizache, Imperial Motor Hotel, Eurotel Plaza, and Lienzo Charro Prof. Enrique González).

Taxis: Taxicabs are plentiful in the downtown area near Plaza Acuña and at the larger hotels. A typical ride within the downtown area

costs around US$4, to the city outskirts US$6-10 depending on the distance.

Driving: With a map it's fairly easy to find your way around the city. Narrow streets in the older downtown district aren't a problem for the average sedan, truck, or van; motorists driving large RVs may want to park on the larger avenues at the edges of town, then use public transport (or walk) downtown.

The city has devised a system of pentagonal, numbered street signs that are intended to help motorists reach their destinations more easily. Signs marked "1," for example, lead to Blvd. V. Carranza and Mexico 40 East, while those marked "23" lead to Mexico 54 and Calle M. Abasolo. With so many different options, however, it's very difficult to associate numbers with destinations unless you're a long-term visitor or resident.

AROUND SALTILLO

Ramos Arizpe

Only 12 km northeast of Saltillo via Mexico 40, Ramos Arizpe became a virtual city suburb with the opening of the Aeropuerto Plan de Guadalupe, the only commercial airport serving the Saltillo area. The town is regionally famous for *pulque,* an alcoholic beverage made with fermented maguey (agave) extract, and for *pan de pulque.* If you've had trouble finding this substance, look no further than the **Pulque Restaurant** on Calle Gral. Charles between Morelos and Ocampo, three blocks south of Arizpe's Plaza Principal.

Other local attractions include the nearby *balneario* at **Ojo Caliente,** and the abandoned **Hacienda de Santa María** four km northeast of town.

Arteaga

The foothills of the Sierra Madre Oriental, rising east of Saltillo along the Nuevo León border, are little explored by out-of-state visitors but are highly favored by Saltillo residents, many of whom have built vacation cabins in the area. A good starting point for an excursion into the mountains (here called the Sierra de Arteaga) is the small ranching and farming town of Arteaga, 17 km (11 miles) east of Saltillo via Mexico 57. Flanked by picturesque Arroyo Seco and Arroyo Blanco, Arteaga is known for the production of apples and handicrafts, particularly ceramics. A small state tourist office on Mexico 57 just west of town toward Saltillo has ample information on the area.

Farther east and southeast, narrow paved roads off Mexico 57 ascend the sierra to **El Parque Forestal El Chorro, El Cañon de la Roja,** and the quaint mountain villages of **Los Lirios, San Juan de Dolores,** and **San Antonio de las Alazanas.**

TORREON TO SALTILLO

TORREON

Founded in 1887 as a rail center by Mexican, American, British, and French interests, Torreón is the largest of the Región Lagunera cities and an important cotton, wheat, vinifera, mining, and dairy farming center. In spite of being well within the borders of the Chihuahuan Desert, this area has managed—with irrigation help—to become one of Northern Mexico's economic strongholds.

Torreón attained official city status in 1897, at which time engineers carefully laid out an urban plan. What was intended to be a "modern and very practical" community has actually turned out to be quite an attractive and livable city of 440,000 residents. Wide avenues with palm-lined medians in the city center give the impression of what Pasadena, California, might have looked like if it had been built by Europeans, while several downtown parks and plazas contribute splashes of green to the cityscape.

Parks
Perhaps Torreón's most impressive asset is its large and leafy parks, which provide an easy respite from summer heat and a refuge for migrating birds. Food and beverage vendors hawk their wares on warm evenings and on weekends, adding a festive atmosphere.

The city's largest park, **Bosque Venustiano Carranza,** covers 30 square blocks bordered by Av. Juárez, Av. Bravo, Calz. Cuauhtémoc, and Calle Juan Pablos in the middle of the city. Large casuarinas, fan palms, and other tree varieties provide shady paths for walkers and joggers, and benches are distributed throughout for more sedentary park visitors and kissing couples. The park also contains a small zoo, pool, theater, children-oriented amusement park, and the **Museo Regional de la Laguna.** This INAH-sponsored museum (open daily 10 a.m.-5 p.m.) houses permanent exhibits on regional archaeology; a collection of Mesoamerican ceramics; ethnographic displays from Coahuila, Oaxaca, Puebla, Hidalgo, Chiapas, Chihuahua, and Guerrero; a small library; and occasional traveling exhibits. Toward the north end of the park and less interesting (at least to nongeologists) is the **Museo de la Minería,** which contains exhibits on various minerals native to the region.

Second in size is six-block-square **Alameda Zaragoza,** west of Bosque V. Carranza between calles Ortega and Guerra off Av. Juárez. Smaller yet is the **Plazuela Juárez,** farther west between calles Corona and Galeana off Av. Morelos, where a statue of Benito Juárez always seems to have a bird sitting on its guano-crowned head.

Accommodations
Built within the last two decades, most of Torreón's hotels are modern, boxy affairs. If you're planning on stopping over to see some of the city, one of the downtown hotels would be a good choice since driving in and out of the city from Mexico 40 and Mexico 49 can be an ordeal (see Torreón's "Transport" section for details); conversely, if you're just passing through and need a place to sleep, a hotel or motel on the outskirts of the city might be more suitable. Downtown hotels are considerably less expensive than highway motels.

Downtown: Most of the better hotels are found in the vicinity of the Plaza de Armas on Av. Morelos or Av. Juárez. The six-story **Hotel Calvete** (tel. 17-16-10-10), on the southwest corner of Av. Juárez and Calle Corona, has good rooms with a/c and TV for US$25-30 s/d, and a parking garage a block away. A block north and three blocks west at Av. Morelos and Treviño, **Hotel del Paseo** (tel. 16-03-07) is similar at US$26.60 s, US$30 d, with parking at nearby Hotel Río Nazas (same owners).

Somewhat less expensive at US$18-25 per night are the basic but adequate **Hotel Galicia** (tel. 16-11-11), facing the east side of Plaza de Armas on Calle Cepeda; **Hotel Naves** (tel. 16-15-15), south of the plaza at Av. Hidalgo and Calle V. Carrillo; and **Hotel Arriaga** (tel. 16-10-55), a block east at Av. Hidalgo and Calle Cepeda. **Hotel Francia** (tel. 16-18-20), at Calle Ramos Arizpe and Av. Carranza four blocks southwest of the plaza, is a bit noisy due to a busy location but costs just US$15-18 for a spartan room with private bath.

The clean and comfortable **Hotel Río Nazas** (tel. 16-12-12, fax 12-61-77) near Hotel del Paseo is a large step up with a/c, TV, phones, a basement parking garage, a restaurant-bar, and a travel agency (with car rental) for US$37 s/d.

The city's top downtown hotel is the **Hotel Palacio Real** (tel. 16-00-00, fax 16-86-08), a stately, nine-story, European-style hotel facing the north side of Plaza de Armas. Completing the effect is the hotel's atmospheric **Café de Paris** on the ground floor. Rooms with all the amenities cost US$60 s, US$78 d. Hotel facilities include a swimming pool, disco, travel agency, car rental, parking garage, restaurant, and bar.

East End (Near Mexico 40): On Diagonal Reforma just north of Av. Juárez (about five blocks northwest of Blvd. Revolución/Mexico 40), **Motel La Villa** (tel. 20-15-12) offers standard, air-conditioned rooms around a parking lot and pool for US$30 s/d. On Blvd. Revolución, two blocks west of Diagonal Reforma, **Hotel Posada del Sol** (tel. 20-25-71) has similarly priced rooms but no pool.

© MOON PUBLICATIONS, INC.

Very near Motel La Villa on Diagonal Reforma is **Motel Paraíso del Camino** (tel. 13-99-30, tel./fax 20-03-33), where pleasant rooms with a/c, refrigerator, TV, and phone, around a pool and parking lot go for US$44 s, US$48 d.

A bit east from the center of town yet not quite on the outskirts is **Hotel Del Prado** (tel. 21-24-24, fax 21-29-58) on Paseo de la Rosita, two km south of Blvd. Revolución opposite the Club Campestre La Rosita (Rosita Country Club). Plush rooms with servibars, a/c, satellite TV, etc., cost a steep US$92 s/d. The hotel has a pool, restaurant, coffee shop, and disco.

West End (Near Mexico 49): Motel Paraíso del Desierto (tel. 16-11-22), at Blvd. Independencia and Jiménez, is the motel equivalent of the downtown Palacio Real, offering spotless, modern rooms with a/c, refrigerators, satellite TV, and phones, plus a pool, security parking, and coin laundry, for US$77-83 s, US$80-88 d.

The friendly **Motel Campestre** (tel. 14-27-81, fax 14-07-43) is on Blvd. Miguel Alemán 251 Ote., next to a PEMEX station west out of town on Mexico 49/40. Technically speaking, this motel is within Gómez Palacio city limits, but it's actually closer to downtown Torreón. Rooms around a pool and parking lot are in the US$33-40 range.

RV Parks

RVers and campers may park their rigs in the **Motel Campestre** lot and pay a nominal fee for the use of showers in unoccupied rooms. See also the Gómez Palacio section in the Durango chapter for details on the Quinta Colina Trailer Park.

Food

Prosperous Torreón supports restaurants of every menu and budget. Many inexpensive and medium-priced eateries can be found along Av. Morelos between Hotel Río Nazas and Plaza de Armas, including the popular *cafetería* at **Benavides Farmacia,** just east of the Río Nazas at Av. Morelos and Calle Treviño. The Benavides menu features Mexican standards, inexpensive breakfasts, sandwiches, soups, and salads; it's open 7 a.m.-9 p.m. Another good spot for breakfast or an afternoon coffee is **La Copa de Leche** on Calle Carrillo a half block south of the Plaza de Armas.

The **Restaurant Naturista** on Av. Morelos between Calle L. Vicario and Calle Corona is a typical natural foods grocery with a small vegetarian cafe and bakery attached. Another good bakery—and one where you can get coffee as well as pastries (a rarity outside Mexico City)—is **Cafetería y Pastelería Star Cake** at Av. Hidalgo Pte. 274, three blocks south of Plazuela Juárez.

Eng Woo's is a decent and inexpensive Chinese restaurant on the north side of Av. Morelos between calles Blanco and Falcón. **Restaurant El Vitral,** on the south side of Av. Morelos between Blanco and Acuña, offers a good Mexican and continental menu in a semi-elegant atmosphere. **Restaurant El Cairo** at Av. Morelos 1011 between Acuña and Rodríguez serves slightly expensive Arabic food along with a few Mexican plates. For more upscale Chinese, try **El Dragón del Oro** opposite El Cairo.

Facing the east side of Alameda Zaragoza, on the corner of Calle D. Guerra (Calle 16) and Av. Morelos, **Pollos Santos** is a popular outdoor fried-chicken place that serves beer.

Cabritolandia Chilo, at the corner of Av. Matamoros and Calz. Colón, about four blocks east of Plazuela Juárez, specializes in *cabrito al pastor* (spit-roasted kid goat). **Restaurant La Majada,** on Blvd. Independencia at Calle 16, is an old standby for American-style steaks, *carne asada,* and *cabrito al pastor.*

Recreation

Bullfights: Corridas are periodically held at the **Plaza de Toros Torreón,** at Calle Blanco and Av. Simón Bolivar, northeast of Av. Independencia. The state tourist office should have a current schedule, or you could stop by the bullring itself for a look at posted schedules.

Festivals: The city's biggest annual celebration is the **Feria del Algodón y Uva** or "Cotton and Grape Fair," held each September (usually the second and third week of the month). Parades, exhibits, concerts, dances, and various other activities take place at different venues around town, although the main events are held at the Instalaciones de la Feria on the intersection of Periférico Norte and Mexico 30 on the northern outskirts of the city.

Radio: Torreón's radio station 96.3 FM is one of the most progressive stations in Northern Mexico, with a varied format of jazz, world music, and regional styles.

Information

Tourist Office: The state tourist office (tel. 17-16-98-88), at Calle Rodríguez 7401, distributes maps and brochures on Torreón and Coahuila.

Post Office: The city GPO is in the large, virtually unmarked Palacio Federal facing Av. Juárez between calles Corona and Galeana.

Transport

Air: Aero California (tel. 17-22-18-88; Blvd. Independencia 15 Ote.) has nonstop flights between Torreón and Ciudad Juárez, Durango, Tijuana, and Mexico City.

Aeroméxico (tel. 12-70-21; Blvd. Independencia 565 Ote.) flies direct to/from Chihuahua, Durango, Guadalajara, and Mexico City.

The lowest air fares are those published by **SARO** (tel. 800-83-224, airport), which flies daily to/from Culiacán, Mazatlán, Mexico City, and Monterrey; and by **Noroeste** (tel. 16-56-79, airport), with direct flights to/from Durango and Monterrey (and other northern cities via Durango).

Torreón's **Aeropuerto Internacional Francisco Sarabia** is right on the northeastern edge of town, about 15 minutes by car from the city center. Taxis cost US$10 from downtown Torreón, while *colectivos* are US$2.60 per person.

Bus: The modern **Central de Autobuses de Torreón** is near the eastern end of Av. Juárez off Av. Presidente Carranza. **Omnibus de México** and **Transportes del Norte** serve most large cities in Northern Mexico as well as Mexico City and Guadalajara. For inter-city travel within the state, **Transportes Frontera, Autobuses Blanco** and **Autobuses El Aguila** provide most bus services.

Around town, city buses ply main east-west avenues Revolución, Juárez, and Allende, and north-south Calle Ramos Arizpe, Calz. Colón, and Calz. Cuauhtémoc.

Train: The División del Norte trains arrive at and depart from the FNM railway station at the southern end of Calle Galeana (about five blocks south of Blvd. Revolución). This line runs from Ciudad Juárez to Mexico City; only second-class seats are available between Ciudad Juárez and Torreón. The fare is US$8 and the trip takes 14 hours. (For further details, see "Railway Schedule," pp. 86-87.)

Driving: Torreón is laid out like a large grid broken into partial grids separated by diagonal boulevards to form a large triangle (if this sounds confusing, it's nothing compared to the street configuration itself). Calz. Cuauhtémoc bisects the peak of the triangle formed by Blvd. Independencia and Diagonal (Blvd.) Reforma, while Blvd. Revolución forms the triangle's base. When driving across these diagonals from one "shard" of the triangle to another, it's very easy to

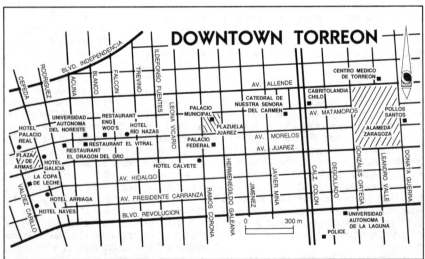

become lost. Keep a map handy; without one you're liable to spend an inordinate amount of time driving in angled circles.

Adding to the confusion is a system of one-way streets and a decided lack of signs pointing the way in or out of the city from Mexico 40 or 49. Remember that Calle Ramos Arizpe is the way out of the city toward Mexico 49 North (actually west at this point), while the way in (south/east) is via Calle M. Múzquiz one block west. Another hint: heading out of town toward Mexico 49, follow signs for "Durango" even if you're heading south (e.g., to Zacatecas). At the east end of town, accessing Mexico 40 East is somewhat easier. Use the *periférico* (bypass) that arches north over the city to go from Mexico 49 to Mexico 40.

Car Rental: Cars can be rented from travel agencies at the Palacio Real and Río Nazas hotels. Since Torreón doesn't get many tourists, rental volume is low and rates tend to be higher than average.

Fuel: Several PEMEX stations in Torreón pump Magna Sin.

VICINITY OF TORREON

Viesca
Set amid a desert oasis of sand dunes and date palms, Viesca (77 km/47.5 miles east of Torreón) looks like a scene plucked from *Beau Geste* or an Indiana Jones epic. *Datiles* (dates) are in fact a primary agricultural product of the area, along with cotton, corn, and wheat. The town itself has just over 3,400 inhabitants and was named for the first governor of the former Province of Coahuila y Texas, San José de Viesca y Bustamante.

Each July Viesca residents celebrate the **Feria Regional de Aniversario** in honor of the town's 1830 founding. No accommodations are available in Viesca but food is available from cafes off Av. Hidalgo (Mexico 40) and from vendors near the town plaza.

PARRAS DE LA FUENTE

Founded in 1578 as Santa María de las Parras, this town of 26,000 makes a convenient midway stopover on Mexico 40 between Torre-

ón (152 km/94 miles west) and Saltillo (146 km/90.5 miles east). Parras is known as the "cradle of North American viticulture," since the oldest winery on the continent (San Lorenzo) was founded here in 1626 and the area is still an important winemaking center. Parras's other claim to fame is that the republic's first president after the Mexican Revolution, Francisco I. Madero, was born here.

Sights And Activities
Madero's family home, **Recinto Madero** (at the corner of Calle 16 de Septiembre and Alameda del Rosario), has been turned into a small museum chronicling the revolutionary leader's life. More interesting perhaps is the **Museo del Vino,** which contains exhibits of the crushing, fermenting, and aging processes used in local winemaking. The museum is housed in the 300-year-old **Hacienda de Urdiñola,** a few km north of town off Coahuila 35, the road to La Paila. For those interested in wine culture, the best time of year to visit Parras is during the **Festival de la Vendimia** ("Vintage Festival"), which coincides with the annual grape harvest.

Wineries: Vinifera is cultivated in fields surrounding Parras, but in town several wineries maintain *bodegas* (storage and distribution facilities) where wines may be tasted and purchased:

- **Vinos Caseros Santo Madero**, Calle Ocampo near Fco. J. Mina
- **Bodega de Perote**, Av. Fco. I Madero, west end of town
- **Vinos Caseros Fuantos**, Calz. del Marqués north of Blvd. Tapia
- **El Vesubio**, Calle Ramos Arizpe and Benavides

Accommodations And Food
The town's least expensive hotel is the simple **Hotel Parras** (tel. 842-2-06-44), near the main plaza at the corner of calles Ramos Arizpe and Reforma, where rooms are around US$10-15. The three-star **Hotel Posada Santa Isabel** (tel. 2-05-72) on Calle Fco. I. Madero (a block west of the plaza) has comfortable, clean rooms for US$30-33 s/d.

Parras's most famous hostelry is the resort-style **Hotel Rincón del Montero** (tel. 2-05-40, fax 2-23-47; A.P. 37, Parras, Coah.), 22.5 km

(14 miles) south of Mexico 40 on Coahuila 125. Situated on 57 shady acres, the resort features a nine-hole golf course, tennis courts, horseback riding, a spring-fed pool, restaurant, bar, and spacious rooms with kitchenettes for US$68-80 per night. There are also 12 RV spaces with full hookups and showers available for US$15 per night.

Restaurant El Colonial (facing the south end of Plaza de Reloj on Calle Ramos Arizpe) and **Restaurant Maracay** (near Vinos Caseros Santo Madero) serve good *platillos típicos*.

Parras is famous for *dulces* (sweets) made from cactus fruit (*tuna*), nuts, and honey, and there are at least a half dozen *dulcerías* downtown. One of the most typical is **Dulcería Re-gionales Doña Gayita** at the corner of calles Ramos Arizpe and Arriaga.

Information
Parras has an informative state tourist office (tel. 842-2-08-76) at Km 4.5, Mexico 30 (north of town on the road to La Paila).

The telephone area code for Parras and immediate vicinity is 842.

Transport
Buses to Torreón and Saltillo leave frequently throughout the day from the main bus terminal downtown on Calle Ramos Arizpe (Mexico 40) near Calle M. Múzquiz.

BOB RACE

THE STATE OF NUEVO LEON

Of the five Northern Mexican states that border the U.S., Nuevo León is the smallest, with a 19-km (12-mile) sliver of border abutting Texas northwest of Laredo. With a literacy index above 95%, it has one of Mexico's top three most educated populations (along with the Federal District and Baja California), largely due to the influence of its state capital, Monterrey. In many ways the whole state is but a capital suburb, trading labor and raw materials for Monterrey money and initiative. Of 25 stockbrokers licensed in Mexico since 1975, 17 have been based in Nuevo León.

Under Spanish rule, the territory was called Nuevo Reino de León and was a colonial backwater devoted to cattle ranching. Hostile natives prevented regional development until the end of Spain's tenure in Mexico, after which the state had to deal with years of border disputes and war with the Republic of Texas and the U.S. before the industrialization of Monterrey at the turn of the century brought a sudden measure of prosperity.

Today most of the state's population is concentrated in the Monterrey metropolitan area, which includes the surrounding municipalities of San Nicolás de los Garza, San Pedro Garza García, Ciudad Guadalupe, Gen. Escobedo, Santa Catarina, and Apodaca. The state's second most populated region is the agricultural zone around Allende, Montemorelos, and Linares in the southeast. Currently the biggest producer of citrus in the nation, the Allende-Linares area is also a major source of sorghum, alfalfa, corn, wheat, cattle, pigs, and poultry.

MONTERREY AND VICINITY

The self-titled Sultana de Norte ("Sultan of the North") sits on the Río Santa Catarina flood plain, 539 meters (1,765 feet) above sea level and surrounded on all sides by distinctive peaks of the Sierra Madre Oriental. The saddlelike profile of **Cerro de la Silla** ("Saddle Hill")—often considered a symbol of the city—rises to the east; to the south is **Loma Larga** ("Long Slope"), to the west **Cerro de las Mitras** ("Bishop Hats Hill"), and to the north **Cerro del Topo Chico** ("Little Mole Hill").

Over the last century the city has become Mexico's industrial capital due to its strategic location at a mountain pass near the U.S. border; well-developed transport connections; access to petroleum, coal, natural gas, and other nearby natural resources; and its skilled and highly educated workforce. The city is also an important supply-and-market center for nearby ranching, agriculture, and poultry production, as well as the site of a large military base. Yet another important source of metropolitan revenue is the steady influx of tourists and investors from Texas. A new tollway has brought San Antonio within 4½ hours' drive instead of six.

According to Mexico's 1990 census (the next won't be out until 2000), 2.6 million people live in the Monterrey metro area; the city's chamber of commerce claims that the number tops out at three million. Either figure makes it the nation's third largest metro area after Mexico City and Guadalajara. Restricted to Monterrey city limits, the population numbers just over a million.

Often described as the nation's most forward-looking city, Monterrey has the country's largest number of colleges, universities and institutes of technology on a per capita basis and owns over 20% of Mexico's computers. Before the oil boom of the '70s, Monterrey also claimed an astonishing 25% of Mexico's GNP and nearly a third of its exports. With such a strong footing in the world of commerce, it's no surprise that the Partido Acción Nacional (PAN) has a firm grip on the city and surrounding state. Local workers belong to company-sponsored unions which provide inexpensive housing, daily commute transport, and a variety of leisure activities, from weekend baseball to beach vacations, making the average PRI-subsidized labor union look quite shabby by comparison.

Monterrey is also unique in its strict enforcement of local littering and seat-belt laws.

GLASS AND BEER

Two companies exemplify Monterrey's aggressive economy and demonstrate how Mexico is moving ahead with an updated international trade agenda. Vitro, a maker of glass and household appliances and one of the city's first major manufacturers, purchased failing American company Anchor Glass in 1989, introduced new (and more advanced) technology to the company, and turned it into a profit maker. More recently the firm has entered into equal-partner (not *maquila* or in-bond) ventures with Whirlpool, Ford, and Dow Corning to sell glass components to these companies. As a result, Vitro is now Mexico's largest industrial group (with $4.4 billion in assets) and the nation's first multinational; more than half its sales are in U.S. dollars.

Visa, a consortium owned by the Garza Sada clan, is doing so well with the Cervecería Cuauhtémoc and other endeavors that it was able to buy a major share in Bancomer (Mexico's second largest bank) in 1991. The company is in the process of modernizing barley cultivation, harvesting, and processing so that it can compete with the U.S. beer industry. The only thing protecting the current Mexican market from a U.S. beer invasion is high tariffs; with a drop in tariffs virtually guaranteed by the passage of NAFTA, Visa executives know Mexican beer doesn't stand a chance against the American giants unless production can be stepped up.

HISTORY

Monterrey was founded on the banks of the Río Santa Catarina in 1596 by a group of 700 Spaniards who had fled Mexico City because the Inquisition suspected them of adhering to Judaism—an offense then punishable by death. The settlers named the colony in honor of the Viceroy of Nueva España at the time, Gaspar de Zúñiga Acevedo, Conde de Monterrey.

Franciscan missionaries arrived in 1603 but had little success in converting the native Amerindian population, and by 1672 the colony had only 685 inhabitants. It wasn't until the beginning of the 18th century that the natives were sufficiently "pacified" to allow movement into the more fertile areas of the valley. After minerals were discovered in the surrounding mountains in 1715, trade with booming Zacatecas to the south increased, the population mushroomed to 3,000, and a Jesuit college was founded.

Monterrey's development, however, suffered a serious setback when a major flood in 1752 inundated the town and almost totally destroyed the fragile economy. Many Monterrey residents left for better climes in neighboring Tamaulipas, and the area was in danger of losing its entire population until the opening of nearby Mina de la Iguana in 1757 began attracting a new wave of settlers.

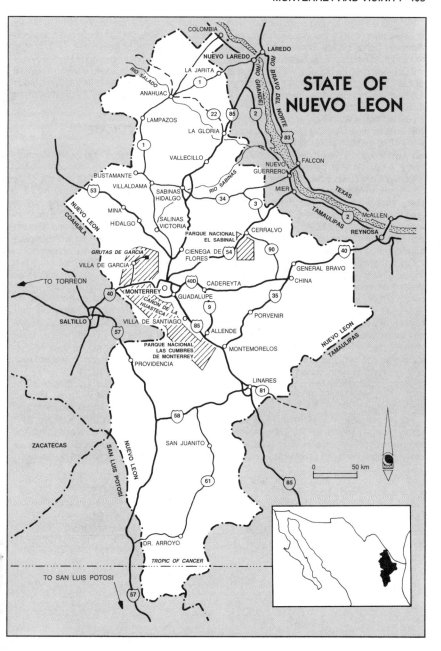

STATE OF
NUEVO LEON

COLOMBIA
LAREDO
NUEVO LAREDO
LA JARITA
RIO SALADO
ANAHUAC
RIO BRAVO DEL NORTE (RIO GRANDE)
22
85
2
LAMPAZOS
LA GLORIA
83
1
VALLECILLO
FALCON
NUEVO GUERRERO
TEXAS
BUSTAMANTE
VILLALDAMA
SABINAS HIDALGO
RIO SABINAS
MIER
53
NUEVO LEON
COAHUILA
34
3
TAMAULIPAS
2
McALLEN
MINA
HIDALGO
SALINAS VICTORIA
Parque Nacional EL SABINAL
CERRALVO
REYNOSA
GRUTAS DE GARCIA
CIENEGA DE FLORES
54
90
40
VILLA DE GARCIA
GENERAL BRAVO
TO TORREON
40D
CADEREYTA
CHINA
40
MONTERREY
GUADALUPE
CAÑON DE LA HUASTECA
9
35
PORVENIR
SALTILLO
VILLA DE SANTIAGO
85
ALLENDE
NUEVO LEON
TAMAULIPAS
57
Parque Nacional LAS CUMBRES DE MONTERREY
PROVIDENCIA
MONTEMORELOS
LINARES
81
58
0   50 km
ZACATECAS
SAN JUANITO
85
SAN LUIS POTOSI
NUEVO LEON
61
DR. ARROYO
TROPIC OF CANCER
TO SAN LUIS POTOSI
57

In 1792 a major turning point for the city's fortunes arrived with the establishment of a Monterrey bishop's office. The civic-minded second and third bishops, Fray Rafael José Verger and Don Ambrosio de Llanos y Valdés, arranged for the construction of a number of important public works, including an aqueduct to supply a steady water supply for the city.

Just as things were looking rosy for Monterrey, another major disaster struck in the shape of the 1836 partition of Texas from Mexico, an event which led to a drastic decline in local commerce. A decade later, before the city had time to recover from Texas independence, the Mexican-American War erupted. On Oct. 8, 1846, after a three-week battle in which the Mexicans used the Obispado as a fort, 6,200 U.S. troops under the command of Gen. Zachary Taylor took control of the city and remained as an occupation force until July 8, 1848.

Once the war was over and the U.S. had granted statehood to Texas, however, Monterrey wisely took advantage of its proximity to the world's largest economy as both endpoint and relay point for burgeoning U.S.-Mexico trade. If revenge was ever a Monterrey intention, it took form during the U.S. Civil War (1860-66), when Monterrey profited heavily from the traffic of supplies and armaments to the Confederacy (a rather ironic position, considering that Texas originally seceded from Mexico in part because slavery had been declared illegal in all Mexican territories).

The industrialization of Monterrey took place rapidly between 1882 and 1910. Using national and international (especially U.S.) capital, Monterrey entrepreneurs first constructed a railroad (1882) between Monterrey and the border, a major boost for U.S.-Mexico trade. Next they built one of the world's largest breweries (Cervecería Cuauhtémoc, 1890), a huge iron and steel foundry (Fundidora de Fierro y Acero Monterrey, 1901), a major cement plant (Fábrica de Cementos Hidalgo, 1906), and a state-of-the-art glass factory (Fábrica de Vidrios y Cristales, 1909, today Vitro). These four industries became the cornerstones of Monterrey's modern economy and remain so today.

After the Mexican Revolution, the city's population exploded, rising from 88,000 in 1920 to 333,000 by 1950, and exceeding 2.5 million 40 years later. In spite of its size, the city has the highest per capita standard of living in Mexico today; televisions (an admittedly one-sided measure) are in 60% of the homes. All indicators point to increasing prosperity for Monterrey residents, as the city has added banking, financial, and information services to its traditional industrial base with the intention of further diversifying the economy.

CLIMATE

Chamber of commerce and tourist literature published in Monterrey readily confess that when it comes to climate, this is a city of extremes. The mean temperature in July is 27.2° C (81° F), with daytime highs climbing into the 30s C (90s F), sometimes higher. The most uncomfortable months are August and September, when humidity rises along with temperatures. During these months the occasional inversion layer holds suspended particulate over Monterrey, and the surrounding mountains are cloaked in a haze.

If you plan to travel to Monterrey during the winter months, don't expect balmy weather. Though winters tend to be mild, the occasional *norte* blows across the Great Plains, down through Texas, and right into the Valle de Monterrey, forcing residents to don gloves and overcoats for a week or so at a time.

Monterrey's mean annual precipitation is 49.6 cm (19.5 inches). As in South Texas, May and September are typically the rainiest months.

In terms of weather, the best overall months to visit Monterrey are October, March, and April when it's usually dry, sunny, and temperate. Second best are May, June, and November.

SIGHTS

El Obispado (Bishop's Palace)
Construction of Monterrey's most striking prerevolutionary structure, at the west end of Av. Padre Mier, began in 1787 for a residence for Don Fray Rafael José Verger, the city's second bishop. Fray Rafael died before its completion in 1797, however, and the massive domed building was used as a service annex by the local diocese until 1819, when it was converted into military barracks. During the 1846 U.S. invasion, Mexican soldiers used it as a fort because of

its strategic hill position overlooking the city; Pancho Villa later made it his temporary headquarters during revolutionary campaigns in northeastern Mexico.

El Obispado was declared a Colonial Monument by the Mexican government in 1932 and now houses the **Museo Regional de Nuevo León.** Among the displays contained in the museum's eight rooms are a small collection of pre-Hispanic artifacts from northeast Mexico, an exhibit on the Spanish hacienda era, 18th- and 19th-century religious art (mostly of local provenance), and exhibits on Mexican independence and the 1910-20 revolution, focusing on roles played by Nuevo León citizens.

The museum is open Tues.-Sat. 10 a.m.-1 p.m. and 3-6 p.m., Sun. 10 a.m.-5 p.m.; admission is US$3.30 Mon.-Sat., free on Sunday. Even if you're not interested in the museum, El Obispado's grounds are worth visiting for views over the city. Laid out along the slopes below the Bishop's Palace is **Colonia Obispado,** a neighborhood of huge mansions built in the '40s and '50s.

Catedral De Monterrey
Facing Plaza Zaragoza (the south end of the Gran Plaza), the Monterrey Cathedral is similar in overall design to the cathedral in Saltillo, with an ornate, late baroque facade flanked by two towers of asymmetric height. Construction began in 1770 under Franciscan supervision, and the main structure—including the facade—was completed in 1791. The shorter clock tower was added in 1817 (the clock itself, made in Mexico City, dates to 1786), and the neoclassical bell tower was fashioned in 1899. Cathedral status was bestowed in 1833.

The somewhat austere cruciform interior contains several altars and 19th-century religious paintings. The lower section of the main altar is adorned with a mural painted by Mexican muralist Angel Zárraga in 1945. Depicting the life of the Virgin Mary, this is one of the few public works of art that Zárraga—who was quite popular in France and Spain—executed in Mexico.

Barrio Antiguo
Behind the Catedral de Monterrey, the "Old Neighborhood" consists of 15 blocks bordered by Río Santa Catarina along the south, Calle Dr. Coss to the west, Calle Matamoros to the north, and Calle Naranjo to the east. Representing the best-preserved parcel of 18th- and early 19th-century architecture in the city, the colonial-style casas here are a mix of residences, warehouses, art studios, and antique shops—Monterrey's equivalent of Manhattan's Soho. During summer, the city sponsors live outdoor music and theater in the neighborhood.

Along with the Bishop's Palace and the cathedral, one of the most impressive examples of viceregal architecture in Monterrey is the Barrio Antiguo's **Casa del Campesino** at Calle Mina 1101 between Ocampo and Abasolo (three blocks east of the cathedral). Originally built as a residence for the governor of Nuevo Reino de León (Nuevo León's former provincial name) around 1750, it was converted into the city's first hospital in 1791 and is now used by various agrarian organizations. The building covers an entire city block, surrounding three patios with high-ceilinged rooms in the typical colonial style. The largest room in the building, a neogothic auditorium, contains a classic Mexican revolutionary mural painted in the 1920s.

El Obispado

19th- And 20th-Century Architecture

With its modern glass-and-steel skyscrapers and neat suburban tract homes, Monterrey looks more like a North American city than any other city in Mexico. Even the city's 19th-century downtown has U.S. roots, due to the prominence of the work of architect Alfred Giles. Though born in London in 1853, Giles immigrated to the U.S. and established his career in San Antonio, Texas.

During the 1890s, at the beginning of Monterrey's industrialization, Giles was contracted to design the **Banco Mercantil** (corner of Morelos and Zaragoza), **Edificio La Reynera** (Morelos and Parás), **Casino Monterrey** (Zuazua and

Abasolo), **Arco de la Independencia** (Av. Pino Suárez and Calz. Madero), and the house of Don Joel Rocha (today the **Centro Cultural de Monterrey,** Av. Padre Mier 545), as well as many other buildings that have since been razed. Designed in beaux arts style, these elegant turn-of-the-century buildings are quite similar to architecture found in downtown San Antonio, several of which were also Giles endeavors.

Moving west from the downtown area (toward the Obispado) and chronologically into the 20th century, the *colonias* (neighborhoods) of **Mirador** (built in the '20s) and **María Luisa** ('30s-'50s) contain many *neocolonial* (the Mexi-

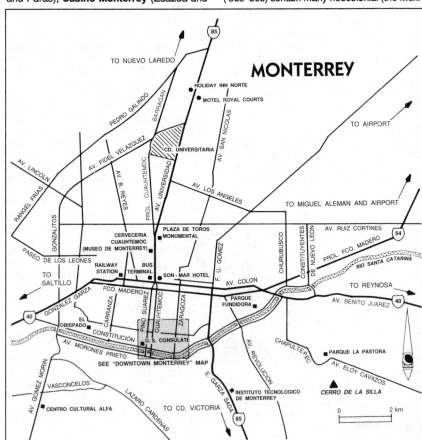

can term for Victorian and Georgian styles) houses that could have been taken from any number of cities in the southeastern United States.

Southwest of downtown Monterrey, the newer **Del Valle** district (part of **San Pedro de Garza García,** the wealthiest municipality in all of Mexico) has drawn its inspiration from Texas and the U.S. Southwest with modern, boxy, flat-roofed homes mixed with peaked-roof two-story bungalows, often with Chevy/GMC Suburbans parked in their driveways. In Monterrey this housing style is sometimes referred to as "neo-McAllen" (a descriptor that raises the south Texas city's architectural status considerably). Except for the preponderance of surrounding trees, the rows of satellite dishes sprouting from virtually every rooftop make residential Del Valle look like a satellite tracking station at first glance; Calz. Del Valle, the main avenue through the district, could almost pass for a Dallas suburb.

Gran Plaza

Sometimes referred to as "Macroplaza" for its size, the Gran Plaza actually joins several smaller plazas and parks into a lengthy north-south pedestrian corridor running parallel to calles Zuazua and Zaragoza from Av. 5 de Mayo to the river. Carried out between 1980 and 1985, the project severed several east-west avenues, including Morelos, Padre Mier, Matamoros, Ramón, and 15 de Mayo.

At the south end of the plaza toward the river looms the huge, concrete-and-glass **Nuevo Palacio Federal,** built in 1973. Just north of the federal building is the oldest plaza section, **Plaza Zaragoza,** flanked by the cathedral and Barrio Antiguo to the east, and the 19th-century downtown to the west. Opposite Calle Ocampo from the cathedral, the relatively new **Museo de Arte Contemporáneo de Monterrey** (see the separate MARCO entry for a description) faces the 1930s **Círculo Mercantil Mutualista** and modern **Condominio Acero** on the west side of the plaza; together with the Nuevo Palacio Federal, the three buildings form a wall of concrete, glass, and steel around the south end of the Gran Plaza.

In the middle of this end of the plaza stands a 70-meter-high, 12.5-meter-wide, 1.8-meter-deep vertical slab known as the **Faro del Comercio** ("Lighthouse of Commerce"). Designed by cele-brated Mexican architects Luis Barragán and Raúl Ferrera, the structure was erected in 1984 as part of the ambitious Gran Plaza project and is the tallest monument in the country. A green laser beam projected from the top of the red, prismatic tower focuses on different city symbols, including El Obispado, Cerro de la Silla, and the Palacio de Gobierno. Beneath this section of the Gran Plaza is a subterranean shopping center and parking lot.

Northward, about halfway up the plaza on the east side, the **Teatro de la Ciudad** is one of Mexico's premier theatrical venues. Facing the theater on the opposite side of the plaza is the huge, angular **Torre Administrativa,** built in 1984 as headquarters for the state congress and other state government bodies. On the plaza between the Teatro de la Ciudad and Torre Administrativa, the simple **Parque Hundido** offers passersby a retreat from the sharp angles and glaring surfaces of modern Monterrey with trees, benches, modern sculptures, and a fountain.

Farther north in the plaza is the **Explanada de los Heroes,** a large, empty square flanked by stone fountains and balustrades decorated with urns and masks in the Greek style. Monuments to revolutionary heroes Juan Zuazua, Antonio Villareal, Pablo González, Benito Juárez, and Miguel Hidalgo y Costilla break up the space toward the north end. The plaza ends at the impressive turn-of-the-century **Palacio de Gobierno.**

Basílica De La Purísima

Designed by renowned Mexican architect Enrique de la Mora, this church is considered one of the most significant modern religious structures in Mexico if not all of Latin America. A 19th-century *templo* on the site was demolished in 1942 to make way for Mora's 1946 project, which is based on a system of parabolic shells—a technique now copied around the world.

The slender, 43-meter bell tower bears a terra-cotta sculpture of the Immaculate Conception executed by sculptor Adolfo Laubner in 1946 and fired by the famous Ladrillos Monterrey brickworks. It is purportedly the largest terra-cotta sculpture on the American continent. The church's three facades feature 15-meter parabolic arches surmounted by onyx window frames. The striking bronze *Christ and the apos-*

tles sculpture over the principal facade was done by German sculptor Herbert Hoffman Ysenbourg.

During the day, the interior of the church is bathed in natural light filtered through modern stained glass windows fashioned by Mexican, German, and American artists. Modern religious paintings of the Virgin of Guadalupe, San Felipe, the Four Evangelists, Santa Teresita, and others hang on the walls.

Sitting on the main altar is the most sacred religious image in Monterrey, the **Virgen Chiquita** or "Little Virgin." A crude wooden image standing only 17 cm (6.6 inches) high, the Virgen Chiquita was originally housed in a small chapel (on the same site as the current basilica) built by a Tlaxcalteca woman known as "La Zapatera" (the "Shoemaker") in the mid-1700s. According to legend, the great flood of 1756 receded from the city when La Zapatera brandished the little image before the floodwaters. During his 1990 visit to Mexico, Pope John Paul II bestowed sainthood on the Virgen Chiquita, thereby officially recognizing the miracle.

The basilica is on the corner of Av. Hidalgo Pte. and Serafín Peña, west of Av. Pino Suárez. Barrio de la Purísima, the surrounding neighborhood, dates to the turn of the century and features many neoclassical-style residences known for their conservative inhabitants.

Basílica Del Roble

Another church associated with a mythic holy image, the Basílica del Roble is at Calle Juárez and 15 de Mayo, a few blocks south of the Mercado Juárez. According to legend, in 1592 Franciscan Padre Andrés de León came upon an oak tree (*roble*) that bore an image of the Virgin Mary on its trunk. Believing it to be an omen, he founded a mission nearby; the settlement of Monterrey was established four years later. In 1853 the Iglesia del Roble was built on the spot, and in 1963 it was given basilica status. To many Monterreienses it is the city's "mother church" because of its associations with the founding of the city.

The church resembles a Roman temple in design, with a peaked roof and portico supported by marble-tiled columns. A colorful mosaic over the main door depicts the legend of the Virgen de Roble ("Virgin of the Oak Tree"). Inside are three large, column-supported naves;

the main altar is crowned by an ornate bronze *baldaquín* (altar canopy) similar to those found in Italian basilicas.

Museo De Arte Contemporáneo De Monterrey (MARCO)

This US$11 million museum, designed by Mexican architect Ricardo Legorreta, opened in 1991. Set around a central courtyard, the two-story building contains a permanent collection of contemporary Mexican and Latin American art, plus traveling exhibits. The MARCO shop carries a very good collection of books on Mexican art, plus a few posters and quality handicrafts. Also on the premises are a *cafetería* and courtyard cafe.

The museum faces the east side of the Gran Plaza at Zuazua and Ocampo. Hours are Tues., Thurs., Fri., Sat. 11 a.m.-7 p.m., Wed. and Sun. till 9 p.m., Mon. closed. Admission is US$3.30 for adults, US$1.50 for children 6-12, free for students and children under 6; Wednesday admission is free for everyone. For further information call 83-42-48-20.

Museo De Monterrey And Salón De Fama (Cervecería Cuauhtémoc)

The original brick warehouse of the Cervecería Cuauhtémoc on Av. Universidad Nte. and Av. Luis Mora has been converted into an art museum containing exhibits of contemporary art by Latin American artists. The museum's collection of over a thousand works includes such masterpieces as "El Maizal" by Gerardo Murillo, "El Grande de España" by Diego Rivera, "El Lanceado" by José Clemente Orozco, and "La Mujer Dormida" by David Alfaro Siqueiros. Temporary exhibits have featured works by Henry Moore, Giacometti, Frida Kahlo, Rufino Tamayo, Picasso, and other superstars of the Latino art world. Two large copper brewing vats hang through the museum's upper floor, the only beer-related exhibit. A cafe on the upper floor offers coffee and snacks. The museum is open Tues.-Sat. 9:30 a.m.-9:30 p.m., Sun. 9:30 a.m.-8 p.m. Admission is free.

Outside the warehouse, in a shaded corner of the grounds, is a pleasant outdoor beer garden that's open in warm weather. In a small cement, steel, and glass structure in the west section of the grounds is the **Salón de Fama,** Monterrey's Sports Hall of Fame. One room is dedicated entirely to the evolution of Mexican baseball, while two other rooms contain trophies, uniforms, autographed pictures, and other artifacts from a variety of sports played in Mexico. Hours are Tues.-Fri. 8:30 a.m.-6:00 p.m., Sat.-Sun. 10:30 a.m.-5:30 p.m.; admission is free.

The Museo de Monterrey is within walking distance of the "Cuauhtémoc" Metro station.

Museo De História De Nuevo León

Housed in a striking, 1818-vintage building next to the Hotel Monterrey Clarion on Zaragoza, this historical museum was inaugurated in 1989 and contains various exhibits on the historical and cultural evolution of Northeastern Mexico. Artifacts on display range from the pre-Hispanic era to Monterrey's period of industrialization. One room is also set aside for temporary displays of painting, sculpture, and other visual arts.

Hours are Tues.-Sun. 10 a.m.-6 p.m.; admission is free.

Centro Cultural Alfa

Located in posh San Pedro Garza García, the Centro Cultural Alfa is funded by the nonprofit arm of an industrial consortium and devoted to expositions of the sciences. The complex's most striking architectural feature is the Pabellón El Universo or "Universe Pavilion," a building in the shape of a huge, toppling cylinder. Among the facilities are an exploratorium-type exhibit, planetarium, aquarium, aviary, garden containing pre-Cortesian art, and Omnimax theater. For the most part, the offerings are oriented toward children rather than adults.

The center is open Tues.-Fri. 3-9 p.m., Sat. 2-9 p.m., and Sun. 12-9:30 p.m. Admission is US$4 per person. Occasionally the center sponsors morning and evening events with different hours and admission charges.

To reach the CCA from downtown Monterrey, follow Av. de la Constitución west along the river to Av. Gómez Morín and turn south (left), then continue on Av. Gómez Morín to Av. Roberto Garza Sada; the CCA is left on R.G. Sada (look for the Pabellón El Universo). Free shuttle buses to the CCA are provided from the Alameda on Av. Pino Suárez in the city center every hour Tues.-Fri. and every half-hour Sat.-Sunday.

Instituto Tecnológico De Monterrey

A group of local engineers led by Don Eugenio Garza Sada founded this citadel of higher education in 1943, and it soon distinguished itself for academic excellence in Mexico. Among the campus buildings is the boldly designed 1988 **Edificio de Tecnología Avanzada** (Advanced Technology Building), which consists of two eight-story wings linked by a lower three-story building and "tilted" in opposite directions so that they form a 60° angle between them—purportedly a reflection of the Cerro de la Silla and a modern representation of a classic Mesoamerican ceremonial motif. From a distance they look like half-toppled skyscrapers.

ITM is now the mother campus for the Instituto Tecnológico de Estudios Superiores (ITESM), a system with 26 campuses in 25 cities around Mexico with a total enrollment of 48,000 (the Monterrey campus enrolls around 1,500). The campus also participates in visiting scholar/professor programs with 27 foreign universities. ITM's strongest programs are in engineering, business administration, "informatics" (computer science), food sciences, natural sciences, and

Instituto Tecnológico de Monterrey

BOB RACE

education. Since 1990, ITESM has developed a system of "hallmark courses" designed to balance the sciences with studies in the humanities for the purpose of developing values, improving communication skills, and fostering a "spirit of enterprise."

Among other sports programs, ITM sponsors a collegiate American-style football team, the Borregos (Bighorn Sheep).

ITM is southeast of the Río Santa Catarina and city center off Av. E. Garza Sada.

Cintermex

One of the largest facilities of its kind in Latin America, the Centro Internacional de Negocios Monterrey (International Trade Center of Monterrey), also known as Cintermex, was inaugurated by Pres. Carlos Salinas in 1991 following the signing of the North American Free Trade Agreement. In addition to 40,000 square meters of first-class exhibit space, the center contains a section with posh retail shops, a bank, and secretarial services.

City officials and local investors hope that, in the wake of NAFTA, rapidly increasing trade will make Cintermex an important focus of Mexican national and international trade.

Cintermex is in the Parque Fundidora, east of the city center via Av. F.I. Madero. The "Parque Fundidora" Metro station is within easy walking distance.

MONTERREY ACCOMMODATIONS

Budget

Several of the city's least expensive hotels are found in the general vicinity of the busy intersection of Av. Colón and Av. Universidad, near the bus and train stations. This location is also convenient to the "Cuauhtémoc" Metro station and the Museo de Monterrey (Cervecería Cuauhtémoc), as well as city bus lines to anywhere in the city. None of these hotels have parking lots, so they're more practical for visitors using public transport than for the self-propelled.

Three on Calle Amado Nervo (two blocks west of, and parallel to, Av. Pino Suárez) that cost US$23-28 for decent rooms with private bath include **Hotel Amado Nervo** (tel. 83-72-35-90) at No 1110, **Hotel Nuevo León** (tel. 74-19-00) at the corner of Calz. Madero, and—best

of the bunch—the well-kept and quiet **Hotel Posada** (tel. 72-39-08) at No. 1138 (Amado Nervo and Reforma).

Along the same street is the cheaper (US$18-20) but spartan **Hotel Virreyes** (tel. 74-66-10) at Calle Amado Nervo 902 Norte. Nearby at Av. Universidad 1114 Nte., **Hotel America** (tel. 74-18-20) has plain but not-very-quiet rooms in the same price range.

Least expensive of all is the **Villa Deportiva Juvenil** (tel. 43-08-08), a 400-bed hostel in the Parque Fundidora near Cintermex on Av. Madero Antiguo (east of downtown). The cost is US$4 per night per bed; as always, you must have an International Hostelling (AYH/IYH) membership or be willing to sign up on the spot to be admitted. Downtown Monterrey is only 10-15 minutes west of the hostel by city bus or Metro (use the "Parque Fundidora" Metro station).

Medium-priced Hotels

In the US$45-60 range are several good hotel choices, including some that are in or near the Zona Rosa—the shopping/eating/hotel district west of the Gran Plaza. The top choice here is **Hotel Colonial** (tel. 83-43-67-91), an older building in the heart of the Zona Rosa at the corner of Av. Hidalgo and a small fountain plaza. Rated at three stars, all rooms are clean and offer a/c, TV, phones, and carpeting for US$45 s, US$48 d; a parking lot is attached to the hotel and you'll find a restaurant downstairs. Be sure to book ahead for this popular hotel.

El Paso Autel (tel. 40-06-90, fax 44-46-47), about a dozen blocks north of the Zona Rosa at Calle Zaragoza 901 Nte. (at Calle R. Martínez), is a clean, well-run place with a/c, TV, pool, restaurant, and basement parking for US$40-45 s/d.

About the same distance west of the Zona Rosa, near the Basílica de la Purísima, is the equally pleasant and similarly priced **Hotel Los Reyes** (tel. 43-61-68), Av. Hidalgo 543 Poniente. Facilities include a restaurant-bar and ample parking.

The reliable, five-story **Son-Mar Hotel** (tel. 75-44-00, fax 72-50-77) at Av. Colón and Av. A. Reyes Nte., quite near the "Cuauhtémoc" Metro and main bus stations, has large a/c rooms for US$35-45 and a restaurant-bar; parking is available. Also in this general vicinity, **Hotel Jandal**

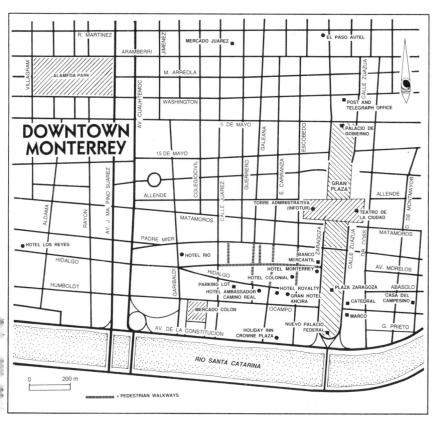

DOWNTOWN
MONTERREY

0   200 m

‖‖‖‖‖‖‖‖‖ = PEDESTRIAN WALKWAYS

(tel. 72-46-06) at Av. Cuauhtémoc 825 Nte. (between Arteaga and Salazar) has small but pleasant rooms with a/c and satellite TV for US$32-40, plus attached restaurant and parking. Also along Av. Colón but on the other side of Av. Pino Suárez closer to the bus and railway terminals, the seven-story **Fastos Hotel** (tel. 72-32-50) has modern a/c rooms in the US$45-50 range. Night owls may like the Fastos for its 24-hour restaurant.

South of the "Cuauhtémoc" Metro station at Calle Jiménez 1120 Nte. (east of, and parallel to, Av. Cuauhtémoc) is the modern, no-frills **Hotel Soles** (tel. 75-25-83) with a/c rooms and parking for US$35-38.

The cozy **Hotel Royalty** (tel. 40-28-00, fax 40-58-12), squeezed between the lofty Ambassador and Ancira hotels in the Zona Rosa at

Av. Hidalgo 402 Ote., straddles the gap between medium-priced and luxury hotels at US$66 s/d for rooms with all the amenities.

Also stretching the upper end of this price range is the pink, three-story **Hotel Royal Courts** (tel. 76-20-17, fax 76-27-10), at Av. Universidad 314 Nte. near the Ciudad Universitaría in the northern part of the city. Comfortable rooms with cable TV, a/c, heating, and phones cost US$54-70 s, US$66-80 d. Facilities include parking and a heated pool.

Farther north, off Mexico 85 at Km 15.5 (just south of the Infotur office and Saltillo bypass), the comfortable, motel-style **Hotel Nueva Castilla** (tel. 76-67-70) has rooms with a/c, heat, phones, and satellite TV around a parking lot and pool for US$40-55.

In Parque Chipinque, atop Meseta de Chipinque overlooking southwestern Monterrey, **Motel Chipinque** (tel. 78-11-00) offers recently renovated rooms with satellite TV for US$50-60; facilities include restaurant, pool, and tennis courts.

Luxury Hotels

Three of Monterrey's hotels have earned *gran turismo* ratings, while six boast five-star ratings, more than any other city in Northern Mexico. Although tourists make up a significant portion of the guests at these hotels, the majority are business travelers. Because most business travel takes place during the week, all of the hotels listed below run regular weekend specials with discounts of 40-50% below rack rates. To get the best rates, always ask about possible discount programs; even during the week you should be able to get a "corporate" discount.

Starting at a mere five stars, the stately and historic **Gran Hotel Ancira** (tel. 83-45-75-75; 800-333-3333 in the U.S./Canada; fax 83-44-52-56) at Av. Hidalgo and Escobedo (a block east of the Ambassador) was built in 1911 in the beaux-arts style and augmented in 1952 in the then-fashionable "Streamline" (California deco) style. A local anecdote featuring this hotel tells how Pancho Villa, upon arrival in Monterrey with his troops during the Mexican Revolution, entered the spacious Ancira lobby on horseback—one of the deeds that no doubt helped earn him the epithet "Centaur of the North." At the moment operated by the Radisson chain, Ancira's elegant rooms come with a/c, heat, satellite/video TV, and phones, and cost US$75-85 s/d.

The imposing **Hotel Monterrey Clarion** (tel. 43-52-20; 800-221-2222 in the U.S./Canada; fax 44-73-78) faces the Gran Plaza at the corner of Zaragoza and Morelos. Rooms with the usual five-star amenities cost US$100 s/d; some have better views of the plaza than others. **Hotel Río** (tel. 44-90-40, fax 45-14-56), at Av. Padre Mier and Garibaldi a few blocks northwest of the Zona Rosa, has similar rates and facilities; it's popular with tour groups from Texas.

For location and service, Monterrey's best *gran turismo* is **Hotel Ambassador Camino Real** (tel. 42-20-40, fax 45-19-84) at Av. Hidalgo 310 Ote. in the Zona Rosa. Spacious, international-class rooms with a/c, heating, refrigerators, satellite/video TV, and 24-hour room service cost US$100-135 s/d during the week, around US$60 on weekends. Hotel facilities include security valet parking, heated pool, indoor tennis court, health club, two restaurants, coffee shop, and bar.

Around the corner, between Hotel Colonial and Sanborn's, is the subdued **Santa Rosa Suites Hotel** (tel. 42-42-22, fax 42-33-44), a quiet, executive-oriented place where spacious junior suites with all the amenities are US$130-150 per night (rack rate). On the small plaza opposite Santa Rosa Suites, the new **Howard Johnson Plaza Suites** is currently under construction; rates will probably be similar.

Hotel Fiesta Americana Monterrey (tel. 63-30-30, fax 63-42-07) is a landmark unto itself at Av. Vasconcelos 300 Ote. near the junction with Lázaro Cárdenas, not far from the Centro Cultural Alfa in the San Agustín neighborhood of San Pedro Garza García. This huge, modern hotel has the largest number of rooms in Monterrey, with the usual international-class amenities plus a heated indoor pool, outdoor tennis court, spacious public areas, and courtyard with waterfall. Regular rates are US$155 s/d.

At last pass, the Holiday Inn chain (91-800-00-999 toll free in Mexico) had three properties in Monterrey. Rated at five stars and costing US$100 per night, **Holiday Inn Monterrey Norte** (tel. 76-65-66), at Av. Universidad 101 Nte. (on the north side of the city toward Mexico 85), features rooms with a/c, refrigerators, satellite/video TV, and phones, plus a pool, two lighted tennis courts, and a free airport shuttle (most hotels in Monterrey charge a fee for airport transport). The recently renovated **Holiday Inn Crowne Plaza** (tel. 19-60-00, fax 44-30-07), downtown at Av. Constitución 300 Ote., has five-star rooms with the usual amenities, plus a heated indoor pool, outdoor tennis court, health club, and disco for US$100-110 per night. Rumor has it this hotel may soon be taken over by Fiesta Americana.

In the exclusive Contry residential neighborhood close to ITM, the newish, four-star **Holiday Inn Express** (tel./fax 29-60-00) at Av. E. Garza Sada offers pleasant modern-colonial architecture and rooms with all the amenities (and balconies) for US$75-85 per night. Rates include a complimentary breakfast every morning and complimentary beer in the early evening.

RV Parks

Hotel Nueva Castilla (see "Medium-priced Hotels," above) has a number of spaces with electrical/water hookups for RVs, campers, or trailers at US$13 per night for two people, US$1 each additional person.

Bahía Escondida Resort (tel. 83-85-11-12), 36 km (22 miles) south of Monterrey on Presa Rodrigo Gómez (commonly called "Presa de la Boca") near Santiago, has electrical/water hookups for US$10 per night, plus a restaurant, tennis courts, and barbecue grills. Normally the resort is open only to members, but if there is space they will usually accept nonmember RVers.

FOOD

As you would expect from Mexico's third largest city, Monterrey has a wide variety of restaurants and cafes. Nuevo León is prime ranching country, so local specialties include many beef dishes. Among the most typical are *agujas asadas a las brasas* (charcoal-broiled spare ribs), *machacada con huevos* (dried beef, eggs, and *salsa picante* mixed together and served with flour tortillas), *carne soasada* (dried meat marinated in lime juice, baked till it turns a golden hue, and served as an appetizer or snack), and *cortadillo norteño* (cuts of beef stewed in a spicy tomato sauce).

Many vendors and small restaurants specialize in Monterrey-style *tacos al carbón* (often simply called *taquitos*), a plate of small, open corn tortillas topped with shredded *carne asada* and served with a variety of salsas; a local theme for several *taquito* restaurants revolves around waitresses and cooks dressed as *monjas* or Catholic nuns! In the Zona Rosa a section of Av. Hidalgo has been turned into an open pedestrian mall where several taco stands are open nightly.

Goat also occupies a special place in Nuevo León cuisine, and the classic *cabrito al pastor* (kid goat roasted over mesquite coals) is found in many Monterrey restaurants.

Burgers, fried chicken, and other fast food are amply available at U.S. franchises like **Carl's Jr.** (Colonia Del Valle, Colonia Contry), **Burger King** (Las Torres, Colonia Villa los Pinos), **Kentucky Fried Chicken** (13 locations, including Alameda, Cuauhtémoc, Cumbres,

Tecnológico, San Agustín, Centro, Del Valle, Madero, Contry), **Wendy's** (Zona Rosa, Del Valle, Cintermex), and **McDonald's** (Zona Rosa, Galerías Monterrey, Gómez Morí, Del Valle, Tecnológico).

Those on a tight budget will find the cheapest eats downtown at the huge *lonchería* section in the west end of **Mercado Colón**, at avenidas Juárez and Constitución. **Mercado Juárez** (ten blocks north at Av. Juárez and Aramberri) also has a substantial collection of *loncherías*.

Though many hotels offer bottled or filtered water, the tap water in metropolitan Monterrey is considered quite potable.

Regional

$$ **Restaurant Avenida** (tel. 83-51-09-61), Av. Los Angeles 412 Ote., San Nicolás de los Garza. Well northeast of the city center, this *cabrito* house is worth a mention since it serves *pollo al carbón* (charcoal-grilled chicken) as well as goat and *carne al carbón*.

$$ **Restaurant Los Castores** (tel. 46-29-39), Calle Gonzalitos 325 Sur. Los Castores specializes in *machacada con huevos* and other local-style *almuerzos*, plus *carnes al carbón* and *cabrito*.

$$ **Chivito** (tel. 75-77-25), Zaragoza and Treviño, north of the Alameda. At least 15 different restaurants in the city serve almost nothing but *cabrito*, but this is one of the only places with nightly live music. Besides *cabrito al pastor*, regional *botanas* (snacks) are also a specialty. Open daily noon-midnight.

$$ **Restaurant El Pastor del Norte.** This no-frills eatery is thought by many to serve the best *cabrito al pastor* in the city. *Carne asada* is also on the menu. There are two locations: Calz. Madero Pte. and Av. A. Reyes (tel. 74-04-80), and Calz. Madero Pte. and Av. S. Bolivar (tel. 46-89-54). Both are west of Av. Cuauhtémoc and open daily noon-midnight.

$$ **El Rey de Cabrito** (tel. 45-32-32), Av. Constitución 817 Ote., at Calle Dr. Coss (behind MARCO). This three-story restaurant convenient to the Zona Rosa and Gran Plaza is another strong contender for the local *cabrito* crown. Open daily, noon-midnight.

$ **Las Monjitas,** Calle Galeana 1018, off Hidalgo pedestrian mall, Zona Rosa. One of the better *taquito* places with staff dressed as nuns. There's even a church bell near the entrance for customers to ring as they enter. Nearby on Hidalgo is the similar **La Parroquía.**

$$-$$$ El Tio Restaurante (tel. 46-28-18), Av. Hidalgo and México, Colonia Obispado. In business since the 1930s, this colorful, colonial-style place has a garden dining area with trees, fountains, and waterfall, and is one of the best places in the city for an introduction to regional cooking. House specialties include *carne asada, cabrito al pastor,* and *fritada de cabrito,* but there are also Mexican standards and international dishes on the menu. Open daily 1 p.m.-midnight.

National

$$ Cenaduría San Marcos (tel. 83-78-97-97), Av. Bosques del Valle 110, Plaza Londres, near Alfa Cultural Center in the Garza García district. *Pozole* (hominy soup) and other *antojitos* are *muy típico* in this indoor-outdoor place. Open daily 7 a.m.-midnight.

$$ Restaurant La Fe Palenque (tel. 45-13-47), Av. Morones Prieto 2525, a kilometer east of Av. Gonzalitos. Nightly mariachis, folkloric dancing, and cockfights are the main draw at this festive amphitheater-style restaurant serving standard *platillos mexicanos.* Open daily 1 p.m-1 a.m.; shows begin at 5 p.m.

$$ La Fonda de San Miguel (tel. 42-96-87), Av. Morelos 924 Oriente. A casual restaurant-bar in the Barrio Antiguo that specializes in *botanas.* Open daily noon-midnight.

$$ El Jardín, Calle Ocampo at Plaza Zaragoza. Also in the Barrio Antiguo, this little courtyard restaurant close to MARCO is a nice place for drinks and Mexican *antojitos;* the art on the walls is for sale. Open daily 11 a.m.-11 p.m.

$$-$$$ El Molino Restaurante (tel. 56-56-12), Av. Bosques del Valle 110, Colonia Bosques del Valle. This somewhat upscale Mexican restaurant in an old house with high ceilings serves such creative dishes as *crepas de flor de calabaza* (squash-flower crepes), *pulpos al ajillo* (octopus in garlic sauce), and *huachinango a la tikin-chik* (Yucatán-style red snapper). Several regional dishes, such as *agujas norteñas* (Northern-style short ribs) and *cabrito,* are also on the menu. *Mangos al tequila* is one of several tasty desserts. Open daily 1 p.m.-midnight.

$-$$ Plazuela de los Antojitos, Centro Comercial Galerías Monterrey, Av. González Garza. In one wing of this huge mall in western Monterrey is a reasonably priced food court with several vendors selling Mexican food. Open daily 11 a.m.-8 p.m.

International

$$ La Cabaña Regiomontana (tel. 83-42-48-13), Calle Matamoros 318 Poniente. Originally opened in 1953, this is a favorite local venue for a broad cross-section of Monterrey residents. In spite of the restaurant's name, the menu features a range of moderately priced continental, North American, and Mexican dishes. Open Sun.-Thurs. 11 a.m.-1 a.m., weekends 11 a.m.-2 a.m.; live music 2-5 p.m. daily.

$$-$$$ Das Bierhaus. This popular chain serves German standards in a beer-hall ambience at six locations, the most conveniently located of which include: Calle Escobedo 580 Sur, Centro; Av. Hidalgo and Rayon, Centro; Av. Revolución 800 Sur, Colonia Contry; Av. E. Garza Sada 2408, near ITM.

$$-$$$ Restaurant Luisiana (tel. 43-15-61), Av. Hidalgo 530 Ote., Zona Rosa. A Monterrey institution close to the Ancira, Monterrey, and Ambassador hotels, the Luisiana combines reliable continental and North American cuisine with impeccable service and an elegant decor. Open daily noon-midnight except Christmas Day and New Year's Day.

Coffee Shops

No-nonsense, American-style *cafeterías* have become an institution in Monterrey. Four chains—Sanborn's, Benavides, VIP's, and Martin's—dominate the scene. All are good values any time of day but are especially popular for *desayuno* and *almuerzo.* The similar menus feature a wide list of Mexican and American dishes along with soups, salads, pasta, and sandwiches; all are open around 7 a.m.-10 p.m.

$ Benavides. Overall, this *farmacia*-attached chain has the lowest prices. Zona Rosa: Morelos and Escobedo; Centro: Av. Pino Suárez 602 Sur; Colonia Del Valle: Mississippi 129 Pte.; Bosques del Valle: Av. Vasconcelos 404 Pte.; Colonia Las Cumbres: Paseo de la Victoria 2200; Galerías Monterrey: Gonzalitos 625; Colonia Roma: Av. Garza Sada 2410 Sur; Madero: Calz. Madero 3350 Pte.

$-$$ Martin's. Very good, but mostly limited to the suburbs. Contry: Av. E. Garza Sada; Las Cumbres: Alejandro de Rodas 3102; Lincoln: Av. Lincoln and Gonzalitos.

GETTING YOUR GOAT

The art of breeding, herding, and eating goats came to Nuevo León with early Spanish settlers—most likely either Basques or Sephardic Jews—who were originally introduced to the animals by their Moorish conquerors from North Africa prior to the 16th century. Like arid North Africa, Northern Mexico has turned out to be perfect goat country, and no one else in the world relishes goat cuisine like Monterreienses.

By far the most common goat dish in Monterrey is *cabrito al pastor,* kid goat roasted whole on an iron spit angled toward (but not directly over) a fire pit filled with glowing mesquite coals. Before cooking, the *cabrito* is marinated in a mixture of herbs and spices for up to eight hours; the marinade used by each *cabrito* house is a closely guarded secret. At least 15 restaurants in Monterrey specialize in *cabrito al pastor,* not to mention the many other eateries that list the dish on their menus.

All parts of the goat, including the head *(cabecita)* and internal organs, may be served. Diners order by the cut; most popular because of the abundance of meat are the *pierna* (leg) and *paleta* (shoulder). *Cabrito guisado* is a thick stew of shredded *cabrito* and slightly spicy *salsa jitomate* (tomato sauce). Also cherished but harder to find outside restaurants that specialize in goat are *cabrito en su sangre* (cabrito stewed in its own blood), *machitos* (cooked goat tripe rolled into flour tortillas with *salsa picante*), and *fritada de cabrito* (fried, ground goat blood

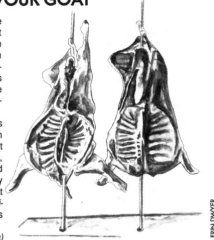

ERIN DWYER

cabrito

cooked with pieces of goat meat). More appetizing to the average visiting gringo are *glorias,* chewy candy made from nuts and/or seeds cooked with sweetened goat's milk.

The prime season for goat-eating is May-Oct., when fresh *cabrito* is available. Other times of year, frozen *cabrito* or older goats—not nearly as tasty—may be substituted.

$-$$ **Sanborn's.** Pricier than the others but the food is generally tastier, more creative. The Zona Rosa branch has a separate bakery area with counter stools, good for a quick pastry and coffee. Zona Rosa: Calle Escobedo 920; Plaza San Agustín: Real San Agustín 614 Sur, next to Hotel Fiesta Americana; Galerías Monterrey: Gonzalitos 625.

$ **VIP's** has the most efficient service of the chains. Zona Rosa: Av. Hidalgo 402 Ote.; Tecnológico: Av. E. Garza Sada 1711; Universidad: Av. Universidad and Colón; Del Valle: Av. San Pedro 110.

Asian

$$ **El Dragón Chino.** This large, banquet-style Chinese restaurant serves reliable Cantonese and Mandarin cuisine at three locations (each is open daily 11 a.m.-11 p.m.): Centro Comercial

Patio Santa Rosa: Calle Escobedo 928 Sur, between Morelos and Hidalgo; Del Valle: Av. Vasconcelos 65 Pte.; Tecnológico: Río Panuco and Tecnicos.

$$ **Gran Plaza** (tel. 83-42-04-57), Calle Escobedo 480 Sur. Similar to El Dragón Chino; open daily noon-11 p.m.

$$-$$$ **Hei Sei Sushi Bar** (tel. 63-10-86), Av. Real San Agustín 222, Residencial San Agustín. A reasonable facsimile of a real sushi bar, with plenty of fresh fish. Try the Tampico Roll (sort of a Mexican version of the California Roll). Open daily 1-11 p.m.

Pizza

Pizzas Josephino's and **Pizza Hut** make the most reliable pizzas in town; Josephino's is slightly less expensive and has several downtown locations.

$$ Pizzas Josephino's. Gran Plaza: Zaragoza 840 Sur; Obispado: Av. Hidalgo 1612 Pte.; Patio Santa Rosa: Calle Escobedo 930 Sur; Centro: Padre Mier and Av. Cuauhtémoc; Del Valle: Plaza San Pedro, Humberto Lobo 520.

$$ Pizza Hut. Centro: Av. Pino Suárez 725; Madero: Calz. Madero and Guadalajara; Universidad: Av. Universidad 320 Nte.; Del Valle: Av. Vasconcelos and Bosques del Valle.

Vegetarian
Monterrey's vegetarian restaurants all fall into the typical Mexican mold, i.e., natural foods stores with small cafe areas attached. Offerings include whole-grain breads, yogurt, salads, soups, and standard Mexican dishes using soy and gluten for meat substitutes.

$$ La Naranja (tel. 83-58-47-37), Calle Filósofos 207, Pasaje Tecnológico.

$$ Mana Vegetariano (tel. 78-48-15), Av. Vasconcelos 143, Colonia Del Valle.

$-$$ Restaurant Vegetariano, northeast corner of Calle Ocampo and Av. Cuauhtémoc.

$$ Señor Natural (tel. 44-57-68), Calle Escobedo 713 Sur, Centro.

$$ Superboom (tel. 45-26-63), Av. Padre Mier 300 Ote.

Groceries
Supermarkets are abundant in the suburbs, but noticeably lacking in the city itself. On the north side of town, the large **Soriana** chain has a branch at Av. A. Reyes and F. Bartolomé. Another Soriana can be found at Calle Humberto Lobo and Capellanéa in Colonia Del Valle. **Gigante** has a branch near ITM at Av. E Garza Sada 699, Colonia Florida.

Downtown there are several daily markets with fresh produce; for locations, see "Markets" under the "Shopping" section, p. 418.

RECREATION

Bullfights
Although the *fiesta brava* is not as popular in Monterrey as in some parts of Mexico, there are ample opportunities to view bullfighting. The main venue, **Plaza de Toros Monumental** (tel. 83-74-04-50), is just east of Av. Universidad (also known as Av. A Reyes here) at Priv. del

Prado, north of the Arco de la Independencia. Originally built in 1937 and renovated in the '70s, this concrete-and-steel stadium has a retractable roof so that the *sombra y sol* can take place in any kind of weather. The Monumental season runs during May and December; tickets (US$15-30) are available through the Infotur office next to the Gran Plaza. Events are typically held on Sundays except during the occasional festival, when a three-day corrida may be scheduled.

If you're in town on a weekend during the season when no corridas are scheduled at Plaza Monumental, you may be able to attend one at the **Plaza de Toros Cuauhtémoc** in Guadalupe, a suburb east of Monterrey. The Cuauhtémoc ring is within walking distance of the "Expo Guadalupe" metro station, a 20-minute ride from downtown Monterrey. Typical ticket prices here are US$10 on the sun side, US$13 for shade. The Infotur staff will be able to reveal the current Cuauhtémoc schedule.

Cadereyta (33 km/20.5 miles east of the city via Mexico 40) also has a *plaza de toros* should both the Monterrey and Guadalupe rings be inactive when you visit.

Charreadas
Monterrey has several *charro* associations which practice *charrería* in various locations around the city. The premier venue for the sport is **Cortijo San Felipe** in the Garza Garcia district. Inquire at the Infotur office for schedules and *lienzo charro* locations.

Theater
The arts are heavily subsidized in Monterrey and the city has the best live theater resources outside Mexico City. Since 1988 the city has been the permanent home of the Muestra Nacional de Teatro (under the auspices of the Instituto Nacional de Bellas Artes and the Consejo Nacional de la Cultura y Arte), and has been a three-time host (alternating with Guanajuato) of the internationally renowned Festival Internacional Cervantino, considered the most significant dramatic arts festival in Latin America.

Major theatrical venues include **Teatro de la Ciudad** (tel. 83-43-30-11, Matamoros and Zuazua near the Gran Plaza), **Teatro Monterrey** (tel. 43-64-66; Av. Constitución and P. Díaz,

Centro), **Teatro Calderón** (tel. 75-12-20; Juárez and Tapia, Centro), **Teatro del Maestro** (tel. 75-13-20; Washington 802 Pte., Centro), and **Aula Magna** (tel. 42-45-07; Universidad Autónoma de Nuevo León, Av. 5 de Mayo between Juárez and Colegio Civil, Centro).

For the latest theatrical offerings, check the "Teatro" page of *El Norte's* "Gente" section or inquire at Infotur.

Bars And Discos

All the major hotels have nightclubs, although these are not as heavily frequented by local club-goers as in most other Northern Mexican cities.

Outside the hotels, both locals and tourists make plenty of noise at **Señor Frog's** (Plaza Fiesta San Agustín, Av. L. Cárdenas and Real de San Agustín) and **Iguanas Ranas** (Plaza Versailles Cumbres, off Paseo de la Victoria, Colonia Las Cumbres). One of the more interesting bars downtown is **La Fonda de San Miguel** (tel. 83-42-96-87), at Av. Morelos 924 Ote. in the Barrio Antiguo; the San Miguel features live folk and jazz music Wed.-Sat. evenings.

Among the most popular discos are **Onix** (E.C. Livas 201 Pte.), **Koko Loco** (Av. Pino Suárez 849 Sur), **Kaos** (Av. E. Garza Sada), **Pistacho's** (Río Tamazunchale 306 Nte.), **Baccarat** (Grijalva 150, Colonia Del Valle), and **S.S.** (Río Orinoco 105 Ote.).

Cinema

Monterrey is the movie-viewing capital of Northern Mexico, and local movie houses show a remarkable number of first-run foreign (including American) films. The "Cine" page of the "Gente" section in *El Norte* daily newspaper provides a comprehensive list of what's showing around town, along with cinema addresses and starting times. Admission prices are a bit higher than elsewhere in Mexico, about US$3.

The **Alliance Française** (tel. 83-42-48-05; Av. 20 de Noviembre 651 Sur, Colonia María Luisa) screens French films on Saturday nights at 6 p.m.; admission is free. The auditorium at **MARCO** occasionally shows foreign art films.

Shopping

For many North American visitors, shopping is the name of the game in Monterrey. Just about

---

MONTERREY'S WHEEL OF FORTUNE

Of the many traditions and customs that distinguish Monterrey from other Mexican cities, one of the most unique is the "Sorteo Tec," a municipal lottery that began in 1947 with the raffling of a 1947 Lincoln sedan. The Sorteo has escalated to four raffles a year in which the first prize is a newly built, fully decorated and furnished, air-conditioned house with two new cars in the garage and a pool; second prize is a new car (1993 offerings included Dodge Ram Chargers and Chrysler New Yorkers).

The money earned by the lottery supports around 25% of the students enrolled in the ITESM university system; tickets cost US$100 each (yes, foreigners may participate). Many of the autos raffled off in the Sorteo Tec are supplied by local auto factories. Mercedes Benz recently joined the award lineup; the German auto manufacturer opened a Monterrey plant in 1994 which produces 2,000 vehicles per year.

---

anything available in Mexico City (or San Antonio, Texas, for that matter) can be found in the markets, shops, department stores, and malls dotting the cityscape.

Shopping Areas: Many Mexican-made, fully licensed, designer goods—Ralph Lauren Polo, Calvin Klein, Gucci, Louis Vuitton, etc.—are sold in shops in the Zona Rosa, especially along the **Av. Hidalgo** pedestrian mall. These kinds of items are also available in the various shopping centers in well-to-do Garza García Garza, southwest of the city.

Of the larger shopping plazas for which the city is famous, the most impressive are the **Mall Del Valle** (off Av. Vasconcelos in the posh Del Valle area) and the **Galerías Monterrey** (off Av. González Garza, west of the Gonzalitos loop); the latter contains over 100 shops and department stores. There is also a modest shopping center with a pay parking lot beneath the **Gran Plaza.**

The Zona Rosa branches of **VIP's** and **Sanborn's** have good magazine sections with plenty of English-language reading material (VIP's is better organized).

Galerías Monterrey

JOE CUMMINGS

Markets: Filling an entire block between avenidas Juárez and Cuauhtémoc (east-west) and Calle Ocampo and Av. Constitución (north-south), **Mercado Colón** is a traditional urban Mexican market with row upon row of vendors purveying live birds, herbs, fresh-dressed *cabrito,* inexpensive pottery, kitchen utensils, curios, fruits, vegetables, baskets, and *artículos religiosos.* In the vicinity of this market, especially along Calle Ocampo between Juárez and Cuauhtémoc, are many small shops selling inexpensive clothes, umbrellas, and household goods; on the north side of Ocampo is a smaller market called **Mercado San Luis.** Farther north from here on Av. Juárez, between calles Aramberri and Ruperto Martínez, is **Mercado Juárez,** another large market with many of the same items as Mercado Colón.

Arts and Crafts: A good spot for regional handicrafts is **Casa de las Artesanías de Nuevo León** (tel. 83-45-58-17), at Dr. Coss and Allende, where there is a large selection of glass, ceramics, copper, brass, leather, and carved wooden items.

Carapán (tel. 45-44-22), at Av. Hidalgo 305 Ote. (opposite Hotel Ambassador), is worth checking out for its tasteful assortment of rugs, homespun cottons, hand-blown glass, silver, and other arts and crafts selected for their high quality. The **Sanborn's** at Galerías Monterrey and at Plaza Fiesta San Agustín have small but high-quality *artesanía* sections that include, for example, Talevera ceramics. The Zona Rosa

Sanborn's also stocks arts and crafts, though the selection is not as good as at the aforementioned branches.

Other handicraft shops in downtown Monterrey include **Quetzal Artesanías** (tel. 42-00-49; Dr. Coss 1217 Sur, Centro), **Mercado Indio** (tel. 48-50-20; Simón Bolivar 1150 Nte., Mitras Centro), and **Unión de Artesanos de Nuevo León** (tel. 75-17-05; Morelos between Zaragoza and Escobedo, Zona Rosa).

World-renowned crystal glass producer **Kristaluxus** (tel. 51-63-96) has a factory outlet at Calle José María Vigil 400 in Colonia del Norte where crystal can be purchased at discounted prices. The plant also invites visitors to have a look at glass-producing processes; guided tours are available at 10:30 a.m. Mon.-Sat. The shop is open Mon.-Fri. 9 a.m.-6:30 p.m., Sun. 9 a.m.-2 p.m.

Pharmacies: Monterrey is well equipped with modern *farmacias,* with locations throughout the city. **Farmacia Las 24 Horas Benavides** (tel. 45-14-35), opposite the Hospital Civil at Av. Madero 3350 Pte., is open round-the-clock.

Parque Chipinque

Atop Meseta de Chipinque at 1,500 meters (4,920 feet), this forested park 20 km (12 miles) southwest of downtown Monterrey is always a few degrees cooler than the city below and as such is an especially popular picnic spot during hot summer months. When the air is clear there are good aerial views of Monterrey. The restaurant-bar at the Motel Chipinque is a good spot for pre-sunset drinks, but take care on the drive back down, especially after dark.

Other Parks
The Río la Silla, which runs east and south of the city, is a favorite waterway for local canoe enthusiasts. Canoes can be rented at the beautiful, 108-hectare **Parque La Pastora** on the banks of the river in Guadalupe (follow Av. Chapultepec southeast off Av. Revolución).

Parque Canoas, southeast of the city on Av. E. Garza Sada (past the Av. Revolución junction), is a small, shady park with canoes for rent on the same river.

Tennis
Visitors can play tennis for hourly rates at **Chipinque Racquet Club** (tel. 83-35-33-76; Av. Lázaro Cárdenas 97, Residencial San Agustín) and **Sierra Madre Tennis Club** (tel. 78-47-70; Prol. de los Angeles 617, Colonia Jerónimo Siller). Several of the larger hotels in the city also have courts.

Festivals
Monterrey's biggest annual event is the two-week **Feria de Primavera** or "Spring Fair" in April (beginning Palm Sunday), when a number of commercial expositions, parades, concerts, and sports events are held at various venues around the city.

Of more interest perhaps to foreign visitors is the **Northern Mexican Fair** ("Feria del Norte de México") held in conjunction with the traditional **Fiesta Guadalupana** during the second week of December. One of the most impressive religious processions takes place at the Basílica de Roble, culminating in an all-night mass the evening of Dec. 12 (the feast day of the Virgin of Guadalupe); other events include handicrafts, agricultural, and food exhibits celebrating *norteña* culture.

MONTERREY INFORMATION

Tourist Offices
The main branch of the state tourist office (tel. 83-40-10-80) is on the fourth floor of Edificio Kalos at Av. Constitución and Zaragoza, at the

---

MONTERREY TELEPHONE NUMBERS

Local Police: 42-45-46
Highway Patrol: 43-25-76
Green Angels: 40-31-14
State Tourist Office: 44-43-43
Red Cross: 42-12-12
U.S. Consulate: 43-06-50
Monterrey Area Code: 83

---

south end of the Gran Plaza. For everyday inquiries, the smaller Infotur office (tel. 45-09-02), on the subterranean level of the Torre Administrativa along the west side of the Gran Plaza at Zaragoza and Matamoros, is more than sufficient.

If you're approaching Monterrey from Mexico 85 North (i.e., from Nuevo Laredo or Colombia), there's a small but well-marked Infotur office on the highway at Km 21 just north of the city near the Aeropuerto del Norte. On the eastern approach from Cadereyta via Mexico 40, there's another Infotur office at Km 35. If you're driving from either direction, it's a good idea to stop and get exact directions to your intended Monterrey destination; this could save you as much as an hour of frustration and wandering around in the city!

Infotur has two toll-free telephone numbers for information on Monterrey and Nuevo León: 800-235-2438 from the U.S./Canada; 91-800-83-222 in Mexico.

For information on travel elsewhere in Mexico, visit Monterrey's **SECTUR** office (tel. 54-20-44) on the third floor of the Palacio Federal, Av. Presidente Juárez y Corregidora.

Media
English-language newspapers available at the Zona Rosa hotels or at most Sanborn's and VIP's department stores include the *Mexico City News, USA Today, Laredo Times,* and *Wall Street Journal.*

Mexico's highest-quality Spanish-language newspaper, *El Norte,* is published in Monterrey. Even if your Spanish is minimal, *El Norte* is a good source of information on local cultural events, often listed in easy-to-follow columns.

The very informative *Monterrey Review,* a quarterly bilingual magazine oriented toward business as well as leisure travel, is distributed free in major hotels. The smaller-format and more tourist-oriented *Spotlight on Monterrey* is also widely available in hotels.

Standard Monterrey television consists of eight channels—three from Mexico, plus five local networks. Many residents also use satellite dishes to receive U.S. cable stations. The city boasts 45 radio stations, with a higher than usual number of Top 40-style formats.

Maps

Good city maps of Monterrey are difficult to find. At Sanborn's and VIP's you can purchase the *Guia Roji* map, which is very detailed but doesn't pinpoint landmarks, hotels, monuments, tourist attractions, parks, or the like—just streets and neighborhoods. Infotur distributes free sketch maps that depict the main avenues for cross-city traffic and are useful for general touring. What this city sorely needs is a map similar to those once published by HFET or those now published in the neighboring state of Coahuila.

Monterrey has two INEGI offices, one at Av. Garza Sada 1702 Sur, Colonia Nuevo Repueblo (tel. 83-45-01-38, fax 83-45-01-98), and another at Av. Colón Pte. 1505, Colonia Industrial (tel. 72-50-33, ext. 136, fax 75-37-60). These carry topographical maps for all of northeastern Mexico.

Immigration Office

If you've somehow made it as far as Monterrey without a tourist card or other immigration documents, you can make yourself legal at the city immigration office (tel. 83-44-44-70) at Av. Pino Suárez 330 Sur downtown.

Money

As elsewhere, the best banks for foreign exchange are **Banca Serfin** (Av. Hidalgo 330 Pte.; also at the airport), **Banamex** (Av. Padre Mier 102 Ote.), and **Bancomer** (Av. Padre Mier 480 Ote.).

There are several *casas de cambio* in downtown Monterrey and in the Del Valle and San Agustín districts. The greatest con-

CONSULATES IN MONTERREY

AUSTRIA

Río Orinoco 105 Pte.
tel. 56-90-15

COLOMBIA

Monte Palatino 120 Nte., Col. Fuentes de Valle
tel. 78-54-60

DOMINICAN REPUBLIC

Av. Lázaro Cárdenas Pte. 2475, Col. San Agustín
tel. 78-62-27

ECUADOR

Calz. del Rosario 286
tel. 38-15-27

FRANCE

Padre Mier and E. Carranza, Centro
tel. 35-17-84

GERMANY

E. Carranza 1215, Col. Palo Blanco
tel. 35-17-84

GREAT BRITAIN

Priv. Tamazunchale 104, Col. del Valle
tel. 78-25-65

HONDURAS

Av. Insurgentes 1717, Col. Santa María
tel. 33-39-84

ITALY

Dr. Coss Sur 465, Centro
tel. 44-32-50

NETHERLANDS

Av. Morelos 867 Ote., Centro
tel. 42-50-55

NICARAGUA

Profra. Rosa Gómez Sur 250, Centro
tel. 38-53-77

PANAMA

Pedro Quintanilla 390, Col. Chepe Vera
tel. 46-33-71

PERU

Loma Alta 606, Col. Loma Larga
tel. 40-42-44

UNITED STATES

Calle Constitución 411 Pte., Centro
tel. 45-21-20

centration is along Av. Ocampo Ote. near the Zona Rosa, where you'll find the convenient **Casa de Cambio Monterrey, Casa de Cambio Toledo,** and **Casa de Cambio Cadeca.** Hours of operation are generally around 9 a.m.-7 p.m.

American Express (tel. 83-45-26-28, 43-04-60) has an office at Av. Padre Mier Pte. 1424 where you can report lost/stolen traveler's checks or receive a cash advance on an American Express card.

Post And Courier

The city's main post office is at Av. Zaragoza and Washington downtown. **DHL** has offices at Av. Hidalgo 1295 Pte. (tel. 83-79-49-30) downtown and Carr. Miguel Alemán 205 Ote. (tel. 79-49-20) in Colonia Linda Vista (east of the city on the way to the airport). A bit farther out at Km 16.5 on Mexico 54 is a branch of **UPS** (tel. 86-22-77).

GETTING THERE

Air

Because of its role as Mexico's economic center, air services to Monterrey are extensive. The best choice from most of the continental U.S. is **Continental** (tel. 800-525-0280 in the U.S.; 800-231-0856 in Canada/Europe; tel. 83-33-26-22 in Monterrey; Galerías Monterrey), which operates direct flights to/from Atlanta, Chicago, and Houston, with connections to many other U.S. cities as well as Vancouver.

For Texans, **Aeroméxico** (tel. 44-63-99; Av. Padre Mier and Av. Cuauhtémoc) is more convenient, with direct daily flights from San Antonio for US$78 each way. Aeroméxico also flies to Monterrey via Aguascalientes, Chihuahua, Hermosillo, San Luis Potosí, and Tampico.

Mexicana (tel. 40-55-11; Av. Hidalgo 922 Pte.) flies direct to Monterrey from Chicago, Mexico City, San Antonio, San Luis Potosí, and Tampico.

Among the smaller airlines, **SARO** (tel. 91-800-83-224; airport) has flights to/from Acapulco, Culiacán, Mazatlán, Mexico City, Tijuana, and Torreón, while **Aeromonterrey** (tel. 56-56-16; Calz. San Pedro Sur 500-3, Fuentes del Valle) operates turboprops to/from San Antonio, Harlingen (Texas), Tampico, Matamoros, and Veracruz. **Noroeste** (tel. 44-74-29; Av. Hidalgo 480 Pte.) fields direct flights to/from Torreón,

with connections to Durango and Mazatlán.

Airport Transport: Aeropuerto Internacional Mariano Escobedo is 25 km (14.8 miles) northeast of the city center via Mexico 54, around 40 minutes by car. The standard *sitio* taxi fare out to the airport is US$18, while a *colectivo* costs US$8 per person. Better—if you don't have much luggage—are the green VW Eco-Taxis, which charge according to meter readings. A ride to the airport from downtown Monterrey in an Eco-Taxi should cost US$6-7 if taken during off-commute hours. Buses also run between the main downtown bus terminal and the airport several times a day for US$1.60.

Bus

Autotransportes Elite, Transportes Frontera, Omnibus de México, Transportes del Norte, and **Transportes Tamaulipas** all offer several buses per day to/from Nuevo Laredo and Reynosa near the Texas border for around US$10 each way, as well as buses to/from Matamoros (US$11-16), Tampico (US$19), San Luis Potosí (US$18), Torreón (US$12), and Zacatecas (US$13-15). Omnibus de México and Transportes del Norte also operate buses to/from Chihuahua for US$26-28 one-way.

Buses to Monterrey can be booked through **Greyhound Trailways** in Texas for links with Transportes del Norte from San Antonio (US$29), Houston (US$50), Austin (US$37), and Dallas (US$60). For details, contact Greyhound Trailways anywhere in the United States.

Transportes Monterrey-Cadereyta-Reynosa (tel. 83-75-44-55) does a route along the lower Texas-Mexico border via McAllen (Texas), Matamoros, Reynosa, Río Bravo, Camargo, Díz Ordaz, Ciudad Miguel Alemán, Cadereyta, and Monterrey that ends up in Matehuala, S.L.P. (a convenient terminus for Real de Catorce)! Except for Matehuala (US$15), none of these tickets costs more than US$8-10.

For service to/from Piedras Negras, you'll want **Autobuses Blanco,** which operates four buses a day for US$14 each way.

Transportes Monterrey-Saltillo (tel. 48-49-73, 75-57-44) has a monopoly on the route to Saltillo, with buses running every 15 minutes 5 a.m.-9 p.m. for US$3 ordinary class, US$6 *ejecutivo.*

Towns and villages in Coahuila, San Luis Potosí, and Tamaulipas—e.g., Ciudad Victoria

(US$10), Monclova (US$14), and Ciudad Valles (US$18)—are served by **Transportes Tamaulipas** (tel. 75-32-09).

Bus Terminal: Monterrey's busy Central de Autobuses (tel. 75-32-38; Av. Colón near Av. Universidad) has all the usual services, including a *cafetería*. Several city bus lines terminate here; the "Central" Metro station is within walking distance.

Train

Two *primera especial* trains to Monterrey from the U.S.-Mexico border were available as we went to press. **El Tamaulipeco** operates between Matamoros and Monterrey via Reynosa. The one-way fare of US$11 from Matamoros or US$8 from Reynosa includes a box lunch and soft drinks served by uniformed train employees. Second-class seats on the same trains cost US$5.50 and US$2.30 respectively. The trip takes around 6^{1}/$_{2}$ hours from Matamoros, 2^{1}/$_{2}$ hours from Reynosa; see the "Railway Schedule," pp. 86-87, for departure and arrival times.

You can also ride a train to Monterrey from Piedras Negras via Saltillo on **El Regiomontano.** See the "Piedras Negras" section for details on this train between the border and Saltillo. From Saltillo the train takes 2^{1}/$_{2}$ hours and costs US$11.

From Monterrey, **El Regiomontano** continues southward to San Luis Potosí (US$15) and Mexico City (US$29).

A third train, the second-class-only **Del Golfo,** runs between Monterrey and Tampico on the Gulf of Mexico coast via Ciudad Victoria. The train leaves Monterrey daily at 8 a.m. and arrives in Tampico at 7 p.m.; arrival and departure times are the same in the reverse direction. In either direction the train stops in Ciudad Victoria at 1 p.m. The fare is US$2.50 between Ciudad Victoria and either Monterrey or Tampico, i.e., US$5 one way for the Monterrey-Tampico (or vice versa) run.

Railway Station: The impressive Monterrey railway station, off Av. Colón west of the bus terminal, has gift shops, a **casa de cambio,** clean restrooms, schedule boards (rare in Mexico), and a restaurant. The nearest Metro station is "Central."

Driving

Nuevo León 1 (from Colombia), Mexico 85 (from Nuevo Laredo or Ciudad Victoria), Mexico 54 (from Ciudad Miguel Alemán), and Mexico 40 (from Reynosa or Saltillo) all converge at Monterrey. The new eight-lane bridge, warehouse, and customs complex at Colombia is mainly used by cargo-carrying traffic as a way to bypass the congested Nuevo Laredo crossing. If you plan to follow Nuevo León 1 to Monterrey rather than Mexico 85, the Colombia crossing is quicker and more efficient than the Nuevo Laredo crossing. Count on around 3^{1}/$_{2}$ hours between Colombia and Monterrey, more if you slow down to look at historic Bustamante and Villaldama.

The Mexico 85-D tollway begins 69 km (43 miles) south of Nuevo Laredo and costs a stiff US$21.30 (in 1993) for the 165-km (102-mile) ride; the speed limit is 110 kph (68 mph), which makes the total Nuevo Laredo-Monterrey driving time (including those stretches not covered by the tollway) about two hours. From San Antonio the driving time is around 4-4^{1}/$_{2}$ hours. There has been some discussion of lowering the toll since the tollway is very much underused. The original two-lane *libre* (toll-free) road is in good condition but truck traffic can be heavy at times; count on around three to four hours.

The shortest way to Monterrey from the border is from the crossing at Roma, Texas, via Ciudad Miguel Alemán and Mier (Tamps.), a distance of 171 km (106 miles) along two-lane Mexico 54; from Nuevo Laredo it's 230 km (143 miles) total, from Colombia 299 km (186 miles). When traffic is light, the Roma-Monterrey route can be done in about three hours.

Approaching Downtown Monterrey: Coming from the north via **Mexico 85** or **Nuevo León 1,** the quickest way downtown is to take the "Monterrey Via Rápida" bypass off the highway (Nuevo León 1 merges with Mexico 85 14 km/8.7 miles north of the city), then follow signs for "Zona Centro" to Av. M. Barragán, which becomes Av. Cuauhtémoc, then Av. Universidad, before merging with Av. Pino Suárez downtown.

From the northeast (**Mexico 54**) there is no bypass, so stay with Mexico 54 till it becomes Blvd. Miguel Alemán, then Calz. Madero; Madero leads into the heart of downtown via Av. Colón. From Cadereyta/Reynosa, **Mexico**

AUTO RENTAL AGENCIES IN MONTERREY

ALAL

Airport
tel. 48-93-86
Hidalgo 400 Ote.
tel. 40-78-48

AUTO RENTAS EJECUTIVAS

Escobedo 930 Sur
tel. 43-65-65

AVIS

Airport
tel. 445-67-26
Galeana 1050 Sur (at Ocampo)
tel. 42-81-25
Berim del Norte
Matamoros 210 Pte.
tel. 44-29-37

BUDGET

Airport
tel. 45-40-45
Hidalgo 433 Ote.
tel. 40-41-00

CAR EJECUTIVO

Hidalgo 1550-C Pte., Col. Obispado
tel. 40-48-80, fax 42-36-44

CENTENARIO

E. Carranza (south of Hotel Ambassador)
tel. 44-64-63, fax 42-00-65

CAR RENTE UN AUTO

Zacatecas 307, Col. Independencia
tel. 40-48-85, fax 45-52-89

CORPORATIVOS DE AUTOMOVILES DE RENTA

Hotel Crowne Plaza, Av. Constitución 300 Ote.
tel. 19-93-00

DOLLAR RENT-A-CAR

Hidalgo 498 Ote.
tel. 42-05-01

HERTZ

Airport
tel. 44-72-00
Hotel Ambassador
tel. 45-61-95
Garibaldi 814 Sur
tel. 44-80-65
Hotel Río
tel. 45-61-36, fax 40-15-47
Holiday Inn Norte
tel. 76-24-00

KARPE AUTO ARRENDADORA

Hidalgo 1612
tel. 45-77-00

MAZDA RENTE UN AUTO

Airport
tel. 43-05-49
15 de Mayo 860 Ote.
tel. 42-98-68

NATIONAL

Escobedo and Hidalgo
tel. 44-63-63

OPTIMA RENT-A-CAR

Ocampo 531 Ote.
tel. 42-86-99

RENEE

Hidalgo 418 Ote.
tel. 42-06-04

ZERGO RENTA AUTOS

Airport
tel. 440-660-82
Garibaldi
808-A Sur (next to Hotel Río)
tel. 42-81-11
E. Carranza 1011 Sur
tel. 42-88-11

40 East becomes Av. Benito Juárez, then merges with Calz. Madero and Av. Colón as above.

From **Mexico 54 South** (Montemorelos, Ciudad Victoria), the highway becomes Av. E. Garza Sada, which leads directly across Río Santa Catarina to Av. Constitución; turn left on Constitución to reach the city center.

From Saltillo (**Mexico 40 West**), follow "Centro" signs for a fairly smooth transition to downtown Monterrey via Blvd. Díaz Ordaz.

GETTING AROUND

Bus
An extensive city bus system covers the metro area, with main routes along Av. Cuauhtémoc-Av. Alfonso Reyes (south-to-north), Av. M.L. Barragán-Av. Pino Suárez (north-to-south), Av. Colón (east-to-west and west-to-east), Av. Constitución (east-to-west), and Av. Morones Prieto (west-to-east). Most of downtown Monterrey is within walking distance of points along these routes.

Metro
Monterrey has recently begun building and operating an elevated tramway called "Metrorrey," more commonly known simply as "El Metro." The first line, Línea 1, was inaugurated in 1991 and runs 17.5 km (10.8 miles) from San Bernabé (northwest of the city proper) to Guadalupe (east of the city). It was financed by a combination of private and public funds, and its most outstanding feature so far is the cavernous steel-and-plexiglass "Cuauhtémoc" Metro station near the intersection of Av. Colón and Av. Cuauhtémoc.

When the Metro is running smoothly, it only takes around 20 minutes to run the entire line—a considerable time savings over any other mode of transport. Ticket cards are dispensed from machines in each station in denominations of 80 centavos, N$2, N$3, N$5, N$7, and N$8; the shortest journey—between two consecutive stations—costs 80 centavos, and there are 17 stations in all.

The next line—as yet unbuilt—will probably run northeast-southwest from San Nicolás to Garza García.

Taxis
As usual, taxi *sitios* (stands) are concentrated around the bus and train terminals, major hotels, and market areas. The average hire (e.g., from the bus or train terminal to the Zona Rosa) for a large taxi from one of the *sitios* is US$6-7 per trip. A less expensive alternative is to take one of the new metered "Eco-Taxis," green VW bugs that burn only unleaded gas and cost around US$2.60-3 for the same trip (US$0.85 at flagfall plus per-km charges). To the airport, a metered Eco-Taxi would only cost about US$6.60, while a *sitio* taxi would charge US$18. Eco-Taxis must be flagged down on the street—outside of the city center they are sometimes few and far between.

Driving
Although Monterrey is not the easiest of cities to drive in, it's not nearly as difficult as, for example, Torreón, Zacatecas, or Guanajuato. City streets are wide and mostly well marked, and there are few of the diagonals that make the traditional Spanish grid so maddening; in fact the city plan is closer to that of a large North American city than that of a typical Mexican city.

Still, as with any large city, you should plan your routes with a map before setting out from point A to point B. Several city streets bear the family name of the local Garza Sada technocratic dynasty, which leaves many Mexican as well as gringo motorists racking their brains to distinguish one Garza Sada (Francisco, Roberto, Eugenio are three of them) from another.

Blue-and-white signs point the way to tourist attractions in and around the city. Unfortunately, they're not always in place from start to finish and may leave you stranded (as the El Obispado signs left the author); don't count on them.

Street Numbers: The central point for the city street-numbering system is the southwest corner of the Mercado Juárez at Av. Juárez and Aramberri; streets running east and west of Juárez are Ote. and Pte. respectively, while those to the north and south are Nte. and Sur. Thus Av. Hidalgo 310 Ote. is, theoretically, three blocks east of Juárez; the system isn't perfect but it serves as a good general guideline.

Rush Hours: Monterrey's heaviest traffic generally occurs 8:30-9 a.m., 1-2:30 p.m., and 6-7:30 p.m. To avoid delays and frustration, avoid driving during these times of day when you have a choice.

Traffic Laws: The four-lane section of highway that forms Av. Constitución (along the Río Santa Catarina at the south edge of downtown Monterrey) has separate speed limits for each lane, an absurd idea that almost no one pays any attention to! Note, however, that a law requiring the use of seat belts in Monterrey is enforced.

Parking: Except in the Zona Rosa, parking isn't that much of a problem. There is a convenient 24-hour parking lot off Av. Hidalgo Ote., just west of the Hotel Ambassador, in the Zona Rosa; fees are very reasonable. Beneath the Gran Plaza is another large pay lot.

Auto Rental: Several auto rental agencies have offices in the Zona Rosa along Av. Hidalgo Ote. (near the Hotel Ambassador). See the "Auto Rental Agencies in Monterrey" chart for names, addresses, and telephone numbers.

TOURS

From San Antonio
Alamo Coaches (tel. 210-271-0047) in San Antonio, Texas, offers a convenient three-day shopping/sightseeing tour of Monterrey and Saltillo. The tour departs San Antonio at 5:45 a.m. Friday morning and arrives just after noon in Monterrey for hotel check-in (usually the Hotel Río). In the afternoon the tour continues to Cañon de la Huasteca, the Basílica del Roble, and the Palacio de Gobierno. On Saturday the tour moves on to Saltillo to see the Catedral de Saltillo and market square, and on Sunday returns to San Antonio with a shopping stop in Nuevo Laredo. The trip costs US$99 per person including transport, tours, and lodging. All tour leaders are bilingual. A similar tour is also run by San Antonio's **Fiesta Tours** (tel. 512-222-8687).

City Tours
In Monterrey itself, **Osetur** (tel. 47-15-99) leads half-day tours of the city (departing 9 a.m. from behind the Gran Hotel Ancira) and nearby attractions (departing 1:30 p.m. from behind the Ancira). The tours run daily Tues.-Sun. except on Sunday afternoons; each day involves a different itinerary for a total of 11 possible tours. All tours cost just US$8.50 regardless of the itinerary. Sample city destinations include the Gran Plaza, Kristaluxus, Cervecería Cuauhtémoc, and Galerías Monterrey; Monterrey-vicinity tours might include Cola de Caballo ("Horsetail Falls"), Centro Cultural Alfa, or the Grutas de García.

VICINITY OF MONTERREY

Parque Nacional Las Cumbres De Monterrey
The most extensive national park in Mexico, Las Cumbres covers 246,500 hectares (609,000 acres) at the northern end of the Sierra Madre Oriental near Monterrey. The limestone mountains, some reaching over 3,000 meters (9,800 feet), are cut with numerous streams that provide water for the city of Monterrey and form major canyons, including La Huasteca, San Juan Bautista, Santa Catarina, and La Mielera. Several of metropolitan Monterrey's most popular recreation areas—Horsetail Falls, Cañon de la Huasteca, Grutas de García, and Meseta de Chipinque—fall within park boundaries.

Since national park status in Mexico does not forbid human habitation or exploitation (with the proper permission only), don't go to these places expecting untrammeled wilderness. Still, with some effort you can find satisfying wilderness areas near the main attractions.

This area is honeycombed with over 500 known limestone caves, some of which offer the best caving experiences in North America. Permission to explore many of the caves is difficult to obtain; if interested, your best bet is to work through a caving association in Texas.

Cascada Cola De Caballo
"Horsetail Falls" is 42 km (26 miles) southeast of Monterrey via Mexico 85; the turnoff is three km (two miles) south of Villa de Santiago. The last few kilometers of road wind through an attractive wooded area.

Because the park is around 2,000 meters (6,500 feet) above sea level, temperatures tend to be several degrees lower than on the plains below; a near-constant mist from the falls keeps the surrounding area green and lush. Osetur, a Monterrey tour operator, manages the nicely landscaped grounds, which include picnic tables with grills alongside streams formed by the falls. The 25-meter (82-foot) falls themselves are about 500 meters (550 yards) from the ticket booth at the entrance, along a stone path that can become slippery with spray at times. Stone steps climb alongside the falls to about a third of its height. Another trail farther to the side goes to the summit of the falls.

On summer weekends and holidays the park can become quite thick with city residents escaping the heat; come early in the day to beat the crowd. The falls are practically deserted in the winter yet still a worthwhile visit for the misty mountain atmosphere.

JOE CUMMINGS

Cola de Caballo

Entry to the park is US$2 for adults, US$1 for children under 12. You can ride a horse to the top of the falls for US$4, or a horse cart for US$3.60; horses for general riding can be hired for US$8.30 per hour.

There is a small, free parking lot at the entrance to the falls, about 50 meters beyond the Motel Cola de Caballo entrance. The motel charges US$3.30 to park in its lot. The motel itself is in a state of disrepair and not a recommendable place to stay.

Beyond the falls, the road continues past a few mountain villages to the less-visited **Cascada Chipitín.** Watch for animals and pedestrians along this road.

Villa De Santiago

Santiago began as a hacienda established in the fertile Valle de Guajuco, in the foothills of the Sierra Madre Oriental, in 1650. By the beginning of the 18th century, the hacienda had grown to "Villa" status and its cobbled streets and simple colonial buildings are now a local tourist attraction. Most of the architecture dates to the 1800s but there are still several casas—particularly along Calle Morelos off the town plaza—that were built as early as 1745.

The clean and friendly **Restaurante Las Palomas** on the plaza serves typical regional cuisine.

Santiago is 36 km (22 miles) south of Monterrey via Mexico 85. To reach the plaza from the main exit off Mexico 85, follow signs marked "Palacio Municipal" near the entrance to town.

Cañon De La Huasteca

Sixteen km (10 miles) west of Monterrey via Mexico 40, this steep-walled canyon was once used by Spanish settlers as well as local Amerindians as a refuge from marauding Apaches. Dramatic rock wall formations caused by erosion, as well as native petroglyphs and pictographs, attract visitors from all over the northeast. One cavelike formation is known as the "Cueva de la Virgen" because at certain times of day, light from a crack in the wall projects an image of the Virgin Mary onto another wall.

In Mexico the canyon is famous for its use as a location setting for the film *Cuando Lloran los Valientes* ("When the Valiant Cry"), starring Mexican movie idol Pedro Infante as the legendary *regiomontano* bandit Agapito Treviño. Treviño, known as "El Caballo Blanco" for his white mount, used the canyon to hide from prerevolutionary soldiers in pursuit.

To explore this area on foot, obtain a copy of INEGI's G14-7 (Saltillo) topographical map.

Grutas De García

Among the largest known caverns in Mexico, the Grutas de García are eight km (five miles) east of Villa de García, which is 41 km (25 miles) west of Monterrey off Mexico 40 (on the way to Saltillo). The main entrance measures 12 meters (36 feet) tall by 15 meters (49 feet) wide. Passages through the caves—16 caverns in all—are lighted so that visitors can admire the highly visual crystalline formations with names like Mano del Muerto ("Hand of Death") and Teatro (named for is heavy, curtainlike shapes). A cable car runs nearly a kilometer from the parking area to the caves, which are 1,110 meters (3,700 feet) above sea level in the side of Cerro del Fray ("Friar's Mountain").

The caves are open daily 8 a.m.-4 p.m. A US$3 entry fee covers admission, cable car ride, 90-minute tour, and use of a children's playground and swimming pool near the parking area.

The narrow and winding road between Villa de García and the caves is not suitable for RVs. Villa de García itself was founded in 1577, but the standing architecture dates to the mid- to late-19th century.

Villaldama

A Franciscan mission was established here in 1690 on the mission road between Zacatecas and San Antonio; following the discovery of nearby gold and silver veins, a town named San Pedro de Villaldama was settled in 1826. Local mines were abandoned after North American mining interests fled the violence of the 1910-20 Mexican Revolution.

Of minor interest is the neoclassic **Ex-Templo de San Pedro de Boca de Leones,** a church built at the beginning of the 19th century on the site of the original Franciscan mission. The building is now used as a cultural center. Calle de Rangel Frías joins the two town plazas and is lined with examples of typical regional architecture.

Villaldama is 91 km (56.4 miles) north of Monterrey via Nuevo León 1.

Bustamante

Seventeen km (10.5 miles) farther north along Nuevo León 1, Bustamante began as Misión San Miguel de Aguayo in 1686, founded in 1686 by Tlaxcaltecas from Saltillo. The traditional houses—of which few are left—feature walls of adobe and brick topped by peaked, thatched roofs. Another local style is characterized by long, shallow pilasters that run alongside windows and doors from foundation to roof.

On Calle Independencia near the town plaza, the art deco **Hotel Ancira,** built in the '50s as a residence, doubles as simple lodge and town bus terminal.

Six km (3.7 miles) south via a gravel road are the **Grutas de Bustamante,** a little-explored network of caves. One of the largest, Gruta del Palmito, is 45 meters (150 feet) wide, 30 meters (100 feet) high, and 160 meters (525 feet) long.

Cerralvo

Roughly halfway between Monterrey (152 km/71 miles southwest) and the Texas border, Ce-

rralvo is the oldest town in Nuevo León. Founded as a mining community named Ciudad de León in 1577, the town was renamed in 1629 after the 15th viceroy of Nueva España, the Marqués de Cerralvo. Several buildings in town date to the early 1600s, including the partially ruined **Antigua Casa de la Moneda** (the Old Mint) on Calle Mina. As in Bustamante, the elongated door and window pilasters are typical of regional colonial architecture during the 17th and 18th centuries.

The **Antiguo Hospital** on the corner of calles Hidalgo and Zaragoza was constructed at the end of the 18th century in a grand "C" shape around a central patio. The unique entrance facade features a floral-carved stone arch extending over short columns that are mounted on large stone pedestals.

Good food and lodging are available at **Hotel El Paso,** Calle Morelos 617 Oriente. Several blocks west at Calle Morelos 222 Pte., **Restaurant Noreste** offers regional cooking.

Parque Nacional El Sabinal: Just southeast of Cerralvo off Mexico 54, this eight-hectare (20-acre) national park preserves old stands of sabinos (Montezuma bald cypress) along a scenic arroyo, forming a cool, wooded oasis in this arid region. Birding is excellent during the winter months, and picnic tables and grills are available for public use.

Linares

This town 83 km (51.5 miles) southeast of Monterrey, at the junction of Mexico 85 and Mexico 58, is the center of the state's "Zona Naranjera" where most of northeast Mexico's *naranjas* (oranges) are grown.

Citrus cultivation was introduced to the area by American Joseph Robertson at the beginning of the century, but the town has been around since its founding in 1712 by Spanish soldiers. Linares attained official city status in 1777 along with Nuevo León's first bishopry. The **Catedral de San Felipe Apostol** on the town plaza was built in 1779; a cupola and tower were added in 1805 and 1853. Several other 18th- and 19th-century structures can be found in the vicinity of the plaza. A modern building of interest is the post-revolutionary, neo-Aztec **Botica Morelos** at Morelos and Madero, facing the plaza's west corner.

Near Los Altares, 32 km (20 miles) west of

Linares via Mexico 58, is scenic **Cañon de Santa Rosa,** on whose vertical rock walls the sculptor Federico Cantú has carved a 650-square-meter (7000-square-foot) relief.

In Linares, the **Hotel Guidi** (Av. Morelos between Allende and Zaragoza) offers adequate rooms for US$15-20 per night, while **Hotel Plaza Mira** (Calle Hidalgo and Juárez) is a bit nicer for US$25-30. Both have attached restaurants. **Restaurante Cabritos** (Av. Suárez between Hidalgo and Allende) serves its namesake, while **Restaurante El Herradero** (Calle P. Salce and Independencia) concentrates on *carne asada.*

THE STATE OF TAMAULIPAS

History

Meaning "High Mountains" in a Huastec dialect, Tamaulipas was inhabited by descendants of the Olmec culture when the first Spanish navigators explored the upper Gulf of Mexico coast five years before the Conquest. In 1516 Hernández de Córdoba sailed from Cuba and entered the mouth of the Río Pánuco, only to turn back upon sighting Huastec villages along the river banks.

A more extensive exploration of the coast was carried out by Capt. Alfonso Alvarez de Piñeda, who followed the course of the Río Bravo (Rio Grande). Alvarez named this wide waterway Río de las Palmas because it was profusely lined with native sabal palms (virtually the only wild palms left today are in the Sabal Palm Grove Sanctuary near Brownsville on the U.S. side). Alvarez was killed by Huastecs while exploring the Río Pánuco in 1519. Later explorations of the Tamaulipan coast continued to focus on the mouths of the Bravo, Soto la Marina, and Pánuco rivers.

Under Spanish rule the area became known as the Province of Pánuco. Spain's *empresario* program, which encouraged the colonization of

Northern Mexico, Texas, and Louisiana by offering generous land grants, attracted Capt. José de Escandón to what is now northern Tamaulipas. Escandón had arrived in the New World at age 15 as a cavalry soldier, and was commissioned in 1746 to survey the lands between Tampico and the Río San Antonio. In 1748, after obtaining permission to distribute land grants in the Río Bravo area, he helped establish 23 settlements in this region, including the present-day towns of Laredo, Dolores, Mier, Camargo, Reynosa, San Fernando, Soto la Marina, and Ciudad Victoria. Under Escandón's governorship the province's name was changed to Nuevo Santander; this name held through Mexican independence but was changed to Tamaulipas following Texas secession in 1836.

Tamaulipas Today

Due to the abundance of water, farming (cotton, cereals, tobacco, sugarcane, coffee) and cattle ranching are the prime inland economic activities, while fishing and shrimping predominate along the coast. Petroleum and natural gas from the Pánuco Basin near Tampico is also an important source of state revenue, as are the *maquiladoras* of Nuevo Laredo, Reynosa, and Matamoros—three of Mexico's largest border communities.

During Spanish rule, Tamaulipas became the cradle of cattle ranching in North America and today the ranchero culture arches over virtually everything Tamaulipan, from the music (polka and *chotis* in the north, *huapango* in the south) to the traditional Tamaulipan costume of fringed chamois and calfskin.

Land And Sea

Tamaulipas boasts 430 km (267 miles) of Gulf coastline, cut by the Bravo, Guayalejo, Pánuco, Soto la Marina, and San Rafael rivers, among the largest. The intersection of river and sea has created an extensive network of estuaries, lagoons, *bocas,* beaches, and saltmarshes that make the Tamaulipas coast of considerable interest to naturalists.

The eastern escarpment of the Sierra Madre Oriental extends northwest-southeast through the southwestern part of the state, where it meets the coastal plains to form several unique environments, including cloud forest and Tamaulipan tropical/subtropical thorn forest. Latitude is another contributor to the landscape, as the lower third of the state falls below the Tropic of Cancer.

Tamaulipas borders the state of Veracruz to the south, the Gulf of Mexico to the east, Texas to the north, and the states of Nuevo León and San Luis Potosí to the west. Geoculturally, the state can be divided into three major regions: the semi-industrial north, the sparsely populated coast, and the primarily agricultural inland valleys.

Climate

The northern part of the state has a climate much like that of South Texas, with a warm, humid coastline and a temperate, semi-dry *matorral* inland with scattered rain year-round. To the southeast, the climate is tropical/subtropical with rain falling mostly in the summer. The Sierra Madre Oriental region to the southwest is warm and semi-dry, moderated by moist Gulf breezes from the east and protected from the interior desert by high peaks to the west. In most of the state you can expect high June-Sept. temperatures.

RECREATION

Beaches

The best beach areas in the state are, from north to south, **Bagdad, El Mezquital, El Barrancón, Carbonera, La Pesca, Tepehuaje, Barra de Ostiones,** and **Barra del Tordo.** They all share a broad, flat profile—much like beaches along the Texas Gulf Coast but with fewer crowds. Facilities are often limited to *palapas* and a few trash receptacles.

Fishing

The state hosts more than 20 annual fishing tournaments and maintains over 50 *parques turísticos* on its lakes, rivers, and beaches. Among the lakes frequented by keen anglers are the **Vicente Guerrero, Falcón, Gómez, Caballero, Méndez, San Lorenzo,** and **Real de Borbón,** all of which primarily contain freshwater bass (striped, black) and catfish.

Saltwater/Lagoons: Lagoon fishing along the Tamaulipan coast is especially productive. In the calm, easily accessible "flats"—shallow, sandy lagoons on the leeward side of the barrier islands (*barras*)—anglers can hook flounder, sheepshead, croaker, redfish, and speckled trout.

Crabbing

Lagoons are also a major source of saltwater crabs. All you need for a crabbing expedition is a length of twine equal to the water's depth, crab bait (chicken meat is recommended), and a hand net; net the crab *before* you pull it from the water or it'll release the bait.

Onshore/Offshore

Surf casting on the Gulf-facing beaches and islands is a bit more challenging and offers a wide variety of redfish, speckled trout, black drum, whiting, and sandtrout. Offshore catches include marlin, sailfish, yellowfin tuna, kingfish, yellowjack, tarpon, amberjack, pompano, and red snapper; you'll need to launch your own boat—or hire a local boat—to take advantage of this fishery.

Hunting

The most popular hunting areas are found near Miguel Alemán, Reynosa, Matamoros, San Fernando, Padilla, Ciudad Victoria, Soto la Marina,

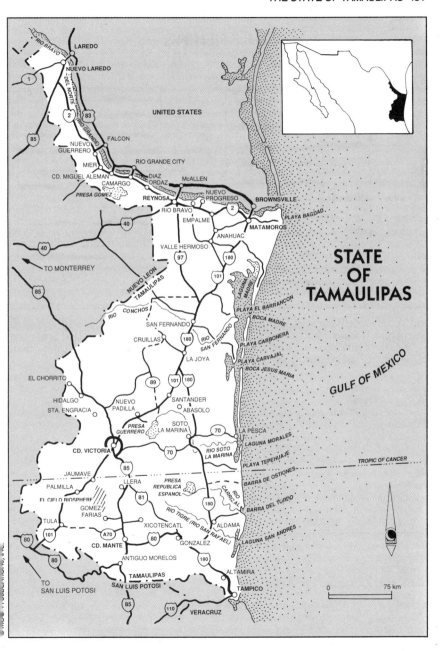

STATE OF TAMAULIPAS

GULF OF MEXICO

UNITED STATES

RIO BRAVO

LAREDO

NUEVO LAREDO

DEL NORTE

FALCON

NUEVO GUERRERO

MIER

CD. MIGUEL ALEMAN

CAMARGO

DIAZ ORDAZ

RIO GRANDE CITY

McALLEN

PRESA GOMEZ

REYNOSA

NUEVO PROGRESO

BROWNSVILLE

PLAYA BAGDAD

RIO BRAVO

EMPALME

MATAMOROS

ANAHUAC

VALLE HERMOSO

TO MONTERREY

NUEVO LEON

TAMAULIPAS

RIO CONCHOS

SAN FERNANDO

CRUILLAS

RIO SAN FERNANDO

LA JOYA

PLAYA EL BARRANCON

BOCA MADRE

PLAYA CARBONERA

PLAYA CARVAJAL

BOCA JESUS MARIA

LAGUNA MADRE

EL CHORRITO

HIDALGO

STA. ENGRACIA

NUEVO PADILLA

SANTANDER

ABASOLO

SOTO LA MARINA

PRESA GUERRERO

LA PESCA

CD. VICTORIA

RIO SOTO LA MARINA

LAGUNA MORALES

PLAYA TEPEHUAJE

TROPIC OF CANCER

JAUMAVE

PALMILLA

LLERA

PRESA REPUBLICA ESPANOL

BARRA DE OSTIONES

EL CIELO BIOSPHERE

GOMEZ FARIAS

RIO TIGRE (RIO SAN RAFAEL)

RIO CARRIZAL

BARRA DEL TUNDO

TULA

XICOTENCATL

ALDAMA

LAGUNA SAN ANDRES

CD. MANTE

GONZALEZ

ANTIGUO MORELOS

TAMAULIPAS

SAN LUIS POTOSI

ALTAMIRA

TAMPICO

TO SAN LUIS POTOSI

VERACRUZ

0   75 km

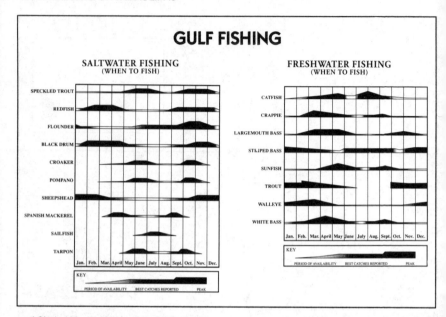

and Ciudad Mante. White-winged dove (*paloma alas blancas*, in season mid Aug.-Nov.) is the favorite game of *tamaulipecos*, followed by quail and wild turkey (*codorniz* and *guajalote*, same season as dove), white-tailed deer (*venado de cola blanca*, Dec.-mid Jan.), and goose and duck (*ganzo* and *pato*, mid Oct. to mid-February).

NUEVO LAREDO

Mexico's quintessential border town receives more daily visitors from the north than any other city along the U.S.-Mexico border (Tijuana has slightly higher vehicle counts but the statistics contain proportionately more passers-through). Partially this is due to the city's location—only 2 1/2 hours from one of the 10 largest cities in the U.S. (San Antonio, Texas); another reason is that the city offers a well-developed downtown with everything from elegant dining to street vendors to cut-rate liquor stores, plus two leafy public plazas, all within walking distance of the International Bridge.

Although Nuevo Laredo's population of 278,000 has outpaced that of "Old" Laredo's 120,000, the two cities are closely linked by culture and economics. Holidays as culturally distinct as Washington's Birthday and Mexican Independence Day are celebrated on both sides of the border, and the twin cities share a single pro baseball team, Los Tecolotes de los Dos Laredos, which plays in both Mexican and American minor leagues.

Tariff and customs revenues collected at Nuevo Laredo are greater than at any other port of entry in Mexico, and along with Ciudad Juárez and Tijuana, Nuevo Laredo is one of the most important business centers along La Frontera. The *maquila* industry that plays such an important role in other large border towns is integrated here into a more diverse area economy that includes import-export operations, transportation, cotton farming, cattle ranching, and tourism.

HISTORY

"Los Dos Laredos" ("The Two Laredos") started out as one when *empresario* Don Tomás Sánchez established a colony on the north bank of the Río Bravo in 1755. In honor of his sponsor José de Escandón, who hailed from Laredo, Spain, Sánchez named the settlement Villa de San Agustín de Laredo. Founded as the first nonmissionary, nonmilitary Spanish settlement in North America, the town served as a center for the North American continent's first cattle ranches.

Laredo found itself caught between the two wars of national liberation in the early 1800s, first Mexican independence from Spain (throughout which most Laredo residents remained Spanish loyalists) and then Texas independence from Mexico. When neither of the newly formed republics of Texas and Mexico would provide protection against marauding bandits and Apaches, Laredo joined the states of Tamaulipas, Coahuila, and Nuevo León in declaring their own "Republic of the Río Grande" in 1840. Laredo was made the capital of the new republic, which lasted only 10 months before Mexican troops brought the area back under Mexican rule.

In 1845, when the Republic of Texas was annexed to the U.S., Laredo was again abandoned in a no-man's land between the two countries, since the U.S. and Mexico disagreed over the boundary line between Texas and Mexico. The Treaty of Guadalupe Hidalgo, signed at the end of the Mexican-American War, established the Río Bravo (Rio Grande) as the border; those Laredo residents who wanted to remain Mexican citizens moved across the river and established Nuevo Laredo in 1848.

In the late 1800s the founding of two new railroads made Los Dos Laredos a major transportation link between the U.S. and Mexico. The Texas-Mexican Railway connected the city with the deep-water port of Corpus Christi on the Texas Gulf coast, while the Missouri Pacific joined the midwestern U.S. with Mexico's national railway and Mexico City.

The city's transportation role was further strengthened when the Pan-American Highway (Mexico 85) was completed in 1935, establishing a continuous roadway between Laredo and the Panama Canal via Mexico and Central America. Another boost to the local economy arrived during the U.S. Prohibition years, when Texas residents began slipping over the border to the Cadillac Bar and other Nuevo Laredo watering holes for a legal drink, thus introducing tourism to the area. By the end of WW II, Nuevo Laredo was one of the most prosperous cities in Mexico.

SIGHTS

As Nuevo Laredo is a relatively new city by Mexican standards (see "History," above), it offers virtually nothing of historical interest to see. For Texas residents it's a place to shop and party on weekends and holidays, though most visitors never get farther than a few blocks down Av. Guerrero, the main tourist strip that runs directly south from the bridge.

If you're just going for the day, it's easy to walk over International Bridge No. 1 from downtown Laredo near Hotel La Posada—you can park your vehicle in the free lots off Laredo's Zaragoza St., below Riverdrive Mall. Those who are driving across will use International Bridge No. 2. Parking in downtown Nuevo Laredo is tight but pay lots are available.

Parque Arqueológico Morelos
This park three blocks east of International Bridge No. 1, between calles Bravo and 15 de Junio, exhibits some 50 replicas of historical sculpture representing the seven major pre-Cortesian cultures in Mexico and Mesoamerica. Many have been copied from artifacts at Mexico City's famous Museum of Anthropology as well as from the Mayan ruins of Chichén Itzá and Teotihuacán.

Plazas
Three plazas strung out north to south along Av. Guerrero are the focus of public life in Nuevo Laredo: **Plaza Juárez** (two blocks from the bridge at calles Victoria and Galeana), **Plaza Hidalgo** (Av. Guerrero and Calle González), and **Plaza México** (Guerrero and Independencia). Plaza Hidalgo is the largest of the three and serves as city center, flanked by the Palacio Federal on the east and various restaurants and hotels to the west.

NUEVO LAREDO ACCOMMODATIONS

Hotels and motels in large border towns are typically expensive by Mexican standards. Those in Nuevo Laredo are a pleasant exception, representing some of the best bargains along the border.

Budget Hotels
One of the best deals in town is the friendly and efficient **Hotel Rendon** (tel. 871-2-05-32), a classic Mex-deco hotel on the southeast corner of calles Juárez and González two blocks west of Av. Guerrero near Plaza Hidalgo. Tidy rooms with private bath cost US$21.60 s, US$25-26.60 d; the only drawback for motorists is that the hotel has no parking lot (24-hour pay lots are available nearby). Another border classic is the well-worn **Hotel Regis** (tel. 2-90-35) at Calle Pino Suárez 3013 (corner of Matamoros toward the bridge), where rooms are also in the US$20-30 range. As at the Rendón, parking must be arranged outside.

A few blocks west, at the northwest corner of calles Pino Suárez and Ocampo, is the well-kept **Fiesta Motor Hotel** (tel. 2-47-27), which has a small parking lot and 35 rooms for US$33 s/d.

Cheaper downtown hotels with basic but adequate rooms for US$17-21 include **Hotel Calderón** (tel. 2-00-04), at Calle Juárez 313 between Hidalgo and Pino Suárez toward the bridge; and **Hotel Sam's** (tel. 2-59-32), a block east at the corner of Calle Hidalgo (2903) and Matamoros. In the same price range but a notch down in overall maintenance are **Hotel Texas** (tel. 2-18-07), at Av. Guerrero 837 near Plaza Hidalgo; and **Hotel Reno** (tel. 2-18-44), at Calle Ocampo 335 near the bridge.

Medium-priced Hotels
Nuevo Laredo's two top (four-star) hotels are reasonably priced and conveniently located for motorists on the east side of Av. Reforma on the way south out of town, five and seven km respectively from the International Bridge. The first, **Del Río Motor Hotel** (tel. 871-4-36-66) on Av. Reforma at Obregón, has rooms with a/c, satellite TV, and phones for US$45 s, US$50 d. The hotel has a good restaurant and two swimming pools, and is within walking distance of Gigante and Soriana supermarkets.

Two km farther south on Av. Reforma, the similar **Motor Hotel Hacienda** (tel. 4-46-66) has rooms for US$40 s/d; all rooms face away from Av. Reforma, a design that promotes quiet accommodations. The Hacienda also has a pool and restaurant.

The **Santa Monica Motel** (tel. 4-21-16), at Av. Reforma and Candela nearby the Hacienda

and Del Río motels, offers fair two-star accommodations for around US$30 s/d.

Laredo, Texas

On the Texas side of the border just off I-35 on San Bernardo Ave. are several motels in the US$30-40 range, including the **Monterrey Inn** (tel. 210-722-7631, 4820 San Bernardo Ave.) and the **Siesta Motel** (tel. 723-3661, 4109 San Bernardo Avenue). **Motel 6** has rooms for around US$30 at two Laredo locations: 5310 San Bernardo Ave. (tel. 725-8187) and 5920 San Bernardo Ave. (tel. 722-8133).

The most comfortable and convenient place to stay in Laredo for walks across the border is **Hotel La Posada** (tel. 210-722-1701), on Zaragoza St. at San Agustín Plaza. Laid out in the classic Mexican colonial style around a courtyard and pool, it's a short walk from International Bridge No. 1. Facilities include a security parking garage. Rooms are US$60-80 per night (senior discount available).

FOOD

Regional Cuisine

Northern Tamaulipas food specialties include a dish whose fame has spread from the border, across Texas, and throughout the U.S., Canada, and even Europe: *fajitas,* marinated and mesquite-grilled skirt steak served with flour tortillas, grilled onions, salsas, and various other condiments. Traditionally speaking, *fajitas* are most often cooked and served while on a picnic outing, but Nuevo Laredo has several restaurants where they can be purchased by the kilo.

The easiest to find is **Restaurant La Palapa** (tel. 871-4-00-68), at Av. Reforma 3301 not far from the Hacienda and Del Río motor hotels; it's open daily for dinner and is slightly upscale. **Las Tablitas** (tel. 2-16-90), at calles Degollado and H. de Nacataz east of Plaza Hidalgo downtown, also specializes in *fajitas,* as well as *queso flameado* (Mexican-style cheese fondue); it's open daily noon-midnight. Both restaurants serve acclaimed *carne asada, norteña*-style steak.

Goat (*cabrito*) is also quite popular in the Nuevo Laredo area. The original source of the northern tradition of naming at least one goat eatery "Principal" in every town is the Cantú-family-owned **Restaurant Principal** (tel. 2-13-01) at Av. Guerrero 624, just north of Calle Dr. Mier—look for the skewered *cabritos* roasting *al pastor* in the window. This clean, inexpensive restaurant also serves *pollo asado, carne asada,* and *machitos* (goat-tripe burritos), with *frijoles rancheros* (ranch-style beans) on the side. The Principal is open daily for lunch and dinner. The nearby **Restaurant Nuevo León** at Av. Guerrero 508 (just north of Calle Pino Suárez) is another authentic *norteña* place with *cabrito al pastor, fajitas,* and *machitos.*

A bit more upscale is **El Rincón del Viejo** (tel. 2-25-23), at Calle González 4834 near Parque Mendoza. Regional dishes, including *cabrito al pastor,* are served in an inside dining room as well as in a courtyard dining area where tables are arranged along shallow ponds. El Rincón is open for lunch and dinner daily.

National

For tacos of all kinds, Nuevo Laredo's most renowned restaurant is **Restaurant El Rancho** (tel. 871-4-87-53), also known as **Su Majestad El Taco** ("His Majesty the Taco"), at Av. Guerrero 2134 just north of Av. Lincoln. In addition to a huge selection of tacos, El Rancho specializes in *carnitas, pozole, birria estilo Jalisco* (Jalisco-style stew), *carne asada,* and a wider-than-average selection of Mexican beers. It's open daily 11 a.m.-midnight.

México Típico (tel. 2-15-25), on the west side of Av. Guerrero between Mina and Canales, is the place to go for traditional Mexican atmosphere, mariachis, and an extensive menu of national standards, plus a few regional specialties (such as *carne asada a la tampiqueña,* one of the restaurant's best dishes). Open daily for lunch and dinner.

For quick Sinaloa-style barbecued chicken with beans, tortillas, and salsa, stop at **El Pollo Loco** at Av. Guerrero 2454 (just north of Carranza) or at Calle Matamoros 702 downtown.

Breakfast

Another regional specialty, *machacado con huevo* (dried beef with eggs) is available at two inexpensive coffee shops on the northwest and northeast corners of Ocampo and Dr. Mier on the north side of Plaza Hidalgo. **Cafetería Modelo** on the northeast corner is the cleaner of the two, and offers pastries as well as egg break-

EL DORADO BAR & GRILL

Nuevo Laredo has been a favorite eating and drinking spot for South Texans since the 1920s Prohibition, and the longest running border joint of them all is alive and well under its latest moniker, El Dorado Bar & Grill (tel. 871-2-00-15). Originally founded as a casino and restaurant named El Caballo Blanco in 1922, the restaurant became the Cadillac Bar in 1926 after being purchased by New Orleans native Mayo Bassan. Bassan's Creole style of cooking influenced restaurant cuisine throughout the Rio Grande region with such dishes as roast quail, fried soft-shelled crab, red snapper *en papillote,* and braised frog legs. *Cabrito* and several Northern Mexican standards were later added to the menu.

Perhaps Bassan's most famous innovation was the Ramos gin fizz (listed on the current drink menu as "New Orleans gin fizz"), a sweetish cocktail made with frothy egg whites and gin. The house drink list encompasses 99 items, including such antiques as sherry and egg, absinthe frappe, Sazerac, and the "popper," a savory tequila concoction served in a large shot glass with a loud flourish—in which a white-jacketed waiter slams the glass onto the bar (or table), then stands back while you down the drink in one swallow.

In 1958 Bassan turned the Cadillac Bar over to his Texan son-in-law Porter Gardner, who operated the restaurant until his retirement in 1980. Gardner left the Cadillac to his employees and it was eventually sold to the Longoria family, who changed the name to El Dorado Bar & Grill in 1992. A franchise operated in the U.S. under the name "Cadillac Bar" has no relation to the original Nuevo Laredo location other than the name and a drink called the "slammer," inspired by the original Cadillac's popper.

Nothing much has changed at the legendary Belden and Ocampo location (two blocks south, one block east of the bridge); the El Dorado has the same white-coated waiters, the same piano-player, the same funky smell you'd expect from a 70-year-old bar, and the same menu featuring quail, *cabrito,* frog's legs, and Mexican standards. The sturdy wooden bar, with not a blender in sight, is still the restaurant's greatest asset. The large, guarded parking lot in back of the restaurant is useful for downtown shopping sprees; as long as you eat or drink at El Dorado, parking is free. The restaurant is open daily 10 a.m.-11 p.m.

fasts. Both *cafeterías* are open for breakfast, lunch, and dinner.

If you plan on making your own breakfast and need to stock up on coffee, search out **Café Bola de Oro** at Calle Matamoros 444 (at Hidalgo), not far from the international bridges. Bola de Oro roasts and grinds several varieties of fresh coffee.

Seafood And International

Mariscos Mandingo (tel. 871-3-12-05), at Calle Obregón 1307, bills itself as "a little corner of Veracruz in Nuevo Laredo," and specializes in fresh *huachinango* (red snapper) as well as other fish and shellfish from the Gulf.

Popular with border-hopping gringos are two elegant restaurants near the international bridge, **Victoria Restaurant and Bar** (tel. 2-08-95) on the northwest corner of Victoria and Matamoros; and **The Winery Pub and Grill** (tel. 2-88-95) at Calle Matamoros 308 (between Victoria and Belden). Both restaurants serve a variety of continental, North American, and Mexican dishes, and are open daily 11 a.m.-11 p.m.

RECREATION

Racing And Sports Book

Nuevo Laredo Downs (Hipódromo-Galgódromo Nuevo Laredo, tel. 871-2-38-02; 210-726-0549 in Texas) is 11 km (seven miles) south of town off Mexico 85 and features greyhound racing Wed.-Fri. and horse racing on weekends. The funky **Nuevo Laredo Turf Club,** at calles Bravo and Ocampo (only a block from the bridge), offers off-track and sports betting on U.S. and Mexican sports events in a bar setting.

Bullfights

Plaza de Toros La Fiesta, on Mexico 85 just past the airport south of town, hosts Sunday *corridas* between Washington's birthday (Feb. 15) and early September. For scheduling information, contact the Nuevo Laredo state tourist office next to the International Bridge or call the Laredo Convention and Visitors Bureau (tel. 210-722-9895; 800-292-2122 outside Texas) in Laredo, Texas.

Discos

Nuevo Laredo's discos are crowded with bouncing bodies on weekends. A few blocks down Av. Guerrero and west one block on parallel Calle Matamoros (next to The Winery Pub and Grill) is **Lion's Den,** a disco that's popular with tourists. **Vivanti's,** opposite the Del Río Motor Hotel; and **Firenze's,** two blocks down from Vivanti's, get a mix of young people from both sides of the border. More in the middle of town is the equally popular **Tom & Jerry's** at Av. Guerrero 3011. All are open Wed.-Sun. till 2 a.m.

Radio

A Tejano station in Laredo, 92.7 FM, broadcasts a good variety of border music and can be picked up on either side of the border.

Shopping

One of Nuevo Laredo's major tourist draws—for Mexicans as well as foreigners—is that it offers the best shopping anywhere along the U.S.-Mexico border. In large part this is due to its position at the head of the Pan-American Highway; all cargo heading north or south passes through Nuevo Laredo, a major convenience for wholesale buyers and sellers.

Tourist-oriented gift shops line the north end of Av. Guerrero near the bridge. Except for liquor and cigarettes (which cost about the same anywhere in town), prices aren't always that good, so it pays to shop around. Overall, the best selection and prices are at the **Nuevo Mercado de la Reforma,** a collection of around 100 shops which take up an entire block on the west side of Av. Guerrero (look for a red sign reading "MERCADO"). The **New Juárez Market,** a small mall at Av. Guerrero and Calle Bravo with around ten shops, is also good. Most of the shops in both of these malls accept credit cards.

For handicrafts alone, your best bet is the **Mercado M. Herrera,** a collection of around 50 shops located 1½ blocks east of Av. Guerrero at calles Ocampo and Hidalgo. The **Centro Artesanal,** at Av. Guerrero and M. Herrera a few blocks farther south, also offers arts and crafts for sale.

La Mansión, at Av. Guerrero 206, has very good prices on picture frames, whether ready-made or custom. Including glazing and matting, prices run as much as 80% cheaper than in the U.S. or Canada. La Man-

sión also sells handicrafts, patio furniture, and planters.

Marti's (Calle Victoria 2923 at Av. Guerrero) is a boutique that specializes in custom-designed clothes along with high-end furniture and handicrafts—with boutique prices to match.

Reyes, on the east side of Av. Guerrero just south of Calle Hidalgo, offers boots, saddles, and other handmade leather goods at decent prices.

NUEVO LAREDO INFORMATION

Tourist Offices

The state tourist office (tel. 871-2-01-04), just to the west of International Bridge No. 1, has a list of Nuevo Laredo hotels and a few informational brochures.

On the U.S. side of the border, the **Laredo Convention and Visitor's Bureau** (tel. 210-722-9895; 800-292-2122 outside Texas) works closely with the Mexican side and can provide information on both Laredos. They have an office in the Laredo Civic Center at 2310 San Bernardo Ave. as well as an information center in El Mercado at Flores and Hidalgo, near Laredo's Hotel La Posada.

Post Office

Nuevo Laredo's main post office is in back of the Palacio Federal, just east of Plaza Hidalgo.

Maps

The **INEGI office** (tel. 871-5-59-74) at Calle Chilapa 2549, Colonia Guerrero, carries topographical maps for Tamaulipas, Coahuila, and Nuevo León.

U.S. Consulate

There is an American consulate (tel. 871-4-06-

NUEVO LAREDO TELEPHONE NUMBERS

Police: 2-37-37
Highway Patrol: 4-12-84
State Tourist Office: 2-01-04
Club Cruz Ambar (medical emergencies): 2-89-54
Nuevo Laredo Area Code: 871

96; after hours 210-727-9661 in Laredo) at Av. Galeana and Madero, about 12 blocks south of the bridge.

NUEVO LAREDO TRANSPORT

Air

Although no direct flight service is available to Nuevo Laredo, **TAESA** (tel. 210-725-8414) operates daily flights between Laredo International Airport (Texas side) and Mexico City daily. Taxi service between the Laredo airport and Nuevo Laredo is available for US$25.

Bus

The busy Nuevo Laredo bus terminal is west of Av. Reforma on Calle G.L. Velarde (off Av. López de Lara). Facilities include left-luggage service and a *cafetería*.

Transportes del Norte handles first-class buses to/from Tampico (US$26), Ciudad Victoria (US$13), Ciudad Valles (US$30), Monterrey (US$10), Saltillo (US$20), San Luis Potosí (US$32), Chihuahua (US$42), Durango (US$56), Mazatlán (US$54), Mexico City (US$60), and Zacatecas (US$35). For 30-40% above these fares, **Turistar** has *ejecutivo* buses to/from Ciudad Victoria, San Luis Potosí, Durango, Mexico City, Guadalajara, Monterrey, and Zacatecas.

Less expensive second-class buses to towns and cities in Tamaulipas and Nuevo León are operated by **Autobuses Blancos** and **Transportes Frontera.**

From Laredo, Texas: For US$3 you can take a Transportes del Norte or Transportes Frontera bus from the Greyhound Trailways bus depot at Matamoros and San Bernardo Ave. in downtown Laredo. You can also buy through-fares for buses to/from other U.S. cities as well as into Mexico.

City Buses: The most useful lines for getting around Nuevo Laredo run north and south along Guerrero, Juárez, and López de Lara between the city bus depot at Matamoros and Belden and the Central Camionera off Av. López Lara.

Taxis: Cabs are abundant but not inexpensive. A taxi from the Central Camionera to Plaza Hidalgo, for example, costs about US$10. A taxi across the bridge between Nuevo Laredo and Laredo (from the northernmost end of Av. Guerrero and Water St.) costs US$5.

Train

Passenger service out of Nuevo Laredo is operated on the Mexico-Monterrey-Nuevo Laredo line (sometimes called the **Aguila Azteca** or "Aztec Eagle"), which reportedly hasn't missed a day of service since the Mexican Revolution. Train No. 2 departs Nuevo Laredo at 6:55 p.m. and makes stops in Monterrey, Saltillo, San Luis Potosí, San Miguel Allende, and Querétaro before reaching Mexico City at 7 p.m. the next day.

First-class reserved fares are available only between San Luis Potosí and Mexico City; the rest of the line offers second class only. The second-class fare between Nuevo Laredo and San Luis Potosí is US$7 each way; other one-way fares include Monterrey US$2.50, Saltillo US$3.50, San Miguel Allende US$8.30, and Mexico City US$10.

Advance tickets can be purchased at the FCN railway station at Av. López de Lara and Calle Gutiérrez.

Driving

Traffic in Nuevo Laredo isn't all that bad as long as you avoid the bridge during ordinary commute hours and on Sunday afternoons. There's a convenient parking garage in the same building as The Winery Pub and Grill at Matamoros and Belden near the bridge; rates are US$0.85 per hour.

AUTO RENTAL AGENCIES IN NUEVO LAREDO

AVIS
Av. Reforma and E. Zapata
tel. 4-25-51

BUDGET
Arteaga 3025 (at Juárez)
tel. 2-42-41

HERTZ
M. Herrera 2348
tel. 3-33-73

FAST AUTO RENT
Chihuahua and López de Lara, Col. Anáhuac
tel. 4-32-32

Note that Av. Guerrero merges with Av. Reforma just south of Calle Campeche, about five km (three miles) from the bridge, and Av. Reforma in turn merges with Mexico 85 South.

If you're only using Nuevo Laredo as a Mexico gateway and don't plan to stop over, you can avoid the city altogether by using the relatively new Puente Internacional Solidaridad (Solidarity International Bridge) at Colombia, N.L., 40 km (25 miles) west of both Laredos. From Colombia it's a short drive to Mexico 2 (which leads northwest to Piedras Negras, southeast to Nuevo Laredo) and Nuevo León 1 (south to Lampazos, Bustamante, and Monterrey).

Mexican Vehicle Insurance: If you don't already have Mexican insurance (highly recommended), you can purchase a temporary auto policy in Laredo, Texas, at **Bravo Insurance** (tel. 210-722-0931, fax 210-723-3657; 2112 Santa Ursula).

Border Formalities

The Nuevo Laredo and Colombia crossings are open 24 hours. Bridge tolls run about US$2 in either direction (depending on the value of the peso). See the "Entry Regulations" section, p. 100, for important information on Mexican immigration and customs requirements.

Tours

Olé Tours (tel. 210-726-4290) in Laredo, Texas, offers half-day, shopping-and-lunch van or bus tours of Nuevo Laredo for around US$12 per person.

NUEVO LAREDO TO MATAMOROS (LA CARRETERA RIBEREÑA)

Known as La Carretera Ribereña or "River Highway," the 330-km (205-mile) stretch of Mexico 2 that runs parallel to the Río Bravo (Grande) from Nuevo Laredo to Matamoros passes through the most historic section of the state. Early Spanish land grants for farms and ranches along the river plains that became the province (and later state) of Nuevo Santander, and then the states of Tamaulipas and Texas, have endured centuries of wars, revolution, and Apache attacks. While the larger border cities of Nuevo Laredo, Reynosa, and Matamoros today reflect a modern, hybridized Mexican-American culture, the smaller towns along the river are proud guardians of their Hispanic heritage.

This is a route best chosen by motorists with the time to explore rather than visitors in a hurry (US 83 on the American side is a faster ride) or those relying on public transport. Straight through, the drive takes around 3 1/2 hours; count on a half day if you plan to stop along the way.

GUERRERO VIEJO AND PRESA FALCON

The original town of Guerrero was founded in 1750 under the Spanish *empresario* plan, but the entire town of 4,000 packed up and relocated when the Presa Falcón (Falcon Dam) was built in 1953 and the town was flooded with the impounded waters of the Río Bravo.

Some of the original buildings in Guerrero Viejo (Old Guerrero) can be seen when the lake level drops. Guerrero Viejo is 32 km (20 miles) north of Nuevo Guerrero (or 85 km/52.5 miles southeast of Nuevo Laredo)—watch for a small "Guerrero Viejo" sign on the east side of the road at about Km 163, then drive 30 km (18 miles) east on a rocky road through several open gates. What can be seen of the old town, when the lake level permits, are the tops of several sandstone buildings, including the 1750-vintage **Misión Ampuero** church and the top of the plaza *kiosko*.

Near Nuevo Guerrero, on the southwest edge

of the 87,000-acre lake, is a *parque turístico* with facilities for camping, fishing (black, white, and striped bass; crappie; and catfish), boating, and picnicking (grills, tables, and trash receptacles). Falcon State Park on the U.S. side just across the border also has facilities for tent camping (US$6 per night) and RVs (full hookups US$10), plus screened shelters (US$15), picnic areas, and a boat launch.

MIER

This quiet town of 6,000 is 19 km (11 miles) farther south along Mexico 2. Founded in the 1750s under José de Escandón's *empresario* program, downtown Mier features the typical sandstone architecture and narrow, cobbled streets of the era. On one side of a large shady plaza is a Catholic church designed by Spanish-German architect Enrique Portcheller in 1798. (Using his trademark blend of Spanish and French Creole styles, Portcheller designed many of the larger 18th-century buildings in Roma and Rio Grande City across the border.) Near the highway junction is **Capilla San Juan,** a nicely restored chapel built in 1752.

Among Republic of Texas historians, Mier is infamous as the execution site of 17 Texas independence fighters in 1842. Captured by Mexican troops during an unsuccessful raid north of the Río Bravo, 176 Texans were on their way to Mexico City when they made an unsuccessful escape attempt near Salado, Texas. Upon their recapture, they were taken to Mier and forced to draw beans from a pot. The 17 rebels who drew black beans (10% of the band of 176 rebels) were executed on the spot.

Lodging And Food
Few tourists spend the night here, but simple rooms costing less than US$20 per night are available at **Motel Barrera** (Terán and America) and **Hotel Garza** (Palacios and Morelos). Slightly nicer and pricier is **Motel Asia** at Obregón and Matamoros.

Libations and Mexican food can be taken at **Restaurante La Mansión** or **Restaurante Casa del Sol,** both on Calle Allende.

CIUDAD MIGUEL ALEMAN AND PRESA GOMEZ

Fifteen km (9.5 miles) southeast of Mier along Mexico 2, Ciudad Miguel Alemán has little to interest the visitor in terms of history or architecture. Its chief draw is that this is the fastest road route between the border and Monterrey (see the "Getting There" section under "Monterrey" for more details). For residents of Roma, Texas (on the opposite side of the river within walking distance), Ciudad Miguel Alemán is also a place to eat Mexican food and shop for curios.

On the outskirts of town, off Mexico 2, is **Balneario Santa Lucia,** a rustic resort with thermal baths and pools.

In mid-March the local chamber of commerce hosts a "Winter Texan" fiesta for all the North American snowbirds who spend their winters across the river in the Rio Grande Valley. Av. Hidalgo is closed off to vehicular traffic to allow vendors and strolling mariachis to create a festive atmosphere.

Practicalities

Ciudad Miguel Alemán has its own state tourist office on Av. Hidalgo, not far from the bridge. A PEMEX station in town pumps Magna Sin. At Km 1 on Mexico 2 (on the southwestern outskirts of town), **Motel California** has adequate rooms for US$21-24 per night.

The Roma-Ciudad Miguel Alemán border crossing is open 24 hours.

Mexican vehicle insurance can be purchased at Roma's **Guerra Insurance** (tel. 210-849-1261; corner of Franklin and US 83).

CAMARGO

Along with Mier, this is another of the more historic towns along Mexico 2. Founded in 1749, Camargo has always been the more prosperous of the two; during the 19th century, steamboats plied the Río Bravo (Rio Grande) between Camargo and the river's mouth at the Gulf of Mexi-

co. Today the town of 7,000 inhabitants is a center for farming, ranching, and brick-making; a legacy of the latter occupation is the many brick buildings interspersed with older pastel-colored adobe and stucco houses.

The oldest section of the tidy downtown near the main plaza (**Plaza Hidalgo**) has charming, narrow streets. Tall Washington palms surround the plaza, where a block of three buildings (including the 18th-century **Palacio Municipal**) to one side have been nicely restored for use as local government offices. On another side of the plaza is **Parroquía de Nuestra Señora de Santa Anna**, a small, single-towered, 18th-century church. The church is the focus of much celebrating each year on July 26, the town's patron saint day.

On the opposite bank of the river is **Rio Grande City**, Texas, originally founded as the Spanish colony of Carnestolendas in 1768. In 1852, following the end of the Mexican-American War, an army of Mexicans and Texans who were dissatisfied with national governments on both sides convened in Rio Grande City and led an unsuccessful attack on Mexican troops in Camargo in an attempt to establish a "Republic of the Sierra Madre" in Northern Mexico.

Practicalities

Tourists are a rare sight in Camargo but the local citizens are friendly. A shop at one side of the plaza stocks liquors and curios. Should you become hungry while visiting, the clean, air-conditioned **Restaurant Miramar** (a block southwest of the plaza) offers seafood, tacos, and Mexican standards.

Camargo is 24 km (15 miles) southeast of Ciudad Miguel Alemán. Just outside of Camargo on Mexico 2 toward Ciudad Miguel Alemán, a roadside booth collects a US$1 toll even though Mexico 2 doesn't widen or improve in either direction along this stretch!

The Camargo-Rio Grande City border crossing is open weekdays 7:30 a.m.-9 p.m., weekends 8 a.m.-4 p.m.

PRESA MARTE R. GOMEZ

Also known as Presa del Azúcar ("Sugar Lake"), this impound of the Río San Juán is 24 km (15 miles) southwest of Camargo via a paved road. An old favorite with Texan anglers, Gómez still produces a fair number of largemouth bass as well as crappie, dagger, and catfish.

Practicalities
Simple rooms and cabins with kitchenettes can be rented on the lake at **El Azúcar Motel** (tel. 897-2-21-96, 2-17-03 in Ciudad Miguel Alemán), which also has a restaurant, bar, pool, boat ramp, rental boats, ice, and a few RV spots with full hookups.

Also in the vicinity, but not as well equipped as El Azúcar, are the similarly priced **Motel Loma Vista** and **Motel Ess.** Other camping, fishing, and boating facilities are available nearby.

Club de Caza y Pesca de Monterrey on the lake is a decent restaurant that serves Mexican food and fresh fish at *palapa* tables.

GUSTAVO DIAZ ORDAZ

Continuing southeastward 32 km (20 miles) south of Camargo, the next town along Mexico 2 is nondescript Gustavo Díaz Ordaz, a small cotton- and sorghum-farming center. The town's claim to fame is the unique *chalán* or vehicle ferry that runs across the Río Bravo to and from Los Ebanos, Texas, the only such service anywhere along Mexico's borders.

To use the ferry or to watch it in action, take Av. Hidalgo, the main street into Díaz Ordaz from the highway, then turn right at the sign marked "El Vado Los Ebanos" and follow this street past the plaza (about 2.9 km/1.8 miles from the highway) until it becomes a dirt road. From the plaza it's 2.2 km (1.4 miles) to the ferry crossing. The ferry runs daily 9 a.m.-5 p.m. and costs US$1 per auto; only three cars can cross at a time. Pedestrians may ride for US$0.25 per person. There are immigration checks on both sides of the river.

The state government has tentative plans to replace the unique Vado Los Ebanos ferry with a bridge at some point in the future.

Accommodation
The two-star **Motel San Miguel** at Calle Morelos 220 has adequate rooms for around US$24 per night.

REYNOSA

This modern, industrial city of 300,000 is the least interesting of the larger border towns in the touristic sense but is an important business destination due to its *maquilas* and huge PEMEX facility.

The second Escandón settlement on the Río Bravo, the city was founded in 1749 as Nuestra Señora de Guadalupe de Reynosa and became an important post for salt trade in early Nuevo Santander. A flood in 1800 destroyed the town and forced the residents to move to the current site (hence the lack of historical sights). Directly across the river is the small town of Hidalgo, Texas, which is about 16 km (10 miles) south of larger McAllen.

Los Ebanos ferry

Reynosa's main square, market, and cathedral sit atop a small hill about a kilometer from the bridge via Calle Zaragoza. Between the bridge and the square along Zaragoza and Allende are a string of tourist-oriented shops, *casas de cambio,* restaurants, bars, discos, and hotels.

Flanking the city are several industrial parks as well as one of Mexico's largest petrochemical refineries.

Accommodations

Reynosa has over 30 hotels and motels, most of them rated by the state at two stars (see p. 62 in the "Introduction" for rating information) but featuring above-average room rates. Among the better downtown choices is the well-located **Hotel Rey** (tel. 892-2-62-32) at Calle Díaz between Méndez and Madero, where clean rooms with a/c and TV cost US$27-33. Similar in price and features is **Hotel San Miguel** (tel. 2-21-70) on Av. Colón between Mina and Terán.

Visitors on a budget will find **Hotel Nuevo León** (tel. 2-13-10), very near Hotel Rey on Calle Díaz, adequate for US$12-20 s/d.

More upscale accommodations are available at the four-star **Hotel San Carlos de Reynosa** (tel. 2-12-80) at Calle Hidalgo 970 Nte., where large a/c rooms with TV and phones cost US$36-45 per night. Another four-star choice is **Hotel Virrey** (tel. 3-10-50) at Blvd. Hidalgo (Mexico 40) and P. Balboas, four km (2.5 miles) southwest of the International Bridge. Rooms with all the amenities plus private terraces cost US$36 s, US$46 d; there is also a pool on the grounds. Both the San Carlos and the Virrey have their own restaurants.

One of Reynosa's better accommodation deals is **Motel Engrei** (tel. 3-17-30) at Km 104 on Mexico 40, seven km (4.3 miles) southwest of the bridge on the outskirts of town. Well-maintained rooms with a/c, phones, and satellite TV are US$26-30 s, US$30-35 d. On the premises are a pool, tennis court, and restaurant (open daily 7 a.m.-11 p.m.).

McAllen, Texas: Across the river in McAllen, hotel and motel rates are the highest in the Rio Grande Valley. At the budget end, the best bargain is in nearby San Juan (west of McAllen proper) at the family-owned **San Juan Hotel** (tel. 210-781-5339; 125 US 83 Business). Simple rooms in a restored 1800s house cost just US$22-25 s, US$28-40 d. At the upper end, the place to stay is the **Casas de Palmas Hotel** (tel. 631-1101 or 800-4-COMPRI; 100 N. Main), where rooms in a 1918-vintage colonial-style inn are US$60-80 s, US$70-80 d.

RV Parks

Reynosa has nothing catering to the RV-camper crowd, but Texas's Rio Grande Valley, just across the river, is a national RV headquarters.

From Mission east to Brownsville is a string of over a hundred RV parks. In the McAllen area, you'll find **Ashworth Trailer Park** (tel. 210-686-0221, Ash and Sixth); **Casa de Mobile** (tel. 686-1836, 2022 11th St.); **Citrus Valley RV Park** (tel. 383-8189, State 107 and Rooth); **Handke's Mobile Park** (tel. 686-3076, Taylor Rd.); and **VIP Motel & RV Park** (tel. 682-8384, 3501 US 83). Rates run around US$10-13 per night. There are dozens more RV parks in the nearby communities of San Juan, Mission, Pharr, Alamo, and Penitas—many of these have the lowest rates in the valley. (If you're interested in learning more about South Texas and the Rio Grande Valley, read Moon's *Texas Handbook.)*

Food

Reynosa bears the distinction of having the largest number of restaurants per capita in the state of Tamaulipas, many of which are along paralleling calles Zaragoza, Aldama, and Allende in the town's *zona rosa* or tourist district. **Sam's** (tel. 892-2-00-34) at Allende and Ocampo is famous throughout the area for its inexpensive steak dinners, Mexican platters, and border specialties such as quail. The pricey **La Cucaracha** (tel. 2-01-74) at Aldama and Ocampo is a border-hopper's favorite for Mexican and continental cuisine.

Gorditas are a regional specialty, and the place to try them is **Las Gordas de Don Vicente** (tel. 2-74-84) at Calle Zaragoza 223 Ote. *Cabrito* and *carne asada* are house specialties at **Restaurante El Pastor** (tel. 2-41-91) at Calle Juárez 710 Norte.

Fried-chicken lovers will find seven branches of **Pollos Frito Buenos Aires,** at Díaz and Guerrero, Blvd. Hidalgo, Ramírez and Guadalajara, Ramírez and Nayarit, Prol. Paris and G.L. Velarde, Balboa and Río Mante, Blvd. L. Cárdenas and Paraguay.

Two hotel eateries worth mentioning include the restaurant attached to the **Motel Virrey,** which is popular for *cabrito, carne asada,* and Gulf shrimp; and the **Café San Carlos,** the Hotel San Carlos's bustling coffee shop—good for breakfasts. (See "Accommodations," above, for locations.)

Recreation

Bullfights: Though Reynosa is not a big town for the *fiesta brava,* the Plaza de Toros off Matamoros and Zapata, about 10 blocks west of the main plaza, hosts occasional corridas. Check with the tourist office in town for scheduling.

Bars: Among the several bars in the *zona rosa* catering to gringos, the most classic hangouts are **Dutch's** at Calle Ocampo 1020 Nte. (look for the windmill out front) and **Hostelería del Bohemio** on Zaragoza Oriente. The latter features live music in the evenings. **Treviño's Bar,** located in a gift shop of the same name near the International Bridge, usually has mariachis.

Shopping: The usual vendors and souvenir shops line the tourist streets near the bridge. **Mercado Zaragoza,** a block south of Plaza Hidalgo off Calle Hidalgo, is a large market with handicrafts.

Information

Tourist Offices: SECTUR (tel. 892-2-46-60) has an office at Calle Oaxaca 360, Colonia Rodríguez. A state tourist office also is attached to the immigration/customs office at the International Bridge.

Money: The greatest concentration of *casas de cambio* is along Calle Hidalgo near the plaza.

Telephone: Reynosa's area code is 892.

Getting There

Air: Aeroméxico (tel. 892-2-90-14; Av. Guerrero 510, corner of Portes Gil) operates daily flights to/from Mexico City. Taxis between downtown Reynosa and the airport, 15 km southeast of city center, cost US$13; a *colectivo* is US$5.

Bus: Reynosa's Terminal de Autobuses is off Calle Colón west of Mina. **Valley Transport Company** (VTC) and **Transportes Monterrey-Cadereyta-Reynosa** buses run between the McAllen and Reynosa terminals for US$3 each way.

Autotransportes Elite, Transportes Frontera, Omnibus de México, Transportes del

Norte, and **Transportes Tamaulipas** all offer several buses per day between Reynosa and Monterrey for around US$10 each way.

Transportes Monterrey-Cadereyta-Reynosa also operates second-class buses on a circular route that links towns along the border (Matamoros, Reynosa, Camargo, Díaz Ordaz, Ciudad Miguel Alemán) with Monterrey, N.L., and Matehuala, San Luis Potosí. Except for Matehuala (US$15), all legs along this route cost less than US$10.

Transportes Fronteras and **Transportes Tamaulipas** offer long-distance buses to cities throughout San Luis Potosí and Tamaulipas as well as to Mexico City and Querétaro. Service to Zacatecas, Guadalajara, Durango, Chihuahua, and other points west is provided by **Omnibus de México** and **Transportes del Norte.**

Train: El Tamaulipeco runs between Reynosa and Monterrey for US$8 first class, US$2.50 second class. See the "Railway Schedule," pp. 86-87, for departure and arrival times.

Driving: The traffic in Reynosa can be thick during commute hours (early morning, midafternoon, early evening), especially at the junction of Mexico 2 and Mexico 40.

For **Green Angels** assistance, call 2-11-19.

If you're heading toward Reynosa from the U.S. and need Mexican vehicle insurance, one of the oldest and most reliable agencies along the entire border is **Sanborn's Mexican Insurance** in McAllen (tel. 210-686-0711, fax 210-686-0732; 2009 S. 10th). In Hidalgo you can also arrange a Sanborn's insurance policy at **Patty's Insurance** (tel. 843-2863; 309 S. Bridge).

Border Formalities: See the "Entry Regulations" section, p. 100, for important information on Mexican immigration and customs requirements. The Reynosa bridge crossing is open 24 hours.

Getting Around

City Bus: Buses and *colectivos* link all sections of the city; most have their destinations prominently displayed on a marquis over (or whitewashed onto) the windshield. Fares are US$0.30-0.60.

Taxi: Cabs are plentiful in the Plaza Hidalgo area, near the International Bridge, and at upscale hotels. Count on around US$5 for a downtown hop, US$7-9 between the bridge and the junction of Mexico 2 and Mexico 40.

AUTO RENTAL AGENCIES IN REYNOSA

AVIS

Hidalgo 370 Nte., Centro
tel. 2-12-37
Blvd. Morelos 1230, Col. Rodríguez
Aeropuerto Internacional Lucio Blanco
tel. 2-12-37

HERTZ

Km 103, Mexico 2, Col. El Anhelo
tel. 3-99-33
Aeropuerto Internacional Lucio Blanco
tel. 3-00-40

DOLLAR

Juárez 1050 Nte.
tel. 3-00-20
Aeropuerto Internacional Lucio Blanco
tel. 2-33-30

BUDGET

Aeropuerto Internacional Lucio Blanco
tel. 3-01-96
Blvd. Morelos 275
tel. 2-56-93

Auto Rental: Underscoring the city's importance as a business destination, Reynosa has more car rental agencies than any other city along the border. See the "Auto Rental Agencies in Reynosa" list, above, for names and addresses.

REYNOSA TO MATAMOROS

East of Reynosa, Mexico 2 veers away from the Río Bravo (Rio Grande) and passes through the farming centers of Río Bravo and Ramírez before returning to the river at Matamoros. The rich alluvial soils of the Río Bravo plains were virtually ignored until the turn of the century, when river levees and underground irrigation systems were developed. Before that, periodic floods made farming along the river a risky proposition. Also, although the soils were intrinsically rich, the naturally high evaporation rate made it almost impossible to farm the flood plains without irrigation. As a result of controlled watering and mild year-round temperatures, the area now enjoys a 330-day growing season and is an important truck-farming center.

The spread-out town of **Río Bravo,** 16 km (10 miles) southeast of Reynosa, has several small hotels, including the budget **Hotel Papagallo** (Calle 5 de Febrero 105 Sur), the moderate **Hotel La Mansión** (Madero and Galeana) and **Hotel Posada San José** (Calle 5 de Mayo 203), and the *clase económica* **Hotel Río** (Madero 709). Restaurants, including several fast-food places, are abundant along the town's main avenues.

A gravel road north off Mexico 2, 32 km (20 miles) east of Reynosa, leads north 13 km (eight miles) to the tiny community of **Nuevo Progreso,** opposite Progreso, Texas. The latter is linked to US 83 by paved road. On the Mexican side, **Restaurant Arturo's** is a favorite border hop for quail and other game platters. The bridge at this crossing is open weekdays 7:30 a.m.-9 p.m., weekends 8 a.m.-4 p.m.

MATAMOROS

History

Founded under the Escandón *empresario* plan as San Juan de los Esteros Hermosos in 1765, Matamoros was originally a cattle ranching colony. In 1820, the port of Bagdad was established at the nearby mouth of the Río Bravo (Grande) and the town quickly became a regional trade center. Renamed Matamoros in 1826 in commemoration of Mexican independence hero Mariano Matamoros, it's one of only four cities in Mexico whose names are preceded by the honorific "H," which stands for the English equivalent of "Heroic, Loyal, and Unconquered" (hence Mexican traffic signs in the area read "H. Matamoros").

Following the annexation of Texas, the U.S. government established Fort Taylor on the Texas side of the river in 1846, thus sparking the Mexican-American War. In Matamoros, Mexican troops quartered themselves at Casa Mata; Matamoros was briefly occupied before war's end in 1848.

The city prospered during the American Civil War by supplying Confederate troops in Texas via the port of Bagdad, thus avoiding the Union stockade along the Texas Gulf coast. Bagdad didn't last because of the almost continuous on-

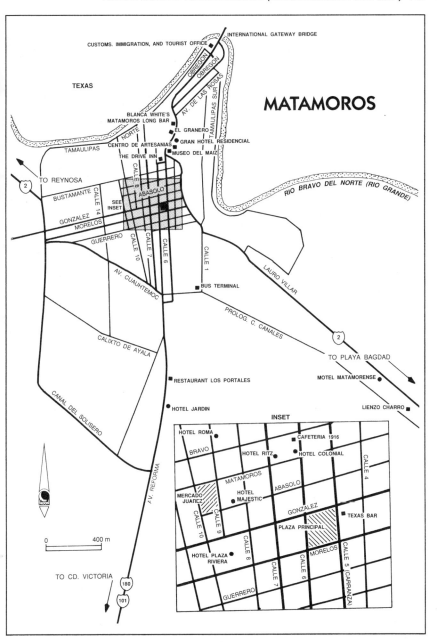

slaught of hurricanes, bandits, and pirates. In 1904 the St. Louis, Brownsville, and Mexico railway was routed to Brownsville, thus reestablishing Matamoros' importance as a commercial center.

Matamoros Today

The area now supports over 80 *maquiladoras,* and a Union Pacific rail terminus has replaced the old St. Louis, Brownsville, and Mexico line. The Gateway International Bridge joins Brownsville and Matamoros (pop. 305,000) and leads to the clean and well-lit Av. Alvaro Obregón, which is lined with bars, restaurants, and souvenir shops. To get a feel for nontourist Matamoros, walk a few blocks down Obregón and make a left at Calle 5 (Carranza) or 6, which lead to the **Plaza Principal,** the main public square. Day or night, this is the city's downtown heart.

LOWER RIO BRAVO CORRIDOR

The U.S.-Mexico borderlands contain some of the richest and most diverse natural environments in either country. With more species per square kilometer than anywhere in the United States, the lower Río Bravo (Rio Grande) corridor in particular represents a fortuitous cross section of Gulf coastal plains, Río Bravo river delta, and Tamaulipan inland plains—a unique blend of humid, subtropical conditions and brush country.

Ten biotic communities have been identified in the area: Tamaulipan thorn forest, upper valley flood forest, *barretal,* upland thornscrub (*matorral*), mid-delta thorn forest, mid-valley riparian woodland, woodland potholes and basins, coastal brushland potholes, sabal palm forest, and *loma* (coastal clay) tidal flats.

These habitats together support over 115 unique vertebrate species, including four of the six remaining wildcats in the U.S. and Mexico—cougars, bobcats, and the endangered **ocelot** and **jaguarundi** (50 years ago the Río Bravo plains were also home to the jaguar and the margay cat, but these may have since disappeared from the area). These habitats also provide important nesting and migratory grounds for around 400 bird species, since this is where two North American migratory paths—the Central and Mississippi flyways—converge.

Sights

Museo Casa Mata: Built in 1845 to defend Mexico from invading U.S. soldiers, this former military quarters contains exhibits of local historical artifacts, Huasteca ceramics, and weapons from the Mexican Revolution era. It's located at the corner of Guatemala and Santos Degollado (take Calle 1 south to Santos Degollado and make a left) and is open Tues.-Sun. 9:30 a.m.-5:30 p.m. Admission is free.

Museo del Maíz: Inaugurated in 1986, this museum devoted entirely to corn is a short walk from the International Bridge at Calle 5 (Calle Carranza) and Av. Constituyentes, a block from the Gran Hotel Residencial. Exhibits detail the history of maize cultivation in Mexico from pre-Cortesian times through the present, as well as traditional folkloric and medicinal uses of the maize plant. There's a strong underlying political message accompanying some of the displays, focusing on criticism of national land distribution policies (Mexico was self-sufficient in corn until 1965 and is now a net importer). The exhibits are fairly easy to follow even if you can't understand the Spanish-only labels.

The museum is open Tues.-Fri. 9:30 a.m.-5 p.m. and Sat.-Sun. 9:30 a.m.-3 p.m. Admission is free.

Accommodations

Budget Hotels: Several of the city's cheaper, one-star hotels are found along Calle Abasolo downtown, including **Hotel Majestic** (tel. 891-3-36-80, Abasolo and Calle 9), **Hotel El Rey** (tel. 2-01-44, Abasolo and Calle 14), and **Hotel Mexico-Frontera Norte** (tel. 2-08-56, Abasolo and Calle 9). These have basic rooms (no a/c) with private baths for US$15-18, but little besides price to recommend them.

Moving up just a notch, **Hotel Colonial** (tel. 2-19-10), on the northwest corner of Calle 6 and Matamoros, is an older hotel with atmosphere and street noise for US$18 s, US$20 d. The Colonial has no parking lot.

Quieter, less central, and about the same price is the string of budget motels along Av. Lauro Villar (Mexico 2), the road southeast toward Playa Bagdad. Two of the better choices on this avenue are the **Fontana Motel** (tel. 6-41-23) at Km 3 and **Motel Matamorense** (tel. 3-30-95) at Av. Lauro Villar and Voz de la Frontera.

Rooms with a/c cost US$20-22 and both motels have parking lots.

Medium-priced Hotels: Hotel Ritz (tel. 2-11-90), at Calle 7 and Matamoros, is a classic border hotel with large a/c rooms for US$35-45 per night; a parking lot is attached. If the Ritz is full, **Hotel Fronterizo Roma** (tel. 3-61-76), nearby at Calle 9 and Bravo, has similar rates but doesn't have quite the charm.

Out on Av. Lauro Villar at Fco. Villa, **Hotel Road Runner** (tel. 3-26-13) has rooms with a/c, TV, and phones for US$36-45 a night. The Road Runner also has its own restaurant and parking lot.

The new and efficient **Hotel Jardín** (tel. 7-07-23, fax 7-07-22), at Calle 6 and Bilbao toward the south end of town and Mexico 180, has very good rooms with a/c, heat, satellite TV, phones, and refrigerators in the US$40-60 range. The hotel also has a restaurant and room service. Similar in price and amenities is **Hotel Plaza Riviera** (tel. 2-07-75), at Calle 10 and Morelos downtown (two blocks from Mercado Juárez).

Luxury Hotels: Top of the heap is the **Gran Hotel Residencial Matamoros** (tel. 3-94-40, 3-94-92), formerly the Del Prado (and before that El Presidente), on the east side of Calle 5a near the Museo del Maíz and Centro de Artesanías. Conveniently located within walking distance of several of the city's best restaurants, the colonial-style Gran Hotel Residencial has a spacious lobby with a dramatic entrance and modern rooms catering to visiting business executives, plus a pool amid landscaped grounds. Rates run US$80-100 during the week, around US$60-70 on weekends.

Camping: Self-contained campers will find plenty of space on the beach in the vicinity of Playa Bagdad, 38 km (23.5 miles) east of town via Mexico 2 (see "Recreation," below).

Accommodations In Brownsville, Texas

On the U.S. side, **Motel 6** (tel. 210-546-4699), off US 77/83 at the FM 802 exit, has single rooms for US$26 per night, plus $7 for each additional adult. The next least expensive motel is the nearby **Best Western Rose Garden Inn** (tel. 546-5501; 845 US 77/83 N), where rooms are $35-45 s, $45-55 d.

There are also a couple dozen apartment complexes in Brownsville that take winter Tex-ans for a few weeks or months at a time (rates are much lower than at the hotels). The **Brownsville Tourist Information Center** (tel. 210-541-8455) at US 77/83 and FM 802 maintains a list of these and can assist with reservations.

RV Parks: Like the rest of Texas's Rio Grande Valley, Brownsville is well equipped for RV and mobile-home drivers. Most of the RV parks are scattered throughout an area east of town, off Boca Chica Blvd. and Minnesota Ave. (FM 313). Several reputable parks that belong to the Brownsville Recreational Vehicle and Mobile Home Association (which represents approximately 1,900 RV spaces) include: **Autumn Acres Trailer Park** (tel. 210-546-4979, 5034 Boca Chica); **Blue Bonnet Trailer Park** (tel. 546-0046, 2404 Las Casas); **Citrus Gardens Trailer Park** (tel. 546-0527, 2225 S. Dakota); **Crooked Tree Campland** (tel. 546-9617, 605 FM 802); **Four Seasons RV & MH Park** (tel. 831-4918, 6900 Coffee Port); **Los Amigos Trailer Park** (tel. 542-8292, 3350 Boca Chica); **Paul's Trailer Park** (tel. 831-4852, 1129 N. Minnesota); **Río RV & MH Park** (tel. 831-4653, 8801 Boca Chica); **Stagecoach RV Park** (tel. 542-7048, 325 FM 802); **Tip-O-Tex** (tel. 350-4031, 6676 N. Frontage); and **Trailer Village** (tel. 546-8350, 5107 Boca Chica). Rates tend to be a uniform $10-12 nightly, $100 monthly, $200-225 for three months, $450 for six months.

Food

As in Nuevo Laredo, *cabrito* and *carne asada* are specialties. Matamoros also prides itself in serving the best tacos along the border. Along Calle 5 are several inexpensive outdoor taco places popular with locals.

One of the nicer taco huts is the newish **El Granero,** just south of Blanca White's Matamoros Long Bar on Av. Obregón near the intersection of Calle Gardenias. In a diminutive, air-conditioned building, El Granero's kitchen turns out over a dozen kinds of moderately priced tacos (among the best are smoked chicken, *rajas poblanas,* and *carne asada),* all served with *frijoles a la charra* and three kinds of salsas in a very clean, low-key atmosphere. El Granero is open Tues.-Sun. 11 a.m.-10 p.m.

Blanca White's Matamoros Long Bar (tel. 891-2-18-59), just north of El Granero at Av. Obregón 49 at Gardenias, is another outpost in the ubiquitous Grupo Anderson chain. As usual, the menu features dishes inspired by local recipes but turned out with an original flair. Unlike the typically rowdy Anderson restaurants found at Mexican beach resorts, Blanca White's has both good food and a fairly restrained ambience. It's open daily noon-midnight.

Nearby at Calle Obregón and Las Rosas is the airy, fern-style **Oscar's Café,** with a broad selection of Mexican, North American, and continental dishes. Oscar's is open daily for breakfast, lunch, and dinner. The clientele is a mix of border-hoppers and businesspeople.

Dark and velvet-lined, **The Drive Inn** (tel. 2-00-22) at Calle 6 and Hidalgo has been a border institution since 1916. Steak, seafood, continental and Mexican choices are well represented on the menu; some border aficionados swear by the place while others abhor it.

On weekend nights the border-hoppers outnumber the locals at the funky **Texas Bar** (tel. 3-13-49), at the southeast corner of Calle 5 and González opposite Plaza Principal (also known as Plaza Allende). Though mainly a drinking establishment, it serves border-style Mexican food.

Out toward the Hotel Jardín on the east side of Calle 6 at Calle J.S. El Cano, the straightforward **Restaurant Los Portales** (tel. 2-33-38) specializes in *cabrito* and *carne asada,* served with *frijoles rancheros,* for lunch and dinner daily.

Breakfasts: For hearty *desayunos* and *almuerzos,* Matamoros has several downtown coffee shops worth trying. One of the more popular ones—day or night—is the **Cafetería 1916** on Calle 6 at Matamoros, near the Hotel Colonial; the menu covers just about all the standards. Farther north on Calle 6 at Galeana is the equally popular **Cafetería El Faro.** Several other *cafeterías* are located in the vicinity along calles 6 and 7.

For something different, scan the local markets for *micharro,* the sweet, gelatinlike kernels of the sabal texana or sabal palm—a delicacy that's becoming increasingly difficult to find.

Recreation

Bullfights and *Charreadas:* Matamoros has a Plaza de Toros at the southern outskirts of town off Av. Reforma. Local *charro* associations practice and compete at the **Lienzo Charro La Costeña,** also south of town on the high-

way. Check with the Matamoros tourist office at the International Bridge or with the Brownsville Convention and Visitors Bureau in Brownsville, Texas, for scheduling information. Bullfight season generally runs May-Sept., while *charreadas* are held year-round.

Theater: The city's historic **Teatro de la Reforma,** built in 1864 and recently restored to all its original glory (and then some), hosts ballet, live theater, and other highbrow entertainment. The theater is on the east side of Calle 6 between Abasolo and Gonzáles, near Plaza Principal.

Bars: Matamoros's main restaurant and bar area, or *zona rosa,* extends southeast from the bridge to the main plaza at Calle 5 (Carranza) and González. **Blanca White's Matamoros Long Bar** (see "Food" in this section) is well stocked and well serviced, a very reliable choice, if a bit pricey by Mexican standards. The clientele is a mix of well-heeled locals and gringos. On the same street, the more local **Garcia's** (tel. 891-3-15-66; Ave. Obregón 2) features live Latin music most nights.

The **Texas Bar** (Calle 5 138, opposite the plaza) has become something of an institution for border-hoppers. The atmosphere borders on the seedy but prices are quite moderate. The nearby **U.S. Bar** is similar.

The lobby bar and disco at **Gran Hotel Residencial** are popular on weekends.

Festivals: One of the oldest and biggest events of the year is a cross-border celebration involving Brownsville, Texas, as well as Matamoros, **Días de los Charros** ("Charro Days" in Brownsville). A local version of the pre-Lenten festival (à la Carnaval and Mardi Gras), it's held for three days in late February at various venues in each city and features parades, costume balls, food, music, and dancing.

Diez y Seis or Mexican Independence Day (Sept. 16) is also big in both cities; on the weekend nearest the 16th they cooperate for **Fiesta International,** a bicultural weekend of fireworks, parades, and *mucho* celebration. For scheduling details on either event, contact the Brownsville Chamber of Commerce (tel. 210-542-4341 in the U.S.).

Día de Nuestra Señora del Refugio, the city's patron saint day (July 4), is confined to the Mexican side and features a pageant of *matachine* and other folk dances.

Shopping: Though not as popular a shopping venue as Nuevo Laredo, Matamoros sees many Texans looking for quick south-of-the-border bargains. The shops along Av. Obregón are not the cheapest, since they cater to day tourists who don't venture very far into town, but some of their folk art is decent.

Two large markets in town carry a wide selection of Mexican arts and crafts and are more susceptible to negotiation. **Mercado Juárez,** stretching across Abasolo and Matamoros between Calles 9 and 10 (about three blocks east of the plaza), is the biggest; a smaller version is on Bravo between Calles 8 and 9. The **Centro de Artesanías** on Av. Obregón near the Gran Hotel Residencial contains several shops selling glassware, boots, clothing, and other handicrafts.

Radio: For some great border radio, tune in 96.1 FM (KIWW), a Tejano station received on both sides of the river. Bilingual DJs play a hot mix of Tex-Mex, *norteña,* and Tejano pop.

Playa Bagdad

Formerly known as "Playa Lauro Villar," this Gulf of Mexico beach 38 km (23.5 miles) east of Matamoros stretches north some 16 km to the mouth of the Río Bravo near the abandoned port of Bagdad. This is one of the most pleasant coastal recreation areas along the Gulf, only a small portion of which has been developed. *Palapas* (US$1.60 per day) extend for a couple of hundred meters north and south of the road's end, with a modest seafood restaurant at the north end. Freshwater showers are available, as is a first-aid clinic and parking lot (also US$1.60 all day).

Windsurfing is tops all along the Gulf shore and, except in storm conditions, the beach is very suitable for swimming. Camping is permitted north or south of the public area.

Surf casting is fair anywhere along the beach, and anglers also have the option of fishing in an inland lagoon. The best saltwater fishing in the area is 22 km (13.6 miles) south via the sandy coastal flats at the *escolleras* (jetties), beyond the fishing village of Conchillal (eight km/five miles south). This is also where the best surfing action is.

Getting There: The highway to the beach from Matamoros is in fair condition all the way. If you don't have your own wheels, you can catch one of the blue-and-white *colectivos* that run from Plaza Allende (Plaza Principal) downtown all the way to Playa Bagdad three or four times daily.

Information

Tourist Offices: The state tourist office (tel. 891-2-36-30) at Puerta México (the customs-immigration building next to the International Bridge) distributes brochures, maps, and information on local sights and activities.

A limited amount of information on Matamoros can also be obtained at the **Brownsville Information Center** (tel. 210-596-3721; 800-626-2639 outside Texas), at the junction of FM 802 and US 77/83. It's open Mon.-Fri. 8:30 a.m.-5 p.m., Sat. 8 a.m.-5 p.m., Sun. 9 a.m.-4 p.m.

Matamoros Transport

Air: Aeroméxico (tel. 891-3-07-01; Av. Obregón 21) has daily flights between Matamoros and Mexico City. The airport is 12 km (7.5 miles) south of town off Mexico 180; taxis cost US$15, *colectivos* are US$8, and buses from the Central de Autobuses are US$0.60.

Bus: The city's Central de Autobuses is off Calle Canales between Calle Aguilar (Calle 2) and Calle 1. The main regional bus lines are **Tres Estrellas de Oro, Oriente,** and **Transportes Frontera,** which serve cities and towns throughout the states of Tamaulipas, Nuevo León and San Luis Potosí.

Transportes del Norte and **Omnibus de Mexico** have daily *ejecutivo* buses to Monterrey for US$15 each way. Express and first-class buses to Tampico are operated by Transportes del Norte and **Oriente** for US$12-16.

MATAMOROS TELEPHONE NUMBERS

Police: 6-07-00
Highway Patrol: 7-01-34
Green Angels: 2-36-30
State Tourist Office: 2-36-30
Cruz Roja (medical emergencies): 2-00-44, 6-65-62
U.S. Consulate: 6-72-70, 6-72-71; after hours (210) 546-1611 (Brownsville)
Matamoros Area Code: 891

Buses to Matamoros from Brownsville leave frequently throughout the day from the **Greyhound/Valley Transit Co. (VTC)** station (tel. 210-546-2264), at 1305 E. Adams. The fare is US$3.

Train: El Tamaulipeco takes 6¹/₂ hours to complete its daily run between Monterrey and Matamoros, with a stop in Reynosa. Reserved first-class fares for the journey are US$8 Monterrey-Reynosa, US$11 Reynosa-Matamoros, US$19 Monterrey-Matamoros; second-class fares are US$2.50, US$3, and US$5.50 respectively. See the "Railway Schedule," pp. 86-87, for arrival and departure times.

Driving: Matamoros is one of the easier border cities to drive through because of its wide, well-planned avenues, which link the border crossing directly with Mexico 2 and Mexico 180.

To reach Mexico 2 east (to Playa Bagdad) from the International Bridge, follow Av. Obregón south and bear left onto Calle 2 (Blvd. Lauro Villar) at the sign marked "A Playa Bagdad." Blvd. Lauro Villar becomes Mexico 2 within a couple of kilometers.

For Mexico 180 south (to La Pesca and Tampico), stay on Av. Obregón until it merges with Calle 6, which becomes Av. Reforma south of Calle Canales; Av. Reforma eventually turns into Mexico 180.

Border Formalities: See the "Entry Regulations" section, p. 100, for important information on Mexican immigration and customs requirements. The Matamoros bridge crossing is open 24 hours.

AUTO RENTAL AGENCIES IN MATAMOROS

AVIS

Av. A. Obregón 1
tel. 3-54-61

BUDGET

Av. A. Obregón 33-A (and airport)
tel. 3-48-80

DOLLAR

P. Cárdenas 100, local H-15
tel. 7-35-25, 7-45-83

RALLY AUTO RENT

Calle 6 (Bustamante) and Herrera 202-1
tel. 3-19-96, 3-57-08

Tours

Gray Line (tel. 210-542-8962) operates a five-hour sightseeing/shopping tour of Matamoros from South Padre Island, Texas, for U$15 per person. A Brownsville operation, **Bro-Mat** (tel. 544-6292), offers similar tours.

MATAMOROS TO TAMPICO

The 504-km (312-mile) coastal route between the Texas border and the Gulf port of Tampico is scenic and lightly trafficked. Mexico 101 leads southeast from Matamoros through San Fernando, then links with Mexico 180, which zigzags farther south via Aldama to Tampico. Along the way several roads branch east off Mexico 101 and Mexico 180 to the vast Laguna Madre and Gulf of Mexico shores, where there is mile after mile of undisturbed *loma* tidal flats, salt-marshes, and sandy beaches.

Although there has long been talk of developing a modern "mega-resort" somewhere along this stretch, so far the entire coast has been blissfully neglected by mass tourism. Birding, beaching, windsurfing, surfing, and fishing are superb in many spots but are best enjoyed by self-contained visitors who travel with their own shelter and supplies. The only hotels north of Tampico are in La Pesca, San Fernando, Aldama, and Barra del Tordo. The typical *laguna* branch road terminates at a local fish camp, not always the most attractive of places but a source for minimal supplies.

Magna Sin is available only in San Fernando, so be sure to top off the tank before continuing southward.

Playa El Mezquital

This broad beach area on a long barrier peninsula wedged between the Gulf of Mexico and vast Laguna Madre has many similarities to Padre Island National Seashore along the Texas coast except that it's even more remote from human intervention. Although there are no facilities to speak of, access to both Gulf and Laguna Madre beachcombing, fishing, and camping is superb for well-equipped visitors.

The turnoff for El Mezquital is 21 km (13 miles) south of Matamoros off Mexico 180, after which it's another 57 km (35 miles) on a paved surface to the coast. The scenic road bridges the Río El Tigre (the first of two Río Tigres along the coast) and the north end of the Laguna Madre. Vehicles equipped for sand-flats driving can continue south some 60 km (37 miles) or more along the peninsula.

Other names for this barrier peninsula include "Punta La Capilla" and "Barra San José."

San Fernando (Fernando De Presas)

This small town on Mexico 180, where the highway crosses the Río San Fernando, is a popular restaurant and fuel stop for long-distance motorists. It's also a staging point for excursions to the Laguna Madre beaches of El Barrancón, Carbonera, and Carvajal, and for hunting trips in the *matorral* surrounding the Río Conchos. In the center of town near the plaza are several buildings that date to the mid-19th century, including the **Palacio Municipal, Mercado Hidalgo,** and stone **Iglesia de San Fernando.** The latter is very much in the style of the San Antonio missions in South Texas.

Accommodations: Several motels along or near the highway offer basic but comfortable lodgings. One of the better choices in town is **Motel La Serena** (tel. 894-4-02-65; Calle Zapata), which offers clean a/c rooms and a swimming pool for US$24-30 per night. **Motel La Hacienda** (tel. 4-04-99), at the north end of town at Km 174, has similar facilities for around US$5 less. Clustered in this same area along the highway are **Hotel San José** (tel. 4-17-29, Km 173), **Hotel Las Palomas** (tel. 4-04-85, Km 178), and **Hotel Paso Real** (tel. 4-10-36, Km 172), all in the US$20-30 range.

RV Park: Attached to the Motel La Serena is **La Serena RV Park,** with full hookups for US$11 per night.

Food: Of the several highway eateries, only **El Granero Grill** is open 24 hours. Other highway spots include **Pollo Frito Buenos Aires, El Esfuerzo, Davila,** and **Boca de Catán.**

Fuel: A PEMEX station on the highway pumps Magna Sin, the last available until Tampico.

Hunting Resorts: El Tejón, outside San Fernando off Mexico 180, hosts hunters shooting for white-winged dove, quail, duck, and goose along the Río Conchos. Facilities include landscaped grounds, restaurant, pool, and tackle shop. Farther southwest near the village of Criullas (39 km/24 miles south on Mexico 180, then west about 25 km/15.5 miles), **La Loma** specializes in quail and white-winged dove. For information on either resort, contact Sunbelt Hunting & Fishing (tel. 800-876-4868; P.O. Box 3009, Brownsville, TX 78520).

East of town 40 km (25 miles) on Lago la Nacha, a natural lake fed by the Río Conchos, is the **Laguna Vista,** a hunting and fishing resort with a/c rooms, restaurant, and pool. For further information contact Laguna Vista (tel. 210-421-4401, 800-274-4401; P.O. Box 44, Combes, TX 78535).

Playa El Barrancón And Playa Carbonera

Almost any road heading east from Mexico 180 between Matamoros and San Fernando leads to the Laguna Madre western shore. Most are unpaved and lead to saltmarshes—great sites for birding.

Along this western shore, intrepid beachgoers and sportfishers can ferret out at least two sandy beaches, both of which are suitable for camping and lagoon fishing. **Carbonera** is the most accessible; a paved road leads east from the town of San Fernando all the way to the lagoon shore, a distance of about 52 km (32 miles). From Carbonera an unpaved road sand road continues south to **Playa Carvajal,** a beach at the tip of Punta Barranco Amarillo where the estuarial Laguna el Catán branches west off the Laguna Madre. Both beaches have *palapas,* picnic tables, cooking grills, and trash receptacles; Carbonera also has an area set aside for camping.

To find **El Barrancón** you must make an eastward turn off Mexico 180 about 18 km (11 miles) north of the Mexico 180/Mexico 97 junction, just three km south of the small town of Alfredo V. Bonfil. The first road is paved as far as Santa Rita (about 23 km/14 miles), after which it forks into two dirt roads. Take the left fork for El Barrancón. Beach facilities include *palapas,* grills, tables, and trash bins; camping is permitted.

SOTO LA MARINA-LA PESCA

La Pesca ("Fish") is the name generally given to an area at the mouth of the Río Soto la Marina, where river and sea meet to form a network of estuarial lagoons. Starting with the southernmost extension of the Laguna Madre, named *lagunas* also include La Sal, Almagre, Tulosa, Santa Rita, Contadero, Chovenosa, and Morales. These lagoons, along with the Gulf and the wide Río Soto la Marina itself, offer a seemingly endless variety of venues for fishing, boating, birding, and simple enjoyment of the estuarial environment.

For years there has been talk of establishing a government-funded, Cancún-style resort here, but for now the area safely remains a sleepy backwater with a bit of seasonal fishing and small-scale tourism. Perhaps the area's saving grace is that, though beautiful in its own right, the Gulf tidal flats don't fit the palm-fringed, crystal-sands image required to compete with Mexico's Pacific or Caribbean coastal resorts. A more realistic objective would be the condotel-style development found at South Padre Island along Texas's south coast, though many frequent visitors would rather see La Pesca preserved the way it is today.

The small town of La Pesca, a jumble of unfinished or decaying breeze-block architecture near the end of the 54-km (34-mile) paved road from Soto la Marina, is the least attractive aspect of the area. Visitors normally stay in vacation homes or small resorts along the estuary, or else they camp on the beach well away from town. The beach at the end of the road has *palapas,* wooden shelters, trash receptacles, and a breakwater jetty. Another road continues north behind the dunes for a couple of kilometers before giving way to hard-packed sand.

Soto la Marina is the main supply center for La Pesca visitors and residents. One of the original Escandón settlements dating to the mid-18th century, the town's main historical claim is that it hosted northeastern Mexico's first printing press, installed and operated by Bostonian J. Samuel Bangs in 1816.

Geography And Wildlife

Typified by barrier islands, barrier peninsulas (or *barras*), and coastal lagoons, the topography surrounding La Pesca is similar to that found all the way along the Gulf coast from Galveston Island, Texas, to Tampico. The major differences are that the Mexican portion is much less developed and the average temperatures significantly milder, thus allowing for a greater variety of flora and fauna to flourish.

Barra Soto la Marina: Extending northward from La Pesca nearly 200 km (124 miles), this thin wedge of sand and tidal clay separates the Gulf of Mexico from the Laguna Madre. The entire length of the Gulf side is sandy beach—one of the longest on the North American continent. The beach is backed by a coastal dune ridge, which is held in place by salt-tolerant vegetation such as sand verbena and red or black mangrove. On the lagoon side of the dunes are coastal grasslands and saltmarshes of varying width; in some places the dunes extend all the way across the *barra,* while in others the land behind the dune ridge is submerged by wash-over channels.

Laguna Madre: Separating Barra Soto la Marina from the mainland, this vast, shallow, brackish lagoon is fed by fresh water from the Soto la Marina, El Carrizo, and Conchos rivers mixed with salt water from the Gulf of Mexico. Because of the greater number of rivers emptying into Mexico's Laguna Madre, the average salinity is significantly lower than that of Texas's Laguna Madre. The lagoon's median depth is around a meter (three feet); in some places the lagoon barely covers the tidal flats underneath.

Silting near the mouth of the Río Soto la Marina has created a land bridge across the *barra,* thus dividing the Laguna Madre from the Laguna Morales to the south.

Fauna: The aquatic interplay of rivers, lagoon, tidal flats, marshes, wash-over channels, and Gulf waters produces a perfect environment for the spawning, foraging, and nursing of fish and shellfish species. Many local species spawn in one area, nurse in another, and feed in yet another, participating in a cycle that wouldn't be viable anywhere else. Redfish, for example, spawn in the Gulf but spend most of their lives in the lagoons; young shrimp nurse in the lagoons but move into the Gulf as adults.

Manatees are sometimes seen at the mouth of the Soto la Marina river in the fall (when they begin migrating toward the Yucatán Peninsula for the winter), while roseate spoonbills, pelicans, marsh hawks, snow geese, and other colorful waterfowl often frequent the edges of the lagoons and marshes in winter. Easy to spot are white pelicans, which attain wingspans of up to three meters (nine feet), and the frigate bird, whose wingspan is often 2-2½ meters (seven to eight feet).

Occasionally visitors may catch glimpses of bottle-nosed, spotted, or bridled dolphins swimming close to shore. Sea turtles—including the loggerhead, hawksbill, green sea turtle, giant leatherback, and Kemp's (Atlantic) ridley, were once common but due to over-harvesting are now rarely seen near shore.

Climate

La Pesca is just north of the Tropic of Cancer (but farther south than the Florida Keys), which means mild temperatures most of the year. The average low for January is 10.5° C (51° F), while the average high for the same month is 21° C (70° F). In July, La Pesca temperatures range from 24° to 34° C (76° to 93° F). In general, summer highs in the area are two or three degrees lower than in Matamoros or Nuevo Laredo.

Average annual precipitation in the area is around 65 cm (25 inches), or about half the average rainfall in Miami. September is the wettest month, averaging around 13 cm (five inches) of rain. The hurricane season begins in May, peaks in August and September, and fades out by the end of October, but most of the *barra* suffers little or no damage during tropical storms or hurricanes—just rain and high winds (there's only a one-in-eight chance of a hurricane striking this far south in any given year). With an eye to the weather, the best time of year for a visit is Oct.-May.

On hot summer weekends and extended holidays, crowds fill the central beach area at La Pesca. April's Semana Santa, in particular, is a time to avoid if enjoying the beach is your primary objective.

Accommodations

Most of the places to stay in the area are strung out along the Río Soto la Marina, off the south side of the road before you reach the town of La Pesca itself. All have their own piers or boat launches and can arrange fishing trips. There is no telephone service in the area but some places maintain reservation/information lines in Reynosa, Soto la Marina, Tampico, or McAllen, Texas.

El Refugio Motel, on the estuary just before La Pesca between Km 43 and 44, provides comfortable rooms for US$40, RV spaces with full hookups for US$10. Next door, the **Hotel Villa del Mar** (tel. 132-7-00-65) offers 11 basic rooms with a/c for US$35; new rooms under construction will probably cost more. Villa del

Mar also has RV spots for self-contained rigs for US$5-7 and a pleasant *palapa* sitting area by the river.

A hundred meters east of Km 44 is **La Marina del Río Campo Turista** (tel. 892-2-06-72 in Reynosa; 210-630-0138 or 800-284-1286 in the U.S.), an eight-room Mediterranean-style lodge with a/c that costs US$60 per double including meals. La Marina has the best all-around reputation for comfort and service in the area, as well as the best boat-launching facilities. Nearby is the similarly priced, 24-room **Hotel El Pescador** (tel. 12-13-13-33 in Tampico), which has exceptionally well-kept grounds—quite an accomplishment given the fast-growing flora along the estuary.

La Gaviota Trailer Park (tel. 210-380-1240 in Texas) on the estuary at Km 48 has two-way hookups for US$8, tent spaces for US$5, a private pier, *palapas,* and barbecue pits.

In the same vicinity is **Campo la Pesca del Río** (tel. 800-331-0479 or 210-632-6849 in the U.S.), a 15-room, Mediterranean-style, hunting-and-fishing lodge with doubles for US$95 up, including all meals. It's also known as Hotel La Pesca and La Pesca Lodge; the restaurant has a good reputation.

A new place called the **Hacienda El Contadero** on the opposite side of the river has recently opened—for information on how to get there (a ferry ride across the river is necessary), check with the state tourist office in Matamoros or Ciudad Victoria.

In the ramshackle village of La Pesca, the basic **Motel La Isla** (tel. 11-7-01-67 in Soto la Marina) has rooms for US$15 per night.

Camping: Most of the resorts along the river will allow tent camping on their grounds for a nominal fee. Camping on the beach is free.

Soto la Marina: Should you find yourself in need of lodging in Soto la Marina, **Hotel María Cristina** (tel. 7-00-51) and **Hotel Chicago** (tel. 11-7-03-51), near the junction of Mexico 180 and the road to La Pesca, offer fair rooms for US$25-30 s/d.

Food

All of the resorts have restaurant service. In La Pesca itself are several well-stocked mini-markets and a couple of basic seafood places; ice is readily available. A greater selection of groceries is available in Soto la Marina.

Recreation

Fishing: Most visitors to La Pesca are interested in trying their luck with the area's namesake. Among the gamefish species common to the Laguna Madre are redfish, black drum, flounder, sheepshead, speckled seatrout, skipjack, and striped mullet. Several of these are also found on the Gulf side, along with pompano, mackerel, manta ray, seabass, shark, corvina, tarpon, sand trout, and, farther offshore, grouper, bonito, kingfish, red snapper, marlin, and sailfish. A variety of oysters and crabs make their home among the island's intertidal zones. Crabs are especially plentiful, with perhaps 20 species commonly seen.

Even at its most crowded, La Pesca has plenty of room for every angler. Any of the resorts mentioned under "Accommodations," above, can arrange guided fishing trips by boat, although there is no guide industry comparable to that in Port Isabel/South Padre Island north of the border. A couple of local fishing associations organize annual fishing tournaments, most notably the international tournament hosted by the Club Tiro, Caza y Pesca Tamatán through Hotel El Pescador in mid-November.

Boating: Trailered or car-topped boats can be launched at any of the resorts mentioned above. Shallow, flat-bottomed boats are best for river or lagoon boating. Boating in Gulf waters should only be undertaken by persons experienced in open-sea boating, as salvage and rescue services are scarce.

Surfing: The surf near the beach jetty is very good at times, comparable to wave action in Port Aransas, Galveston Island, and other Texas surfing destinations where artificial hard shores are available. In general, the best times of year for surf are spring and late summer/early fall.

Windsurfing: Novices will find the Laguna Madre or Laguna Morales perfect for working on turns or for long sails in one direction; the mouth of the Río Soto la Marina offers stronger breezes suitable for intermediate boardsailors, while the Gulf has stronger winds yet and offers the added surf challenge.

Hunting: Inland from the estuarial system are hunting areas for white-winged dove, quail, duck, goose, wild turkey, wild boar, and white-tailed deer. Most of the resorts can advise and arrange hunts; contact **Hotel El Pescador** or **Campo la Pesca del Río** for information. Hunting regulations in Mexico are very strict; be sure to read the section on hunting in the "Out and About" chapter (see p. 43). Going through a Mexican hunting broker is the simplest way to clear the necessary red tape.

Getting There

Air: La Pesca has its own 2,070-meter (6,800-foot) airstrip for small planes. If arriving pilots buzz the strip once or twice, someone will drive out to provide taxi service.

Bus: Between Soto la Marina and La Pesca there is only one slow bus daily—count on a three- to four-hour ride and a US$4 fare. Buses to Soto la Marina leave frequently from Matamoros, Reynosa, Ciudad Victoria, and Tampico.

Driving: Due to the road conditions and the number of towns encountered along the way, it's nearly a full day's drive from Matamoros (254 km/157.5 miles) or Tampico (279 km/173 miles) to La Pesca, four to five hours from Ciudad Victoria (180 km/111.5 miles), and about two hours from Soto la Marina (54 km/33.5 miles)—if you obey the speed limits and make stops for food and gas along the way. (The state tourist office claims it only takes two hours from the border, a time record that would surely mean violating speed limits the entire way.) From any direction, it's two-lane highway all the way; the last leg between Soto la Marina and La Pesca is particularly slow, in spite of scant traffic, due to long stretches of potholes and patched road, plus an extensive middle section of rolling hills with tight curves.

Ciudad Victoria-Soto la Marina: The 1 1/2- to two-hour, 121-km (75-mile) drive from Ciudad Victoria to Soto la Marina along Mexico 70 is particularly scenic; the eastern half of the Victoria-Soto road passes through the rolling Sierra Tamaulipas and some of the state's best examples of Tamaulipan thorn forest. Here you can truly begin to make sense of the "tropical/arid" description geographers have bestowed upon this type of terrain. Mexico 70 is heavily patched in places but overall is in fair condition; traffic is light. You'll pass several ranches along the way; **Rancho El Cone** near Km 80 features a small roadside restaurant in a stone house.

Fuel: La Pesca has one PEMEX station, with Nova and diesel only, near the estuarial fishing harbor. The nearest stations with Magna Sin are in Ciudad Victoria and San Fernando; if

your vehicle takes unleaded gasoline, top off in one of these towns before approaching La Pesca. By the time you read this, the PEMEX station in Soto la Marina may have added a Magna Sin pump, but don't take a chance.

SOTO LA MARINA TO TAMPICO

Beaches North Of Tampico

South of Soto la Marina, several roads branch east off Mexico 180 to coastal zones with flat, sandy beaches much like those found farther north. The turnoff for **Playa Tepehuaje** is 56 km (35 miles) south of Soto, from which it's 40 km (25 miles) by paved road to the beach. *Palapas,* tables, grills, and trash collection are provided by the state. By this point, you've left the Tropic of Cancer behind and are firmly within tropical Mexico.

Well off the beaten track, **Barra de Ostiones** (also known as El Brasil) is the next beach south, 98 km (61 miles) south of Soto and then 36 km (22 miles) east via a gravel road. Facilities are nil but there is plenty of space for camping; the small Río Carrizo empties into the Gulf here, providing an estuarial zone of interest to naturalists.

About 18 km south of Barra de Ostiones along the coast is **Barra Vicente,** (also called Rancho Nuevo), the only known area where the endangered Atlantic ridley sea turtle still nests and lays eggs in any sustainable numbers. At one time the Atlantic ridley nested all along the western Gulf coast (in 1947, a film recorded some 40,000 ridleys laying eggs at Rancho Nuevo), but its numbers have been in drastic decline over the last 30 years. Since 1978 a team of Mexican and U.S. marine biologists have been attempting to restore the population by habituating the turtles to new nesting areas.

Barra del Tordo is 50 km (31 miles) northeast of Aldama, which is 148 km (92 miles) south of Soto la Marina. This long stretch of mostly undeveloped beach at the mouth of the Río Carrizal is popular on hot weekends and on holidays. Facilities include a long line of *palapas;* between April-Oct. **Hotel Playa Azul,** a mediocre restaurant-hotel concession, may be open. During Semana Santa the beach is thick with food vendors.

Small fishing boats are available for rent year-round for trips up the scenic Río Carrizal. Francisco Haces (tel. 210-350-4986 in Brownsville or 12-13-14-26 in Tampico) operates a fishing resort on this river.

South of here at the mouth of the Río Tigre, where it feeds into the **Laguna San Andrés,** is a fishing lodge called **Pelifinos** with rooms overlooking the river. For information on rates and reservations, contact Trips Unlimited (tel. 210-399-8800; Route 1, Box 81M, San Benito, TX 78586). A rock reef offshore offers interesting diving possibilities.

Aldama

Originally founded as Presas del Rey in 1790, Aldama today is a ranching, farming, and hunting center that serves as a supply and staging point for excursions to Barra del Tordo, Rancho Nuevo, Barra de Ostiones, and **Presa República Española.** The latter is a reservoir 40 km (25 miles) north of town with facilities for camping and fishing (large black bass are plentiful).

Aldama is known by gastronomes throughout the state for *barbacoa* and cheeses, especially *queso panela* (often served grilled). The town has also earned a reputation for skillfully made saddles, *chaparreras,* and other leather *vaquero* gear.

Practicalities: On the highway, **Motel El Greco** (tel. 127-4-03-71) offers nine very basic rooms for around US$15 per night. In town at Méndez and Reforma, **Hotel Rancho Viejo** (tel. 4-01-84) has better-kept rooms in the US$18-30 range.

Restaurante Las Trojas and **Restaurante Los Motivos,** both near Km 35 on the highway, feed passing motorists. A PEMEX station pumps Magna Sin.

At Presa República Española, **El Paraíso Fishing & Hunting Lodge** (tel. 12-13-14-26 in Tampico; 210-350-4816 in Brownsville, Texas) and **Campo Española** (James Mayo, tel. 318-323-8612; 505 Martin St., Monroe, LA 71292) offer a/c lodging and meals.

TAMPICO-MADERO

Modern Tampico is a curious mixture of upscale shopping malls and seedy waterfronts, classy suburban homes and downtown blocks whose air of romantic decay, though often compared to New Orleans, is perhaps more reminiscent of a monsoon-blasted South China Sea port.

Surrounded on three sides by water—the Gulf of Mexico to the east, the Río Pánuco to the south, and a patchwork of lagoons to the west—Tampico is most of all a mariner's city. The second oldest and largest port in Mexico (after Pajaritos, Ver.), the Río Pánuco harbor handles over 10% of all offshore cargo in the country. Sea freight lines terminate in the U.S. at Galveston, Texas, and New Orleans, Louisiana (for transshipment of Mexican goods by road throughout the U.S. and Canada), and to various ports in Europe.

There is also considerable shipping traffic between Tampico and other ports in Mexico's "Faja de Oro" or "Gold Belt" for oil production, which extends from the central Tamaulipas coast southeast to Campeche. Annexed neighbor city Ciudad Madero is home to the biggest PEMEX facility in Northern Mexico; an oil pipeline runs northeast from Madero through Ciudad Victoria to Cadereyta for use by industrial giant Monterrey. Despite local industry, the city itself is surprisingly clean.

Including its Siamese twin, Ciudad Madero, metropolitan Tampico currently counts 545,000 inhabitants and is the nation's eighth largest metro area. The city's principal livelihood remains the storage, refining, and shipping of oil (centered in Ciudad Madero), with transport, chandlery, textiles, food processing, military service, and fishing close behind. Shrimp—in addition to being harvested by offshore Gulf trawlers—are raised in the many lagoons that dot the inland landscape.

Both short-term visitors and longer-term snowbirds will be glad to hear that Tampico has Mexico's second lowest consumer price index among the country's 35 largest cities.

HISTORY

Exploration And Settlement

Spanish conquistadores came upon the confluence of the Río Pánuco, Río Tamesí, and Gulf of Mexico—the site for today's Tampico—early in their Gulf coast explorations. Explorer Alfonso Alvarez de Piñeda, who surveyed much of the upper Gulf, met his demise at the hands of Huastec Indians when probing the Río Pánuco in 1519. *Misionero* Fray Andrés de Olmos had more peaceful contact with Huastecs living on the south bank of the Río Pánuco (at present-day Ciudad Cuauhtémoc) in 1530, 1532, and 1544. It wasn't until 1554, however, that Franciscan friars were able to establish the ranchería of Villa de San Luis de Tampico on the north shore, populated by a mix of Spaniards and Tlaxcaltecas from the settlement of San Esteban de Pánuco (present-day Pánuco, Ver.) farther southwest; this colony, along with the newer ranchería, was razed by pirate Sir Laurent Graff (known as "Lorencillo" among the Spanish) in 1684.

French mariners, Spaniards, indigenous tribes, and pirates battled over control of the estuarial harbor throughout the remainder of the 17th and 18th centuries, preventing permanent settlement by any single group until late in the northern *empresario* program. Antonio López de Santa Anna finally transferred a sizable chunk of land (which he had been granted in return for his successful campaign against Emperor Agustín de Iturbide) to ranchers along the north bank of the Río Pánuco in 1823. At the time, a Huastec settlement called Tampico sat on the south bank; thus the new settlement was named Santa Anna de Tampico. The town was occupied by U.S. troops in 1847 during the Mexican-American War, and when Santa Anna fell in 1854, the unpopular dictator's name was quickly removed. Tampico was also briefly occupied by the French during France's 1862-63 naval invasion.

TAMPICO

TO SOTO LA MARINA

HOTEL POSADA DE TAMPICO
PLAZA TRES ARCOS
PLAZA CRYSTAL
LIVERPOOL

0   3 km

AV. TAMAULIPAS

BLVD. COSTERO

PLAYA MIRAMAR

GULF OF MEXICO

AV. UNIVERSIDAD
LOPEZ MATEOS
AGUA DULCE
AV. HIDALGO
FRANCITA
EJERCITO MEXICANO
CUAUHTEMOC
CALLE 1 DE MAYO
AV. OBREGON

BUS TERMINAL
MUSEO DE LA CULTURA HUASTECA

HOTEL CAMINO REAL

LAGUNA DEL CARPINTERO

RIO PANUCO

70

SEE INSET

TO CD. VALLES

TO VERACRUZ

180

INSET

MENDEZ
DR. MATIENZO
S. J. INES DE LA CRUZ
S. DIAZ MIRON
20 DE NOVIEMBRE
COLON
F. I. MADERO
RIBERA

V. CARRANZA
F. A. OLMOS
ALTAMIRA
A. OBREGON

HOTEL CAPRI

PLAZA DE ARMAS

HOTEL IMPALA

B. JUAREZ
ADUANA
LOPEZ DE LARA

HOTEL INGLATERRA

SUPER CREAM

HOTEL MONTE CARLO

HOTEL TAMPICO

CAFE MUNDO

HOTEL JALISCO

HOTEL BUENA VISTA

HOTEL PLAZA

HOTEL COLONIAL

MARKET

HOTEL POSADA DEL REY

RESTAURANT INSURGENTES

RESTAURANT LA GRAN MURALLA CHINA

PLAZA DE LA LIBERTAD

A. SERDAN

PORTAS GIL

SALON PALACIO
RESTAURANT DILIGENCIAS

H. DEL CANONERO

0   100 m

RIO PANUCO

ADUANA

RAILWAY STATION

© MOON PUBLICATIONS, INC.

Growth And *La Bonanza Petrolera*

Fishing and chandlery were the primary occupations for the remaining 19th and early 20th centuries. Because of the abundance and high quality of crabs harvested in the huge estuarial system, Tampico soon earned the nickname Puerto Jaiba or "Crab Port." The town also offered a secure harbor for ships moving along the Gulf coast between Mexico and the United States.

Crabbing quickly took a back seat following the discovery of petroleum in the Pánuco Basin in 1911. During the early years of oil exploration in the 1910s and '20s, Tampico was a boomtown that attracted workers, speculators, and hangers-on from all over the Western world. North American and British companies flocked to the area and flooded Northeastern Mexico with U.S. dollars, turning Tampico into the "New Orleans of Mexico." During the city's pre-nationalization heyday, a quarter of all the crude petroleum extracted in the world came from Tampico. In the 1920s the city was so far ahead of the rest of Mexico in terms of technology and modernization that the nation's first commercial airliner left the ground not from Mexico City or Monterrey but from Tampico.

Nationalization And Diversification

Largely due to an oil workers' strike in Tampico, Mexican President Lázaro Cárdenas expelled all foreign companies and nationalized mineral resources in the mid-1930s. The city's short-lived glory faded as the new Petróleos Mexicana (PEMEX) failed to maintain the quality and growth of regional oil exploitation. When the oil boom of the 1970s boosted the city's fortunes again, Tampico's city government wisely used the windfall to diversify the economy, improving and extending local infrastructure for manufacturing, food production, and shipping.

Although a preponderance of Tampiqueñas still work in PEMEX-related jobs, the city is no longer entirely oil-dependent. Altamira, 20 km to the north, is currently being developed to become the most important cargo port in Latin America.

SIGHTS

Plazas And Historical Buildings

The city's heart is the **Plaza de Armas,** bound-

Plaza de Armas

ed by calles Fray Andrés de Olmos, Colón, Carranza, and Mirón. Surrounded with palms, the plaza's huge, tile-domed *kiosko* frequently hosts live mariachi or marimba music on Sundays. Any day of the week—unless it's raining—the park is packed with people strolling or sitting. Facing the north side of the plaza is the imposing **Catedral de Tampico,** built in 1931 with money donated by an American oil mogul on the site of an earlier 1823-vintage church.

Two blocks southeast at Juárez and Madero, the slightly smaller **Plaza de la Libertad** dates to the turn of the century and is flanked by Porfiriato-era, beaux arts-style architecture—the prime example of which is the **Correos y Telégrafos** building on the north side. On the west side of the Plaza at Madero and Juárez, the **Hotel Posada del Rey** bears the typical wrought-iron balconies of the era that have inspired comparisons with New Orleans.

Museo De La Cultura Huasteca

The little-known Huastec Culture Museum, in the Instituto Tecnológico de Ciudad Madero, houses the best exhibits on the history and archaeology of the Huastec civilization outside

Mexico City. Displays include extensive examples of Huastec ceramics, architecture, painting, clothing, copper and shell crafts, lapidary arts, and sculpture. The museum (tel. 12-5-63-39) is located at Calle 1 de Mayo and Juana Inés de la Cruz in Ciudad Madero and is open Mon.-Fri. 10 a.m.-5 p.m., Sat. 10 a.m.-1 p.m.; admission is free.

Waterfront
Visitors interested in the maritime realm may want to explore the Río Pánuco riverfront along the southwestern edge of downtown Tampico, parallel to the rail line. Like many waterfronts around the world, Tampico's projects a classically seedy atmosphere, characterized by cheap taco bars, bustling markets, street vendors, seamen's hotels, and congested traffic—in fact the waterfront looks much like it did during the 1948 production of *The Treasure of the Sierra Madre*, parts of which were filmed on location here.

The best streets for exploration are Héroes del Cañonero and Ribera where they cross Méndez, Aduana, Juárez, Olmos, and Colón. The occasional whiff of Chinese incense wafting down the narrow streets comes from the home altars of buildings inhabited by descendants of Chinese immigrant merchants and workers who arrived 80 years ago. It's quite okay to wander around this area during the day, but at night it could be a tad rough.

At the south end of Calle Aduana on the waterfront (two blocks south of the Plaza de la Libertad) is the **Aduana Marítima,** a huge brick Victorian built in 1880 as the city's first customs house.

Puente Tampico
This graceful, ultra-modern suspension bridge, completed in 1988, arches high over the Río Pánuco to link the states of Tamaulipas and Veracruz—and Northern Mexico with Southern Mexico. At the south end of the bridge you are actually farther south than the northern tip of the Yucatán Peninsula. Before the bridge was built, southbound travelers had to cross the wide river by ferry or take the long way around west of Laguna Chairel.

From northeast Tampico, Av. López Mateos leads to the bridge, which affords a bird's-eye view of the river and city—worth the US$3.60 bridge toll.

TAMPICO ACCOMMODATIONS

Because of the city's relatively low cost of living, hotels in Tampico typically cost less than hotels and motels in comparably sized Mexican cities. There also appears to be a price war going on; when the author visited, rooms with posted rates of US$40-45 per night were typically going for US$26-28, especially midweek.

Budget Hotels
Several tattered hotels near the waterfront on calles H. de Cañonero and Ribera cater to merchant mariners, transient oil workers, and a few intrepid budget travelers. Among these are **Hotel Monterrey** (tel. 12-12-43-71, H. de Cañonero 515 Pte.), **Hotel Río** (tel. 12-58-31, H. de Cañonero 608 Ote.), **Hotel Buena Vista** (tel. 12-29-46, H. de Cañonero 112 Ote.), and **Hotel Progreso** (tel. 12-39-13, H. de Cañonero 218 Ote.). Rooms cost US$12-17 and are very basic (hot water is usually unavailable) but secure for male visitors; solo female travelers might find their occupations misconstrued and hence would best avoid these hotels.

A gem floating in the middle of the colorful but congested market area on the waterfront is the clean and efficient **Hotel Jalisco** (tel. 12-29-24) at Calle La Paz 120 Poniente. Plain, comfortable rooms with a/c and hot water cost US$20-25 s/d. The nearby **Hotel La Paz** (tel. 14-03-82) at Calle La Paz 307 Nte. is very similar.

North of the Plaza de Armas in the center of town are a couple of other decent cheap hotels, **Hotel Capri** (tel. 12-26-80) at Calle Juárez 202 Nte. and **Hotel Nuevo León** (tel. 12-43-70) at Calle Aduana 107 Nte. The Capri is the least expensive at just US$15 per night for spartan but clean rooms with fan and bath; the Nuevo León adds TV for US$15-18 s/d.

Moving up a notch, **Hotel Tampico** (tel. 12-49-70), at Calle Carranza 513 Ote. downtown, is a grand old dame that has seen better days but is nonetheless atmospheric and well located for sightseeing and restaurants. Spacious, plain rooms with private hot-water showers and TV cost US$23-30 s/d. The ballroom on the first floor is often used for private parties, so the higher your room is, the quieter your stay is likely to be. The hotel has its own security parking lot in back.

Although it has no parking lot (24-hour pay parking can be arranged at nearby lots), the historic and well-run **Hotel Posada del Rey** on the Plaza de la Libertad at Calle Madero 218 Ote. has small but comfortable rooms with TV and a/c for US$19 s, US$22 d. Rated at three stars, this is one of Tampico's best hotel values under US$25; ask for an inside room (*habitación al dentro*) to avoid the street noise below.

Practically next door to the Posada del Rey at Calle Madero 210 Oriente., the friendly and efficient **Hotel Colonial**, (tel. 12-76-76) offers well-maintained rooms with a/c and TV for US$20 s, US$24 d—another real bargain. If the Colonial is full, try the similar **Hotel Plaza** (tel. 14-16-78) up the street at Madero 204 Ote. Weekend rates for the Colonial and Plaza may be higher than those quoted here.

Medium-priced Hotels

On Calle Díaz Mirón near the Plaza de Armas are two traditional favorites among business travelers and middle-class Mexican tourists. **Hotel Impala** (tel. 12-12-06-84) at Calle Mirón 210 offers sheltered parking and comfortable, spacious rooms with a/c and TV for a reasonable US$27 s, US$33 d (if you belong to Sanborn's Mexico Club you may receive a further 20% discount). **Hotel Monte Carlo** (tel. 14-10-93) at Av. López de Lara 107 Nte., a block west of the Hotel Tampico, has similar facilities and costs about the same as the Impala.

There are several rather dilapidated beach hotels at Playa Miramar, Ciudad Madero, including the **Mirador, Los Pinos,** and **Ritz.** Pricewise they fall into the US$25-35 range, but the accommodations themselves are strictly bottom-dollar. During the cooler months (Oct.-March), they're generally closed.

Luxury Hotels

Hotel Inglaterra (tel. 12-12-56-78, fax 12-14-05-56), opposite the Plaza de Armas at Calle Mirón 116 Ote., is rated at five stars by the state government (to be taken with a grain of salt); it features basement parking and rooms with all the amenities—a/c, TV, phones, mini-bar/refrigerator—for US$50-60.

For true five-star luxury it's necessary to move away from downtown Tampico to the newer sections of the city. The efficient **Camino Real** (tel. 13-88-11), at Av. Hidalgo 2000 (about two km northwest of downtown), has 100 well-appointed rooms on tropical landscaped grounds for US$94 s/d. Facilities include a/c, satellite TV, video, phones, restaurant, coffee shop, car rental agency, travel agency and swimming pool, plus tennis and golf course privileges at a local country club.

Farther out along Av. Hidalgo beyond the Plaza Crystal shopping center (about seven km/four miles northwest of downtown), **Hotel Posada de Tampico** (tel. 28-05-15) has 140 modern rooms at the same rack rates as the Camino Real, but room specials of US$60-75 s/d are often available; the pool is larger than the Camino Real's, and the hotel also has a lighted tennis court, putting green, restaurant, and disco on the premises. A new wing is being added.

RV Parking

Motorists with RVs or campers may park overnight in the airport parking lot for a small fee.

FOOD

Tampico's seafood restaurants are much admired by Mexicans from Matamoros to Veracruz. Known throughout Mexico as "Puerto Jaiba" ("Crab Port"), the city harvests around 20 different crab species from the rivers, lagoons, and Gulf. For Tampiqueñas the favored method of preparing crabs is simply to boil them whole in salted water to produce *jaiba al natural,* which is cracked and eaten with flour tortillas and special salsas of lime, chile, and garlic. Another popular dish is *jaiba relleno,* crab shells stuffed with shredded flounder, shrimp, or striped mullet.

Striped mullet (*lisa*) is also commonly served as ceviche, in which small pieces of the raw fish are marinated in lime juice, onions, cilantro, chile, and tomatoes, and eaten as a *botana* or snack. Shrimp (*camarón*) is as common as crab, and comes boiled, barbecued, or fried; or in *empanadas de camarón* (shrimp turnovers), *tortas de camarón* (shrimp sandwiches), and *tamales de flor de calabaza y camarón* (steamed with squash flowers inside a wrapper made of banana leaves instead of the usual corn husks).

The city is also widely known for *carne asada a la tampiqueña,* often called "Steak Tampico" or

"Tampico Filet" on English-language menus. Much favored by *mexicanos* and gringos alike, this dish consists of thin, butterflied fillets of beef quickly seared and served with *enchiladas verdes,* pickled chiles, *frijoles a la charra,* and a square of grilled cheese (usually *panela*), with salsa and cubed avocado (or guacamole) on the side—the original Mexican combination plate. It was probably this dish—carried in the memories of U.S. oil workers returning home in the '30s—that introduced North Americans to Mexican food (and the infamous Mexican "combination platter") on a large scale.

Many of the foregoing dishes can be sampled quite inexpensively at streetside vendors in the market area along Calle P.J. Méndez at calles 20 de Noviembre and Colón, near the Recinto Fiscal (customs area). Tacos, for example, cost just US$0.25 apiece here, US$0.40 elsewhere in the city.

For higher quality but still moderately priced *cocina típica,* you'll find numerous restaurants—several of them quite unique—in the area between Hotel Tampico and Plaza de la Libertad.

Seafood

$$ Restaurant de Mariscos Diligencias (tel. 12-14-12-79), corner of Calle H. del Cañonero and López de Lara near the Plaza de la Libertad. Although the Diligencias looks very weatherworn, both inside and out, this classic waterfront eatery still receives raves for its Gulf coast-style seafood, which has strong affinities with coastal cooking along the entire Gulf crescent from Tampico to Tampa. The large, moderately priced menu includes all types of fresh fish and shellfish, including the belt-buster "Seven Seas Plate" (*Fiesta de Siete Mars* on the Spanish side of the menu), which comes with seven types of seafood—including the best *pulpo* (octopus) this author has ever eaten—all fresh, all fried. Portions for all entrees are sizable. Open daily 11 a.m.-10 p.m.

A slightly nicer branch of the restaurant can be found at calles Mayor and Ayuntamiento (tel. 12-76-42).

$$-$$$ Restaurant Jardín Corona (tel. 12-42-45), Av. Hidalgo 1915 (a block south of the Hotel Camino Real). At the other end of the scale in price and ambience, this marble-floored eatery offers fresh seafood in a variety of ways—baked, broiled, fried, and steamed—plus steak platters and Mexican standards. Open daily noon-11 p.m.

$ Restaurant-Bar Pikio (no phone), Playa del Mirador (south end of Playa Miramar near the mouth of the Río Pánuco). One of two seafood restaurants parked near the outer harbor, Pikio specializes in tasty *brocheta de pescado adobado,* chunks of marinated fresh fish barbecued on skewers. Open Wed.-Sun. 11 a.m.-8 p.m.

Regional

The *café y nevería* (coffee and ice-cream shop), a downtown Tampico tradition, usually serves far more than just coffee and ice cream. Open long hours, the shops attract a steady clientele throughout the day by offering inexpensive, filling meals and a place to hang out for an hour or two with friends.

$$ Café y Nevería Elite (tel. 12-12-03-64), Calle Díaz Mirón 211 Oriente. Popular with a broad cross section of office workers, politicos, and coffee dreamers, the Elite offers an assortment of Mexican and seafood dishes, including delicious *brochetas de camarón* and stuffed crab, as well as breakfasts. Open daily 7:30 a.m.-11 p.m.

$ Café Mundo (tel. 14-18-31), corner of López de Lara and Mirón. Old, funky, and open 24 hours, the Mundo is especially popular with students and workers. The menu covers the gamut from *desayuno* to *torta milanesa.*

$ Café-Nevería El Globito (no phone), Calle Andrés de Olmos, at one corner of the Plaza de Armas. Also open 24 hours, the Globito is strong on ice cream and fruit drinks.

$-$$ Restaurant Insurgentes, Calle Mirón between Av. López de Lara and Calle Aduana. Very popular, inexpensive spot with *enchiladas huastecas* and seafood. Open daily noon-11 p.m.

$$ Restaurant-Bar Salón (Saloon) Palacio (tel. 12-18-77, Aduana and H. de Cañonero Ote., near Plaza de la Libertad). Established in 1897, this once-rowdy cantina (which appears in the Tampico bar scenes in *The Treasure of the Sierra Madre*) has been somewhat tamed by tourism. Although the restaurant badly needs a paint job on the outside, the marble floors and brass-and-wood bar inside are clean. The menu—a cross-section of *mariscos, carne asada a la tampiqueña,* and other Tampico specialties (including *huachinango* or red snapper stuffed with shrimp and crab)—is a reasonable value given the historic surroundings. Open Mon.-Sat. 11:30 a.m.-midnight.

$$ Restaurant La Troya (tel. 14-10-24), Hotel Posada del Rey, Calle Madero 218. This popular, reasonably priced hotel eatery specializes in seafood and *gringas* (burritos filled with cheese and chorizo). Open daily 11 a.m.-11 p.m.

Chinese

Tampico is known to have the best Chinese restaurants along Mexico's entire Gulf coast. Several are found along Av. Hidalgo (Mexico 80/180) in the vicinity of the Camino Real and Posada de Tampico.

$$ La Gran Muralla China, Av. Hidalgo 5201 (tel. 12-28-19-19); and Av. López de Lara 107 Sur (tel. 12-47-59) downtown. Both locations specialize in high-quality seafood prepared in the Southern Chinese style with just a bit of Mexican influence. Open daily noon-midnight.

$$ Imperio Chino (tel. 3-12-77), Blvd. Hidalgo 3302 near the Hotel Camino Real. This huge, banquet-style place has a menu to match. Open daily noon-11 p.m.

Other

A number of American-style fast-food places, including **Pollo Loco, Super Cream del Camino, Super Burger Hidalgo,** and **KFC,** are lined up along Av. Hidalgo. Two shopping centers on Hidalgo, **Plaza Crystal** and **Tres Arcos,** have well-stocked food courts with good Mexican food.

Super Cream is worth a special mention because it's one of the few sit-down bakeries— and one of the few to serve coffee—in Northern Mexico. The downtown location on Calle Carranza, a block west of Hotel Tampico between Calle Aduana and Av. López de Lara, is open daily 7:30 a.m.-10 p.m.

RECREATION

Tampiqueñas count themselves lucky to live in a city that is practically surrounded on all sides by lagoons, rivers, and the Gulf of Mexico, creating abundant opportunities for fishing, swimming, boating, and other aquatic activities.

Laguna Del Carpintero

This lagoon in the middle of the city provides public facilities for picnicking, swimming, water-skiing, or simply strolling along the water's edge. A small zoo and children's park are also on the premises. Certain sections of the shoreline are still under development and will reportedly feature water slides and other more elaborate diversions at some point in the future.

Playa Miramar

Known locally simply as "La Playa," this 10-km (six-mile) stretch of packed sand washed by Gulf surf is northeast of Tampico proper at the edge of Ciudad Madero. *Palapas* (with wooden chairs beneath) line the length of the central beach, which is backed by a stand of casuarina trees and seafood kiosks. A few run-down concrete beach hotels of 10-20 rooms each stand well back from the beach toward the north end. By all appearances, the water along most of Playa Miramar seems amazingly clean considering the proximity of the harbor entrance and PEMEX facility.

Driving on the beach is permitted; the main part accessible by vehicle extends 3.7 km (2.3 miles). At its southeast end, near the mouth of the Río Pánuco, the beach ends at a long concrete pier for fishing or strolling. At the north end, the sand becomes too loose for driving and hence this is the nicest area for lounging around. *Palapas* at the north end rent for US$5 a day; a large *palapa* restaurant offers fresh seafood.

The central part of the beach—where the *palapas* are—becomes quite crowded with Mexican families on warm-weather weekends and holidays. Tampiqueñas practically headquarter themselves here all week to celebrate Semana Santa. During the fall and winter, though, you'll have the place almost all to yourself.

Framed by grassy dunes and beach houses (some of them abandoned), the beach continues for several kilometers north. A poor, broken-asphalt road on the landward side of the dunes meanders for a few kilometers, after which you must continue by foot. This area is worth exploring for its natural flora (prickly pear, live oak, verbena, casuarina), less-visited beaches, and cleaner water.

Getting There: From downtown Tampico it's 15 km (nine miles) to Playa Miramar. If you're driving, simply follow Av. López de Lara from Tampico till it becomes Av. Obregón, which in turn leads through Ciudad Madero (past the huge PEMEX facility and naval base) to the beach. *Colectivos* and *taxis de ruta* labeled "Tampico-Playa" run back and forth along this route for US$0.33 per passenger; the No. 24 city bus plies the same route for US$0.20.

Laguna Tamiahua

Across the state line in the state of Veracruz, this huge estuarial lagoon paralleling the coast is known for fishing and shrimping, as well as for uninhabited islands, mangroves, and wildlife. Buses to Naranjos, Ver., will drop passengers off in Horconcitos near the north end of the lagoon, where boats can be rented; or you can ride all the way to Naranjos and switch to a Tamiahua-bound bus. Motorists can drive themselves to the lagoon via Mexico 180 South. The town of Tamiahua, at the south end of the lagoon, is the main supply center.

Entertainment

Bars and Dance Clubs: Many of the bars, cantinas, and *salones* downtown are frequented by men only. **La Tasca,** attached to the Restaurant La Troya in the Hotel Posada del Rey, is an exception and is reasonably atmospheric, as is the long, stool-less bar at the **Salón Palacio** (see "Food," above).

Turning up the heat a bit, the **Centro Nocturno Tropicana** at Av. López de Lara 111 Sur downtown features a mix of live and recorded Latin dance music nightly. Out on Av. Hidalgo are a couple of discos, including **Lib-Lam** (tel. 12-13-17-18, Av. Hidalgo 3400) and **El Porvenir** (tel. 13-05-62, Av. Hidalgo 1403).

Radio: Tune in 94.5 FM (broadcast from Poza Rica, Veracruz) for an invigorating blend of *norteña* and *tropicale* musics.

Shopping

Tampico doesn't have much of interest in the way of traditional markets or handicrafts, but for Mexicans in the region it's highly prized for its modern malls and shopping plazas. The **Plaza Tres Arcos** and **Plaza Crystal** malls, next to one another on Blvd. Hidalgo toward the Posada de Tampico and airport, are stuffed with upscale stores. (Cinemas Gemelos, in the latter, shows recently released American films for only US$2.30 admission.)

Across from Plaza Crystal on Blvd. Hidalgo is **Liverpool,** a plush, Macy's-style department store with imported foods (on the second floor) and a small handicrafts section.

Festivals

March/April: Throughout these two months both Tampico and its neighbor, Ciudad Madero, celebrate a string of festivals, beginning with **Carnaval** (see "Festivals and Events," p. 56, in the "Out and About" chapter for details on this holiday) the week before Lent.

During the third week of April, Tampiqueñas celebrate the **Aniversario de la Repoblación de Tampico** with art, culture, and sporting events. A special emphasis is placed on folkloric dancing, and the city hosts a regional conference on *huapango,* a traditional dance indigenous to southern Tamaulipas's Región Huasteca. This festival more or less merges with Semana Santa, which involves fireworks and *matachine* processions centered at Playa Miramar in Ciudad Madero.

December: Día de la Virgen de Guadalupe, Dec. 12, attracts many *indígenas* from the southern part of the state who come to worship and dance at various churches dedicated to Guadalupe, including the Catedral de Tampico on Plaza de Armas.

Other: The city honors the Virgen de San Juan de los Lagos twice a year, on Feb. 2 (Candelaría) and Aug. 15 (Ascension Day), at the Iglesia Nuestra Señora de Guadalupe.

TAMPICO INFORMATION

Tourist Office

The Tamaulipas State Tourist Office (tel. 12-12-26-68), in the Palacio Municipal at Calle Olmos 101 Sur Altos (opposite the northwest corner of the Plaza de Armas), distributes hotel

---

TAMPICO TELEPHONE NUMBERS

Police: 2-14-37
Highway Patrol: 28-05-42
Green Angels: 13-85-78
State Tourist Office: 12-26-68
Red Cross: 12-13-33
U.S. Consulate: 13-22-17
Tampico Area Code: 12

brochures, a Spanish-language tourist newspaper, and a cartoon-style chamber of commerce map.

Telephone

Hotel Posada del Rey houses a convenient, 24-hour LADA office where long-distance national and international calls may be paid for with a credit card (Visa, MasterCard, or American Express).

U.S. Consulate

Tampico has a U.S. consular post (tel. 12-13-22-17) at Av. Hidalgo 2000, next to the Hotel Camino Real. The consulate is open Mon.-Fri. 9:30 a.m.-1:30 p.m.

TAMPICO TRANSPORT

Getting There

Air: Aeroméxico (tel. 12-17-06-56; Plaza Tres Arcos) operates direct flights daily between Tampico and Mexico City, Monterrey, Poza Rica (Ver.), San Luis Potosí, and Veracruz. **Mexicana** (tel. 13-96-00; Av. Universidad 700-1) has direct flights to/from Mexico City, Monterrey, and Veracruz.

Aeropuerto Francisco Javier Mina is nine km northwest of downtown Tampico off Mexico 80/180, about 15 minutes by car. A taxi to central Tampico will cost around US$10, a *colectivo* US$3.50.

Bus: Tampico's **Centro de Autobuses** is on Calle Zapotal and Av. López Mateos (off Av. Ejército Mexicano), 2.4 km (1.5 miles) east of Av. Hidalgo.

Autobuses de Oriente (ADO) and **Servicios de Huastecos** operate thrice-daily, first-class buses from Matamoros and Reynosa for US$18 each way; classier ADO *ejecutivos* on the same routes run once a day for US$24. To/from Veracruz, first-class buses cost US$22 and run 10 times daily.

Transportes Frontera has second-class buses to/from Monterrey (US$18, eight daily), Nuevo Laredo (US$26, four daily), and Ciudad Victoria (US$8, eight daily); and both first-class and *ejecutivo* buses to/from Monterrey for US$23 and US$32 respectively.

Vencedor Río Verde has cornered the market on second-class buses between Tampico and Río Verde (US$8, once daily), Xilitla (US$7, once daily), and San Luis Potosí (US$14, four daily).

Train: Two lines offer passenger rail service to Tampico from elsewhere in Mexico. From Monterrey, the slow, second-class only Del Golfo runs via Ciudad Victoria daily, leaving Monterrey at 8 a.m. and arriving in Tampico at 7 p.m.; the fare is US$5 each way.

El Huasteco, a second-class train between San Luis Potosí and Tampico, also costs US$5 each way and takes around 11 hours (for scheduling information, see the San Luis Potosí "Getting There" section). The railway station faces the Río Pánuco waterfront on the southwestern edge of downtown Tampico.

Driving: From the southern outskirts of Matamoros to Tampico is about a six-hour drive under normal road conditions. Av. Hidalgo slices into the northwest corner of the grid at a diagonal and links the downtown district with Mexico 80/180 North and the airport. Av. López Mateos links Mexico 80/180 North with Mexico 180 South via Puente Tampico over the Río Pánuco. If you're heading toward San Luis Potosí, you'll want Av. Universidad, which leads to Mexico 110/70 West.

Getting Around

Taxis de rutas and *colectivos* circulate all over town, especially along main thoroughfares Hidalgo, López de Lara, Obregón, and López Mateos. The standard passenger fare for these is around US$0.33. The city bus system costs a bit less but is more complicated.

Taxis in the downtown district cost US$4-6 per trip.

Driving: Tampico's neat downtown grid is easy to follow, but the one-way street system that keeps traffic moving so well also sometimes forces newcomers to drive around in circles in order to reach a given destination.

More than in any other city in Northern Mexico, local residents tend to run red lights with regularity. Whether on foot or in your own vehicle, always look both ways before entering an intersection.

Car Rental: Three agencies handle the demand for rental vehicles, **National** (tel. 12-13-54-34, Hotel Camino Real, Av. Hidalgo 2806), **Dollar** (tel. 28-05-87, Av. Hidalgo and Río Guayalejo), and **Budget** (tel. 13-71-00, Av. Hidalgo 3400).

CIUDAD VICTORIA AND VICINITY

CIUDAD VICTORIA

Tamaulipas's state capital was founded in 1750 as Santa María de Aguayo under José de Escandón's *empresario* program. In 1825 it was made state capital and the name was changed to honor Mexico's first president, Guadalupe Victoria. In 1846 the city was briefly occupied by U.S. troops during the Mexican-American War, and it also played a key role in the 1910-20 Mexican Revolution.

Today this bright, clean, and prosperous little city at the intersection of Mexico 101, 70, and 85, shadowed to the west by the Sierra Gorda, has a population of 213,000, most of whom are supported by government service, education, construction, and manufacturing, or by supplying surrounding farms and ranches. One of the premier local crops is henequen, an agave plant used to make twine, burlap bags, floor mats, and upholstery interiors. The city is also known for leather crafts, especially the *cuera tamaulipeca,* a fringed chamois jacket with white calfskin patterns on the shoulders and cuffs and the state coat of arms on the back. Other Victoria products include furniture fashioned from *ebano* (Texas ebony), mesquite, pine, and palm.

Situated at nearly 300 meters (980 feet) above sea level, Ciudad Victoria is blessed with a mild climate most of the year; the occasional summer heat wave or winter freeze are departures from the norm. Hunting, fishing, and nearby El Cielo Biosphere Reserve are major local attractions for Mexican and foreign visitors alike.

SIGHTS

Museo De Antropología E História
In the rectory of the Universidad Autónoma de Tamaulipas downtown on Av. Colón, this small museum contains the usual photos from the revolutionary era, along with pre-Hispanic artifacts (mostly ceramics and arrowheads) and early portraits of noteworthy men of local provenance. It's open Mon.-Fri. 9 a.m.-5 p.m.; admission is free.

Parque Recreativo Tamatán
This huge pastoral park at the southwestern edge of town along the Río San Marcos contains a playground, zoo, artificial lake, and *lienzo charro* along with acres of woods.

Paseo Méndez
Of the three public plazas in town, this is the largest and leafiest. Open-air theatrical and musical performances are occasionally held here. The *paseo* is at calles 5 de Mayo and Rosales, just west of the tourist office.

ACCOMMODATIONS AND FOOD

Budget
Best of the lower-priced places is the tidy **Hotel Posada Don Diego** (tel. 131-2-12-79), on Calle Juárez between calles 9 and 10. Basically furnished rooms surround a courtyard in the colonial style and cost US$18-21 s/d. The hotel has its own parking lot (one of the only places under US$45 that does) and **Restaurant La Carolina.** Similarly priced, but not as nice, is **Hotel San Juan** (tel. 2-79-93) at Calle Colón 427 Nte. (north of the Hotel Santorín).

Casa de Huéspedes Amelia (no phone), at Calle Hidalgo 1053 between calles 7 and 8, has 15 spartan but adequate rooms for as little as US$10 per night; weekly and monthly rates are also available.

The well-located **Hotel Los Monteros** (tel. 2-06-40), at Calle Hidalgo 962 Ote., facing Plaza Hidalgo just a block off Blvd. J.B. Tijerina (the main north-south avenue through town), offers a quiet, classic Mex-deco interior around two courtyards for US$24 s/d; the downstairs restaurant is good. The hotel doesn't have a parking lot but there is a 24-hour pay lot around the corner.

At the north end of town where Mexico 85 North meets the *periférico,* **Motel Jardín** (tel. 6-15-55) has 15 run-down rooms for US$15-18 per night—recommended only as a last resort.

Medium-priced
Next door to the Hotel Los Monteros on Hidalgo is the busier (and noisier) **Hotel Sierra Gorda**

TO MONTERREY

TO MATAMOROS

85

101

PERIFERICO A. LOPEZ MATEOS

TAMAULIPAS

MOTEL JARDIN

PARADISE INN

VICTORIA TRAILER
PARK RESORT

MOTEL
LA VILLA

BUS TERMINAL

LIBRAMIENTO DE TRANSITO PESADO

EL MESQUITE
GRILL

SAN ANTONIO
MOTEL

BERRIOZABAL

CARRERA TORRES

RIO SAN MARCOS

RESTAURANT
EL GRANERO

COLON (9)

JUAN B. TIJERINA

TORRE
GUBERMENTAL

STADIUM

V. CARRANZA (22)

FCO. I. MADERO

MATAMOROS

MORELOS

JUAREZ

TO SOTO LA MARINA

70

5 DE MAYO (16)

SEE INSET

RAILWAY STATION

SANTUARIO LA VIRGEN
DE GUADALUPE

85

HOTEL
PANORAMICO

MOTEL LAS FUENTES

TOURIST
OFFICE

TO TAMPICO

CIUDAD
VICTORIA

PASEO PEDRO
J. MENDEZ

PARQUE
RECREATIVO
TAMATAN

TO SAN LUIS POTOSI

101

0   700 m

INSET

CARRERA TORRES

MATIAS S. CANALES

LAURO AGUIRRE (11)

HNOS. VASQUEZ (13)

COLON (9)

JUAN B. TIJERINA

PORIFIO DIAZ (7)

JOSE N. DE CACERES

HOTEL
SAN
JUAN

ABASOLO

GASPAR DE LA GARZA

EMILIO P. NAFARRETE (14)

MANUEL GONZALEZ

PALACIO
FEDERAL

MUSEO ANTROPOLOGIA
E HISTORIA

MERCADO MUNICIPAL

ZARAGOZA

ALLENDE

FCO. I. MADERO

PLAZA HIDALGO

BRAVO

5 DE MAYO (16)

HOTEL EVEREST

HOTEL SIERRA GORDA

HOTEL LOS MONTEROS

PINO SUAREZ (18)

GUERRERO

CAFE CANTON /
EL PATIO MEXICANO

RIO SAN MARCOS

MATAMOROS

HIDALGO

HOTEL POSADA
DON DIEGO

MORELOS

JUAREZ

PALACIO DE GOBIERNO /
CENTRO CULTURAL

RESTAURANT LA
POSTA PLAZA

0   200 m

(tel. 131-2-20-10, fax 131-2-97-99). The staff is very helpful with tourist information. Most of the rooms have been remodeled and now include a/c, phones, and satellite TV. Rates are US$30-38 s, US$36-43 d; be sure to request an inside room if you're bothered by street noise. The Sierra Gorda has no parking facility of its own but there is a pay lot attached to the hotel.

On the west side of the plaza at Av. Colón 126 is **Hotel Everest** (tel. 2-40-50), where rooms with a/c, satellite TV, in-house video, and phones go for US$38 s, US$47 d. As at the foregoing hotels, you must pay for parking.

Several motels on the northern and northeastern outskirts of town offer convenient lodging for motorists. At the north end of town off Mexico 85, the recently renovated **San Antonio Motel** (tel. 6-26-16) has comfortable a/c rooms around a pool and parking lot for US$38-40 s/d. The well-run **Paradise Inn** (tel. 2-99-88) at Km 1 on Mexico 101 (the highway from Matamoros), on the northeast edge of town, and the nearby **Motel La Villa** (tel. 6-80-11) have similarly priced rooms. **Motel Las Fuentes** (tel. 2-56-55) at Km 227 on Mexico 85, with rooms with a/c, mini-bars, TV, and phones, costs US$40-45 per night. The San Antonio, Paradise, La Villa, and Las Fuentes all have attached restaurants and free parking.

Down on the southern edge of town off Mexico 85, the heavily advertised **Motel Panorámico** (tel. 2-55-06) sits on a hill overlooking the city. Rooms with a/c, phones, satellite TV, and in-house video are US$39-45 s/d. Facilities include a pool and restaurant.

Luxury
The newest hotel in town is the modern **Best Western Hotel Santorín** (tel. 131-2-89-38, fax 2-83-42) at Av. Colón 349 Nte., two blocks north of Plaza Hidalgo. Comfortable rooms with all the amenities cost US$47-57 s, US$54-64 d Jan. 1-May 15, about US$10 higher in summer and fall, and US$10 lower the last two weeks of December. Non-smoking rooms are available on request, and the hotel has its own parking garage, a National Car Rental office, restaurant, and lobby bar.

Resort
Hacienda Santa Engracia (tel. 131-2-43-56), a half-hour drive north of the city off Mexico 85, is a quiet, peaceful lodge with a swimming pool,

tennis courts, and facilities for horseback riding. Rooms come with fireplaces and Tamaulipas-made furniture; rates are in the US$45-65 range. Guests dine together at huge, family-style meals. The Hacienda has a reservation and information office in Ciudad Victoria at Calle Aldama 1062 Ote.

RV Parks
The **Victoria Trailer Park Resort** (tel. 131-2-48-24), on the Mexico 85 bypass one km (0.6 mile) west of the Mexico 101 intersection, has 150 sites with full hookups on 10 acres. Slots are US$8-10 per night per rig for two persons, plus US$1 extra for use of a/c and US$2 for each additional person. A small market sells groceries on the premises; shower facilities are also available.

At the junction of Mexico 85 North and the *periférico,* the **Motel Jardín** has a small trailer park with 10 RV sites with full hookups for US$8 per night, plus showers and toilets.

Food
Gorditas Estilo Doña Tota has become famous throughout the state and there are now three branches in town. The original, a funky eatery with photos of old-time Mexican actors on the walls, is at Av. Berriozábal 1748 between calles 5 and 6. Other branches are at Calle Juárez 205 Ote. and Calz. Luis Caballero 520. All serve the trademark *gorditas* (thick tortillas stuffed with shredded beef, *nopales,* and scrambled egg) along with *nopalitos con salsa* (strips of prickly pear cactus served with salsa) and quesadillas. Prices are low.

Near Plaza Hidalgo are several inexpensive and moderately priced restaurants, including the U.S.-style **Daddy's Restaurant** (tel. 131-2-40-50) next door to the Hotel Everest at Av. Colón 148 Norte. Daddy's menu features a broad range of steaks, seafood, burgers, sandwiches, salads, soups, and Mexican standards. Down the street a bit at Colón 124 Sur, **El Patio Mexicano** (tel. 2-68-71) serves good Mexican platters amidst a traditional Mexican decor.

At Calle Colón 114, the humble **Café Canton,** two doors north of El Patio Mexicano, provides a decent *comida corrida* for US$3.50 as well as inexpensive Mexican breakfasts. The home-style enchiladas and *entomatadas de pollo* are particularly good here.

Moving upscale a bit, the semi-elegant and long-running **Restaurant El Granero** (tel. 2-61-55) at Carrera Torres 509 Ote. serves Mexican and international cuisine; house specialties include *carne asada* and seafood. **La Posta Plaza** (tel. 2-14-44), at Calle Zaragoza 701 at Calle 11, has a similar menu but is decidedly classier (and more expensive) with its fountain and garden dining areas.

El Mesquite Grill (tel. 2-61-55), just north of the San Antonio Motel on the east side of Blvd. Tamaulipas, is a very reliable restaurant with a Mexican and international menu. A large breakfast buffet is served daily, and delicious cookies (not the usual bland *pan dulce*) come with breakfast coffee orders. On Sundays *cabrito* is available.

RECREATION

Shopping
Artesanía Tamaulipeca (tel. 131-2-19-54), Calle Pino Suárez (Calle 18) 402 Sur near the Centro Cultural, carries a selection of regional handicrafts, including the *cuera tamaulipeca*. A smattering of folk crafts is also available at (and around) the **Mercado Municipal** at Calle Díaz (Calle 7) and Av. Morelos.

Along the south end of Calle Madero (Calle 17), a pretty divided boulevard with trees along the median, a number of modern shops and boutiques offer a variety of purchasing possibilities.

Events
In October the city holds an **Exposición Agrícola, Ganadera, Comercial, Industrial y Turística,** a large state fair of sorts that features events and exhibits having to do with farming, ranching, trade, industry, and tourism.

TRANSPORT AND INFORMATION

Air
Aeroméxico (tel. 131-6-91-91; Carrera Torres and Abasolo) fields daily flights to/from Mexico City. In the past, Aeroméxico has also operated flights between Matamoros and Ciudad Victoria, but for the time being all flights now operate via Mexico City.

The airport is 20 km (12.5 miles) east of town off Mexico 70.

cuera tamaulipeca

Bus
The Central Camionera is at the east end of Carrera Torres where it meets the *libramiento de tránsito pesado* (and inner ring road for bus and truck traffic). All the major bus companies based in Reynosa, Matamoros, Tampico, and San Luis Potosí operate buses to Ciudad Victoria for US$0-10 second class, US$10-15 first class, or US$18-21 *ejecutivo*. Buses to/from Mexico City cost around US$26. **Transportes Tamaulipas** has frequent buses to/from Monterrey (US$7) and Nuevo Laredo (US$15). **Transportes del Norte** buses ply between Ciudad Victoria and Ciudad Valles (US$8) and San Luis Potosí (US$11).

Train
Travel to Monterrey and Tampico by train takes twice as long as by bus, but it's cheaper and

the scenery is better. **Del Golfo** No. 171 departs Tampico at 1:10 p.m. for Monterrey, arriving at 7 p.m. In the opposite direction, No. 172 arrives from Monterrey at 1:30 p.m. and departs at 1:50 p.m. for Tampico, with a 7 p.m. arrival on the coast. The fare for either leg is just US$2.50 (second class only).

The railway station is at the west end of Av. Hidalgo at Calle Carranza (Calle 22).

Driving
The central portion of the city is laid out in the same neat grid designed by city planners in 1895. From the north, Mexico 85 turns into Blvd. Tamaulipas, which then becomes Blvd. J.B. Tijerina through the city proper. A ring road around the city is well marked and leads to Mexico 101 South (for San Luis Potosí, Mexico 101 North (to Reynosa), Mexico 70 East (for Soto la Marina), and Mexico 85 South (for Ciudad Mante and Tampico).

PEMEX stations with Magna Sin are plentiful in town as well as along the highway junctions on the outskirts.

Auto Rental
Cars can be rented at **National** (tel. 131-9-22-75, Blvd. Tamaulipas 1507 Nte.; or Hotel Santorín) and at **Budget** (tel. 6-50-16, Carrera Torres between calles 11 and 12).

Information
The **Dirección General de Turismo** (tel. 131-2-10-57, fax 131-2-11-11), at Calle Rosales 272, is the head tourist office for the state and a good source of information on Ciudad Victoria and vicinity.

Radio: *Victorenses* are very proud of their Tamaulipan heritage, and the university-sponsored "Radio Tamaulipas," 107.9 FM, plays

---

CIUDAD VICTORIA
TELEPHONE NUMBERS

Police: 2-01-95
Highway Patrol: 6-47-79
Green Angels: 2-10-57
State Tourist Office: 2-10-67
Red Cross: 6-20-77
Ciudad Victoria Area Code: 131

---

mucho local and regional music (with no advertising).

VICINITY OF
CIUDAD VICTORIA

Presa Vicente Guerrero
An impoundment of the Soto la Marina, Corona, Pilón, and Purificación rivers, 47,000-hectare Presa Guerrero is known as one of the best bass-producing lakes—possibly *the* best—in Mexico. The main supply and lodging center for the lake is **Nuevo Padilla,** 54 km (33.5 miles) northeast of Ciudad Victoria via Mexico 101 (about 200 km/124 miles/four hours southwest of Reynosa). The original town of Padilla, founded by José de Escandón in 1749, appears in historical footnotes as the place where Mexican emperor Agustín de Iturbide was executed in 1824. The town was flooded when the dam was constructed in 1970; during periods of low water you can catch glimpses of old Padilla architecture above the water near the mouth of the Río Purificación. The original highway (Mexico 101) was also inundated; a new road now curves around the north end of the lake to Nuevo Padilla, where Mexico 101 continues southward.

Villa de Casas, on the southern end of the lake off Mexico 70 (44 km/27 miles east of Ciudad Victoria), is another lakeside center where a *parque turístico* offers picnic tables, grills, and *palapas.*

Along the undeveloped east shore of the lake is **Rancho La Lajilla,** designated a "protected natural area" by the state of Tamaulipas because of its exemplary flora (primarily Tamaulipan thorn forest) and fauna (including the endangered jaguar). Hunting for quail, white-winged dove, wild turkey, and white-tailed deer in season is permitted in the area.

Along untouched sections of nearby rivers, especially along the Río Corona, venerable Montezuma bald cypress (sabina or ahuehuete in Mexico) and Texas ebony (ebano) grow in abundance.

Fishing: The large lake offers many different types of shore terrains in which to hook catfish, tilapia, and several varieties of largemouth bass; the lake record is held by a lunker weighing over 7.2 kilograms (16 pounds). Recommended tackle includes medium-action rods,

17- to 20-pound test monofilament line, large plastic worms, slab spoons, spinners, and buzz baits. Fish are generally biting year-round, though Dec.-Feb. are considered the best months for trophy-sized bass, April-June for sheer numbers.

A limited supply of bait and tackle, along with simple accommodations and food, are available in Nuevo Padilla and Villa de Casa. Several lakeside fish camps also offer lodging, food, and fishing (and/or hunting) packages that can be booked through Texas offices. The typical one-night, two-day package for a Texas-affiliated lodge includes a comfortable a/c room, meals, and an English-speaking fishing guide for US$175 per person. At more rustic Mexican-run camps you usually pay as you go, with separate (and lower) fees for lodging, food, and guide.

At the northeast end of the lake near where old Mexico 101 was submerged, one of the premier facilities is **Big Bass Lodge** (on the lake) and its associated **Club Exclusivo** (inland). Each has a hotel, pool, restaurant, and bar; Big Bass also has a private airstrip and boat ramp (guests at one lodge may use the facilities at either). Three-day hunting/fishing packages start at US$900, fishing packages are US$175-200, and minimum room-and-meals packages are US$85 per person per day. For information or reservations, contact Big Bass Tours (tel. 800-531-7509, fax 512-687-8514; 1418 Beech St., Suite 122, McAllen, TX 78501). Big Bass Tours has recently begun sponsoring an annual Big Bass Fishing Tournament at Presa Guerrero in October.

Also on the northeast end of the lake, **Hacienda Alta Vista** (tel. 210-423-2234; P.O. Box 1511, Harlingen, TX 78551) offers a 35-room hotel, full RV hookups, pool, Jacuzzi, private airstrip, boat-launching facilities, and similar multiday fishing packages.

Around the northwest edge of the lake, on the north bank of the Río Purificación (east of Nuevo Padilla), **Campo El Sargento** has 20 rooms, RV slots with full hookups, a restaurant-bar, pool, private airstrip, and boat ramp. Rates for room and board only are US$75 per day, fishing packages are US$175 per day, and typical hunting packages run US$500 per day. For further information or reservations, call or write Sunbelt Hunting and Travel (tel. 800-876-4868,

210-546-9101 in Texas; 131-2-43-56 in Padilla; P.O. Box 3009, Brownsville, TX 78520).

The nearby **Campo La Reforma** (tel. 131-2-56-11 in Ciudad Victoria) has simple cabins and fishing guides. A bit farther south near Padilla Viejo (Old Padilla), at the mouth of the Río Purificación, the Mexican-operated **El Pelicano** (tel. 131-2-15-50 in Ciudad Victoria) has five cabins, a restaurant, full hookup RV sites, a boat ramp, and moderately priced package deals. **La Tortuga,** just south of Padilla Viejo on the lake, has a few simple cabins and RV sites with full hookups.

Toward the southwest end of the lake, on the north bank of the Río Corona, **La Isla** (tel. 800-327-3574, P.O. Box 3763, Brownsville, TX 78520) features a 12-room lodge, two-way RV hookups, showers, pool, *palapa* bar, gravel airstrip, and hunting/fishing packages.

At the south end of the lake (actually along the Río Villa de Casas, which feeds into the lake) are five fish camps of varying costs; signs in the town of Villa de Casas point the way to each. Closest to Casas is **Chato's,** which features several cabins, a pool, rustic restaurant-bar, boat launch, and parking for RVs and trailers. **Croix,** west of Chato's, and **Chico's,** to the east, offer places to camp, RV parking, and boat launches, but that's about it. Southwest of Croix, **El Dorado** (L&J Outdoor Tours, tel. 131-2-30-24 in Ciudad Victoria; tel. 800-533-8687, 210-631-3665 in the U.S.; P.O. Box 4906, McAllen, TX 78502) has a lodge with 10 a/c units, full-hookup RV sites, showers, toilets, restaurant-bar, pool, and boat ramp; hunting/fishing packages are available.

Northeast of Villa de Casas on a separate road is **Campo Charly Morris** (a.k.a. Victoria Bass Club; contact L&J Outdoor Tours), with several a/c cabins, a restaurant-bar, and hunting/fishing packages.

El Chorrito

The most important religious pilgrimage site in northeastern Mexico, El Chorrito ("Little Stream") is a shrine to the Virgen de Tepeyac, whose image appears in a votivelike cave formation. The formation itself is at the rear of a *templo-gruta,* a large, domed chapel with a volcanic cave at the rear; skeptics will note that the image looks as if it has had the temporal assistance of a sculptor. The site is doubly sacred because it is also the source of a spring which feeds into slender El Chorrito waterfall, set amidst lush surroundings and impressive valley and mountain views.

Annual pilgrimages and *matachine* dance processions to honor the Virgen del Chorrito are held March 17-19, then again during April's Semana Santa, and yet again for Fiesta Guadalupana (Dec. 12). An average 50,000 pilgrims visit the shrine every year. The village of El Chorrito has several shops selling shrine paraphernalia and a few places to eat; during festival times the enterprising villagers set up trailer parks, *palapa* restaurants, and more souvenir stalls.

Getting There: El Chorrito is 25 km (15.5 miles) west of El Tomaseño (near Villa Hidalgo), which is 77 km (48 miles) northwest of Ciudad Victoria via Mexico 85 (or 78 km south of Linares, N.L.).

Reserva De La Biosfera El Cielo
About 50 km (31 miles) south of Ciudad Victoria is North America's northernmost cloud forest, a rare area of extreme biodiversity known as El Cielo ("The Sky"). Because of its scientific value, in 1985 the Mexican government declared 144,530 hectares (360,000 acres) of land surrounding El Cielo in the Sierra de Cucharas (a subrange of the Sierra Madre Oriental) to be a Biosphere Reserve. The following year the United Nations added the reserve to its "Man and the Biosphere" program.

El Cielo represents a transition zone between tropical and temperate zones that has produced four basic ecosystems: **tropical caducifolia jungle** in the eastern third of the reserve, at an elevation of 200-800 meters (650-2,600 feet); **mesophilic montane forest** or **cloud forest** (*bosque de niebla* in Spanish), an area covering about 18% of the reserve that receives rain around six months a year and produces a fantastic variety of flora—including over 30 types of orchids—at an elevation of about 800-1,400 meters (2,600-4,600 feet); **pine-oak forest** over about a third of the reserve at 1,400-2,400 meters (4,600-8,000 feet); and **chaparral-matorral** on the sierra's lower western slopes, an arid area of dwarf oaks and heaths.

Throughout El Cielo—but especially in the cloud forest belt and along the Río Sabinas—a unique and profuse mixture of flora grow side by side, including native palms, North American

cacti, cedars, tropical orchids, oaks, ferns, lianas, Spanish moss, acacias, willows, cottonwoods, poplars, four species of sugar maples (twice the number found in New England!), sweet gums, dahlias, roseapples, and magnolias.

Both neoarctic and neotropical animal species inhabit the reserve, among them jaguar, ocelot, *temazate* (red deer), white-tailed deer, gray fox, and black bear, plus 21 species of amphibians, 60 reptiles, and 40 bats. Bird counts have confirmed 255 resident bird species (including quetzal, elegant trogon, collared forest falcon, crested caracara, chachalaca, curassow, bluecrowned motmot, and ferruginous pygmy owl) and 175 migratory bird species, or roughly half of all bird species known in Mexico.

Just over half of the reserve is located in the *municipio* of Jaumave, with smaller portions divided among Gómez Farías, Llera, and Ocampo. Around 2,500 Mexicans still reside on lands within the reserve; for now the government prefers that they leave on their own rather than be forced out.

Visiting El Cielo: The reserve is closed to the general public but permission to visit may be granted on a case-by-case basis. Permission is usually granted as long as visitors are accompanied by guides registered with the government. Permits may be requested in person at the Desarrollo Urbano y Ecología office on the third floor of the Torre Gubernamental in Ciudad Victoria.

Prospective visitors may also call or write in advance to: El Biologo Hector Zamora Treviño (tel. 131-2-97-77, ext. 124-139), Dirección Desarrollo Urbano y Ecología, Torre Gubermental José López Portillo, Ciudad Victoria, Tamaulipas.

During the rainy season, May-Oct., El Cielo's cloud forest layer is almost perpetually veiled in mist.

Rancho Cielito
On the banks of the scenic Río Sabinas, at the eastern edge of El Cielo, this private, 150-acre ranch is popular among birders and naturalists. The river is lined with Montezuma bald cypress and offers several good swimming areas. Simple accommodations and campsites are available. For further information, write Larry Loff (Texas Southmost College, Brownsville, TX 78520), or call Jack Berryman (tel. 210-546-5131) in Texas.

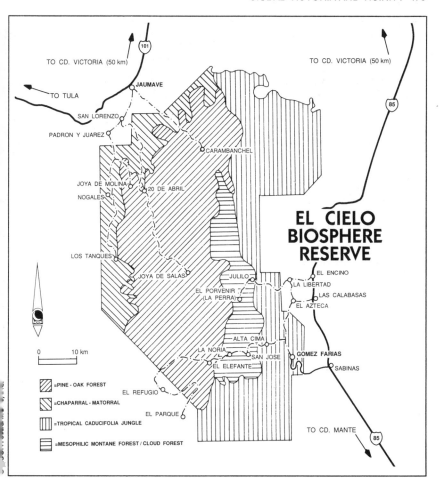

TO CD. VICTORIA (50 km)

TO TULA

101

JAUMAVE

SAN LORENZO

PADRON Y JUAREZ

CARAMBANCHEL

JOYA DE MOLINA

20 DE ABRIL

NOGALES

LOS TANQUES

JOYA DE SALAS

JULILO

EL ENCINO

LA LIBERTAD

LAS CALABASAS

EL PORVENIR
(LA PERRA)

EL AZTECA

TO CD. VICTORIA (50 km)

85

**EL CIELO
BIOSPHERE
RESERVE**

ALTA CIMA

LA NORIA

SAN JOSE

GOMEZ FARIAS

EL ELEFANTE

SABINAS

EL REFUGIO

EL PARQUE

TO CD. MANTE

85

0   10 km

⬜ = PINE - OAK FOREST

⬜ = CHAPARRAL - MATORRAL

⬜ = TROPICAL CADUCIFOLIA JUNGLE

⬜ = MESOPHILIC MONTANE FOREST / CLOUD FOREST

Ciudad Mante

Few travelers stop off in Ciudad Mante, a sugarcane center southeast of Ciudad Victoria about halfway to Ciudad Valles, S.L.P. Visits to either of two active sugar mills south of town may be arranged through almost any hotel in town.

Ciudad Mante serves as a supply point for excursions to two nearby lakes. **Presa Ramiro Caballero,** 25 km (15.5 miles) east of Ciudad Mante via Mexico 80, then four km south on a dirt road, is a favorite local camping and fishing spot.

The 7,000-acre **Presa San Lorenzo,** about 48 km (30 miles) northeast of Ciudad Mante (127 km/79 miles southeast of Ciudad Victoria), near the town of Xicoténcatl (about midway between Mexico 85 and Mexico 81), turns out a fair number of largemouth bass. The state provides grills, *palapas,* tables, two boat ramps and camping areas. At least two lakeside fish camps with accommodations are currently being developed under North American auspices.

Accommodations: Several *clase económica* hotels provide basic lodging for around US$15 a night, including **Hotel California** (Km

9, Mexico 85), **Hotel America** (Privado del Mercado 14), **Hotel Riestra** (Av. Juárez 317 Pte.), and **Hotel Jardín** (Calle Galeana 103 Nte.). In the US$20-25 range are the nicer **Motel Río** (tel. 123-2-19-24; Blvd. González and Azuceña), **Motel Los Arcos Courts** (tel. 2-08-70; Blvd. L. Echeverría and Quintero), and **Hotel Monterrey** (tel. 2-27-12; Calle Juárez 503 Nte.).

The most comfortable place in town is **Hotel Mante** (tel. 2-09-90; Av. Guerrero and Sidar), which has four-star rooms with a/c and TV for US$27-36.

Tula

Founded in 1617 by Franciscan missionaries, Tula is the oldest town in the state and the first place in southwestern Tamaulipas that begins to show Huastec influence. Many 18th- and 19th-century buildings have survived, and there are minor Huastec ruins in the nearby *ejidos* of **La Laguna, Potrero de Palma, El Coronel,** and **Las Pintas.**

Tula is known for handcrafted leatherwork, including *cueras tamaulipecas.* The city's **Centro Artesanal** is housed in a two-story, 19th-century building in the old section of town.

Accommodations and Food: Two basic hotels, the **Rossana** (Calle Hidalgo 7-B) and the **Mesón de Mollinedo** (Calle Morelos 1), provide simple rooms for US$10-15 per night.

The local cuisine has more in common with that of San Luis Potosí than with Tamaulipan styles. Specialties include *enchiladas tultecas* (chile-dipped tortillas smothered with cheese, chorizo, lettuce, onions, tomatoes, and *chile pequín* sauce), *pipián* (a currylike preparation of chiles and pumpkin seeds), tamales, *nopalitos,* and *atole.* Regional cooking is available at **Restaurante Tulteco** at Km 40 on Mexico 101 on the outskirts of town. **Restaurante Las Perlitas,** on Calle Hidalgo near the Hotel Rossana, serves Mexican standards as well as a few local dishes.

SPANISH PHRASEBOOK

English is occasionally spoken by merchants, hotel staff, and travel agents in state capitals and beach resorts—but even in these cities, you can only count on finding English-speaking Mexicans within each city's tourist districts. Outside the tourist areas, and even in smaller border towns, it is somewhat rare to encounter anyone who speaks more than a few words of English. Sometimes a few words is enough, sometimes it isn't.

Hence it is incumbent upon the non-Spanish-speaking visitor to learn at least enough Spanish to cope with everyday transactions. Knowing a little Spanish will not only go a long way toward mitigating communication problems, it will also bring you more respect among the local Mexicans, who quite naturally resent foreign visitors (usually Americans) who expect Mexicans to abandon their mother tongue whenever a gringo approaches. A popular sign seen in tourist restaurants reads, "We promise not to laugh at your broken Spanish if you won't laugh at our broken English." Out of courtesy, you should at least attempt to communicate in Spanish whenever possible.

The type of Spanish spoken in Mexico is usually referred to as "Latin-American Spanish" (in contrast to the Castilian Spanish spoken in Spain), although the Spanish here differs significantly from even that of other Spanish-speaking countries in the western hemisphere. In Northern Mexico especially, many Anglicisms have crept into the language. For example, the common Latin-American Spanish term for "car" is *el coche,* but in the North you'll more often hear *el carro;* signs at automotive stores may read *auto partes* rather than *refacciones.*

PRONUNCIATION GUIDE

Consonants
c like 'c' in "cat" before 'a', 'o', or 'u'; like 's' before 'e' or 'i'

d as 'd' in 'dog', except between vowels, then like 'th' in "that"

g before 'e' or 'i', like the 'ch' in Scottish "loch"; elsewhere like 'g' in "get"

h always silent

j like the English 'h' in "hotel" except stronger

ll like the 'y' in "yellow"

ñ like the 'ni' in "onion"

r always pronounced as strong 'r'

rr trilled 'r'

v similar to the 'b' in "boy" (not like English 'v')

z like 's' in "same"

b, f, k, l, m, n, p, q, t, as in English

Vowels
a as in "father" except shorter

e as in "hen"

i as in "machine"

o as in "phone"

u usually as in "rule"; when it follows a 'q' the 'u' is silent; when it follows an 'h' or 'g' it is pronounced like 'w' except when it comes between 'g' and 'e' or 'i', when it is also silent

USEFUL WORDS AND PHRASES

Greetings And Civilities
¡Hola!—Hello!

Buenos días—Good morning

Buenas tardes—Good afternoon

Buenas noches—Good evening, good night

Buenas—can be used when you're not sure of the time of day

¿Cómo está?—How are you?

Muy bien—Fine

Así así—So-so

Muchas gracias.—Thank you very much.

De nada—You're welcome (literally, "It's nothing")

Sí—Yes

No—No

Yo no sé.—I don't know.

Está bien—It's fine; okay

Bueno—Good; okay

Por favor—Please

¡Salud!—(To your) health! (used in toasting or after someone sneezes)

Dispénseme—Excuse me

Perdóneme—Pardon me

Lo siento—I'm sorry

Adiós—Goodbye (can also be used as a passing hello)

¿Mande?—What? (as in "Could you repeat that?")

Terms Of Address

yo—I

usted—you (formal)

tú—you (familiar)

él—he/him

ella—she/her

nosotros—we/us

ustedes—you (plural)

ellos—they/them (all male or mixed gender)

ellas—they/them (all female)

señor—Mr., sir

señora—Mrs., madam

señorita—miss, young lady

Communication Problems

No hablo bien español.—I don't speak Spanish well.

No entiendo.—I don't understand.

Hable más despacio, por favor.—Speak more slowly, please.

Repita, por favor.—Repeat, please.

¿Cómo se dice . . . en español?—How do you say . . . in Spanish?

¿Entiende el inglés?—Do you understand English?

¿Se habla inglés aquí?—Is English spoken here? (Does anyone here speak English?)

Getting Directions

¿Dónde está . . . ?—Where is . . . ?

¿Qué tan lejos está a . . . ?—How far is it to . . . ?

de . . . a . . .—from . . . to . . .

¿Conduce a . . . este camino?—Does this road lead to . . . ?

la carretera—highway

el camino—road

la calle—street

la cuadra—block

kilómetro—kilometer

milla—mile (commonly used near the U.S. border)

el norte—north

el sur—south

el oeste—west

el este—east

al derecho or *adelante*—straight ahead

a la derecha—to the right

a la izquierda—to the left

At A Hotel

¿Hay un hotel cerca de aquí?—Is there a hotel near here?

posada—inn

casa de huéspedes—guesthouse

¿Puedo (podemos) ver un cuarto?—Can I (we) see a room?

¿Cuál es el precio?—What is the rate?

¿Están incluídos los impuestos?—Does that include taxes?

¿Acepta tarjetas de crédito?—Do you accept credit cards?

solo efectivo—cash only

un cuarto sencillo—a single room

un cuarto doble—a double room

con camas gemelas—with twin beds

con una cama de matrimonio—with a double bed

con baño—with bath

sin baño—without bath

baño colectivo—shared bath

agua caliente—hot water

agua fría—cold water

calentador—heater

aire acondicionado—air conditioning

toalla—towel

jabón—soap

llave—key

cubierta or manta—blanket

papel higiénico—toilet paper

hielo—ice

Post Office

la oficina de correos (or el correo)—post office

Quiero unas estampillas.—I'd like some stamps.

Quiero mandar esto . . . —I'd like to send this . . .

por correo aéreo—by air mail

certificado—certified mail

Quiero mandar este paquete.—I'd like to send this parcel.

¿Hay correo para mí? Me llamo . . . —Is there any mail for me? My name is . . .

Telephone

caseta de teléfono—telephone office

Quiero llamar a . . . —I want to make a call to . . .

por cobrar—collect call

persona a persona—person-to-person

una llamada de larga distancia—a long-distance call

Quiero hablar con . . . —I want to speak with . . .

¿Está . . . ?—Is . . . there?

No está.—S/he's not here.

La linea está ocupada.—The line is engaged.

Changing Money

Quiero cambiar dinero.—I want to change money.

cheques de viajero—traveler's checks

¿Cuál es el tipio de cambio?—What's the exchange rate?

¿Hay comisión?—Is there a commission?

banco—bank

casa de cambio—currency exchange office

Making Purchases

Necesito . . . —I need . . .

Deseo . . . or Quiero . . . —I want . . .

Quisiera . . . —I would like . . . (more polite)

¿Hay . . . aquí?—Is/are there any . . . here? (Do you have . . . ?)

¿Cuánto cuesta?—How much does it cost?

¿Puedo ver . . . ?—Can I see . . . ?

ésta/éste—this one

ésa/ése—that one

Me llevo éste.—I'll take this one.

caro—expensive

barato—cheap

más barato—cheaper

Driving

Lleno, por favor.—Full, please (at a gasoline station).

Se me ha descompuesto el carro.—My car has broken down.

Necesito un remolque.—I need a tow.

¿Hay un garage cerca?—Is there a garage nearby?

¿Puedo pasar con este carro (esta troca)?—Is the road passable with this car (truck)?

¿Con doble tracción?—With four-wheel drive?

No hay paso.—It's not passable.

el semáfora—traffic light

el señal—traffic sign

gasolina—gasoline (petrol)

gasolinera—gasoline station

aceite—oil

agua—water

llanta desinflada—flat tire
llantera—tire repair shop

Auto Parts
banda de ventilador—fan belt
batería—battery
bomba de gasolina (agua)—fuel (water) pump
bujía—spark plug
carburador—carburetor
distribuidor—distributor
eje—axle
embrague—clutch
empaque, junta—gasket
filtro—filter
frenos—brakes
llanta—tire
manguera—hose
marcha, arranque—starter
radiador—radiator
regulado de voltaje—voltage regulator

Public Transport
la parada del autobús—bus stop
la central camionera—main bus terminal
la estación de ferrocarril—railway station
el aeropuerto—airport
la terminal del transbordador—ferry terminal
Quiero un boleto a . . . —I want a ticket to . . .
Quiero bajar en . . . —I want to get off at . . .
¡Aquí, por favor!—Here, please.
¿Cuánto le debo?—What do I owe?

Hiking And Camping
¿Dónde empieza la vereda (el sendero)?—
  Where does the trail (path) start?
¿Se puede acampar aquí (allá)?—Is camping
  permitted here (there)?
¿Hay agua potable?—Is there drinking water?
¿Hay agua allá?—Is there water there?
la tinaja—water hole
el ojo de agua—spring

el pozo—well
la mochila—backpack
la bolsa de dormir—sleeping bag
la carpa—tent
la leña—firewood
el carbón—charcoal
el fuego—fire
los cerrillos or *los fósforos*—matches
el cruce—crossing
a pie—on foot
a bestia—by horse, mule, or burro
Quiero rentar (comprar) . . .—I want to rent
  (buy) . . .
un burro—a burro
un caballo—a horse
una mula—a mule

Geography
la isla—island
el cerro or *la colina*—hill
la montaña—mountain
la sierra—mountain range
el bosque—forest
la barranca—large canyon
el cañon—medium-size canyon
el arroyo—streambed, wash, small canyon
el valle—valley
la catarat—waterfall
el río—river
la laguna—lagoon or lake
bahía—bay
el mar—sea
la playa—beach
la punta—point, headland

Numbers
0—*cero*
1—*uno* (masculine) *una* (feminine)
2—*dos*
3—*tres*
4—*cuatro*

5—*cinco*
6—*seis*
7—*siete*
8—*ocho*
9—*nueve*
10—*diez*
11—*once*
12—*doce*
13—*trece*
14—*catorce*
15—*quince*
16—*diez y seis*
17—*diez y siete*
18—*diez y ocho*
19—*diez y nueve*
20—*veinte*
21—*veinte y uno*
30—*treinta*
40—*cuarenta*
50—*cincuenta*
60—*sesenta*
70—*setenta*
80—*ochenta*
90—*noventa*
100—*cien*
101—*ciento y uno*
200—*doscientos*
1000—*mil*
2000—*dos mil*
20,000—*veinte mil*
million—*millón*

Days Of The Week

domingo—Sunday
lunes—Monday
martes—Tuesday
miércoles—Wednesday
jueves—Thursday
viernes—Friday
sábado—Saturday

Time

¿Qué hora es?—What time is it?
la una—one o'clock
las dos—two o'clock
a las dos—at two o'clock
las tres y diez—ten past three
las seis a la mañana—six a.m.
las seis a la tarde—six p.m.
el mediodía—noon
la medianoche—midnight
hoy—today
mañana—tomorrow
ayer—yesterday
esta noche—tonight
anoche—last night
esta semana—this week
la semana pasada—last week
el próximo año—next year
el mes pasado—last month
hace dos años—two years ago

Miscellaneous

más—more
menos—less
mejor—better
un poco—a little
un poquito—a very little
grande—large
pequeño—small
caliente—hot (temperature)
picante—hot (spicy)
frío—cold
rápido—quick
malo—bad
difícil—difficult
fácil—easy

LANGUAGE STUDY

Dictionaries And Phrasebooks

One of the best dictionaries of a portable size for the Spanish student is the paperback *University of Chicago Spanish-English, English-Spanish Dictionary,* which emphasizes New World usages and contains useful sections on grammar and pronunciation. If even this small volume is too large for your backpack, the *Collins Gem Dictionary: Spanish-English, English-Spanish* comes in a tiny 4 by 3.25 by 1-inch size with a sturdy plastic cover and over 40,000 entries.

Berlitz's *Latin-American Spanish For Travellers* is a small phrasebook divided by topics and situations (e.g., Grammar, Hotel, Eating Out, Post Office) that some people find very helpful. Not all of the phrases and terms it contains are used in Mexico but it's better than nothing.

One of the best references for off-the-road adventurers is Burleson's and Riskind's *Backcountry Mexico: A Traveler's Guide and Phrase Book* (University of Texas Press). Although it's rather bulky for carrying in a backpack, it contains many words and phrases that could be of value to hikers and campers if studied before taking an extended backcountry trip.

Advanced Spanish learners may be able to improve their command of idiomatic Spanish with Frances de Talavera Berger's *¡Mierda!* (Plume: New York). Subtitled *The Real Spanish You Were Never Taught in School,* the book's copious *vulgarismos* or slang expressions have a decidedly scatological slant and should probably be aired in public only after practice with a trusted native speaker.

Language Study

Those who plan to spend an extended period of time in Northern Mexico should seriously consider enrolling in an intensive Spanish course. Night classes at an adult community school or summer university courses are a fine introduction, but the most time-and-cost-effective study program is one that immerses you in the language and culture within Mexico. The *Centro de Idiomas* in Mazatlán is a long-running private language school with reasonable rates (see the "Mazatlán Information" section for details).

If your travels will take you through Baja California, you might consider the friendly, family-owned **International Spanish Institute of Ensenada (Colegio de Idiomas)**, tel. 6-01-09, 6-65-87, at 377 Boulevard J.A. Rodriguez in Ensenada. This school offers a choice of one-day, weekend, and six-day (or longer) courses, with six hours of language class per day. Tuition is US$20 per day (a bargain at less than US$4 an hour) weekdays, US$50 per weekend, and classes are always limited to five or fewer persons. For an additional US$20 per day they can arrange a homestay with a local Mexican family that includes a private room and three meals per day. This is considerably cheaper than staying in even the cheapest hotel and eating out; staying with a Mexican family also gives students plenty of opportunity to practice Spanish after class. ISIE can also be contacted through Kathy Luna (tel. 619-472-0600), P.O. Box 536, Bonita, CA 91908.

In the U.S., excellent eight- to 10-week Spanish summer programs are open to the public at the University of California, Berkeley (Department of Spanish & Portuguese, Dwinelle Hall, University of California, Berkeley, CA 94720, tel. 510-642-6000); and at the San Antonio branch of Mexico's Universidad Nacional Autonoma de Mexico (600 Hemisfair Park, P.O. Box 830426, San Antonio, TX 78283, tel. 210-222-8626). Many other colleges and universities in the U.S. and Canada offer similar summer intensives. In investigating a program, be sure to ask what type of Spanish—Latin American or Castilian—will be taught.

GLOSSARY

abarrotes—groceries

aduana—customs service

antojitos—literally "little whims," quick Mexican dishes like tacos and enchiladas

arroyo—canyon, dry wash, or stream

atole—thick, flavored corn beverage popular in San Luis Potosí and southwestern Tamaulipas

autopista—freeway

bahía—bay

balneario—spa or bathing resort, usually associated with natural springs

barrio—neighborhood

basura—trash or rubbish; the sign No Tire Basura means "Don't throw trash."

boca—literally "mouth," a geographic term describing a break in a barrier island or peninsula where sea meets lagoon

bolsón—desert depression where rainwater collects

cabecera—*municipio* capital, roughly equivalent to a county seat

calle—street

callejón—alley or lane

cañon—canyon

cardón—*Cereus pringelei,* the world's tallest cactus

casa de huéspedes—guesthouse

cerro—hill or mountain

cerveza—beer

charreada—Mexican-style rodeo

charro/charra—horseman/horsewoman

CONASUPO—Compañía Nacional de Subsistencias Populares (National Company for Popular Subsistence)

Churrigueresque—*churrigueresco* in Spanish, named for Spain's Churriguera family of architects, a late baroque style in neo-Hispanic churches and cathedrals characterized by heavy ornamentation

cigarro—cigarette

colectivo—van or taxi that picks up several passengers at a time for a standard per-person fare, much like a bus

comedores—small diners, often near bus stations or in municipal markets

comida corrida—fixed-price afternoon meal

correo—post office

corrida de toros—"running of the bulls" or bullfight

COTP—Captain of the Port

curandero—traditional healer

curios—novelties

D.F.—Distrito Federal (Federal District), a special federal entity that grants Mexico City an administrative status similar to that of a state

desertland—biotic community with an average annual precipitation of 25 cm (10 inches) or less

efectivo—cash payment

ejido—collectively owned agricultural lands

ensenada—cove or small bay

FONART—Fondo Nacional para el Fomento de las Artesanías (National Foundation for the Development of Arts and Crafts)

FONATUR—Fondo Nacional de Fomento del Turismo (National Foundation for Tourism Development)

forest—biotic community dominated by trees over 15 meters (49 feet) in height, usually with a closed and/or multilayered canopy

Gral.—abbreviation for "General" (rank)

grassland—biotic community dominated by grasses and/or other herbaceous vegetation

gringo—Mexican slang for Caucasian foreigner

hectare—equal to 2.74 acres

IMSS—Instituto Mexicano del Seguro Social (Mexican Social Security Institute)

INAH—Instituto Nacional de Antropología e História (National Institute of Anthropology and History)

ISSTE—Instituto de Seguridad y Servicios Sociales para Trabajadores del Estado (Security and Social Services Institute for Government Workers)

laguna—lagoon, lake, or bay

llano—plains

lomerías—hilly desert grasslands of southern Chihuahua and northern Durango

maguey—agave or century plant; maguey extract is often fermented and distilled to produce alcoholic beverages, including mescal and tequila

maquiladora (maquila)—a "twin-bond" or "in-plant" manufacturing enterprise where foreign components may be imported and assembled, then exported to a foreign country, free of customs duties in each direction; now that NAFTA has passed U.S. Congress, the *maquiladora* may become extinct.

malecón—waterfront promenade

mescal/mezcal—alcoholic beverage distilled from maguey extract

mariscos—literally "shellfish," but often used as a generic term for seafood

matachine—a type of religious dance procession popular in the north

mochila—knapsack or backpack; (*mochilero*: backpacker)

municipio—the next administrative unit below the state, Mexico's equivalent to a county

mercado—market

nopal, nopales—prickly pear cactus; with the spines removed it is commonly served as a side dish—parboiled or grilled—throughout the north; *nopalitos* are strips of cooked or pickled *nopal.*

palacio municipal—literally "municipal palace," equivalent to city or county hall in the U.S.

palapa—thatched, umbrellalike shade shelter or roof

panadería—bakery

parrada—bus stop

PAN—Partido Acción Nacional, the main opposition party to the ruling Partido Revolucionario Institucional (PRI)

PEMEX—Petróleos Mexicanos (Mexican Petroleum)

periférico—highway loop or bypass

peyote—*Lophophora williamsii,* a hallucinogenic cactus used for religious rituals among certain Amerindian cultures

pensión—boardinghouse

playa—beach

plaza—town square

plazuela—smaller plaza

pre-Cortesian—a reference to Mexican history before the arrival of the Spanish conquistador Hernán Cortés, i.e., before 1518; other terms with the same meaning include "pre-Columbian" and "pre-Hispanic"

punta—point

Porfiriato—the period during which Porfirio Díaz was president of Mexico, when many foreigners purchased land and established businesses in Mexico

presidio—military garrison

PRI—Partido Revolucionario Institucional

Prol.—an abbreviation for "Prolongación," an extension of an older avenue/boulevard

puro—cigar

ramal—branch road

ranchería—a collection of small ranching households, most often inhabited by *indios*

ranchito—small ranch

rebozo—traditional handwoven Mexican shawl; the best are made in the state of San Luis Potosí.

refresca—soda or soft drink

retablo—altarpiece; also, a devotional carving (usually tin or wood) presented as a shrine offering

sarape—traditional all-purpose blanket; the most famous are from Saltillo

scrubland—biotic community dominated by shrubs and/or multistemmed trees generally under 10 meters (31 feet)

SECTUR—Secretaría de Turismo (Secretariat of Tourism)

SEDESOL—Secretaría de Desarrollo Social (Secretariat of Social Development)

SEDUE—Secretaría de Desarrollo Urbano y Ecología (Secretariat of Urban and Ecological Development); now subsumed under SEDESOL

s/n—*sin número* or "without number," used for street addresses without building numbers

Solomonic—an architectural term applied to Spanish baroque columns—common on 17th- to 18th-century church facades—with spiral motifs

tahona—wooden mill for grinding ore to separate gold; sometimes hand operated, sometimes powered by burro or water-wheel

tianguis—open-air market

tienda—store

tinaja—pool or spring

topes—speed bumps

trago—slang for a "swallow," i.e., a quick drink

ultramarinos—delicatessen-liquor store

viceregal—*virreinal* in Spanish; a reference to the 300-year period (1521-1821) when a Spanish viceroy ruled Mexico as Nueva España; as a historical term, "viceregal" is often synonymous with "colonial."

woodland—biotic community dominated by trees not exceeding 15 meters (49 feet) in height with an open (or interrupted) single-layer canopy

REFERENCES

DESCRIPTION AND TRAVEL

Bowden, Charles. *The Secret Forest*. Albuquerque: University of New Mexico Press, 1993. A captivating social, historical, and ecological evocation of the Sonoran tropical deciduous forest surrounding Alamos, Sonora.

Burleson, Bob, and David H. Riskind. *Backcountry Mexico: A Traveler's Guide and Phrase Book*. Austin: University of Texas Press, 1986. Part guidebook, part anthropological study of Northern Mexico with useful tips on backcountry travel.

Hancock, Richard. *Chihuahua: A Guide to the Wonderful Country*. University of Oklahoma Press, 1978. This hard-to-find, out-of-print book has good historical notes on some of the state's smaller towns.

Lumholz, Carl. *New Trails in Mexico*. Tucson: University of Arizona Press, 1990. A re-publication of Lumholz's classic 1912 volume on Sonora's Papagueria (Tohono O'odham homelands) with historic photos and sketches. Contains marvelous descriptions of the native medicinal uses of such common Sonoran Desert plants as saguaro and greasewood, even snippets of Papago songs.

Morris, Mary. *Nothing to Declare: Memoirs of a Woman Traveling Alone*. Boston: Houghton Mifflin, 1988. Mostly a very personal journey but sprinkled with insights into daily Mexican life.

Nelson, Mike. *Mexico from the Driver's Seat*. Oak Park, MI: Scrivener Press, 1991. A collection of Nelson's humorous, homespun columns from the *McAllen Monitor*, *Mexico City News*, and other periodicals, based on his extensive motor travels around Mexico researching road conditions for Sanborn's Mexican Insurance. Although cheaply produced, with many typesetting gaffes, Nelson's unique and infectious prose levels the myths about driving in Mexico.

Pfefferkorn, Ignaz. *Sonora: A Description of the Province*. Tucson: University of Arizona Press, 1989. Originally published in German in 1794-95 and translated into English by Theodore Treutlein in 1949, this complete description of northern Sonora (including present-day southern Arizona) was written by a German Jesuit missionary who spent a decade among the Pima and Papago Indians prior to the Jesuit expulsion in 1767.

Wallace, Dillon. *Beyond the Mexican Sierras*. Chicago: McClury & Co., 1910. Well-written, humorous account of the author's travels along Mexico's Pacific coast at the turn of the century.

HISTORY AND CULTURE

Artaud, Antonin. *The Peyote Dance*. New York: Farrar, Straus & Giroux, 1976. An interesting piece of participatory anthropology in which the notorious founder of *théâtre de cruel* dares to live the Tarahumara myths in the face of possible insanity. Much of this work was in fact written from a Paris asylum upon Artaud's return to France after spending eight months with Tarahumara shamans.

Bierhorst, John. *The Mythology of Mexico and Central America*. New York: William Morrow, 1990. A good introduction to Mexican mythology, with passages on Yaqui, Mayo, Tarahumara, Cora, and Huichol myths among others.

De Vaca, Cabeza. *Adventures in the Unknown Interior of America*. New York: Collier Books, 1961. The classic account of De Vaca's nine-year journey on foot through the American Southwest and Northern Mexico.

Gershman, Suzy, and Judith Thomas. *Born to Shop Mexico*. New York: Bantam Books, 1989. Delightful shopping guide written by two very savvy Texas women. Includes sections on border towns.

Herzog, Lawrence A. *Where North Meets South: Cities, Space and Politics on the U.S.-Mexico Border.* Center for Mexican American Studies, University of Texas at Austin, 1990. Sociologist Herzog postulates a new urban paradigm, the "transfrontier metropolis." The text focuses mostly on the San Diego-Tijuana area, with plenty of demographic and economic statistics and maps to illustrate the author's points.

Reavis, Dick J. *Conversations with Moctezuma: Ancient Shadows over Modern Life in Mexico.* New York: William Morrow & Co., 1990. This collection of observations by an American foreign correspondent living in Mexico is full of insider information on political and social organization in modern Mexico, with special reference to Monterrey and the 1988 presidential election.

Paz, Octavio. *The Labyrinth of Solitude: Life and Thought in Mexico.* New York: Grove Press, 1961. Paz has no peer when it comes to expositions of the Mexican psyche, and this is his best work.

NATURAL HISTORY

"Biotic Communities of the American Southwest—United States and Mexico," *Desert Plants,* Vol. 4, Nos. 1-4. Superior, AZ: University of Arizona Press (for the Boyce Thompson Southwestern Arboretum), 1982. A carefully team-researched study of Greater Southwest biomes with plenty of detail on northwestern Mexico (including Durango and Chihuahua). Although it's tough going, this is a definitive work for those with a serious interest in the typology of Mexican vegetation.

Davis, L. Irby. *A Field Guide to the Birds of Mexico and Central America.* Austin: University of Texas Press, 1972. A good supplement to the Peterson guide (see below).

Ives, Ronald L. *Land of Lava, Ash, and Sand: The Pinacate Region of Northwestern Mexico.* Tucson: Arizona Historical Society, 1989. Edited by Karen J. Dahood. This collection of excerpts from the prolific writings of Ronald Ives (1919-82), who specialized in environmental research on northwest Mexico, presents an admirable synthesis of the geography, geology, meteorology, volcanology, history, and anthropology of the Pinacate region.

Peterson, Roger Tory, and Edward L. Chalif. *A Field Guide to Mexican Birds.* Boston: Houghton Mifflin, 1973. Despite being a bit outdated, this is still the most popular and useful guide to birding in Mexico.

Steinhart, Peter. *Two Eagles/Dos Aguilas: The Natural World of the United States-Mexico Borderlands.* Berkeley: University of California Press, 1994. Pre-publication material for this book, which examines the borderlands as a "distinct province of the hemisphere," looks very good. Includes excellent photography by Tupper Ansel Blake.

Wauer, Roland H. *A Naturalist's Mexico.* College Station, TX: Texas A&M University Press, 1992. Although only 65 pages are devoted to Northern Mexico (plus 14 pages on Isla Tiburón), this anecdotal, travelogue-style narrative of Mexico's natural environment is a good read. Birding activities receive more emphasis than other aspects of the author's Mexican explorations, so those with a keen interest in Mexican birds will enjoy this book most.

FOOD

DeWitt, Dave, and Nancy Gerlach. *The Whole Chile Pepper Book.* Boston: Little, Brown and Co., 1990. Written by the editors of *Chile Pepper* magazine, this compendium of fact, lore, and recipes is the definitive culinary guide to chiles.

Esquivel, Laura. *Como Agua Para Chocolate* (*Like Water for Chocolate*). New York: Doubleday, 1993 (available in either Spanish or English language versions from the same publisher). Each chapter begins with a different recipe. See "Film and Video" below for a description of the magical story.

Peyton, James W. *The Cuisine of Northern Mexico.* Santa Fe: Red Crane Books, 1990. A good introduction to the border cuisines of Sonora, Chihuahua, Coahuila, and Nuevo León, complete with 150 easy-to-follow, mouth-watering recipes.

SPORTS AND RECREATION

Franz, Carl, with Steve Rogers. *RV Camping in Mexico.* Santa Fe: John Muir Publications, 1989. A bit out of date, but the introductory chapters would be useful for anyone planning their first RV trip to Mexico.

Lehman, Charles. *Desert Survival Handbook.* Primer Publishers, 1990. A no-nonsense guide to desert survival techniques that ought to be part of every pilot's or coastal navigator's kit.

Oleksak, Michael, and Mary Oleksak. *Béisbol: Latin Americans and the Grand Old Game.* Master's Press, 1991. The best reference available on baseball south of the border.

Wyatt, Mike. *The Basic Essentials of Sea Kayaking.* Merrilville, IN: ICS Books, 1990. A good introduction to sea kayaking, with tips on buying gear, paddling techniques, safety, and kayak loading.

THE TARAHUMARAS

Since most books on the Tarahumaras were written 20 or more years ago, it's difficult to judge how authoritative or relevant any of them are with respect to today's Tarahumaras. On top of that, descriptions of customs and ceremonies differ so completely from book to book that it almost seems as if the author-researchers are describing different tribes—and in a way they are, since there is no "standard" Tarahumara group.

Bennett, Wendell, and Robert Zingg. *The Tarahumara: An Indian Tribe of Northern Mexico.* Glorieta, NM: Rio Grande Press, 1976. Republished from the original 1835, pioneering work, this is the best source on mid-19th century Tarahumara life.

Fayhee, M. John. *Mexico's Copper Canyon Country.* Evergreen, CO: Cordillera Press, 1989. Humble and humorous, this anecdotal guide gives a good feel for what Sierra Tarahumara hiking and backpacking is all about, although details on transport and accommodations are rather out of date.

Fontana, Bernard L. *Tarahumara: Where Night Is the Day of the Moon.* Flagstaff, AZ: Northland Publishing, 1979. A nicely photographed, large-format work containing some of the most current (but far from up-to-date) anecdotal research on the Tarahumaras. Both the text and photographs (by John P. Schaefer) refer to the highland Tarahumaras east of the Continental Divide, an area peripheral to the geographic and cultural heart of the Sierra Tarahumara.

Kennedy, John C. *The Tarahumara of the Sierra Madre: Beer, Ecology, and Social Organization.* Arlington Heights, IL: AHM Publishing, 1978. Great title, fair but outdated information.

Kennedy, John C., and Raúl López. *Semana Santa in the Sierra Tarahumara: A Comparative Study of Three Communities.* Berkeley: University of California Press, 1981. A good source for understanding the cultural variation among different Tarahumara villages.

Lumholz, Carl. *Unknown Mexico: Explorations and Adventures Among the Tarahumara, Tepehuane, Cora, Huichol, Tarasco, and Aztec Indians,* volumes 1 and 2. New York: Charles Scribners & Sons, 1902. A pioneering piece of research by the legendary Norwegian ethnologist. Information on the Sierra Tarahumara is mostly contained in volume 1.

Pennington, Campbell W. *The Tarahumar [sic] of Mexico: Their Environment and Material Culture.* Salt Lake City: University of Utah Press, 1963. Considered by many to be the seminal work on Tarahumara culture.

FILM AND VIDEO

El Mariachi. Directed by 23-year-old Robert Rodriguez, at the time a UT-Austin film student, on a budget of US$7000 in Ciudad Acuña, Coah., this film stars Carlos Gallardo as a young guitarist mistaken for a hit man in the world of *narcotraficantes.* The unique combination of a poetic tone with in-your-face realism had critics jumping out of their seats. In Spanish with English subtitles; slated for video release.

Like Water For Chocolate (Como Agua Para Chocolate). Based on Laura Esquivel's succulent novel and adapted for the screen by her director husband Alfonso Arau, this is one of the most successful transitions of Latin American literature's magic realism movement to the screen. The story takes place during the Mexican Revolution years in the vicinity of Piedras Negras, Coah., where the film was shot on location. Tita, the youngest of three daughters, is condemned by tradition to taking care of her mother in old age rather than marrying the man she loves; the novel follows the way in which she sublimates her romantic passions in the kitchen.

In the book, each chapter begins with a recipe containing classic border motifs. The title is a Mexican expression that describes a passion akin to boiling water ready for the addition of ingredients to produce hot chocolate. Distributed in the U.S. by Miramax (producers of *Enchanted April, Mediterraneo*). In Spanish with English subtitles, available on video.

INDEX

Page numbers in **boldface** indicate the primary reference. *Italicized* page numbers indicate information in captions, charts, illustrations, maps, or special topics.

Parroquia de la Purísima Concepción (Real de Catorce): 358
Parroquia de San Fernando (Guaymas): 158
Parroquia de San Juan Bautista (Sombrerete): 334
Parroquia de San Miguel Arcángel (Tancanhuitz): 370
Parroquia de Santo Cristo de Burgos (Ciudad Jimenez): 264
pensiónes: see guesthouses
people: 35-38, *36, 130;* criollos 36-37; cultural customs 116-118; immigrants 37-38; *indígenas* 37; mestizos 36-37; *see also* Amerindians; *specific people*
Pershing, John "Blackjack": 29, 237
pesos: 111-112
pets: 100-101
peyote: 358
Picacho San Onofre mountain: *6*
Pico El Pinacate: 124
Piedras Negras: 379-382, *381*
Pima: *36*
Piñeda, Alfonso Alvarez de: 429, 459
Pirámide Votiva: 334
Pitiquito: 136
Plan de Iguala: 26
Plateros: 334
Playa Angel: 219
Playa Bagdad: 451
Playa Carbonera: 454
Playa Carvajal: 454
Playa Cerritos: 195
Playa El Barrancón: 454
Playa El Mezquital: 453
Playa El Tambor: 189
Playa Escondida: 195
Playa Gaviotas: 198
Playa Huatabampito: 175
Playa Las Arenitas: 189
Playa Las Cabras: 219
Playa La Tambora: 219
Playa Maviri: 182
Playa Miramar (Guaymas): 158
Playa Miramar (Puerto Peñasco): 130
Playa Miramar (Tampico): 465-466
Playa Norte: 198
Playa Olas Altas: 198
Playa Sábalo: 195
Playa San Nicolás: 156
Playa Tepehuaje: 457
politics: *see* government
population: *36,* 37
Posada Barrancas: 288-289
postal service: 114
pottery: 61, 240, *243,* 253
precautions: 119; driving 93-94; fishing 47;

snakebite prevention *108-109;* surf conditions *195*
precipitation: 11-12, *11*
Presa Alvaro Obregón: 168
Presa Comedero: 190
Presa de la Amistad: 377
Presa Fancisco I. Madero: 263
Presa La Boquilla: 264
Presa Lázaro Cárdenas: 315
Presa López Mateo: 189
Presa López Portillo: 190
Presa Marte R. Gómez: 442-443
Presa Ramiro Caballero: 475
Presa Sanaloa: 189
Presa San Lorenzo: 475
Presa Venustiano Carranza: 383
Presa Vicente Guerrero: 472-473
Pueblo Indian Revolt: 228
Puente Tampico: 462
Puente Tampoán: 367
Puerto Peñasco: 128-137, *129, 130, 134, 135;* accommodations 130-132; climate 128; food 132; information and services 133-134; recreation 132-133; sights 130; transportation 133; vicinity of 134-137
Punta Chueca: 156
Punta de las Clavadistas: 198

QR
Quevedo, Rodrigo: 237
Quírare: 286
radio: 114
Rafael Buelna Airport (Mazatlán): 214
railroads: 86-89
rail travel: 79-80, 86-89
rainfall: 11-12, *11*
Ramos Arizpe: 394
ranching: 32, 224
Rancho Cielito: 474
Real de Catorce: 40, **357-360,** *359*
rebozos: 350, *362*
Recohuata Hot Springs: 280-281
recreation: 41-52; fishing 44-47; hiking and backpacking 41-43; hunting 43; water sports 47-52; *see also specific recreation*
recreational vehicles: 91-92
Región de las Quebradas: 312
Región Huasteca: 40, **363-374,** *364, 366, 368, 372-373;* Ciudad Valles 367-369, *368;* El Consuelo 369-370; Río Verde 365
Región Lagunera: 6, 40
religion: 38; Catholicism 38; Mennonites: 248-249; Seri 157; *see also* Amerindians
reptiles: *17-19, 108-109,* 272
Reserva de la Biosfera El Cielo: 474, *475*
Reynosa: 443-446, *446*

MOON HANDBOOKS—THE IDEAL TRAVELING COMPANIONS

Moon Handbooks provide travelers with all the background and practical information he or she will need on the road. Every Handbook begins with in-depth essays on the land, the people, their history, arts, politics, and social concerns—an entire bookshelf of introductory information squeezed into a one-volume encyclopedia. The Handbooks provide accurate, up-to-date coverage of all the practicalities: language, currency, transportation, accommodations, food and entertainment, and services, to name a few. Moon Handbooks are ideal traveling companions: informative, entertaining, and highly practical.

To locate the bookstore nearest you that carries Moon Travel Handbooks or to order directly from Moon Publications, call: (800) 345-5473, Monday-Friday, 9 a.m.-5 p.m. PST.

THE PACIFIC/ASIA SERIES

BALI HANDBOOK   by Bill Dalton
Detailed travel information on the most famous island in the world. 428 pages.   **$12.95**

BANGKOK HANDBOOK   by Michael Buckley
Your tour guide through this exotic and dynamic city reveals the affordable and accessible possibilities. Thai phrasebook. 214 pages.   **$10.95**

BLUEPRINT FOR PARADISE: How to Live on a Tropic Island   by Ross Norgrove
This one-of-a-kind guide has everything you need to know about moving to and living comfortably on a tropical island. 212 pages.   **$14.95**

FIJI ISLANDS HANDBOOK   by David Stanley
The first and still the best source of information on travel around this 322-island archipelago. Fijian glossary. 198 pages.   **$11.95**

INDONESIA HANDBOOK   by Bill Dalton
This one-volume encyclopedia explores island by island the many facets of this sprawling, kaleidoscopic island nation. Extensive Indonesian vocabulary. 1,000 pages.   **$19.95**

JAPAN HANDBOOK   by J.D. Bisignani
In this comprehensive new edition, award-winning travel writer J.D. Bisignani offers to inveterate travelers, newcomers, and businesspeople alike a thoroughgoing presentation of Japan's many facets. 950 pages.   **$22.50**

MICRONESIA HANDBOOK: Guide to the Caroline, Gilbert, Mariana, and Marshall Islands
by David Stanley
Micronesia Handbook guides you on a real Pacific adventure all your own. 345 pages.   **$11.95**

NEW ZEALAND HANDBOOK   by Jane King
Introduces you to the people, places, history, and culture of this extraordinary land. 571 pages.
$18.95

OUTBACK AUSTRALIA HANDBOOK   by Marael Johnson
Australia is an endlessly fascinating, vast land, and *Outback Australia Handbook* explores the cities and towns, sheep stations, and wilderness areas of the Northern Territory, Western Australia, and South Australia. Full of travel tips and cultural information for adventuring, relaxing, or just getting away from it all. 355 pages.   **$15.95**

PHILIPPINES HANDBOOK   by Peter Harper and Evelyn Peplow
Crammed with detailed information, *Philippines Handbook* equips the escapist, hedonist, or business traveler with thorough coverage of the Philippines's colorful history, landscapes, and culture. 600 pages.   **$17.95**

SOUTHEAST ASIA HANDBOOK   by Carl Parkes
Helps the enlightened traveler discover the real Southeast Asia. 873 pages.   **$21.95**

SOUTH KOREA HANDBOOK   by Robert Nilsen
Whether you're visiting on business or searching for adventure, *South Korea Handbook* is an invaluable companion. Korean glossary with useful notes on speaking and reading the language. 548 pages.   **$14.95**

SOUTH PACIFIC HANDBOOK   by David Stanley
The original comprehensive guide to the 16 territories in the South Pacific. 740 pages.   **$19.95**

TAHITI-POLYNESIA HANDBOOK   by David Stanley
All five French-Polynesian archipelagoes are covered in this comprehensive guide by Oceania's best-known travel writer. 235 pages.   **$11.95**

THAILAND HANDBOOK   by Carl Parkes
Presents the richest source of information on travel in Thailand. 568 pages.   **$16.95**

THE HAWAIIAN SERIES

BIG ISLAND OF HAWAII HANDBOOK   by J.D. Bisignani
An entertaining yet informative text packed with insider tips on accommodations, dining, sports and outdoor activities, natural attractions, and must-see sights. 350 pages.   **$13.95**

HAWAII HANDBOOK   by J.D. Bisignani
Winner of the 1989 Hawaii Visitors Bureau's Best Guide Award and the Grand Award for Excellence in Travel Journalism, this guide takes you beyond the glitz and high-priced hype and leads you to a genuine Hawaiian experience. Covers all 8 Hawaiian Islands. 879 pages.   **$15.95**

KAUAI HANDBOOK   by J.D. Bisignani
Kauai Handbook is the perfect antidote to the workaday world. Hawaiian and pidgin glossaries. 236 pages.   **$9.95**

MAUI HANDBOOK   by J.D. Bisignani
"No fool-'round" advice on accommodations, eateries, and recreation, plus a comprehensive introduction to island ways, geography, and history. Hawaiian and pidgin glossaries. 350 pages. **$14.95**

OAHU HANDBOOK   by J.D. Bisignani
A handy guide to Honolulu, renowned surfing beaches, and Oahu's countless other diversions. Hawaiian and pidgin glossaries. 354 pages.   **$11.95**

THE AMERICAS SERIES

ALASKA-YUKON HANDBOOK   by Deke Castleman and Don Pitcher
Get the inside story, with plenty of well-seasoned advice to help you cover more miles on less money. 460 pages.   **$14.95**

ARIZONA TRAVELER'S HANDBOOK   by Bill Weir
This meticulously researched guide contains everything necessary to make Arizona accessible and enjoyable. 505 pages.   **$16.95**

**BAJA HANDBOOK: Mexico's Western Peninsula
including Cabo San Lucas**   by Joe Cummings
A comprehensive guide with all the travel information and background on the land, history, and culture of this untamed thousand-mile-long peninsula. 356 pages.   **$15.95**

BELIZE HANDBOOK   by Chicki Mallan
Complete with detailed maps, practical information, and an overview of the area's flamboyant history, culture, and geographical features, *Belize Handbook* is the only comprehensive guide of its kind to this spectacular region. 263 pages.   **$14.95**

BRITISH COLUMBIA HANDBOOK   by Jane King
With an emphasis on outdoor adventures, this guide covers mainland British Columbia, Vancouver Island, the Queen Charlotte Islands, and the Canadian Rockies. 381 pages.
$15.95

CANCUN HANDBOOK   by Chicki Mallan
Covers the city's luxury scene as well as more modest attractions, plus many side trips to unspoiled beaches and Mayan ruins. Spanish glossary. 257 pages.   **$13.95**

**CENTRAL MEXICO HANDBOOK: Mexico City, Guadalajara,
and Other Colonial Cities**   by Chicki Mallan
Retrace the footsteps of Cortés from the coast of Veracruz to the heart of Mexico City to discover archaeological and cultural wonders. 350 pages.   **$15.95**

CATALINA ISLAND HANDBOOK: A Guide to California's Channel Islands
by Chicki Mallan
A complete guide to these remarkable islands, from the windy solitude of the Channel Islands National Marine Sanctuary to bustling Avalon. 245 pages.   **$10.95**

COLORADO HANDBOOK   by Stephen Metzger
Essential details to the all-season possibilities in Colorado fill this guide. Practical travel tips combine with recreation—skiing, nightlife, and wilderness exploration—plus entertaining essays. 416 pages.   **$17.95**

COSTA RICA HANDBOOK   by Christopher P. Baker
Experience the many wonders of the natural world as you explore this remarkable land. Spanish-English glossary. 574 pages.   **$17.95**

IDAHO HANDBOOK   by Bill Loftus
A year-round guide to everything in this outdoor wonderland, from whitewater adventures to rural hideaways. 275 pages.   **$12.95**

JAMAICA HANDBOOK by Karl Luntta
From the sun and surf of Montego Bay and Ocho Rios to the cool slopes of the Blue Mountains, author Karl Luntta offers island-seekers a perceptive, personal view of Jamaica. 230 pages. **$14.95**

MONTANA HANDBOOK by W.C. McRae and Judy Jewell
The wild West is yours with this extensive guide to the Treasure State, complete with travel practicalities, history, and lively essays on Montana life. 393 pages. **$15.95**

NEVADA HANDBOOK by Deke Castleman
Nevada Handbook puts the Silver State into perspective and makes it manageable and affordable. 400 pages. **$14.95**

NEW MEXICO HANDBOOK by Stephen Metzger
A close-up and complete look at every aspect of this wondrous state. 375 pages. **$14.95**

NORTHERN CALIFORNIA HANDBOOK by Kim Weir
An outstanding companion for imaginative travel in the territory north of the Tehachapis. 765 pages. **$19.95**

NORTHERN MEXICO HANDBOOK: The Sea of Cortez to the Gulf of Mexico
by Joe Cummings
Directs travelers from the barrier islands of Sonora to the majestic cloud forests of the Sierra Madre Oriental to traditional villages and hidden waterfalls in San Luis Potosí. 500 pages. **$16.95**

OREGON HANDBOOK by Stuart Warren and Ted Long Ishikawa
Brimming with travel practicalities and insiders' views on Oregon's history, culture, arts, and activities. 461 pages. **$15.95**

PACIFIC MEXICO HANDBOOK by Bruce Whipperman
Explore 2,000 miles of gorgeous beaches, quiet resort towns, and famous archaeological sites along Mexico's Pacific coast. Spanish-English glossary. 428 pages. **$15.95**

TEXAS HANDBOOK by Joe Cummings
Seasoned travel writer Joe Cummings brings an insider's perspective to his home state. 483 pages. **$13.95**

UTAH HANDBOOK by Bill Weir
Weir gives you all the carefully researched facts and background to make your visit a success. 445 pages. **$14.95**

WASHINGTON HANDBOOK by Archie Satterfield and Dianne J. Boulerice Lyons
Covers sights, shopping, services, transportation, and outdoor recreation, with complete listings for restaurants and accommodations. 433 pages. **$15.95**

WYOMING HANDBOOK by Don Pitcher
All you need to know to open the doors to this wide and wild state. 495 pages. **$14.95**

YUCATAN HANDBOOK by Chicki Mallan
All the information you'll need to guide you into every corner of this exotic land. Mayan and Spanish glossaries. 391 pages. **$15.95**

THE INTERNATIONAL SERIES

EGYPT HANDBOOK   by Kathy Hansen
An invaluable resource for intelligent travel in Egypt. Arabic glossary. 522 pages.   **$18.95**

MOSCOW-ST. PETERSBURG HANDBOOK   by Masha Nordbye
Provides the visitor with an extensive introduction to the history, culture, and people of these two great cities, as well as practical information on where to stay, eat, and shop. 260 pages. **$13.95**

NEPAL HANDBOOK   by Kerry Moran
Whether you're planning a week in Kathmandu or months out on the trail, *Nepal Handbook* will take you into the heart of this Himalayan jewel. 378 pages.   **$12.95**

NEPALI AAMA   by Broughton Coburn
A delightful photo-journey into the life of a Gurung tribeswoman of Central Nepal. Having lived with Aama (translated, "mother") for two years, first as an outsider and later as an adopted member of the family, Coburn presents an intimate glimpse into a culture alive with humor, folklore, religion, and ancient rituals. 165 pages.   **$13.95**

PAKISTAN HANDBOOK   by Isobel Shaw
For armchair travelers and trekkers alike, the most detailed and authoritative guide to Pakistan ever published. Urdu glossary. 478 pages.   **$15.95**

STAYING HEALTHY IN ASIA, AFRICA, AND LATIN AMERICA
by Dirk G. Schroeder, Sc D, MPH
Don't leave home without it! Besides providing a complete overview of the health problems that exist in these areas, this book will help you determine which immunizations you'll need beforehand, what medications to take with you, and how to recognize and treat infections and diseases. Includes extensively illustrated first-aid information and precautions for heat, cold, and high altitude. 200 pages.   **$10.95**

TIBET HANDBOOK: A PILGRIMAGE GUIDE
by Victor Chan
This remarkable book is both a comprehensive trekking guide to mountain paths and plateau trails, and a pilgrimage guide that draws on Tibetan literature and religious history. 1104 pages. **$30.00**

MOONBELTS

Made of heavy-duty Cordura nylon, the Moonbelt offers maximum protection for your money and important papers. This all-weather pouch slips under your shirt or waistband, rendering it virtually undetectable and inaccessible to pickpockets. One-inch-wide nylon webbing, heavy-duty zipper, one-inch quick-release buckle. Accommodates traveler's checks, passport, cash, photos. Size 5 x 9 inches. Black.   **$8.95**

**New travel handbooks may be available that are not on this list.
To find out more about current or upcoming titles,
call us toll-free at (800) 345-5473.**

IMPORTANT ORDERING INFORMATION

FOR FASTER SERVICE: Call to locate the bookstore nearest you that carries Moon Travel Handbooks or order directly from Moon Publications:

(800) 345-5473 • **Monday-Friday** • **9 a.m.-5 p.m. PST** • **fax (916) 345-6751**

PRICES: All prices are subject to change. We always ship the most current edition. We will let you know if there is a price increase on the book you ordered.

SHIPPING & HANDLING OPTIONS: 1) Domestic UPS or USPS first class (allow 10 working days for delivery): $3.50 for the first item, 50 cents for each additional item.

Exceptions:
- **Moonbelt** shipping is $1.50 for one, 50 cents for each additional belt.
- Add $2.00 for same-day handling.
- UPS 2nd Day Air or Printed Airmail requires a special quote.
- International Surface Bookrate (8-12 weeks delivery):
  $3.00 for the first item, $1.00 for each additional item. Note: Moon Publications cannot guarantee international surface bookrate shipping.

FOREIGN ORDERS: All orders that originate outside the U.S.A. must be paid for with either an International Money Order or a check in U.S. currency drawn on a major U.S. bank based in the U.S.A.

TELEPHONE ORDERS: We accept Visa or MasterCard payments. Minimum order is US$15.00. Call in your order: (800) 345-5473, 9 a.m.-5 p.m. Pacific Standard Time.

ORDER FORM

Be sure to call (800) 345-5473 for current prices and editions or for the name of the bookstore nearest you that carries Moon Travel Handbooks • 9 a.m.–5 p.m. PST
(See important ordering information on preceding page)

Name: _____ Date: _____

Street: _____

City: _____ Daytime Phone: _____

State or Country: _____ Zip Code: _____

QUANTITY	TITLE	PRICE

Taxable Total_____

Sales Tax (7.25%) for California Residents_____

Shipping & Handling_____

TOTAL_____

Ship: ☐ UPS (no PO Boxes)   ☐ 1st class   ☐ International surface mail

Ship to: ☐ address above   ☐ other _____

_____

_____

Make checks payable to: **MOON PUBLICATIONS, INC**. P.O. Box 3040, Chico, CA 95927-3040 U.S.A. We accept Visa and MasterCard. **To Order**: Call in your Visa or MasterCard number, or send a written order with your Visa or MasterCard number and expiration date clearly written.

Card Number: ☐ **Visa**   ☐ **MasterCard**

☐ ☐ ☐ ☐   ☐ ☐ ☐ ☐   ☐ ☐ ☐ ☐   ☐ ☐ ☐ ☐

Exact Name on Card: _____

expiration date:_____

signature_____

THE METRIC SYSTEM

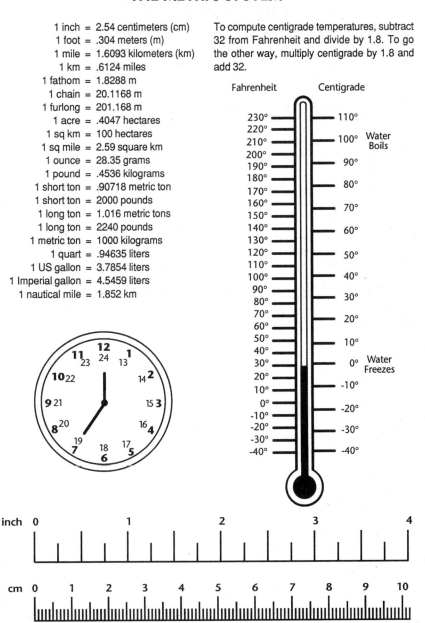

1 inch = 2.54 centimeters (cm)
1 foot = .304 meters (m)
1 mile = 1.6093 kilometers (km)
1 km = .6124 miles
1 fathom = 1.8288 m
1 chain = 20.1168 m
1 furlong = 201.168 m
1 acre = .4047 hectares
1 sq km = 100 hectares
1 sq mile = 2.59 square km
1 ounce = 28.35 grams
1 pound = .4536 kilograms
1 short ton = .90718 metric ton
1 short ton = 2000 pounds
1 long ton = 1.016 metric tons
1 long ton = 2240 pounds
1 metric ton = 1000 kilograms
1 quart = .94635 liters
1 US gallon = 3.7854 liters
1 Imperial gallon = 4.5459 liters
1 nautical mile = 1.852 km

To compute centigrade temperatures, subtract 32 from Fahrenheit and divide by 1.8. To go the other way, multiply centigrade by 1.8 and add 32.

Fahrenheit   Centigrade

230° — — 110°
220°
210° — — 100°   Water
200°   Boils
190° — — 90°
180°
170° — — 80°
160°
150° — — 70°
140°
130° — — 60°
120° — — 50°
110°
100° — — 40°
90° — — 30°
80°
70° — — 20°
60°
50° — — 10°
40°
30° — — 0°   Water
20°   Freezes
10° — — -10°
0°
-10° — — -20°
-20°
-30° — — -30°
-30°
-40° — — -40°

inch 0   1   2   3   4

cm 0 1 2 3 4 5 6 7 8 9 10

ABOUT THE AUTHOR

Joe Cummings has written about travel and culture for over a decade. Attracted to geographical extremes, his first in-depth journeys involved the river deltas and rainforests of Southeast Asia, where he worked as a Peace Corps volunteer (Thailand) and university lecturer (Malaysia), and later contributed to popular guidebooks on Thailand, Malaysia, Singapore, Burma, Indonesia, and China.

Joe became infatuated with desert terrains while exploring the Sierra del Carmen and Chihuahuan Desert reaches of Texas' Big Bend Country for Moon's *Texas Handbook*. His love of South Texas border culture, including *norteña* music and food, eventually spilled over into Mexico; in preparation for his research travels in Baja California and Northern Mexico, he undertook an intensive Spanish language course and lived with a Mexican family. Joe is now a confirmed Mexico fanatic.

When not on the road or sequestered with his word processor in Alta California, Joe likes to cook, play guitar, swim, boogie-board (preferably in tropical surf), read/re-read Graham Greene novels, and ride mountain bikes.